HOOLIGANS

The A-L of Britain's Football Gangs

Nick Lowles and Andy Nicholls

MILO BOOKS LTD

First published in September 2005 by Milo Books

ISBN 1 903854 41 5

Design and layout by e-type

Printed and bound in Great Britain by the Bath Press Ltd, Bath BA2 3BL

MILO BOOKS LTD
info@milobooks.com

Contents

Dedicated to Maci and Freya.
You make me happy when skies are grey.

Introduction

FOOTBALL HOOLIGANISM HAS been a prominent feature of British society for more than 40 years. In its "heyday", in the late Seventies and early Eighties, tens of thousands of young men were involved all over the country, every week. It was not uncommon for mobs of over 1,000-strong to face each other inside a ground. Vast police resources were committed to prevent disorder, while acres of newsprint and miles of film were devoted to covering the antics of those involved. Even today, with British hooliganism in possibly terminal decline, thousands of would-be yobs still turn out every Saturday. At the time of writing, almost 4,000 were on banning orders, with more joining the list every week. Without the huge operations and intelligence gathering that is a feature of policing football today, hooliganism would undoubtedly be very much alive.

Violence has been present at football for over 100 years, but it was in the late Fifties that hooliganism as we know it today was born, probably in the North West of England, where train-wrecking became a weekend pursuit among supporters of the bigger clubs. Its emergence coincided with the birth of British youth culture among a post-war generation that sought to be different from its elders and with the money to follow football independently of their parents. This new identity and self-confidence exploded onto the terraces with the skinheads of the late Sixties. Tough, fashion-conscious, territorial and violent, the skinhead was the working-class antidote to the middle-class hippy. Ends formed and pride was earned by taking opponents' "ends" whilst holding onto one's own.

The early hooligans were young; most were in the teens. By contrast, many of today's hardcore element are in their thirties or forties and have been active for 20 years or more; a 56-year-old man was convicted of involvement in an end-of-season riot at Millwall in May 2002. Many of these youths were indulging in copycat behaviour. They had read about the seaside clashes of the Mods and Rockers, and heard stories of skinheads, bootboys and "aggro". They wanted to sample the anarchy for themselves.

Instances of hooliganism appear to have dipped briefly in the very early Seventies as the first generation of terrace fighters grew, but soon they were replaced by a new generation and the issue was very much back in the news. In 1973, the London listings magazine *Time Out* produced a special feature on the London ends, mocking Chelsea and Spurs for being the weakest of the big teams – something that would quickly change. Years later, sarcastic Liverpool fanzine *The End* and music/style magazine *The Face* would report on changing hooligan fashions and tactics. Television coverage and pitch invasions and fighting on the terraces were avidly studied. Throughout the entire period, the media, police and government wrung their hands in despair at continuing disorder. The dates and fixtures might change but the expletives have remained the same.

By the late Seventies, the most important change in the hooligan subculture was underway. The football casual, neatly decked out in labelled clothes, replaced the skinhead, the mod revivalist, the punk and the greaser on the terraces. Suddenly hooligans were recognisable not by their scarves, badges, rosettes and boots, but by the absence of the same. Image became increasingly important. Football gangs began to choose lurid names and print calling cards. The likes of West Ham's I.C.F and Chelsea's Headhunters were soon widely known, though it seemed to take the police several years to cotton on.

The authorities eventually fought back. Steel-toe-capped boots became viewed as offensive weapons (even though they had long since been discarded by the gangs), segregation within grounds and enclosed areas became universal. By the late Seventies, with it becoming increasingly difficult to take opponents' ends, the hooligans began to move around the ground in the search of confrontation. The casuals often took up residence in the seats rather than standing areas, both as a status symbol but also because these areas were less policed. By the early Eighties violence was increasingly occurring outside the grounds.

The Heysel disaster in 1985, the televised riot of Millwall fans at Luton, the persistent misbehaviour of English fans abroad, and the deaths at Hillsborough in 1989, proved to be defining moments in British football. Hooligans became pariahs. English teams were banned from European competition in the wake of Heysel. The Thatcher Government promised a crackdown and police were given new powers to reign in troublemakers. A series of police undercover operations, coupled with the emerging rave culture, saw a rapid decline in hooliganism within many clubs. Officers began to use CCTV and hand-held video cameras in a bid to identify troublemakers.

Membership schemes were introduced. Football fanzines and inflatables replaced terrace fighting. The effects of the rave scene proved to be short-lived but by now football was becoming big business and hooliganism was a threat to profits. As the game became more respectable so the fanbase became more affluent. Prices went up and many in traditional working class communities, where most hooligans have derived, became priced out. Post-Hillsborough, all-seater stadiums and the Premier League cut capacity and hooliganism amongst the leading clubs. Chelsea, Leeds and West Ham were replaced by Cardiff, Stoke and Hull as hooligan strongholds. Millwall remained Millwall.

In May 2002, fearing a repeat of widespread trouble at a match two years before, over 2,000 police were needed to keep order at Stoke's play-off game against Cardiff. In the same month, over 900 Millwall fans rioted for four hours after their own play-off defeat to Birmingham. Fifty-six police officers were injured, more than 100 fans were later convicted and the local football intelligence officer described it as worse that the Brixton, Broadwater Farm and the Poll Tax riots. Such events are, however, now the exception rather than the rule. In the Seventies, as this book will show, trouble on such a scale occurred regularly, but those days are

A 1973 edition of London magazine Time Out *identified some youthful-looking leaders of the main 'ends'.*

gone. Football violence still hits the headlines but sweep away the media spin and the trouble itself is relatively isolated, if sometimes vicious. In 1977, the Home Secretary expressed concern at the six convictions and fines totalling just £160 for a Chelsea football riot that saw Charlton's ground ripped apart and local houses attacked. In 2004, over 20 Chester fans were imprisoned for an attempted fight against their Wrexham opponents in which some did not even throw a punch.

Since the new millennium, yet another wave of younger firms has begun to worry the authorities. More dismissive of police tactics and possible capture, these "youth" firms are quicker to use weapons and attack ordinary fans. But, as is graphically illustrated in Burnley, a concerted police effort can remove dozens from football grounds. In bygone years the hardcore of hooligans would amass dozens of convictions. Now it is a one-strike policy.

This book intends to be an accurate as possible

history of the gangs who participated in British hooliganism during its most active period. It records trouble from those who participated in the disorder, from the authorities, from newspaper archives and from the perspective of those whose lives were blighted. There is no exact history of hooliganism, and as is clear in many of the accounts recorded here there are very different memories of a single incident. It is a book that could not have been written 20 years ago, when hooliganism was at its height, because many of the more than 200 hooligans interviewed during this project would still have been active. Most talk now because they have moved on.

The media and authorities scream blue murder at every outbreak of disorder, especially when it involves the England team abroad. To the government it brings shame to the nation, while to the largely right-wing tabloid press it is a further indictment of the worst aspects of our permissive liberal society, where the rule of law and respect has collapsed. Hooliganism has heaped shame on this country and, despite the denials of the hooligans themselves, thousands of completely innocent people have been caught up and affected by it. But 40 years after the media first began to report trouble on our terraces, there still remains little understanding of why hooligans do what they do. Laws have become increasingly draconian, to the point where people are regularly banned from football grounds for several years for simply being drunk and imprisoned for two years for threatening behaviour without actually hitting anyone.

The question of why is perhaps even more pertinent now. Penalties for getting caught are almost certain imprisonment and a lengthy ban from football grounds. There are two answers. The first is that many hooligans find it fun, pure and simple. Football hooliganism is far more than just fighting. It is about a day out, a weekend away, a holiday. It is about drinking, being with your mates and having a laugh. The tribal nature of football, town against town, city against city, only increases the bond between fans and rivalries with one another. Even when trouble does occur, it is often little more than pavement dancing. This is not belittling the severity of the violence, but without understanding why it has continued in the face of increasingly severe laws society will never eradicate it. Yes, hooliganism is decreasing, but just as terrace violence largely replaced inter-town and school fight-ing in the Seventies and Eighties, as young lads came together to fight for their football team, we may now be seeing a return to more localised disorder. Stricter laws without getting to the root cause simply displaces trouble.

A more serious explanation is that Britain has a drink-fight culture. Drinking to excess is part of our culture. Middle class university students are no different from the ordinary Joe in the street. Getting drunk is part of having a good time. In many communities, men who don't drink are considered weird and soft. Fighting is another dominant feature of many communities, where being hard gives social standing. The decline of traditional industries and the de-industrialisation of many areas has if anything intensified the importance of masculinity amongst males.

In 1996, one of the present authors spent a weekend in a former pit village in South Wales. The mines had long closed and unemployment, drugs and violence ravaged the area. His hosts were five Cardiff hooligans and the conversation consisted of the weapons they had at their disposal, who was the hardest bloke in the village and tales of football hooliganism. Driving back into Cardiff, one of the lads turned round to their guest and asked him what he thought of the weekend. He replied that they were a good bunch of lads and he'd had an interesting time.

The Cardiff lad looked quizzical and with heavy eyes said, "It's all a bit sad really. We've got nothing else to do. Football fighting's a laugh but it's all we've got."

The author shrugged his shoulders and remained silent, but he knew what was meant. On a Saturday afternoon, as he marched around city and town centres across England terrifying shoppers and rivals supporters, this young man was important. The drudgery and struggle of day-to-day life was forgotten as other people now had to take notice.

A year earlier, the same author had met Chelsea face Andy Frain, better known as "Nightmare", in the Mitre pub in Reading. It was only a few days after the Dublin football riot and the media was in hooligan overdrive. Frain was predictably scornful of the media. He railed at its hypocrisy. "There's always been people like us, cannon fodder. Two hundred years ago they would be putting on our red tunics and sending us out into the front line."

And in a way he was right. During several wars over the last two centuries, Britain's prisons would be emptied and the hardest, meanest men would be let loose on the battlefield. The 1960s liberal society didn't create hooliganism and the people involved, they have always existed. Football simply became an arena because it was a popular working class sport.

The final word on "why" must be left to the football hooligans themselves. Over 20 years ago, two academics looked at the origins of football hooliganism and working class youth culture in their seminal book *We Hate Humans*. An Arsenal fan gave a simple explanation for his involvement in violence.

It is as pertinent now as it was then: "You could have a terrible week, a bust-up with your girl, row with your old man, lose your job, everything could go wrong … But when you go down there, on the terraces, you're shouting along with the rest … Your worries fall away, you're top of the world."

For all that football violence is shocking and disruptive, hooligans are ordinary people drawn from ordinary society. Believe it or not, there are a good number of journalists, MPs and even police officers who once upon a time ran on the terraces. *Hooligans* is the story of the many thousands of people who have done exactly that over the past 40 years.

Nick Lowles and Andy Nicholls

A

ABERDEEN

Ground: Pittodrie
Firm: Aberdeen Soccer Casuals
Rivals: Dundee, Motherwell, Hibs, Rangers

It didn't get much bigger than Liverpool in the European Cup. The Scottish champions against the English champions, with the latter arguably the best team in Europe at the time, was built up in the press as a Battle of Britain. Liverpool took the first leg at Pittodrie by a single goal, and would run out 4–0 winners at Anfield, but it was the Scouse fans rather than their all-conquering team that caught the imagination of many of the younger Aberdeen lads.

"The young ruffians observing and waiting for the opposing fans saw in the visiting section groups of young Scousers with strange hairstyles, leather jackets, trainers and, more importantly, no club colours," recalled one fan in the book *Casuals* by Phil Thornton. "It baffled the home contingent."

The away match was little different, as Aberdeen's Jay Allan described in *Bloody Casuals,* a landmark hooligan memoir written in 1989. "Just next to us at the Anfield Road End were 500 to 600 young lads. None of them had scarves on, and they all had their hair in a side-shade. I didn't know then who they were, but I now know they were the early dressers … these lads were the Liverpool Scallywags."

Clothes had not been important to Aberdeen's rougher element, with many still wearing regulation Harrington jackets, tight jeans and shaven heads. A few months later West Ham and Manchester United travelled up to Aberdeen for a pre-season tournament and, while the Londoners still wore the skinhead fashion, the Mancs looked exactly the same as the Liverpool fans the Scots had seen in the European match. By the time Aberdeen played

Ipswich in that year's UEFA Cup, the look had caught on among their younger lads. It united youths from different areas of the Granite City at a time when the club, under manager Alex Ferguson, was enjoying unprecedented success at home and in Europe.

Scotland's first casual mob was born in Aberdeen that season and its history was intrinsically linked to fashion. The casual image gave the young lads a unifying bond that differentiated them from older lads in the city and, for a while, from every other football mob in the country. Yet they were forced to travel down to London, Leeds, Manchester or York to buy their clothes, as few Scottish stores stocked the labels they sought. Often the lads would make a weekend of it, taking in a game and a hooligan fight. Aberdeen lads became regulars at Spurs, Arsenal and Leeds. In the days before the Internet, watching, listening and chatting was the only way the word was spread. It was also common for lads to use Aberdeen matches in England as an excuse to make a week of it, drinking, fighting and shopping their way to or from a game. With their team's dominance of Scottish football in the early 1980s, there was certainly enough travelling to do.

In 1983, Aberdeen played at Old Trafford for Martin Buchan's testimonial. It was a meaningless game for the players but momentous for the fledgling Aberdeen Soccer Casuals. "We'd been looking forward to this all summer," recalled Allan. They stopped at Glasgow on the way, where a small group of 15 ASC joined up with 100 Tottenham, who were there to play Celtic. From there they took a train to Preston, where they met up with 50 more Aberdeen who had come down on a direct train. Some went straight on to Manchester, while others took a day in Blackpool. To their disappointment, there was no welcoming committee for them in Manchester, and even after the game, when small pockets of United hung around street corners, there was no trouble. The 100 ASC went home untested but growing in confidence.

A year later, small numbers of ASC set off for a pre-season match at Leicester. The Leicester Baby Squad was beginning to earn a reputation which the now seasoned fighters of Aberdeen were keen to test. By the afternoon of the game there were 65-70 Aberdeen together and a Leicester lad told them to head for the seats. They were again to leave England disappointed as the police shepherded them to and from the ground. A group of Aberdeen also travelled to Newcastle for the visit of Chelsea. The game was all-ticket but the Aberdeen were there to watch the two mobs in action. They went home amazed at the age of some of the Newcastle lads. Trips like these were highly educational for the pioneers of the casual culture in Scotland.

In 1982, the ASC announced their dominance on the Scottish scene by running riot in a cup final in Glasgow. With no rival casual firms around and the Scottish police totally unprepared for these scarf-shunning hooligans, the ASC marauded around the streets of Glasgow at will.

Oil brought outsiders to Aberdeen and prosperity to the city. New money was matched by confidence and the combination led to greater investment in Aberdeen Football Club. A young Alex Ferguson was the manager and the team included captain Willie Miller and a youthful Gordon Strachan. The club won three League and Cup titles in the 1980s and a European Cup Winner's Cup trophy. The oil industry also meant that many of the young lads who followed Aberdeen were able to afford the travel, match tickets and eventually the clothes, at a time when the rest of Scotland was suffering economic recession and industrial decline.

A rivalry with Dundee stretched back to the 1970s, largely because it was the closest game Aberdeen could call local. There was also regular trouble when Aberdeen fans stopped off in Dundee on their way back from matches further south. However, Motherwell replaced Dundee as Aberdeen's main hooligan rivals during the early 1980s when their Saturday Service emerged as Scotland's second casual mob. The fashion rivalry, coupled with a few instances of blade carrying amongst the Motherwell crew, worsened an already fractious relationship and led to several years of

trouble. "These cheeky chappies from Motherwell had made a challenge to Aberdeen's credibility and position in the trendy stakes, and the war with the Saturday Service was to become a special feature on our battle calendar," wrote another Aberdonian, Dan Rivers, in his *Congratulations, You've Just Met The Casuals*. In 1983, Aberdeen twice got into the Motherwell home end, once during the game, causing chaos on the terraces, while Dons fans in their own end threatened to invade the pitch. Referee Andrew Waddell blew his whistle and led the players and linesmen to the tunnel.

Fashion marked Aberdeen out from the other supporters in the early 1980s. Even when other firms adopted the casual look, Aberdeen liked to boast that they were still years ahead of their rivals. There was an element of truth in this, largely because their European adventures brought them into contact with new fashions and hooligan trends in England and the Continent. Aberdeen enjoyed mocking their rivals, as in a flyer aimed at Dundee fans in the early 1980s: "This has been printed for the benefit of you Dundee shits, some of whom think are now Casuals. It was only a few months ago that you were still skinheads. In fact, you still have more skinheads than you have so-called Casuals. Do you remember that for the last two or three years how you used to try and slag us and sing 'where's your scarves' while all the time we were laughing at your silly 'Y' cardigans and 'sta-press' trousers along with your denim jackets and about 10 scarves. It seems that you have discovered names such as Fila, Tacchini and Ellesse. Wow. We were wearing that gear when we went stealing them in Hamburg on our way to Gothenburg."

At its peak the ASC could mobilise 600-1,000 lads for a tasty home game and regularly took 3-400 for a game in the big two cities. On one occasion, they had a 700-strong mob at Celtic. And as early as 1982, they were clashing with Hibs, though their opponents were still skinheads and punks. In one fight, a top Aberdeen lad was struck around the head by a skinhead wielding a chain. By 1984, the casual craze had taken hold in Edinburgh and, while the trip to the capital had long had the potential for trouble, the newly formed Hibs Capital City Service made it a more equal contest.

The first proper clash took place at a League match in the autumn of 1984. More than 300

Aberdeen lads made the trip down in quite appalling weather conditions. Dan Rivers was new to the scene when he boarded the train. He had been to games at Rangers and Celtic but this was his first on the fringes of the ASC, and he later captured the atmosphere perfectly: "Some of the older lads were having a walk about the carriages and geeing the boys up, almost like a team talk … At the same time, though, there were also a few of the main faces going among the younger lads and telling them, 'If anybody runs, they'll get it back on the train' … As Haymarket came and went, everybody was up and ready to go, doing up jackets and double-tying laces. Some lads were even removing their watches. All these mad little elements helped to build up the atmosphere on the train to absolute boiling point."

The Aberdeen boys had the doors open and were hopping off the train at Waverley Station even before it had come to a halt. But the day proved to be a massive anti-climax for the ASC. As they passed the St James's shopping centre and headed towards Easter Road, there was no sign of the CCS. It was only when they reached the ground they were told the game had been called off because of the weather. Some other Aberdeen did find the enemy, however. As they returned to the train station to begin their journey home, a small group of Hibs appeared and threw bricks and stones. Aberdeen took a few casualties but charged forward and their attackers were quickly on their toes without a punch being thrown.

The rearranged game was played a few days later, meaning that only a handful of ASC could either take time off or afford the trip. Almost as soon as a small group of just 22 Aberdeen disembarked an early evening train, they came under a hail of missiles. Hibs were keen on revenge. As with the postponed match, the walk to the ground was uneventful, but they knew that the post-match proceedings would be different. After the game the Aberdeen crew was confronted by about 50 CCS and another 250 punks, skinheads and assorted lumps who were all eager to have a piece of the action. Despite the overwhelming odds, the visitors still charged forward, initially forcing the Hibs fans to retreat more out of surprise than anything. Hibs regained their composure and charged and there were running battles all the way back to the station.

Aberdeen had escaped what appeared a certain canning, and for this reason alone there was euphoria at the train station. Jay Allan said, "We went into the rail bar and you wouldn't believe the scene. Although all of us were cut, bruised and sore, we were handshaking and hugging each other. We did our city proud, we did it for Aberdeen. You would have thought we had just won an Olympic gold for our country in a relay race."

Aberdeen returned to Hibs the following March in a mood of steely determination. The last big trip had been a washout in every sense but now the ASC wanted to put on a show. Hundreds travelled down on the train and there was little of the joviality of the earlier trip; the mood was one of grim determination. The ASC mob filled the road as they left the station, gradually breaking into a jog, and found their quarry at London Road. A hail of missiles announced the presence of 300 Hibs CCS. They charged, and then backed off as Aberdeen came back at them. Scores stood and fought.

One of the Hibs mob was tripped as he tried to get away and was set upon by a number of Aberdeen lads. He was so badly hurt that he was rushed to intensive care. If that wasn't bad enough, their team lost 5–0. The home fans showed their disgust by throwing coins, cans and missiles at the referee and the players. Hibs were to get their revenge at the home encounter later that year when a petrol bomb was thrown into the ASC crowd. There was little let-up on the following trip, this time with a flare being fired into the Aberdeen mob. Hibs were prepared to use weapons to capture Aberdeen's title of Scotland's worst hooligans.

Aberdeen played Motherwell for their first home game of the 1985/86 season and it was decided to teach their Casual rivals a lesson. Aberdeen were at the pinnacle of their power, buoyed up by events in Edinburgh. Thirty of their top boys met up in a city centre pub to hatch their plans. Some thought of catching a train south with the aim of intercepting Motherwell en-route, while others proposed taking a fleet of cars to the beach boulevard and catching them close to the ground. It was finally agreed to meet up in Daisy's bar and ambush the Motherwell mob as it was escorted from the station. The Under-Fives (a name many hooligan gangs used for their younger element, first adopted by West Ham in the early Eighties) were to create a diversion near the station in order to draw some of the police away.

Word spread quickly throughout Aberdeen and by the Saturday morning, as 200 excited casuals began mobbing up, few in the town did not know of the plan. Unfortunately for the ASC, the police were also well informed. After an ASC spotter delivered the news that 70 Saturday Service were on their way, the Aberdeen lads left the bar in a state of high excitement – and ran straight into a police trap. Forty-seven Aberdeen fans were arrested, and while another 700 were still on show inside the ground, the day was a psychological setback for the gang. Of those arrested, five were found not guilty, four had their cases deferred for good behaviour, 30 received fines of between £100-£500 each and eight Aberdeen Casuals, including Jay Allan, were given custodial sentences.

The failed ambush coincided with a crackdown on hooliganism by police and the train was ditched in favour of buses and vans. Even this proved to be a short-lived solution as the police net widened. When they did manage to get to their destination, policing was usually so heavy that nothing occurred. Aberdeen's remote location made it virtually impossible for visiting mobs to arrive undetected. In addition, prison sentences and beatings pushed some into early retirement. Taking the odd punch was an occupational hazard but the increasing use of weapons, particularly by Hibs, was something altogether different.

Dan Rivers recalled getting a severe beating at the hands (and boots) of the CCS at a match in Edinburgh in 1988. The ASC were attacked as they wandered down Leith Walk on their way to Easter Road. In a brief but vicious assault, he found himself alone and was set upon and stabbed. He did not discover the bleeding wound until he was inside the ground, quickly sought medical attention and was rushed to hospital. As he was boarding an ambulance, a Hibs lad popped his head around the door and said: "I hope ye die, ye bastard." Even in the emergency ward, Hibs lads wandered around looking at who had been brought in. That was his last day out to Hibs with the lads – the ferocity of their attack had spooked him and some of the other ASC, as he later admitted.

The rave scene decimated the mob further and the numbers fell to 150 to 200 for big games. "Acid house arrived slowly but surely, and that's where most of us ended up," recalled Aberdeen fan Ade in

Casuals. "The football was never fully packed in, but many had had enough and were more interested in the pills and parties. It seemed a bit pointless all of a sudden, and the clothes took a nosedive."

The gang were also facing more concerted police surveillance and, before long, they had to switch to coaches to evade detection and seek confrontations away from the ground. Even then, travelling anonymously was not guaranteed and in 1994 coaches ferrying the ASC to the capital for games against Hibs were twice intercepted. The Aberdeen boys were held for up to six hours on each occasion before being released, so ensuring that there was no opportunity for trouble.

Throughout the history of the ASC there has been a close link with Spurs. This relationship was formed in those early days of the 1980s when Aberdeen lads would observe the big English firms and solidified when Tottenham played in the pre-season match at Celtic in 1983. "The friendship with Spurs is and has been strong for years with mobs from both sides travelling to each other's big games every season," said Paul, an ASC founder member. For one match against West Ham it was reported that as many as 70 Aberdeen made the trip, believing that Glasgow Rangers were also to be present. The Scottish *Daily Mirror* claimed the Aberdeen leader was William Watson, arrested with 47 other fans at the London game for throwing a bottle at riot police.

While few English firms have brought firms as far north as Aberdeen, Everton were an exception, in 1996. Paul admitted, "It was not one of our better days, we were not expecting what they brought up and loads of our top lads were at an Oasis concert that weekend. But I'll give the Scousers credit, they were the best firm to bring it to us from down south. Despite what has been written before about it elsewhere, I still say we backed them out of Clarkie's Bar." Despite missing a few main faces, Aberdeen fought to gain some respectability throughout the day and there were serious outbreaks of violence long into the night. The police were jubilant when CCTV picked up three such incidents and a total of 14 known hooligans from both firms were arrested and charged with mobbing and rioting, a very rare charge which carries lengthy custodial sentences. Nearly twelve months after the arrests the trial collapsed and just one individual received community service, and a handful of others were fined. Six years after the trouble, the clubs arranged another friendly at Pittodrie, but both police forces were unimpressed and the fixture was cancelled immediately.

More recently, Aberdeen have had a number of other clashes with English firms during pre-season friendlies. At a match at Rotherham scores of Aberdeen lads spent the weekend in Sheffield where they fought with United's Blades Business Crew. In July 2000, Aberdeen played at Hartlepool and fighting broke out on the terracing after just five minutes of play and spilled onto the pitch. The trouble began after a small group of ASC got into the home end and, when fighting broke out with Hartlepool fans, the away contingent were joined by dozens of others who came across the pitch. The game was halted for several minutes until order was restored and, while no-one was arrested, 30 Aberdeen were ejected from the ground. About 250 Aberdeen fans had made the journey down, including about 60 ASC.

A match at Bradford also saw trouble. "The ASC took ninety lads down and most stayed in Leeds," said Paul. "We caught a really early train to Bradford on the Saturday morning, hoping to get some sort of action with the Ointment. They knew we were coming and a couple of lads were in contact with them but, to our disappointment, they never really showed before the game. We sat drinking around the city centre, unchallenged and headed up to the stadium to see if they would show there. There was a small scuffle with around six or seven Ointment lads at a pub beside the ground but police got involved very early. It was agreed with them to meet after the game in Manningham, away from the CCTV and we told them we were not interested in anything in the centre.

"We lost the police, got into Manningham and walked about looking for them. Calls were made but Bradford now told us to come to the centre as they would not come to us. We headed into town but picked up an escort and now in the range of the CCTV, most lads wanted nothing to happen. While we were walking to the station, around thirty Bradford charged up the road, and seventeen ASC who were a bit in front of the main mob ran down to meet them. By now the police had stopped most ASC from joining in, so it was left to the seventeen lads, who stood and took it to Bradford, but against

larger numbers and an array of weapons, including bottles and pub signs."

Aberdeen's current rival is undoubtedly Glasgow Rangers. There has been trouble between the two sets of supporters since the Sixties, when Rangers fans regularly overran the northern conurbation. In 1967, the Chief Constable of Aberdeen warned visiting Rangers fans befor the New Year's Eve match that anyone arrested would spend the weekend in the cells because of the Bank Holiday period. The two sides met in the Skol Cup Final in 1979, when the disputed sending off of Aberdeen's Doug Rougvie infuriated Aberdeen fans. The hostility was reciprocated during the early Eighties when Aberdeen were clearly the leading team in Scottish football, though for a while it appeared that their rivalry with Dundee was marginalizing the Old Firm clash. An attack on Gordon Strachan by a Celtic fan seemed to indicate that they too grew a strong dislike of the Dons.

At a game at Ibrox in 1985, Rangers fans acted angrily to their team's 5–0 drubbing. As Aberdeen fans left the ground, they were greeted by a couple of thousand unimpressed Glaswegians. "It was like a scene from *Zulu*," remembered Dan Rivers. "The Rangers outnumbered us by thousands and were making this constant droning, booing sound, like the Zulus in the film, in between the angriest chorus of 'You're gonna get your fucking heads kicked in' that I had ever heard." The Rangers mob poured towards Aberdeen as they tried to leave the ground, the sky filled with flying bottles, and full-scale fighting went on for what seemed like an age.

The appointment and then success of Graeme Souness as Rangers' player-manager in 1986 re-ignited the hatred felt towards the Glaswegian side, especially because it was at the expense of their own club's fortunes. In May 1987, Rangers won their first League title for many years away at Aberdeen and there was a huge pitch invasion as thousands of fans celebrated their success. The goalposts were snapped and home fans goaded as the pitch, ground and city were overrun. Aberdeen resented this success, especially as it signalled the end of their own domination.

Aberdeen's frustration with Rangers' rise was best summed up in the outrageous tackle by Aberdeen's Neil Simpson on Ian Durrant in 1988. The challenge put the Rangers midfielder out of the game for over two years, and almost ended his career. The fact that some Aberdeen fans celebrated the incident by rushing out souvenir tee-shirts did little to heal the wounds, and they have been re-opened at regular intervals ever since and plied with salt. The following year Aberdeen beat Rangers in the Skol Cup Final, with the ASC running the Rangers ICF before the game. During the match a group of 60 Rangers got into the Aberdeen end but they were soon beaten out by hundreds of Aberdeen, both casuals and "scarfers", after they celebrated their side's equaliser.

Into the Nineties the rivalry became so intense that Rangers' head of security described fixtures between the two teams as worse than Old Firm derbies. At a League game at Pittodrie on 1 April 2000, a pre-arranged fight took place over an hour after the football match had finished between almost 200 fans. Police had to clear the surrounding streets and 17 people were arrested in raids a few weeks later.

In 2002, the League match at Pittodrie between the two was held up for 20 minutes as home fans climbed on to the pitch after a player was hit by a coin thrown from the away end. Clashes between rival fans in the seats spilled onto the pitch, further delaying the game. A subsequent police investigation identified 20 hooligans, most from Aberdeen, and several fans received custodial sentences.

Even when they were not playing each other but when Aberdeen were in Glasgow or nearby they would often still pick a fight with Rangers. "Recently, the ASC were coming back from a Cup game at Dumfries with 19 lads when we bumped into around 40 Rangers," said Paul. "A fight ensued with both sides going back and forth, with the 19 Aberdeen eventually running Rangers back to their bar. An ASC was put in hospital and eight lads were imprisoned for between three and 20 months."

The heyday of the ASC is now just a memory for most of those involved. Old rivalries are now set aside and once sworn enemies are now friends. In 2001 some of the old ASC faces joined together with their counterparts in Motherwell's Saturday Service to form the Independent Football Casuals. The link came about through the Internet, stories were shared and numbers swapped. A meeting of the two groups took place in Motherwell, where the visitors

were put up by their hosts; the hospitality was later reciprocated. This new friendship caused some consternation between the current generation of hooligans from both clubs, but, given the size of some of those involved in the IFC, there was very little they could do.

The Aberdeen Soccer Casuals continue to be a major force in Scottish hooliganism but numbers are well down on their Eighties high. "The ASC today is not what it used to be, largely due to police hassles and jail sentences," said Paul. "The average turnout tends to be between fifty and sixty, with about 150 for big games. Only Hibs and possibly Rangers could match this number. The Scottish scene in general is picking up again, with some youth crews emerging, but the police are well clued up and getting any kind of action is very difficult. They are also beginning to introduce the banning orders you have in England and this will hit some mobs very hard." The legacy, however, is as much about fashion, entertainment and lifestyle as fighting.

Further reading: *Bloody Casuals*, Jay Allan (Famedram); *Congratulations, You Have Just Met the Casuals*, Dan Rivers (Blake Publishing)

AIRDRIE UNITED

Ground: Shyberry Excelsior Stadium
Firm: Section B, Red Army Firm
Rivals: Motherwell, Partick Thistle
Police operations: None
Website: www.airdriehooligans.tk

"A horrible little town, full of headcases," was how one football hooligan author described Airdrie, which lies on the outskirts of Glasgow. A tough little place, it's soccer gang, Section B was formed as early as 1977 by some Airdrie punks who were fed up with Old Firm fans riding roughshod over them when they visited their town. The name came from a local punk band. Section B replaced smaller, less organised mobs such as the Broomfield Boot Boys, Tiny Mob, Tamla Hill and Reos, all housing estate gangs who would turn out against teams from Edinburgh, Kilmarnock and Falkirk, but even when combined could not raise the numbers to tackle the two Glasgow giants. Section B were not immediately accepted by the old boys and had to prove their worth, but before long the young lads emerged as the gamest, boldest and sometimes the maddest of the Airdrie fans. They stood in the same end as the old bootboy mob and led the charges against anyone who dared intrude on their covered terrace.

One day when Celtic came, the police tried putting Airdrie behind the goals while giving the visiting fans the covered end. Airdrie were not impressed and there was fighting throughout the match as they tried to force their way back in. For the next Celtic visit, Airdrie got into the ground early and were in the covered terrace before the Celtic hordes had hit town. Once the Celts came into the ground the local youths were surrounded by away fans hurling bricks, bottles and cans, but the 200-strong Section B did not move an inch. That was it. Nobody ever took their pen again and the covered terrace continued to be their home until it was demolished in the 1990s.

Section B had earned their spurs and the smaller mobs fell into line, although splinter groups continued to exist, one being the Airdrie Wig-heads, a firm of loons who wore women's wigs when they attacked rival fans – a craze that failed to catch on. The late Eighties saw an outfit emerge using the name the Red Army Firm, but it didn't survive for long, and the chant, "One, two, three, who are we? We are the mental Section B," remained the Airdrie battle cry.

Section B were creating headlines within a year of their formation. Following a home game against Hibernian in 1978, William Gray, the Airdrie chairman, made a public plea in a match programme after an attack on the Hibs team coach. "Officials and staff of Airdrieonians Football Club are horrified by the senseless attack by hooligans on the Hibernian team coach on the outskirts of the town last Wednesday," he said. "This attack resulted in injury to one of our opponents who had just won admiration and praise for their display in defeating us. If this action was intended to be an expression of support, we want none of it. Such conduct may be commonplace in other parts of Britain, but it will be a sorry day if we have to accept it as part of the Scottish football scene. Vendettas appear to be springing up between local gangs and the lunatic fringe of the support of certain other clubs. I am aware that there are rabble-rousers who find enjoyment in creating disorder and then disappearing

before the police arrive, but I appeal to our supporters to provide either names or descriptions."

Section B achieved greater notoriety after a televised Scottish Cup game against Albion Rovers in 1982 was held up for thirty minutes by fierce fighting on the terraces. Rovers' home average attendance was only 500, but 7,000 spectators crammed in to watch this match. Among the crowd were a sizeable number of Old Firm supporters, including a contingent from the Coatbridge Celtics, with whom Airdrie battled behind one goal. Many of these supporters wore their own club colours, which further riled Section B. An appeal for calm over the loudspeaker system was ignored, but the arrival of extra police did subdue the crowd.

The Airdrie mob was one of the first in Scotland and later became one of the biggest, yet despite this, they have never had a major clash with the Aberdeen Soccer Casuals, arguably Scotland's largest casual firm during the 1980s and 1990s. There were a few rows with the ASC's predecessors in the late 1970s, but little after that. In the mid-1990s, Section B took more than eighty up to Aberdeen for a cup game, but the police were firmly in control and the Airdrie mob was escorted straight to the ground. They once mobilised 400 lads for a midweek League Cup game at home against Aberdeen in the early 1980s, at the height of ASC numbers and superiority, but the ASC did not show.

Local footballing rivals Motherwell were for many years of little concern to Airdrie's sizeable mob. In 1982 the clubs met in the Lanarkshire Cup Final and Airdrie handed out what was described as a "flurry of unprovoked violence". During the late Eighties, however, Motherwell caused a few upsets. In 1990 they got the upper hand at Airdrie when they turned up 200-strong and took it to Section B after the game. Airdrie had better numbers, but for some reason a few of the lads at the front panicked and ran, something that caused serious grief in the ranks of the mob for some time afterwards. A week after this debacle, Morton brought a 100-strong mob to Airdrie but the home firm whacked the visitors as they tried to take the terrace. There was no mistaking the determination of Section B at this game as they were a proud firm and they knew that a second home humiliation within a week could have signalled a terminal crisis in their ranks.

Ten years later, Airdrie once again faced a

Motherwell mob in a midweek League Cup game at Broomfield and the word went round that they would show. One Section B veteran recalled, "It was an hour before the game and the lads were beginning to gather. Our two spotters, Mr T and JR, had followed them all the way and told us they'd soon be here, the latest update put them ten minutes away. Motherwell at Airdrie is big anytime but a cup match increases the stakes. The word went out and lads scattered around the town knew it was time to come together to put on a reception committee. We were about fifty-strong, which was disappointing, considering we have pulled out far bigger firms in the past. Even more worrying was that half the group were young, inexperienced pups. We knew we could be in for a difficult night. We marched down back alleys to escape the watchful eye of the Old Bill and the CCTV cameras as we headed to meet them outside Safeway. Our mob moved on in preparation for our ambush. Before long we could hear the Motherwell mob chanting confidently, oblivious to our presence. Everybody was getting excited, the adrenalin was pumping, and we were all supporting each other. 'Everybody, no fucking about; get right into these cunts,' whispered one of our top lads. 'Come on, we're fucking Airdrie,' I added. We broke into a gallop; there was no going back now.

"A lad turned the corner and our element of surprise was gone. The roar went up and the sound of shattering glass filled the early evening air. With missile stocks exhausted, it was down to the real action. We got the first push, forcing the fifty-strong Motherwell back up the street, but they had some experienced lads and, after their initial surprise, they regrouped and came back into us. It turned into trench warfare, with neither side budging an inch for the next five to ten minutes. Bins, shopping trolleys and traffic cones were all used as makeshift weapons or battering rams. Eventually, the police arrived but not before my head was split open with a cosh. Dazed and covered in blood, I managed to evade police attention and staggered off to the local hospital. It was quite a battle and initially it all seemed too much for me. After a skin graft and many arguments with my wife later I retired – for nearly two weeks. I might have had a sizeable chunk taken out of my head, but some things are just too important."

The intervention of the police was a relief to many of the top lads on both sides. Fighting was a tiring business and they had been going at each other for almost ten minutes without a break. Most Section B followers will cite this battle as their fiercest ever. However, the fact that Motherwell came in numbers and fought it out on the High Street was a major irritation for the Airdrie boys, and one that they still smart about. The fact that Motherwell performed well on what was supposed to be a revenge mission was even more annoying.

A few days later Airdrie were away at Partick Thistle, where there was always trouble. Section B numbers were depleted by injuries and arrests from the Motherwell game, but they still had enough to travel and their numbers were boosted by friends from the Wigan Goon Squad who came up for the match. There were a few skirmishes before the game but the real clashes occurred afterwards with 20 Partick hooligans fighting 40-50 Section B and Goon Squad. The police separated them and directed the away fans to the station, but failed to give them an escort and further fighting broke out. Airdrie claimed victory, a point contested by the home fans. Over the past few years the animosity to Partick Thistle has grown to the point where they are despised as much as Motherwell. One Airdrie leader said, "They have taken liberties with a couple of our boys in Glasgow and they smashed up a pub we used in Airdrie, thinking our mob was in it, when it was occupied at the time by Rangers fans. Although Motherwell is our main rival, this one has become something of a grudge match."

A mob of up to 80 gathered for the return home fixture against Thistle. There was no opportunity to get at them before the game, so Section B decided to ambush them on their way home. They jumped in taxis and headed for a small town outside Airdrie called Coatbridge. The police arrived shortly before Thistle and it took some explaining as to why 50 men were sitting in trees overlooking the railway station.

Section B was attracting large numbers for a club with crowds of less than 2,000. However, on the pitch, financial problems were bringing Airdrie down. When the team travelled to Ayr Utd for the final game of the season, many thought it would be the club's last ever game. The match was given extra friction by the fact that Ayr's chairman owned the company that built the new Airdrie ground, which was the source of their financial problems. When

Ayr scored their second, the shout, "On the park," went up and over 100 Airdrie stormed the pitch and headed towards the Ayr contingent that had been most vocal in their abuse. Though the police soon shepherded the Airdrie supporters off, a goalpost was snapped and the game was abandoned. Afterwards, 30 Section B being escorted back to the station were confronted by a rival mob, which was a surprise as Ayr had never really put on a show before. The roar went up and the two groups charged at each other, with two startled police officers desperately calling for assistance. When they were only feet apart the two mobs recognised each other as Airdrie. They stopped dead and shook hands, adding to the police officers' bemusement.

The club closed, but before long was back in existence after some directors bought Clydebank, moved it to Airdrie and changed its name to Airdrie United. The scenes of chaos at Ayr had been largely forgotten, but with the club reforming, pressure grew to deal with the hooligans and three Airdrie lads were sent to prison. While Section B has never suffered the police operations of certain English firms, the new ownership signalled a tougher police response. A few of the older lads retired and others picked their games more selectively. Life in the Second Division meant there were few opponents with significant firms anyway.

During the 1970s and 1980s, Airdrie's key rival was Hearts, who had the biggest mob around. Falkirk had their fair share of slaps from Airdrie and there were rows at Kilmarnock, Dundee, Morton and Ayr. Airdrie even claim a couple of "results" against the Hibs Capital City Service. One was after a cup game at Easter Road in the 1990s, when the CCS were at their peak. The Old Firm, meanwhile, no longer offered much threat: Section B claim no Celtic firm has done them since they formed in 1977 and, indeed, in the 1995 Cup Final, a mob of over 100 Airdrie, aided by a few Millwall, took it to the Hoops. There have, however, been clashes with Rangers, both at games between the two and on the way to or from other matches. In 1987, when 150 Airdrie were returning from Partick Thistle and Rangers were playing at home, they clashed outside Glasgow's Queen Street station. Bricks, bottles and fireworks were exchanged in front of shocked and terrified shoppers before police separated the factions and escorted Airdrie on to the train.

In 1991 Airdrie travelled to Clydebank. "Nazi thugs bring terror to town – Airdrie followers go on the rampage," ran the headline in the local paper. The story continued, "Families huddled together in terror as members of Airdrie's notorious travelling support – feared the length and depth of the country – brought mayhem to the Atlantis pub in Kilbowie Road. And the sickening behaviour did not stop once they were inside New Kilbowie for Saturday afternoon's ill-tempered First Division game. Throughout the match, one section of Airdrie's infamous fan base gave Nazi salutes and sang 'Rule Britannia', much to the disgust of the real football fans in attendance. The bother broke out just minutes before the game, which Airdrie won by the odd goal. Bar stools were hurled against the windows and glasses were pitched across the packed dining area."

Airdrie has only played one European fixture, but it became one of their most important fights. Over 150 Section B made the journey to Sparta Prague and gave what they describe as "an excellent show" in town and in the stadium before and during the game. They took special delight in dispatching the neo-Nazi Sparta hooligans before battling it out with the Czech riot police.

As with most mobs, the size of the turnout depends on the opposition, the history, the location, the time of year, the position in the league and the weather. In the late Seventies the travelling mob would be between 70 and 100, mostly young punks and skinheads. At home in the Pen there would be a few hundred, including many drunks and younger watchers. In the Eighties, away numbers increased to 200 for big games and as many as 400 at home, a sizeable portion of an average home crowd of 5,000. Declining team fortunes did little to reduce the hardcore as the lure of a decent fight and drink kept everybody happy. This was, however, before cellphones were in common usage, and Airdrie were never the best for turning out on time or even in the right location for a pre-arranged meet. Being one of the most drink-orientated firms around, booze often dictated where and when they turned out. With the onset of the "happy culture" of the rave scene, numbers dropped but they still maintained 50-plus at away matches and 100, mostly older lads, at home.

Like many Scottish firms, Airdrie have had links with several English teams over the years. In the 1980s they formed a friendship with the Bolton Cuckoo Boys and travelled down to a number of Bolton games. More recently, Wigan's Goon Squad attracted numbers of Section B down south. In between they turned out mobs of over 50 for Millwall v Leeds, Burnley v Millwall, Everton v West Ham, Carlisle v Plymouth, and Man City v Leeds. Some are friendly with Cardiff's Soul Crew. One link over the years has been with a Millwall lad called Paul who once arrived for a Partick game and was sitting drinking with a group and exchanging stories of days gone by. One of Airdrie's lads, Albert, was telling him about a recent midweek match at Brechin City. Paul listened and asked how many went to the game.

"About two hundred," said Albert.

"Two hundred?" said Paul. "Not a bad mob for a Tuesday night."

"No, there were two hundred at the game."

Albert took a few kicks under the table for his honesty.

Today, Airdrie's numbers depend on the opposition but for a key game they can still pull out 60-100 away and a few hundred if needed at home. The core is about 30 but many older lads will come out if required. "We are not the biggest and we are not the best, but we have been here for almost thirty years and we will give it a go when the opportunity arises," declared one of their leaders. "Anyone who says different is a fucking liar."

ALDERSHOT TOWN

Ground: Recreation Ground
Firm: A Company
Rivals: Reading, Brighton, Hereford

Aldershot Town FC is not the club it was. In fact, it was formed as late as 1992, after Aldershot FC became the first club since Accrington Stanley in 1962 to close down whilst in the Football League. It signed off in front of 6,000 fans at Cardiff City – and was reborn into the Diadora Isthmian League, five divisions below. Under the guidance of former Aldershot player Steve Wignall, the team won the championship by 18 points. A further promotion was gained in the following season as well as an appearance in the quarter-final of the FA Vase, and

five years later they gained promotion to the Conference.

While in the Football League, Aldershot saw regular trouble at matches with both Bristol clubs and with Southampton, but with a relatively small fan base they were frequently overrun. There was especially trouble with their main rivals during this period, Reading, and in one game in 1979, more than 70 fans were arrested, many for attempting to carry weapons into the ground. Obviously, the drop out of the League ended the regular games between the two clubs.

Life in the Conference has reduced the opportunities for large-scale disorder, but A Company, as their firm is known, claim to be one of the most active non-league firms about. The name was coined in the Eighties by a lad who remains active today, although he is currently on a banning order. "It's a poor town with young lads who have nothing to do," said one current A Company lad, Jak. "Most of the old faces from back then are still on the scene now, especially for the big fixtures." The town is perhaps best known as the home of the Parachute Regiment, hence the name of the firm. The Army culture has undoubtedly spilled over into the town and late-night brawls between squaddies and locals have for years been a regular feature of Aldershot life.

Aldershot have a close friendship with Portsmouth; many of Pompey's top boys come from Aldershot and have been known to turn out for some of Aldershot's bigger games. After one recent clash with Carlisle, five Aldershot lads received prison sentences. The link with Portsmouth has obviously meant hostility with Southampton but you have to go back many a long year to when the two clubs played a competitive match.

In the first round of the FA Cup, in November 2000, Aldershot were at home to Brighton, who, after Reading, must be considered the A Company's biggest rivals. An NCIS report on the game said, "Aldershot supporters assaulted a group of Brighton supporters in the build up to this match. Other Brighton supporters witnessed this. This led to a public house containing Aldershot supporters being attacked with bottles and glasses. One Aldershot supporter received serious facial injuries. During the match the supporters threw numerous missiles at each other across the segregation area. A strong police presence prevented any disorder at the end of the fixture." Jak admitted it was a bad day for the A Company, made worse by someone being on hand to photograph the assault on their pub. "Only a few lads came outside to front sixty Brighton. We were poor that day."

Taunton and jumped on the local train to Exeter Central. The Old Bill stopped sixty us at the station and sent us back to Taunton, so we drank there all day. However, at about nine o'clock that evening, we drove back to Exeter. There were only ten proper

Nick Harvey

Aldershot and Brighton fans clash violently outside a pub before a game in November 2000.

In more recent years Hereford have emerged as Aldershot's main non-league rivals. "They are always up for it, home and away," said Jak. "A couple of Aldershot lads were recently imprisoned for a forty-man off inside their ground." There was also disorder at the home fixture, despite extra police being drafted in from across Hampshire. Fifty Aldershot clashed with 40 Hereford but police believe that their preventative actions deterred greater disorder. The two clubs played one another again in the conference play-offs a few weeks later and an even bigger police operation was launched. Fifty officers were on duty, including two dog handlers, two officers from West Mercia Police who followed the Hereford mob, and the Force Support Unit, the specialist riot police more commonly deployed at Portsmouth and Southampton games. The police picked up the 60-strong Aldershot crew and escorted them to the ground. On the way they passed Hereford's crew but they were also hemmed in by police and the game passed off peacefully. The police's only complaint was the racial chanting aimed at the Asian referee by some Aldershot fans.

Exeter's more recent relegation has led to the renewal of hostilities. "We did them twice in the 2003/04 season," claimed Jak. "They were on the phone all day saying they were in Farnborough and that they were coming to Aldershot with thirty-five lads. They took so long about it that fifteen of us, all young lads, drove over there and battered them. Half of them ran. Then we drove the minibus to

lads. I was twenty-one and the second oldest, the rest were between fifteen and seventeen, but we attacked their boozer, and really did a good job. We got a lot of respect from Exeter for that, and it was the youth lads' first real off."

A few years earlier, the two sides met in the FA Cup in Exeter. The away end was severely over-crowded, and to avoid a crush many Aldershot fans spilled onto the pitch. The A Company used this as an opportunity to try to attack their counterparts, and several missiles were thrown, including a smoke bomb. It took police 30 minutes to restore order.

There was more trouble on the first day of the 2003/04 season with the visit of York. "York showed with a decent mob," recalled Jak. "There were a few little offs, and one very big one." As a result a mutual respect has now developed between the two.

ARSENAL

Ground: Formerly Highbury, now Arsenal Stadium
Firm: Gooners, the Herd
Rivals: Tottenham Hotspur, Manchester United
Police operations: Evild, Barron

To look at the current fan base inside the Arsenal Stadium, it is hard to believe that they once had one of the most feared hooligan mobs in London, and possibly the most organised anywhere in Britain.

Where the rows of seats are now occupied by middle-class season-ticket-holders, the North Bank was once home to Johnny Hoy, Nick the Hammer and Leggo, all early Arsenal legends. For many years in the late 1960s and early 1970s, the North Bank was virtually impregnable. Many tried to take it and all but a few failed. While football violence has not totally disappeared at Arsenal, few who politely applaud their title-winning teams of today can fathom the intimidation of the place that was the North Bank.

Founded in the 1880s by workers from the Woolwich Arsenal, Arsenal FC became a bastion of British football in the Thirties, winning four titles in five seasons between 1931 and 1935 and the FA Cup twice. More than 50,000 people packed into Highbury every fortnight to watch their hugely successful side. Arsenal carried on in similar vein after the war, winning the League in 1948 and 1953 and the FA Cup in 1950. Yet things had changed. War had ravaged a once-great squad, and the huge evacuation of people from London badly affected the club's support. Once the immediate post-war euphoria had died down, attendances were regularly only half the Thirties level. Floating supporters who once rushed to share in Arsenal's glory were increasingly making the short hop to White Hart Lane. "The bulk of Arsenal's drop in attendance occurred amongst the wartime generation of middle-aged working men, and their departure opened up a space for the kids on the terrace," wrote Philip Cohen and David Robins, the authors of *Knuckle Sandwich*. "Boys would no longer attend matches in the company of their fathers or uncles but now they went with each other. The lure of misbehaviour was now greater."

The occupants of entire estates were moved out of Islington in the immediate post-war years as the bomb-ravaged area was rebuilt but while the parents reconstructed their lives in new surroundings, many of the youngsters found the transition difficult. These were inner-city boys dumped in suburbia, and many did not like it. Some dabbled in local gang life and delinquency, but many others returned to their home, Arsenal. By the mid-Sixties football was fashionable, especially for the young. The World Cup had transformed the image of the game and at Arsenal players like Charlie George would become superstars. The exiled youngsters made the North Bank their real home.

In the 1966/67 season, the North Bank end – an "end" was a large, hooligan-oriented following who adopted one partricular end of the ground as their home – formed. They were a collection of small mobs reflecting the areas from where Arsenal support was drawn. So the local Essex Road, Chapel Street and Packington mobs were joined by groups from Basildon, Borehamwood, Uxbridge and Elstree. The emerging skinhead culture gave the North Bank an identity separate from the rest of the fans and intrinsically linked to violence.

The violence came thick and fast and in the very first year of the North Bank's existence as an "end", the club's hierarchy met to discuss containing the trouble. One idea suggested in October 1967 was for a concrete wall around the pitch to prevent supporters rushing on and disrupting the game. "The barrier, probably about four feet high, would be about six feet inside the existing retaining wall and would consist of pre-cast concrete slabs slotted into concrete posts," noted *The Times*.

The most infamous North Bank leader was Johnny Hoy. While each mob had their own top faces, Hoy ruled the end, and under his leadership the North Bank proved impregnable until 1972, when Manchester United took it. Hoy was said to be six feet two and 14 stone, though such was his reputation that many swear he was a lumbering giant. He was born close to the Highbury stadium and was believed to have had links to the Big Highbury, a notorious local gang. So concerned was the club at his ability to organise trouble that staff at the North Bank turnstiles were issued with his description in the hope of keeping him out. Invariably, they failed. There were perhaps some sympathetic stewards on the gates, because the North Bank leader was clearly noticeable in his long white butcher's coat, with "Arsenal" written all over it.

Before home matches, Hoy would gather together his core followers in the Long Bar of the Gunners pub. Plans would be hatched and weapons compared and passed around. Sometimes these included meat cleavers, sharpened combs and knuckledusters studded with broken razor blades. Waiting on the fringes of the bar and in the street outside were the young 'uns, eager to share in the plans.

Alongside Hoy there were a number of other prominents on the North Bank, each usually running their own small mob. Leggo led the Packington skins, while Nick "The Hammer" Russell boasted of leading an army of 400 hooligans who can "dish out more aggro than anyone else in the country." His sidekick, Pat Stone, added, "Russell never runs, he slugs it out with anyone. He's our leader." The leader of the Arsenal Bromley Boys was Jenko, who remained an Arsenal face into the early 1980s.

Arsenal also exported violence. In 1967 an FA Cup match took them to Bristol Rovers, where they hammered the locals and took the Tote End. Arsenal fans caused havoc twice at Leicester City and on the second occasion, the first game of the 1974 season, their exploits were extensively documented in the national press. They also overran Portsmouth in a FA Cup tie in 1971, as well as Wolves's own North Bank.

In April 1970, Arsenal took the Tottenham's Park Lane terrace at 2.15 p.m. and, to the now all too familiar chant, "Where are you?" they prepared themselves for the inevitable. Fifteen minutes later Tottenham arrived and mayhem broke out. Despite ten minutes of chaos, Arsenal could not be moved. "We took the Park Lane," Arsenal mocked their bitter rivals. They also won the game 1–0, before the fighting transferred into the neighbouring streets.

An even more satisfying result at White Hart Lane occurred the following season, when Arsenal arrived for the final game of the season needing one point to win the title. They won 1–0 and for every Arsenal fan there could not have been a more perfect ending to the campaign. The Gunners took over White Hart Lane and swarmed on to the pitch at the final whistle. With Spurs' fans long gone, some contented themselves by digging up the pitch. Five days later, Arsenal beat Liverpool in the FA Cup to complete the Double and then ran the Scousers ragged outside the ground.

Another London team to fall victim to Hoy's manoeuvres was Chelsea, who for four consecutive years had their Shed taken by their North London rivals. An Arsenal lad, who declined to be named, was involved in one of these assaults and recalled how they met at St Pancras Station and how he was shocked when Arsenal left the train wearing Chelsea scarfs. "What the fuck? I thought. But I was given a Chelsea scarf and told to put it on. I told them where to go, but they insisted and told me we would need them to get into the Shed. While on the train to Earls Court we met other Gooners with Chelsea scarves and one told us that Chelsea's main mob was about to board one of the following tubes. How he knew that I'll never know but he was spot on. The next train arrived and was what we were waiting for, the main mob was here. The doors opened and they were staring us in the face: 'Stockwell, Stockwell, Stockwell,' and 'Arsenal, where are you?' echoed through the station. Then the doors shut and up went the roar of 'Arsenal, Arsenal' and we battered them big time on the platform. One of our well known lads was fighting with one of Chelsea's main boys, the black fella with one arm missing, and the fighting carried on to the live rails. The Old Bill came from everywhere and the current was cut off and all trains stopped.

"We then set about walking to Chelsea, where we got a police escort straight into the Shed, so the trick with the blue scarves worked. We were in. 'Chelsea, Chelsea,' we sang, and before long we were joined by more and more Arsenal who had employed the same trick. The banter was great. 'Arsenal where are you?' we sang. The talk going around was of Arsenal getting a hiding at Earls Court – don't make me laugh. I was there. One of our old faces was recognised by a few Chelsea, but before anything could happen he or one of his mates pulled out a can of yellow paint and sprayed it all over them. It kicked off big time. We won one-nil that day and took the Shed."

Arsenal and Chelsea were bitter rivals on and off the pitch and several fights were arranged well away from football days. One was pre-planned in June 1974 for the West End of London, and hundreds of bootboys battled it out amongst the shoppers and tourists. This was the heyday of Arsenal hooliganism, but it was not to last. Their reputation was an invitation to others and the decline of the skinhead scene weakened the bond that held together the North Bank's different groups. Success on the pitch, which peaked in 1971, attracted floating supporters who were hardly likely to defend their end. Finally, age caught up with many of the early Arsenal leaders. Johnny Hoy was banned from the terrace he had made his own and was forced to take up residence in the Clock End, while Leggo earned a lengthy spell in Borstal. The North Bank became less cohesive. The big leaders were replaced by smaller, more independently minded mobs, and while they would come together when faced with bigger opponents, there was also an increased tendency to fight each another. The average age of the end also dropped, from 15-17 between 1968 and 1972 to 13-15 by 1973.

In 1972 Manchester United became the first team to take the North Bank and they did it in some style. Over 1,000 of the Red Army marched the mile or so to Highbury from King's Cross, wreaking havoc along the way. They steamed the North Bank and held it for the entire game. Chelsea, so long dominated by Arsenal, also took the North Bank. The decision to launch a major assault on Arsenal's home end was made on the day of the yellow paint incident. Arsenal claimed that day as a victory but so did Chelsea. The West Londoners admit that they initially backed off to avoid the lunatic with the paint, but their surge kept the intruders out of the heart of their end. "The Shed interpreted these events as a great victory," recalled Martin Knight. "Greenaway and Eccles [two Chelsea leaders] shook hands and slapped one another's backs. 'Next season, we take the North Bank,' announced Eccles."

By 1974, the North Bank still retained a hardcore of 500 lads but the action was gravitating more towards the opposite Clock End. Fewer police and the displacement of many of the early North Bank hard nuts meant a new end was born at Highbury.

As Arsenal's firm stuttered, others were getting older and more organised. Gunners fan Colin Ward, in *Steaming In,* gives a powerful account of difficult away trips to Middlesbrough and Bristol City in the 1976-77 season. He also recalls the changing mood at Highbury. "Watching Arsenal became a chore," he said. "They had become a diabolical team and in the season 1975-76 were almost relegated. On the terraces they had lost their credibility and people began taking liberties with them."

That season Arsenal played West Ham in the FA Cup. The Hammers came in huge numbers and took over the ground, even outnumbering Arsenal two-to-one in the North Bank. This was the fourth consecutive humiliation at the hands of the Hammers. One old-timer remembered, "We headed towards the ground and managed to walk straight into a huge mob of West Ham who had just smashed up the Arsenal Tavern and then walked with them hoping we wouldn't get sussed out. I took my scarf off and I don't think it went back on at all that day. We got into the ground about two o'clock. West Ham always got into opposition ends early. They

used to do the same at Spurs and at Chelsea. Their tactic was to fill it up with their mugs and idiots then wait for the home team firm to show up. The North Bank was already packed with them, so we headed down to the front where a load of younger Arsenal was grouping up. A large group of Arsenal came into the North Bank from the station entrance and steamed into West Ham. We ran up and joined them and took back a large part of the North Bank. We headed to the back where the younger Hammers were. Loads of West Ham were sitting down chatting and reading programmes when we hit them. Fun time. We all got digs in on the one we caught and for a few minutes it was a massacre. It sounds funny but the sound of Doc Martens running on terraces is a sound that loads of us old gits will remember. Nothing sounds quite like it.

"The OB formed lines on the North Bank, keeping both sets apart. I thought we had the upper hand and would get them out of the North Bank, I thought wrong. The idea lasted until West Ham came at us from behind and battered us at the back of the North Bank. As I said, we were the younger Arsenal and the Hammers were all big bastards. I had my jacket pulled over the top of my head and I was kicked to bits. I managed to protect my face but the rest of me was black and blue. There was a big surge and somehow I got away and found the rest of the Arsenal who were fighting West Ham on both sides. I got punched full in the face by a bloke twice my age and at least twice my size, it was the same all around me, men against boys and I knew we were well fucked.

"The game was one of the most one-sided I've ever seen. We just kept on scoring. I can't remember much of the detail as so much was happening around me. I got sussed out by some Hammers but one of them, seeing how young I was and knowing that I'd already been given a hiding, stopped the others from attacking me. He then told me to fuck off, so I did. After one of the goals, a group of about fifteen Arsenal standing to my right got steamed from behind by a huge group of Hammers. We were now getting done all over the place and my bottle had gone. It was time to keep quiet and to try and look unhappy as goal after goal went in. West Ham were going mental as the humiliation on the pitch got worse and worse."

The next season began no better. The first game

was at home to Bristol City and they too came in huge numbers and took over the North Bank, where they stayed throughout the game. Spurs were also beginning to emerge as a major force after several years in the doldrums and had twice taken the North Bank. At the away fixture in 1976, Arsenal received a pasting, inside and outside the ground. On Boxing Day 1977, it was the turn of Chelsea to take the North Bank, which they did in huge numbers. Apart from West Ham's appearance in the FA Cup game, this was the worst humiliation in their history. From that day Chelsea became the dominant of the two groups.

Arsenal improved as a team in the late Seventies, reaching the finals of both the FA Cup and the League Cup. Their success pitted them against Liverpool, then arguably the best team in Europe. Off the pitch Arsenal faced a torrid time at the hands of the Scousers. In 1978 the teams met in the League Cup semi-final and Arsenal packed two double-decker coaches for the first leg at Anfield. They stood and fought after the game, but the home firm won the day. There was further trouble between the two teams at the 1979 Charity Shield, and again Arsenal got battered.

It was at that match that many Londoners first saw the casual look amongst opposing fans, as Paul Webster noted in the book *Casuals*. "They were flicking their fringes out of their eyes like they all had nervous tics and were sporting some rather natty threads that I must admit looked quite impressive," he recalled. "It took some time for the new look to catch on but, just over a year later, it did. London went casual crazy after that, with every team in the capital having their well-turned-out crew. It quickly became more important to be seen as the best-dressed mob than to be the hardest." While West Ham adopted Burberry and diamond Pringle jumpers, Arsenal preferred Fila, and, in 1982, Nike trainers.

Another long-running feud began with Ipswich, largely as a result of the Norfolk club beating the Gunners in the 1978 FA Cup Final. Arsenal fans were incensed and attacked their rivals furiously outside Wembley. When the Londoners travelled to Ipswich in March 1979, there were 57 arrests and widespread disorder. This feud continued into the Eighties.

By the late Seventies, Arsenal also saw the emergence of a large number of black lads in their mob.

Their hooligans of the late Sixties had been largely white and many had been racist. They clashed with young black gangs on the local estates and the club was targeted for recruitment by both the National Front and the British Movement. This reflected both the area at the time and the lack of interest in football amongst the first generation Afro-Caribbean community. This changed. The composition of the local estates began to alter as immigration continued, and many of the more racist families moved out of London altogether. A preference for football over cricket brought a young generation of black lads on to the terraces. When Arsenal invaded Middlesbrough's Holgate in 1980, the majority of the 60-strong crew were black.

Arsenal's mob enjoyed a resurgence between 1979 and 1983 as a result of this new generation of lads coming through. Two separate mobs emerged, the Gooners and the Herd. The main face of the Gooners was a man called Denton Connor, known throughout the hooligan scene simply as Denton. The name Gooners actually originated with a group of Spurs hooligans who intended to chant it as a term of abuse (a play on the Goons and Gunners) but this was overheard by an Arsenal fan and adopted before it could be used by their opponents. Denton and some of the other leading Gooners were later to provide security for the Pet Shop Boys band, one of whom was a big Arsenal fan.

After a rearranged FA Cup game at Shrewsbury, a few of the Gooners went for a drink in the Three Fishes pub in the town centre. There were only half a dozen and they occupied their time chatting up local women and offering them free tickets for a forthcoming Pet Shop Boys gig. Several lads from the local English Border Front were so outraged that they mobbed up 30-handed and attempted to storm the pub. After an initial flurry of thrown glasses, one of the Arsenal lads, a large-framed black man, stood up and pulled out a blade from under his coat. The story that swept Shrewsbury at the time was this was a machete, but this could simply be the EBF trying to save face. It was men against boys and several of the Shrewsbury lads gladly handed themselves over to the police on their arrival.

The Herd was led by a white lad called Miller. They were separate mobs but, of course, came together for big matches. The Gooners followed old legends like Hoy into the Clock End and by 1980 this was firmly established as their end. It was into here, in September 1980, that a 15-year-old Stoke City fan ventured. Mark Chester was to grow up to be one of football's big men and to lead the notorious Naughty Forty, but back in 1980 he was taught a lesson in hooligan in what he described as "the theatre of hate" in his memoir *Naughty*.

"We were embedded in the heart of the Clock End, surrounded by sarcastic remarks and throat-slitting motions and having cigarette ends flicked at us continually. Instead of punching or kicking us, the Arsenal lads toyed with us, like a cat that has all the time in the world to terrify a mouse before moving in for the kill. Throughout the day I had seen dozens of old Stoke faces that normally would be high-spirited and irrepressible. Down in the tea bar, as I stood with my back to the wall, I could pick them out all trying to look inconspicuous and doing it so poorly that they would receive one straight punch in the nose from out of nowhere, and then be left to chew on it. It was nothing short of torture and the cockneys loved it. It was plain to see that Stoke were not ready for this new decade of football violence."

A memorable 3–2 FA Cup Final victory over Manchester United took Arsenal into Europe. Wins over Fenerbache, FC Magdeburg, IFK Gothenburg and Juventus led to the final, where they faced the Spanish team Valencia. Unlike Liverpool, Leeds, Manchester United or local neighbours, Tottenham, Arsenal caused little trouble in Europe, with the exception of the second leg of the semi-final where a group of Italians were repelled. That was to change in May 1980 in the Belgian capital, Brussels. There was sporadic disorder before the game as many of the 20,000-plus Arsenal fans began arriving. The city was on a high state of alert and the arrest of 39 Englishmen on this first night did little to reassure its people. Arsenal lost the game on penalties and the locals' worst fears materialised as thousands of Londoners went on the rampage.

Arsenal re-established themselves again in London and the early 1980s saw a number of frightening clashes with West Ham's ICF. These occurred both inside their respective grounds and also at a number of clubs across London. West Ham took the North Bank on numerous occasions during the late Seventies and humiliated the North Londoners

when their clubs met in the FA Cup Final at Wembley. However, the most infamous battle for the North Bank was in 1982. The match is remembered for the death of a young Arsenal fan who was stabbed near Finsbury Park station shortly after the game.

There is little that both sides agree on about that day. West Ham claim that Arsenal were picked off as they arrived in small groups, and were eventually chased right out of the North Bank, with many spilling onto the pitch. A smoke grenade added to the chaos, and when the smoke had cleared, West Ham were firmly in control of the back of the terrace, with three separate East End mobs uniting in victory.

"Our numbers were strengthened further by other mates who had been ejected from the ground only to pay to come back in again," remembered West Ham face Terry Sherrin in the book *Congratulations, You Have Just Met the I.C.F.* "We were all rightly full of ourselves and taunted Arsenal rotten. We conducted our own musical, singing the 'ICF, ICF' chant and winding them up with, 'Thank you very much for the North Bank Highbury, thank you very much, thank you very, very, very much.'"

The West Ham account has been challenged by Arsenal lads. "We had firms on both the right and left sides, and try as they might, the ICF could not get past them," claimed one. "The ICF on the right as you face the pitch got smashed, and I never saw them again. After the smoke bomb, the ones in the middle and those on the left got together and all hell had broken loose. Everyone was into 'em, firm, shirts, scarves, old, youth, nobody was backing down. They got pushed up and slightly to the left, about sixty, where they were surrounded by OB. Arsenal had a serious go at getting through the Old Bill, but there were so many that it couldn't be done. Bloody ICF, spent all their lives trying to avoid the Old Bill, I bet they were glad of them that day. Anyone remember the chant echoing from the North Bank: 'We thought you were hard, we were wrong, we were wrong'?"

What was not in question was that Arsenal were back as a major mob. The early Eighties saw them give it and take it. They ambushed Spurs at Birmingham's New Street Station on the day they were away at West Brom and their rivals were playing an FA Cup semi at Villa Park. They rioted in York during an FA Cup game in 1985, clashed away at Watford, stopped off in Northampton on their way back from a game in the Midlands, and had a long-running feud with QPR that often involved the firms fighting at central London nightspots. They were one of the few firms to walk from Liverpool's Lime Street Station to Goodison Park undetected by the police, on a Friday night on the eve of the Grand National, and put up a spirited show after the game, refusing a police offer of public transport and returning to the station as they had left it, on foot.

Arsenal had rarely met Millwall in the early Seventies, as the South London team languished in the lower divisions. They more than made up for it in the late Eighties and early Nineties. In 1988, Arsenal drew Millwall at home in the FA Cup, and between late September 1992 and January 1995, the teams played each other five times in the FA and League cups. The ties are remembered for the hatred directed at Arsenal striker Ian Wright, but events off the pitch were much worse.

Millwall arrived early in North London for the 1988 cup tie, taking over a couple of the pubs normally frequented by Arsenal. When the Gooners finally appeared, they were a motley band of about 100, though many were untested and hangers-on. Arsenal pushed aside the police and went for the pub but a bottle thrown by a younger lad at the window only alerted the occupants to their presence and gave them time to counter-attack. Few Arsenal present will forget the Millwall fan who came from the pub using a petrol-filled Ronson lighter as a makeshift flamethrower. While one Arsenal lad was set alight and was rushed to hospital, reinforcements meant the Gooners' overwhelming numbers gave them the edge. The police managed to regroup and, despite a few minor skirmishes, managed to see out the day without further mass disorder.

The hostility aimed at Ian Wright only intensified the rivalry. In January 1995, Arsenal travelled to the New Den for another FA Cup match. The two mobs clashed outside the Blind Beggar pub in East London and in the neighbouring Sainsbury's car park. The police, when they eventually arrived, forced the groups apart, lining up Arsenal on one side of the road and Millwall on the other. Arsenal

claimed the day, which made the replay, eleven days later, a certainty for trouble. Millwall turned up in huge numbers, taking over the streets and most of the Highbury ground. The 500 officers on duty could do little to prevent the South Londoners over-running the place. Forty-three arrests were made and a further 73 were ejected from the ground. To add to Arsenal's demoralisation, Millwall won the game 2–0.

The disorder with Millwall was the trigger for the Met's investigation into Arsenal's mob, and Operation Evild was born. While some undercover operations lasted months, Evild took only a few weeks. In the first week of February, 90 officers from the Met and the British Transport Police raided 26 homes across North London and the Home Counties and arrested 19 men. Among the items seized, which were proudly shown off to the press as an obvious sign of guilt, were rifles, flick knives, a crossbow and coshes. A number of diaries, photographs and scrapbooks were also displayed for the eager press. "By arresting these people we hope to have broken the back of a core element bent on violence at Arsenal matches," said Detective Superintendent Graham Howard, who led the investigation.

With little of the same fanfare that accompanied their arrest, the charges against the men were dropped a few months later, following the collapse of a Chelsea trial that threw the entire police undercover operation into question.

As several prominent Arsenal lads awaited their legal fate, West Ham were still dishing out the punishment. A league game towards the end of the season saw the ICF launch a ferocious attack on a tube train full of younger Arsenal lads. Perhaps it was coincidence, but the previous tube, full of older lads, was missed. One Gooner gave this account of the terrifying attack: "When it pulled into Plaistow, the entire platform was full of blokes and I must admit I did not realise what was going on until the doors opened and I heard the ICF cry go up. Simultaneously, loads of windows got put through, with everything from bricks to fire extinguishers. Then they all piled on and started hitting out indiscriminately. I even saw some fella who I knew was West Ham get hit by one of the long light bulbs you get on the tube. Unfortunately for those in the carriages, the doors then shut and the tube continued its journey. It was unfortunate in that the ICF were still on the train."

By 1990, Arsenal were once again a hooligan force to be reckoned with, though their opportunities for trouble were diminishing, especially in the capital. In 1993, NCIS claimed that Arsenal were the main firm in London, a view unlikely to be shared by Spurs and Chelsea. At one game at Stamford Bridge they bought 100 tickets for the home end from a tout, but unbeknown to them, Chelsea had been alerted, and as Arsenal entered they were unceremoniously beaten back. The following season it was Chelsea's turn to make a show, this time buying 200 tickets for the Arsenal end from the same tout. Three hundred Chelsea thugs made the journey across London and the two mobs clashed outside a Gooner pub. Two further clashes occurred before the game but the main event happened afterwards as Chelsea searched for an Arsenal pub where they were told a mob was waiting. The Chelsea crew splintered as they failed to find the pub, while others lost interest and slipped away to the tube. According to Chelsea, an Arsenal mob of 200 then attacked a small but tidy mob of 50. "It was murder," said one Chelsea fan. "They were picking up anything – traffic bollards, the lot – and we were getting hammered." One

Chelsea fan called Marcus was slashed down his back and needed 200 stitches.

The following season Chelsea returned for revenge. "The mood was nasty," recalled Chelsea's Martin King. "This was going to be no ordinary ruck. What had been done to Marcus had personalised things." In the event there was no major disorder as the police were alert to the trouble the previous year and were out in force. A few Chelsea went into Arsenal's main pub and demanded to know who had knifed up their friend, but no-one stepped forward.

The Arsenal firm's forays out of London were becoming few and far between. The gravity of hooligan strength was shifting out of the top division and certainly out of London. Arsenal, like most of the other London firms, had been affected by the police undercover operations, and though many collapsed, the prospect of several years in jail did concentrate the minds of many. In January 1990, Arsenal drew Stoke City away in the FA Cup. Many in London saw Stoke as one of *the* emerging mobs in Britain, though they'd had a sizeable hooligan following since the Seventies. Conversely, the lads of Stoke probably didn't think much of Arsenal before the game, which is why they were so surprised with the Gooner turnout that day.

"We had a bit of a shock when about 400 game-

Mirrorpix

Supporters of Arsenal and Turkish team Galatasaray fight in a square in Copenhagen before their UEFA Cup final in 2000.

as-fuck Gooners steamed us back into the paddock," recalled Stoke leader Mark Chester. "We had nothing else to do but fight back. This lasted for just a few seconds when the rest of the assembled Stoke nutters – casuals, scruffs, old blokes in donkey jackets – joined us and drove the masses of Gooners back up the road. I remember everybody shouting, 'Where's Denton, the big black bastard?' as he was singled out as their top lad."

During the 1990s Arsenal had numerous clashes with a resurgent Spurs, though the scale of the disorder was nothing on the scale of fights in the Seventies. The pendulum was swinging back and most of the incidents were caused by Tottenham's rising mob. In one, thirty lads from each side exchanged bottles, glasses and other makeshift weapons during a late-night fight at the Gas Light pub in Finsbury Park. "They set up fights using mobile phones," commented Superintendent Andy Smith. Earlier, a police operation involving 250 officers prevented major disruption during the game.

The *News of the World* was in condemnatory mood when it reported yet another Arsenal v Spurs encounter. "Yesterday's outbreak of violence suggests that what used to be London derby rivalry is now something a hell of a lot worse. It's hatred. When Wright tucked his penalty away at Highbury, the ensuing violence proved that a football match had turned into a battle zone. Wright saluted his strike, the Spurs fans wanted to rip him apart. Has it got so bad in North London that a footballer cannot celebrate a goal without fear of inciting scenes of hatred? What happened at Highbury cuts to the core. A thug mentality has taken over this once great derby and scarred it beyond belief."

In the nineties, a ritual war of words between Arsene Wenger and Alex Ferguson was matched by growing hatred between the two sets of supporters. While Arsenal were never able to properly compete with Man United's combined mobs, there have been a few small, nasty clashes between the two in recent years. At a league game in August, 1999, a United fan was dragged off a train and badly beaten on the platform by a group of Arsenal thugs. A subsequent court case heard that the Gooners had shadowed a rival mob out of Highbury after their club's 1–0 defeat. The fight was caught on CCTV and the police immediately launched Operation Barren to identify those responsible. A few months later they raided the homes of a number of Arsenal fans. "We have got more than twenty very, very bad alleged Arsenal hooligans who picked on a particular Manchester United fan," the officer in charge of the operation boasted. He believed that, for the first time, the organisers rather than the foot soldiers had been implicated.

Arsenal were back at the top of British football, trading trophies with United, while both mobs traded punches at every given opportunity. After an FA Cup semi-final defeat at Villa Park, famous for a Ryan Giggs wonder goal, thugs clashed on the pitch, and a few years later, after Arsenal again lost in the same competition at the same venue, a mass brawl outside was regarded by many as one of the worst fights between the two firms in 20 years.

However, Arsenal's soaring club success did not translate to any significant increase in hooliganism. Football had become trendy and nowhere more so than Arsenal, where Nick Hornby's *Fever Pitch* epitomised the massive surge of middle-class interest in the game. The support base of those attending Arsenal games changed dramatically, and all-seater stadiums and a six-year waiting list for season tickets kept out a new generation of hooligans.

But Arsenal fans could still cause trouble. In May 2000, the club was in the UEFA Cup final against the Turkish side, Galatasaray, in the Danish capital, Copenhagen. For once, most lads across England were rooting for the Gunners. The reason was simple: Galatasaray had played Leeds United in the semi-finals and two Leeds fans were killed before the game. A plethora of hooligan websites urged Arsenal into battle. Two thousand police were on duty for the game, a fifth of the city's entire force, but that did not prevent fierce fighting in the central square before the game which left serious casualties on both sides. One Arsenal fan was stabbed in the stomach and a Turk had his ear almost severed. The injuries could have been worse; a small group of Turkish fans found themselves surrounded by a much larger group of Arsenal and were only rescued when police drove a fleet of riot vans into the middle of the fight and let off teargas. Thirty-seven Arsenal fans were later banned from attending games after being identified from photographs and television footage in Copenhagen.

In another sign of the changing world of football and Arsenal, this trouble was beamed live into homes across the world, and media overkill brought an inevitable police clampdown. Newspapers ran "name and shame" campaigns, and images of dozens of Arsenal lads were plastered in most of the national dailies. Many arrests followed, creating an air of distrust among the ranks of the Herd that persists to this day.

Further reading: *Knuckle Sandwich*, Philip Cohen and David Robins (Penguin), *Steaming In*, Colin Ward (Simon & Schuster)

ASTON VILLA

Ground: Villa Park
Firms: The Steamers, C Crew, Villa Hardcore, Villa Hardcore Apprentices
Rivals: Birmingham City, West Bromwich Albion

"This day was a long time coming. Yes, we'd have our offs in town every now and then, but this was the first league meeting since 1987 and every fucker was out for it: C Crew, Steamers, Villa Youth and Hardcore." So one member of the Villa Hardcore described their most infamous fight in recent memory, against hated rivals Birmingham City. The so-called Battle of Rocky Lane, in November 2002, led to arrests and jail terms – and several different versions of events. For the Villa mob, it was a day to remember.

"About eight of us arrived in New Street, none the wiser as to where the top lads had decided to meet. We were waiting for a phone call, so we decided to have a wander down to City's side of town. Caps and Stone Island badges removed, two of us had a walk into Hurst Street and taxi after taxi was pulling up, stopping outside PJ's [a Birmingham City meeting place]. Naturally we had a walk past and a quick look in through the window and straight off clocked about a dozen of their main lads at the bar, mostly their prominent black lads.

"We got the call to go to Sensations. We'd never heard of the place but it was right in their back yard in Moseley and we jumped in a taxi. We walked in and were met by one of *the* main Villa faces of the C Crew and realised none of 'our lads' [Villa Hardcore, a separate group] were in this place. En route we had been told that Hardcore were firming

up in O'Reilly's. In Sensations was every face from C Crew and the Steamers, fifty-plus with more taxis arriving. We knew this firm weren't going just to show their faces. The two main faces of the C Crew had actually walked and timed the route to perfection from the club to the ground to land on the Zulus. Military precision at its finest.

"The best part about this was that the Zulus were scouting O'Reilly's, they had a couple of black lads driving past and knew that our top man was in there and approximately 250 lads. What they didn't know though was that there was a firm of now 100-plus sitting right in their manor. We were about to hit the fuckers from two ways.

"We jumped in a taxi for O'Reilly's to go on the mooch for tickets. We pulled up in the middle of a load of lads running towards us. As we turned, we were bombarded by bottles, glasses, ball bearings, an exhaust pipe, carburettors and wheel trims. The fucking gypos had robbed a scrapyard on the way up. I got hit by a ball bearing and the lad next to me had his head gashed by an exhaust pipe bracket.

"Once their barrage had gone we ran down to them as they started shouting their predictable war cry. Initial punches were thrown and after that there seemed to be a force field between everybody and a bit of a stand-off; it was as if no one wanted to commit and go in first. We knew the OB were standing there filming and everyone was conscious of it, punches here and there were thrown and we could see their main faces were there straight from the off.

"These were the main players on both sides at it and trying to get it on. It developed into minor scuffles from there really, Blues would shout, 'Zulus,' and come forward, a couple of their main faces would throw some punches and then retreat as Villa stood and vice versa, all accompanied by the obligatory bouncing. In my opinion a right tear-up was spoilt by OB and more and more lads were trying to pull caps down, hoods up and scarves round their faces as OB were lapping it up and taking plenty of footage. You can't knock anyone for not going full pelt with them wankers stood about twenty foot away filming. I still can't believe the prison sentences handed out for that.

"Funniest thing I saw was one of our lads sneak round the side behind some railings with a drainpipe or something and just start hitting them with it. I can't say how long it went on for but it seemed ages but in reality it never is. As the stand-off ensued, OB were arriving by the vanload, and it was game over as I felt an extendable truncheon across my shoulders and was told to fuck off. One thing that has to be cleared up though. Blues keep telling us how their forty stood against our 250. What did they think it was, Rourke's Drift? It was numbers even, forty a side. As people in O'Reillys realised the Zulus had turned up, more and more lads were running down but were stopped by meat wagons blocking the road. People were slow to react out of the boozer because of the numerous shout of 'Zulus' in the day, all the others being false alarms, so the cry-wolf element had set in.

"So what could have been ruck of the century developed into a bit of a Mexican stand-off. Score draw. Both firms had tried to get it on but it didn't work out. Old Bill rounded everybody up and pushed us back on to O'Reilly's car park and started their filming and checking for match tickets in preparation for the escort to the Sty. We got thrown out because we hadn't got tickets so decided to walk the back way in to town.

"As we approached the Sty we could see the helicopter buzzing and that going-off roar. What a sight to see the Zulus running across the road as the C Crew landed. Blues had been turned over on their own manor. They tried to come the crack about their top boys weren't there but they fucking were. The fact of the matter is most of the Zulus who turned up at Rocky Lane were at the McDonalds island. The ones who stood got done and the others ran. Lovely seeing the C Crew rounded up by the Old Bill and escorted to the Sty past us singing, 'One-nil to the Villa Boys,' as we gave them a salute. Blues had their chance and blew it."

* * *

The Third Division was an insult for a club of Aston Villa's size. They might not have had the most successful footballing record in the country but a club that could attract crowds of over 55,000 should not have been here; it wasn't right. As if to show their disgust at their new opponents, Villa fans ran amok, starting with their opening game away at Chesterfield. There was, to some Villa fans, simply no other way to behave.

Villa fans continued to cause trouble at away matches but did not always come out on top. In early September 1972, they came badly unstuck at Cardiff. The Quinton mob, mainly skins from the Quinton area of Birmingham, managed to get into the Cardiff end before the game and while they held their own for a while, the sheer power of angry Welshmen forced them out and viciously ran through them by the time the referee blew for half-time.

Villa's away trip to Midlands rivals Forest in 1973 was another difficult game, as one Quinton veteran remembers. "It was a manic day start to finish. Villa were near the top of league and took about 6-8,000 to Forest. Only two weeks earlier there had been a lot of trouble at a night League Cup match, with Villa getting the better of it. Villa got marched to ground, with not a lot going on, then at the ground the fun started. First their East Stand mob had a go before kick-off and got battered down the terracing to the corner of the Trent End and several attempts were made to get into the Trent End, but no way would they let us.

"About ten minutes from the end, both Forest and Villa piled out of the ground at the same time. We ran round the back of Trent End by the river and chased what we thought was the complete Trent End. They ran up the ramp to the ground end of Trent Bridge and turned and blocked the ramp and couldn't be shifted. Turned out about 100 Forest were holding us up. Meanwhile the remainder had charged into the middle of Villa from inside the Trent End, where they had been hiding. Some Villa were forced into the river, most notably an Asian lad who nearly drowned until he was fished out by a Forest skingirl. There was now chaos and Villa got split into small groups on and around the bridge and it ended up as everyone for themselves to reach the station. Arkwright Street became a mass of little offs all the way to the station and some Villa at the station were in a right mess. It has to go down as the worst doing I have ever seen the Villa get.

"However, Boxing Day the same season, revenge was sweet. What few Forest brought made their way into the Witton to be met by one of the most horrendous gatherings I have ever seen. Poor bastards, I almost felt sorry for them – only almost."

Villa also came unstuck away to Oxford in 1973, despite taking two full special trains of 800 on each. They went straight into the home end and for a while faced little opposition. Then they fell for a classic diversion as ten Oxford came on to the pitch and taunted their opponents. Villa moved forward, unaware that a sizeable Oxford firm had mobbed up behind them and they too surged forward, forcing Villa out of their end and onto the pitch.

The team was enjoying a rich vein of form and in April 1975 they won promotion back into the First Division away at Sheffield Wednesday. Villa not only took the home end, which was no mean feat as Wednesday had a decent reputation, but all the other stands as well. After the final whistle at least 2,000 fans swarmed onto the pitch in peaceful invasion, many dropping to their knees to worship manager Ron Saunders.

A new mob was emerging at Villa called the Steamers. They made their first appearance when 100 got into Man City's Kippax and ran the home fans – hence the name Steamers. Another big battle was against Manchester United's Red Army at a service station in 1975. There was such mayhem that football coaches were subsequently banned from service stations unless approved by the police. The Steamers' main faces included Woody, Melvyn, Foxy, Mouse, Big H, Dennis, Goddard, Rosco, Johnny Green, Dewar, Ginger, Dave, and Pete the Greek. They drank in the Hole in the Wall pub in Birmingham city centre and before big home games, such as those against the Blues, literally thousands would congregate and walk from there to St Andrew's. Such was their connection to the pub that for many years a plaque with over 100 of their names hung over the bar. They were mates, drinking partners and comrades in battle.

While Melvyn was the Steamers' leader, and remained active until the mid-Nineties, better known was Pete the Greek. "At one game he head-butted a police horse which was part of the barrier keeping our boys from getting at Man U fans at a home game," recalled a Villa old-timer. "He was charged and it made front page of *Evening Mail*." Another lad remembered a Third Division game at Preston in the early Seventies: "We were discovered by the Preston boys who trapped us in a residential cul-de-sac. Pete was with us and whereas most of us thought things were looking grim, he set about smashing the wooden fences down and handing us all out planks for our last stand. The Preston boys, while outnumbering us big time, started to lose a bit of their aggression. Pete had had enough and

decided we should get into them. There was chaos but suddenly we were on top and Preston were scattering – those that weren't dropping. What had happened was that the next train had arrived full of Villa, who had somehow stumbled across our predicament and attacked Preston from the rear."

Villa were given a timely reminder that not all days were as successful as the trip to Man City when they got a taste of "Tartan Terror". In October 1976, the club played host to Scottish giants Rangers in a mid-season friendly. Nearly 100 people were arrested and the game had to be abandoned after Rangers fans stormed the pitch (see GLASGOW RANGERS). It was a salutary lesson in terrace mayhem from the Glasgow hordes, though the *Birmingham Post* partly blamed Aston Villa, saying that they should have known that any match with Rangers was likely to attract trouble. "Villa were not obliged to play the game," wrote journalist Ian Williams. "Indeed, if the club had conducted a quick survey among the residents of Aston, it would have received an abrupt answer. And that answer would have been NO – never in a month of Sundays."

Almost exactly a year later, it was Villa's turn to feel the media spotlight after their fans wrought havoc at Leicester. The police were unprepared for the thousands of Villa fans who travelled, and with the away end already full and another two specials on their way, packed with Villa's boys, the club was forced to open up another section of the Kop which was supposed to be for home fans. The police formed a human line to separate supporters engaged in missile tennis.

The day was covered extensively in the *Leicester Mercury*:

Police sensed the rising fear of aggression and were preparing for bigger than usual trouble outside the ground at the final whistle. So, as is standard procedure men inside the ground were pulled out to take station at predetermined spots to keep the two sides apart in the streets.

The City were now losing 2-0 and the game was 'dead'. As the missiles became more frequent there was an outbreak of fighting on the terraces and Leicester fans surged up the low wall, over the advertising boards and on to the pitch.

Police and stewards tried to hold them back but in vain and Referee Robinson had no option but to take the players off the pitch for several minutes until order was restored.

But now the situation on the terraces had deteriorated. In Pen One, Villa fans, some of them drunk, smashed the huge reinforced glass panels at the back with their feet, elbows and even with their hands to get further ammunition for the fusillade.

Police, who had been outside, or should have been moving out, had to stay put and the situation meant that the defences at the final whistle were not as strong or as complete as normal.

The policemen worked valiantly and their main aim was to keep the rival fans apart at all costs. In one spot, one spot alone, there was a huge hole in the police lines and through it poured the hooligans bent on terrorising the streets. At least 200 fans charged down Sawday Street, kicking cars, hurling bricks at windows and building up into frenzy. When they arrived in Aylestone Road the battle was near. They found that they were in an unpoliced area between two units of officers, one heading Leicester fans on to and around Almond Way and the other taking villa fans across the Black Pad between the Tigers ground and the Fosse Industrial Unit.

Here the hooligans saw their chance and when one of the police lines was broken briefly it was a battleground. Bottles, cans, stones, coins, nuts and bolts ... there was a rain of missiles that injured many people including police officers.

And there was some frenzied fighting, mainly with the boot being used as the major weapon and one supporter was kicked for almost two minutes by a group of a dozen Villa followers and was out cold until just before the ambulances arrived. The police waded in and separated the gangs but there were several more confrontations on a lesser scale in the next few minutes. There was little doubt that Villa hooligans began the trouble but Leicester's lunatic fringe seemed determined to finish it and every available policeman was at stretch until buses, private cars and trains left.

Disorder had become so common that in September 1978 the club was forced to issue an appeal to its own supporters. "The message this week from Aston Villa to a section of our supporters is, IF YOU CAN'T BEHAVE, STAY AWAY. There is no point in beating about the bush in this matter because we are talking

about the people coming to Villa Park who, quite simply, we do not want. And it will come as no surprise to know that we are talking about some of the so-called fans who frequent the Wilton End of the ground. There is no doubt in our minds that, on occasions, people wearing Villa colours have provoked opposition fans in that section of the ground."

There was no need to provoke Chelsea when they arrived later that season. The Londoners were already relegated and their hardcore wanted to go out in style. Rather than target the Wilton End, they aimed for the huge – and inviting – Holte End. Chelsea infiltrated the Holte in small groups and then, on the signal from Chelsea legend Eccles, the roar went up and the home fans were cleared out. There was also trouble outside the ground. In one of the more horrific attacks, some Asian shopkeepers were attacked with motorbike chains by a group of Chelsea from Hounslow, who would become known as the Headhunters. Twenty-five years on, many of those involved in that attack were still active at Chelsea.

Chelsea was not to be the only London club to take the Holte. The following season a small group of young West Ham fans, including one Andy Swallow, decided to make a name for themselves by entering the Villa kop. To roars of approval from the rest of the club's travelling army, they scattered the home fans, a victory that saw the birth of West Ham's Inter City Firm.

In March 1980 Villa had the chance for revenge when they played at West Ham in the quarter-finals of the FA Cup but the C Crew were to receive one of their worst beatings, as one lad remembers. "We were playing a Second Division side and with 8,000 Villa we thought we'd be OK. We had never taken that amount before and been turned over, sheer weight of numbers would make it impossible, or so we thought.

"We came in behind the goal and all you could hear was, 'Come on you Irons.' About 100 of their finest had infiltrated our end at about 2.45 p.m. and did what could be best described as rabbit manoeuvres – they came in, belted a few, caused chaos and then fucked off. I looked and saw the same kids in their section but every fifteen minutes or so they came back in, via the help of the stewards. All the kids getting nicked were Villa.

"In the second half it got worse. There were stewards at the gates turning a blind eye as they rushed in and out and many to this day believe they were in on the planned attacks. It was a bit hit and run by West Ham throughout, then they attacked en masse. As Villa tried to get out they were met by mobs of them waiting underneath the stands and loads of Villa lads were wandering back in, bemused and covered in claret.

"Generally none of us had ever seen this before. They were organised, we were naïve, and fear set in for many. It was as bad as it gets when you're seeing people you look up to getting swarmed over and battered. On the pitch was no better and they scored in the last minute, a disputed penalty, which should have led to a reprieve but outside they still came at us, hundreds of them, and there was no hiding place. Everyone was scattered as only a few were holding it together.

"Four of us made our way back to the car. We got spotted by around fifty lads who proceeded to smash the car. After a couple of attempts we managed to get it going, though we had two smashed windows and one dented side panel – and they had won." Congratulations, you have just met the ICF.

The 1980/81 season saw Villa dominate the domestic league. They won their first championship since 1901 with the bonus of doing the double over their fierce rivals Birmingham. The following season, the team won the European Cup, and in 1983, the European Super Cup. It was a good time for one side of Birmingham but success did little to reduce the violence, much to the anger of residents who had to endure repeated battles down their streets. The problem became so severe that they even suggested setting up a vigilante group to protect their houses. To head off this growing resentment, the club announced, in October 1980, plans to create a new coach park and a policy to shepherd away fans straight to the ground on their arrival and back again immediately after the match, thus reducing the possibility of them clashing with locals.

The surrender of the Holte End to Chelsea and West Ham was a huge humiliation for Villa lads. While they had traditionally concentrated on piling into the away fans in the Wilton, they had left their own kop vulnerable. A new mob emerged to prevent further incursions. Called the C Crew, it took its name from the bottom right corner of the Holte,

the first line of defence against enemy infiltration. In its heyday it could muster 500 lads. Main faces included Brownie, Billy, Black Danny, Heaffy, Coley and Fordie.

Black Danny was to earn infamy among the Villa lads. A founder member of the C Crew, he was tall, skinny, and game. "He, along with two others, made assault on Scunthorpe's home in a League Cup game in the late Seventies at half-time, clearing their end," remembered one Villa lad. "He used to box at a place called Alcan Plate in the Birmingham area of Lee Village. The Zulus heard he was there and forty of them came down to the venue after the boxing had finished. They were outside waiting for him, giving it large, but he only pulls a fucking sword out, cue no fucker came near him and probably that's when he was started to be taken seriously. I wouldn't say that he was the leader but he had a very game firm around him."

With Villa challenging Liverpool's dominance of domestic football, it was not surprising that their fans clashed repeatedly during this period. "Our major rows in the late Seventies always seemed to involve Liverpool," said one ex-Steamer. "We always took a large following up there and always seemed to get split up, either on the buses from the station, or walking through the park to and from the coaches. Away games didn't come much worse than Anfield and in the return match at Villa Park, there was always an 'equaliser'."

C Crew continued where the Steamers left off. In 1980, soon after the mob was formed, Villa took a hammering at Liverpool, none more so than Black Danny, who was also targeted because of his colour. For the next Liverpool visit, they were out for revenge. "After the shit we had at Anfield in 1980, especially Black Danny, C Crew decided we would hit 'em and hit 'em early," recalled one member. "We waited for the train to come in, allowed them to get up the escalators, then wallop, we hit them from everywhere, though unfortunately there was a lot of steel on show. Liverpool lads were running into shops, Villa running after them slashing and stabbing. Loads of them were cut and Black Danny was nicked but being six foot four he wasn't hard to pick out. It wasn't just him but he was charged with doing six of them. The Liverpool lads actually had more numbers but the Villa lads were wild and were slashing every fucker they could catch, there was blood flowing on the pavement and shop doorways. To make it worse it was going on in full view of shoppers, who were screaming."

Fearing reprisals, C Crew took seven coaches to their next away game at Liverpool. They were, says one Villa lad, "tooled up to fuck. That gives an indication of the hatred for Liverpool then." Black Danny received a hefty prison sentence but C Crew were on a high, following their team across England and into Europe. So confident that 100 lads even got into the Birmingham kop and took it to the Zulu mob higher up the terrace.

In April 1982, they hit international headlines after kicking off in the semi-finals of the European Cup against Anderlecht. Hundreds of C Crew made the trip, many without tickets, but with touts and locals only too willing to sell, getting into the ground was easy. The tone was set an hour before kick-off when two Anderlecht supporters came on the pitch with their club's flag. Two Villa fans jumped out of the crowd and began punching and kicking them. The police did not intervene and allowed the English fans to climb back into the crowd. Encouraged by the police inaction, and furious at the anti-British Falklands chants of some locals, 100 Villa began moving towards the home fans behind a goal. Small skirmishes broke out almost instantly until eventually the police moved in wielding batons.

Twenty minutes into the game, mass violence erupted as rival gangs exchanged punches and kicks behind the goal. Supporters spilled onto the pitch, some to escape, others to give chase. Several Villa players went over in a bid to calm down the fans and it worked – temporarily. The game was held up for eight minutes while riot squads moved in. One policeman was carried out unconscious. The game finally continued with a line of riot police behind the goal to separate the rival fans. Forty fans were arrested and twenty-six injured.

Villa's manager warned that the behaviour of the fans could cost the club its place in the final with Bayern Munich, while chairman Ron Bendall claimed, "These weren't our supporters. Thy came here and slept rough in the park. We saw some wandering around about carrying bottles of whisky. We took all the precautions we could with forms and photographs and passports. We can't be blamed."

A spokesman for the Brussels police was not convinced. He called Villa fans "animals" and said, "They are a disgrace to the English flag. They are not the sort of people we want back in this country. All they want to do is drink and cause trouble." Three years later, at the city's Heysel Stadium, his words came back to haunt the football world.

The following day, as Villa and the English footballing authorities prepared for disciplinary action, Anderlecht's club secretary, Michael Verschueren, demanded that the English club be kicked out of Europe. "We sympathise with clubs who take every step possible but slowly and surely we are getting into deeper trouble. Something has to be done." He said that the halt in the game disrupted his side's concentration and demanded that either Villa be booted out or at the very least the game be replayed.

There was an agonising wait for UEFA to decide their punishment. Many feared that the club would be made an example of because of years of riots involving English clubs abroad. Meanwhile, UEFA's disciplinary committee secretary added his concern over the behaviour of the English in Europe. "Brussels has been hit three times," he told reporters, and the city would soon ban matches with English fans. In an echo of what was later to be heard after Heysel, a rumour was also spread that the trouble was caused by small groups of Londoners. In the end UEFA agreed the result should stand and Villa went on to win the European Cup.

One of the Villa characters during this period was Cockney Dave, also known to some as "Raincoat Dave". Many have a story to tell about their number one fan who was Villa to the core and would do anything he could to stop others taking liberties at Villa Park. Normally dressed in a long dirty raincoat, old flared jeans and steel toe-capped boots, Dave was a Seventies throwback, but loved nevertheless. "Let's just play it by ear," was one of his catchphrases when on enemy territory.

"I knew Dave from the Crown," wrote Skittle of the Villa Hardcore. "He's a cracking bloke who acted like a beacon to all us young lads in the early Eighties with his hilarious repertoire and obvious knowledge of terrace trouble throughout the Twentieth Century," according to the Villa Hardcore veteran. "When we were younger, Dave kept an eye on us. I remember once in about 1983, we'd played

Albion and a big black guy is offering Villa out in the middle of the road, no-one seemed to want to go near him. Next thing you know Dave calmly walked up to him and kicked the bloke in the shins with his steelies. You'd have heard him scream in the Home Counties [where Dave originates], the bloke was just writhing on the floor, his shin obliterated. Dave continues down the road as if nothing had happened, just an oldish bloke on his way home, but seeking his next victim."

In 1984 Aston Villa played Everton in the semi-finals of the Milk Cup. Villa brought one of the biggest away followings witnessed at Goodison, including hundreds of lads. They got into the Blue House pub early, taking what in those days was an Everton stronghold. A furious Everton mob eventually steamed the pub and a horrific fight followed. The *Liverpool Echo* reported that ten people were slashed, including eight from the Midlands. Everton won 2–0 and though Villa took the second leg by a single goal it was not enough to get to Wembley. There was also fighting at that game as hundreds of Scousers invaded the pitch at the end, which carried on long into the night in the surrounding areas of the ground. Over 70 visitors were arrested, though the violence did not reach the intensity of the first leg. When the accused travelled down for the court case a fortnight later, they were met by a mob of Villa at New Street Station and received a police escort to court.

During the mid-Eighties a firm of younger Villa lads emerged. Called Villa Youth and later Villa Hardcore, these were right-wing, loyalist and white. Heavily influenced by the National Front, the rise of this mob signalled even greater hostilities with the Zulus who, as their name suggested, were a multi-racial firm. While the Villa despised their City rivals, they were also in their hooligan shadow. The Zulu Warriors were creating headlines across the country, headlines brought further support, and the two together brought confidence. This showed in their clashes with Villa. Over 100 people were arrested in what the press described as another day of shame when the two teams met in September 1985. The worst fighting took place around the Central Fire Station in Lancaster Circus and mounted police were used to separate the warring groups. Both sides agree that the Zulus took the day.

The leader of the Villa Hardcore was Stephen

Fowler, who was to become a recognisable face abroad with England. Over the next few years he was to be kicked out of France during the 1998 World Cup, and denied entry to Belgium in 2000 and Japan in 2004. He is credited with putting Villa on the hooligan map in recent years, but the Hardcore have also earned the reputation as arguably the most racist gang active today. After an initial link with the National Front, several members of the firm had close associations with the nazi group Combat 18 and more recently with the British National Party. Several were also involved in British support groups for the Ulster Loyalist paramilitaries.

Villa's right-wing link naturally antagonised the Zulus but it also proved to be a break from earlier Villa mobs, for whom characters like Black Danny had played such a prominent role. Many of the older Villa lads had little time for racist views but accepted that Fowler was "game" and had a following. "Fowler now accepts that it caused a division within Villa ranks for years, hence the split of mobs the night we played Blues [at Rocky Lane in 2002]," said one of the old Villa crew. Fowler also had his enemies around the country. Huddersfield, with several black lads involved, have had a particular hatred of him. Everton, hardly the most multi-racial of outfits, also dislike him and his followers after an incident at a Liverpool pub that left an Evertonian needing 160 stitches in his face.

Villa continued to suffer against the Blues, though this time it was on the pitch. Later the same season they suffered the humiliation of a 3–0 home defeat in what was a key relegation clash. A furious Graham Turner said after the match, "Some defeats are unacceptable, but not the manner in which we lost. Birmingham deserve credit for being so organised but the sad truth is that they even attacked better than we did." Words which summed up their off-field activities too.

West Brom, Birmingham and Villa occupied the bottom three places in the league. Turner's words obviously had some effect because Villa managed to squeeze out the points to pull themselves up a couple of places. There was some fighting before the game as 70 Villa clashed with 40 Zulus who had slipped away from the police escort. Villa avoided relegation, unlike their City rivals, and hostilities were brought to a temporary halt.

Villa's escape was to be shortlived and the following season they were relegated. This brought them together with City but now the Villa Hardcore were a couple of years older, and braver, while the Zulus were having their front doors kicked in by the police. The first fixture, at Villa Park, passed off uneventfully but the Villa decided to put on a show for the return match. The police had carried out dawn raids on the Zulus only a few weeks before and consequently there were few Blues in any organised mob. Feeling confident, a group of 70 Villa got into the giant Kop, and emboldened by their presence, hundreds of other fans in the away Tilton End began clambering over the fence to have a go. Chaos ensued for several minutes as police attempted to force their way through the crowd to separate the mobs. Twenty-six people were injured and 23 arrested inside the ground. The police would later say that for ten minutes they feared the violence would be on a level similar to the fatal 1985 riot against Leeds. After the match, Birmingham finally managed to get a mob of 300 lads together but the police ensured that nothing happened.

The day is regarded by Villa lads as a great victory. This is how one Villa lad remembered it: "Villa were going for promotion and basically our fans filled the allocated areas, forcing the police to let hundreds of Villa fans into the side of the Kop. Naturally our fans see Villa's firm in their section and the old 'Villa Youth' chant comes up. Zulus attack them, which then starts a stampede as Villa then climb over the fences and more and more of our lot are coming over and from the back. You see this mass running of Blues as they are scattered across the side of the Kop. Now we are not saying we took the end but we were in it and they ran."

The Blues had a different view. "Numbers and organisation just didn't happen," said a Zulu veteran. "People had been scared off [by the dawn raids] and undercover OB following you around. About 80 Blues met in the Iron Horse pub, which was a fucking squeeze as it was the size of your living room, just down from McDonalds ramp. No Villa came into town and nothing happened on the way to the ground. Yet when we got there some of the cheeky fuckers for the first time in years had paid into the Kop, and a few others jumped over when it went off. None of our lads were there when it all originally happened, they were fighting our drunks and shirts. Eventually they climbed back into

the Tilton. Yes, they were brave, but would they have done this without the nickings?"

"After the match we headed towards them. People had finally shown, 3-400 of us charging the OB on Garrison Lane trying to get them, but they were having none of it. Everyone went to Boogies after waiting for them to show, but not this time, not when they know a Blues firm will be in there."

Whatever the truth, events in the ground served as a warning to the infamous Zulu Warriors that on the streets of Birmingham the tide was turning. Villa view the 1987 clash as the first in a hat-trick of "victories". It was to be six years before the two teams met again and by now the power had definitely shifted away from the Zulus. The two mobs met at Garrison Park, close to St Andrews. For Villa there was only one winner.

"Hundreds of Villa mobbed up in two pubs. We had been in an escort from Birmingham town but we had broken out of it to wreck their pubs on the way. They then met us at the park. The old 'Zulu, Zulu' chant went up and bottles and everything came flying at Villa. When they had run out of ammo they were steamed and run everywhere. I can remember the Villa lad on the floor fighting with a big rasta and when they were parted he had his dreadlocks in his hands. Their main mouthpiece was knocked clean out."

The Blues only lasted a season in the Premiership and the rival gangs had to wait nine years before they met again. When Birmingham were promoted in May 2002, there was talk of little else. Word went around the pubs and estates, with the Zulus mocking Villa's chances and promising payback for Garrison Park. Such was the buzz of anticipation that a number of "observers" from other clubs came into town to watch, including an infamous Chelsea head, a small group from Wolves, and even West Brom. The day was to become known for the Battle of Rocky Lane, but the real clash happened a short time later, and for Villa, there was only one winner.

The game at St Andrew's was a night match but that did not stop 400 Villa mobbing up in two pubs. The largest of the groups was Villa Hardcore, who gathered in O'Reilly's bar, while a smaller firm, of 150, were in a club in Moseley, in the heart of City territory. These were old school Villa, the C Crew and even a few Steamers, not a person under thirty-five years. One Villa lad recalled it as "the tightest firm we have put together in fifteen years." Their confidence was bolstered when one of the main faces stood up and made a Churchillian speech. "This is it," he said. "Anyone who doesn't fancy it, fuck off now, 'cos anyone who runs is going to get a slap. All the bullshit you have heard for years, all the bullying in town of ones and twos, ends tonight. They bring it on and we stand, this is our top firm."

Adrenalin flowed as the mob poured out of the pub. There was not a copper in sight as they set off towards the ground. A few lads kept order, walking alongside the mob to make sure everyone stayed tight and tight-lipped. Word soon reached the group that 250 Birmingham were at the island near the ground. All their main faces were there.

Bricks and bottles came flying into the Villa group and there was a temporary step back. Then Villa charged into the Zulu mob. "All their main faces take hits," recalled one Villa lad. "I didn't see Cuddles go down but the others did and one of ours, Big Ginger, takes a punch but knocks the Cage Fighter straight out. They are then on the back foot and Villa go through them, scatter 'em. They can't believe it because in their eyes Villa's main firm was at Rocky Lane. One Villa lad had stun grenades apparently but never needed to use them, but I tell you it was their main faces and they were on their toes. Villa are known as being NF, well at the island there were five top Villa black lads with us.

"The next day Cuddles rings our main black lad and says, 'Fair play to you, but who the fuck was your back-up?' No back-up, he is told, just all the old cunts came back out to play. Sky filmed our mob walking into the ground with us singing, 'One-nil to the Villa,' and they were pissed off big time."

The Rocky Lane affray was filmed by five police spotters standing only yards away, and a few weeks later, after a local paper ran a rogues' gallery, doors went in across the city. The rival gangs had been caught on camera brandishing knives, snooker balls in socks, CS gas canisters, batons and bricks. Eleven Villa and eight Zulus were sent to prison and five others were given community service. They were banned from football grounds for up to ten years each. Among the Villa lads was Stephen Fowler, leader of the Villa Hardcore. Fowler was also a recognisable face abroad with England and had been kicked out of France during the 1998 World Cup, and denied entry in Belgium in 2000 and Japan in 2004.

Birmingham would later claim that they were heavily outnumbered at Rocky Lane, but privately some admitted they had been humiliated. For the return fixture, over 300 Zulus mobbed up and marched on Villa Park. Villa had made their mark at the first game but didn't have the numbers to compete with the Blues before the match. During the game dozens of Zulus spilled onto the pitch as fighting broke out in the seats. It proved to be costly bravado as they were again caught on camera and many were later dealt with by the courts.

West Brom also came up against a rejuvenated Villa mob on their return to the Premiership in August 2004. Following the match between the two sides at The Hawthorns, eighty fans fought outside the Uplands pub in Handsworth. The battle involved many well-known faces from both mobs and once again was filmed by police. A local paper reported the aftermath:

60 fans rounded up after big clash

Almost 60 West Bromwich Albion and Aston Villa fans are facing court appearances after clashes between supporters.

On Monday, 22 Albion supporters were charged at Wednesbury police station and 36 Villa fans were due to be charged today at Digbeth police station.

The fans are all male and aged 17-49.

Detective Inspector Claire Mason said she hoped it would send out a "strong message" to anyone who may be thinking of causing trouble ahead of this weekend's game between the two sides at Villa Park.

She said the "major" seven-month investigation showed the police were keen to tackle allegations of football hooliganism.

If 60 of a group of 80 had been arrested, it indicated that the intelligence being gathered by West Midlands Police was very accurate.

In early August 2005, five Villa hooligans were sent to prison for a fight with Chelsea fans in North London a few months before, while another eight were given community service or fines. The court heard how traffic was brought to a standstill as yobs hurled bottles, glasses and traffic cones at one another. Sentenced to one year was Villa Hardcore leader Stephen Fowler, who, the court was told "was snarling and shouting before trading blows with a Chelsea rival." Also imprisoned was 23-year-old Gareth Howells, who gave nazi salutes while shouting "Youth!" The judge said true football supporters were "the rock on which the game is built. But beneath that rock, as there has been beneath rocks since the dawn of time, lurks lower life. They are the mindlessly violent attaching them-selves to the soft underbelly of football as a convenient rallying point."

While hostilities between Villa and the likes of Birmingham City may continue in similar vein for some years to come, the Birmingham courts and police have always been regarded as the worst in the country when dealing with hooligans, and are likely to deal severely with further disorder. So for many, retirement from the scene may be forced rather than voluntary.

B

BARNSLEY

Ground: Oakwell
Rivals: Middlesbrough, Cardiff, Leeds United, Sheffield (United and Wednesday)
Firm names: Inter City Tykes, BHS, Five-0
Police operations: Sherwood, Tyke, Barstool and Bolivia

Barnsley is one of the smaller South Yorkshire towns; its population is lower than neighboring Rotherham and Doncaster and less than half that of Sheffield. An old mining area, it has always had a rough, close-knit community. Young men are brought up to look after themselves. This has been highlighted over the years with the reputation gained by the various mobs who have attached themselves to Barnsley FC.

Brian was one of the youths who enjoyed a "proper day out" in the early Seventies as football violence spread across the country. "Whenever trouble broke out at matches or in town, lads who didn't know each other would stand side by side, battling together dressed in their National Coal Board donkey jackets," he said. "Trouble would break out most weekends when Barnsley played at home. It was never organized and there were no early gang names, we were all Barnsley and if anyone came into our town we would fight them regardless if they came for the football or were lost on their way to Leeds or Sheffield for a night out. Basically we don't like outsiders in our town."

Throughout this era, the main problems occurred with neighboring teams whose close proximity meant they came mob-handed to Barnsley, and vice versa:

1968/69: Violence at an away game at Doncaster. Throughout the day rival fans clashed in the town centre. A length of timber was hurled through a coach window carrying Barnsley supporters. Both sets of fans also clashed in the bus station as visiting fans were waiting for the service bus home.

1971/72: Police drafted in extra officers when Barnsley played Rotherham and made six arrests, including one fan for pinching pool balls from a pub with the intention of throwing them. Other arrests were for disorderly behaviour and one for carrying a smoke canister.

1973/74: Thirty-six arrests were made during the worst violence of the season. Fans clashed before and after the game with Bradford City. A police horse lost an eye after being hit with a brick thrown as a group of Bradford fans were attacked near the bus station.

1978/79 season: Violence broke out on the streets of Barnsley when a coachload of Sunderland fans stopped in the town on their way back from playing Sheffield United. Trouble began in several pubs, then spilled out on to the streets. Barnsley magistrates handed out fines totaling £3,375 to 13 men and one woman involved in the fracas

A couple of years after the Scousers and Mancunians had ditched wool for casual cotton, even the small Yorkshire communities began to latch onto the fashion. It was not an overnight transformation, like in Liverpool, where hundreds of lads could be seen walking around flicking their fringes and squeezing into skin-tight Lois jeans, as Brian recalled. "The casual scene first hit Barnsley around 1980. About half a dozen lads turned up at some game and the majority thought they looked like puffs. Yet before long the lads in the donkey jackets and toe-cap boots were the minority as more and more Barnsley fans, some who had fought for years at matches, turned up wearing Pringle jumpers and bright-coloured tracksuit tops. At the same time up and down the country, firms were beginning to give themselves names, and Barnsley decided on Inter City Tykes. Some lads even went under the title of the Barnsley Hooligan Squad.

"Throughout the early Eighties, on a big game, the firm could call on numbers well over 200, plus normal supporters who would join in, although these were frowned upon by some as they were still walking around dressed like cavemen. At the end of the day these miners who didn't own Fila or Lacoste could hit very hard, so they were more than welcome by many of us."

Early rivalries were forming and one of the first mobs to cross swords with the ICT were the Boro Frontline. "We had literally hundreds of lads out looking for them. At one stage the firm stretched about 400 yards down the street as they moved from one pub to another before the game. Boro were a force though and despite our numbers a small group of them got into the home section of the ground and taunted the Barnsley supporters."

This was the start of a rivalry that would reach its nadir in a clash that resulted in some of the heaviest sentences ever handed out to football hooligans. For years the Boro lads had been regarded as hard but fair, and had frowned on mobs who used knives. There is no irony lost with the Barnsley lads when Boro make that claim, as Brian recalled the horror that unfolded that day.

"After our show at home we decided we would have to turn out at their place, so for the away game we took around 120 lads on the train, knowing that Boro had a good mob and we would have to be on our guard. We arrived and headed straight to the Wellington pub, near the train station. A couple of lads stood outside in case our rivals showed, and after a while the shout went up that they were heading down the street. We pushed our way to the door, but only one was open, slowing our exit. With only a few of us outside, Boro were on top of us, easily outnumbering us.

"We backed off against the pub wall, heads down and arms swinging. After what seemed like ages of throwing punches and kicks at whoever came near enough, I looked up just as a blade was being pushed into one of my mates' arms and being pulled

downwards. I froze and took a hell of a crack on the chin, bringing me back to my senses. I can't remember whether the police arrived first or the fight broke up before they appeared.

"The Boro lads had disappeared and we were lined up against the pub wall with the Old Bill stood in front of us trying to suss out what had gone off. It became clear that seven of our lads had been cut up and they were shipped off to hospital, whilst we were questioned, still outside the Wellington. The Boro lot must have been crazy, as before long it kicked off again. The Middlesbrough mob returned again and stood at the top of the road. The police were pushed aside as we ran at them. They never moved and a toe-to-toe ruck took place before the police managed to get in between. Both firms were split up and we were pushed back down the road.

"Before long we were being herded onto a coach and into vans. I saw these big gates being opened, but instead of the ground we were at the police station. You would have thought that we had used the knives, as we were fingerprinted, photographed and asked to give statements, before being allowed to head home well after the game had finished. We were even warned about defacing the Queen while playing toss the coin nearest to the wall as we waited our turn.

"Three of our lads were detained in hospital overnight; one needed thirty-five stitches in a wound across the forehead and three blood transfusions. During the court case it was stressed that the charged Boro lads had deliberately stolen the knives from a shop when they heard the Barnsley lads had arrived in town. Thirteen of Boro's mob were jailed for a total of thirty-nine years. So after years of listening to Middlesbrough pulling other fans down for using blades, particularly at Everton, the message from Barnsley is, don't forget your firm sank just as low in 1984."

Boro are not the only firm to use knives against Barnsley fans. In September 1986, a 20-year-old Portsmouth supporter was charged with slashing a Barnsley fan with a craft knife across the back after the match. A court heard how the victim's jumper and shirt had a slash mark from the left shoulder to the right waist. Despite denying the charge and also being a member of the 6.57 Crew, the Pompey thug was found guilty and sentenced to two years' youth custody.

A couple of years earlier after a League Cup match at Anfield, a 21-year-old Yorkshireman was slashed eight times across his back with a trademark Stanley knife, leaving him with 60 stitches. His picture was featured in many national newspapers to highlight the increasing use of this weapon at football grounds. Unfortunately it turned into an advertisement rather than a deterrent and soon many hooligan mobs were brandishing the razor-sharp blades.

Around 17,000 Barnsley supporters travelled to Liverpool that evening, in terrible conditions. The fog was that thick that fans were still arriving during the second half and once inside the ground, those arriving late told tales of how they had come under attack outside by groups of locals. Following a 0-0 draw, the attacks and ambushes continued as thousands of Barnsley fans tried to find their transport. Before the replay back in Barnsley, the club's walls were daubed in paint reading "STAB A SCOUSE" in three-foot letters. There were no reports of the threat being carried out but the visiting Liverpudlians were given a rough ride before and after the game.

During the early days of organised gang warfare, Barnsley town centre saw very little violence as few opposing mobs came looking for trouble. One exception was when the Geordies rolled into town, as Brian recalls. "I can't think of many firms or mobs that have come to Barnsley and take over the town completely, but the one that does come to mind is Newcastle, back in the early Eighties. I had just stepped off the bus in town and before my feet could turn me in the direction of the pub, I took one hell of a punch to the jaw. I didn't have a clue who had struck me but by the time I had entered the pub, most of the lads were telling similar stories. Throughout the day pubs were getting smashed up during fights, pool balls and cues were thrown through windows, cushions were put on coal fires along with aerosols, filling the pub full of smoke before the canisters exploded. There was even a rumour going round that in one pub the pet parrot had been thrown on the fire and left to burn because it wouldn't say 'Newcastle', but this was never proven!

"I can't recall coming up against a firm, but the Geordie beer monsters were quite willing to fight everyone and anyone. After the match, which saw hundreds of Newcastle fans locked out of the away end, Barnsley mustered a mob of around sixty and clashed with a large group of their fans. Police moved in quickly and both mobs were parted but we regrouped and kept counter-attacking as the police escorted the away supporters to the train station. Despite making twenty arrests and being stretched to the limit, the police reported no major violence had occurred! All I can say is, fights broke out all over town and all day so either the police were blind or scared to get amongst the Geordies. I'll go for option two, and I don't fucking blame them."

It was about this time when the perils of visiting Barnsley were highlighted, and it was not opposing fans that made the local news but visiting players. Police arrested five youths when the Port Vale reserve team were attacked after they had played at Oakwell. They had left the ground and pulled up at a fish and chip shop at the edge of town. Two of the players suffered broken noses.

Barnsley has several other clubs within spitting distance. None are more despised than Leeds United and Sheffield Wednesday, though both enjoyed prolonged spells in the top flight, keeping clashes with the lower-division Tykes to a minimum. But there were usually plenty of other derby matches in a season. "One of our favourite away games was the short trip to local rivals Rotherham. We would set off on our short trip at around 9 a.m., meaning we would be there long before the pubs opened. By the time the bar shutters did come up, most of the town centre pubs would be full of Barnsley fans, not just firm but normal supporters as well. Trouble would break out as the home lads got their act together, scuffles would kick off in the pubs and spill out on to the streets. Up at the ground it became a ritual to go in the home end. Season after season, more and more Barnsley fans would do this, not in one large group but in smaller ones. As the match got underway, the home end would erupt on numerous occasions as groups of lads would let the locals know who they were. Police would then march the visitors around the pitch to the away end to the sound of 'Reds are here, Reds are there, Reds are fucking everywhere.' Every visit was the same, so you would have thought the police and club would have done something about it but no, they never did, so each time we took the piss."

One surprising rival emerged during this time: any match at Grimsby would guarantee trouble. "We once travelled there by train, around 100 of us, only to find out the game had been called off. We thought we would have a good day out in Cleethorpes, and with the pubs not yet open we had a walk around and went past an amusement arcade where a few of our lads were abused by a group inside playing pool. They ran inside to front them and in no time the windows were through, the pool cues were snatched and wrapped around the locals' heads. We had a couple more scuffles before heading into a pub.

"The police were quickly onto us and tried to order us out of the bar, the landlord stuck up for us, so the Old Bill left us there. A collection went round to say thanks, but not long after a couple of Grimsby lads walked in and all hell broke loose, with chairs and tables flying around. The police returned and this time there was no second chance, we were taken to the train station and surrounded by police until a train arrived that would get us out of their town. The police were not as stupid as their friends in Rotherham and the following year when we returned, Barnsley's entire mob got nicked and held all night before being put on a coach and under police supervision brought home."

By the early Nineties the older lads were settling down and the firm's numbers began to drop. Despite this Barnsley kept a hardcore of around 50 lads and went under the new name of Barnsley Five-0, which is still used.

Nottingham Forest visited Oakwell in the 1993/94 season. Around 50 Forest fans were drinking in the Old Court House pub when 200 home fans gathered on the road nearby, then charged towards the pub throwing glasses and bottles. The Forest fans ran out of the doors and began hurling missiles back. Four police spotters tried to hold the two factions apart until reinforcements restored calm. Nineteen arrests were made that day. The police, however, weren't happy with that and launched Operation Sherwood. After a month-long investigation, 14 fans were arrested in dawn raids when a team of police officers swooped on houses in Barnsley, Doncaster and West Yorkshire.

The following season, old rivals Middlesbrough came to town. Boro hung around two pubs only 100 yards apart, the Beer Engine and the Yorkshireman. Just after 2 p.m., Barnsley's mob made their move and attacked the Beer Engine throwing bricks, glasses and bottles through the windows. The pub

emptied and punches were exchanged, then Boro fans in the Yorkshireman ran out, trapping the Barnsley lads in the middle. No-one backed off. One away lad hit the pavement with a thud after one of Barnsley's main lads connected with a punch, and a police dog which had just arrived ripped chunks out of his leg, leaving him covered in blood. He was then thrown into the back of a police van and arrested.

Police intelligence was growing on hooligan mobs all over the country and Barnsley were becoming very active during a period when at many more of the notorious clubs the scene was relatively quiet. A major crackdown was planned for the Euro 96 Championships, and during the tournament police pulled over a coach full of Barnsley fans just minutes after it had set off for the England v Scotland game. They found plenty of drugs on board but just one match ticket between the entire coachload. A vehicle inspection then revealed a "mechanical fault" and the coach was deemed unsafe to continue. Nine people were arrested, questioned and then released without charge. The operation was part of an overall plan to prevent disorder at the game.

By the 1997/98 season, Barnsley had gained promotion to the Premiership, the first time the club had played in the top league of English football. Every match was a sellout, with no tickets up for grabs on the day. During the close season, supporters queued around the ground to make sure they had their season ticket for this historic year. It brought some heavy defeats on the pitch, 6-0 at home to Chelsea, and away to West Ham, 7-0 away to Manchester United and 5-0 at Arsenal. Off the pitch, Barnsley's hooligans were very active. Although their mob was still as the Five-0, hundreds of lads would turn out, sometimes split into many different groups.

The first game of the season saw West Ham at Oakwell and a large turnout of older lads who had not been involved in violence for years. Sharp policing limited any disorder to a few West Ham fans being attacked in the car park. One incident which made the local papers was when a home supporter ran onto the pitch and was arrested, which led to his season ticket being annulled by the club. He argued that he had been waiting years to watch his team in the Premiership but the club was unmoved. Unless Barnsley's fortunes change dramatically, he will go to his grave having watched less than one hour of Premiership football.

The slashing at the hands of Liverpool had not been forgotten, and at Anfield trouble broke out after the match. A number of Barnsley fans required hospital treatment following a series of clashes. Barnsley claim their mob found no opposition, but instead Liverpool thugs ambushed normal fans on their way back to their transport. The local paper reported that fans returning to cars needed hospital treatment for injuries including black eyes, severe bruising, and broken ribs. One minibus had its windows smashed and tyres let down while the occupants attempted to flee Stanley Park. Even the team coach was bricked before it left the City of Liverpool.

The return game at Oakwell saw several pitch invasions when three Barnsley players received red cards. After the second dismissal, a fan trying to attack referee Gary Willard was wrestled to the floor by Barnsley striker Jan Aage Fjortoft. A steward then had a word with the ref, who left the pitch, leaving both fans and players wondering what was going on. He eventually returned and the game restarted. Following the third sending off, more fans invaded the pitch trying to get to the official. One was brought to a halt by Liverpool's Paul Ince, whilst police and stewards fought to stop the others. Some Liverpool supporters also ran on the pitch when Steve McManaman scored the winner.

Police and security staff had to surround the turf at full-time while the referee and linesman were escorted off. Outside the ground the away fans were attacked and pelted with missiles as they left the ground, and in the bus and train stations police had to use horses to keep fans apart. Referee Willard received a police escort to his car and out of town two hours after the game finished. Some Liverpool players, at the time known as the "Spice Boys", allegedly goaded Barnsley fans from the team bus by rubbing their fingers together, implying they had plenty of money. Police had to disperse angry fans who were trying to attack the bus and throughout the day 17 arrests were made for public order offences.

Police were now monitoring the Five-0. Two outbreaks of violence involving Barnsley fans stopping off at other towns on their way back from matches led them to investigate leading firm members, and before long raids were carried out.

The first incident came after the Five-0 had trav-elled to Leeds for a league game. Over 100 rival fans clashed in Wakefield in a pre-arranged meet almost three hours after the game. It was captured on CCTV and both West and South Yorkshire Police studied the footage to identify the offenders. Operation Tyke was set up, and after months of sifting through evidence, police launched dawn raids on a number of homes in the Barnsley area, arresting 15 men – in addition to 16 who had been arrested during the violence.

Police also made arrests post-Operation Barstool after a coachload of known Barnsley hooligans had stopped off in Darlington on their way back from the FA Cup tie at Newcastle. Violence at two pubs, Bertie's Bar and Yates's Wine Lodge, caused extensive damage and left a doorman with a broken arm. Once again CCTV cameras filmed the fracas, and after a six-week probe officers from Durham travelled to Barnsley to help arrest twelve men. Three later received prison sentences, while others received community service orders.

Police were now trying desperately to break up Barnsley's firm, with the help of banning orders stopping targets from attending the matches and in some cases entering the town centre on match days. The last home game of the season saw police make another 17 arrests when Manchester United visited town, including one individual who headbutted a steward who was ejecting him from the ground.

At the end of the season Barnsley supporters were branded the worst behaved fans in the Premier League at both home and away matches in a table released by the FA and the National Criminal Intelligence Service. They were the only club to average fewer than seven out of ten on a behaviour rating by Premier League observers. Twenty-six of their fans were detained for assault, almost a quarter of the total arrests for that charge at all 92 league clubs. It included a serious assault on a Chelsea fan outside the ground.

Relegation saw old rivalries rekindled and after one melee a barrister at Sheffield Crown Court dubbed Barnsley the punch-up capital of the UK, while police in the town admitted they were struggling to cope with the rise in violence. The Five-0 were cheered by the news and taunted the local football intelligence officers by sending a postcard from Thailand, signing it from the "Bangkok Five-0".

Around this time, many soccer firms were forming

mutual friendships, but Barnsley remained an insular crew. "Barnsley is a close-knit town that is very wary of strangers and finds it hard to take to them," said Brian. "When all this joining-up crap started all over the place, one of Barnsley's lads had friends who ran with the Falkirk Fear. They decided to come down for a game. They entered the pub along with their local mate, however they were soon back in their minibus and making their way out of town when none of the other lads would accept them and refused to even get to know them. Their safety couldn't be assured."

After two seasons in the lower league, Barnsley reached a play-off final at Wembley against Ipswich, and one of their largest-ever mobs arrived in London. It was the proudest day in the club's history for many, even hooligans like Brian who had watched them through thick and thin. "I stood on Wembley Way and was approached by a police officer who told me he recognised me from an incident years ago when we clashed with QPR at Loftus Road. He laughed as he told me how lucky I had been not to be arrested. I joked that it was all in the past and he wished me well. Minutes later, as we made our way up the ramps towards the stadium, a group of Ipswich started mouthing and the next thing they were being knocked all over the place. All this happened in front of the police, including the officer who had clocked me earlier. I managed to get inside and watch the game."

In the season leading to the play-offs, Manchester City had been among their visitors, and the police had made the mistake of putting the visiting City fans in a town centre pub, the Regents Park. Word got round and a large mob of Barnsley lads headed for the Courthouse pub, 100 yards down the road. By the time the police decided to escort the visiting supporters up to the ground, hundreds were outside the Courthouse. They greeted the passing escort with a hail of glasses and bottles, then a charge. One Barnsley lad went down and lost a new Rockport boot, but undeterred was later seen wearing a cheap pair of trainers in another battle. Scuffles broke out all over the bus station area before the police managed to get the City fans to the ground.

Inside the stadium the City lads clashed with police in the concourse of a stand. Officers were called in after catering staff were abused and threatened and had to draw batons. One officer

was rescued by colleagues when he was dragged in to toilets by a mob. After the match the club assessed the damage to the stand and found toilets smashed, cisterns pulled off the walls, a cubicle door missing, panelling missing, signs ripped off walls, a shutter on a refreshment kiosk bent and flooding underneath the stand. Three Barnsley and ten City fans were arrested, including one in Sheffield later that night for having a police baton from the match in his possession.

At the end of the season, Barnsley fans were branded the second worst in the First Division; only Manchester City had more fans banned.

Millwall visited the following season, and again old faces turned out. By early morning, spotters were out waiting for the Londoners to arrive. They were put in the Queens Hotel and surrounded by police. Barnsley drank in two pubs across the road but nothing happened before the game. Afterwards it was a different story. The Millwall lads who had come by train walked up the car park back towards town, whilst the Barnsley lads headed up a road adjacent. At the top of the road a group of home boys ran at the mob of cockneys, who stood, as expected.

In town the group of Millwall, which had now grown in size, walked past the train station and up through the bus station. A number of counter-attacks were made by Barnsley and each time they were thwarted by baton-wielding police in riot gear and numberless uniforms. With the Millwall fans safely on the station, the Barnsley fans and police continued to fight.

The season ended in relegation. There had been 44 arrests of Barnsley supporters, compared with 38 the year before. The local police inspector stressed that he was worried that the lack of intelligence about the clubs in Division Two would make policing games harder. The inspector's worries were to prove right as trouble did break out at quite a few home and away games.

The first major violence of the year occurred when Barnsley played Wigan at home. When the visitors scored their third goal, a number of away supporters ran onto the pitch. At the end, Wigan's Goon Squad mobbed up near the underpass which leads to the town and stations. The police were caught out when around 40 of them clashed with a larger mob of locals, with missiles being pulled up out of gardens and thrown. When the police did arrive in number and with horses as back up, the fans turned on them, pelting them with bricks and stones.

In November, the Five-0 were among 300 hooligans who attacked police and fought running battles in Sheffield city centre. Police with riot shields came under a barrage of missiles as they tried to keep rivals apart. The Barnsley mob had stopped off in Sheffield on their way to Chesterfield; after a few drinks they decided to give the game a miss. Also in the city were Wednesday hooligans, a Derby County mob who had no intention of attending their game at Hillsborough, and later on Sheffield United fans returning from Nottingham. At the height of the trouble the police helicopter was scrambled to warring groups.

Following a home game against Sheffield Wednesday, police with batons drawn, horses and dog handlers forced a large mob of home supporters through the town centre to prevent clashes. Violence first erupted when police penned in the Wednesday fans at the train station. The home mob reacted by throwing bottles and other objects at police from outside the Groggers Rest pub forcing the police to form a line and begin to push the mob back through town. As they stood face to face in Peel Square, a police dog handler collapsed and died of a heart attack. No fans were in the immediate area when the officer fell, but photos were printed in the local papers of suspects the police wanted to question in connection with the violence. Seven men later appeared in court and two were jailed.

Despite the bans and court cases, around 25 Barnsley and Luton fans clashed on Regent Street at lunchtime, while Chesterfield and Mansfield both brought sizeable hooligan contingents to Oakwell. The two most serious outbreaks, however, came at both the home and away games against Cardiff City. For weeks before the November game, police were planning their operation to keep fans apart. Over 300 officers were on duty, the largest number ever for a Barnsley game. They were also worried that hooligans from Leeds and Huddersfield would travel to carry on their rivalry with the Welsh after recent clashes.

Separate Barnsley mobs drank in pubs all around the town, with the biggest, the Five-0, settling in one called The Room from early on. Cardiff's Soul Crew arrived via Chapeltown, between Barnsley and Sheffield, left their coaches and caught the train.

They headed up Eldon Street towards the Five-0, but the police forced them back. At the same time, riot police blocked all the doors and windows of The Room to stop the Barnsley lads getting out. Some thought they would try an old trick and set the pub on fire, so a blaze was lit in the toilets. The police still wouldn't let them out despite the pub filling with smoke. In other parts of the town, coaches were dropping Cardiff supporters off away from the ground causing tension and taunting between the two sets of fans. The odd fight broke out as both sets of fans made their way to the ground.

During the match a group of Cardiff stayed outside the stadium and clashed with a small group of local lads. Inside the ground, police and stewards had to form a line in front of the away end to prevent the two factions from getting to each other. At the final whistle the line had to hold firm as some of the away contingent tried to get onto the pitch and coins and other objects were thrown at the Barnsley players as they headed to the tunnel. Brian witnessed the scenes all day. "Now you don't have to have a degree in rocket science to know that what had been going off throughout the day was only minor to what was about to happen. But for some reason the old bill never saw it coming or if they did they weren't ready. Both sets of lads were well up for it, Barnsley had hundreds waiting outside, and made several attempts to get at the Cardiff fans as they left the ground, every available officer fought to keep them apart.

"Trouble was kicking off all over as the visitors made their way back to their transport and eventually the police started forcing the Barnsley mob away from the stadium and back towards town, but when they reached the railway crossing, next to the station, everything went wrong for the police as they came under attack. Bottles, glasses and bricks rained down on them, thrown by a large baying mob containing some very young wannabes. For the next hour Barnsley fans and riot police clashed throughout the town in running battles. At the height of the violence, police reinforcements were drafted in from West Yorkshire. Eldon Street and Pontefract Road had to be closed off until the vast amount of glass and debris were cleaned up. The Room pub was closed until the fire damage was repaired, however the manager blamed the police for starting the trouble when they blocked off the main doors using a riot van parked across it. Amazingly just seven arrests were made on the day but police promised more after they had studied CCTV footage."

The away fixture was in February and it was a day when the Five-0 took the Soul Crew by surprise. Around 130 arrived in the Welsh capital at 10.30 a.m. by train and headed straight to the bars. When the Cardiff crew found out they were about they mobbed up and headed down St Mary's Street looking for the Yorkshire firm. Dozens of riot police and officers on horseback had to move in as both sets of lads clashed in two bars and then in the street, sending shoppers running for safety. The Barnsley firm were rounded up and taken to the ground by bus but throughout the game, riot police fought to hold them back. They then left early despite requests over the PA system for them to remain in the ground. A line of police with batons drawn tried to stop them leaving via Sloper Road, where Cardiff were congregating. Missiles were thrown between the two groups, including a wheelie bin and metal rods.

On the day only four arrests were made, but the police were determined more would follow and set up Operation Bolivia. South Yorkshire and South Wales Police together studied footage to identify the lads involved. Within a month arrests were being made in the Barnsley area, and local papers were printing pictures of others police could not put names to. On the day police released pictures of seven men they wanted to talk to, the first three dawn raids were carried out. In all, 23 Barnsley fans and 16 from Cardiff were arrested and charged with crimes ranging from violent disorder, affray and public order offences. Around ten months after the violence, all 23 Barnsley fans were banned from attending football matches for three years and some received hefty fines. Twelve Soul Crew members were convicted and received banning orders.

Once again at the end of the season, Barnsley fans were branded one of the worst behaved groups in the division. Twenty-four had been arrested for being involved in acts of violence, out of a total of just 61 for the whole of the league. Cardiff, however, finished top of the overall arrest figures with 149 fans detained; Barnsley were fourth with 59. Unlike other seasons, most of the arrests were at away matches. The police took this as a small victory for

their policy of exclusion orders preventing trouble-makers from attending the town centre and ground on match days. The firm claimed that fewer mobs were turning up in Barnsley and they were having to travel in pursuit of their fix of football violence.

In May 2004, the police said that all but six of the original fifty from the Five-0 had been banned from watching football. This did not take into account the other lads that were willing to get involved but didn't go under the Five-0 banner, but certainly the 2004/05 season was relatively quiet, with no major incidents and few arrests and banning orders. Brian, however, warned, "The local police and magistrates may have banned most of the older boys, but Barnsley still have a lot of young, game lads coming through. You will never change the way people are in this town. Unless you are a local lad and part of this tight-knit community, you won't be made fucking welcome."

BIRMINGHAM CITY

Ground: St Andrew's
Firm: The Zulu Warriors, Zulu Juniors, Junior Business Boys
Rivals: Aston Villa, Millwall, Leeds
Police Operations: Red Card

"Eight in the morning at Geno's cafe in the Bullring. The Blues aren't playing but Villa are away at Coventry, so there's fun to be had. The Juniors have already had a little brawl at the top of the escalators coming up from New Street, the Yardley lot, and a game bunch too.

"A few more older lads showed and about fifty of us were on the train to Coventry with no OB in tow. As we arrived, there were no home lads or Villa in sight. About half a mile from the station we reached a subway and came to a halt; someone knew some-thing. After hanging round what seemed like an eternity, a decent firm of 150 Villa showed. This, I thought, is gonna be tough. Their famous black face was at the front. We charged out the subway and the Zulu shout went up, 'ZUULUUU.'

"One or two stood but the rest of their firm fucked off. A few of their lads got hurt as the boot went in and items of designer gear were removed, as was the norm in those days. Some came back, so we regrouped and charged again. This time we didn't stop and ran them back into the station. It was fucking hilarious as they grappled with one other to get over the ticket barriers. The OB showed up and the Birmingham chant went up again and echoed around the station to remind them who we were.

"They got escorted away and we are put in the waiting room on the platform with strict instructions to fuck off back to Birmingham. But the Euston-bound train from Brum arrived opposite us with a big mob on board. It's the cavalry, and the law wouldn't let them off. Some managed it and ran up the grass banks and out of the station. We went out to meet them, but the OB were well pissed off, threw a load of us into the wagons and took us back to Coventry station all the way back to Birmingham.

"At six o'clock on the same evening, 400 hooligans were casually sitting in the Midland Red bus station waiting for Villa to get back. One copper walked through and eventually clocked on to what was happening and we dispersed to meet back up at Colmore Row and hide in the fifteen or so bus stops up there. One of the Juniors told us they were on their way up, by the side of Rackhams. Most of us were in the bus stops but a few standing by the church called Villa over. As soon as they came near us we charged out. Up went the chant, 'ZUULUU,' and for the second time in the day Villa were run stupid."

* * *

Birmingham City's Zulus are known for the large number of black lads within their ranks, but this was not always so. Until the 1982/83 season, the Birmingham mob had been almost exclusively white. A large skinhead gang took Bristol Rovers' Tote End in the late 1960s. While black players came to the fore in English football, and a generation of young Afro-Caribbeans began to identify more with football than cricket, racism remained rife on the terraces, and Birmingham was no exception.

Sociologist David Robins quoted a Birmingham fan in his book, *We Hate Humans*, saying, "We went to West Brom this Saturday with the Blues and they were all singing National Front. There was this coloured player, Regis [for West Brom]. They were all singing, 'Regis, Regis, gimme that banana'. Then they were singing, 'Nigger, nigger, lick my boots',

'Tarzan want a monkey', and stuff like this. After that they ran round the town after the match singing, 'We hate wogs'." The Blues have got a song about Wolves, "The Molyneux is colourful, the Molyneux. Full of blacks, full of coons, full of niggers, the Molyneux is colourful." Yet years later, it would be the multi-racial Birmingham mob that was singled out by racists up and down the country.

There was fighting at Birmingham City matches throughout the Seventies, with visiting fans trying to take the Tipton End and Birmingham, for their part, trying to take home ends on their travels. March 1973 saw 35 arrests and ten injured during the visit of Manchester United. There were also regular clashes against Villa: in September 1975, 35 people were arrested at the away match, and another 50 at the return game later in the season. In March 1977, 300 home fans ran riot after a match against Spurs. Coaches were damaged and there were several injuries from bricks being thrown. Early in the following season five buses were wrecked and 30 fans arrested in the Birmingham derby at Villa Park and another 37 at St Andrew's. Between the two matches, Blues fans clashed with police during the visit of Leeds.

The 1978/79 season was particularly violent. An away fan died at an early season home game against Chelsea and the same month saw the first of several clashes with Liverpool. Five police and 30 fans were hurt as gangs threw darts, bricks, bottles and coins at each another, and 48 were arrested. At a home match against Villa in October, ten people were injured and 55 arrested. The return match saw a further 27 arrests and several shop windows smashed.

During the Seventies, several smaller mobs made up the Birmingham Kop. They came together on match days to protect their end and led assaults on the opposition at away games. But there was also conflict as estate fought estate and school fought school. At the end of the Seventies the different mobs came together under the name The Apex, Birmingham's first proper mob. The name came from a building firm of the same name and many of their main faces were second-generation Irish from Acocks Green. They marked themselves out from other mobs and even other Birmingham fans by their unique hairstyle, a wedge on one side and shaved on the other. It was a largely white mob, which was surprising given the ethnic make-up of the Acocks Green area.

"ZS" recalls one Birmingham derby in the early Eighties when the Apex took it to Villa. "They came in the Kop," he said. "Two mobs of Apex come charging across the pitch five minutes apart. They had to scale the Kop fence before they could have a pop at the Villa. Another was a few months earlier, at Joe Gallagher's testimonial. They left the ground early, came round the Kop and met the Apex head-on along the Coventry Road. This was a proper row with both sides claiming the result to this day."

This was the last big battle for a while as Villa's C Crew disappeared, to be replaced by Villa Youth, who couldn't match their city rivals. The Blues were also experiencing change within their ranks and a new mob appeared at a game at Maine Road in 1982.

"The Zulus got their name at the Man City game," recalled Brains, a long-time Zulu, in *Top Boys* by Cass Pennant. "It started off as a rugby song, believe it or not. We were at Maine Road and there was all this singing in the ground. I think we were getting beat four-nil, like we always used to, and a couple of lads started singing this rugby song, 'Get them down, you Zulu Warriors...' which was started off as a crack. Then, after the game, we came out of the ground into all the back streets and somebody among the mob we were with shouted 'Zulu' and it echoed all down the entries and it sounded as though there were hundreds and hundreds of us coming and everyone started shouting, 'Zulu!' And that's how it took off, the name Zulu Warriors, from a rugby song."

The leader of the Zulus was a 43-year-old known as Cuddles. "He was regarded as top lad after the opening game of the 1983 season at West Ham when 236 of ours were nicked at Euston," recalled another Blues fan. "He and about seventy Blues carried on to Upton Park and after the game made a stand against big numbers of West Ham. He got cornered and had about three one-on-ones without budging until West Ham finally let him go."

The black lads arrived en masse during the 1982/3 season and this created tension with the all-white Apex crew. During one home match there was a big fight between a white mob and a large mixed group at the bottom of the Tilton, though this might have also been initiated by two rival areas of the city having a pop at one another. Either way, the Zulus quickly

gained the ascendancy and some Apex switched their allegiances, while others dropped out. There have been odd cases of Blues fans switching over to Villa because of the dominant role of the black lads in the Zulus. Villa had, by the mid-1980s, become an all-white mob with strong right-wing links.

One Zulu remembers the day he first saw the firm in action. "I realised the direction I wanted to take during the 1982/83 season. I'm sure it was the Villa game. As usual, at the end of the match the Tilton emptied and all the boneheads headed round to the park. There were hundreds there and everyone started the usual walk to the bottom of Garrison Lane. I went along, adrenalin pumping, looking around, amazed at how many were there. I looked back up the road and saw another mob of Blues appear. I was in two minds what to do, but in the end I went back to see who this other lot were. There were about 300 of them, walking slowly and quietly, minding their own business. At the front was this tall, lean, black kid. In fact there were loads of blacks. Where the fuck did this lot appear from, I thought to myself. The clothes they were wearing were different to the Bulldog gear the other lot were in. Half of them must have been wearing Fila, the rest all Pringles and Lyle and Scott. To a fourteen-year-old they were the dog's bollocks and I was hooked."

In the early 1980s, Birmingham and West Ham fought on several occasions. In October 1981, they battled on the pitch at St Andrew's and there were 30 arrests, and two season later came the trip to East London at which Cuddles made his name against far superior numbers of ICF. The biggest clash between the two, however, came in February 1984, when they met at St Andrew's in the FA Cup. Trouble kicked off inside the ground after Billy Wright's penalty put Birmingham 3–0 ahead. Hundreds of West Ham fans streamed onto the pitch in an attempt to halt the game. The police restored order but with five minutes to go West Ham broke through a 50-strong police cordon and fights broke out all over the main stand. Trouble continued outside and a police motorcyclist was hit in the face with a brick. The final tally was 30 injured and 109 arrests, 32 inside the ground.

There are differing recollections of this day. West Ham have written it up as another ICF triumph, but whoever you believe, there is no doubt that lesser firms than the ICF would have come unstuck that day and very few, if any, would have had the courage to do what they did at a place as hostile as St Andrew's.

Birmingham see it quite differently, as one Zulu recalled: "Yes, West Ham did come round to the Railway End shortly before another mob of West Ham invaded the pitch, but they were soon on their toes when some of us went out to confront them. I remember this because after we had run the Hammers off I found myself locked out of the Railway End and had to go back into the Kop and climb over the fence to get on the pitch, as the second pitch invasion was just starting. Blues went on the pitch and after about sixty seconds of brawling, pushed West Ham off the pitch and back towards the paddock. Fair play to the Hammers for coming on, not many teams would – Leeds didn't get as far – but they are not invincible and they got done in the end. The way they go on you'd think everybody was terrified of them, well we weren't."

The FA ordered an immediate inquiry into the trouble and Birmingham City came in for criticism for not having fencing at the away end. The home side responded that they could not be blamed for the violence of West Ham supporters. FA Secretary Ted Croker was present at the match and quickly gave his views. "These are some of the worst scenes I have witnessed at a football ground," he said. "It was the unfenced areas, of course, from which the so-called supporters came. You could say if they had been fenced in then it would not have happened."

Despite airing his thoughts publicly, Croker then announced that he had no intention of offering himself as a witness to the FA inquiry. This did not go down well with the local paper. "Any man with a bit of spine and in his elevated position in the football world would want to do something," blasted its editorial. "If men like him will not stand up and be counted then what hope is there of seeing an end to this hooliganism which has meant putting fans behind bars like some dangerous primates." The FA found both clubs at fault and handed out a suspended two-year ban from the FA Cup. Any future trouble would trigger the ban. However, both clubs successfully appealed and the threat was lifted.

The early Eighties saw the increasingly active Birmingham mob cause trouble across the country. In August 1982, 50 Blues fans smashed up a pub during a pre-season friendly at Walsall. The team

lost a League Cup match at Burnley and their fans wrecked a local hotel bar, causing £1,000-worth of damage. The final game of the season, away at Southampton, saw hundreds of Zulus battle it out in the streets with home fans after the game. Early the following season the Zulus had to repel an attack by Spurs inside their own seated end and 23 were arrested.

This period also saw further confrontations between Birmingham and Villa. Both teams were in the First Division but the Blues had to endure their neighbours lifting the title and then the European Cup. Unsurprisingly, there was trouble at every game between them. In February 1982, 50 fans were arrested after city centre clashes following a match at St Andrew's. In October 1983, 48 were arrested and one Villa fan was stabbed. The same season saw Birmingham relegated but any hope that hostilities would be put on hold were soon dashed.

One former Zulu remembered, "It was the middle of the 1984/85 season, the Blues had been relegated, so playing the Villa was a no-no and we had to find other ways. Aston Villa's C-Crew changed their name to the Villa Youth, and they were not really up to much. They were OK as the C-Crew and the battles with the Apex were probably even, but the Blues were definitely now the daddies.

"A few weeks after the ambush of Villa at the Coventry game [see above], Birmingham were at home to Shrewsbury and Villa were hosting West Ham. We left the game early when the gates opened and about 300 of us headed to Pigeon Park with the hope of meeting someone, anyone. Two Blues had a straightener on the way up, though fuck knows why, so this put everyone in the mood. We got to the park, which is really a subway, and once again lay in wait. After ten minutes this huge firm appeared at the top of the road, there were about 400 of them. We thought it had to be the ICF, as surely Villa couldn't raise that many. We could see them but they couldn't see us. As they walked around the top of the island we came out of our little hiding place and met them head on, but they weren't West Ham, they were our neighbours, and the look of horror on their faces was a peach as the ambush went perfectly. Not one of them stood, their whole firm scattered, and so did we, as the law showed up within seconds. They must have been escorted from Villa Park. But why did they not make a stand? They had more than us but, once again, they showed themselves up."

Trouble continued at Birmingham games. In March 1984, 44 fans were arrested at an away match against Coventry. The trouble started within minutes of the kick-off when hundreds of supporters spilled on to the pitch. Fans swapped punches and it took the police several minutes to get both sets of supporters back into the stand. After the match, hundreds of away fans went on the rampage and had numerous clashes with locals. Police condemned the troublemakers as "mindless morons". The violence was a blow to Coventry City, who believed their all-seater stadium would eradicate hooliganism. Two months later Birmingham were again up against Southampton at the end of the season, though this time at home. Five hundred Birmingham fans battled with police outside the ground.

The following season took off where the previous one had finished. An away game at Oldham in August saw 300 Zulus battle locals and police before the game and smash down the gates to the ground. Two months later, 400 Zulus threw bricks, stones and lumps of wood at police as they tried to ambush visiting Oxford United fans. In the same month, Brighton manager Chris Cattlin was in angry mood after Birmingham fans created havoc at the Goldstone Ground. A hundred of them left the game early after police blocked them getting onto the pitch, only to walk around the ground and re-enter at the back of the home stand. Bricks, planks of wood and bottles were just some of the weapons thrown by the Zulus, fighting broke out between rival gangs in the streets around the ground and five people were badly hurt. Cattlin criticised the police and called on them to stop opening the gates early.

There were 14 arrests at the return fixture against Oxford in early March as hundreds of Birmingham fans went on the rampage at a vital promotion game for both clubs. A huge police operation managed to round up 400 Zulus who had travelled down early by train and escort them to the ground, but there was little the authorities could do to prevent trouble during and after the match. Dozens of Blues climbed onto the pitch after their side went three-up and taunted home fans. Several Oxford fans came over the moat wall and ran to meet them in an ugly clash with fists and flying kicks. After the match ended, Blues fans leaving the visitors' Cuckoo

Lane end smashed down fencing in the narrow passage behind the stand at the Manor Ground. They spilled into the John Radcliffe Hospital grounds, where two unattended police vans were overturned. Police also quelled trouble between opposing fans in the Headley Way area, close to where Birmingham coaches were parked, and there were several other disturbances across the city. A couple of weeks later, Birmingham were at home to Man City and 200 Zulus attempted to attack a large group of City fans outside the ground.

On the final day of the season, Birmingham needed a win against Leeds to secure promotion to the First Division, while the visitors still had an outside chance of getting third place. This, coupled with being an end-of-season match between the two biggest hooligan mobs in the division, virtually guaranteed trouble. But no-one could have foreseen the carnage to come. It was, quite simply, some of the worst public disorder ever witnessed at a sporting event.

"I remember attacking the Aussie Bar at half-eleven in the morning," recalled Blues hooligan KN. "We had heard Leeds were in there, so off we went. It was mainly younger lads. There were only forty Leeds and there must have been a 150 Juniors as well as a handful of elders who wrecked the pub.

"As for the game, Leeds started smashing the ground up just before half-time and then the Blues invaded the pitch just as the ref blew. The break lasted forty minutes. Our lot then went berserk, every lunatic in south and east Birmingham was out that day. I think Leeds bit off more than they could chew, though they'll never admit it. The Old Bill took their hiding for them and most of the day went by in a blur of violence."

Six thousand Leeds fans packed themselves into the ground, so many that the police had to open up the terracing that was supposed to create a space between rival fans. As Leeds sang "Yorkshire Republican Army", news filtered through that Manchester City, another promotion hopeful, had gone two-up, so realistically ending Leeds' chances. The catering shop at the back of the stand was set alight and planks of wood were handed down to supporters at the front of the terrace to hurl on to the pitch. The real flashpoint was the forty-fourth minute when Birmingham's Martin Kuhl scored what was to be the only goal of the game. Referee

Joe Worall instantly blew for half-time and hundreds of Leeds fans poured onto the pitch. As police, including sixteen mounted officers, tried to chase the visiting fans back, they faced a hail of bricks, bottles and planks of wood. Then, from behind them, Birmingham fans streamed forward hoping to clash with their Leeds rivals. A dozen red distress flares were fired into police lines as home fans from two other stands joined the fray. Leeds boss Eddie Gray and Blues secretary Andrew Waterhouse walked towards the Leeds terrace and tried to restore calm. They ended up fleeing under a torrent of abuse and threats.

The loudspeakers carried appeals for order. Spectators were told that the game would continue regardless of how much trouble there was. Eventually, sense prevailed and a temporary calm was restored. As hundreds of police officers disappeared to get their riot helmets, some Leeds fans actually tidied up the missiles strewn across the pitch. Non-violent Leeds fans also began to get their voice and chanted, "You're the scum of Elland Road."

The peace did not last. The final whistle was the signal for an even bigger pitch invasion, this time led by home supporters. Leeds fans, meanwhile, ripped up their seats and threw them on to the pitch. One hundred officers, backed by horses, formed a line across the pitch in an attempt to prevent rival gangs fighting. Advertising boards, planks of wood, seats and even iron stanchions were among the weapons aimed at them by Blues. "In the name of football please go home," shouted the announcer over the loudspeaker system. He was joined by Birmingham manager Ron Saunders, who also pleaded with fans to go home.

"Outside, by the old ticket office, about sixty of us had a row with seventy Leeds," said one Zulu. "They stood and had it with us but we ended up running them back past the ground. I think Leeds see smashing a ground up as a result. It's up to them, but proper mobs won't respect them for it."

The statistics for the game made chilling reading. One young Leeds fan, attending his first game, was killed when a wall at the back of the ground collapsed. Some reports estimated that over 2,000 people were involved in the trouble at its height. Eighty spectators were hurt, as were 96 police officers and 125 people were arrested on the day, with many more arrested in the months to follow. Yet reaction was muted, overshadowed by even more horrific events 100 miles away: 56 people died and many more were injured in a fire at Valley Parade, the home of Bradford City.

Leading football figures queued up to condemn the events at St Andrew's. "I was hoping that the violence was coming to an end," said FA chairman Bert Millichip. "But it seems a new wave of violence is spreading throughout the country. We have to stamp it out straight away. It just cannot be allowed to continue any longer." Ron Saunders again called for the reintroduction of the birch. "Football became an obscenity on Saturday," wrote Leon Hickman in the Birmingham Evening Mail. "It was anti-police, anti-society, and anti-civilisation. Bloodlust was given a stage that was watched in revulsion by those who could stomach it, or risk it. Hundreds among the Leeds supporters came with premeditated ideas of how they would make Birmingham City pay. Hardly had the first shot been delivered than a tea point was set alight – shades of the horror of Valley Parade – and soon ammunition was being handed down the terraces to within firing range of the pitch. It was the final bean feast of the season, a chance for the Leeds louts to show again the bloodied flag of anarchy."

A blame game soon developed, with all the usual suspects: liberal society, fascists, delinquent youths. Local MP Dennis Howell, a Minister for Sport in the late 1970s, claimed to have information putting the blame at the door of the National Front. One commentator even suggested that Chelsea fans could have infiltrated the game. The local Conservative Party latched onto a claim by one Evening Mail reader that some underprivileged young kids, given free tickets by the council, were involved, to push for the end of subsidies for the unemployed, old and poor.

Most Zulus kept their heads down in the days after the riot. For those who were not arrested on the day, there was the constant worry that their door would go in at any moment. But for some, the idea of melting back into normal society wasn't possible. They had been involved in possibly the worst ever disorder within a football ground and now, to their chagrin, the children of unemployed families, and Chelsea fans, were getting the "credit".

For one young Zulu it was too much. Seven days after the riot, the local paper stumbled on to an exclusive: "Riot at Blues 'caused by organised gangs'." The article was based on an anonymous letter sent to the paper from a hooligan who claimed to be the first on to the pitch. It read, "I am one of the Junior Business Boys and I think Saturday's violence at St. Andrews was the best I have ever been involved in, and the best I have ever seen. After the game we threw chairs and rocks and sticks at the Old Bill because we could not get at Leeds. If the law did not stop us we would have done the business on Leeds instead." Enclosed in the envelope were calling cards emblazoned with the words, "Junior Business Boys, Pride of the Midlands."

The club said they were aware of the Zulu Warriors but had not heard of the Junior Business Boys until the game. The police also only heard of the Juniors on the day of the Leeds game when they arrested one Michael Cotterill for threatening behaviour. During his trial, at which he was given four months' youth custody, the court heard that he came to the aid of a black youth grappling with police. "Look what the bastards are doing to him," he shouted to a ten-strong group. "Come on Zulu Juniors." Cotterill told police, "Us young white lads are Zulu Juniors." Pointing at two West Indians, he added, "They are Zulu Warriors." The police admitted their lack of knowledge to the local paper. "We knew Zulu Warriors were the hooligan element of Birmingham City supporters but we did not know of a junior element. We now understand that they are called Junior Businessmen."

Various criminal trials now brought the Zulus into the local media spotlight. "Police and soccer clubs are becoming increasingly concerned about the Zulu Warrior faction of young fans at Birmingham City matches," reported the Evening Mail. "'They chant a war cry at Blues games which they attend faithfully, home and away. The group takes its nickname from the well-known film, Zulu, and they mimic the warrior chant to try to instil fear in their opponents."

A police spokesman said: "There must be hundreds of them in the faction, but the trouble for us lies in identifying the lads because they have no badge or insignia. They claim to be supporters defending the name of the Blues, but basically they are yobs. Whenever we have arrested any hooligan at a Birmingham City match, invariably he denies being a Zulu Warrior, although I think the group contains the main contingent of troublemakers. The Warriors are lads aged from 18 into their 20s, the juniors are kids about 15 and 16 and they often carry calling cards which they pass out. The youngsters are also known as the Junior Business Bovver Boys from the expression 'doing the business' when you beat someone up."

After the Leeds riot, the club appealed through the Evening Mail for the Zulus to come forward to talk to officials. "Unfortunately, it met with virtually no response," admitted the Blues' Secretary. "The Zulus are probably more noticeable at our away games and membership is almost a cult. I think they believe they are sticking up for the Blues and defending the name of the club. All the youngsters in schools seem to know about the Zulus, it's just a subversive side of city life."

The authorities still knew little about the organisation of football hooliganism in Birmingham. The Juniors became active in the 1983/84 season. "Some of the maddest and gamest fuckers belonged to this lot," said ZS. "They were a bunch of thieving fuckers as well. They couldn't afford the gear most of the time so had to relieve our rivals of it. This lot destroyed the Australian Bar on their own before the Leeds riot, as the older lads stood back and watched. I had a few pre-season days out with them, to Stratford, Sutton and Lichfield, and they always ended up the same – thieving and Villa-bashing. During the next couple of seasons they mingled with the older lads and quite a few of them were nicked in 1987/88 as part of Operation Red Card. A few dropped out but most of those I knew well still go to this day."

Dozens of Zulus and Leeds were imprisoned for their part in the riot. Almost six months after the match, 19-year-old Mark Hewitt was sentenced to six months youth custody for being an alleged ringleader after he was identified throwing a six-foot piece of wood at police. Others, worried about their own liberty, dropped out of the scene voluntarily, but the vast majority felt the riot had put them on the map and many new faces emerged.

The new season kicked off with parts of the St Andrew's ground still under repair and an early home game against West Ham confirmed the authorities' worst fears when further violence broke out. A couple of weeks later, 200 rival Blues and Villa fans fought in the city centre. A 50-strong mob of Zulus attacked a pub, smashing windows. Eight people were seriously injured and there were over 100 arrests. "The game passed off peacefully but trouble erupted when rival gangs met outside the Central Fire Station in Lancaster Circus in what the police considered a pre-arranged fight," reported the *Evening Mail*.

Ron Saunders said that the arrests were a bitter disappointment after the efforts the club had made to combat violence, including new fencing and a £25,000 video security system. He launched the Save Our Society (SOS) campaign, which involved bringing football and showbusiness stars into the fight against hooliganism. Yet over the next few months three people were stabbed at Luton, a West Brom fan was attacked with a hammer and 18 were arrested during a visit to Coventry in which a train was damaged and missiles thrown at locals and the police.

When Birmingham travelled across to Villa Park later that season it was a big game for both clubs. The Blues were second from bottom with just 25 points and Villa were one place above them with 26. KN recalled, "A huge firm met in the Bull's Head, Newtown, and we headed off to the Crown and Cushion pub at Perry Barr to meet our mates. An Old Bill car appeared and was attacked, so the Blues then fucked off quickly. The law was going to land, so we had to get to the pub as soon as possible. We heard sirens but they hadn't reached us as we approached Perry Barr Island. We saw Villa and charged down the road towards them, but the Old Bill then came round the island in our direction so nothing major was going to happen. Most Blues were rounded up and put in an escort towards the ground, but not yours truly and twenty other lads, including the top man. We stood back and acted innocently as the main Blues mob was led away.

"So twenty of us were on their manor with a few OB still about and around three hundred Villa. This was moody. We made our way under the subway and came out on the other side of the road by the old Crown and Cushion. A firm of about forty Villa to our left ran as soon as they saw us. To our right were about seventy lads standing there staring at us. We headed towards them. They had their backs up against the wall and were frozen with fear. They could have hurt us, but chose not to. Our lads in the front started to get edgy and the old Zulu chant quietly started to psych us up. Some of them came towards us and we slowly walked towards them and then, sure enough, it kicked off.

"We scrapped for a good minute or so and, for the first time in a while, they had a go back. This was a proper row with the two sets of lads going for it. The police soon showed, though, and so did a lot more Villa from over the road. Truncheons were drawn to beat a few Villa back and we fucked off up the road and jumped on a bus to the ground, unscathed. They should have battered us, but didn't, we definitely held a fear factor over them."

Birmingham won the game but still got relegated and Villa hauled themselves to safety. A week later, the Blues were at home to Manchester United. Relegation loomed as 500 rival fans clashed at Birmingham New Street station after the game and 40 arrests were made.

Back in the Second Division, the Zulus were once again up against Portsmouth's 6.57 Crew, and there were several major clashes between the two mobs. In April 1985, 20 were arrested during major disturbances following a Blues visit to the south coast. In October 1986, another visit to Portsmouth saw further running battles. At the return fixture at St Andrews, the Fox pub, full of Portsmouth, was attacked by a large mob of Zulus armed with pool cues, bricks and bottles.

Despite the severity of the fighting, a friendship based around mutual respect formed between the two mobs. According to the recent book *Rolling With The 6.57 Crew*, by Cass Pennant and Rob Silvester, "The police were starting to sew things up and dawn raids were commonplace around the country. The Zulus didn't seem to give a fuck about any of this and brought a good mob down who did the business in some style on Fratton Bridge after the game. Against the odds, they broke up some fencing and went to work with some pieces of wood and, to be fair, we took a slapping. They battled really well that day and continued this all the way up to the Air Balloon where, again, a small but bang-up-for-it crew of them really performed. They had jogged all the way from Fratton Bridge to the pub for a fight, a distance of about three miles. The Zulus were like men possessed that day and we were second best. Even the most biased of our boys will agree to this. Birmingham gave the best man-for-man display ever seen at Fratton."

The misbehaviour of Birmingham fans could not continue forever and on the morning of Wednesday, October 7, the doors of 36 fans went in. "Swoop on the Zulus," declared the headline in the *Evening Mail*. "36 arrested in move to end soccer terror." Those arrested came from Birmingham, Warwickshire and Staffordshire and their ages ranged from late teens to mid-40s. The raids were the culmination of an eight-month undercover operation, dubbed Red Card, by a fifteen-strong team who operated out of Steelhouse Lane police station. Several of the officers went undercover. "Evil 'Zulu' soccer gang snared by mole cops," crowed *The Sun*.

The raids had a debilitating impact on the Zulus. In addition to the 40 arrested, many more kept their heads down in the following months. Heavy policing at the matches after the raids compounded the pressure on the gang. When the Blues played Villa a couple of weeks later, the Zulus were a shadow of their usual organised selves, and their rivals took advantage with a raid on the home end.

"The lads got raided and things went quiet on our front, naturally," said KN. "But not Villa. For the first time in years, a couple of Saturdays after everyone had been pulled, they came into one of our boozers. They knew everyone was banned from town and also that the Blues were away that day so no-one would be about. Fifty of them came into Boogies and bullied seven or eight Blues who were in there for the happy hour. They left the bar and charged at Edwards No 7, next door, which had none of our lads in it, just drinkers on their happy hour."

Three years after being relegated from the top flight, Birmingham dropped again. The club's fate had been sealed by the time they travelled to Crystal Palace on the final Saturday of the season. The manager was already promising new faces for the forthcoming campaign but the Zulus were more interested in signing off in their own style. The match was held up for 27 minutes after a pitch invasion by Blues fans. Sixteen people required hospital treatment and 24 were arrested. Hours later, Birmingham fans rampaged through Toddington Services, throwing food and crockery and smashing furniture. One fan was arrested there while another 42 were picked up when police stopped their coach.

There was more trouble on a train bringing fans home, with seats ripped out and thrown around. "One wonders, in the light of Hillsborough, what on earth these mindless idiots were thinking," commented Deputy Chief Constable Paul Leopard.

Seaside towns have proved attractive to Blues fans over the years. During the Eighties, they misbehaved at Torquay, Great Yarmouth and Brighton, but the worst trouble occurred at Blackpool in October 1989 when hundreds went on a day-long rampage. Following the trouble at Crystal Palace, the club had been ordered to introduce an identity card system for away matches, but this did not stop hundreds making the trip without tickets. Fifty-seven fans were arrested as 300 ran amok, smashing windows and looting shops. Riot police were deployed for the first time in Blackpool to prevent 500 hooligans from smashing their way into the ground, and after the match Blackpool Pleasure Beach had to be closed for the first time in its 100-year history as 400 laid siege to the resort. Later that evening some Birmingham fans broke into Blackpool's ground, smashed the goalposts and scattered glass across the penalty area. The *Birmingham Post* described the weekend's events as "the shame of Blackpool". Labour's Shadow Sports Minister demanded new charges of conspiracy and riot be levelled at football hooligans, and the FA's Bert Millichip declared, "We cannot ignore this – we have to rid ourselves of this unwanted element." Birmingham City Council wrote a public apology to Blackpool Council. The club faced further embarrassment when it emerged that their managing director, Ken Wheldon, had sold a number of match tickets to fans outside the ground.

The rave scene might have effectively killed off some hooligan firms but not Birmingham's. Police raids, mass arrests and media attention had come and gone but the Zulus continued unabated. The month after Blackpool, they clashed with Northampton and Manchester United at home and Rotherham away. In January, more than 300 Zulus tried to ambush Bristol City with bricks, bottles and stones in revenge for violence at Ashton Gate earlier in the season. The following month hundreds of Zulus clash with Bolton. Reading away was the final match of the season and, like so many seasons before, the game was marred by a Birmingham pitch invasion, during which a home player was attacked. Nineteen fans were arrested and dozens of seats ripped out or damaged.

During the mid-Eighties, a bitter rivalry developed with Stoke City, arguably the second biggest mob in the Midlands after the Zulus. At a match in August 1986, 100 Zulus battled an equal number of Stoke before the game and there was further trouble inside the ground. The following season, Blues thugs attacked Stoke City coaches with bricks and stones. February 1992 saw yet another major riot by Blues fans after visiting Stoke City scored a hotly disputed goal. Minutes after the Stoke strike, Birmingham thought they had equalised and dozens of fans spilled onto the pitch in celebration. The goal was disallowed, but rather than return to the stand, the fans remained on the pitch. Others joined them and together they attempted to storm the Stoke end. Birmingham fans poured across to the away section in what one journalist described as a "human wave of bloodlust", while others attacked the referee and a Stoke City player. They were fought back at the fences by a line of Stoke's own hooligans. "Only the referee's decision to abandon the match with 50 seconds to go ended the insanity," wrote the journalist. With order eventually restored there was one final twist. After consultations between the referee and both managers it was decided to restart the game – 15 minutes after it had been abandoned. Thirty-five seconds after the game resumed, the final whistle was blown.

"Mindless morons – you shamed Blues and our City," read yet another front-page editorial in the *Evening Mail*. "Birmingham City are in the dock again, dumped there by a mob of brain-deadened fans. No matter how the club may plead mistaken identity – and they have every cause to do so – they are now the focus of hatred and loathing throughout the nation."

Yet as police again hunted those responsible, Birmingham City's chairman lashed out at the referee, claiming that his poor decisions led directly to the trouble. Those comments put him and his club in front of the FA, while Stoke City's chairman called for Birmingham to be docked points rather than face a fine or ground closure. "Deducting points may be the only way of shocking the hooligans into line," he said, though he strenuously denied that his views were influenced by the fact that both were promotion hopefuls. His delight in the behaviour of his own

supporters was matched by the pride felt by Stoke's hooligan leader, Mark Chester, though for diametrically opposed reasons – the Stoke lads were chuffed that they had held off the Birmingham attack.

Trouble receded at Birmingham after the Stoke game. Despite 30 arrests at the last game of the season at Stockport, the following season, for the first time in many years, there were no major incidents, and 1993/94 saw only two noteworthy events, a home match against Villa with 40 arrests and 46 arrests at an end-of-season fight in Southport after the Blues played at Tranmere.

The year 1995, however, saw an upsurge in disorder, beginning with two games against Liverpool in the FA Cup in January. After a goalless draw at St Andrew's, Blues fans pelted away coaches with stones and bricks, while the replay was accompanied by six stabbings, large-scale violence and 30 arrests. Towards the end of the season there was a pitched battle inside St Andrew's during the visit of Cardiff and trouble in Southend before Birmingham's Auto Windscreens Final against Carlisle. After the latter game, a pub in the Paddington area of London was attacked. For the final game of the season City travelled up to Huddersfield and 23 fans were arrested after fighting.

In November 1995, Birmingham played Millwall. Seats were ripped out and thrown as fans rumbled inside the ground. Outside, a large group of Zulus, several hundred strong and armed with bricks, bottles, knives and baseball bats, attempted to ambush their rivals. One of several coaches attacked belonged to the Millwall team and a visiting player was hit. The FA ordered yet another inquiry as Birmingham City and the police disagreed over the events. The police put the blame on the shoulders of home fans, claiming that the missiles were thrown from the Railway Stand, above the visiting supporters. Karen Brady, City's managing director, claimed that not only did CCTV footage not reveal any missile throwing, but that it would be virtually impossible for their fans to be responsible. "The front two rows in the upper part of the stand are kept empty and a line of stewards stops the supporters from hanging over. Therefore they cannot be held responsible." She also claimed that all the broken seats were from the away section of the ground.

The attack on the Millwall coach began a pattern of behaviour at City. A few weeks later more than £3,000-worth of damage was caused to Charlton Athletic

Birmingham Evening Mail

The infamous riot by Birmingham City fans at a game at St Andrew's in 1986. One young fan was killed when a wall collapsed.

coaches and, early the next year, Leeds United players were attacked by a snooker ball, coins and other missiles. A linesman was struck during a match at home against Wrexham in February 1997, and in October 1998, the Huddersfield team coach was pelted with missiles. In between, an away match at Maine Road saw widespread disorder inside and outside the ground. The trouble broke out at the end holding the Birmingham fans after the referee awarded the home side a penalty late in the game for a handball.

The club's owner, David Sullivan, threatened to close St Andrew's and ban fans from travelling to away matches. "If there is any trouble at home I will have no hesitation in playing matches in front of an empty stadium," he said. "It is very disturbing that the trouble was caused by season ticket holders who took up the whole of our 2,500 allocation. These people, fifty to eighty of them, are dragging our reputation into the gutter. They are idiots ruining the club."

At the last game of the 1997 season, at Ipswich, Blues fans went on the rampage in Great Yarmouth, pelting the police with bottles and bricks. A pre-season friendly with Villa was anything but, as fans clashed before and after the game and there were 28 arrests. The following season saw four people seriously injured when more than 100 fans fought after a home match against Notts Forest. More trouble followed home and away against Huddersfield.

On May 13, 1999, police raided the homes of suspected hooligans following the local derby against Wolves the previous month, at which 200 Blues had attacked their rivals outside the ground. Police made their intention to wipe out the Zulu Warriors perfectly clear. Superintendent John Perkins, of West Midlands Police, said the group was using football as a "cover for their gratuitous violence". He went on, "They don't commit the actual acts of violence in the ground necessarily, it's afterwards. It is organised and sometimes at locations we don't become aware of until it has actually taken place. We've got to stamp it out." Another officer added, "They wear expensive baseball caps, Burberry tops, various types of designer labels costing several hundred pounds, and they all like to conform to a sort of a designer image. They're not down-and-outs who are hard up, they're people with a bit of money to spend."

The following season there was more trouble at a Wolves match, but this time it was the visitors who claimed the "result". One Birmingham fan was jailed for five years for attacking a Wolves fan with a house brick.

Millwall again caused a headache for West Midlands Police when the two sides were drawn together on the opening game of the 2001/02 season. The police mounted a huge operation after receiving intelligence that Millwall were coming in numbers to have a go at the Zulus. Hundreds of police met the South London hooligans off a train and marched them directly to the ground. After the match the Zulus attempted to attack the escort and the police operation was thrown off course with the arrival in the city centre of more than 100 Wolves hooligans on their way back from a match at Coventry.

Trouble has become increasingly rare at Birmingham as "retirement", banning orders and better policing have dictated the agenda. "The last five years have definitely gone quiet," said ZS. "It still happens every now and then, and a lot of those faces from 1982 haven't grown up yet, but it will never be as bad as it was. We can still pull a firm of 200-plus, as proved with our trips to Millwall, Spurs, Leeds, Sheff United and the Villa, but on most occasions now you know the Old Bill will have it sewn up. An effort is made to lose the law, but there is so much at stake nowadays. People have been nicked for looking at each other in an aggressive manner."

It is impossible to end this account without Birmingham's take on Rocky Lane, the fight in November 2002 at which Villa claimed to have humiliated their rivals. "About ten punches were thrown at the infamous Rocky Lane brawl," said KN, dismissively. "But some of ours later bumped into this older Villa firm by the ground. Blues numbered around thirty and there were a good eighty Villa, both sets of lads brawling again like the old days. The only real winners were the police who, rather than stop the trouble, stood back and let the two

mobs go for it while they filmed the whole affair. Many were jailed and many more banned for what would have been regarded during the Zulus' heyday as a fuck-all event."

Another Zulu added, "Let the [Villa] have their five minutes of fame, then ask every hooligan firm in the country who they rate, the Zulus or the Villa, and let me know the result. I bet even Villa vote for us."

Further reading: *Top Boys*, Cass Pennant (Blake Publishing); *Zulus*, Caroline Gall (Milo Books – forthcoming)

BLACKBURN ROVERS

Ground: Ewood Park
Firm: Darwen Mob, H Division, Tool Bar & Mill Hill Mob, Blackburn Youth
Rivals: Burnley, Liverpool

The history of hooliganism at Blackburn has closely mirrored the fortunes of the club. During the late 1960s it was a feared place to visit, its greasers and bikers notoriously hot-headed, but from the late Seventies, as the team declined, so did the combativeness of its followers. By the Eighties they were a shadow of their former selves. Jack Walker might have brought the club a lone, albeit historic, piece of silverware in 1995 but the rebuilt Ewood Park has not seen a return to its ferocious heyday of the late 1960s and early 1970s.

As early as 1963 there were national newspaper reports of violence in Blackburn, with many fans arrested after fighting at the home game against Liverpool. At a match at Millwall in August 1967, nine Blackburn lads, all but one from Accrington, were arrested after fighting during and after the game at the Den. "Rival gangs facing each other on the terraces, innocent people threatened by an iron bar and cars smashed: that was the legacy of the first Saturday of the football season," reported an article in *The Times*. "This was nearly a riot," declared local magistrate St John Harmsworth. "It is quite outrageous when peaceful citizens who want to go to a football match on a Saturday afternoon cannot do so because of gangs of hooligans like you." The nine lads had been ejected from the Den for using threatening behaviour and then fought a gang of locals in Deptford. One struck a Millwall supporter with an iron bar while others attacked cars and smashed shop windows.

Their toughest group at this time came from a small town just south of Blackburn. "I started going in 1968 when I was thirteen years old and the main mob then was the Darwen Mob," said Carl, who is now the wrong side of 40. "For a good game we could rustle up a 400-strong mob of greasers. Nobody took our end until Bolton in 1973, but we had already taken their end in a League Cup match at Burnden Park. The Darwen Mob were led by three Hells Angels, who called themselves Moses, Jesus, and God, all big grizzly fuckers with beards and full of homemade tattoos. They were scary-looking men. We took many ends, including Burnley, Oldham, Bolton, Preston, Blackpool, Port Vale, Doncaster and Rochdale.

"By 1970 we had a few skinhead firms from Little Harwood, Great Harwood, Queens Park, and Audley. The top skinheads were Mick from Great Harwood and Dennis from Darnhill. We had mobs in the Riverside paddock, the Darwen end, and the Blackburn end. By the mid-Seventies, most of the original greasers had settled down and teams began coming to Ewood with confidence, but between 1968 and 1975 very few escaped a kicking."

Ewood Park was not impregnable. Bolton and Manchester City both took the home end in 1973 and Burnley shared it on a number of occasions. Burnley are Blackburn's main rivals and there has been trouble at virtually every game between the two clubs. In recent times Burnley's Suicide Squad have dominated, but back in the 1970s it was Blackburn who were on top.

"Despite what Burnley might like to believe, Blackburn did have the upper hand in the late Seventies," said Andrew "Wellsy" Wells, the leading Blackburn face over the past 20 years. "You have to remember the mentality of Burnley fans. The hatred towards Blackburn that still exists to this day is because in that era we used to batter them. Most Blackburn fans have forgotten where Burnley is, as we have left them behind in the football world; most kids around here think it's somewhere in Yorkshire.

"One of the biggest battles with Burnley was a Saturday game in the late Seventies. In those days we used to come into Burnley on the old Accrington Road and meet in the Mitre pub, 500 yards from the town centre. When I arrived there was already a large group of Mill Hill inside, and then the H-Division and the Toll Bar mob increased our numbers to about 200, all in their Stan Smith tennis shoes and Slazenger jumpers. The casual scene had still not hit Burnley, and they were still dressed like Christmas trees.

"We got into our cars and vans and began the convoy through the town centre. As we approached the bottom of Manchester Road we got stuck in a traffic jam and then noticed about 60 Burnley fans drinking outside the Swan pub. The back doors of one of our Transits opened and fifteen of us jumped out and charged at them. In seconds all the others were doing the same and the element of surprise had Burnley running back into the pub and locking the doors.

"The same thing happened at the next two pubs we passed, The White Lion and The Boot, which is now Yates's Wine Lodge. I will always remember an old guy with his dog who had been walking up and watched the three battles. As we got back in the van for the third time, he shouted over, 'You lot should be in the SAS.'

"We then came to a roundabout, close to the Turf Hotel, and Burnley lads came out of the pub and hurled bricks and bottles at us. We clashed but neither firm was really getting on top, then the police baton-charged us and we were marched to the ground. It was mad, because when the fighting broke out we left our vans and cars parked all along the route, which meant the journey home might be on foot.

"At the end of the game, all the Blackburn got together and walked towards the town centre. As 100 of us made our way along the subway, we paused because we knew hundreds of Burnley were following us. The difference in accent between Blackburn and Burnley is distinctive even though the towns are only ten miles apart, so we told our lot to be quiet. As Burnley entered the subway the shout of 'Blackburn' went up, and it took them completely by surprise. We kicked and punched anything that moved. The noise from the subway alerted the rest of their mob, who were waiting by the bus station. As Burnley ran into the bus station, 100 Blackburn poured out behind them. The sight of hundreds of lads charging out of the subway sent the crew at the bus station off, so Burnley were chasing Burnley, with Blackburn chasing the two lots.

"Once the penny dropped that they were chasing each other, they re-grouped and then 3-400 Burnley cottoned on that they heavily outnumbered us and got their courage back. Somehow we got to St James Street and the police were arriving from everywhere, which was not such a bad thing. Then Burnley appeared and bricks, bottles, everything came at us. The noise was unbelievable as missiles hit shop windows and cars.

"One lad, Mac, had his head split open very badly and we were all over the place trying to get it together. Everyone was shouting at each other to turn and face the Burnley and during a break in the 'brick rain' we charged into them and cleaned their front-line. They backed off a bit but more and more Burnley arrived, their numbers were awesome. This happened four or five times along St James Street before the police got between us and managed to baton-charge them away from where we had told them we were parked. Our van was missing, so 20 of us broke away from the main firm to go looking for it.

"As we got near Manchester Road Station we saw ten Burnley on the other side of the road. They were older than your average soccer hooligan, big blokes in their thirties and forties and we were all aged nineteen or twenty. But we went for it. The fight seemed to last for about ten minutes but it was probably two. With no-one getting anywhere, the fighting stopped, and both groups stood staring at each other with bloody faces and ended up shaking hands. We had both had enough and went to pick up our injured from Burnley General Hospital before heading off back to Blackburn, happy with the day's events.

"That is the difference between us and them, we did well against huge numbers of them and we give them credit because we think they earned it. Ask them about us and they will deny it happened, deny they ever ran, deny they were tooled up. In fact they will probably deny we ever played them that night. That's why we hate them; they're forever in denial."

Since the early Eighties, Burnley's Suicide Squad have taken the initiative in encounters with their neighbours. A bigger, rougher and more active crew, they became too much for Blackburn to compete with. Burnley's off-pitch supremacy was established at an infamous game at Ewood Park in 1983 (see BURNLEY) and was reinforced at a testimonial match the following year.

In 1988, 50 Blackburn ambushed Burnley as their train passed through Darwen on the way back from an away game at Bolton. Several smashed windows left those on board ducking for cover. However, Burnley emphasise that their attackers did not wait around long enough to fight them on the platform. It would also appear that this was the exception to the rule of modern Burnley dominance. Two years earlier, Blackburn had failed to appear at an arranged meeting in Burnley on the return from a match at Bradford.

Two local cup games in Burnley saw Blackburn bring only token mobs into town and when 200 Burnley travelled to Blackburn for the 1993 Youth Cup Final there were few locals out. The two sides met twice in the League in 2000 but heavy policing meant both matches went ahead without incident. The two mobs have also clashed at England games, most notably in the Grand Place in Brussels in June 2000.

Bolton, Preston, Blackpool and Oldham have also been local rivals for 30 years, with encounters with Bolton being especially fierce. Early mobs at Blackburn were Mill Hill and H Division, the former being a particularly rough area of Blackburn and the latter so named because its members came primarily from the Higher Croft area of the town. For several years in the Seventies there was hostility between the two groups and regular battles in Blackburn town centre. The hatchet was buried later that decade and the two came together. Leaders of the Mill Hill mob were Anthony Macallion and Baz Turner. Wells and Brooksy ran the H Division. Wells said, "Nowadays the firm go under the name of Blackburn Youth but the numbers can never be compared to the late Seventies and early Eighties. Now it consists mainly of men aged between twenty-five and thirty, but there is also a younger group of around twenty, aged between eighteen and twenty-five."

The Blackburn Youth emerged in 1982 and was the club's first casual firm. With Blackburn nestled between Liverpool and Manchester, they claim the fashion arrived earlier than in a lot of other towns. "Us older skins laughed at them with their silly hair-cuts and baggy jeans," said Carl. "They were more into the look than the aggro. By the time they were on the scene Blackburn were no longer a big hooligan force, although we would turn out and give these weird-looking youths a hand for the big games against Man U, Liverpool, Everton, City, and, of course, Burnley."

Blackburn's catchment area includes a number of small towns like Clitheroe, Darwen and Accrington and there has been an uneasy relationship between the lads from each place. Even the name of the local council, Blackburn with Darwen, reflects a civic attempt to treat others as equals and not junior partners, but hostility did exist. In the Seventies there was trouble between Higher Croft and Mill Hill and there has often been an uneasy relationship between Darwen and Blackburn lads and, more recently, fighting between Clitheroe and Accrington. These tensions partly explain the inability of Blackburn's mob to draw big numbers together regularly.

These towns are also home to small mobs from bigger clubs, most notably Manchester United, but also Leeds, and it was the friction between a group of Accrington Whites and Blackburn's Accrington mob that was the basis for a fight when Leeds travelled to Blackburn in 1990, shortly after being promoted back into the First Division.

"Every game we took loads away and sold out our own end, and whenever we could lads would get tickets for the home end," remembered one Leeds lad. "Blackburn was a nothing game to us. But a few Accrington Whites had a deep hatred for Blackburn. I think they'd had a few run-ins on nights out around the area. So we met them in their local in Accrington on the day of the game, and shortly after lunch about thirty of us went in two Transit vans into Blackburn. We went straight to Yates's Wine Lodge, where we knew the Blackburn lads would be. We steamed straight into them, battering them all over. Some ran into the bogs and locked themselves in and the rest received a kicking and fled up the road. We were rounded up by the law and held near a shopping precinct. The Old Bill kept us there for ages and then marched us up to the ground but, as we arrived, the escort seemed to vanish. We all had tickets for their end but nothing happened as Blackburn were nowhere to be seen."

A new rivalry has emerged in recent years with Liverpool. "It began in the 1999/2000 season," said Wells. "We spotted before the home game that Liverpool had a big firm with them, so we made some calls and got all our lot who hadn't come to the match to meet in the Ewood Arms. We were getting reports from people in the ground that Liverpool seemed to have lads everywhere and were taking the piss a bit. We decided that the best place

to ambush them after the game was under the railway bridge by Kwik Save on Bolton Road, a favourite place of ours because the railway over the top obscures the view of police helicopters and there are two huge sloping banks at either side, so the only escape is to the rear, where the police would be behind them.

"About fifty of us made our way up to the bridge and, as we got underneath, the Scousers spotted us and began to speed up to get that vital few seconds in front of the police. By this point I had pulled away from our mob to have a closer look at what they had and was across the road walking towards them. I was on my own in front of the Liverpool firm and one of the Scousers came towards me on his own, but a police van going about five mph was more or less next to us. I told him to keep walking and that it was on top when suddenly the stupid twat lunged at me and threw a punch, which missed. I caught him with a left hook and he went down. Before he was up the Scousers charged towards me, but the police blocked them off. Some Liverpool lads came around the side of a bus, but luckily for me, there was only enough room between the bus and the banking for five or six of them to get through at once, even though forty were trying. I ran down the side of the bus with them punching and kicking me and somehow I got my little finger caught in some bastard's buttonhole and couldn't get my hand free. I threw punches with the other hand while frantically trying to free myself and get myself some room, making a sort of one-armed tactical withdrawal.

"I was joined by a lad called Gindle, who ran into the Scousers, kicking and punching them, and finally I got my hand free. Two police officers came between us, and one WPc screamed at us to stop and whacked people with her baton. At this point the rest of the Blackburn saw what was happening, ran down and steamed into the Scousers down the side of the bus. Fighting then spread to the other side of the road, I punched a couple more of them then got on to the canal banking because there was a police horse right behind me and the copper was shouting, 'Get down Wellsy or you're nicked.' He ignored the fighting all around him, only had eyes for me and followed me everywhere. I ran along the side of the bus and everyone was going mad, I looked round and the horse was about a foot behind. I grabbed the emergency exit handle on the bus and opened it outwards, the horse trotted right into it and I was away.

"By now the police had a grip and we all went to the town centre, because we knew the Scousers would head for a pub near the station. We holed up in the Jubilee and half an hour later someone said the Sun was full of Scousers, so forty of us left and walked down Northgate. We could see them outside the Sun, with beers in hands, thinking they had the run of the place. As we went past the bookies, a local hardcase, Roy the Dog, clocked what was going on and joined us.

"All the usual crew were there, me, Brooks and all the old lads, a really solid forty. As we got under the car park ramp, the Scousers clocked us and came forward. One of them, the same dumb fuck from the side of the bus earlier in the day, jogged in front of the rest of them so he was put down straight away. His mates then ran towards us with glasses and bottles, stopping the Saturday afternoon mix of football and shopping traffic.

"The noise of smashing glass had people running for cover and we eventually drove the Scousers backwards into the doorway of the pub, where fighting was intense with even numbers. Roy the Dog was in his element, taking on all comers, forcing them back into the pub. We all moved in behind Roy. The Scousers were fighting frantically, trying to stop us getting into the pub, as they knew if we had all got in we would do them. They were hitting Roy with bottles, chairs, fists, anything they could get their hands on.

"This had been going on for two minutes when we heard police sirens, so we backed out of the doorway, leaving two Scousers unconscious in the road. As the police arrived, we all walked back up Northgate. They caught up with us and noticed Roy had a head wound and blood was pouring out. Knowing he was not associated with the football lads, rather than nick him they asked him if he wanted to go hospital. He declined and said he was off for a pint, like your old-fashioned caveman types do.

"It was a right result, both against the Scousers and with not getting nicked, as half a dozen times that day I thought my number was up. But the joy was shortlived. The dickhead Scouse superhero had kicked it off before we were out of sight and the helicopter had filmed the whole incident. The footage was used as evidence to ban eighteen of us

and is available on the Internet for those of you who think Blackburn don't have a firm."

Blackburn's mob has been closely linked to the far Right, which is hardly surprising given the strength in the town of first, the National Front and, more recently, the British National Party. In the Seventies, Blackburn was the only town with two far-Right councillors, who belonged to the National Party, a local offshoot of the National Front. In 2002, a BNP branch was formed and 160 people attended its first meeting, including forty of the Blackburn mob. This group, led by Wells, has been the mainstay of the BNP in the town ever since and probably explains a link with Oldham's Fine Young Casuals in recent years. Despite the clear allegiance with right-wing politics, the Blackburn mob has one Asian lad within its ranks and there is little antipathy towards him. The BNP peaked in Blackburn in 2004 when it polled 9.6 per cent across the town in the European elections, but it has since declined sharply and this has been matched by a drop of interest in the party by the Blackburn Youth.

In 2002, Blackburn played Celtic in the UEFA Cup and there was trouble at both games. A large Blackburn mob travelled to Scotland and, for the home match, they were joined by a few lads from Middlesbrough, Halifax and Leeds. Some Celtic fans were attacked on their way from the train station to Ewood Park.

In early 2004, Blackburn were drawn at Burnley in the FA Cup. The match was switched to a Sunday afternoon on the advice of the police and the game was broadcast live on TV. A huge operation involving more than 600 officers saw the game pass off relatively peacefully, with the exception of one Burnley old head who ran on the pitch and tried to attack Rovers star Robbie Savage. A large mob of Blackburn made their way over on the train, arriving late in Burnley, but were quickly picked up by the police. A fight in Accrington was arranged for after the game and 100 of an impressive 300-strong Burnley mob made the trip, only to find no Blackburn. The game ended in a draw and there was another large police operation for the replay at Ewood Park. Burnley brought several mobs into town, numbering about 250. Afterwards, the two mobs squared up to one another but police comfortably kept them apart.

Into the new Millennium, the Blackburn mob had been whittled down to a core of 25 lads, with a similar number on the periphery. It was no surprise that when the police made applications for 17 civil banning orders, it hit their small mob hard. A local magistrate turned down the first application, but in the autumn of 2004 the police successfully re-applied. Wells was one of those banned for three years.

"From 1968 to 1975 we feared nobody," claimed Carl. "The odd teams that took our end got sorted after the match, but we took many ends and we defended our end many times. In the late Seventies we lost our edge and in the Eighties and Nineties, sadly we were not a force. The Premiership has killed off most of the originals and unfortunately, since our one year of glory, we now attract the new modern fan, all scarves and replica shirts, not forgetting those annoying bastards with the drums."

BLACKPOOL

Ground: Bloomfield Road
Firms: The Rammy, Benny's Mob, Bisons Riot Squad
Rivals: Preston North End, Bolton Wanderers

The evening after the infamous Millwall riot at Luton in 1985, the BBC's *Six O'Clock News* carried a special report on the hooligan gangs wreaking havoc across the country. It singled out five clubs for mention: Millwall, Chelsea, Leeds United, Bristol City – and Blackpool. 'Even a club like Blackpool, with only a few thousand on the terraces, has a big hooligan problem,' said the report. For those young members of the Pool mob who were watching, it was national recognition of their terrace exploits over several riotous years as the most active gang in the lower divisions. As one of the casual mobs to emerge around the UK as the Seventies turned to the Eighties, they had stepped from the shadow of older bootboys, greasers, punks and skins to usher in a more organised, streamlined era of soccer hooliganism.

During the Tangerine glory years of the Forties and Fifties, when Blackpool fielded all-time greats like Stanley Matthews and Stan Mortensen, the club's following was led by Syd Bevers and his Atomic Boys, a group of fans famed for their bizarre dress and humorous stunts. The town itself, Britain's busiest holiday resort, was known for rowdy fun and was a favourite destination for visiting fans.

The late Sixties at Bloomfield Road reflected terrace trends elsewhere with the formation of "ends", Blackpool's being their large Kop, and growing "aggro" with opposing supporters. Derby matches in particular became tense, often chaotic affairs. Blackpool's rivalry with Bolton Wanderers dated from the historic Matthews Final, when Blackpool beat their north-west opponents to win the 1953 FA Cup, but had generally been good-natured. Then on Boxing Day 1973, Blackpool "took" the Lever End at Burnden Park, one of the few times they got the upper hand against their bigger rivals.

Events took a tragic turn the following season, when a confrontation at the back of the Blackpool Kop left a young Pool fan, Kevin Olsen, stabbed to death. It was widely reported as the first hooligan-related death at a football match in the modern era, and, together with the rampages that season of Manchester United's Red Army, ushered in the dark age of soccer violence. The tragedy may well have had its roots in an even earlier confrontation in the 1969/70 season, when a Blackpool fan had stabbed a Bolton fan on the Lever End. Reprisals that day in 1974 were immediate. "Bolton got hammered the day Kevin Olsen died," said one Blackpool veteran. "Everyone went mad, understandably, and they were cowering in a corner of the Kop."

Blackpool's original football firms gathered together at the George, a large, old-fashioned, spit-and-sawdust pub close to the ground. Most of them came from the Central and Revoe areas of the town, and would march past walls emblazoned with "Blackpool FC – Kings of Deepdale" graffiti and commemorations to Kevin Olsen before taking on the likes of West Brom, Notts Forest and Chelsea on the Kop.

A 1974 game at home against Manchester United, then spreading carnage during their legendary season in Division Two, saw thousands of scarf-bedecked Reds flood the resort. So many arrived on the Friday before the game that they were herded onto the beach to spend the night, where several skirmishes broke out. Legend has it that the George firm, their numbers swelled to 2-300 for this huge fixture, were alerted and fought a pitched battle with United fans opposite the Manchester pub, where many Reds who lived in Blackpool would gather. Although not making an impression on the vast ranks of United, they held their ground. At the game, the club gave the visitors Blackpool's Kop, much to the fury of the Pool lads. At the end of the game when the gates opened some United tried to get in the South Paddock, but were chased out by the home support.

The nucleus of what would become the club's first named mob, the Ramsden or "Rammy", came from around the Queenstown area of Layton, east of the town centre. The OK Scooter Club was one focal point; another was Layton Boys' Club, where local youths congregated. Older lads drank in the Victory pub, but it was only when they moved to another boozer, the Ramsden Arms, that they received their name. Overlooking Blackpool North train station, and run by the father of one of their friends, the Ramsden became a meeting place and drinking den for a rough, booze- and barbiturate-fuelled crew of 30-40 main members, swelled on big-match days by many others.

The fearsome Tom Throup (pronounced *troop*) was perhaps their hardest lad but others became equally notorious: Fogs, Big Bird, Jenks and many others. "We're the Tangerine fighting machine!" shouted Fogs as he led 25 Blackpool into 100 Blackburn – and ran them. The Rammy would occasionally also plot up in Roland's Bar, a small piano bar (now demolished to make way for the soulless Houndshill shopping arcade) in Victoria Street in the centre of town which was ideal for launching ambushes on passing mobs.

Inside the ground, the hooligans would assemble on Bloomfield Road's large Kop, which was usually divided down the middle: away fans on one side, home fans on the other. Missiles would fly in both directions. When the home section of the Kop was permanently closed for safety reasons, many of the lads relocated to the East Paddock, known as the "Scratching Sheds", where again they were next to the visiting fans. On the day of a 5-2 victory over local rivals Blackburn Rovers during the 1977/1978 season, a firm of Blackburn tried to take the Scratching Sheds but were "absoloutely crushed", according to one Pool hooligan, while trying to climb safety and segregation barriers to get away. Blackburn fans had been the first to throw home-made ammonia bombs at Blackpool fans during an encounter in the 1969/70 season.

Blackpool's last throw of the dice in the First Division had been 1970/71. For most of the Seventies they performed well in Division Two but could not quite make a promotion spot. All the while they had to contend with enormous visiting contingents from Sheffield, Manchester and other big cities, who would come not just for the game but for a beano weekend in the pubs and clubs. The George and the Rammy cut their teeth in the days of mass brawls with hundreds on each side, storming coaches, charging down the seafront.

Their successes included chasing Arsenal across the bridge of a motorway service station while stopping off on the way to a game at Charlton. Yet perhaps the Rammy's finest moment was the Italy v England game in Turin in 1980. They had travelled across Europe in Transit vans to get there, and led the charge of England fans into the Italians. At least one of them later appeared on the jacket of one of the earliest hooligan books, *Hooligans Abroad*, his face painted, roaring defiance.

A feature of Blackpool life was the amount of fighting away from football: the town was a battleground for those who wanted it, especially in the summer months, when it filled to overflowing with mobs of men from the rougher areas of Scotland, the north-east and elsewhere, full of ale and up for a brawl. "The town bred violence," recalled one older lad. "We would go football training on Tuesday nights, then jump in the van and go up town Jock-bashing. It was there every night of the week if you wanted it, and it was not unusual to have four or five fights a night in the height of the season. It was a mental place."

One active local gang was the Mecca Mob, who hung out at Blackpool's Mecca ballroom, which rivalled Wigan Casino as the premier Northern Soul venue. They would often fight coach parties visiting the club from different parts of the country. The punk scene also became popular and some of the main punks would become football lads. A Dickies concert at Blackburn was the scene of carnage, and was followed by even worse trouble on 6 May 1978, at a Vibrators gig in Preston. One young man from Preston died during fighting between locals and visitors from Blackpool, which sparked a new era of intense rivalry between the two near neighbours.

In 1978, Blackpool fell to Division Three. Three years later, they were in Division Four, playing the likes of Halifax, Rochdale and Torquay. Yet, as it has done many times before, relegation seemed to galvanise the club's hooligan element. Blackpool began to take large numbers to minor grounds, where there were few police and poor segregation.

On occasion their away following dwarfed the home crowd – and many of that away following were there for a brawl. In particular, the name of "Benny's Mob" was heard more and more.

"We used to hang about at the Boys' Club in Layton," said Benny – not his real name. "We were messing about around the flats there and giving some shit to this fat woman who lived there, and she said to me, 'Don't you take the piss, you look like Benny off *Crossroads*.' I had the same black curly hair. Anyway, the lads picked up on it and that was that, a nickname for life.

"I used to go to the games with my uncle. I remember seeing Blackpool chase Preston out of the ground in the Seventies. I also went against Man United, again with my uncle. They had taken over the whole Kop and I got booted in the head. Then a bloke punched me in the face and nicked my scarf. I was only about twelve.

"Once I got into it I was hooked. I'd actually go to Preston some games just for a fight. A pal of mine was Nipper from Leyland, a Preston fan, and he was game as fuck. We'd go anywhere to get a fight. I also had a close mate who was a massive Chelsea fan and often followed them everywhere too. They had an awesome mob in the Seventies and Eighties."

Having grown up observing the fights of older youths and occasionally joining in, by his mid-teens, Benny wanted to lead his own gang and, with his older brother and a core group of schoolfriends, eventually gathered a mob of perhaps 60-80, bolstered to a maximum of about 150 by other firms from around the Fylde Coast. "By 1976, we were Benny's Mob and we were on our own," he said. "Blackpool played Preston in a testimonial and we set the end on fire and I had a fight outside and that was the start of it."

Powerfully built and charismatic, Benny led from the front. His mob's formative early encounters included a full-scale pitched battle with hordes of Pompey Skins on the coach park at Bloomfield Road in August 1980, with Benny leading the charge. Portsmouth brought an enormous following all the way up from the south coast for the game, many of them the feared Pompey Skins. "I looked across and I had never seen a mob like it in my life," said Benny. "They all seemed to be boneheads. We had about 150, mainly our lot. They must have had 1,000 on that car park. I had a one-on-one with a big guy at

the front and then I heard, 'Benny's Mob, let's do it,' and everyone poured in. What a fight it was, and despite their numbers, they never did us."

Relatively quick to pick up on the casual scene because of the proximity to Liverpool and Manchester and the many visitors from those cities, particularly during the summer season, Benny's Mob travelled away in their own early version of the fashion. "We went to Huddersfield in 1980 and again there were hundreds of skinheads waiting for us, while we were all in baggy jeans with narrow belts, baseball shirts and chunky jumpers. And we ran them." Like many casual mobs, Benny's Mob eventually took to the seats rather than go on the terraces, specifically a section of Bloomfield Road's South Stand, particularly Q Block. The match-day meeting place became the Fleece, a recently converted "fun pub" in the town centre. It would remain hooligan central for the Blackpool firm for many years.

In the lower divisions, the off-field action could be more regular and more intense than at bigger clubs, and many lower league mobs would be fighting every week. Occasionally it backfired. Man United cleared out the Blackpool fans when Harry the Dog jumped into their enclosure in a 1981 friendly attended by the usual hordes of Reds. A small mob of Blackpool got ragged through the streets at Sheffield United. "Twenty of us came out of a pub and they all came out after us, tooled up," recalled Benny. "We got chased all the way down the road, getting attacked by every pub we went past."

But in March 1982, Sheffield United came to Bloomfield Road. "About fifty of them came in the South Paddock," said a Pool veteran. "We were going in the seats by them but there was still a few in the Paddock. Eventually there was about thirty of them in a corner and we were going in and pulling them off individually and feeding them to the sharks. One Blackpool lad stabbed three of them that day. They came on the pitch to try to help their mates but couldn't get over the fencing."

In March 1984, Blackpool, who had finally been rejuvenated on the pitch, played at Rochdale. Rumours of trouble were so strong in the week before the match that a representative of Blackpool FC phoned Rochdale's secretary and also tipped off the police. But on the day the local force, used to dealing with crowds of 1,300, were overwhelmed by the 3,000 attendance, mostly from Blackpool. With little local opposition, a Tangerine mob of 200 went on the rampage down Spotland Road after the game. "A trail of havoc," declared the *Manchester Evening News* headline. "Altogether, 21 cars were damaged by bricks and kicks. Two parked vehicles were over-turned. Four police cars also suffered damage."

For a brief period, anarchy reigned. "Two to three hundred Blackpool fans came stampeding down the road smashing everything in sight," one eyewitness told reporters. "They were hurling bricks at cars with kiddies inside. They overturned one car and one idiot was about to toss a lit cigarette into the spilling petrol only thirty feet away from nine parked coaches. Luckily the police with dogs arrived."

By April 1984, police were complaining that an army of about 200 hooligans had latched on to the club. "Police and Blackpool Football Club have vowed to drive out a horde of foul-mouthed, beer-swilling louts who are wreaking havoc at Bloomfield Road," reported the local *Evening Gazette*. It said this hooligan element had occupied a section of the South Stand and "driven out" lifelong supporters.

The following month it was Torquay's turn to host Blackpool's large travelling support for a late season game. The match was a 7.30pm Saturday night kick-off but most of Blackpool's hooligan element travelled down to the south coast for the Friday night, resulting in 24 hours of carnage. "SOCCER MOB STORMS RESORT," declared the local newspaper. The town saw 61 arrests, five people treated for stab wounds – including a Liverpudlian whose stomach was slashed open with a carpet knife, leaving a 15-inch wound – and thousands of pounds' worth of damage. The Yacht public house was wrecked and a nightclub frontage was demol-ished with a large rock. Two Blackpool fans were later convicted of stealing a four-poster bed from a luxury hotel, hiding it in a field and then loading it into their van. Many of Benny's Mob spent the Saturday night in the cells, where they sang songs into the night.

With Blackpool developing a team capable of winning promotion, the 1984/85 season promised to be a wild ride. It began badly for Benny's Mob at a midweek League Cup game at Chester that September. Over-confident, twenty of them went in a home paddock, where most of Chester's boys gath-ered. Heavily outnumbered, they were attacked from all sides in a Custer's Stand-type encounter that

saw one of them receive a broken leg and three need hospital treatment.

Payback was planned for the next league fixture at Sealand Road, in February 1985. The game was halted for fifteen minutes when, as if to a signal, 200 Pool lads jumped out of the away end and ran across the pitch to attack Chester's mob in the paddock. Police reinforcements, summoned to help quell the mini-riot, were met by bricks, bottles, broken terrace barriers and even a corner flag used as a spear. "Blackpool is a disgrace to let that shower follow the club," said Chester secretary Bert Eckersley, who was hit in the face by a fan wielding a heavy bag. The referee, who was also assaulted, feared a fatal incident and took both teams back to their dressing rooms while the battle raged. "We've never had to deal with anything like this at a football match," said a Chester police officer. "It was frightening." Two crash barriers were uprooted, a refreshment hut was wrecked and stand seats were torn out. The FA instituted an inquiry into the incident but subsequently exoner-ated Blackpool as a club.

The dust had barely settled when Blackpool took 3,000 fans to Bury in March. This time the trouble was, if anything, even worse. "An orgy of violence, theft and destruction turned Blackpool's match at Bury on Saturday into a nightmare," reported the *Evening Gazette*. A minibus full of Blackburn Rovers lads was attacked and trashed en route by a vanload of Blackpool, several hours before kick-off. At the game itself, one stand was wrecked – to chants of "smash it up" – seats were ripped out and hurled onto the pitch and a wall outside the ground was pushed over onto parked cars. Sixty-four people were arrested out of a crowd of less than 8,000 and five police officers hurt. It led to the club's second disciplinary tribunal within a month, but again they were cleared. The hearing was told that Blackpool FC had barred some troublemakers from the ground and had published a "hall of shame" in their programme.

In April, Mansfield Town's mob came to the away end of the ground to put up a show and were promptly chased all the way back to their own town centre by a coachload of Benny's Mob. Darlington away on May Day and a promotion clash before 7,000 fans saw more fighting, with 17 arrested and 27 thrown out of the ground. The day had another element of revenge, this time for a small group of Blackpool fans who had come off worst in a fight in Covent Garden, in London, a couple of weeks before against a mob of Darlo. This time a coach of Benny's Mob ran Darlington's boys before the game. One of Darlo's lads later told a rival that Blackpool had brought easily the "best crew of the season". Other battles around this time included the likes of Stockport – who slashed a number of holidaymakers at Blackpool Pleasure Beach – and Tranmere, as well as a surprise visit to Bolton when Wanderers were playing Wigan, which led to mayhem at the train station where Bolton's lads were waiting.

At around this time, a ruthless younger mob appeared in Blackpool. The Bisons Riot Squad (BRS) are believed to have taken their name from the noise they made when running at rivals. Close-knit and suspicious of outsiders, they soon became known for using knives. In one episode at Brighton, four people were slashed, and there is a story that a main Blackpool lad had taken a gun off one of the Bisons before they went down there. Three young Blackpool fans were subsequently banned from every Football League ground for their actions that day, the first time such powers were used by the courts. Other active mobs were based at the Farmers Arms pub in South Shore, in the Bispham/Cleveleys area and in the nearby port of Fleetwood. There were also the Grange Park Winos, from Blackpool's largest council estate, and mobs from neighbouring Lytham St Annes and Freckleton.

The fixture list for the 1985/86 season promised several hooligan slugfests including Derby (however some of their firm couldn't make it due to bad weather), not least Bolton Wanderers at home on Boxing Day. A large turnout of Rammy veterans, Benny's Mob, Bisons, Farmers, Fleetwood and others assembled in a pub near the train station and first set off to attack the Ramsden Arms itself, which had been occupied by a group of Bolton. "Windows were smashed as louts hurled snooker balls and cues through the expensive lead-weighted windows," reported the Evening Gazette. "Glasses and lights were also smashed." Pool's mob numbered hundreds that day, as it was the first time the two clubs had met in years. Several more major battles, including one outside the Foxhall pub on the promenade and another outside the Bolton end before the game, marred the day, and weapons were found

dumped outside the ground after police were seen to be searching people at turnstiles.

This was the Blackpool firm's hooligan heyday. Rarely bested on a full turnout, they mixed it with the likes of Manchester City, against whom they played three home and two away games in various cup competitions during the mid-Eighties. At the home games Blackpool turned out big firms, backing off City on Bloomfield Road at the second, a night game. For the third, Blackpool's firm numbered 200, with the main group attacking City at their end, only to be pushed back by the police, while other groups skirmished in the town centre and at the Bloomfield pub.

"We always had big fights with Man City," said Benny. "In fact my most frightening night was at Maine Road in the cup. We came out after the game and I said, 'We're going into Moss Side, go right.' There was about thirty of us and about 150 City and we went into them. We did them but then more and more came. The police went straight into our firm. Every house in the street emptied and I swear there was 400 following us. They brought in the riot vans while we were jogging down the road. They had to bring a special bus into the middle of Moss Side to get rid of us." Other groups also skirmished with City fans in the dark streets.

Another feature of the mid-Eighties was the arrival of Leeds Service Crew in Blackpool every Bank Holiday weekend. It seems to have begun around 1983 and continued for several years, with the Yorkshire casuals arriving by train, Head sports bags slung over their shoulders, and booking into cheap B&Bs before heading out for a weekend "on the piss". They tended to gather around a pub opposite the Central Pier and at a nightclub called Shades. Inevitably it led to continual clashes with the hometown hooligans. At Easter 1985, the Blackpool firm plotted an assault on them that led to a major riot, with Leeds smashing up the Crown pub and slashing a police dog. More than 50 were arrested. The following Spring Bank Holiday saw more fighting and a Leeds fan slashed, while the Summer Bank Holiday saw running battles in the Central car park and more than 40 arrests, with the Leeds mob estimated at hundreds strong. Nineteen eighty-six brought major clashes on three more Bank Holiday weekends, with two students and one Leeds fan slashed with craft knives and an affray in McDonalds

Blackpool fans at the gates of Bury's away end after a wrecking spree inside the ground in March 1985 that sparked an FA inquiry.

restaurant. Finally a Blackpool fan was sliced so badly down his back by a Leeds mob that his internal organs were visible. After a home game with Bristol Rovers in 1987, two vanloads of visitors looked on open-mouthed as 200 Blackpool from a crowd of less than 3,500 made their way into the town centre to confront Leeds.

To the hardcore lads like Benny, testing yourself against the likes of Leeds and Manchester City was what it was all about. "I still believe, honestly believe, that in the early Eighties we could have taken any firm in the country," he said. "When I was twenty, twenty-one, I thought no-one was going to do us. I was itching to meet the bigger firms to see how we would do, but it rarely happened. That Leeds mob used to come regularly and they were up there with the biggest firms in the country, and yet they never had it over us. Myself and another of the lads used to have competitions, who could knock the most out, a fiver a head.

"What people have to understand about Blackpool is that the town is full of mobs, especially in the summer. So you could literally be fighting every night of the week. For example, one night at the Dixieland [a large nightclub on Blackpool's Central Pier] a full firm of Chelsea were in. They'd played Stoke that day. I took forty in there and their main geezer was giving it the big 'un, so I butted

him straight in the face and the whole place went up. And we did them.

"I lived and breathed it. But it meant the police got to know who everyone was and that made it increasingly difficult for the lads on match days. The police at Blackpool are very good at crowd control because they are so used to it."

Wigan, whose mob was respected by Blackpool's, arrived firm-handed in 1986 with 80-100 on a train. Blackpool had been tipped off, but only a small number had gathered in a bar on Talbot Road when Wigan showed earlier than expected. A short but fierce fight in the pub doorway ended with the arrival of police and the pub landlord bringing out his two rottweiler dogs. By lunchtime Blackpool's mob was up to equal numbers and caught up with the Wigan crew on Central Drive, smashing into them and scattering them in several directions. One was hit by a car and rolled over the bonnet with a Blackpool lad still holding his coat and punching him.

"The police arrived quickly and Blackpool disappeared, allowing both sides to regroup," said one of the Pool lads present. "After meeting up at a pub and getting everyone back together, we then went hunting their mob again, hoping they would have the sense to try to escape their police escort. With it being Wigan, who were always up for a row, they had. We found them on Central Promenade and had another

pitched battle across all four lanes of the road, the central reservation, the tram tracks and the prom. Again Blackpool had the better of it but every time Wigan ran, they regrouped and came back for more."

Brawling continued right up to the start of the game and the cells at Blackpool police station soon filled up with those arrested. "Fighting between rival soccer fans halted promenade traffic and trams," reported the *Evening Gazette* the following Monday. "My favourite fights in the early Eighties were with Wigan," said Benny. "They were a good mob, like us, and we had some great rows."

Indeed, Wigan and Bolton were regarded as sterner opposition than Blackpool's main rivals, Preston North End. For most of the Eighties, Blackpool claim to have had Preston's number, something confirmed in another Boxing Day match, this time in 1987 at Deepdale. If police thought the 11 a.m. kick-off would avoid trouble, they were wrong. "The word was to meet at a certain pub car park in Blackpool, going in cars and vans," said one of those present. "We had at least 200 lads in a procession of forty or fifty vehicles. We drove to Preston, came off at the Tickled Trout Hotel, up Ribbleton and parked – not our normal route. The cars disgorged their passengers and we marched to the ground, coming behind the Pavilion and the Town End. It was quite a big gate for that time, with about 5,000 Blackpool. Sometimes we took more there than our home gates.

"Preston were queuing up to get in the ground. They all started shuffling in tighter and looking at their shoes. There was a big debate about whether we should stampede them, with some saying, 'No, they're just normal fans,' and others saying, 'But some of the their boys are hiding in amongst them, and besides, they're Preston, let's do them anyway.' In the end we left them.

"We poured round the car park and into the Town End. Their lads used to go in the paddock next to it and the seats above and they were all there, DD and his firm. When they saw us they shouted across, 'Town centre afterwards, the Red Lion.' We gave them the usual abuse back. We were winning for most of the game but in the end lost two-one, which didn't improve anyone's mood. We came out together to see police in force, so we headed down Deepdale Road towards the town centre.

"A young copper shouted, 'Where are you lot going?'

"'Pummelling heads,' was the reply.

"The police managed to round us up and herd us back towards our vehicles. We loaded up then drove round a convoluted way and ended up on Deepdale Road by a triangle of parkland. I was in the fifth or sixth car and coming up I saw DD and Crooks with about fifteen of their leadership. One of the Blackpool lads in a car ahead of us jumped out and shouted, 'Get everyone out now!' This was a once in a lifetime opportunity.

"They saw us coming. DD worked with one of the Blackpool lads and he pointed at him and said, 'You're dead,' then appeared to reach down towards his sock for something. Then they realised how many of us there was. Everyone had parked up and we filled the street. They ran everywhere and we were trying to catch them and trip them up. People were fighting with each other to get at the ones we caught.

"Their leader lost the belt that he was swinging round his head, together with the knife which had saved him from a severe beating. The belt later hung on the wall of a Blackpool pub as a trophy. He managed to get away and had to run off holding his trousers up with one hand. The others were chased down various streets. One or two were still shouting, 'Red Lion, go to the Red Lion.' We were shouting back, 'No, now.' The Old Bill turned up, held us for a while, searched a few people and cars, then let us all go."

At a home game in the same period, Preston brought two vanloads to Talbot Square in central Blackpool, only to be attacked from three pubs simultaneously. "They tried to claim some sort of result when a group of them caught Benny on his own near a shopping centre but in truth they had been run ragged all day," said another Blackpool lad. "Wayne P, a Blackpool legend who sadly died not too long afterwards, led one massive charge into them on Central Drive. The following year we caught up with their firm near the police station and ran them all the way to the ground."

Middlesbrough at home in 1987 was considered one of the all-time confrontations. "When we played the north-east teams in the Seventies, the likes of Sunderland, we simply couldn't handle them," said a Pool veteran. "There were just too many. But we held our own against Boro.

"We were in the Bloomfield pub, near the ground, before the game when a crew of them

jumped out of a couple of cars and a taxi. We poured out of the pub and completely ironed them out, but they were very, very game. They ran in the end but you could tell they didn't want to. We then got to the ground and went round their end but most of them were already inside, so we were just getting abuse and cut-throat signs over the fence. We carried on walking, chanting, 'Sea, Sea, Seasiders,' and heard a mob of them outside responding, "Tee, Tee, Teessiders." They must have thought we were singing the same and that we were Boro, so we ploughed into them. Neither side held back, then it just went off all over the place.

"Some of them came into the South Stand and were wiped out. Another lot came into the South Paddock and hats off to them, they were dead game. Loads steamed into them but they didn't get done. The police pulled them out and as they walked round the pitch they were looking up and clapping. Others tried to come across the pitch to help them but the cops held them back. After the game we were nowhere really, while they were going mad, storming the police lines. But we'd been brilliant that day against one of the roughest firms in the country. One of our lads who was nicked was talking to one of theirs in the van. 'Your lot are game as fuck,' said the Boro lad. 'You just haven't got the numbers.'" There were, however, more brawls with Boro into the following early hours.

That was becoming increasingly true at Bloomfield Road: organised hooliganism was slowly dying. Things had probably started to change after the Heysel Disaster in 1985. The increasing severity of sentences for hooligan-related offences also deterred some. Other main lads left the area to look for work, succumbed to drugs, or died in a variety of circumstances. Dance music turned many more away from the terraces and into the clubs. CCTV cameras were installed inside and outside the ground, making it easy for police to identify any locals fighting, and a membership scheme was instituted.

Old habits died hard however. In 1989, in Pool's first major match since the Hillsborough Disaster, they played Bolton in the Northern final of the Sherpa Van Trophy at Bloomfield Road. The Bolton team coach was attacked, police twice had to clear the pitch of invading fans and the streets around the ground saw several fights with some of the 4,000 visiting fans. A cup match at Queens Park Rangers saw a young

Rangers firm ragged out of the Blackpool seats, several of them minus items of clothing.

This period also saw games in both league and cup against Lancashire rivals Burnley. At Turf Moor two gates of over 18,000 were swelled by 5-6,000 Pool fans. At the first, a night game, because Pool's following could not all fit in the away section of the old Longside, about 1,000 Seasiders occupied seats in the Cricket Field stand, to chants of "What's it like to see a firm?" directed at 40 Burnley lads who had earlier gone to attack a couple of Pool lads on their own. A Burnley firm came unstuck at a cancelled Boxing Day fixture in 1995, when they ran into an assortment of younger lads and Rammy. But in 1991, Benny, whose face was by then well known to the local police, was banned from attending football matches for three years for fighting with Spurs fans. It signalled the end.

For the past decade and more, there have been few clashes of any note involving Blackpool fans. Their hooligans would still produce the odd "turnout" throughout the Nineties and into the Noughties -- Cardiff at home, Wigan at home and away and Leicester City away -- and "liberty takers" have occasionally found themselves on the end of an old-school backlash, including a small but cocky Peterborough firm who were annihilated in a pub near the ground. And like many clubs, there have been stirrings of a "youth" element, though how dedicated such groups are is open to question. Blackpool can still turn out a mob, but the truth remains that visiting mobs arriving in the resort in large numbers looking for trouble are now more likely to find it with out-of-town mobs than locals.

BOLTON WANDERERS

Ground: Reebok Stadium
Firms: Mongy's Cuckoo Boys, Tonge Moor Slashers, Billy Whizz Fan Club, Horwich Casuals, Astley Boys
Rivals: Man Utd, Burnley, Wigan
Police Operations: Gamma

"Dawn Swoop on Soccer Fans," screamed the headline of the *Bolton Evening News* on 1 March 1989, as 24 Bolton supporters were targeted in what the newspaper called a "commando raid". It was the culmination of a six-month undercover operation

codenamed Gamma, aimed at smashing various Bolton gangs who had caused trouble up and down the country. It had been sparked by a riot by hundreds of Bolton fans on the first day of the season at Southend, an event that received national media attention and had been used by the then-Sports Minister as evidence to support his desire for compulsory ID cards. Greater Manchester Police knew that they had to act, and six Merseyside-based officers were selected to travel with Bolton fans. Their eyewitness evidence, and accompanying film footage, formed the basis of the arrests and subsequent convictions. Six weeks later, a further 16 fans were raided.

The police proudly displayed an array of weapons, including smoke bombs, chair legs covered with nails, rings with spikes and knuckle-dusters. The press reported that the raids targeted several active gangs, including the Billy Whizz Fan Club, the Tonge Moor Slashers, the Mongoose Cuckoo Boys, the Horwich Casuals and the Astley Bridge Mob. It was these firms, the police alleged, that were behind the trouble that had followed Bolton for several years.

"The Mongoose Cuckoo Boys," laughed one Bolton veteran. "That shows how clueless they all are. We were Mongy's Cuckoo Boys, named after a lad who was a bit of a loon, a 'mong'. The police thought it was mongoose and the papers reported it, but it was a name we never used. To begin with there were only a dozen of us from various areas of Bolton but the name caught on, especially in recent years on the Internet.

"The other groups did exist. The Tonge Moor Slashers were drawn from the Tonge Moor area of town and were by far the naughtiest of the little firms that followed Bolton in the Eighties and Nineties. They were aptly named, as at least three or four of them would rather slash than anything else. The Billy Whizz Fan Club was a ragtag mob from all over with only a few of them respected for football violence. The Horwich Casuals were again a very naughty set but they also contained some top lads. Unfortunately, as with quite a few at BWFC, a few took to skag [heroin]. The Astley Bridge boys were a younger bunch of lads but were nevertheless formidable, especially when targeting people using Bolton as an interchange on their way to Blackburn, as the more reliable Forest lads will tell you."

The police had been forced to act after three years of almost non-stop trouble by Bolton fans. The

national media might have focused on the likes of Leeds, Millwall and Chelsea, but Bolton fans had been causing mayhem on an almost weekly basis, something reflected in the reports of the *Bolton Evening News* between 1984 and 1988:

Bradford away, Dec 1984
Sections of the huge away support threw missiles into the Bradford crowd. Bolton fans ambushed the Bradford players with a barrage of missiles as they went to salute their fans.

Preston away, Mar 1985
Play was held up after Bolton had a goal disallowed. Fans climbed the safety barriers and invaded the pitch.

Hull away, April 1985
Repeated violence broke out on the terraces and fans clashed on three sides of the ground. The fighting spilt onto the pitch, and while the referee continued with the game, police sent dogs and horses into the Bolton end. This was regarded as a major "result" for the hooligans at Bolton, as Hull were a formidable mob. Wanderers went up there on a Friday night needing a win to clinch promotion. Bolton fans turned up en masse and eventually were allocated three sides of the ground. One well-known member of The Cuckoo Boys said, "Although there were plenty of pitch invasions and problems with the police, no Hull came near us all night."

Walsall away, Sept 1985
Walsall fans were attacked before and during the game. Police dogs were needed along the length of the pitch to restore order.

Wigan away, Dec 1985
An hour before kick-off, a group of Wigan fans attacked a town centre pub containing away fans. Bricks, bottles and other improvised weapons were launched through the pub windows and Bolton supporters returned fire with throwing chairs and tables. As they tried to leave the pub they were greeted by knife-wielding Wigan hooligans. "It was absolutely horrifying," said an eye-witness. "People were running about with their shirts ripped off and blood pouring from their backs." This was one of a series of incidents before the game that left two people hospitalised and 20 arrested. An exasperated

club secretary, Des McBain, said, "We still have not learnt the lessons of Heysel."

Bury away, February 1986

A group of Bolton fans ransacked a jeweller's during a rampage through the town after being turned away from Gigg Lane. Inside the ground, Bolton fans ripped out seats and hurled them on to the pitch while others attempted to invade the home end as their side went down 2–1. Twenty-four people were ejected from the ground. A double-decker bus transporting Bolton fans was vandalised, with every upstairs seat being thrown out of windows and the driver threatened with a knife as he tried to radio for help. A second bus was also slightly damaged but in this case the driver did call for help and was given a police escort back to Bolton.

Darlington away, Freight Rover Cup quarter-final, May 1986

Throughout the match there were clashes on the terraces and these spilled onto the pitch at the final whistle, leading to 16 arrests. On the way home, some Bolton fans stopped in a village pub and stole the charity box on the bar. Club secretary, Des McBain, said, "It's diabolical. This incident is a disgrace and an embarrassment to the club and Bolton as a town."

Fleetwood Town away, pre-season friendly, August 1986

Louts fought pitched battles with rivals from Blackpool using stones, bottles and other missiles. There were minor scuffles between rival groups of Bolton inside the ground but the real disorder occurred when Bolton learnt that a group of Blackpool fans were gathering in a nearby park. About 100 Bolton fans climbed out of the ground and into Memorial Park, where the clash occurred. "We don't want them to come and watch us," said Bolton's player-manager, Phil Neal, later. The club secretary, Des McBain, added, "We are absolutely disgusted with the performance of our so-called fans. We will be discussing it at some length shortly to see what can be done about it."

Swindon at home, Aug 1986

Clashes in the street outside the ground. One scared driver hit two pedestrians while attempting to escape the trouble.

Rotherham away, Oct 1986

Bolton fans invaded the home end.

Tranmere at home, Dec 1986

A mob of 100-150 Bolton fans chanted "Kill, kill, kill the Bill" before attacking police officers with stones, bricks and bottles after the game.

Swinton v Wigan, Rugby League Cup Final

Bolton fans ambushed Wigan fans with bricks near Trinity Street station.

The Rugby League Cup Final was often staged at Burnden Park and Bolton's hatred of Wigan started at these matches, according to the Cuckoos. "Wigan's football lads latched onto the rugby following and always took the opportunity to come to Bolton with a big crowd and played up with safety in numbers. It was at this game that the Swinton lads did a jewellery shop."

Chesterfield away, Feb 1987

Police used dogs and drew truncheons to quell disorder on the terraces. There was trouble before, during and after the game as fans threw stones, bricks and bottles at one another. Thirty-two people were arrested.

Port Vale away, Feb 1987

A Vale fan was stabbed in the neck and throat outside a pub in Burslem before the game. Home supporters attacked the pub where Bolton fans were drinking and the local man was attacked after the fight spilled out into the street. Part of his ear was cut off and he lost the use of two fingers after his wrist was also slashed. He required 40 stitches to his wounds.

Middlesbrough at home, April 1987

Bolton fans threw missiles through the window of the Sweet Green Tavern as rival fans inside returned the missiles along with chairs, tables and pool balls. Landlord Malcolm Pilkington said, "I have never seen anything like it in my life. Almost every window in the place was smashed. The amazing thing is that nobody was hurt. It was a cowardly way to fight without a single punch being thrown." Trouble continued all day as 150 Middlesbrough hooligans arrived early in minibuses and a further 200 travelled on the train. A frustrated police officer said, "The problem is that we seem to have more

problems finding the Middlesbrough fans than the Bolton hooligans do."

The *BEN* editorial was scathing. "What a shameful, self-destructive weekend display from the shower who masquerade as Bolton Wanderers' fans." Dismissing the hooligans as "howling demi-brains" and displaying the courage of a "magpie with a sparrow's egg", it concluded, "It must be some curious form of retardation which makes man-children form into packs for the specific purpose of harming people who visit the town to watch a soccer game. Sadly, the harm comes home. By the end of Saturday, a Bolton pub had been badly damaged, Bolton barmaids frightened out of their wits, Bolton Wanderers followers branded prats, Bolton shoppers intimidated, Bolton lives risked. The team lost, the town lost."

York away, May 1987
The police were forced to move in after disturbances broke out in the Bolton end during half-time.

Scarborough away, August 1987
The home side won 4–0 and there was trouble on the terraces during both halves. More trouble occurred afterwards as both sets of fans were allowed out together. The police and the club both blamed alcohol. The club promised to redouble their efforts to end the trouble linked to the club. "The violence did the club no good whatsoever," said Mr Davies. "It is also very embarrassing for the town of Bolton itself." The newspaper expressed calls for troublemakers to be banned from Bolton games, and its letters page was full of condemnation from ordinary supporters. "The louts who go to matches hell-bent on causing trouble would, I'm sure, think twice about going if they knew they would get a few lashes of the birch," wrote one.

Rochdale, Oct 1987
Nine Bolton fans were convicted and banned from domestic and international matches after trouble at local rivals Rochdale.

Burnley, Nov 1987
Forty fans were arrested, one police officer was injured and three cars overturned after Bolton's 1–0 Cup victory. Two hours before kick-off, Burnley fans attacked Bolton in the Stork Hotel with bricks and bottles. Trouble then broke out after the final whistle after Burnley fans reacted angrily to pitch celebrations by away fans. Police sent mounted officers on to divide fans and restore order. Club secretary Des McBain promised a life ban for every Bolton fan convicted of the trouble. Again, the editorial spat fury. "So conditioned are we to mindless soccer violence in this country that Saturday's disgraceful scenes between Burnley and Bolton fans are unlikely to rate a mention when they read out the Requiem for our once-proud national game. Equally, there can be no doubt that the Burnley fans who invaded the pitch were spoiling for trouble, harassing visiting supporters and terrorising families by charging them into the Bob Lord stand after being driven off the field by mounted police ... If such incidents can occur at a first round FA Cup tie between two Fourth Division clubs, the football authorities must shudder to think what is going to happen when our big clubs are allowed back into Europe."

Fearful of official sanctions that would accompany further violence, the club rushed through a raft of measures to limit hooliganism. The "Out With the Lout" campaign, set up a year earlier to challenge racist chanting amongst Bolton fans, was resurrected and an £800 grant from the Football Trust allowed them to install another CCTV camera in the ground. Violence within the ground had fallen drastically after the first camera was installed. In an attempt to reduce trouble away from home, the club asked all coach parties to book through the club. "We do not want to make money out of this but we want to make sure that our name in the game does not get any worse," said commercial director, Alf Davies. To prove their tough approach, the ten Bolton fans convicted after the Burnley trouble were banned for life.

Barnsley away, FA Cup third round, Jan 1988
The Second Division side beat Bolton in a game beset with trouble, despite the presence of 160 police officers, 50 more than usual. Barnsley's second goal was the spark for vicious fighting and it took the introduction of police dogs to restore order. Inspector Richard Gray of South Yorkshire Police said that even before the game groups of Bolton fans were circling the town centre in search of home fans to attack, but stressed that the trouble came from the "mindless minority", as usual. "A lot of idiots follow football teams these days but Bolton seem to have more than

most," he remarked. Bolton fans inundated their paper with claims of police over-reaction. Whatever the basis of these, it appeared that Bolton's record of trouble meant that any sign of misbehaviour was increasingly likely to be met by a harsh response.

Wolves, Feb 1988

Thirty were arrested after trouble before and during the game. West Midlands Police were forced to deploy 70 officers in two rows along the length of the away end, but their actions caused outrage amongst Bolton fans and even the club. "The police were provoking trouble with our supporters," claimed Bolton chairman Barry Chaytow. "All our supporters were doing were making comments, not using foul language, yet the police were going in and taking them away. Our fans were telling us that our team were rubbish and that was a fair comment on the day. Certainly it was no reason to take people away. I went down with our club President, Nat Lofthouse, during the first half and asked to see the officer in charge. I told him that he was out of order and I pleaded with him to let our fans go. I was as good as told I should mind my own business as it was nothing to do with me."

Burnley, April 1988

Tensions were running high after the FA Cup violence earlier in the season and a huge police operation failed to prevent disorder before the game. Four hundred Bolton fans laid siege to a pub holding Burnley fans. Bricks and other missiles were thrown through the windows of the Bradford Arms in a 60-minute reign of terror. Two police vans were damaged and officers from the Greater Manchester Police Tactical Aid Group were drafted in to restore order. "There were women and children inside this pub," said landlady Agnes Hobbs. "It could have been murder." There was further trouble during the game when Bolton fans tried to smash their way through a fire door to reach the visiting fans. A policeman was injured and his helmet was knocked off with a scaffolding pole.

Wrexham, May 1988

Bolton travelled away to Wrexham needing a win to take the title. Four thousand supporters made the trip down to a nervous Welsh town. Pleas to stop pulling down fencing were ignored by sections of the away contingent celebrating their team's promotion. Bolton fans invaded the kop end and wrecked the goalposts and 100 seats, but the police were relieved that the trouble was not worse. "The majority of the fans were very well behaved," said Inspector Richard Jones. "There have been some reports that there were pitched battles after the game. If there were, we didn't see any of them, and considering there was such a large contingent of travelling fans there were very few arrests." His views were not shared by the club. "It was the worst violence I had seen all season," said Wrexham club secretary Stan Gandy. "Regrettably, Bolton fans were the same when they were here last time. At least sixty seats have been broken and we had to cancel a Sunday League game because of the damage to the posts, which are now in several bits."

Southend away, Aug 1988

Rival fans squared up as the players left the pitch at half-time, forcing police with dogs to put on a show of strength in the centre circle. It was the first time in Southend's history that dogs had been brought into the Roots Hall ground but even their presence did not stop a mass pitch invasion at the end of a game, which Bolton lost. There were immediate repercussions, not least because the club had publicly opposed the Government's plans for a compulsory ID scheme. "We were saying that we can handle the problem without a 100 per cent membership scheme but these people are proving that we can't," said an angry Des McBain. "All our objections are being kicked into touch." Sports Minister Colin Moynihan lost no time in highlighting Bolton's problem by listing the Southend incident as one of seven football riots to back up his request for ID cards.

"Wanderers are now in the ranks of the bad boys," said the *BEN* editorial. "They have achieved a certain notoriety and, sooner or later, the FA is going to act. Bolton supporters could soon be subjected to bans or restrictions similar to those imposed on the notorious Wolves followers. At worst there could be a total away ban on Wanderers fans. The cancer has taken hold and drastic action is called for."

* * *

Their next game was at home to Cardiff, a potentially explosive fixture. Before the game started the fans were warned over the public address system

Bolton's mob on the charge at Burnley. Their firms had some strange names, including the Cuckoo Boys and the Billy Whizz Fan Club.

that their behaviour had to improve or the club would be fined. The warning was ignored within a minute of the game starting when trouble broke out on the terraces. There were also clashes between rival gangs of Bolton fans in the Wagon and Horses pub near the ground. According to eyewitnesses, groups from Tonge Moor and Great Lever, both regulars in the pub on match days, fought one another with bottles, glasses, tables, pool cues and balls after one man had spilled a pint over another. "There was an atmosphere of trouble after the drink was spilled," a barmaid said. "The landlord went in to try and calm things down. Then it just went off and there was utter chaos. Everything was flying around the room for about twenty minutes. I have never shaken as much in my life."

With such a litany of violence, the police felt compelled to act. The first raids, catching 27 people, came on 2 March 1989, and a further 16 were arrested a month later. The local press keenly supported their actions; indeed, many hoped that the days of trouble were now over. "The police may have turned the corner in their fight to smash the

organised violence that has besmirched the name of Bolton Wanderers," reported the paper.

A year later, 34 men pleaded guilty at Bolton Crown Court to football-related offences. The police operation spanned several months and targeted the ringleaders of the four main mobs. It combined the use of several undercover officers, backed up by surveillance cameras inside the Bolton ground, providing video evidence. The court heard how the undercover officers infiltrated the gangs as part of the painstaking and dangerous task of gathering evidence. They tracked them around the country, identified their associates, and even secretly filmed some of the violence. The operation was seen as such a success that it was considered a blueprint for other police forces.

One Bolton lad agreed that the firm were sucked in by the undercover policemen. "Call us naive, call us plain fucking stupid, and, thinking about it now, we were. One game, these blokes turned up with Scouse accents, said they were from Warrington and we took it, hook, line and sinker. We had a few lads from that neck of the woods who came with us so it's not as daft as it sounds, and give the coppers credit, they were up for a brawl. A few lads who at the start thought they might be snides saw them attacking rival fans, so before long they were accepted by most of us. It was a nightmare when we were all nicked, we were in the police station and the cunts were there and we thought they had been nicked, too. Next minute they are at the custody desk booking us in."

However, any hopes that the convictions would eradicate hooliganism at Bolton were soon dashed, as the club's fans continued to misbehave the following season, with trouble at Bristol Rovers, Rotherham and Wigan. Mass disorder occurred at the home game against Birmingham as Bolton fans threw bricks at police and away fans after the game. Bolton qualified for the play-offs on the final day of the season, but again the day was marred by violence. Cars were attacked and overturned, one-arm bandits were raided and locals harassed. When Bolton lost the play-off final against Tranmere Rovers in June 1990, 300 of their fans attempted to attack rival supporters.

The police raids and subsequent convictions did in fact signal the end of Bolton's hooligan heyday. That, coupled with the introduction of CCTV, football intelligence and stiffer penalties, began slowly to have an effect. Trouble did persist, such as the 500-strong mass brawl between Stoke and Bolton in October 1990, and the running battles in Cleethorpes four hours after Bolton's away game in Grimsby in August 1993, but was becoming rarer.

After a few years passed off without any major reports of violence, the club were reunited with local rivals, Blackburn, as both clubs' fortunes on the pitch nose-dived. An NCIS report from a Division One game at Ewood Park, on 23 September 2000, read, "Serious disorder was prevented by an extensive policing operation. During the game there were two small fights inside the stadium. A home supporter was also arrested for shouting racist abuse at a player. Post match, police monitored two groups of supporters as they moved away from the ground; the two groups swelled to about 100 Bolton and 50 Blackburn. The two groups shadowed each other on opposite sides of the road, separated by foot and mounted officers. Firm policing and the presence of mounted officers prevented disorder. The Bolton supporters made an attempt to break the escort but again the presence

of the mounted officers was vital in holding them in place. They were escorted to the train station. At 7pm police attended an incident where a group of 15 Bolton supporters were causing problems in a public house near Blackburn's ground. They were removed by police but went to a second pub where they again caused problems. They were again removed and one arrest was made. The remainder were placed in a taxi minibus but 100 yards up the road the taxi stopped and the Bolton supporters alighted and attacked four drunken Blackburn supporters. Three more arrests were made and the group was escorted out of Blackburn. A number of Blackburn supporters were involved in disorder in the town centre later in the evening with other local men."

Another NCIS report stated that there was more violence at the return game that season, on February 2. "This local derby passed without serious incident until the second half of the game, which Rovers eventually won four-one. Each Rovers goal resulted in pitch runners and the match score and celebrations of the Rovers fans led to a marked deterioration in the behaviour of Bolton fans. Just before full-time paramedics requested police assistance as they were treating a Blackburn fan in the south west corner of the ground in view of Bolton fans who were making threats and trying to get through the segregation gates to confront Blackburn fans. Officers intervened and this culminated in a serious confrontation between police and a large number of Bolton fans on the concourse of the Nat Lofthouse Stand. Officers used batons to disperse the crowd from the concourse and to defend themselves from attack. Once outside the stadium, the Bolton fans remained confrontational and hostile, and batons were again used by officers to defend themselves. Mounted officers were deployed to disperse this crowd. As the supporters mingled on the coach park, disorder took place between rival fans."

The same season, scores of Everton fans infiltrated sections of the ground reserved for the home fans in an FA Cup tie marred by sporadic outbreaks of violence. And in November 2002, four Bolton fans were banned for life from the Reebok Stadium. Stephen Barrow, Shane Durham, Graham Knowles and Russell Brookes were banned after being found guilty of attacking Man United fans in a local shopping centre in January that year and were given three-year banning orders.

The NCIS report on the incident read, "A tense stand-off developed in Bolton town centre before the match. More than 40 Manchester United fans gathered in Corks Pub while Bolton supporters packed into Yates's Wine Lodge across the road. Sixty police officers in riot gear blocked off the road and used eight police vans to form a cordon down the middle of the road. Two of Corks' windows were smashed and bottles and glasses were thrown as the hooligan groups tried to get at each other. There were 20 arrests and 20 more fans were ejected from the Reebok stadium during the game."

With trouble once again making the headlines, the club also announced a mandatory five-year ban for anyone convicted of acts of violence but without receiving a banning order from the court.

But it was not just local police and the club who tackled the hooligans from Bolton. "Nine football hooligans have been jailed thanks to the American crime fighting agency, the FBI," said one news report. "The men, all Bolton Wanderers fans, were caught on video tape last February, assaulting a Manchester United fan at Chorley railway station, Lancashire, but the CCTV footage was accidentally wiped by station staff. However, the tape and video recorder were sent to the FBI headquarters in Virginia where scientists were able to restore the images. Preston Crown Court heard three United fans were knocked to the ground and kicked repeatedly at the railway station. Steven Povah, 47, from Leigh, was knocked unconscious, spent several days in intensive care, and needed reconstructive surgery to an eye socket. Mr Povah can only walk with the aid of a stick. Nine men, all from Bolton, pleaded guilty to violent disorder. Ronald Brickles, 31, and Anthony Charnock, 32, were both jailed for two and a half years and 44-year-old Malcolm Cooling was imprisoned for 12 months. The other six, aged between 38 and 48, were given intermittent custody orders to serve time at weekends. A tenth man, aged 43, was given 150 hours' community service."

At least one Bolton veteran admits that the tide at Bolton has turned, and recent seasons have been relatively peaceful off the pitch, whilst on it Sam Allardyce has turned a mediocre mid-table outfit into Champions League hopefuls.

BOSTON UNITED

Ground: York Street
Firm: No organised, named firm
Rivals: Lincoln, Peterborough, Hull

Boston United are one of the few clubs in the Football League with no organised hooligan presence, but with many local derbies and a young fan base. The club was promoted into the Football League in 2002, after finishing top of the Vauxhall Conference. Its biggest success, other than achieving League status, was a 6–1 win over Derby County in the FA Cup in 1955. Nineteen years later, Boston held the then reigning League Champions to a goalless draw at the Baseball Ground.

Boston might not have an organised mob but there has been trouble down the years. As far back as 1967, the club was forced to post warnings to its fans after trouble at a Northern Premier League game with Netherfield. The club was fined £15 and the notices were posted around the terraces and in the club programme.

The club's first season in the old Third Division pitted them against local rivals Lincoln. "Welcome to the League," ran the headline in the local paper. At least 80 of the Lincoln Transit Elite made the trip, and during the game a large group of travelling fans tried to break through police lines to attack home supporters. The local paper carried a photograph of one Lincoln fan being led away with blood pouring from a head wound. Boston fans responded by throwing two smoke grenades on to the pitch. After the game there was further disorder, with police forced to draw batons and use CS gas to contain the Lincoln fans who remained in town.

The following season, an away fixture at Hull saw more trouble for Boston fans. The home side won the game with a last minute goal and, unwisely, a group of Boston fans attempted to storm the Hull end. Retribution was swift and violent and all six of the coaches transporting the away fans were attacked and badly damaged after the game at a cost of more than £10,000.

On 13 June 2004, 100 people ran amok in Boston town centre following England's European Championship defeat by France. The police were called to The Still pub to quell a disturbance but the violence soon spread to other parts of the town.

Police reinforcements were called up from across Lincolnshire and in the ensuing trouble two police cars were overturned and set alight, several shops were looted and another was set on fire. Thirty-nine people were arrested and several were sent to prison. Many of those convicted received bans from every football ground in the country for up to seven years. There was further trouble after England were knocked out of the competition by Portugal. "It was just general chaos," said a local journalist. "Shop fronts were being smashed through and people were trying to loot cigarettes and beer from the local off-licence. I think it was just pure frustration at the football."

Whilst the disturbance was, in a roundabout way, football-related, it seems the rioting and looting was hardly organised. Frustration undoubtedly played a part but it is perhaps relevant that Boston has a Portuguese migrant community, most of whom work in the surrounding agricultural and food-packing industry. Only three days before the riots, more than 46% of voters in Boston backed the UK Independence Party (UKIP) or the British National Party (BNP) in the European Elections. It was the highest combined vote for the two parties anywhere in the country.

The absence of home-grown hooligans has actually attracted the presence of rival fans, with Lincoln, Swansea and Notts County all taking small mobs to Boston during the 2004/05 season. And after a recent game at Notts County, Boston fans clashed with Forest supporters at Nottingham railway station.

BOURNEMOUTH

Ground: Dean Court
Firm: Boscombe Casual Elite
Rivals: Southampton, Reading

"Bournemouth are on the Tote, they're fucking taking it!" So *Bovver* author Chris Brown recalled the day in January 1974 when Bournemouth had the cheek to try to take Bristol Rovers' Tote end. It was a top of the table clash between league leaders Rovers, then unbeaten, and second-placed Bournemouth. When the two sides had last played each other, on the opening day of the season, Rovers fans had rampaged through the southern coastal town and rival supporters clashed on the seafront and in numerous nightclubs. Now Bournemouth were trying their luck by arriving in the Tote early and catching the home fans by surprise. "We couldn't get out quick enough," recalled Brown. "We stormed across the road, eager to displace the intruders who had dared to take our patch. It wasn't as if it was Villa or City we were up against, just a bunch of Tory-voting beach boys who only work in the summer."

Rovers steamed into the Bournemouth lads and after a few minutes of fierce fighting, managed to reclaim their end. But that was not the end of the trouble. After the game there was widespread disorder as rival fans fought and vehicles and property were vandalised.

Hooliganism at Bournemouth first hit the national press in 1967, when the club was forced to post warning notices around the ground after disturbances at home games. During the early Seventies, when the club went through a relatively successful period, the town could be an unpleasant place to visit for a number of away teams. The Cherries, as Bournemouth are known, have long considered Southampton their main rivals and there were a number of dust-ups between their fans in the 1970s and after a League Cup game in 1987.

As Bournemouth's fortunes declined, so Southampton adopted a more paternal attitude to their neighbours. "They try to stir up rivalry but we consider them more a little brother," said Nick, a Southampton lad. "We have gone down there and played friendlies on more than one occasion when they have been strapped for cash, but still a small section of them seem to hate Saints. It is not reciprocated and their results are cheered at St Mary's. Bluntly, they are not on our radar."

Other rivalries exist with Reading and Exeter, and again there has been regular conflict with both. Bournemouth are dismissive of Reading, though their rivalry intensified in 2001 when they travelled to Berkshire needing a win to secure a place in the play-offs and ended up with a draw. The clashes with Exeter have usually involved only small groups from either side but have been fierce and intense enough to earn mutual respect.

Bournemouth's seaside location has attracted many big mobs who have used it as an opportunity to misbehave, the most famous being Leeds in May, 1990, when a sizeable chunk of the 10,000 fans battled with riot police over two days (see LEEDS). While Leeds understandably grabbed the media headlines – 3,000 people fighting was not your usual run-of-the-mill football match – many Bournemouth lads are keen to record their own exploits that day.

"One myth is that there were no Bournemouth giving it back," recalled JB. "But the fact is Bournemouth made sure they got some revenge in isolated incidents." One such incident, where a group of locals attacked two van loads of Leeds in Blandford, is described on the Bournemouth Internet forum. Another post claims that a group of Leeds were also attacked outside the 5th Avenue nightclub. The bitterness of that day still runs deep.

One of Bournemouth's greatest football triumphs in recent years was their 2–0 Cup win over Manchester United. The result did not go down well with a group of Cockney Reds who had made the trip. A few minutes before the end of the match, they left the ground, made their way to the home end and steamed in. Several people were knocked to the ground and injured as others trampled over them after a crash barrier collapsed. The match was held up for five minutes as fans spilled on to the pitch to escape the chaos. One Bournemouth fan said, "There must have been fifty or sixty of them and they just steamed into us. We couldn't get out of the way. Boots and fists were flying and I heard that some of them had knives and I saw people and barriers go down."

One train carrying away supporters home ended its journey unexpectedly early after Manchester fans again went on the rampage. The train crew stopped the Inter-City express at Southampton after United fans forced open a closed buffet bar and wrecked the compartment. "There were about sixty Manchester United supporters on the train, all from the London area," said a BTP spokesman.

Two weeks after the United game, Bournemouth hosted Millwall in the League and again there was trouble. Fifty Millwall went on the rampage after leaving the Gander on the Green pub before the game and several were arrested. One of them was Frank Holding, of Peckham, South London. He was convicted of using threatening words and behaviour likely to cause a breach of the peace after he attempted to stop a fellow Millwall fan from being arrested. The court learned that unemployed Holding had two previous convictions for football violence, which did little to impress the judge. "If you put as much energy into getting a job as you do following football you would probably get one," he told Frank.

The following season, Millwall caused even more trouble. Their fans had recently been banned from travelling to away matches after an infamous Cup riot at Luton, but that didn't deter 2,000 from making the short journey to the south coast and taking over the ground. "They came out of the seats and across the corner of the pitch into the South End, I have never seen a panic like it," remembered one Bournemouth fan. "They were fucking lunatics and apart from one of our lads who had a go, nobody was covered in glory that night. I think most of us ended up hiding in the Supporters' Club Very embarrassing."

A few years later, Bournemouth hosted Millwall again. A couple of Bournemouth fans were on a prison coach, having been sentenced for offences at a game against Fulham, and saw the Millwall yobs mooching around. "We started giving them loads of abuse and hand signals through the coach windows," one later recalled. "The screws on the bus were panicking and telling us to stop. We were killing ourselves laughing at the screws and Millwall were laughing at us when they saw we were hand-cuffed together. Mind you, wild horses couldn't have got me off that coach, there were some right mean-looking bastards with them."

Another fan, JB, remembered, "Some successes and some defeats characterised the 1980s, with the highlights being seeing only the backs of heads of the Reading, Villa, Oxford, Andover and Saints firms, although these successes were put into perspective when we came a not-so-clever second against a couple of obscure mobs." Bournemouth were "turned over" by the then non-league Wycombe Wanderers in an FA Cup tie in 1980, and again three years later at another FA Cup tie at Windsor & Eton, though at this game the non-leaguers' firm was bolstered by a group of Chelsea who gave the Cherries a rough ride. "We were stoned and stalked all night and we were lucky to get home in one piece," recalled a Bournemouth lad.

Others deemed bad days included Bristol City away, when a van that had brought a group of lads

Mirrorpix

Bournemouth riot police clash with some of the 10,000-strong Leeds contingent during an infamous Bank Holiday fixture on the South Coast in 1990

to a match was turned over, getting chased through a snowstorm at Middlesbrough, and the visit of Everton during a sunny pre-season friendly that concluded similarly, but without the snow. The Bournemouth lads felt more confident when six of them started on a similar number of Hull outside the Queens Park pub a few years ago, though their optimism shrank when a second vanload of Hull lads pulled up alongside them.

The hooligan scene in Bournemouth largely died a death after the Leeds game. Bank Holiday fixtures were stopped and the resulting drop in income had a knock-on effect on the club's fortunes. Off the pitch, fewer mobs began to travel down. But organised violence has returned to the club in recent years. "Bournemouth's mob had a quiet period throughout the 1990s, only turning out for really big games," said one lad currently active. "However, the last three years have seen an amazing upturn in our fortunes. Small steps were made with a few lads getting fed up with shitty mobs coming to town and taking liberties, so they loosely mobilised themselves at home and for a few away trips."

The current firm is called the Boscombe Casual Elite and was born in 2001 in Southampton's Yates's, where a dozen Bournemouth lads were drinking after their match at Cambridge was postponed. The name stuck.

The final game of the 2001/02 season saw the largest Bournemouth turnout for some years. A claim that a few Bournemouth had been bullied at Lincoln by far superior numbers attracted about 100 local lads for the return fixture. This was only half the number that Lincoln brought down but an impressive mob for the town. "A big Bournemouth turnout had been coming but the response was astounding and helped seal Bournemouth's return to the world of football violence," declared JB. "While there was no major violence, the BCE were bang up for it all day. A few minor scuffles occurred, with mixed results, but the major incident came when the OB brought the Lincoln Transit Elite escort past the pub where Bournemouth were drinking.

"As soon as they were close, Bournemouth launched everything that wasn't nailed down at them. Traffic came to a standstill as bottles, glasses, bricks and bits of wood were slung across the road towards the Lincoln bullies. Unfortunately, a pub fence stopped what would have been an almighty tear-up but, with hundreds of OB, there would have been dozens more arrests. The OB were extremely baton-happy throughout the day but the BCE constantly gave them the run-around. However, when there are literally hundreds of them accompanying both mobs, then nothing is going to kick-off on a large scale. The closest it came was very nearly a major fuck-up by us. The police had split the home fans into two groups and we roamed the back streets separately and came across each other. Tooled up with lumps of wood and poles, our lot charged them and they piled forward, each thinking the other was Lincoln. It was only as we met in the middle of the road that someone shouted, 'They're Bournemouth.'"

Buoyed by their turnout against Lincoln, the BCE grew and had their first major fight at the club's away match at Bristol City in September 2003. "Twenty-five Bournemouth – virtually all youth – had been drinking all day around town when they bumped into Bristol's City Service Firm lads," recalled JB. "It was a decent brawl and lasted about two or three minutes before the BCE forced the CSF young 'uns onto their toes. It was nothing major and we appreciate it was only Bristol's young lads, but a result is a result and we were having that one."

"Today, Bournemouth has a hardcore of thirty lads who regularly turn out at home, with numbers swelling to as large as eighty for big games," claimed another BCE lad. "It is mostly a game set of youth with a sprinkling of older lads, although more senior members take charge when big opposition is expected. A cup game against Southampton or Leeds would probably push the number nearer to 150. In 2001, there were two Bournemouth lads on bans but this has now risen to fourteen, a sign the police have realised that we have got it going again."

During the 2003/04 season, 40 BCE arrived at Brentford at eleven in the morning but the only fighting was after the game with the police. A similar-sized mob travelled to Yeovil and again fought police. Thirty went to Port Vale and there was a small clash after the game.

Bournemouth's final game of the season was at home to Stockport and the northerners brought a firm of lads down on the Friday evening. "There were small offs on Friday night and Saturday afternoon with Bournemouth largely coming out on top," said a Bournemouth lad. "However, as night drew in the numbers, especially among the older lads, dwindled. Regardless, a suicide mob of fifteen youth lads made their way up to where they had heard sixty Stockport were drinking, knowing full well they were going to take a battering. The EVF [Stockport's Edgeley Volunteer Force] steamed out of the boozer and launched bottles and glasses at the young BCE. Some Bournemouth had it on their toes, with only four or five game lads staying to fight. Despite showing their courage, or foolhardiness, numbers got the better of them and they were forced to do one. However, that night was useful for sorting out who wanted it and who didn't for the following season."

A new rivalry was created in September 2004 following their match against Leyton Orient, when 14 Londoners attacked six Bournemouth fans, of whom only three were lads. They were hit with plant pots, ashtrays and even road signs and, despite the Bournemouth lads holding their ground for a while, the battle left two of them badly injured. "Fucking bullies," said a Bournemouth lad, dismissively.

The same season saw small fights with Bristol Rovers, Peterborough, Brighton, Cardiff, Exeter and Chelsea but none have amounted to much. Following an altercation between a few Bournemouth Youth and some police outside the Blackpool home game, the local media ran a campaign to get them banned and, subsequently, three were handed banning orders. The biggest turnout was the 50 they took to Peterborough but they encountered no opposition.

Very few firms would put the BCE on their priority list, and hence they have encountered little action. It will be the headlines from that May Bank Holiday weekend in 1990 that will be remembered when football hooliganism and Bournemouth are mentioned in the same sentence.

BRADFORD CITY

Ground: Valley Parade
Firms: The Ointment, Bradford Section Five
Rivals: Huddersfield, Leeds
Police operations: Olive

Bradford is a deeply divided city. The 2001 riots only brought into the open what had been happening for some time – a growing segregation between the white and Muslim communities. It is surprising therefore that the Bradford City hooligan gang, The Ointment, is a multi-racial group with little of these frictions. Indeed, on the day of the riots many of the Ointment were present merely as observers, and there is little indication that any of them have become involved in the British National Party, which has since won four council seats in the area. Indeed, it is one of the few mobs to have a number of Sikhs involved.

The first national media report of hooliganism involving Bradford was in May 1969, when the club played at Darlington. It was the final day of the season and both clubs still in with a chance of promotion. Bradford ran out 3-1 winners but the game was overshadowed by crowd trouble, which held up the match for twelve minutes. It began in the fourth minute, just after Darlington had taken the lead. Within a minute hundreds of rival fans were fighting in the cricket pitch end and on the pitch. The players were taken off and appeals were made by both club chairmen, both managers and the players. The *Northern Echo* carried a photo of one fan about to smash a wine bottle over the head of a rival.

The following season saw a number of incidents at home matches, culminating in street clashes with Bristol Rovers fans in early March. Several shop windows were smashed and an away coach damaged as Bradford and Bristol Rovers fans fought. A 17-year-old was arrested for possession of a sheath knife inside the ground. When quizzed by police, he said that he had just been kicked so he pulled out the knife in case anyone tried again. "Until recently crowd behaviour after Valley Parade games has been good but in there has been deterioration which is causing the police concern," said a Chief Supt Long.

Local rivalries included Leeds and Huddersfield, but with the former riding high in the First Division,

most of their animosity was directed at Huddersfield. In 1976 there was trouble at the Tony Leighton testimonial at Leeds Road, while the following year saw clashes both home and away. There were further disturbances at their home game against Huddersfield in 1979, and the trouble between the two continued into the Eighties.

"It was a first ever Sunday game and as always the visit of Bradford made it extra special, both on and off the pitch," said a Huddersfield lad of one such incident. "With the match being on TV, about twenty lads went to one of the lads' houses to watch it and the rest went to the game. At this point it was unclear whether Bradford were here or not. Around seven of us decided to go out just before the match had ended and walk up to by McDonalds. A couple of lads were talking to bouncers up there who said that City were in the Royal Swan, which is around twenty yards from McDonalds.

"As we approached McDonalds we saw a couple of City out on the street having a nose about. One of the lads decided to get in first and went towards them but Bradford must have been stood by the door of the Swan because they were out so quick, chanting the usual 'Ointment Mental', and they had us on our toes. At one stage I was trying to get in McDonalds but pulling the door the wrong way. As it happened quite a few from the flat and who had not been to the game were walking up the road at this time. They came running up but we still did not have the numbers and Bradford were seriously backing Town off.

"By then sirens were ringing round town and there were little scuffles breaking out. When the police got Bradford up to the bus station we went to the Plumbers, which is near the station, but Bradford brought it to us again, trying to break out of the escort.

"On another occasion at home, as the match finished and it got later into the night, most folk were thinking of drifting off to their locals when one Town lad came into the Crescent and said he had seen a mob walking on Bradford Road. We all congregated outside the pub. To get onto Bradford Road there are two ways from the pub and we were discussing which way to go but then the decision was made for us. Bradford came round the corner with the usual chant.

"I think their plan to take us by surprise had

severely backfired as everybody was well pissed off with all the running round earlier in the day. Not one lad from that incident had any hesitation and everybody was straight into them. For a brief moment it looked as though they were going to stand. Some actually did, although getting a quite severe beating – bins over the head and the like. As they seemed to realise the game was up they split into different mobs, going in all directions. To give them credit, they were actually trying to stand, until they saw those caught were getting a hiding.

"By the time the chasing had finished we were on at the Engine pub on Bradford Road, probably a good half a mile from the original incident, and the police were on the way. As we made our way back to the pub we realised that quite a few of their lot had been got at badly, as ambulances were coming as well. One lad was unfortunate enough to be cornered in a Chinese restaurant, ending up as number fifty-three on the menu, and a few were laid out on the top road getting treatment. At the end of the day it was highly unfortunate for Bradford that they were seen by a lad in his car, because I think if they had had the element of surprise it may have turned out differently. We'll never know."

In July 1986, a 17-year-old Bradford fan was stabbed to death during an extraordinarily vicious, three-way fight involving Bradford, Leeds and Huddersfield. Darrell Penney, a trainee baker, was stabbed several times during a clash lasting two hours and involving over 100 people, and died on his way to hospital. Police told the press that numerous weapons had been used in the late night disturbances, including Stanley knives, bricks and bottles. Eleven people were arrested and an 18-year-old youth from Huddersfield charged with the murder.

But by far the most significant and far-reaching event for the club and its supporters was the terrible fire that broke out at Valley Parade on 11 May 1985, at a home game against Lincoln City. It began as a day of celebration, with the Bantams parading the Division Three championship trophy around the ground before kick-off – marking City's promotion into the second tier of English football for the first time since before the Second World War. At half-time, however, a tiny blaze caused probably by a discarded match or cigarette took hold among rubbish piled beneath the main stand, and quickly engulfed the antiquated wooden structure. In the appalling inferno, 56 people lost their lives and more than 260 were injured. The death toll would have been higher had it not been for the courage of police officers and 22 spectators, who later received bravery awards.

The subsequent Popplewell Inquiry led to new safety legislation covering sports grounds. Unsurprisingly, the disaster also had an effect on hooliganism at the club; running around the streets looking to beat up rival fans lost what appeal it may have had for some. Yet others, shockingly, persisted with behaviour that was now ingrained, almost an addiction.

Another set of supporters with a long history with Bradford is Sheffield United. In October 1981, United face Steve Cowens encountered his first real taste of hooliganism at a match at Bradford. One hundred Ointment attacked a pub of United, throwing bricks, bottles and waving bats as they moved in. Cowens says that United rallied and finally managed to get out of the door and as their numbers grew so Bradford's bottle went. There was further trouble on the way to the ground and inside rival fans exchanged missiles, including pool balls and darts. "I have never seen so many people led away with head injuries," he wrote in his book *Blades Business Crew*.

The rest of the Eighties saw regular bouts of trouble between the two clubs in both cities. In 1986, a coach carrying 46 Bradford City fans to Portsmouth was driven straight to a police station in Leicestershire after fighting at a nearby M1 service station with the Blades. One of the Sheffield contingent (who was actually a Villa lad) was badly injured and several of the coach windows were smashed. The fans did not miss much, as Bradford were hammered 4–0 by Pompey, and one of the Ointment received a nine-month prison sentence.

The BBC were up for revenge at the next game in Bradford in early October 1986. One hundred and fifty Sheffield lads made the trip on three coaches and photocopies of a newspaper article retelling the service station incident were put on the seats to gee people up. During the match Bradford fans repeatedly chanted the name of the service station at their rivals.

A clash between a small group of Rotherham Blades and the Ointment resulted in the death of a 17-year-old after he ran into the path of a car as he tried to escape the Blades charge. Richard Joyce suffered serious injuries and died later in hospital. He should not have been at the game, as he was on a ban as part of his bail conditions following the incident a couple of months before in which Darrell Penney was stabbed to death.

At the return fixture, the Ointment took 80 lads down to Sheffield. "We were surprised at the numbers they turned out but agreed it was a show of strength for their deceased friend," recalled Cowens. "We also had sympathy. Although we were all hooligans, no one wanted a rival dead or maimed, that just wasn't what it was all about."

Bradford is a big urban area, and the hooligans could occasionally pull out large numbers. For an away fixture at Derby in April 1985 they took 200 to Derby seeking payback for trouble at the home game earlier that season, when 29 were arrested and one newspaper headline read: "Fans go mad." Once they reached Derby, cars were kicked, fences ripped down and bottles and bricks thrown as the gangs met outside the Jubilee pub.

The Ointment struggled against the Leeds Service Crew in the Eighties, however, and could never match their neighbours' numbers. In 1986, Leeds fans partially wrecked Odsall stadium, setting fire to a chip van and storming the pitch. The resentment towards Leeds was more than just local rivalry, it was racial as well. Leeds had a strong NF influence in the 1980s and many of its active supporters were white lads from Bradford. Unsurprisingly, there was great hostility between the NF-leaning mob and the multi-racial Ointment.

Mark Chester of Stoke's Naughty Forty is less than charitable about the Ointment, dismissing them in his book *Naughty* as brick throwers, bottlers and, on one occasion, informers. He charts a series of incidents during the late Eighties at which Bradford ran each time. These included a clash in the 1987/88 season, when 20-odd Stoke ran 70 Bradford in the Potteries, and another in the early Nineties when seven of Stoke's Under Fives claim to have held their own against 40 Bradford.

Police were on full alert when Bradford visited York City in the early 1990s. Pre-match intelligence suggested that The Ointment were travelling over tooled-up, with a view to fighting inside the ground. Police searched away fans with metal detectors and discovered dozens of concealed weapons, including flick knives, Stanley blades, a metal scribing spike

and chains. Dozens more weapons were found in surrounding gardens and bins as word of the searches spread. There was still trouble inside the ground, with Bradford fans attacking the police with coins and other missiles. Seven men were convicted and fined a total of £1700. The local papers carried photographs of the array of confiscated weapons, while Bradford City attempted to distance itself from the incident by claiming that Leeds United fans were behind any intended trouble. The police, meanwhile, were happy with the day's events. "We feel we were at least successful in preventing these weapons getting on the terraces."

In 1994, the Ointment turned up 50-handed at Cardiff shortly before Christmas and "slapped" a few Soul Crew before the game. Cardiff had not been expecting them to show, and by the time they got a firm together, the Yorkshire crew had moved on towards the ground. The return fixture was on the last day of the season and a mob of Cardiff made the long journey over in search of revenge. "Someone booked two late coaches from a luxury holiday firm, telling them it was for a wedding reception in Halifax," according to Tony Rivers in *Soul Crew*. "There were 110 lads on these buses from all over South Wales: it was the cream of the Soul Crew."

From Halifax, the gang made their way into Bradford by train but they were met at the station by police spotters, including the familiar face of NCIS officer Richard Shakespeare. There were a few minor skirmishes, with Bradford throwing bottles at them but then scattering when Cardiff charged. In one incident, Cardiff caught Bradford in the Market Tavern pub and launched into them with tables and stools.

There was further trouble after the game when a small group of Soul Crew broke through police lines and clashed with the Ointment. "We got to the top of the road and it was full of Bradford. Some Cardiff started barging through, then a big group of dressers passed," wrote Rivers. "Fair play to them, they came steaming into us and it was proper off again, both sides not giving an inch. Two policemen on horseback charged between us, forcing us back down a small alley."

Also in 1994, the Ointment attacked a known Huddersfield pub – but the incident was secretly filmed by the police. Fifteen Bradford fans were

CCTV footage released by West Yorkshire Police of violent clashes between Bradford City and Aberdeen football fans in Bradford city centre in July 2003.

sentenced to a total of 20 years' imprisonment, while the Huddersfield fans escaped punishment after claiming they were innocent victims who only retaliated to an unprovoked attack. Hostilities were renewed on December 2003, when Huddersfield ambushed a train carrying Bradford supporters, hurling missiles through its windows. The attack happened as the train pulled into Halifax station on the Manchester–York line. Thirty men threw bricks and bottles and eight windows were smashed. The Bradford fans were returning from a match at Wigan.

Bradford City were promoted to the Premiership in May 1999, and this brought them up against old foes Leeds. At a subsequent away game, 56 people were held by police after disturbances inside and outside Elland Road. Forty-four people, all Bradford fans, were nicked before the game but all were later released without charge. Eleven people were arrested at the match in Bradford, in March 2000, though only half for public order offences.

There could have been considerably more trouble, as many Bradford fans were furious that their club had given Leeds fans at least 500 tickets for the Ciba Stand, normally reserved for home supporters. "It was just greed," said Paul Snowden, secretary of the Queensbury branch of the Bradford City Supporters Club. "They didn't need to sell them to Leeds fans."

In early 2001, Bradford clashed with both Manchester clubs in the space of two months. In mid-January, a home game against United saw numerous small fights and several arrests, and there was more trouble after the game as the United escort made its way through Centenary Square on its way to the train station.

In mid-March, at the home match against City, a group of Ointment tried to get into a pub where the City mob was drinking. There was further trouble inside the ground when Manchester fans got into a section reserved for home supporters. Four arrests were made for racial chanting aimed at the local community outside the stadium, which resulted in stones being thrown into the stadium from local children. There was more disorder after the game and in total 20 Manchester City and six Bradford fans were arrested.

In July 2003 Bradford's pre-season friendly against Aberdeen led to serious fighting after the game (see ABERDEEN) which was caught on CCTV. A short time later, dozens of police raided the homes of 20 Bradford supporters in a series of co-ordinated dawn raids in what became known as Operation Olive. This was in addition to 21 arrested on the day itself, and the police also sent their sister force in Scotland CCTV images of another dozen people believed to be Aberdeen fans. Among those detained was an accountant, a builder, a window fitter and a machine operator. Chief Inspector David Lunn, in charge of the operation, told the press, "Our message is that Bradford City football club and West Yorkshire Police will not tolerate such behaviour. At the end of the day people have died through football violence. It must stop now."

Eight Bradford fans were subsequently jailed, with sentences ranging from three to five months, and another three were given community service. All were banned from football grounds for several years. The court heard how the fight lasted just 37 seconds before being broken up by police. Eight of the eleven were aged over thirty.

Today, the Ointment is down to a hardcore of thirty people, though this can double for big games, leading the local football intelligence officer to tell one reporter that the gang was using "rent-a-thug" reinforcements. The officer went on to say that they were not paid but attracted by the potential of getting involved in violence. "These are associates of prominents [hooligans] who will come in and give them a hand when they think the need is there," he said. "We see them out and about on match days although they have no particular interest in the team." He added that the core of the Ointment is not growing and that, unlike many other clubs, there were no signs of a new "youth firm" emerging. "It seems that it is the same people who have been involved for years and there are those who are still intent on disorder while in their forties," he said.

BRENTFORD

Ground: Griffin Park
Firms: Hounslow Mentals, TW8 Casuals
Rivals: Fulham, Exeter, QPR

The first recognised firm at Brentford were the Hounslow Mentals, who formed in the early 1970s and were together for about ten years. Their trademark mode of transport dispelled the myth that all Londoners were flash, as they were often seen arriving on enemy territory in the back of an old removal van. Their heyday was 1976-81, when, with numbers averaging 30 to 50, they travelled to most away games.

One infamous trip led to the kidnapping of a Cardiff lad after a Cup game at Ninian Park. The unfortunate Welshman was taken by train back to Paddington and left, tied up with Brentford silk scarves, in the train toilet. Other games where the Mentals left their mark were against Newport, Tranmere, Reading, Swindon and Sheffield Wednesday, where they went into the home Kop. They also travelled to Manchester United and sprayed a bit of graffiti outside the Old Trafford ground which is still there if you look hard enough.

When the Hounslow Mentals' numbers dwindled due to the curse of the Casual era, organised hooliganism at Brentford died down, although, as was the case at most clubs, it never went away completely. Rivalries with certain firms continue to this day, a perfect example being the hatred between Brentford and Fulham which has led to many clashes. The antipathy started in the 1979-80 season, when the teams met for the first time in about 20 years. Fifty Fulham tried to take Brentford's home end but a massive mob chased them onto the pitch in the New Road corner. The return fixture and an FA Cup game the same season saw big fights in Bishops Park, Fulham. The following season, Fulham gained an edge when they brought a big mob to Griffin Park, which provoked a 100-a-side battle before the game. It was the late 1980s before the clubs met again and, over the following few seasons, there were regular clashes.

On New Year's Day, 1996, Brentford took 6,000 fans to Craven Cottage, half of the total attendance. There were Brentford mobs all over the ground and Fulham were well and truly outnumbered. More recently, the clubs met at Griffin Park in a LDV game, with a Fulham mob having a go in the home end. In the last meeting between the sides, three years ago, Fulham tried the same again but were beaten out. Fulham may now have established themselves in the Premiership but there is still a lot of simmering local animosity, especially amongst the older lads.

Brentford have had a complex relationship with Chelsea over the years and quite a few Chelsea faces made Griffin Park their second home, especially as policing and obtaining tickets at Stamford Bridge became tougher. There have been occasions when Chelsea lads have turned up in small numbers to have a go at opposing teams, notably Watford in the late Seventies and Portsmouth in the early Eighties. However, Brentford insist it was always their show. Conversely, Chelsea have had a go at Brentford. When the Bees hosted Windsor & Eton FC in the FA Cup in 1982, a small mob of Chelsea hooligans tried to take over the home end, but were forced out. When they tried again the following week they received an even bigger hammering, although their persistence was admired by the home mob.

These incidents, however, were few and far between and Brentford were regarded as one of the less active firms in the capital – until a new, younger mob emerged in recent years. The TW8 Casuals, named after their London postcode, are mostly in their late teens or early twenties.

QPR are based just around the corner from Griffin Park but the two sets of fans very rarely clash. The new Brentford mob wanted to take on QPR but were told not to by older lads. "There are long-standing reasons for this," explained one. "During the 1980s, QPR used to pop down to our place for the livelier games, as did Chelsea, and a very close rapport was established between the lads. Most are in their mid to late thirties now and do their best to defuse tensions between both sides. As for the younger lads on both sides, that will go off probably sooner rather than later given the amount of pissed-up calls they make to each other. Both sides have been told they can't have it until the next time they play each other. So far they have listened but fuck knows how long it will last. QPR have a very handy youth mob and ours is growing all the time."

Perhaps surprisingly, another rival is Exeter City.

The West Country outfit have not travelled up to Brentford since 1981, but they always turn out when the Bees come to them. A TW8 lad explained, "We always used to travel there because it was a decent train trip, nothing to do with looking for trouble. Simply, it was a good piss-up, as there were loads of good pubs on the way to the ground from the city centre. It then became a bit of a pisstake, they took the hump and one year it went off. So now it's regarded as one of our biggest away games outside London."

This was confirmed when, of the 300 Brentford fans who travelled to Exeter for a midweek LDV Cup match, 50 were the firm. Most came by train, arriving early in the afternoon. They were drinking in a pub on the way to the ground when 20 locals announced themselves at the top of the road. The Bees emptied their glasses and bottles, charged into them and scattered them back up the road. After the game, most headed straight home but a dozen or so went back to the same pub. Exeter were determined to avenge the earlier incident and attacked the pub with CS gas. Those Londoners who weren't rubbing their eyes in pain charged out and forced the home lads on their toes again.

The LDV has proved popular with Brentford lads in recent years. At Southend in March 2001, both sets of fans exchanged missiles and a number of supporters were injured. Southend also tried to get into the away end but were beaten back by police and stewards. After the game there were several clashes between fans and one Brentford lad was stabbed.

One of their best-remembered away days was to Wigan at the turn of the millennium. A mob of 80 made the journey north for what everyone agreed was a nothing game. They left London early and arrived in Wigan at 10.30. Neither the police nor Wigan's Goon Squad were expecting a show and the surprise was clear by the reaction of the sole policeman on duty outside the station. "I didn't know you lot would bring this many," he remarked. It was a sentiment later echoed by members of Wigan's firm. The Bees took over two pubs in the town centre and awaited a home reception committee, but nothing happened. A couple of Wigan spotters told them they had nothing to match them that afternoon and the match passed off peacefully as in a haze of alcohol. Wigan acknowledged the turnout a couple of years later, when for the first time in ages they took a large firm down to Griffin Park.

The biggest outing in the 2003/04 season was to Sheffield Wednesday, when 50 travelled up on a coach and another 20 on the train. They made for the city centre but were intercepted by the Old Bill and taken straight to a pub near the ground. The locals were cleared out and they were given the run of the place until shortly before kick-off. Few of the TW8 minded because the highlight of their trip was a pre-arranged fight with Fulham on the way back. However, this too failed to materialise when their West London rivals claimed they only had 30 lads.

Though it is normally easy to determine most teams' main rivals through locality or history, the same cannot be said of Brentford. Two examples are recent additions to the TW8 hit list. One that emerged from nowhere is Peterborough, with whom there have been regular stand-offs in recent encounters, and the other is Hull City. In 2004, 70 TW8 Casuals chartered two coaches for the trip to Hull and a further 30 went by train. Both groups met in Goole and, after a few hours drinking, made their way into the city. Shocked but undeterred by the away following, 200 Hull were waiting for their return to the station and it kicked off briefly before police, with dogs and horses, restored order. The Londoners were escorted back to Goole, only to find all the pubs near the station closed on police advice. This particularly upset the landlady of the pub they had been in earlier. So impressed had she been by the London boys' earlier behaviour she had prepared a buffet for their return and argued with police when they told her that the lads she was making sandwiches and sausage rolls for were hardened football hooligans.

Being so close to other clubs, it is not surprising that over the years Brentford lads became friendly with other firms and, during the early to mid Nineties, this extended to the fringe political scene, with a couple of Bees being active with the neo-nazi group Combat 18. Even today the more important Brentford games tend to attract one or two guests from other firms, such as QPR and Chelsea, and there are also close connections to Arsenal. The recent cockiness shown by the young members of TW8, however, has meant that these friendships are becoming increasingly strained.

BRIGHTON & HOVE ALBION

Ground: Withdean Stadium
Firm: Bosun Boys, West Street
Rivals: Crystal Palace, Southend
Police operations: Edgar, Facade

Ask any Brighton fan to name the team they hate and they will say Crystal Palace. They may be 50 miles apart, and as a rivalry it does not conjure up the same image as the Old Firm derby or even Portsmouth v Southampton, but the competition between their fans is no less intense. "The rivalry with Palace dates back to a series of games in the 1970s and 1980s," explained Trent, a member of the Brighton firm. "There was loads of trouble at these games."

Brighton's biggest crowd of the season saw their club draw with Palace in October 1976. More than 27,000 people packed into the Goldstone Ground, only to see smoke bombs being thrown on the pitch by Palace supporters. The first was removed by Palace's captain, but a second landed inside the Albion half and play had to be stopped. An announcement was made pleading for no more objects to be thrown on the pitch. Several arrests were made before and after the game.

The following month Brighton drew Palace at home in the FA Cup. It was to end with the visitors twice coming from behind to earn a replay. Nearly 30,000 people watched the game, rival fans fought on the terraces and six people were arrested. The replay was another draw, so a third game was needed to separate the sides, this time on neutral ground, and Palace ran out winners by a single goal.

Before a midweek game in April 1985, up to 200 Brighton fans went on the rampage on the train taking them up to a Palace game, overwhelming the steward and looting the bar. Police made 43 arrests as Palace fans attempted to reach rivals immediately after the match. A further 27 were ejected from the ground as Albion fans hurled lumps of concrete at their opponents, with Palace fans responding with coins.

"In more recent times we haven't played them very much, apart from a couple of pre-season friendlies in the early Nineties," said Trent. "The first friendly was moved from a Saturday afternoon to a Friday night on police advice, but this didn't stop the trouble. Two Brighton lads charged into a mob of seventy Palace lads armed with a crate of milk bottles. The Palace turned and ran before they realised there were only two of them, then the two Brighton bolted, to be greeted by the rest of Brighton's firm coming up the road. The fighting was quelled when the police drove cars between the two mobs. We played another friendly on a week night, found the Palace contingent in a pub and promptly gassed them. The pub was trashed and a bike was thrown through one of the windows. When we played them in the League two seasons ago, Brighton took about 400 lads but were rounded up by Old Bill and taken to the ground. They fought with police all the way."

Another longstanding rivalry is with Southend. There were rows between the two sets of fans throughout the Seventies. Fourteen were arrested in 1974 and, two years later, two Southend fans were stabbed by Brighton. "We've always taken a mob down there," said Trent. "We had a row with them in the late Nineties on the seafront on a glorious sunny day. The year before, loads of us went for the weekend and during the game seats were thrown and big green dustbins were launched into the Southend stands. People tried to force open the gates and there were a couple of small pitch invasions. Another interesting one was when Brighton drew Canvey Island in the FA Cup and, it not being far from Southend, their firm turned up with some old faces from West Ham. This led to battles in the streets around the ground after the game with riot police coming under attack and Brighton coaches stoned on their way from the game."

Many of Brighton's early clashes were against south coast rivals Bournemouth, Portsmouth and Southampton. At a Christmas game at home to Bournemouth in December 1971, 29 were arrested after fighting inside and outside the ground. Before the game a mob of 100 Bournemouth marched through the streets of Hove, smashing car and shop windows. Brighton responded after the game, attacking a coach, smashing several windows and causing £1,000-worth of damage. The coach was about to leave the Greyhound Stadium after it had picked up Bournemouth's directors. "I was just moving slowly out of the park when there was a lot of shouting and I heard glass," the driver said. "I looked round and there was a whole series of bangs, and glass coming in everywhere." The driver took

evasive action and when the attack stopped he chased the lads and caught one. "I gave him what for," he said. Two other coaches transporting away fans were also attacked and other coach drivers refused to move until police agreed to ride aboard their vehicles.

Another 29 people were arrested at a match against Portsmouth in April 1977. Injured fans were carried from the terraces on stretchers as some of the 140 officers on duty pulled fans out of one section of the crowd during a match that Brighton won 4–0. After the game, two cars were overturned and others damaged, and chanting youths smashed windows of shops and houses in Sackville Road. Twenty people were treated for injuries. "We have never seen such ugly scenes at an Albion match," said a St John Ambulance spokesman. "Some people were hell-bent on trouble." Earlier, a train carrying Portsmouth fans was stopped near Bognor Regis after the crew were threatened. British Rail said fans had urinated everywhere except in the toilets and had damaged seats and ripped out light fittings. Trouble then flared at half-time with Albion two goals up, and fighting between Portsmouth fans and the police continued throughout the second half.

The trouble continued as Portsmouth fans headed home, with the 9.50 p.m. football special making a number of unscheduled stops due to vandalism and fighting. It was halted at Shoreham after light bulbs and seats were thrown out of the windows, again at West Worthing after a hammer and a fire extinguisher were thrown out, and then near Chichester for police to remove fans who had broken into the rear cabin. Finally, at Woodgate Crossing and Havant, the train was stopped after the emergency cord was twice pulled. "Unfortunately, Portsmouth's supporters have a bad reputation and you cannot stop them drinking on the way to and from the match," said Brighton chairman Mike Bamber. "Hooligans and drink is a fatal mixture."

In January 1978, 26 people were arrested and at least 56 were injured during violence before and after a game against Southampton. Most of the injuries were caused by missiles, including pieces of broken glass, thrown from a small section of the crowd. Fourteen people were taken to hospital, most suffering from head and facial wounds. Four Southampton fans were arrested in Shoreham after police stopped a bus to search for weapons.

Trouble first erupted at Brighton railway station an hour before kick-off. Police were soon on the scene to quell the disorder but more occurred after the game. A local businessman offered a £500 reward for anyone whose testimony led to the convictions of the four Southampton fans who attacked him in The Lanes. A plate of sandwiches he was carrying for a family party at a London pantomime was knocked from his hands and he was punched and kicked around the head.

Former Sussex police chief Jim Marshall, then a Conservative councillor, told the local paper that it was time to rid the club of the hooligan minority. "These people are the scum of the earth," he declared. "If the club got rid of them, ten times more people would be attracted to the ground." He offered to meet the club to discuss the problem but they were obviously tired of Marshall's interventions, not least because he offered no practical solutions. "There is nothing much more we can do about the situation," remarked club secretary Ken Calver. "But if Mr Marshall would like to come forward with something constructive we would be prepared to listen."

The police were a lot happier when Southampton next visited. Though there were still 29 arrests, there was little of the trouble that had marred the previous fixture and police boasted of their new crowd control measures. "If people were expecting trouble from Southampton fans on a pub crawl during the evening they were pleasantly surprised," said a police spokesman. "Most were headed home before opening time." The worst trouble happened at the Swan Hotel in picturesque Arundel when Southampton fans went through it like the Wild West. Fists flew, glasses were smashed and the visitors clashed with locals and then with police.

Brighton's close proximity to London has encouraged numerous weekend visits from the capital's clubs. In mid-April 1978, Brighton was overrun by thousands of Spurs fans. "Why did the thugs invade?" asked the local paper, as it described the town's worst outbreak of soccer thuggery. Ninety-one people were arrested and 105 were injured, including 20 police officers. A Spurs fan from Essex was stabbed after a fight between eight Spurs and 30 Brighton.

Spurs fans arriving on the Friday night sparked fights all over the area. Ten beach huts on the seafront at Hove had windows smashed and Spurs slogans sprayed on them. There was further trouble before the game, and though twice the normal number of police were on duty, reinforcements were still required. Twenty-nine people were arrested at the ground, including ten Brighton fans. The failure to properly segregate rival fans in the North Stand was seen as the cause of the disorder and play was twice held up for a total of 19 minutes as fans fled the fighting. Efforts to contain the bulk of the Spurs supporters in the north-east corner of the ground failed when early arrivals jumped two barriers into the North Stand, the traditional territory of Albion's heavy mob. Despite the trouble, the referee said that no amount of violence was going to force him to abandon the game. "I shall keep the teams here all night if I have to," he said.

The Albion chairman said that he was considering a £50,000 fence around the ground. But he regretted having to fence in fans, "especially our own, who don't cause trouble."

Six months later it was the turn of West Ham with even more widespread violence. "Hammers hooligans run riot," ran the headline in the *Evening Argus*. More than 600 West Ham fans travelled to Brighton on the Friday night and ran amok. A boat was set alight, a seafront café raided and windows smashed. Seventy-seven West Ham fans were arrested on that night alone. The worst of the violence occurred shortly before 9 p.m., when West Ham and Brighton fans clashed. A Londoner was slashed from ear to ear across the back of the neck and stabbed in the back and arm. A Brighton fan was struck over the head with an iron bar. With most pubs refusing to serve the visitors, many of the Hammers spent the night marauding through the streets, smashing windows and chanting.

Trouble continued on the Saturday. Supporters were searched and no boots, knives, bottles or other offensive weapons were allowed into the ground. However, dozens of West Ham fans got into the home end and surged forward when their team scored, forcing the locals on to the pitch. An elderly Albion supporter, Sidney Harris, collapsed and died in the crush when he was forced against a barrier and fell. A close friend blamed West Ham fans. "West Ham supporters were everywhere," said Ray Bulbeck. "They were mingling with the Brighton fans and there were some very violent scenes. It was the most frightening game I have ever been to. There should have been more police on duty, it should have been an all-ticket match and the West Ham supporters should never have been allowed to mingle with Brighton fans."

With violence from London clubs now becoming a regular occurrence in Brighton, councillor Marshall was again on hand to give the local paper his opinion. "Obviously, Brighton is an attractive prospect compared with a dour, industrial town. What we need is tougher laws to deal effectively with these people." For their part, Brighton's magistrates vowed to set an example. "We are going to make it clear that this town will not tolerate the sort of behaviour we saw on Friday night," said the chairman of the bench, George Parks. "We cannot allow gangs of youths to rampage in the streets, damage property and put people in fear. It's either going to be expensive for the guilty ones or more painful still, particularly if they have previous records."

The authorities' determination to prevent similar scenes again appeared to have paid off when Arsenal visited almost a year later. Thirty-three people were arrested but there was none of the chaos and violence of the Spurs and West Ham games. Dozens of Arsenal supporters were ordered to take off their steel-toe-capped boots if they wanted to get into the ground. Police searched every fan for hidden weapons and trod on their toecaps to test for steel before letting them through the turnstiles. Most of those arrested before the game were immediately dealt with in two special courts which sat throughout the match. Big fines were handed out and the magistrates declared, "We will do our utmost to see that the residents of this town are free to walk the streets without fear. It is our intention to punish as heavily as possible in these cases." The police were also content with the outcome. "I think we can be pleased with the results," said Superintendent Cyril Leeves. "I think we have a successful formula for controlling big crowds."

Brighton & Hove Albion and Sussex Police believed they had turned the corner and the mood of confidence spread to the local paper. At the beginning of the 1983 season, the *Argus*'s football columnist expressed the belief that the worst was over. Twenty-four hours later, he, the club and the

police were proved wrong as 300 Chelsea fans arrived in town the evening before their League match. Before long, two Londoners were in hospital with stab wounds. "It was evil, the worst trouble I have ever seen," said Derek Baker, landlord of the Carpenters Arms. "We tried to keep the fans out but they just swamped us. I had two men on the door but they were just swept aside. The fans kept taking glasses and bottles and went outside to throw them. They were rampaging about, kicking and punching each other. It was awful."

Thirty-four people were arrested on the Friday and petrol bombs were found on the Saturday, supposedly made by two Brighton fans. Another was arrested for firing a starting pistol at Chelsea fans. Inside the ground there were repeated pitch invasions during which several police officers were attacked and kicked around the body and head.

"They swarmed on to the Goldstone pitch in their hundreds, an obscene battle cry on their lips and violence on their tiny minds," reported the *Argus*. "For a few brief seconds it seemed that the hordes who would call themselves Chelsea fans only wanted to salute their team's victory, but the illusion was brutally shattered as first one, then another policeman was felled and then kicked as they lay helpless on the turf. The rampaging thugs, disowned by the club they say they support and the majority of soccer fans everywhere, sensed that they massively outnumbered the officers who tried to hold them back. With all the 'courage' of a pack of hyenas, they pounced, punched, kicked and fled. They moved as a group, like the cowards they are, never daring to stand alone. Throughout the game violence erupted in short bursts as rival fans managed to invade each other's territory and, as always, it was the police who had to go in and stem the trouble. The isolated outbursts were to prove an insignificant curtain raiser for the disgraceful scenes that followed the final whistle."

The paper's editorial agreed that punitive sentences were probably needed but added that a long-term solution was required. It also foresaw severe restrictions in travelling support. "What is worrying now is that there are games ahead where it is possible to forecast more trouble, and public opinion will not tolerate a repetition of the disgraceful scenes at the Goldstone, or any other football ground. If the action they have to take

Lincoln City versus Brighton, and a fierce fight breaks out inside the ground.

Nick Harvey

appears repressive, then that is a price society must pay for letting the situation get out of hand."

The following season, Brighton and Huddersfield fans clashed again. "Before the game we were all over the resort but afterwards it was a different story," recalled a Huddersfield lad. "About thirty of us were heading towards the station when a mob of Brighton came up the road. It went off big style. They were straight into us and fights spread into local gardens. When we finally got to the station we thought it had all calmed down but Brighton came at us again across the tracks, with one lad brandishing a blade. One lad ended up in hospital, minus a prized piece of clothing. Luckily for him, the nurse who treated him knew the Brighton lads and he got his jumper back in the post."

In more recent years, Brighton has also had a terrace rivalry with Oxford. "It stemmed from a

game in the Eighties when hundreds fought in Hove Park opposite the Goldstone Ground with police on horseback having to quell the trouble and it carried on through the next decade," said Trent. "We had a great row with them in the mid-Nineties when twenty-two of us avoided the Old Bill by drinking in Reading and going to a pub in Oxford during the game. Oxford found us and a five-minute battle took place with no police for miles. Snooker cues, umbrellas and dustbin lids were just some of the weapons used by both sides. It was in the middle of a main road and all the traffic got held up. When police arrived, the Brighton contingent were taken straight home, minus one hospitalised and three nicked. There seems to be a mutual respect between the two firms."

During the Seventies and into the Eighties, the main firm was the Bosun Boys, named after the pub the lads drank in. Then in the late Eighties and into the Nineties came the West Street firm. Today, according to Trent, they don't have a name. And he is keen to stress there is no such mob as the Brighton Headhunters. "The name first appeared in one of the hooligan books, but it is complete bullshit," he insisted. In the past there were tensions between the small mobs that make up the Brighton firms which derived from the rivalry between the small towns around Sussex, but this was overcome in the 1990s with everyone coming together.

On Saturday, 4 January 1992, Brighton hosted Crawley Town in the FA Cup. There was huge travelling support for the local derby, including a couple of dozen Chelsea, Spurs, Arsenal and even Millwall hooligans. The reason for this extraordinary show of unity amongst some of London's most fierce rivals was that the leader of the Chelsea Headhunters at that time, Tony Covelle, was from Crawley and was keen to put on a show on the south coast. After the game, this group was attacked and run by a much larger mob of Brighton, with Covelle himself receiving a shoeing. The Chelsea lads felt humiliated, especially after Brighton learned about the representatives from the different London mobs being present. Chelsea's mood soured even further after a few of their mob linked up with Brentford for a home against the Seagulls and also got a slap.

Revenge was sought and the following July, eighteen months after the Crawley FA Cup match, a mob of Chelsea decided to pay their new rivals a visit one Saturday during the close season. Word swept around the football scene and the Blues were joined by Glasgow Rangers, QPR, Millwall, Arsenal and even a German who followed FC Cologne. The police were quickly alerted and on the morning of the trip rounded up and arrested 34 Chelsea. "NCIS foil football riot," ran the headline in one newspaper. A number of weapons were also discovered.

Chelsea had to wait for another few months to get even. Brighton were playing at Brentford, contact was made before the game and a fight was arranged for afterwards at Victoria. Brighton appear not to have known precisely who the representatives of this rival mob were, for if they did they might not have bowled out of Victoria underground with such confidence and run straight into Chelsea's mob. "It was truly the worst hiding I have ever seen one mob dish out to another," recalled Martin King

in the book *Hoolifan*. "They were taught a lesson, one that they would never forget. They had known that day in Brighton exactly who they were slapping up in the air. A cliché, I know, but they fucked with the big boys and they paid for it big time."

In the early Nineties, Brighton, like so many other clubs, were struggling financially. With surging land values in the south-east, the club's chairman decided to sell the ground for a retail park and even mooted the idea of ground-sharing with Portsmouth. With the club's future seemingly doomed at the Goldstone Ground, Brighton played what everyone thought would be their last game there, against York City. Emotions ran high as the supporters packed into the ground for one last time. This is how one Brighton fanzine recalled events: "Just 15 minutes into the game dozens of fans ran onto the pitch, quickly followed by hundreds, which turned into thousands. People of all ages and backgrounds joined in, including the opposing York fans who swapped shirts with their Brighton counterparts and united in chants of, 'Sack the board.' Fans sunbathed in the centre circle, played Frisbee, and a mass beach ball game broke out. Surrounded by a bemused line of fully clad riot police, the crowd refused to leave. The match was abandoned (for only the third time in football history due to crowd involvement). The occupation continued for a symbolic 90 minutes and ended peacefully as subdued fans left the Goldstone for perhaps the last time."

The good nature of the pitch invasion did not stop some hysterical media headlines. "Rampage, soccer shame, football riot," screamed the press. "It's a return to the worst hooliganism of the Seventies," declared the BBC. "Rival fans had to be kept apart. It could have been another Hillsborough." The police set up Operation Edgar and several people were subsequently charged, but the protest worked, at least temporarily. The chairman announced the proposed move to Portsmouth was off the agenda and the club would be staying at the Goldstone for at least another season. While Brighton did move into temporary premises, the inadequate Withdean Stadium, the club remained in Brighton.

One team that has very little time for Brighton is Cardiff. "This all started when we played them in the last season of the Goldstone Ground," remembered Trent. "They brought loads of fans with a massive mob and there were some outbreaks of fighting before the game. Afterwards, hundreds of them were waiting for their coaches when fifty of us fronted them up from the bottom of Hove Park. They came charging down into us and the fighting spread into the road and the tennis courts in the park. Riot police used their batons to split up the two groups and force the Cardiff on to their coaches. There was further trouble at the train station as more Cardiff fans were attacked. We played them a few years later and a good mob of 150 Brighton turned out. There were several fights while the game was going on in the area around the Withdean Stadium, where they were outnumbered but well game.

"Brighton have not taken a mob down to Ninian Park, that is true. Some scarfers were attacked down there, which led to ill feeling. When we last played them their coaches were pelted with missiles on the way to the ground which is probably the reason for their animosity."

There are few stories of the Brighton mob travelling away. With the exception of Palace, most of their incidents of trouble have been at home. One exception was a match at Swindon in November 2001, when a train carrying the Brighton mob was badly vandalised. They were transferred on to a replacement but this too was vandalised.

At the time of writing, a number of Brighton defendants were facing Crown Court trials after an alleged brawl with Leeds United fans.

Further reading: *A Casual Look*, Lorne Brown and Nick Harvey (Football Culture UK)

BRISTOL CITY

Ground: Ashton Gate
Firm: City Service Firm
Rivals: Bristol Rovers, Cardiff, Millwall

As the train pulled into Reading station, hundreds of Tacchini-clad lads buzzed with excitement for the crucial Fourth Division promotion clash. It was nearing the end of the 1983/84 season and Reading were top, with Bristol City second. It was a new dawn for the followers of the club, and word of the importance of this clash had spread around Bristol's pubs in the weeks before. For this particular group, it was something else.

The train doors opened and off they piled, laughing, shouting and singing. Shoppers, commuters and ordinary fans hurriedly stepped aside to let the hordes vacate the train first, fearful of being caught in their stampede or providing someone with an excuse to give them a slap. Outside, local residents moved quietly but quickly into shop doorways and down side streets to escape the attention of the mob. The police tried to contain the group but were pushed aside in the rush. All the way along the route to the ground there was destruction. Cars were vandalised, windows smashed and shops looted, and any ill-advised or unfortunate Reading fan who wandered into the group soon regretted it.

The mob split into two, most going to the away terrace but 100 trying their luck in Reading's home end. Before a ball had been kicked, and taking their cue from the latter bunch who were already attacking any Reading fan they could, dozens of City supporters streamed onto the pitch, taunting their rivals to do likewise. They went off to allow the game to begin, but another pitch invasion greeted Reading's second goal. Meanwhile, inside the away end, bottles, bricks, wooden poles and even lumps of concrete ripped from the terracing were hurled at police and rival fans and various missiles hit the Reading goalkeeper.

With war on the terrace, the referee had little choice but to stop the game in the hope that the police would restore order. But the trouble continued and even an appeal from City boss Terry Cooper over the speaker system halted the chaos only temporarily. Almost as soon as the players returned, the goalie was again attacked and fighting with the police resumed. Cooper was furious. His two daughters sat in the stand, petrified, and the reputation of his club was being destroyed in front of his eyes. Without warning, he leapt from the dugout, sprinted across the pitch and clambered into the battleground. "Their eyes were wild," he later recalled. "All they wanted to do was get the police. I have never seen such hatred in people's eyes." Undeterred, he found the ringleaders and pleaded with them, for the sake of the club and any chances of promotion, to stop. It worked and order was restored. But the cost was high. Forty-eight people were arrested, 13 police officers were hurt and national shame was heaped upon the club.

Not everyone shared that shame. Many of those

involved were proud of their notoriety; they had, after all, made the back page of *The Sun*. It was a defining moment for the hooligans at the club, which received a severe reprimand from the FA. The actions of Terry Cooper probably saved it from a more serious punishment. There had been trouble at City matches before but nothing on such a scale. The City Service Firm had scored on its debut.

Bristol might not have had the frightening reputation of Glasgow or Liverpool but it's a big city and could be an unpleasant place to visit if you weren't welcome, as Arsenal found out in 1976. The Gooners were still top of the hooligan world in the capital but there was no deference shown when the teams met in the League. Bristol had just been promoted to Division One and were taking thousands away to the bigger games. Arsenal mobbed up for the return fixture and, expecting another easy turnover, plotted the taking of the Bristol end on the train.

Colin Ward remembered the contempt he and his fellow Londoners felt for the West Country club in his book, *Steaming In*. But the crew weren't so confident minutes after entering their end, as Ward related. "There seemed too many people milling around for comfort, and suddenly a shout went up, 'There's Londoners in our end. Do the Cockney bastards!' I heard the sound of fist hitting a face … We backed off and some of our group saw the futility of standing our ground and leapt back over the turnstiles. I couldn't see a way out and just concentrated on getting myself away from the shower of blows. The guy next to me got kicked in the face and went down into the gravel.

"A girl ran up and grabbed his hair, pulling it violently while at the same time spitting at him. She was foaming at the mouth. 'You bastard,' she screamed. Apart from the girl, other people were queuing up to get to him and I could hear the sickening sound of boots repeatedly hitting his body. It was indiscriminate and nasty, any part of his torso was fair game. One really vicious guy was trying to stamp on his face with the heel of his boot … We all tried to leave with as much dignity as we could muster, but the leers and the catcalls hit their mark. 'Go 'ome cockneys.'"

Colin Ward was not the only London hooligan author to come unstuck at Bristol. In *Terrace Legends*, infamous Chelsea leader Steve Hickmott claimed that the city was the scene of his worst

beating. "We'd just come out of a pub and four or five geezers walked towards us carrying a sports bag," he said. "They hit me over the head and I was taken to hospital to have my head stitched back up."

Bristol City fans were again under the spotlight when the FA ordered an inquiry after their cup-tie against Swindon in 1981, which resulted in the game being held up for 20 minutes. The referee, John Martin, made the decision after concrete and stones were thrown on to the pitch. Police formed a line in front of the City fans after they came under missile attack.

A couple of years later, the CSF were born. "It was the thing to do at the time," said one of its original members.

After the Reading riot, the CSF had a reputation to uphold, but few mobs were prepared to try their luck in Bristol. However, Middlesbrough's relegation to the Third Division in 1986 gave City a firm to test themselves against. There was a big show from both sides at the home leg, and City promised to turn up in style for the Ayresome Park return, but it was not to be. The local papers reported that flyers calling for a big turnout were being circulated and a few days before the game a number of people in south Bristol were arrested. No charges were brought but it was enough for the CSF to cancel.

In May 1987, Bristol met Sheffield United in the Third Division play-offs. The Blades brought hundreds down for the fixture, which had been moved to a Sunday night, and police ordered pubs to close at 3 p.m. That did not deter the boys and there were serious clashes before, during and after the game on a day when both sides claimed a victory. In his book *Blades Business Crew*, Steve Cowens wrote of how United ran Bristol ragged. Bristol disagree. "Due to the pub restrictions, Bristol City fans took to drinking carry-outs in their hundreds, maybe as many as a thousand," remembered one CSF lad. "They were not all firm but scarfers and general drunks and they swelled the ranks in Greville Smythe Park directly outside the ground. Every so often a shout would go up and hundreds would set off across the park, drunkenly roaring, 'Whooargh, Sheffield, kill 'em,' and the sky was awash with flying Blackthorn cider bottles. It was not pretty."

The following season, Sheffield United returned. Fighting between United's Blades Business Crew and the CSF spread from the terracing to the pitch, with stewards being brushed aside as the mobs battled it out. This time there was little dispute that the Sheffield mob had the upper hand, certainly on the pitch.

Bristol City's most successful recent football season was 1989/90, when the team finished second in the old Division Three, though the fact that it was their arch rivals, Bristol Rovers, who beat them to the title, muted their celebrations. Improving fortunes were matched with activity on the hooligan front. Four hundred CSF travelled away to Birmingham, 350 to Bolton and a similar number turned out for Sheffield United. The biggest turnout that season was early in the campaign at Cardiff, always a crunch match. Five hundred CSF made the journey on two trains from Bristol St. David's. Welsh police were waiting for them but struggled to hold the lines inside the station, allowing small groups of City to slip out, some running through the station office to the astonishment and alarm of the staff. Sporadic fighting with the Soul Crew broke out in and around the nearby bus station, with Bristol later boasting that they had got the upper hand. The main mob then broke free of the police lines and roamed around the city centre in a pack, hunting for Cardiff. When the match started the Soul Crew launched missiles of every description into the away end. Furious at their antics and buoyed up by a victory on the pitch, 200 Bristol steamed out of the ground, broke down a security door and ran past a line of startled police. Cardiff had been visited, lost 3–1 nil on the pitch and were sent to the bottom of the League.

City were promoted in 1990 but their time in the second tier of football was short-lived and after they were relegated their chances of meeting the big mobs were reduced. But a regular diet of Rovers, Cardiff and Plymouth meant the CSF still had some tasty opponents.

In 1995 they were drawn at home in the FA Cup to Everton, who brought down a 50-strong mob, with an average age of about 35. They drank in a CSF-frequented pub before the game but there was no show from locals, although that changed on the way to the ground as the two mobs clashed minutes before the kick-off. City had the better of the game but Everton sneaked a winner in the last minute and when travelling fans piled onto the pitch there were

some minor scuffles. The bulk of the Bristol lads, already furious with the Scousers taking liberties before the game, mobbed up outside the ground. The Everton firm soon joined them and battled every inch of the way back to their coach. At first it was firm on firm, but it soon escalated into a free-for-all. "In the end, Bristol had blokes in their fifties getting out of cars to have a go and loads of old Scousers were ready to join in," said one participant. "The police lost control and it was a miracle that nobody was killed when a mounted officer lost the plot and rode his horse into the middle of Everton's firm as they tried to get across the road and into the Bristol lads. 'Fuckin' mental,' shouted one of the Bristol. He was not wrong."

A year earlier the CSF had turned over Liverpool in their main pub before a League Cup but Everton had definitely bettered them. "They shocked us that day, we had done well at Anfield but Everton were different class, we simply were not at the races when they came down here," said one of the CSF's main faces.

There is no love lost between the two Bristol teams and there has been trouble at local derbies as far back as the 1960s and regular violence at the annual Gloucester Cup in the early Seventies. A new phase of this rivalry began in 1989 as the teams battled for dominance on the pitch and their respective hooligan groups vied for control of the streets. A long-standing criticism raised by many City hooligans is that Rovers do not try against their local rivals. One CSF veteran said, "The North Bristol Long Faces have made it to the likes of Oxford, Exeter, Cheltenham, Yeovil and Torquay, but a couple of miles across Bristol to that red thing? Whoa, fuck that! This rankles with the CSF. It is hard to find any of City's boys below forty who have a good word to say for the sullen Gasheads. Many of City's younger boys have never even seen a Rovers mob."

There was little chance of them avoiding each other in the 1989/90 season, as not only were both sides in the same division, but both were competing for the title. After a 1–1 draw in March 1989, Rovers attacked a City pub with baseball bats. This set off a series of tit-for-tat strikes into each other's communities. A year later it was City's turn to seek revenge and, at their home game against Brentford, word went round that a mob was forming to take it to Rovers at a Sunday League fixture between the Inns of Court and the Essex Arms. A remarkable 250 City answered the call and as their side went 3–1 down, they invaded the pitch. Opposing them were 50 Rovers and several police riot vans.

"The Essex Arms had developed a reputation for bullying, with its Gashead support seeing fit to bring a stretcher along to games as a nice subtle touch," recalled one City lad. "As soon as Inns went three-one down, City invaded the pitch. One player was knocked out and others chased off into a neighbouring housing estate by a mob waving corner flags. The changing rooms were broken into and, in a symbolic gesture, an Essex Arms-Bristol Rovers blue and white kit was burned in a goalmouth." The local Sunday League administration acknowledged that the problem was caused by outside football hooligans but suspended Inns of Court from the league all the same.

A few weeks later, the two Bristol clubs faced each another with the title at stake. It could not have been scripted better. City went into the match as division leaders, but a 3–0 defeat handed the title to Rovers. All too predictably, City fans attempted to wreck the ground and hoardings were ripped out and thrown on to the pitch. A few months later, as City were returning from a match at West Brom, some of their supporters even attempted to burn down Rovers' temporary ground at Twerton Park in Bath. The ground survived but substantial damage was caused. The gang responsible became known as the "City Fire Brigade" and T-shirts with a picture of the burned-out stand were sold at City matches. The arsonists were caught, and after their names and addresses were reported in the local paper, retribution was quickly sought.

The derby games went away when Rovers were relegated from the Second Division but the police's relief was short lived as, two years later, City followed them, so by 1995 the cross-city rivalry was back on. That year, City fans rioted at the home match against Rovers after a ticketing mix-up resulted in 2,000 season ticket holders being locked out. The club accepted responsibility and was punished accordingly. The following season Sky Television decided to screen the Ashton Gate tie live and the match was switched to a Friday night, but the decision to televise the game only increased local tensions and hostilities. In the days leading up to the game the local paper hyped up the fixture and, with so much now at stake, violence was almost inevitable.

With only seconds left and City leading by a single goal, the home fans were celebrating. In Rovers' last attack, a cross came over and, to the horror of the home crowd, the ball was knocked into the back of the net. Rovers' fans went delirious, City's apoplectic, and 300 CSF stormed on to the pitch to confront a handful of jubilant away supporters who were dancing on it. Fighting broke out in the goalmouth and mounted police were brought on to the pitch to restore order. The match was restarted five minutes later for little more than the final whistle. Bristol Rovers' players ran for the safety of the tunnel as City supporters invaded the pitch yet again. Defender Lee Martin was punched on the back and three others took refuge in the old tunnel under the main stand as the CSF chased opposition players. Ten minutes after the end of the match, 50 City fans ran through the back entrance of the Wedlock Stand throwing bottles and stones at petrified away fans, many of whom were forced on to the pitch to escape the barrage of missiles.

Rovers manager Ian Holloway fled for his life when the mob invaded the pitch. "I thought I was going to die," he said later. "All sorts of thoughts were going through my mind as I ran off the pitch. I thought they were after me and if they caught me I could get kicked to death." City manager Joe Jordan shared Holloway's outrage: "It was a disgrace. It was the first time for a number of years that we had enjoyed national coverage like this. We had a good opportunity to show what good football there is in the Second Division but all that will be overshadowed by other events."

The FA, PFA, the club and the police all promised to hold their own investigations. The *Bristol Evening Post* declared the events, "A win for thugs." Its editorial continued, "After years of trying, football had become the family game once more. But yesterday, as the nation watched on TV, Bristol hooligans took it back to the dark days."

Bristol City fan Steve Clutterbuck blamed a small group of City fans for the trouble. "The game was the culmination of all the stupid hate there seems to be among some of our supporters towards Rovers," he said. "It's been happening for the past few months now, irrespective of the opposition. There are forty or fifty louts in the Carling Stand who start up the chant of, 'Stand up if you hate the Gas.' Lots of people stand up and block your view but if you try to complain they shout you down and call you a Gashead."

"At the moment I just feel like walking out of the place, shutting the door and never coming back," said City chairman Scott Davidson. "We have dug this club out of a hole but all that hard work has been undone in just a few moments. I sat there and watched what was going on and couldn't believe it. I don't want to be part of a club where that sort of thing happens." The following day, he changed his mind. "After long, hard, reflection, I've decided to stay and fight it out. Not to do so would be giving in to the thugs. They have already done enough damage. Here, we are facing all sorts of enquiries and possible punishments because of the actions of a mindless few, but they cannot and must not be allowed to win, ever."

Trouble continued away from the ground. After a series of tit-for-tat attacks on pubs and houses, a family in South Bristol was forced to flee their home after prolonged abuse and harassment culminated in the murder of their two cats. During this period it is widely accepted that City had the bigger mob and, as though to illustrate their domination, the CSF decided to celebrate their 1998 derby win at Ashton Gate by going on a pub crawl in the Rovers end of town.

But two years later, Rovers carried out a surprise attack on City on their return from a match in Oxford. It was the first time in a decade the "Gas" turned southwards towards the Bristol City stronghold of Bedminster and a pub called the Three Lions. One drinking there remembered, "There were fifteen of us plus a few couples enjoying a Saturday night drink unaware of sixty Rovers heading our way. A well known City character called the Paratrooper ran in shouting about a mob, but it being him, everyone dismissed this as nothing more than cider talk and carried on socialising. A couple of minutes later the first unwanted guests appeared. A few made it through the door but were beaten back by fists and a volley of glasses. One hapless Gashead was left prone on the floor while his mob tried to smash the double-glazing. For once, the Paratrooper had been talking sense and Rovers were well and truly south of the river.

"City's boys defended the front door and armed themselves with furniture until the windows of the pub imploded. This was the cue for City to hurl the contents of the cooler shelf, furniture and anything

not nailed down at the sea of Gas faces looking through the smashed windows. Missiles of all kinds were exchanged until Rovers backed away from the windows and doors under the ferocious barrage and City's boys ran into the street, some armed with chair legs and bottles. The Gas decided to stand as only a small number had emerged from the pub, but were beaten back down the road. For the next ten minutes City continued to walk into Rovers who, despite the advantage of numbers, could not push us back. The police stood back from what was later described as a full-scale riot until they had sufficient reinforcements. Rovers fled, some on a passing bus, and attempts were made to drag them off.

"The police finally arrived in numbers and tried to separate the factions using dogs, CS gas and batons, but the battle continued, now some 300 metres from the Three Lions. City then called it off, dropped their weapons and walked back to the pub. They pointed out that Rovers were now under the protection of the police. Only four arrests were made after the Rovers attack, all City supporters. All those requiring hospital treatment were Gasheads, apart from one City boy bitten by a dog."

Bristol City's rivalries extend into Wales and they have clashed repeatedly with Cardiff and Swansea. City believe that they have matched Cardiff over the years and many expressed annoyance at what they saw as bias in a book about the Soul Crew. In October 2000, more than 200 City lads went on the rampage in Swansea four hours before the game and three pubs were smashed up as rival fans exchanged bottles, bricks and glasses. The police bore the brunt of much of the missile throwing, with police dogs and their handlers getting particular attention. Police admitted that they were unprepared. Superintendent David Jenkins said, "All the indications were that we were going to have a peaceful match. We accept we got it wrong and there will be a major inquiry. All the indications were that there would be no prominent troublemakers and we expected families to attend the game." No arrests were made.

City's other main rival is Millwall, the most ferocious mob ever to visit Ashton Gate. This feud goes back to 1984. After accepting an invitation to Millwall v Swansea, one of Bristol City's boys announced to all at Millwall's Barnaby pub that they would be putting in an appearance later that year at the Den. One of the locals was so taken aback by this that he rounded up the disbelieving Millwall in the pub, saying, "Come and listen to this cunt." A short time later, after watching a south Bristol boxer at Wembley in the ABA finals, the same Bristol man went to see his pals in south London and daubed slogans in yellow paint around the ground.

On the day, City's intrepid painter navigated a course for two coaches back to the Barnaby and got lost. Confirmation came that they were finally heading in the right direction in the form of one of Millwall's main boys standing directly in front of the oncoming coaches, arms outstretched, leaving the driver with two options, stop or run him over. He stopped, and that was the moment Millwall put the windows through on both coaches with whatever they could lay their hands on.

"City's boys were straight off the coaches through the now missing windows and for the next ten minutes there was a hectic battle which continued right up to the turnstiles of the ground, City being led by their painter and decorator now armed with a car aerial," said one CSF lad. One of Millwall's boys suffered the indignity of having his jewellery stolen at his own turnstiles, while City's mob began to brick Millwall's end from the car park. In seconds, Millwall's entire end rushed in their thousands to the turnstiles trying to get at City outside. In all fairness to Millwall, paint man admitted later, had they managed to get out, he would never have been able to tell his tale.

The return in 1985 saw Millwall come to Bristol with the meanest mob City have ever seen. Hundreds of City's boys met at the Black Horse pub but most had left by the time Millwall arrived. They attacked the pub with weapons including an axe. Two City supporters were slashed and two Millwall fans hospitalised in the fighting, during which a stolen white van was deliberately driven at three Millwall boys. City lost the game but most in the ground preferred to watch the violence centred on City's Dolman Stand, neighbouring the away terrace. Bristol City's firm caused thousands of pounds of damage to their own ground by ripping out hundreds of their seats and hurling them at the away end, along with darts, pool balls, bolts and even a toilet cistern. Millwall attempted to climb out of the away end and one of them broke his leg in an unsuccessful attempt to negotiate a 15-foot drop. The post-match battle saw

fighting in Greville Smythe Park, Winterstoke Road and Coronation Road, with no winners. Six City hijacked the car of TV and radio football commentator Jonathon Pearce, which explains why a man who claims to support Bristol City is never seen anywhere near Ashton Gate.

The disorder across the city resulted in 73 arrests, 250 seats ripped out, and thousands of pounds' worth of damage. Darts, snooker balls, chunks of wood and milk bottles were all used as weapons and two men were slashed across the back with Stanley knives. Millwall fans had arrived at the ground to see "Millwall die – F-Troop die – CSF" painted across walls. After the game, the trouble spread to Bedminster where sledgehammers and pickaxe handles were used to smash open a barricaded pub. Fans captured a milk float and used the bottles as weapons.

Bristol City secretary Bob Twyford, a former policeman, said he was so disgusted that he was ready to quit football altogether. "If I was offered another job tomorrow I would take it," he said. "I have seen as much as I can stand of football hooliganism and my post could well soon be in the situations vacant column. It was the worst crowd disturbance I have ever seen at a football match. The most sickening thing of all was that most of the damage in the stand was done by so-called City supporters."

Seven years later, in 1991, Millwall were back and in an even more destructive mood. One bruised CSF members recalls the day as the worst rout his mob ever had to endure. "Around 250 boys left the Hen and Chicken pub headed for fewer than 100 Millwall who were half a mile away at a pub called the Orchard, near the harbour. By the time we arrived we were anything but tight, stretched over hundreds of metres with the front nearing the pub and the older, slower lumps still crossing a footbridge over the river. The front went to attack the unsuspecting Millwall who were sitting outside the pub.

"The Millwall mob were proper blokes, including most of their major players, and they all stood. It went totally septic for City. When Millwall came at them, some City stood and some ran. They were a bloody rabble, all over the fucking shop against opposition who came as one, only stopping to use rubble from a nearby skip to batter the game blokes who did stay. City got legged down the road to the footbridge and some ran right, some left and some went up the steps of the bridge, blocking the way across. CSF had to watch Millwall doing the business to their CSF mates while being trapped on the footbridge, unable to get involved because of people trying to escape. It was a total shambles and quite a few suffered more than just wounded pride after getting the treatment with bits of four-by-two from that skip.

"Since then it has simmered on, with an ambush by Millwall near London Bridge and rows at London Bridge Station, Paddington, Bristol's Redcliffe Hill, under Millwall's East Stand, at Ashton Gate, and even the site of TV's *Only Fools and Horses*, Mandela House, which is actually in Bristol. Simply, nobody is respected more by Bristol City and the CSF than Millwall."

At a 2001 battle, Millwall fans threw seats inside the City stadium in a midweek clash that had been switched from a Saturday after police fears of crowd disorder. Police were punched, kicked and faced a hail of missiles as they attempted to prevent Millwall throwing seats and other improvised weapons at home supporters. A month later, police asked for assistance from the public to nail the hooligans and published video stills of 15 men they claimed were involved in the trouble. "It is clear that a group of people travelled to the match for violence, not for the football," said a detective. "The videos show a small hardcore of ringleaders and agitators who encouraged other people to get involved."

In recent years, City have struggled to find adequate opponents in the new Second Division, especially at home where very few mobs bother to travel. There were turnouts by Cardiff and Plymouth but both have now been promoted. In October 2001, Cardiff brought a large mob over the river but, despite attempts to meet up, there was little to report before the game. As a mob of up to 500 Cardiff were being escorted out of the ground, Bristol attacked and there were several minutes of confusion before the police restored order.

The return fixture, in late December, saw Bristol take 300 to Cardiff and while there was a half-hearted attempt to ambush them along the route, the Soul Crew were, once more, fairly disorganised at home. However, during the match, Cardiff were clearly present in huge numbers, with hundreds in the seats overlooking the away end. Bristol came from behind to win the game 3–1 and Cardiff were furious.

Throughout the match, Bristol were bombarded with coins and plastic bottles filled with piss. The police apparently did nothing to stop it and their impotence was evident when a WPC got showered by one of the suitably filled bottles. The Soul Crew roared with approval as the police simply stood by. Bristol were escorted straight back to the station while 40 officers faced a rioting mob of more than 1,000. Such was the severity of the trouble that one member of a police surveillance team decided he'd had enough and ran off up the street.

In February 1999, the CSF went to West Brom, where the second half was delayed by 15 minutes as 200 fans clashed during the interval. The police were caught on the hop with no presence inside the ground. Reinforcements were called but by the time they arrived the stewards had the situation under control. The gods were smiling on the CSF when the fixtures put them away at Plymouth on a Bank Holiday Monday. Dozens of Bristol supporters travelled down on the Sunday night and began drinking in pubs around the Hoe and the Barbican in Plymouth city centre. Their presence soon got the attention of locals and police were mobilised to prevent small skirmishes erupting into mass disorder. Fighting also broke out inside the stadium the following day and eight people were arrested. More recently, Bristol were involved in trouble in Blackpool after their game in April 2002. They left the ground early and clashed along the promenade with groups from Leicester and Plymouth.

As some of their main rivals have moved up a division, Sheffield Wednesday emerged as City's most eagerly awaited game of the season. In 2004, after a large showing by Wednesday in Bristol and Internet claims that their mob had gone soft, the CSF decided to mobilise for the return fixture. Two CSF mobs set out, one of 300 heading straight for Sheffield city centre while the other, 70-strong and drawn from Taunton in Somerset, went to a pre-arranged meet with two Wednesday boys on a motorway service station. From there, the slightly apprehensive but excited mob was guided through country lanes to the small village of Beighton and the Gypsy Queen pub. Ten minutes after their arrival a similar-sized mob of Wednesday arrived and attacked the pub with what appeared to be the contents of a building site. Bristol responded by running out of the building with most of its detachable contents. Once everything that could be thrown had been, it was hand-to-hand combat for several minutes before Wednesday were forced, at some pace, back up the street. Back in Sheffield, the larger mob celebrated news of the victory, as did a few Blades who were out drinking with them for the day.

Since Cardiff's Millennium Stadium has been hosting football finals, Bristol has become a major intersection and even a new battleground for firms on their way to or from the Welsh capital. In 2003, Bristol clashed with Sheffield United before the Yorkshire side played against Wolves and a year later, around 80 rival fans were involved in violence in Bristol city centre the night before the Carling Cup Final between Middlesbrough and Bolton. Police used batons and CS spray to disperse the hooligans on Pero's Bridge, which spans the docks near the Watershed media centre. Fans were also involved in disturbances at nearby Brannigan's bar where chairs and other missiles were thrown. Six

people were arrested and more than 150 police officers were drafted into the city centre. Bristol City fans returning from an away match at Sheffield, and a small number of Cardiff travelling back from their match at West Ham also became involved.

Later the same season, Bristol headed to Cardiff for the final of the LDV Vans Trophy against Carlisle. Trouble erupted after the game at a Wetherspoons pub, which, since the opening of the Millennium Stadium, had become a meeting point for hooligans at cup finals. Fighting began inside but spilled out on to the streets where it became a battle with the police. Forty police in riot gear were bombarded with rocks and bottles in several minutes of madness. Sixteen people were arrested on the day and another eleven after their pictures were trailed widely in the Bristol press. A South Wales police spokesman said, "It was a very nasty street battle. The police were saved by their protective clothing. It was basically Bristol fans against the police."

Empics

Bristol Rovers fans run across the pitch towards rival Bristol City fans at a derby game in December 1996.

Nearly 20 years have passed since the riot at Reading, yet as far as the relationship between the CSF and local police forces go, it seems not a lot has changed.

Further reading: *Terrace Legends*, Cass Pennant and Martin King (Blake Publishing)

BRISTOL ROVERS

Ground: Formerly Eastville, now the Memorial Ground
Firms: Tote Enders (at Eastville), the Gas Hit Squad
Rivals: Bristol City, Aston Villa

"Meet the Tote End Mob, third in soccer's League of Violence. Bristol Rovers are their idols. And if the team gets beaten on the pitch this screaming army of followers will win on the terraces. Behind the goal, at the popular end of every football ground in the Third Division, is their battlefield. Here they wage war on rival skinhead supporters, awarding their own fearsome points system. And this young mob, with their steel-capped boots and cropped hair, proudly boast, 'We are third in the league.'"

So reported the *Western Daily Press* in September 1971. The Tote End had formed in January 1967 following an FA Cup tie against Arsenal, when visiting fans invaded and occupied the covered home terrace. It was the first full-scale invasion of Bristol Rovers' ground and a few of the harder lads promised it would be the last. That was to be wishful thinking; over the next few years several teams took the Eastville ground. In August 1969, a huge mob of Birmingham skinheads descended on Bristol for a pre-season friendly, catching the home fans by surprise, and rampaged through the ground.

Three months later, a visit by Aston Villa sparked a war on the terraces. Indeed, with the exception of Bristol City, there was no set of fans more hated by Rovers than Villa. They only had to step out of the train station and fighting would begin. On the day of this League Cup game in November 1969, there was fighting before, during and after the game. It is a day still legendary in old-school hooligan circles at Rovers.

One of the men behind the Tote End was Andy Philips, or "The Bear", as he was nicknamed by Villa fans after one fight. Born in 1950, Philips began going to Rovers at the age of ten. He stood out from the crowd from an early age in his studded leather jacket and winkle-picker boots. "Andy was a paradox," remembered Chris Brown, known as "Browner", in his book *Bovver*. "When just about every other member of the Tote was a spawny-bollocked pubescent skinhead, Andy was 20 years plus, built like the proverbial brick shithouse and, what's more, a greebo – a great ambling hulk with hair down on his shoulders, wearing dirty jeans and a leather jacket. To get a nod of recognition from the big man was a great accolade in itself. What were we, who prided ourselves on our appearance and our manner, doing, being led by him? But led we were, and whenever Andy was around you felt safer, invincible; he was our talisman."

The Tote Enders entered the Seventies the way they left the Sixties – fighting. Luton, Reading, Bournemouth, Plymouth and Aldershot were all overrun in 1970, and in January 1971, before a home match against Villa, there was trouble the moment the Brummies came off the train. It wasn't always an easy ride. Preston North End skins came in early April and took the Tote End, but they were forced on to the pitch at half-time, to the victorious chants of, "You are inferior," from the Rovers fans.

Browner recalled that another tough ride was at Swansea in the 1971/2 season. "Rovers got off to a flying start, we were two-nil up by half-time and the two sets of fans kept up a never-ending tirade of abuse at each other, separated by a long line of coppers and their mean-looking alsatians. The chants got more and more abusive. Then we went too far. There was always one chant guaranteed to get all Taffs absolutely raving, including the coppers, and as soon as we started to sing it we regretted it. 'Aberfan, Aberfan, Aberfan.' It was bang on half-time, always an edgy period and this was like a red rag to a bull. They came pouring up the steps behind us, brushing past the ineffectual coppers, who, I'm sure, actively encouraged them. They were armed with bricks, bottles and metal bolts, and we dropped like flies. Angus, a thick-set older geezer from Lockleaze, had been standing next to me. Now he slumped to the terrace, a pair of scissors poking out of his shoulder blades, blood oozing through his Fred Perry. The Tote fought back, but the Swansea mob were now coming down the terrace at us, always an advantage. The law finally decided to step in and dogs and truncheons quickly restored order, but not before the Celtic warriors had inflicted severe damage on the English invaders."

Confidence was growing in the Tote. Opponents were dispatched with increasing regularity at home and away, but there was still a long way to go to match the big boys and the 1971/72 season brought them to earth with a thud. Rovers hosted Stoke City in the quarter-finals of the League Cup in November. A capacity 33,000 crowd packed into Eastville, hoping for an upset. To the horror of Rovers, a Stoke mob called the Family took and held part of the Tote End. "They were the biggest and ugliest bunch of fans you could ever wish to meet – we had our work cut out," said Brown.

One of Bristol's casualties that day was Andy Philips. A huge Stoke fan who was obviously leading their firm caught the attention of the home lads and Philips moved in, fancying his chances. Brown said, "Andy sidled up to the monster and swung that infamous arm, landing that infamous punch. I winced, but the monster didn't. He just looked at Andy and smiled. Andy landed another. The monster smiled again. Andy knew he was beat and made a swift exit." Rovers lost the tie 4–2 but the fighting wasn't over. A Stoke fan lost his eye and a police horse was stabbed as rival fans clashed after the game.

Two months later, Rovers were drawn away at Leeds in the FA Cup, a huge draw against one of the giants of English football. Thousands of Rovers fans set off early in excited anticipation, as Brown vividly remembered. "Elland Road was the first big ground most of us had been to. It showed too, we were in awe. We thought about having a pop at the Gelderd Road End, yeah, fucking right, I thought about it for a millisecond. Some poor bastards had a go and barely lived to regret it. Still, they got a good reception when the law escorted what was left of them around the edge of the pitch to the comparative safety of the away end. Somebody should have told the Leeds fans this was the away end, there were as many of them as us in there. Rovers lost four-one and we decided to leave the ground before the final whistle but as we did they came up the subway opposite us, hundreds of them, like a swarm of ants. I couldn't believe it. They had beaten us four-

one, what more did they want, blood? Obviously they did."

However, the hiding at Leeds did little to deter the Tote Enders. Three months later their team played away at Aston Villa and this time they decided to have a crack at the huge Holte End Kop. "We sang 'We've got the Holte End in our hands, we've got the Holte End in our hands' and we had," said Browner. "I had never seen so many Rovers fans at an away game, there were thousands of us. Our main mob was facing us at the opposite end of the ground, but about 500 of us had infiltrated the home fans and we had taken the massive, infamous Holte End with surprising ease. We had come charging up the steps at the back and were swift and merciless in our operation. It was virtually bloodless and they ran to the far end of the cavernous terracing, where they stopped to regroup and assess the situation. We knew we were in an unstable position. It was still a quarter of an hour away from kick-off and we felt that if we could stay put for the next fifteen minutes we would be OK, the law wouldn't dare move us off once the game had started, there were too many of us. The minutes ticked away but fifteen were just too many and soon the heavy thud of boots came closer. They appeared behind us, coming up the same steps and emerging through the same tunnel we had not ten minutes before. They also came from our left and the mob that we had just chased off to our right had now recovered. Absolutely incensed, they attacked with real venom, a three-pronged assault that left us with only one way out, the pitch. We fought as much as we could and we could see our comrades-in-arms at the open end facing us, desperately trying to get on the pitch to help us out, but the law massed in front of them held firm. To coin a phrase, we were fucked."

For two consecutive seasons in the early 1970s, Bristol Rovers were drawn away at Chesterfield for their final game. In April 1973, two coachloads of Tote End lads proved enough to clear their opponents' Kop. Rovers won but other results went against them and they missed out on promotion. Two coaches stopped off in Mansfield on their way home and almost instantly bumped into a coach of local fans returning from a match in Cambridge. During three hours of street violence, ten Rovers fans were arrested.

"Most of those on the coaches were youngsters

and they started roaming around the town," said Chief Insp Roderick Grant of Mansfield Police. "Then several coachloads of Mansfield Town supporters arrived back in town and the two factions clashed. Offensive weapons, including staves, bricks and batons were used." Windows of local shops were smashed and cars damaged and overturned.

The new season began with a Watney Cup game at home to the holders, West Ham United. Hammers fans predictably infiltrated the Tote, but at half-time Rovers rallied and steamed down at the invaders from the top of the stand, joined by a second group who came in from the side. Fighting spilled on to the pitch as police raced over with dogs barking and truncheons flailing.

While Rovers rarely played Bristol City in the League, there was the annual Gloucester Cup held at the end of each season. Trouble was a regular feature at these matches in the early Seventies, with Rovers claiming the better of the fights, perhaps spurred on by a resentment of City's better football. For many of the Tote Enders, rucks during the season were merely a prelude to the cup match at the end with City. Time and again they infiltrated City's East End in small groups before mobbing up and charging down the terrace.

Despite their antipathy, there was some common ground between the two, and on a number of occasions they actually came together against an invading force. "We even used to share a pub," recalled Andy Philips in *Terrace Legends*. "It would be City in one bar and Rovers in the other, and we never fell out once. If a big London team came down, we'd join up together and be Bristol against the invaders."

Another complex relationship existed between Bristol Rovers and Chelsea. They ran together but they also fought. In 1973, Chelsea played a friendly at Bristol City as part of the transfer deal that took City's Chris Garland to west London. Several Rovers lads also followed Chelsea and it was agreed that a Tote End mob would link up with Chelsea for the game. Fifty lads met up, an equal number of Rovers and Chelsea, but that's where the equality ended. Leading the Chelsea mob was the legendary Micky Greenaway and from the outset the Rovers lads were in awe.

Their plan was to infiltrate the East End in one and twos, with the Bristolians going first. However,

the City boys were waiting, and no sooner had the Rovers firm entered the ground than they were attacked. Chelsea, seeing this, promptly turned around at the turnstiles and disappeared, to chants of 'You'll never take the East End,' they roared, and for once they were right."

Chelsea lost a lot of friends that night and there was no hint of an alliance when they returned in August 1976 to play Rovers. Chelsea boys headed straight for the home end, helped by having the same blue and white colours of the home side. They camped on the Tote a good hour before play began and even the local newspaper reported on the capture of the home end: "Tote End pride will take longer to repair than the damage to Eastville's dressing rooms following a coup by Chelsea fans last night. It will take the proud Tote Enders a long time to live down the fact that their territory was taken over by three coach loads of Chelsea fans. The Chelsea fans were eventually rounded up by stewards and police for their own protection and escorted to the Muller Road terrace. It was while they were being escorted that they smashed £40 worth of windows at the back of the South Stand."

Three and a half years later, Chelsea were back, and there was more trouble. "All hell let loose in soccer rampage," ran the front page headline in the *Bristol Evening Post*. "In violence rarely seen in Bristol before, 32 people were arrested and 36 injured during an orgy of trouble." Once again the similarity of the teams' colours contributed to a nightmare for the police, as fans mixed throughout the ground. Chelsea again infiltrated the Tote End, this time in even greater numbers than before, tricking stewards and police by giving Bristol addresses and chanting Bristol songs at the turnstiles. Mounted police were used to separate fans and there was trouble on the pitch when fencing at the open end broke and fans spilled out. With so many police required inside the ground, there were too few outside. Chelsea left before the end of the game and stormed through the city centre, smashing more than 20 shop windows in Stapleton Road and stealing £1,000-worth of goods.

There was widespread condemnation of the poor policing. "It was a disgrace," said one kiosk owner. "We were given no protection at all. The fans were like a mob gone berserk. It could have all been stopped if there had been more foot patrols."

Bristol police admitted that they were not fully prepared for the trouble and that the 200 officers assigned to the match was not enough. "I am naturally disappointed by what happened on Saturday and have instructed officers to re-examine our arrangements and make a complete review," commented Assistant Chief Constable Wally Girven.

Rovers fans were still celebrating their promotion to the Second Division when they played City in the 1974 Gloucester Cup. Recent euphoria steeled them to prove that they were the best team in Bristol. A few pre-match skirmishes were the prelude to the main act, planned for ten minutes after kick-off. Rovers infiltrated the East End in their customary way, in one and twos, but rather than congregating at the back of the stand they spread out across the entire end. The signal for trouble came from an emerging Rovers hard-man, Bob Doughty, a biker who until that season had been on the periphery of a Bristol gang known as the Tramps. As the referee blew for kick-off, the City fans mocked their opponents, believing they had opted out of an attempt on their end. Then, cue, Doughty made his move.

"The Rovers, the Rovers," he bellowed.

Like soldiers rising from long grass, 70 Rovers louts tore into the home end, striking anyone within punching distance. "Our surprise attack had the desired effect," said Brown. "The East End was in disarray as more and more Tote Enders joined in the attack. We had infiltrated good and proper, and they came under assault from every angle. It was awesome to see such chaos caused by so few. The City fans could not determine from which way we were coming and neither could the law. We battled our way to the centre of the East End and were joined by the rest of the jubilant Tote Enders. We triumphantly revealed our colours and hitherto hidden scarves were unveiled and hoisted aloft as a sign of victory."

Promotion brought a new excitement around Eastville. The Aldershots, Bournemouths and Torquays were now distant memories as the boys geared up for bigger opposition. Sheffield Wednesday was their first away game and thousands of Rovers fans, including a large number of fighters, made the trip north. Their confidence soon subsided as Wednesday's mob attacked them first before the game and then towards the end when they steamed into the open gates at the back

of the away end. Now they were a small fish in a very big pond.

Another early-season away game was at Luton. "Soccer hooligans run riot at Luton," read the headline in the *Western Daily Press*. Fifteen Rovers fans were arrested after attacking opponents with planks of wood torn from fences, some with their nails still sticking through. Several of the most prominent faces at Eastville were among those arrested and the incident had a sobering effect on the rest of the mob. This, combined with poor on-field performances, led to a decline in violence. Even the home leg of the Bristol derby passed off without major incident, though this was partly the consequence of a very large police presence that ensured the two supporter groups did not meet.

There was a revival towards the end of the season as the Tote End looked forward to home games against Manchester United and Notts Forest and away matches at City and Cardiff. Rovers and United fans clashed before the game but the violence was nothing compared to the mayhem of Forest, and normal service resumed at the away leg of the Bristol derby. City were riding high while Rovers were struggling. Both sets of supporters came on to the pitch at the final whistle but another big police operation kept them apart. The mobs withdrew, only to continue hostilities outside the ground.

The days of being able to walk freely around a ground were long gone, and as a consequence the Tote End ceased to be the centre of operations, as the Rovers hard nuts moved around to the seated North Stand to get closer to the away pen. By 1977, many in the Bristol Rovers mob identified themselves with the National Front. "Rigid arm salutes were a common sight and NF, British Movement and Column 88 badges were de rigueur," said Brown. "The black kids who had followed Rovers in the early Seventies had, understandably, disappeared from the terraces and the dissenters, of whom there were few, either kept a low profile and kept their mouths shut or stayed away entirely." Black players and supporters of opposing teams were singled out for racist abuse. Yet, paradoxically, Rovers fans were horrified when rival support did it to them. During a home match against Sunderland in the 1975/76 season the opposing fans targeted one of the Rovers boys for the colour of his skin. Monkey chants and relentless baiting caused a reaction not only in this one lad but among all the fighters. To them, he was not black but just one of the lads.

The increasing support for the National Front coincided with a decline in the fortunes of both the club and the firm, and their problems were compounded by the relative success of City, who in May 1975 were promoted to the First Division. Gates slumped and many of the original Tote Enders began to retire. The Bristol Rovers mob was even pushed out of its city centre base and replaced by City.

Violence became less frequent at Eastville, though the occasional match brought everyone back out. On 5 November 1977, Rovers were drawn at home to Millwall. The match was given extra edge as it became common knowledge that a camera crew would be following the infamous F-Troop for a BBC *Panorama* documentary. Every loon and retired hooligan came out of the woodwork. Millwall arrived early and smashed up Stapleton Road, the main thoroughfare to the ground, and any Rovers lads they came across. The home boys regrouped inside the ground, helped by the absence of the F-Troop leaders, whose coach had broken down on the motorway.

"We had a good turnout, the best for a number of years," remembered Brown. "It was not as big as the glory days of the early Seventies, but the rumours about the *Panorama* documentary had brought a lot of lads out of retirement. All around I could see kiddies who had not put in many appearances in the last few years. Andy Philips and the rest of the Tramps had now taken a back seat. Bob Doughty was coming to the fore, not because of his physical presence or stylish power, like Andy, but more because of his fearsome image. Bob epitomised the Tote End perfectly, part-fascist, part-biker, part-punk and not in the least bit sophisticated. We stormed down the terrace and fired in as soon as the interlopers dared to appear. The fracas was shown in all its gory detail the following week on TV. We watched with glee as the reporter observed that 'without F-Troop the Millwall invaders got short shrift from the home fans and the tide of battle turned against Millwall's hooligans'."

Hooliganism continued at Bristol Rovers into the Eighties but not on the same scale. Even a Christmas home match against City was reported as trouble-free, which led the Rovers chairman to declare, "I am convinced that the heyday of soccer hooliganism is coming to an end. Being able to come to a local derby and enjoy it without being worried over violence on the terraces should encourage people to come back again." Several groups of supporters tried to infiltrate areas occupied by rival fans but they were quickly escorted out. No arrests were made and only six people were ejected.

Violence, however, continued to be exported away. At a match against Reading in early 1983, Rovers fans got into areas designated for home supporters. Fans then invaded the pitch and there were 19 arrests. Among those convicted were two men caught punching opponents and then stamping on them while they lay on the floor. There was further controversy after Rovers manager Bobby Gould encouraged his players to applaud the travelling contingent at the end of the game. Reading believed this was condoning the fans' behaviour and Gould was forced to admit an error. A few days later the club issued a letter to travelling supporters urging better behaviour. "As players and management," the letter concluded, "all we can guarantee is 100% effort, but if the result does not go our way, we would expect you to behave in the true Bristol Rovers tradition of good sportsmanship."

Rovers were slow to take up the casual look as, according to one of the older lads, fashion was not important in the lives of the old school hooligans. "There was a right old mix of lads who kept it together in what were our glory days," he explained. "In the 1970s, all sorts made up the Tote End, a fair mix of skins, suedeheads and bootboys in the early days, together with the Tramps, a bunch of leather and denim jacketed bikers and pikeys who were to fashion what Harold Shipman was to caring for OAPs. Looking good was not important."

"When the Pringle-clad casuals arrived, the Rovers lads lost their way a bit," recalled Browner. "Never high up in the sartorial stakes, the scruffiness of the ground somehow transferred itself to the fans. The lads in the know, who could tell their Sergio Tacchini from their Lacoste, made brave efforts to keep up appearances and fly the tattered blue and white quartered flag, but in the face of the City slickers from across the river, who by then had tasted the high life of the First Division, they were fighting a losing battle, at least numerically. [City] were generally better organised than the Gas and their stunt in the early Eighties of removing the padlock from the gates at the back of the Tote End the night before a game and replacing it with their own, so they could all get in and have a bundle, took some beating."

An active hooligan at the time was David Jeal. He was drawn to Rovers as a 15-year-old boy and within a couple of years had graduated into a hooligan with a small mob known as the Young Executives. He dressed in the early designer labels and occasionally in smart blazers with the Bristol coat of arms on the pocket. "We must have looked quite a sight," he recalled. "We looked more like players than fans. We used to raise a few eyebrows when we suddenly started fighting." Ten years later, after fighting across England with Rovers and Europe with England, Jeal swapped the terraces for the pulpit and eventually became a pastor at a young offenders' institute. The conversion began when he started having nightmares about being surrounded by City fans slashing him with Stanley knives. In 1992 he witnessed a Swedish hooligan receive a bad beating from England fans, one that continued long after the victim had slumped to the floor. As he stood and watched he thought to himself, Has my life really come to this? "It was a scary time. I felt frightened and alone in a foreign land with no-one to turn to. I decided I had to get to a phone to speak to my mum. She was a member of the Salvation Army and at the time I was really embarrassed by that. But I just had to speak to her. When I got through I shouted, 'I'm really scared, please pray for me.'"

Bristol Rovers hit rock bottom and closure seemed likely when the lease to the ground was not renewed. The club moved to Twerton Park, Bath, in 1987 but lost a lot of their regular support in the process. With a tiny capacity in the new ground, most of the trouble involving Rovers' new mob, the Gasheads, occurred away from home.

The mob got its name, the Gas or Gasheads, as an insult from Bristol City. The old Eastville ground was next to a gasworks and spray from the cooling tower used to envelope the ground and the fans. When Rovers left Eastville for Twerton Park, the Rovers fans turned the insult on its head and called themselves Gasheads as a reminder of their old ground.

The move caused no let up in the rivalry with City and an injury time Rovers equaliser in the Bristol derby at Bath caused a pitch invasion. Players ran for their lives as rival gangs clashed. There were 22

arrests and running battles in the streets around their temporary home. A tit-for-tat battle between the two Bristol mobs resulted in nine City fans being arrested for burning down the Twerton Park ground.

Plymouth and Cardiff City became Rovers' big opponents. Rovers have repeatedly clashed with Plymouth, including one occasion at Plymouth's away game at Torquay. Rovers were playing in nearby Exeter and a fight was arranged over the phone during the second half of their respective games. In 1988, a train carrying the Gasheads back from a match in Cardiff stopped after fans started a fire on board. In February 1989, eleven people were arrested after fighting outside the ground during a visit by Cardiff City.

In one bizarre incident, a wheelchair-bound Cardiff fan leapt up during a game at Bristol Rovers and punched several Bristol supporters. Despite being an away supporter, the man was put in the disabled enclosure in the home end as stewards presumed he would be no threat. He began swearing loudly and when a Rovers supporter complained, he jumped out of his chair. Police were quickly on the scene and the man was bundled back into his wheelchair and taken to the away end. "We couldn't believe it," said one Rovers fan. "It was like watching Lazarus rising from the dead."

In May 2000, 150 Rovers travelled to Cardiff. They were heavily policed before the game but there was trouble immediately afterwards and 22 arrests were made, though much of this was the result of Cardiff clashing with the police. "Streets of fear," ran the headline in the *South Wales Echo*.

In May 2003, Rovers and Cardiff fought at Cheltenham Spa railway station. Rovers were returning from nearby Kidderminster while Cardiff had been at Crewe. As 150 Bristol waited on the platform, a train pulled in from Birmingham carrying 30 Cardiff. Steel benches were torn up and used as battering rams to smash the windows of the front carriage. Those on the train tried to grab hold of them and others let off fire extinguishers. It took police some time to arrive but when they did they came in force. Twelve cars and twelve vans raced to the scene, and even Kent police, who were guarding the US airforce base at RAF Fairford – home to nuclear bombers – were mobilised and order was restored.

A 4–1 FA Cup defeat away at Barnsley, in February 1999, was the scene of further trouble. Fifteen people were arrested as rival fans clashed before and after the match. Trouble initially broke out at O'Neill's pub after police attempted to round up Rovers fans. A cabinet in the middle of the pub was smashed and partitions were pushed over. One hundred Rovers hooligans left the game early and they clashed on the way to the railway station with 30 or 40 Barnsley who were already banned from football grounds. A mounted officer fell from his horse after it was hit by a car. Chief Inspector Tony Murray of South Yorkshire police, said, "As soon as some Bristol Rovers fans started to arrive, it seemed they were intent on causing trouble."

The following season there was further disorder at a match at Oxford. An NCIS report concluded, "A group of 120 Bristol Rovers supporters clashed with police on route to the ground prior to this fixture. A female officer was sprayed in the face with CS spray by a Bristol Rovers supporter. Extra police officers had to be drafted in to deal with this group, who were placed on buses and escorted to Didcot. During this operation a window was smashed on the bus. Twelve arrests were made for public order offences. On their return to Bristol, the Rovers supporters, numbering about 50, made their way to a pub where Bristol City supporters were drinking. They attacked the pub, smashing all the windows with bricks. A large number of injuries were sustained at this time, however only one person attended hospital with a head injury. Police from all over the city had to attend to deal with a series of running fights."

It was small time compared to the Tote days but showed that, like many lower league clubs, Rovers are still active. Browner said, "Of the younger lads who I know are still involved I take my hat off to them, and in the last few years they have got themselves together a decent, tight-knit firm of about a 100 on a good day who have had a fair share of results, but bearing in mind in the Seventies and Eighties, hundreds were battling against the likes of West Ham, Chelsea, Millwall, Leeds and Aston Villa, it's hard to compare when you're up against some of England's finest as in Macclesfield and Cheltenham.

"When the chances have come in recent years it's been good to see a lot of the old faces turning out and making an effort, with the young lads especially out to impress, most noticeably at games at Barnsley, Derby and Liverpool in the FA Cup, when large numbers turned up, caught out the locals and

dished out a few slaps. Many of the lads begrudge paying money to see overpaid, under-skilled third-rate players who aren't fit to tie Bruce Bannister's or Alan Warboys' laces, but will still show for the local derbies against the Shit, the '82ers', the dark side from across the river.

"The two rarely meet now, as the annual Gloucester Cup games have been cancelled, which is not such a bad thing since an enterprising group of lads returned from a game at Oxford and decided on an excursion over the river and gave the Three Lions pub a little visit. In the following weeks the visit was reciprocated with pubs up the Fishponds and Gloucester Road getting a call from the glaziers' friends."

This kind of tit-for-tat attack peaked in the early Nineties and resulted in many areas being avoided by both firms. City had the city centre while Rovers drank on the outskirts, but on several occasions hit squads attacked pubs and casualties were taken on both sides. Thankfully, it all died down but there were clashes at a recent pre-season friendly before and after the game at Rovers, a wake-up to those who thought the rivalry had gone away.

Browner described today's firm as "like a cheap wine". They don't travel well, but bearing in mind they have been stuck in the lowest division now for the last few years, the lads have kept at it and trips to Oxford, Cardiff, Swansea and Plymouth in particular have been eventful, but nothing on the scale of the Tote End days.

Chris Brown summed it up in *Bovver*. "In 1987 Rovers board failed to secure a satisfactory new lease from their landlords and the club found itself staring extinction in the face. The decision to move out of Bristol and ground-share with non-league Bath City was understandable, but it brought cries of dismay and anguish from long-suffering Rovers fans who couldn't bear to leave their beloved, though much-neglected stadium. The move brought about a premature end to the Tote. The atmosphere and ambience of that foreboding terrace had disappeared forever and the Tote End itself was demolished in the Nineties."

"Sadly," said Browner, "a monstrous IKEA store now stands in its place. Where once tribes of youths performed their 'rites of passage' and bodily fluids flowed in the name of love, hate and pride, Justin and Kate now bicker over which wood-flooring they should choose. It fucking kills me. The Tote and its inhabitants may have long gone but it, and they, will never be forgotten."

Further reading: *Bovver*, Chris Brown (Blake Publishing)

BURNLEY

Ground: Turf Moor
Firm: Suicide Squad, Suicide Section Fives, Suicide Youth Squad
Rivals: Blackburn Rovers
Police operations: Fixture

It was ten o'clock in the morning and for over an hour a steady flow of excited men had been slipping into the pub. It was still sixty minutes before official opening time, yet pints flowed, drugs were consumed and weapons concealed as the generals and lieutenants huddled around a table finalising their battle plans. Minutes later police swooped on the pub, closed it down and attempted to disperse the crowd, fearing it would double to over 1,000 by opening time. The officer in command knew he would have his work cut out; one of the most hate-filled football derbies in Britain was still hours away, yet the thugs were restless and one thing was on their minds – destroying the enemy.

It was not Rangers v Celtic or Millwall v West Ham that had brought men in their mid-forties out of "retirement" to join hundreds of active hooligans for the day. The pub was on the outskirts of Burnley, and that day they were playing Blackburn. And to see a mob of that size, in 2005, was proof that, in some towns at least, football hooliganism was far from finished.

Burnley nestles amid the hills of east Lancashire and has a population of about 80,000. Unlike other small towns in the North West of England, where many local youngsters desert their hometown club to follow bigger and more glamorous Premiership sides, Burnley people support Burnley FC and are famously tagged "the most loyal of all". Their club claims they have the biggest support in the country compared to the size of its town (a claim sometimes contested by Middlesbrough), and amongst that

loyal support exists a hardcore hooligan firm called the Suicide Squad.

The SS were formed in 1985. Andy Porter, a founder member who later wrote a book of the same name, recalled how the firm got its name: "It was when suicide bombers started operating in the Middle East that one of the lads came up with the name. We were walking from the Broadswords pub to the White Lion when it suddenly came to him. One of the lads had it printed on cards and we all knew straight away that it was exactly what we wanted: 'Burnley FC Suicide Squad.' It sounded catchy and it sounded good. In a moment the Suicide Squad had been formed. The name just rolled off the tongue and it gave us our anthem, 'Su, su, Suicide!'

"For years we had a firm but no name. Most firms had names by the early Eighties: West Ham's ICF, Chelsea's Headhunters, the Leeds Service Crew and so on. We were just the Burnley crew, and even tried that out as a name, but it didn't sound right. We wanted a tag that everyone would remember and the SS was perfect. Years later the police intelligence believed we were called The SS because of the number of times our small firm went on suicide missions and fought firms with far superior numbers. That's a decent call but, as usual with the police, total bollocks."

The SS was just the latest chapter in the history of hooliganism at Burnley. As far back as 1964, the national media was reporting trouble at a Burnley game with Sheffield United. Three years later, *The Times* reported older Burnley fans complaining about the emergence of a large group of youngsters who had begun to gather inside the ground to sing abuse at rival fans. This growing antagonism coupled with sporadic outbreaks of violence upset the club's traditional support and put some off watching their football. In August 1970, one Burnley fan wrote a letter to the *Burnley Express* complaining about trouble at their away match with Man City:

Within a 15-yard radius of where I was standing I witnessed at least two serious incidents. In one, a fairly long-haired youth was attacked by a group of skinheads, marginally escaping without serious damage to his left eye. In the other, one skinhead maimed another with what used to be called in the era of the teddy boy a knuckle-duster. In each case, three policemen were required to stop the fights. More depressing than even these bare facts was the attitude of the crowd. "The screws [police] start half the so-called hooliganism," a man remarked. In fact the rapid intervention of the police, at considerable risk to themselves was, to say the least, commendable.

But generally speaking, the level of violence at away matches was less than some other clubs, and Burnley was often overrun by Bolton, Blackburn and even Oldham during the 1970s.

Across the North West, travelling fans were known for causing damage to football trains, especially the specials that were laid on to take them to games. The comfort level was minimal but was accepted because the trains were cheap and direct. In January 1973, Burnley fans were afforded a new level of luxury when British Rail agreed that fans travelling to the team's away game at QPR would be able to travel aboard the "League Liner". Fitted with a discotheque, a 42-seat cinema showing football highlights, and two carriages fitted with headphones giving a choice of three pop channels, the football and railway authorities hoped that travelling in luxury would stop the vandalism. Clubs would hire the train from the Football League, fix the level of fares, sell the tickets and make their own catering arrangements.

Football League Secretary Alan Hardacre said that the train was the biggest public relations operation they had engaged in and was part of their wider "brighter football" policy intended to counter hooliganism by encouraging more wives and girlfriends to the game. The League dodged the question of banning drink on board, which many believed caused much of the vandalism on the specials. "We shall not be the Gestapo," said Hardacre. "But I do not imagine that supporters will want to carry drinks on the train with them." He also announced that the team would be encouraged to travel on the train, but this received considerable scorn from *The Times*. "After a particularly lame performance the presence of the losing team could bring a new element of conflict to the robust and traditional pleasures of the British football specials."

Two years later, *The Times* reported a dozen arrests at Burnley's home match with Arsenal, but to the relief of the local police, the violence was not on the scale of previous encounters.

An early Burnley leader was a local character called Norman Jones. During one Boxing Day derby at home to Blackburn Rovers (known as Bastard Rovers to Burnley fans), the home support was busy fighting off an attempted incursion onto their Longside when Jones ran onto the pitch wearing a Blackburn scarf. From a distance, the Blackburn fans applauded the cheek of one of their own. Their appreciation turned to anger when Jones threw off the scarf and began jumping on it, whilst goading a Blackburn player to fight. "There's only one Norman Jones," chanted the home fans as he was led away by police. Years later Jones was to fall out of favour with the Burnley hardcore after he appealed for calm during a major riot at Blackburn. The cheers turned to groans and chants of "Fuck off Norman" as the ground was ripped apart.

The late Seventies saw invasions from Newcastle, Sunderland and Celtic. Newcastle arrived on Boxing Day 1976 in their thousands. There was widespread trouble inside the ground though just between the away fans and the police. The Geordies drove the police out of their end before attempting to rip down the fence separating them from the home end. It took the liberal use of police dogs to restore order. Outside the ground, the two mobs clashed in a ten-minute fight.

Later that season, Sunderland were at Turf Moor for a Cup game and they too arrived in huge numbers. They again attempted to take the Longside but this time it was home fans who repelled them.

In 1978, however, came the match that would be an unforgettable and in many instances formative experience for Burnley's young would-be hooligans. The town of Burnley was literally besieged with the invasion of Celtic for an Anglo-Scottish Cup game. Every national newspaper reported the following day on what the *Burnley Express* called "the most disgusting scenes ever witnessed at Turf Moor". The game was temporarily abandoned as home fans spilled onto the pitch to avoid missiles thrown from the travelling contingent. While Celtic fans were blamed, Burnley fans were more than happy to join in. The Scots had come down in their thousands and took over much of the ground. They swept aside one police line and edged ever closer to the home fans on the Longside. With the police offering little real resistance it took the home fans to defend their end, to chants of "You'll never take the Longside."

"Celtic was something I witnessed that will live with me forever," recalled Andrew Porter, who was then just twelve, in *Suicide Squad*. "Everything was coming over the fence; the air was full of glass and piss. Celtic fans started climbing the fence pulling the bars apart and actually snapping them off. Police retreated to the pitch. It was time for me to get down from my vantage point. Then, when I thought it couldn't get any worse the Celtic fans started using the snapped off railings as spears, pushing through our fence and stabbing at anyone and everyone. All hell broke loose then as the railings started flying through the air."

"They were fighting a battle they were bound to lose," noted the local paper, "and after about half-an-hour there were sufficient Celtic fans on the Longside for them to attempt a takeover bid. They were quickly repulsed with chants of 'they'll never take the Longside,' but the scene had been set. When the Celtic fans tried again ten minutes before the end they were more successful, scattering the home supporters onto the pitch. Even then, they continued to be hit by flying missiles."

Porter, or "Pot" as he is better known, was born in 1966 and from a young age wanted to be a hooligan. In his book he recalled playing Subbuteo as a child, but instead of trying to beat your best mate at the popular game whilst trying not to stand on the fragile players or crease the baize-green pitch, he concentrated on building up an army of fans in the makeshift grandstand, and with the help of toy soldiers would force the games to be abandoned. In an interview for a French television documentary, *Fucking Hooligans*, he states that when he was young all he dreamed of being was "hard" and a soccer thug. He succeeded in his ambition and is still regarded as one of the SS top boys.

He, like every other Burnley fan, professes to hate neighbouring Blackburn and remembered the first time he went to the local derby. "My first derby game against Blackburn, or as everyone I know calls them, Bastard Rovers, was on Boxing Day. The first thing I noticed was the sense of pure hatred. Every lunatic I knew seemed to be on the Turf and the ground was packed with 28,000 people. I was on the top of the Longside near the fence, singing, 'We hate bastards.' Bricks were flying everywhere, hitting the fence, and Burnley fans were trying to entice the police into swaying around. Then Blackburn scored and all eyes went to the Bee Hole end to see if any arms went up in the air or any scarves waved. Some were spotted, prompting an exodus from the Longside as lines of lads flowed into the Bee Hole end looking for away fans."

For Pot, the Celtic game was unbelievable, yet out of character for Burnley's fans of the Seventies. "If the fans had put up a fight like that every week we would have been untouchable. They never, and many times came off second best during that period. I would say the worst lot were Bolton. I'm honest enough to admit that they terrorised us for years, I don't like admitting it but it's true, we simply could not live with them years ago." Burnley's mob was even humbled by tiny Bury before one game in the late Seventies.

In 1978, Burnley were drawn away at Anfield in the cup. The excitement of playing England's top club soon evaporated as Burnley fans were picked off unmercifully in the car park before the game. "The Burnley fans grew silent but the Scousers had their targets in sight and moved in. They gave any Burnley a proper kicking, nicking all their scarves," recalled Pot. There was further trouble after the game as scared away fans made their way back to their cars. "I couldn't believe it but the Scousers were actually dropping out of trees into the Burnley fans and taking whatever they wanted." It proved to be a sobering lesson to many of the younger lads who were later to emerge as hooligans.

Five years later an opportunity to avenge that night came with Burnley drawn away to Liverpool in the Milk Cup. The young lads who had watched the beatings dished out in horror were now five years older and bigger. Norman Jones collected names for the trip and a determined 100 set off in two coaches in search of revenge. By the time they pulled up alongside Stanley Park, the Burnley fans were up for a fight. In the distance they saw the first silhouettes of the Liverpool mob and this time there was no stepping back. It was the youngsters who had witnessed the beatings in 1978 at the front and after a quick engagement the home mob backed off. The police arrived and arrests were made but the Burnley fans were buoyant.

Burnley lost 3-0 and there was little prospect of anything better for the second leg. Liverpool brought a big mob and there was a fierce fight in the Oxford pub, which the away fans won comprehensively. Unwisely, they then decided to go out onto the street, where they were to meet a ferocious reception. The police arrived and the Burnley mob legged it, allowing Liverpool to retreat back into the pub. "It was a rough night but over the two games we had done well and knew if we stuck together could match the so-called big boys," recalled Pot.

Seven weeks later, Burnley travelled to Blackburn on Easter Monday for one of the worst days of violence in their club's history. "The Match that died of shame – 'Animals' on rampage in cauldron of violence," read the front page of the *Lancashire Evening Telegraph*. "Ewood Park became a cauldron of violence when it witnessed the worst crowd trouble ever seen at a ground," it reported. "Hooligan Burnley supporters rained missiles on to the pitch, and police were forced to baton charge the mob when it was feared two women were trapped in a kiosk. Darts, coins and smoke bombs were hurled from the Darwen end, and slabs of asbestos roofing was torn down to provide further ammunition."

Twenty-one people were injured, including five police officers, and 33 were arrested. Many of the casualties were Burnley supporters struck by missiles thrown by their own kind. The trouble started well before kick-off as 200 Burnley fans were being escorted to the ground. Seven away fans were arrested as they tried to break through police lines to attack locals. There was further trouble inside the ground after a group of Burnley fans had infiltrated the home end. After a flare-up between rival supporters, the Burnley fans were led around the pitch to great cheers from their compatriots in the away end.

Major disorder broke out at half-time after police were forced to retreat from the away end after coming under sustained attack from many in the 3,400-strong travelling contingent. Shortly after the restart, the Blackburn keeper was hit on the leg by an empty whisky bottle. The referee was finally forced to take the players off during the second half as Blackburn were leading by a single goal. "An element of Burnley support went berserk," noted

the paper, "and the occasional missile became a torrent. Asbestos roofing panels were smashed from the stands and thrown indiscriminately towards the pitch. During the fifteen minutes the match was stopped, several people were carried unconscious and bleeding from the terraces."

Chief Superintendent Gerald Billingham described the hooligan element as animals. "They are an absolute disgrace," he fumed. Burnley chairman Mr John Jackson disowned the rioting supporters, and manager Frank Casper said over the public address system, "You are a disgrace to Burnley Football Club, and we don't want you at Turf Moor again." Blackburn chairman William Fox blamed the Government. "[They] said they would restore law and order, and they have got to do it," he said. "I do not think there has been anything like this at Ewood before, and incidents like these answer all the questions about why gates are falling."

The feeling of despair was matched by the local newspaper's editorial. "What words do you use to condemn soccer hooliganism – disgrace, shame, outrage? They have all been used time and again; far too often – and still the evil of violence on the terraces remains. Society needs to re-examine the whole phenomenon of soccer violence to find its precise causes, before an effective remedy can be found. We have obviously not come up with the right solution as yet. And sadly, the only way at the moment of tackling the disease appears to be with a policeman's truncheon."

When the police later claimed that the Suicide Squad name came from suicidal attacks on opponents, perhaps they were referring to incidents such as the one at a game against Leicester City. A 22-year-old Burnley fan, William Kerr, was alleged to have launched himself into a group of Leicester City supporters, and begun fighting. Sgt John Halstead declared that he had had a perfectly clear view of what happened, and had not seen any aggressive moves by the Leicester fans. But when charged by police, Kerr said, "Who do you think I am, the Incredible Hulk?" He later testified in court that he had been walking home with his younger brother when they were surrounded by Leicester fans. "They began shouting obscenities and spitting and then one of them grabbed my scarf. I told the youngsters to run as a coloured lad took hold of me. I was on the floor being punched when the police arrived."

The court believed Kerr's version of events and he was found not guilty.

The second half of the Eighties saw several fierce clashes with North West rivals Bolton, Stockport and Wigan. As previously mentioned Bolton clearly had the upper hand over Burnley during the Seventies and early Eighties but life was not as easy as the Suicide Squad got into its stride. The two clubs were drawn together in the FA Cup in November 1987 and it was another game that was remembered for all the wrong reasons.

There was serious disorder in the Turf pub before the game after the Suicide squad came across the group of Bolton sitting in the corner. The away mob was viciously attacked and the only let-up came when the police arrived. There was also considerable trouble during the game and fighting on the pitch at the final whistle. "I like to call it payback time," wrote Pot years later. "More than 200 of us met up in the General Havelock, a pub on the outskirts of Burnley town centre. Everyone was up for it, especially me. I class Bolton as my main rivals. I hate them because I respect them; they have turned us over so many times. Burnley ran Bolton ragged that day and they've never been the same since. I thought they were the top team in Lancashire – until this day. Just a week later Burnley played Bolton in a League match and they didn't turn up."

The 1980s also saw the start of a long-running feud with Stockport County and several nasty encounters saw people on both sides slashed and stabbed. There were differing accounts of Burnley's away match against Stockport in September 1988, when 400 Suicide Squad made the short trip into Greater Manchester. "Riot" was the description given to the events before and during the Friday night league game in several of the national newspapers. "Burnley supporters reduced the on-field action to a sideshow as they fought with police in their own enclosure for 20 minutes before calm was restored," reported the *Daily Mirror*. "Police were heavily outnumbered and a helmet was thrown onto the pitch before reinforcements were called in." Similar articles appeared in many other national newspapers.

Several police officers were injured, including three who were taken to hospital. The most serious trouble took place at the local railway station as police battled with away fans to prevent them from reaching their local rivals. Yet Greater Manchester Police played down the incident and criticised some of the media accounts. "Reports in the national press have blown the trouble out of all proportion," claimed Supt John Hodgson. "You would think the ground was a seething mass of fighting, but that could not be further from the truth. It was not much of an incident and was confined to a small area of the ground." Confrontations between the two sides continued for years, with several occurring at England internationals.

A more surprising rivalry developed with distant opponents Plymouth Argyle. The two mobs first clashed twice in 1984. Ten years later, Burnley beat Plymouth in the play-off Division Two semi-finals. The first leg, at Plymouth, saw a large number of Burnley fans stop off in Torquay for the night and several were jailed after clashes with local doormen. There was more trouble at Plymouth during Burnley's visit in November 1996, then in May 1998 the teams met on the last day of the season with relegation staring both in the face. A 2-1 home victory saw Burnley safe and Plymouth doomed. [For details on this feud see PLYMOUTH in *Hooligans 2*.]

Between 1986-9, the Suicide Squad was augmented by a small but tight-knit group of younger lads who took the name Suicide Section Fives. An attack on two vanloads of Hartlepool brought them to the attention of the older lads and soon they became their firm's recognised "youth" section. The Nineties were quieter on the domestic front for Burnley, though they established a regular and violent presence at England internationals. The form of the team fluctuated, attendances dropped and local derbies were fewer. Two new rivalries that emerged were against Cardiff and West Brom. Cardiff came unannounced in April 1992 and though they took Burnley by surprise the tables were soon turned and the Welsh mob were on their toes. Burnley won the old Fourth Division title that season and the sides didn't play each other for a few years. When they did, 48 Burnley travelled to Cardiff but a huge police escort took them straight to the ground without giving the rival mobs a chance to meet. However, the size of the police operation was seen as a compliment by the Burnley lads.

In 1999, a new generation of Burnley hooligans began to emerge, initially in small numbers but then as their own recognisable mob. The Suicide Youth

Squad (SYS), or Burnley Youth as they were also known, grew to be one of the most active youth mobs in the country. Initially the older lads were suspicious, even dismissive, of these youngsters, many of whom were teenagers, but after they proved themselves on a number of occasions they were gradually accepted. For the police they were to prove a constant worry, not simply because of their numbers, which for a large match could rise to 100, but also because they often ignored hooligan proto-col and appeared to hold the police in far more contempt than did the older lads.

The emergence of the Youth coincided with an upsurge in hooliganism in Burnley. In October 1999, over 50 Burnley clashed with Millwall at London Bridge station. According to the National Criminal Intelligence Service, Burnley gained the upper hand after two or three minutes of fighting, though largely due to bigger numbers. The return fixture saw police attacked with thunder flashes, smoke canisters and other missiles in the town centre before the match. Superintendent Gary Stephenson of Lancashire Police described the actions of a "small number" of Burnley supporters as "appalling and totally unacceptable". Eleven people, five from Burnley and six from Millwall, were arrested for public order offences during the disturbances.

A few weeks after the match at Millwall, over 200 Burnley hooligans travelled to Wigan. There was trouble after the game as Burnley slipped the police escort and were, in the words of NCIS, "involved in a pitched battle with a mob of Wigan lads. All kinds of weapons and missiles are used before police again restore order. Burnley lads are then put on the train home, but get off in Preston but trouble there is prevented by a heavy police presence."

The return game saw even more trouble. "There were ugly scenes in Yorkshire Street as a hard core of 300 Burnley and Wigan Athletic supporters fought it out after most of the capacity 20,000 crowd which had turned up to see Ian Wright's debut had left peacefully," reported the *Lancashire Evening Telegraph*. "Mounted officers and foot and dog patrols were sent in to separate the rival factions. But police say this triggered an unprovoked attack on officers by 200 Burnley fans in which innocent people became caught up. "An eleven-year-old girl suffered a broken arm after she was pushed into the path of a police dog, and police operations manager

Supt Gary Stephenson said, "So-called fans shamed the town and the club with their behaviour during the highlight of this season."

The following season saw Burnley travel to Blackburn for the first competitive game since they ripped Ewood Park apart in 1983. First, however, was their fixture at Turf Moor, which saw Burnley turn on police after failing to get at their rivals. Hundreds of Burnley then made the short trip to Rovers, including huge numbers of "youth". Blackburn were nowhere to be seen but after the game hundreds of Burnley clashed with police in Accrington. "A policeman was dragged into a pub and glassed by soccer hooligans," the local paper reported. "The officer was attacked in the Black Horse in Abbey Street, Accrington, as police trying to go to their colleague's aid faced a barrage of bottles and glasses. Thirty-six people were arrested for football-related incidents during the day by police, who launched the biggest ever operation at a Lancashire football match. Police sealed off the area. One man has been arrested in connection with the incident and was being ques-tioned today.

"The chairman of the Lancashire Police Authority, Dr Ruth Henig also condemned more than 500 Burnley fans who ignored police advice and travelled to the game by train – getting off at Rishton station before being marched to Ewood Park under heavy police guard after being spotted by officers, saying: 'You have to ask why these people got off the train at Rishton, because it is a long walk to Ewood Park. It is obvious they wanted to break away and make their own way there, probably causing trouble on the way before being spotted by the police.'"

Earlier that season there had been trouble at Huddersfield, though as an NCIS report noted, police action prevented mass disorder. "125 Burnley fans got on a train to travel to Huddersfield includ-ing five known hooligans. The fans got off the train at Halifax to seek a confrontation. Good intelli-gence and sufficient police resources prevented serious disorder. As a result of further intelligence the return service was adequately policed and the fans were prevented from leaving the train. A classic example of good police work involving three forces. One man was arrested for a public order offence."

The Youth really arrived during the two matches

Jayne Walsh

Andrew Porter, one of the leaders of the Burnley Suicide Squad, walks his dogs not far from Turf Moor.

of "the racist capital of the north". While support for the BNP has slipped back sharply since then, largely due to their councillors being considered ineffective, there is still a strong residue of support in the town. The BNP polled 16.7% in the 2004 European elections, the party's highest share anywhere in the country, and 10.3% in the 2005 General Election.

The party's success was gained on the back of deep-seated division between local white and Asian people. The Asian community, who make up under 7% of the town's population, are ghettoised in the two poorest wards and a study conducted by Lancaster University found alarming levels of racism were "part of the wallpaper" among young people in East Lancashire. Unsurprisingly, the Burnley mob reflected this deep engrained racism. "Burnley hooligans are predominantly racist, male, white, aged between sixteen and thirty-five," noted a police report.

In late June 2001, Burnley erupted into racial rioting. While most of the media concentrated on the role of Asians in the trouble, there was also considerable violence from the white community. While the Asians mainly targeted the police, the local whites attacked Asians and their property. "A significant proportion of the white offenders were known football hooligans." One man jailed for three years for his part in the trouble was Andrew Porter.

There was further racial violence in June 2002, following England's World Cup match with Sweden. As the final whistle blew on what was another disappointing England performance, many Burnley hooligans attacked Asian taxi drivers before turning on the police. A police report into the Burnley hooligans also noted attempts to link up with hooligans from Chelsea (September 2001) and Stoke City (2002) to attack Asians in the town. The trouble at the Stoke match was only prevented through a massive police operation costing £50,000 and involving 250 officers.

One member of the SYS who received most media attention was Luke Smith. A convicted hooligan, he was elected as a BNP councillor in May 2003 at the age of just 21. His tenure in office was not to last long as four months later he glassed the Leeds BNP organiser during a fight at the party's annual festival in the neighbouring countryside. Smith resigned

against Preston North End. The home leg saw a mob of 300 Burnley, mostly SYS, come together during a night match to face their opponents. The away match saw hundreds of Burnley run amok in Preston city centre before their end of season crunch game. During clashes, Burnley fans smashed windows, threw bottles and overturned bandit machines. One pub worker told the press, "When they first came in we thought 'Oh my God.' I spoke to one fan and he said if anyone aggravated them they would smash the place up."

The past few years have seen the rapid growth of the British National Party (BNP) in Burnley. In 2001, the far-right party polled 11% in the General Election and the following year it gained three councillors and 28% of the town's vote in the local borough elections. May 2003 saw seven more council victories, earning the town the dubious title as a councillor and the BNP was hammered in the by-election. He went on to be banned from town centre pubs after further trouble.

The Burnley Youth were causing real trouble for the local police and the start of the 2002/3 season saw an upsurge in violence. During a fight with Notts Forest fans in December 2002 a 17-year-old, Nathan Shaw, from Nottingham, was hit by a bottle and later died in hospital. The town and both clubs were stunned and the police came under huge pressure to act, especially as a short time earlier an elderly woman had died after she was struck by a flying object during another town centre fight. Why, some wondered, after so many years of monitoring the hooligans, could they simply not seem to know who these younger troublemakers were?

In the immediate aftermath of Shaw's death, the local chief inspector promised to crack down hard on the hooligans. "I want to hurt hooligans and to let everyone else know that we are hurting them," said Richard Morgan. "We also want to build intelligence so that we can hurt them in the future. There is no escape for you." Operation Fixture was born, and over the next twelve months £50,000 of Government funding helped secure convictions and bans against over 100 Burnley hooligans, making it the biggest operation of its kind in the country. [For more on Fixture, see POLICING in *Hooligans 2*]

Op Fixture had a dramatic impact on hooliganism at Burnley, but as was evident during the Cup clashes against Blackburn, there are still hundreds of young men who are keen, willing and able to get involved in trouble. "Despite many of the older lads calling it a day, there are loads more taking over where we left off," said Andrew Porter. "Recently we have turned out 200 for Leeds and well over 100 for Liverpool who disappointed us by bringing no mob at all. The numbers we had out for Blackburn both home and away was unreal. The SS are still active. At the England v Wales game at Old Trafford they had it with Stoke, and on a cup final day battered Blackburn when the two mobs bumped into each other in Blackpool."

Further reading: *Suicide Squad*, Andrew Porter (Milo Books)

BURY

Ground: Gigg Lane
Firms: Interchange Riot Squad, Interchange Crew
Rivals: Rochdale, Bolton, Stockport, York
Police operations: Antelope

There was a commotion outside but few of the punters thought much of it. Shouting and a few lads squaring up to each other was hardly unusual on a Saturday evening. But the shouting grew louder, and then came the crash. A sandwich board came flying through the pub window, sending shards of glass in every direction. Then came the bottles and yet more shouting. Some lads inside the pub composed themselves and returned fire with their own bottles, a few pint glasses and the customary bar stool. It was Bury v Stockport, 17 October 1998.

The pub was only yards from the local police headquarters yet it took 15 minutes for officers to respond. That did not impress many locals, including a Mr Newport, who dialled 999. "I am disgusted," he later told the press. "They sent just two officers and by the time they arrived everyone had disappeared." The police offered the pitiful explanation that the delay may have been a communication problem.

However, Bury town centre is under almost total CCTV surveillance and the entire incident was recorded, providing the police with a golden opportunity to make amends. Even then, it took a pub doorman, who overheard some of the Stockport lads planning the attack, to alert the CCTV operator to follow the unfolding events. Operation Antelope was established and 15 months later, 16 men were found guilty and ten received custodial sentences. It was Bury's biggest hooligan trial.

Events began shortly before midday when Stockport County's Football Intelligence Officer, Steve Chisnall, and a spotter were touring Bury's pubs looking for "prominents", the hardcore of Stockport's hooligan mob. They came across ten but were told that the bulk of the mob had decided to give the game a miss and stay in Stockport. At the same time, PC Steve Orr, Bury's FIO, was doing likewise. For the next couple of hours both officers shadowed their respective hooligan groups. The game passed off peacefully and an hour after it ended the police stood down.

"The Stockport fans left the town and Bury's prominents went to their usual post-match haunts," remembered PC Orr. But, unbeknown to either officer, the main Stockport mob had slipped quietly into town while the match was in progress and made their way by taxi to a pub on the fringes of the town, where they remained until the police stood down.

At precisely 6.45 p.m., one CCTV camera captured a large group of Bury supporters leaving the Old White Lion pub to walk past the George and then return to the first pub. At almost the same time, Stockport were on the move, leaving the Jolly Wagoners, also for the George. It was now that the CCTV caught four Stockport lads chatting to two Bury prominents near Yates's. "At 7.30 p.m., the Stockport fans streamed out of the George towards Yates's where the six lads had begun to fight," said PC Orr. "At exactly the same time, the Bury prominents left the Old White Lion and, as Stockport turned the corner into Market Place, the Bury fans turned and ran back to the Lion and the Stockport supporters started attacking the premises."

Bury repelled the first attack and, despite being outnumbered, even forced Stockport to back off. Their opponents were not put off for long and soon were back with an even more vicious assault. Again their advances were blocked and again they charged. With the Bury lads apparently deciding to stay in the pub, the visitors eventually gave up and began walking away, unaware that Bury had slipped out of the rear door and were mobbing up behind them. Stockport gathered themselves again and backed Bury off, before the arrival of the police.

It took PCs Orr and Chisnall almost two months to sift through the CCTV footage and identify the culprits. Over a couple of days either side of Christmas, doors went in across Greater Manchester. Ten Stockport fans, who the judge believed were the main protagonists, were eventually each sentenced to six months' imprisonment and six Bury fans to 200 hours' community service. Among the Bury lads prosecuted were a soldier, a bailiff and two taxi drivers, and most were considerably older than their Stockport counterparts.

The CCTV turned a public relations disaster into a successful police operation. "Without this video footage we would never have been able to identify or prosecute those involved in this violence," said PC Orr. "CCTV is the new weapon. This case highlights its effectiveness in fighting crime." His Stockport colleague concurred. "Praise must be given to the CCTV operators who were the main players in this incident. Without their awareness of what was going we would have found it difficult to secure a prosecution." Or in other words, thank heavens for the cameras, where would we have been without them? Within months, Chisnall was promoted to "spotting" at Manchester United and England games.

Football violence is uncommon at Bury, a small club rightly proud of its family-oriented policies, and research unearthed fewer incidents of trouble linked to its fans than almost anywhere else in the country. In 2001, Bury was one of only two clubs in the country without a single arrest in and around the ground, and many Bury fans would be shocked and surprised to hear of a hooligan group linked to the club, but there is. The Interchange Crew, formerly known as the Interchange Riot Squad, may only have a core of 30 lads but they are active and have been around for a while.

Most of the violence in Bury has been precipitated by visiting fans. In November 1977, West Brom fans rioted through the streets around Gigg Lane after their team's League Cup defeat. They smashed glass doors and even threw lumps of concrete through windows as they rampaged in the streets. Inside the ground, rival fans crossed swords in the Cemetery Road end of the ground and 15 people were arrested, five from Bury.

The trouble caused an understandable backlash from locals and within a couple of weeks more than 600 had signed a petition calling for the club and the police to prevent any repetition. Leading the protest was Mrs Edna Glover, whose leaded front window was shattered by a lump of concrete. She and the other organisers were convinced that the trouble was getting worse every season. "When West Brom came, it was the worst we had ever known in our eight years here," she said. "But going round with the petition has opened my eyes to just how bad the problem is for people living in the streets near the ground. It has reached the stage where people are afraid to look out of the window or leave their lights on in case the mob should single them out as a target."

The police announced a raft of measures, including a new coach park for away fans much closer to the ground, and greater supervision once they had arrived, with visitors stewarded straight into the ground on arrival. The head of Bury Police was quick to point out that these measures had nothing to do with the petition, but were merely a response to the West Brom violence. Regardless of the reasons, the redoubtable Mrs Glover was no doubt reassured that she could now sit in her front room on a Saturday afternoon and watch the wrestling in peace.

The new arrangements were put to the test only a couple of weeks after their implementation with the arrival of Notts Forest in the FA Cup. Tensions were running high in the build-up to the game, with even the editorial of the local newspaper urging restraint. While accepting that football violence was "a reflection of present-day society", it called for the football authorities to take a lead. "Would it be considered a little namby-pamby for an appeal to be made to the crowd before the match by officials on both sides?" it asked. "It has been reported Mr Clough, the Forest manager, got an encouraging response when he appealed to his team's supporters to cut out the use of offensive language. Perhaps Mr Clough and Mr Bob Stokoe should ask over the loud-speakers that there should be no after-the-match incidents which would be a blot on the memory of a contest that should be packed with enjoyment."

Fortunately for everyone concerned, not least the local residents, their houses were untouched by Forest supporters. There was trouble but this was confined to the ground. Fines totalling £860 were handed out to 14 supporters in the 21,500 capacity crowd. Twenty people were arrested after fighting on the packed terraces. "It was 100 per cent better," said a beaming Mrs Glover. Her views were echoed by Mr Brian Wilde, owner of a newsagent on Parkhills Road. "They were the best behaved supporters we have had in the shop," he said.

Another FA Cup match in 1980, at Liverpool, is one many Bury fans will remember as among the most unpleasant day spent following their side. Anfield was not then as welcoming as it became, and to make matters worse, in those days the police had no objection to Everton and Liverpool playing at home at the same time. This was the case on this occasion and as Bury fans left Anfield for the coaches and trains home, they were confronted by not only hundreds of Liverpool thugs, but also masses of Evertonians looking for Mancunians and

for Wrexham fans who had just visited Goodison. What went on after the match can only be described as carnage. Liverpool's and Everton's mobs at the time used to mix freely and join up to fight visitors, and this was one such occasion when outsiders were systematically beaten and chased all over Priory Road and Stanley Park long into the night. There were many accounts of even Everton and Liverpool supporters being attacked by local youths who by this time had begun to dress without colours and anyone wearing blue and white or red and white was regarded as a target by football's first "casuals" – though that was not a name they used themselves.

The police admitted they were powerless to control the mass brawling and, even before many of the casualties had left hospital, they announced that it would be the last time that Everton and Liverpool would be allowed to play games at home on the same day.

In March 1985, Blackpool arrived with 3,000 fans. "Sickening! Fans orgy of violence," was how the *Manchester Evening News* described what followed, as the visitors virtually demolished the main stand to chants of "Smash it up". A small Bury mob did pick off a couple of isolated Blackpool lads before the match, and sparked a brief punch-up in the club car park just after kick-off, but were utterly routed after the game. At least one was chased into the living room of a terraced house near the ground and punched and kicked in front of a startled family watching *Final Score* – not, one hopes, Mrs Glover. The FA launched a disciplinary tribunal into the Seasiders' wrecking spree and Bury chairman Terry Robinson called for special sentences for football hooligans. "I am at a loss for words to describe their behaviour," he said. "I was sickened."

Bury's closest rivals have traditionally been Bolton, which is a short drive away. Unfortunately, Bolton is a much bigger town and had one of the most active and dangerous mobs in the lower divisions. They came to Bury in February 1986 and it wasn't pretty. "Rampaging Bolton Wanderers fans hijacked a double-decker bus last night and threatened the terrified driver with a knife," ran the opening paragraph in the local paper. "In an orgy of destruction the supporters stripped the top deck, smashing every window and hurling 17 seats into the road. The bus was one of five to be vandalised after the local derby game between Bury and Bolton at Gigg Lane. Trouble had flared during the game when Bolton fans got into the Bury end of the ground. Police ejected 24 people."

In a separate incident in 1987, a group of Bolton fans who had been turned away from Gigg Lane after the match had been cancelled because of bad weather went on a rampage during which a jewellery shop was raided.

Bury lads with hooligan tendencies have often followed either of the big Manchester clubs rather than their own team, while others have been drawn to Bolton and even Burnley. This, combined with the club's playing fortunes, has restricted the number of fighting lads prepared to turn out for Bury, though in recent years older City and United lads who live locally have turned out for the higher-profile games. These are normally against Rochdale, Bury's biggest local rivals. In the 2003/04 season Bury took 100 lads to the away fixture there, an even split of older and younger lads, their biggest turnout in many years.

More recently, there was trouble at Bury's away match against York City. Four travelling supporters were arrested after violence broke out with rival fans after the game. Up to 40 lads were involved in a row in a pub near York railway station and several missiles, including pool cues, were thrown. One eyewitness said, "It was like the OK Corral. The police looked as though they were struggling to control it because there were so many people fighting." A spokesman for Bury FC said, "Just when we are trying to get things on and off the field sorted, we then get a minority of so-called Bury fans who have heaped further shame on our club, we have been let down again and everyone here is disappointed."

This trouble came on the back of repeated racism from sections of the Bury support. At a match against Torquay, the club's own player-manager, Andy Preece, was racially abused by a small section of his own supporters. He said, "I think it's been going on for a while now, but I hadn't been totally made aware of it. The only way to deal with these people is to stand up to them and be strong. I'm not going to tolerate it and I know the fans won't tolerate it."

Unfortunately, this was not an isolated incident. Recent matches against Huddersfield, Millwall, Notts County and Bournemouth have all been marred by a racist minority. At the Bournemouth match the group behind the racist chanting turned up wearing white boiler suits with racist stencilling on them.

C

CAMBRIDGE UNITED

Ground: Abbey Stadium
Firms: The Main Firm, the Young Irish
Rivals: Peterborough, Norwich City, Oxford United, Luton Town

Mention Cambridge United in a hooligan context and the name Les Muranyi immediately comes up. The man they called simply "The General" was born in 1959, became an active soccer thug in the Seventies and received national attention in 1985 when he was sentenced to five years' imprisonment for leading an ambush on visiting Chelsea fans. It was a remarkably violent incident that left 15 people needing medical treatment and 32 arrested. But the coverage Muranyi's subsequent trial received was perhaps as much due to surprise at such a shocking fight taking place in the supposedly genteel surroundings of Cambridge – plus the fact that the victims were the notorious Chelsea.

The publicity surrounding Muranyi's trial provided the public for the first time with an insight into the organising of hooliganism. "By your actions you have ruined the lives of several of your co-defendants," the judge told Muranyi when passing sentence. "Some of them are weaker characters than you and lads of good character. You are the General."

Football hooliganism at Cambridge United was not born on that fateful day in February 1984. Trouble at the Abbey Stadium dates back to the late Sixties, notably in fixtures against local rivals Peterborough. There was serious disorder in 1977 when they played at Peterborough. A heavy police presence for the return fixture prevented further clashes, though Cambridge fans did attempt to pull down the fencing to reach their opponents.

When Oxford visited in 1977, a huge away mob rampaged through the city. The local paper described the travelling fans as in "riotous mood" after they stormed the pitch and broke the goalposts following Oxford's defeat. Cambridge manager, Ron Atkinson, went onto the pitch to plead for calm but quickly withdrew under a hail of missiles. An estimated 600 Oxford fans were involved in the trouble and, while Cambridge offered little resistance inside the ground, an Oxford coach was bricked as it left the ground.

However, veteran Newcastle hooligan Terry Mann recalled Cambridge as having a tidy little mob in the early 1980s. In *Terrace Legends*, he wrote, "Once we went to Cambridge in the old Second Division and went into their end. We had huge numbers but, respect to them, they didn't half give us a good fight. It went on for a good ten minutes. They came from everywhere."

When Cambridge weren't fighting opponents, they were battling with each other. During one home match against Peterborough in November 1977, the local paper reported that five policemen were injured and 20 arrests made as Cambridge football fans battled among themselves. A smoke bomb was thrown from the Cambridge terrace into the penalty area but the referee agreed for the game to continue despite the Peterborough goal being lost in coloured smoke.

Cambridge also suffered from fans stopping off there on their way back from matches. In 1977, a 21-year-old year old Wolves fan was killed after Cambridge lads attacked the coach he was travelling on returning from a match in Ipswich. In 1981, 46 Norwich fans were arrested after wrecking the Still and Sugar Loaf pub in Cambridge on their return from QPR. Eight people were taken to hospital. There were several other serious clashes between the two sides, including the time Norwich came through for a Cambridge v Ipswich game and there was a three-way fight outside the ground. The repeated trouble earned Cambridge respect from the Norwich lads. "Cambridge was always a good trip," one recalled. "Cambridge had a fair mob led by a geezer called the General. I had seen this mob before; they ran a mob of Millwall out of Liverpool Street Station when we were on our way back from Watford."

In the late Seventies, the Main Firm was born. It was the brainchild of Muranyi, a young man of Hungarian-Irish parentage who had thrilled to the violence he saw on the terraces. "We came together in schooldays at the Abbey and grew into a decent mob," he later recalled. "West Ham created a massive impression on me with the ICF in 1979. I'd heard of Millwall's F-Troop, Treatment and Halfway Line, who all featured in a 1977 BBC *Panorama* documentary. I chose the name Main Firm for our crew in 1979. It was a Chelsea schoolboy who gave me the idea when he used the phrase to large himself and his mates up. It had a very authentic ring to it."

The Main Firm quickly grew, attracting youths from the city, from areas such as Romsey Town, the Arbury Estate and Cherry Hinton. Muranyi's charisma and skill as an organiser set them apart. They drank in a notorious city centre pub, the Kings Arms, while on match days they often met at a pub on Newmarket Road, closer to the ground, called the Burleigh Arms. "Early Burleigh" was the catchphrase on Saturday mornings.

The late Seventies was a golden era for Cambridge United. Under the managership of Ron Atkinson, the club won the Fourth Division title in 1977 and were runners-up in the Third the following year. For a club that had only entered the League in 1970, the rise eventually to the Second Division, where they were to play the likes of Newcastle United, Burnley and West Ham, was nothing less than miraculous. A credible mid-table finish meant that the following season they were up against Chelsea for the first time in their history. Thirty-seven people were arrested as rival fans clashed before and after the game, which led Cambridge's chairman to tell Chelsea that he did not want to see their fans ever again.

But there was further trouble at the same fixture the following season, this time with 51 arrests. Dozens of Chelsea infiltrated the home end and fighting broke out as Cambridge rallied to defend it. After the game hundreds of Chelsea fans ran through the streets, attacking property and locals with bricks and stones. Windows in over 30 homes were smashed as rival gangs exchanged missiles. Many locals were furious at what they saw as poor policing. "Football should be banned altogether," said one mother. "So this is the game of football, how did we get involved?" asked another. A petition was drawn up by residents calling for their local MP to demand action be taken to prevent this sort of trouble happening again.

Stung by the fierce criticism at the last encounter, the police prepared a large operation to prevent further trouble at the next visit of Chelsea. In the first home game of the following season 350 police were on duty to shepherd 4,000 travelling Chelsea fans. Officers lined the route from the railway station to the ground and coaches were prevented from dropping fans off in the city centre. Local residents who bore much of the brunt of the violence the previous season were full of praise for the police. Despite this, there was still some trouble. Fifty-one people were arrested, a Cambridge fan was stabbed in the back and several Chelsea fans also required medical treatment.

When the two sides met again in February 1984, their fortunes could not have been more different. Chelsea were sitting pretty at the top of the table, while Cambridge languished in bottom spot. Muranyi and his associates decided to have "one last big pop" at them. Given the history of recent encounters, after weeks of planning and a top brass meeting at their Divisional Headquarters, the police believed they were fully prepared for all eventualities. So serious was the danger to people and property considered that the city police mounted their biggest ever operation, to handle 6,000 of Britain's most notorious football fans. This time 450 officers were on duty for what the local paper called a "police military operation".

Meticulous police planning got off to a bad start after it was discovered a couple of days before the match that several rubbish skips containing bricks littered the route from the train station to the ground. Otherwise, matters appeared to be running smoothly. Traffic police were used in an attempt to escort every coach into the city and twelve double-decker buses were laid on at the train station to ferry people straight to the ground to stop them wandering freely into town. The club did its bit by opening up the turnstiles at 12.30 p.m. Season ticket holders who were made to vacate their seats to make room for visiting fans were given free entrance to other parts of the ground.

What the police could not do much about was the determination of the Cambridge hooligans. The result was 32 arrests around the city, most from Cambridge, and 60 Chelsea arrested on a coach on the M11. A man needed an emergency operation after being slashed across the neck with a broken bottle in Newmarket Road and another fan was stabbed. A police motorcyclist was dragged from his machine and another officer suffered a broken nose. A mother and her baby were trampled under-foot as a mob ransacked her shop in Burleigh Street and 15 people were treated for injuries. The only people smiling that day were Cambridge's account-ants. The top versus bottom clash attracted a bumper crowd of 10,602 packed into the ground, including 6,000 who had travelled up from London. Gate receipts passed the £25,000 figure, £3,000 more than the club's previous best.

Thirteen months later, 25 Cambridge United fans were imprisoned at the Old Bailey for their part in the trouble. Muranyi received five years after plead-ing guilty to riot and Steven Robson, who had four previous convictions, including two for football violence, received four years for wounding (Robson later died in prison while serving a sentence for another offence). The remainder were sentenced to terms of between five and 15 months.

Passing judgement, His Honour Judge Hilliard said the public were sick of soccer violence and that the sentences would teach football fans up and down this country that football violence meant loss of liberty. "This was organised, pre-planned violence which endangered life," he declared. "An experi-enced police officer said that it was the worst series of incidents that he had seen in ten years. The public look to the courts for protection and for an example to be made. Those who are minded to do likewise should be deterred by the sentences the court passes and, after taking all these matters into considera-tion, each of the defendants must lose his liberty. It gives me no pleasure to send away young men of previous good character whose careers today are shattered, whose homes or jobs will go as a result of the sentences which I am about to pass. Some of you wish the clock could be put back and so do I. But it can't, and the damage to your lives is the price that must be paid to teach football fans up and down the country that football violence means loss of liberty, however young, however good, however sad, however hard the effects on individual defendants may be. Single or sober you present one view. But in a mob with drink inside you, you present a very different picture."

The court was told that 80 of "Muranyi's Army" met up in the City Arms pub while others acted as lookouts. Posing as helpful locals, they directed Chelsea fans into a waiting trap. Reassured by the small group of Cambridge drinking outside the pub, the Chelsea fans advanced, but just before they entered, 30 yelling Cambridge fans burst out. "The 'innocent' drinkers closed in behind," the prosecu-tion told the court, "and the Chelsea supporters were set upon with pool cues and bottles. More Chelsea fans were trapped in 'pincer' movements as 150 Cambridge supporters took part in running battles. Passers-by ran for cover, cars were vandalised and one Chelsea fan ran through the thorns of a rose hedge in his panic."

Muranyi paid the price. As the first identifiable gang leader to be jailed after a major trial at the height of football hooliganism, his face was splashed across the pages of every national newspa-per and dozens of column inches were given to discussing terrace warfare. "Organized on military lines and wearing a 'uniform' of expensive designer-label sweaters, the new breed of football louts staged well-planned attacks on rival fans," *The Times* informed its ageing readers. "The members of the gang were mature men, mostly in their mid 20s. Some where married with mortgages and children, and soccer violence was their Saturday afternoon entertainment. Known as the 'Cambridge Casuals', Muranyi's 'Army' all wore the same kind of expen-sive casual clothes – Pringle label sweaters, jeans and Nike training shoes – so they could easily identify their comrades during disorders. Their smart appear-ance gave them a respectable air."

Muranyi, unsurprisingly, recalls the events slightly differently. Twenty years later, in the pages of *Top Boys*, he gave his account. "We finally left the pub at about two o'clock and, within a minute, we walked into a mob of them coming round the corner and it kicked off from there," he insisted. "Quite spontaneously, we've ended up chasing them in two groups and cutting off their retreat. This was later claimed as a pincer movement that I'd planned deliberately before the game, but it wasn't planned. It was totally spontaneous."

Back in Cambridge, there was shock. "Cosy Cambridge should hang its head in shame today," read the editorial of the *Cambridge Evening News*. "We have been sickened by the horrific account of hooliganism recounted at the Old Bailey. That so-called football supporters should be at the Central Criminal Court for what will go down in history as one of the worst episodes concerning vandalism and violence is depressing and degrading in the extreme. Our fair City has been blighted."

Yet the parents of those imprisoned were equally shocked by the sentences and claimed that their sons were being made scapegoats. "Obviously, they have got to be punished and I am not condoning what my son did, what he did was wrong," said one mother. "But no way should they have had to wait fifteen months on a two-day-a-week curfew for the trial. Putting them in the Old Bailey has been to make an example not just in Cambridge but all over the country."

Their objections were not shared by those in authority. Local MP Robert Rhodes welcomed the sentences while the local police chief condemned those clubs who were soft on dealing with hooligans, especially those who proposed the use of "sin bins" – temporary holding cells at grounds. "That is the negative way of dealing with the problem," he said. "Having them dealt with by the courts is the positive way." The local paper had also hardened its view by the following edition. Under an editorial headline "Good judgement", it went on to applaud the verdict. "We can celebrate now that at least some of the rotten apples have been excised from the barrel of this society. We salute the policemen on the front line and we hope the likes of Muranyi and his mates never soil our streets again."

The newspaper was to be disappointed. Despite telling the court that he was now too old to continue hooliganism, Muranyi returned to the fray on his release. He was banned from the Abbey Stadium for life but continued to organise violence away from it. At the age of 45, he was on licence, having just been released from serving three years for football violence.

A few weeks after the Chelsea attack, Cambridge hosted Peterborough in the league for the first time in six years. In the past this fixture would have been accompanied by mass disorder but this match passed off peacefully, due to heavy policing, including officers drafted in from across the county, and a near absence of Cambridge lads because of the mass arrests the previous month.

Seven months after the Chelsea ambush, it was the turn of Millwall to cause trouble in the city. Three hundred Londoners went on the rampage before their match at Cambridge, two city centre shops were raided, and goods worth an estimated £5,000 were stolen from a jewellers. In other incidents, a police officer was injured by a flying bottle and rival fans fought on the pitch. After the game, Millwall fans rampaged down Newmarket Street. Thirty-two fans were arrested. Several local shopkeepers were highly critical of an apparent lack of police presence. While the police chief defended his operation, claiming that the 116 officers on duty was sufficient, local businesses thought the police were unprepared and could have prevented the disorder. The fallout from the trouble reached the local council chamber when a councillor proposed the banning of all away fans in the future.

The local newspaper reported on the story with some humility. Only a week before, an editorial predicted that the likelihood of trouble at Cambridge had receded now that the team had been relegated to the Third Division. "We were writing on the eve of the new football season and we already know that we were speaking too soon," the editor wrote. "The scenes in the City on Saturday afternoon were almost as bad as anything seen last season when United entertained, among others, the infamous followers of Chelsea football club."

The rave scene saw the Main Firm's top faces turn to money-making, and they were behind a string of illicit events in Cambridgeshire and Bedfordshire, running the security and selling drugs, although a nasty fallout with some serious heavies from Leicester curtailed some of their activities. In the meantime their mob has continued to be sporadically active, and the Main Firm was augmented by a new group, the Young Irish, so named because many were the sons of Irish construction workers who had stayed in Cambridge after completing the M11 motorway. Paradoxically, their two main protagonists became active on the England international scene. They numbered about 25 and were generally ten years younger than the Main Firm lads.

In March 1991, the Main Firm launched a serious attack on a pub full of Grimsby, but it was merely a prelude to carnage when they assaulted an Ipswich firm at a pub called the Drum and Monkey in November 1991. "The pub was obliterated while the police were nowhere to be seen," said one of those present. "Ipswich scattered in the first few seconds, leaving the remainder still in the pub to get well and truly sorted. One Ipswich fan lost his ear and another had his legs broken. Chairs were being thrown out of, and then back through, the windows. It was the worst violence I've seen at a Cambridge away match and the biggest firm I've seen away, probably about eighty lads. Norwich also had a little firm there, who were chased at the station."

In October 1995, a pub of Northampton hoolies was stormed before an away match, with CS gas canisters and flare guns used. A coachload of the Main Firm was promptly sent back to Cambridge by the police before the match had started.

Then in 2000, a home FA Cup tie against Bolton saw a major confrontation before the game. A Bolton fan was stabbed in the neck and, after the game, as the away mob sought revenge, Cambridge were given a tough time. A few years later a group of Cambridge, many of them banned from the Abbey Stadium, attacked some Lincoln fans drinking in the Corner House pub close to the ground. Police had to step in to protect the away fans.

Peterborough continue to be Cambridge's big rivals. A meeting of the two teams in late March 2001 saw trouble all day. Ten arrests were made in what was a crucial match, with Peterborough languishing towards the bottom of the League. Moments before kick-off, rival gangs tried to get to each other on the pitch but were kept apart by the intervention of the police.

The Cambridge boys had never forgotten the beating they took at the hands of Oxford in 1977. While few of the people around that day were still active, the simmering resentment was passed down through the years. In 2004, the current lads decided

to get their revenge and 25 made the journey by train into London and then out on the coach to Oxford, led by the head of the Young Irish. Cambridge's version is that phone numbers were swapped on arrival and they were told the home mob were waiting in the Blackbird pub on the Leys Estate.

Cambridge attacked an Oxford mob in the pub car park, and serious fighting ensued, with some sustaining broken ribs from flying chairs. All the while the Oxford mob grew bigger as locals from the estate, which had been the scene of serious rioting some years earlier, ran or drove up to join in. Cambridge held their ground long enough for the police to arrive and, to their surprise, they were put back on a bus and sent straight back to Paddington.

Oxford have strongly contested this version of events. "There was hardly anyone there waiting for Cambridge as they didn't tell us they were coming, and have not bothered before," insisted one Oxford lad. "There were two main faces outside the pub, and five others of the firm inside, but the rest were local pub drinkers. Having said that, the two main bods say it was a top little crew they brought down, well game, but then no firm was present to see just how good they were."

Though little has been heard from United's firm in recent years, their LDV Vans Final against Blackpool at the Millennium Stadium in 2002 showed what they can turn out: one of the hardest and most notorious Main Firm figures, a Mike Tyson type who had just emerged from a long stretch for armed robbery, took a coachload of doormen over to Cardiff and marched them down the main street before the game. Anyone who stopped to watch the burly bruisers march past was greeted with the words, "Come on Cardiff. What are you worried about? We're just a bunch of country bumpkins." There were no takers.

Asked what was the most important lesson he has learnt from his time running Cambridge's mob, Muranyi recently replied, "Motivation. I was one of the few who made it happen. If I had the chance again, I'd put even more planning into it." You can tell he means it and, without him, Cambridge, and specifically the taking of Chelsea, would not be talked about to this day.

Further reading: *Top Boys*, Cass Pennant (Blake Publishing)

CARDIFF CITY

Ground: Ninian Park
Firms: Soul Crew, Valley Commandos
Rivals: Swansea, Bristol City, Millwall
Police operations: Javelin, Base

They began arriving shortly after lunch by train, car and bus. A trickle turned into a stream and by 3 p.m. there were at least 1,000 in town. "We are animals," they chanted as hundreds marched up and down Pride Hill, Shrewsbury's main shopping street. Within an hour, most shops had closed, the locals had disappeared and they had the streets to themselves.

Cardiff City's Littlewoods Cup fifth-round match at Shrewsbury, in November 1986, kicked off in appalling weather. That and the rumours of the throngs of Cardiff who had taken over the town that afternoon meant there appeared to be more away supporters than locals. The game was petering out into a boring draw when Shrewsbury scored from a disputed free-kick a minute from time. "Sheep shaggers, wank wank wank," cried a few foolhardy home supporters, safe behind the fences. Scuffles broke out between a few hundred Cardiff and the police and it took several minutes for order to be restored. But the peace was only temporary.

At most games at Gay Meadow, both sets of fans were released at the same time, but on this one occasion West Mercia Police decided to give the home fans a head start. The temperature was rising and most Shrewsbury fans hurried home, leaving behind an increasingly angry and vocal Welsh army. Even from the top of Wyle Cop, 300 metres from the ground, the cry could be heard. A roar went up and hundreds of Cardiff broke through the police lines. They streamed into the town centre, smashing shop windows and overturning cars. A home fan who stopped by a police van in the belief that it offered him protection was stabbed in the stomach and crumpled in a heap. Six policemen were hurt and 21 people arrested. There was further trouble in towns on the route back to South Wales. "It really does look like wartime," said the President of the local Chamber of Commerce. "It is really appalling and depressing to see something like this happen in such a wonderful old town." Cardiff City blamed the police for failing to keep control at the end of the match.

Luton Town looked on smugly. They had been due to play Cardiff in the previous round and their refusal to allow away fans meant the Welsh club were awarded the tie without a ball being kicked. "I don't wish to gloat about last night's incident because this is another sad day for the sport I love," said Luton's chief executive. "But until such times that clubs like Cardiff change their views on allowing their supporters to travel, then this sort of trouble will continue. If a massive police operation is what they want then football is doomed. Cardiff have had more trouble with their fans than any other club in the League this season and they are going to have to think again."

In the past few years the Cardiff City hooligan group, the Soul Crew, has become virtually a household name. Large-scale disorder against Millwall, Stoke and, more importantly, Leeds, and a best-selling book chronicling their exploits and a prominent appearance in BBC TV's *Hooligans* series left few people unaware of a major hooligan problem in South Wales. But while the media's interest has been fairly recent, the trouble has not.

As far back as the late Sixties, Cardiff fans were running riot all over the country, and in 1969 railway bolts were thrown at Aston Villa supporters. The following year, the prospect of violence during the visit of Millwall led to steel toe-capped boots being confiscated at the turnstiles. In 1974, the club imposed a ban on any person under the age of 17 attending a game without an adult unless they possessed a special pass.

That August, 137 fans were arrested during Cardiff's visit to Bristol City, of whom only six were locals. It was the first time more than 100 people had ever been arrested at a football match in England. The vast majority were arrested in trouble before the game, and of those, five were 13 years old, 14 were 14, and a further 40 ranged between 15 and 18. During the game, some of the home fans chanted "Aberfan" at Cardiff in reference to the disaster at the tiny Welsh mining town, something police later described as "particularly provocative". The club said that they were "horrified and disgusted" with the behaviour of many of the Cardiff fans, claiming that some of the troublemakers were as young as ten. "What is the root cause of so much hooliganism?" asked an editorial in a Bristol newspaper. "Does the fault lie in the homes and in the schools in the first place? Have we, in fact, created a soulless way of life on vast, impersonal estates for so many people who, to obtain a sense of adventure, of excitement, can escape from their boredom and frustration only by going on the rampage?"

The Bristol game was a prelude to one of football's most violent days, the visit to Cardiff a month later by Manchester United. There are different accounts of who came out on top that day but all agree that it was absolute bedlam. United face Tony O'Neill said that the fighting after the match was "indescribable", while Leicester University academics called it a "watershed in the reporting of football hooliganism," the first time pre-match coverage had focussed on the potential rather than the game itself. One Cardiff fan recalled seeing more than 600 United fans rampage through the streets, smashing windows and attacking and turning over cars. The United confidence drained when up to 2,000 Cardiff marched up the road and attacked them.

The mood inside the ground was almost indescribable, with 10,000 Reds taunting thousands of equally hostile locals. "It was lunacy," recalled O'Neill in his book *Red Army General*. "These Welshmen were demented, baying for English blood." The real fighting occurred afterwards, but again who came out on top is hotly disputed. What both sides agree is that it was one of the biggest and most-prolonged instances of mass brawling at a football match up until that time.

Another big team to find Ninian Park an unfriendly place was Everton who visited Cardiff in the fifth round of the FA Cup in 1977. Their football trains were bricked even before they had stopped at Cardiff station. Inside the ground the 4,000 Everton fans camped in the Canton Side stand were picked off apparently at will. When Everton's Duncan McKenzie scored a disputed goal, hundreds of Cardiff steamed into the away end with such ferocity that many decided to leave the ground and head straight back to the station. For some even this was not a wise move, as chasing locals forced them to flee down the track.

"Anyone convicted of carrying an offensive weapon at a football match, even for the first time, will go to prison straight away," said Sir Lincoln Hallinan, the South Glamorgan magistrate, at Cardiff Magistrates Court in the aftermath of the match. One 17-year-old was sentenced to 28 days for possessing a lump of rock, and a man was jailed for 14 days for having a half-brick under his jacket.

Cardiff did not always have it their own way. In September 1972, they had viciously expelled Aston Villa's Quinton mob from the home end at Ninian Park. When they next travelled up to the Midlands, in 1974, the hosts were out for revenge. "It was 1.30 p.m.," remembered one Villa lad. "Cardiff had obviously tried to get in the main end early but got spotted. In fairness, there were no more than 100 of them. Villa lads surounded them and they couldn't get back to the Witton End or move towards the Holte End. The infamous Pete the Greek led the charge and, basically, they were sitting ducks."

Early the following season, Cardiff came badly unstuck at Millwall when the appearance of the players signalled a home charge into the away end. A few Cardiff stood and fought, but most ran to other parts of the ground, even if it meant paying in again. "Even when we thought things couldn't get any worse, Millwall found their way in amongst us," recalled David Jones in *Soul Crew*. "More and more Millwall were mobbing up and when goal number three went in, Cardiff didn't even bother cheering. The result of the match meant nothing to most of us by now; there were far more important things to worry about, like getting out of this shithole alive." The tables were turned the following April: after the game, up to 200 Millwall piled out of the ground, but their confidence evaporated as mob after mob of Cardiff went into them, some attacking them with scaffolding poles from building work at the Ninian Park pub.

The one team whose supporters repeatedly gave Cardiff trouble was Chelsea. During the late Seventies and early Eighties there were at least five major clashes between the two. In 1977, Cardiff fans ripped apart the newly installed scoreboard at Stamford Bridge. Later that season, Chelsea got their revenge when thousands of their supporters ran amok before and after the game. Two years later a coachload of Chelsea, lead by Steve Hickmott, got into Bob Bank and there were further clashes in the park outside. In September 1982, a mob of 500 Chelsea virtually took control of Cardiff city centre, dispatching easily what little opposition there was.

The biggest game was in March 1984, with Chelsea riding high in the League and Cardiff facing relegation. At least 7,000 Chelsea fans made the trip, including more that 1,000 hooligans, dwarfing the home support of only 4,000. There were clashes in the city centre before the game and much more serious disorder immediately afterwards. Cardiff appeared to be coasting after scoring three goals in the first 25 minutes but the Londoners scored three in the final few minutes to level the game. Shortly before the final whistle the core of the Chelsea mob left the ground, only to reappear at the back of the Bob Bank. Cardiff had guessed as much and were prepared, fighting like demons to successfully defend their end.

The tables were turned outside the ground as huge numbers of Chelsea, hooligans and normally peaceable fans, ripped through the 700-strong Cardiff mob. The home fans tried to ambush their visitors on the way back to the train station, but were forced back again. "This was by far the worst trouble I had ever seen at Ninian Park," wrote David Jones. "Chelsea's was also by far the best firm ever to come to Ninian."

Portsmouth was the only club besides Chelsea to consistently do the business in Cardiff. In the late 1970s they came into the Grange End and in October 1982, they had a firm of 400 lads in the city centre as early as 11 a.m. They ran Cardiff ragged and, while there were a few skirmishes on the way to the ground, these were no more than a token effort.

One of the early Cardiff legends was Frankie, a man so well known that songs were sung about him on the terraces. In 1971, he led an attack on Millwall at Paddington station dressed in full *Clockwork Orange* attire and some time later he and a friend charged into 50 Leeds. "I go to a match for one reason only, the aggro. It's an obsession," said Frankie. "I can't give it up. I get so much pleasure when I'm having aggro that I nearly wet my pants. I go all over the country looking for it."

The Soul Crew was formed in the early 1980s by a London hooligan who had recently moved to Cardiff. Nicky Parsons came up with the name because many of the Cardiff lads loved soul music, but there is also a suggestion that previously he had been in a small north London mob called the Soul Firm in the late Seventies. An early Soul Crew outing was to Lincoln and, with Birmingham playing away at Derby, a clash with the Zulus was an exciting prospect. Three hundred and fifty Cardiff made the trip by train and, sure enough, on their return, they came across the Zulus at Derby station. They overran the Birmingham lads, some of whom fled by running down the track. It was a defining moment for the Soul Crew.

They were made up of smaller mobs from across South Wales. The Grangetown Boys, the Docks lads and Ely were from Cardiff. Further west were small groups from Neath, Port Talbot (the Pure Violence Mob), Llanelli and Bridgend. Then there were the Valley boys from the mining communities of Merthyr Tydfil, Aberdare and the Rhondda. When these disparate groups came together the Soul Crew could boast mobs of 500 plus. However, organising these groups was always difficult, and from time to time there were personal and sometimes violent fallouts.

Race has never been a major issue within the Soul Crew. This partly reflects the catchment area of Cardiff supporters, industrial South Wales having a long history of trade union organisation and left-wing militancy, but also the influence of a group of black lads from the Docks area of the city. In the early Eighties, Nicky Parsons attempted to inject some far-Right politics within the firm and was virtually run out of town. Years later, a few of the Soul Crew flirted with the neo-Nazi Combat 18. In 1998, 30 turned up for a C18 meeting in the city but were quickly told in no uncertain terms to leave their "politics" out of football hooliganism.

Cardiff's biggest rivals are clearly Swansea though they have not played one another often over the past 25 years. During the early Eighties, Cardiff fans watched Swansea's meteoric rise up the divisions under John Toshack with disbelief and jealously. More recently, the tables have been reversed, with Cardiff settled in the Championship while Swansea have struggled. Generally, Cardiff have dominated their off-field contests, but that was not always the case. The Soul Crew came badly unstuck at Vetch Park in 1984 after an attempted assault on Swansea's North Bank went badly wrong. In 1988, a small group of the self-styled Pure Violence Mob from Port Talbot were attacked after another game and chased from the seafront into the sea. It was an incident that was to haunt Cardiff for years to come, as not only Swansea but Millwall and Wrexham as well would sing "swim away" at the Soul Crew.

There had been small skirmishes between Cardiff and Swansea over the years but never had the two full mobs met head-on. That changed when, in mid-November, 1991, Cardiff were drawn away at Swansea in the FA Cup, the first meeting between the two in the competition for 78 years. It was a plum draw at a time when the Soul Crew was at the top of its game.

The bulk of the main Cardiff lads met up in Neath and by lunchtime their group had swollen to 150. Instead of travelling into Swansea in a convoy of minibuses, it was decided to stagger the departures in order to lose the police and meet up again in Swansea itself. Surprisingly, there was no visible police presence on the street and almost immediately the small groups of Cardiff clashed with locals. They were soon joined by 300 lads who piled off one of the many trains bringing the Bluebirds into the city. Outside the ground, this group battled with 180 Swansea. A bit further around the ground there was a clash with another 200 Swansea. *Soul Crew* co-author Tony Rivers recalled, "They stood their ground for as long as they could. Cardiff threw themselves into the enemy and the Swansea never really had a chance. I swear I saw tears in the eyes of some of them as they were kicked and punched all over the place. Other Cardiff chased more Swansea past the Queen's, one of their favourite pubs. It was utter annihilation. Some lads at the back of our mob never even saw what was going on, so big was the crowd in front. The Swansea started disappearing, leaving friends strewn on the floor, shop windows smashed and even some cars overturned. There have been Cardiff-Swansea confrontations since then, with mainly the police winning, but I have never seen anything to match that day."

Nor had the city of Swansea. "Had I had double, treble or even quadruple the number of officers, this violence would still have occurred," said Superintendent Mel Poole. Thirty-nine people were arrested, six train coaches damaged and six double-decker buses, transporting Cardiff fans from the train station to the ground, had their windows kicked out. Several motorists had bus seats thrown through their windscreens. After the game hundreds of rival fans, many armed with bricks and bottles, fought pitched battles. The police put the number of Cardiff troublemakers at 900. Of more immediate concern to the authorities was the Autoglass Cup clash between the two teams only 72 hours later. "What happened was absolutely deplorable and beyond belief and I will not tolerate a re-run," added Poole. "I will do everything in my power to ensure the tranquillity of the city is not breached. I will not have it spoilt by sub-human animals such as we experienced on Saturday."

Cardiff battled it out with London's major firms during the Seventies, and the mid-to-late Eighties saw the West Midlands clubs, Wolves and Birmingham, emerge as key hooligan opponents. One leading Soul Crew face, Neil MacNamara, will never forget the game at Molyneux in 1988. Wolves were top of the Fourth Division and Cardiff second, while an equally bitter contest was occurring off the field. MacNamara travelled up in a minibus which was soon surrounded by a mob of 200 Wolves. The van and its occupants were attacked and a breeze block was thrown through a window, catching MacNamara in the stomach. A ruptured spleen and internal bleeding almost killed him.

There were also several major battles with the Zulus. In the early 1980s, they came mobbed up into Cardiff and gave the Soul Crew what some have called "the worst hammering we ever took". This was despite Cardiff having a mob of 600 out. After an initial clash, a small group of Zulus slipped their escort and ambushed Cardiff close to the Philharmonic pub. Word spread that Birmingham were close by and the pub immediately emptied. "Little did we know what awaited us," recalled *Soul Crew* co-author David Jones. "We were immediately met by 25 Zulus wielding blades. They just kept coming at us like robots. All you could see was the whites of their teeth, smiling at us … I was hit on the head with a golfing umbrella and was out of action for the second time that day and, in the end, Cardiff got annihilated."

Several years later the teams met again after Birmingham were relegated to the Second Division. Five hundred Cardiff were on the streets but there was no visible away mob in town. The Soul Crew eagerly awaited the return game, in April 1996, and hundreds made the trip. By 11 o'clock, 100 Cardiff had clashed with 150 Zulus in the city centre. Inside the ground both sets of fans threatened to climb on to the pitch but the police moved in quickly to prevent an escalation. Only a heavy police presence stopped major trouble outside as the two mobs, both numbering about 1,000, attempted to break through police lines.

There was only going to be one outcome at games with Millwall, and that was trouble. The Soul Crew were reaching their peak in the mid-Nineties when Cardiff were drawn away at Millwall in the Autoglass Trophy in November, 1996. To any ordinary football fan it was a nothing game in a nothing cup. To the Soul Crew it was a chance to pit themselves against the best. One hundred and fifty of Cardiff's top boys made the midweek trip, arriving in London unannounced at 4.30 p.m. An hour later the call was made to Millwall that they were there, 150-strong, not a copper in sight and, more importantly, on their manor. Millwall were caught by surprise, with no more than 40 lads, and had little enthusiasm for a bundle. There was a brief clash outside the ground, and whilst the home crowd bayed for Welsh blood inside, even they were forced to admit that Cardiff had taken the day.

Cardiff were at home to Millwall on the first day of the season in 1999. The hooligans couldn't have scripted it better. Within minutes of the fixtures being announced, the Internet was buzzing. Threats and counter-threats flew and interested "observers" from other clubs gave their expert forecasts for the game. "Get Ready Taffies, we're coming to wreck your country," boasted one. "We're flying the flag of St George." A Millwall fan threatened, "Let's get this straight. Cardiff are hard as nails, but you're missing the point, Millwall are coming to town, boys." Another forecasted the "tear-up of the year". On the day there was a virtual running commentary on the Web, proof to the media that "the violence was planned well in advance".

In the days following the match, these Internet postings were posited as a sinister development in hooliganism, coinciding as they did with the release of the latest NCIS annual report which highlighted the use of the Net to communicate. One newspaper noted that "yobs have discovered that going on the Net is faster and more secure than word-of-mouth or post-box campaigns." Quite when Millwall or Cardiff mobilised their forces through direct mail letters was not revealed.

On the morning of the match, Cardiff met up early in a pub in Grangetown. The first Millwall began arriving shortly after 11 a.m. and were immediately escorted to Sam's Bar, close to the station and dangerously near several known Cardiff pubs. The police were obviously hoping to gather the Millwall together in one place before escorting them, *en masse*, to the ground, but before this could happen the pub was attacked by 300 Cardiff. The pattern had been set for the rest of the morning, and as the police battled to contain one fight, another would break out somewhere else. An hour later, another 150 Millwall arrived, and by the time their total numbers had swelled to 300, the police decided it was time to move. It was quite a mob, according to Tony Rivers. "I saw all their faces. It was their best. Again, there weren't many under 30 and they had some right gruesome-looking bastards, but so did we."

Cardiff had decided that town was now too busy with police for another major onslaught, so instead they made their way around the back of the town in order to ambush the Londoners on their way to the ground. A mob of 600 Cardiff was spotted by a police motorcyclist, police reinforcements arrived and a huge battle erupted between them. Overhead, a police helicopter recorded proceedings, and it wasn't pretty viewing. Police logs from that day cite eight hours of disorder. In one incident a large group of Cardiff cornered a small squad of police, including two spotters, in a park near the ground. The police video clearly showed them cowering in terror as the baying mob moved in, chanting. The pilot reacted quickly and turned his helicopter on to its side, creating a wind wall between the two groups. The video was later used in police training into how not to police a match; it showed officers isolated in small groups rather than acting in a co-ordinated manner.

The intensity of the hostility inside the ground was palpable. Millwall snarled and chanted, Cardiff threw missiles and sang. The game ended in a draw but by the time Millwall were ready to leave, 1,500 Cardiff were waiting outside, many trying to force their way into the away end. The police tried to keep Cardiff out and Millwall in but the numbers involved made their task almost impossible. A few Millwall broke through but weight of numbers drove them back. Minutes later, 40 Millwall forced open the Grandstand doors, only to be met by 50 of Cardiff's hardest lads. "I couldn't have handpicked 50 worse people for them to bump into," wrote Rivers. "Millwall got savaged. Two were immediately knocked out, the rest chased back in. Some were caught as hundreds of Cardiff joined in."

The police were rightly worried for the return game in early December. The consensus within NCIS and the Metropolitan Police was that the events in August and the simmering hatred between the two mobs meant that deaths were quite possible. Millwall fans had already contacted the press in South Wales with the chilling message, "Stay away or else." One warned, "I would tell the decent Cardiff supporters, and I'm sure that's most of them, to keep away from Millwall at the next match. We assume that those who do turn up are looking for trouble, and we will give it to them. Every Cardiff fan will be targeted."

The largest-ever police operation for a domestic football match was put in place. It included, for the first time in policing football, the tracking of the movements of one of Cardiff's leaders via his mobile phone by GCHQ, Britain's secret surveillance HQ in Cheltenham. Cardiff fans were encouraged not to travel but that did not stop 700 making the trip. Every move they made was shadowed by hundreds of police and, to prevent them wandering aimlessly around South London, they were allowed into the game without tickets. The police operation worked and, while Millwall fans battled with the police after the match, the two mobs did not meet.

The Second Division that year was a hooligan paradise, containing Stoke, Bristol City and Wigan. Cardiff's away game at the newly opened Britannia Stadium saw one of the largest post-game police operations. Six hundred police could only limit the trouble between two of the largest hooligan mobs around at the time. The Soul Crew, 350-strong, met up in Stafford early doors but police were on the ball and intercepted them as they arrived in Stoke. Cardiff were herded on to waiting coaches with the intention of going straight to the ground but when the hooligans rioted and broke several coach windows, the drivers refused to go and the police were forced to take them to the ground on foot. Searches on other Cardiff coaches discovered a huge arsenal of weapons, including more than 100 Stanley blades and even a circular saw.

Police attempts to segregate the fans inside the ground soon collapsed as Cardiff ripped down tape there to keep some sections of the ground out of bounds. As hundreds of visitors poured through, riot police had to take up residence on the running track. There were sporadic outbreaks of trouble inside the ground and several seats ripped out and thrown. Widespread chaos followed outside. Four hundred Cardiff rushed at fences that had been erected to keep rival fans apart and clashed with police, and CS gas, horses and dogs were released in order to restore calm.

Staffordshire Police subsequently launched Operation Javelin, and over the next 18 months almost 200 people were arrested. In South Wales, ten months after the match, police issued newspapers with 64 photographs of wanted people. Fifty-four handed themselves in and a further 21 were charged after dawn raids. This followed 66 photographs being released to the Staffordshire press and 29 people arrested on the day of the match. Dozens were imprisoned and most were banned from football for between two and ten years. District Judge Graham Richards said, "There were the most appalling scenes of fighting during the course of the game and along Hartshill Road. It looked like the streets of Beirut ten years ago."

That summer, former Wimbledon owner Sam Hammam bought Cardiff City. A wave of anticipation swept through their fan base. Wales had recently achieved partial devolution, and a new sense of pride and nationalism spread across the nation. For many, Hammam's arrival brought hope that finally they would have a football team to be proud of. One of his biggest initial supporters was Cardiff-crazy Annis Abraham, a local businessman and veteran Soul Crew member. He became a bridge between the new owner and the rest of the mob. Hammam promised to run an inclusive club, or "family", as he repeatedly called it, and with Abraham's help organised meetings with supporters, including large groups of Soul Crew, in the Valleys and at the club itself.

The police watched in horror as Hammam employed Neil McNamara, one of the main Soul Crew leaders, as his personal bodyguard. Other hooligans, including some on football bans, became match-day stewards. The press even reported Hammam proudly wearing a "Valley Commando" badge at City board meetings, and in 2001 he celebrated promotion by treating 70 top Soul Crew members to a champagne and shrimp reception at a hotel in Mansfield. Executive coaches were laid on from Ninian Park and, with Hammam on board, the selected hooligans travelled north served along the way with fresh cakes and fruit juice. Hammam was even good enough to pose for photos with his friends. NCIS was incredulous, but by then they had their own internal problems with the Soul Crew.

In February 2001, Birmingham met Liverpool in the Worthington Cup Final in Cardiff. Almost as soon as Birmingham's semi-final had ended, the Internet spewed out threats and counter-threats. Two leagues separated the clubs, but now the Zulus returned to Cardiff 150-strong the night before the game. The running battles lasted almost two hours, several pubs were forced to close, sixteen people were arrested and nine taken to hospital.

Promotion brought Cardiff together with Millwall, Stoke, Bristol City and Huddersfield. Optimism was sweeping the club and the close and somewhat strange relationship between owner and hooligans insulated the Soul Crew from outside criticism. Cardiff opened the new campaign with a home match against Wycombe Wanderers. The game petered out in a disappointing draw but word was already spreading of a more feared opponent in their city. Manchester United were playing Liverpool in the Charity Shield the following day but up to 150 Manchester fans, a mix of Manchester and Cockney Reds, arrived while the Wycombe game was underway and took up residence in Cardiff's main pub, the Prince of Wales. The police quickly surrounded the pub and, as Cardiff streamed back into the city centre after the game, there was initially confusion and then anger. There were a few minutes of fighting between Cardiff and the police along the High Street, but they never really got it together enough to have a proper go at the Manchester mob in the pub.

As the evening wore on, the police presence subsided enough for some Manchester to slip away and both sides agreed to head to Grangetown. "We headed to a pub called Poet's Corner," recalled one Manc. "We had about fifty with more turning up when some Cardiff appeared. A few Reds went over and told them to get it together, as they only had a few, and then come to us or we'd go to them. They started playing up so they got a few slaps. Then more and more of them turned up in cabs and they got run everywhere. By this time everyone was fuming with them for being silly cunts and some even got pulled out of cabs and slapped about, though nothing major. The following day was even funnier. A few Reds, along with a few Hibs who didn't go into the game, bumped into a firm of Cardiff while the match was on. It was equal numbers and they called it on but got run again, with a couple getting caught while the rest left them there."

A fortnight later, Cardiff were drawn away at Millwall in the Worthington Cup. Media fears proved unfounded as few Soul Crew made the midweek journey to London. This did not, however, stop Millwall rioting after the game. A much bigger turnout travelled to Bristol City in early October. Police managed to keep the groups apart before the game, but afterwards 50 Bristol charged at Cardiff, which led to several hundred Welshmen breaking out of their escort. The return fixture, held over Christmas, spoke volumes about the Soul Crew. Three hundred Bristol came on the train and, like Millwall a couple of years before, were put into Sam's Bar. Cardiff hovered around but didn't have the numbers or the inclination to do much in town. At two o'clock, Bristol were marched to the ground and though small mobs of Cardiff mingled in and jostled with the visitors, there was again no real trouble. Inside the ground the Bristol fans came under a torrent of abuse and missiles. A good 800 Cardiff were packed into B Block, the seats closest to the away end, and threw a whole array of makeshift missiles. Riot police stood by as Cardiff fans filled plastic bottles with piss and threw them into their opponents' end. A huge cheer went up when a WPc was struck by one such weapon, but even this did not evoke a response from the police.

Cardiff lost 3–1, much to the joy of the away fans. A massive mob of Welshmen gathered outside the ground, at one stage numbering over 1,000, but rather than going for the Bristol City firm, they fought with the police, whose own operation was a disaster. Whilst the majority of officers escorted Bristol back to the train station, 40 officers were left to deal with the baying mob. Under a barrage of hundreds of missiles, from bricks, stones and even road signs, the police were forced back in more than an hour of trouble. Even the police's own surveillance team ran off. At least 110 vehicles were damaged and a local photographer was beaten unconscious.

A week later, another huge police operation accompanied the visit of Leeds United. The third

*Police stand by with batons drawn during a pitch invasion at the end of the
Cardiff City–Leeds United game in January 2002.*

round FA Cup game was switched to a Sunday and broadcast live on TV. The Leeds Service Crew were intercepted in Hereford and escorted into Cardiff train station before being marched straight up to the ground. There were literally thousands of Cardiff lads out that day; for some it was the biggest game of their lives. Cardiff won and hundreds invaded the pitch, goading away fans. Outside, there was a repeat performance of the Bristol game, as ordinary Leeds fans and their vehicles were attacked in the car park and Cardiff battled with police. The match received national media attention, partly because it was live on TV and against Leeds, but the trouble did not match that of the Bristol game and there was once again no actual fighting between rival mobs.

Much of the press attention related to accusations that Sam Hammam's match celebrations, which included walking around the pitch while the game was still being played and doing "the Ayatollah" in

front of home fans, contributed to the post-match disorder. In truth, Cardiff fans needed little encouragement, and an estimated 3,000 of them were up for fighting that day.

Clashes throughout the rest of the season were small-scale by comparison. There was trouble in Huddersfield despite Cardiff's game being called off due to a waterlogged pitch. Fifty people were involved in a fight shortly before the final whistle at Cardiff's match at Northampton and there were clashes before and after the match at Chesterfield.

According to an NCIS report: "Missiles were thrown and the police came under attack as hooligans from both teams tried to get at each other. The trouble lasted well into the evening."

Cardiff got through to the play-offs, where they met old foes Stoke City. The away leg saw one of the largest police operations at a domestic game, with a staggering 2,000 officers on duty. The match was stopped for seven minutes as police fought with

Stoke fans inside the ground and there was more of the same afterwards. Only 800 Stoke fans watched their side win the play-offs in Cardiff. At the end of the game police had to draw batons to prevent a mob of 600 Cardiff from getting to their opponents.

There must have been a general sigh of relief when the season was over but it was clear that things were never going to be the same again. A combination of the negative publicity surrounding the Leeds United game and the subsequent BBC *Hooligan* series brought the national spotlight onto Cardiff and its owner, the Soul Crew and South Wales Police. Sam Hammam was forced on the defensive after Leeds and promised to rid the club of hooliganism. However, his approach was questioned by the BBC, not least because days after the FA Cup match their undercover reporter secretly filmed a meeting at the club, attended by several of the Soul Crew leaders, and Hammam appeared to make light of the trouble. He was also forced to defend his appointment of McNamara as a personal bodyguard after his hooligan "past" was revealed in the press. Poacher turned gamekeeper, was Hammam's response, though this defence unravelled after McNamara was arrested for setting off a fire extinguisher in the middle of the night in the hotel hosting QPR before a key game at Cardiff.

A month after the programme, the club met the police and agreed a number of new security additions and changes to the stewarding of matches. In addition, the club was told that any hope of the council backing a possible new stadium was dependent on a reduction in trouble. Lord Mayor Russell Goodway said, "I have made it absolutely clear that the club's future aspirations in Cardiff will be supported by the Council only if there is a clear zero-tolerance policy in respect of hooliganism. If Cardiff is to have a new football stadium, and that is a vision we all share, then it means that we start today by banning known individuals identified as trouble makers by any of the partners. A recent television documentary inflicted a great deal of damage on Mr Sam Hammam, his club and the city, and no one can afford to accommodate hooliganism if the commitments to eliminate this threat are to retain any credibility."

The police, meanwhile, launched Operation Base to identify those behind the Leeds and Bristol disorders but a more important development was taking place behind the scenes. For some time other forces had been critical of South Wales Police's handling of football matches and the effectiveness of their Football Intelligence Unit.

In May 2001, a complaint was made by Metropolitan Police officers over the relationship between a Cardiff football spotter and target hooligan leaders. On the day of the FA Cup Final, Sam Hammam was drinking with several Soul Crew faces, including Annis Abraham and Neil McNamara, in Sam's Bar. A Cardiff police spotter was accompanying an Arsenal spotter when they came across the group. The South Wales policeman, in uniform, shook hands with Hammam and accepted a beer, which he downed in one. The incident was caught on CCTV monitoring the Cardiff group. A second complaint came in from a Hartlepool spotter who questioned whether it was right for Cardiff spotters to be seen drinking with Soul Crew leaders the night before a match. An internal South Wales Police inquiry was launched and at least one statement was taken from a sergeant from another force. The inquiry was inconclusive but the police spotters were switched to other duties and a new team was put into place.

"The BBC programme began the end of the Soul Crew," said one lad with over 15 years' experience. "The club, the council and the police all came under pressure to crack the whip – and they did. The final straw was West Ham away when we took the ICF outside the ground. But it came at a cost and a few of our top lads were sent down. The Soul Crew was over."

He was commenting after serious clashes before, during and after Cardiff's first visit to Upton Park for 24 years. One media report described "violent skirmishes all around the ground" and how "battered bodies littered the high road and side streets." The fighting continued until 7 p.m. The report continued, "Earlier in the day police had tried to contain any possible trouble ahead of the game by locking Hammers fans inside pubs. Customers of the Earl of Wakefield on Katherine Road, for one, were held for more than an hour before being released just half-an-hour before kick-off, but only after each and every person inside had their name, address and photograph taken. Despite the best efforts of the Met, they were simply outnumbered by the hooligans, who rampaged freely in some areas despite the continued police presence."

Despite such reports, it was regarded as "just another day at the office" by one Cardiff thug. "West Ham have been decent, don't get me wrong, when they were about in the 1980s they were up there with the best, but it's gone there now, they are finished. We turned up there and they complained they never had numbers. Why? Did they honestly think we would not show at their place? When we met what they did have, they were simply not up to the task and were sent packing in seconds. At one stage they fled through the market and when they all fell over a fruit stall, resorted to trying to keep us at bay by slinging apples and fucking pears. I always thought ICF stood for the Inter City Firm, not I Chuck Fruit."

The police initiated a major clampdown on the Soul Crew and Sam Hammam began to distance himself from them. Bans increased and the police now adopted a more aggressive attitude towards bad behaviour inside the ground. However, the violence continued away. In September 2003, it took 150 riot police to quell trouble at Cardiff's away match at Sheffield United. Extra police were drafted in, along with mounted officers and the force helicopter, after intelligence suggested that Cardiff hooligans were going to arrive early for a confrontation. Clashes broke out in several locations across the city and several people required hospital treatment. Among them were two football intelligence officers, one from South Wales and the other from South Yorkshire. The game was delayed for ten minutes after Sheffield United hooligans, who planned to ambush their rivals, caused traffic chaos.

"The level of violence towards police officers by Cardiff hooligans was extremely high, the worst we have seen in Sheffield for many years," said match commander, Superintendent Martin Hemmingway. "My officers did a superb job in ensuring large scale disorder was averted. In the circumstances, many arrests were impossible but there will now be a full scale investigation to bring these people to justice."

The media was quick to list this as another Soul Crew escapade but Tony Rivers said it was not. "The Valley Rams [fans' group] organise dozens of coaches to away games all over the country now. They are not Soul Crew coaches but, obviously, they contain lads who used to run with the Soul Crew in the past. They are now more interested in getting

pissed and if a fight comes along they happily join in."

Despite their formidable reputation, Cardiff's mob continue to have detractors among the English hooligan fraternity. "I would say they're like the Leeds of Wales, known to have numbers, but not as invincible as they believe themselves to be," was the view of one Darlington lad, though he accepts his team have never taken a decent firm to Wales. "They are a good lower league mob and definitely on a par with Stoke, Hull and Plymouth. Numbers yes, but it doesn't make for the best firm."

His view is shared by Barry, a Northampton hooligan. "They aren't anything special, they just have the numbers. Any good fifty can be as good as any other on their day and lowly old Northampton ran them ragged here in the 1997 play-offs. It was proper toe to toe and they got done. Some of the Dock lads are right handy but every town has tasty geezers. So, to sum it up, yes they have a massive firm but it's twenty years too late to be running round 500-strong."

It's a similar story at Fulham, where one "chap" said, "I have only seen Cardiff in proper action once at Fulham, when the match was stopped for thirty minutes as fighting erupted in the home Stevenage Road enclosure. A mob of them came on and tried to take it. Fulham did really well and backed them off before about 250 Cardiff came over the pitch into the stand from the away end. Pure numbers did Fulham that day, so in that respect I rate them, but it is down to the huge numbers and their lawlessness, rather than the fact they were harder, gamer or better organised than some firms."

The Bristol firms seem to be split on Cardiff. "To our minds they are on a par with ourselves, although they can call on huge numbers," said Mel of City. "However, in the 1980s they sometimes went missing. They seem to attract a lot of the very worst hangers on, vandals, brick throwers and water sports enthusiasts [piss bottle throwers]. Invincible? They have been legged by Wurzel more then once so one would say they are not."

Chris Brown, from Bristol Rovers, is more charitable. "It probably is difficult to judge whether the Soul Crew is up there with the top boys as their reputation has been forged mostly in the lower regions. It's my experience that they certainly are one of the top performers on their day only, whisper it, I've always found Swansea just as much as a handful. I wouldn't say they were the best organised as a lot of their lads come from the valleys, rather than just from Cardiff itself, which probably lends itself to a bit of in-fighting. Any sizeable city with only one team in it is bound to make up a pretty strong outfit. So, were they genuine top boys? Maybe eight out of ten. Or were they more great marketeers with the coolest name who believed their own hype? Ten out of ten!"

Certainly many of the older, more established hooligan groups have little time for Cardiff, particularly those who cut their teeth in the Eighties casual heyday. David Jones recalled West Ham's Bill Gardner dismissing Cardiff when the two mobs bumped into each other at New Street Station. "Get your fucking Toy Town firm off the platform," snarled Gardner "We're waiting for the Zulus and we don't need you spoiling it for us. We'll give you five minutes to fuck off."

Almost twenty years later Manchester United's Tony O'Neill was equally dismissive when he came across Tony Rivers and some of his friends in Cardiff. "Run along little boy," he said, with the disdain of swatting a fly.

However, many of those quick to dismiss Cardiff support bigger teams who rarely played the Welsh side, especially from the Nineties onwards. Cardiff could as easily respond that West Ham's ICF live off a reputation gained in the Seventies and Eighties. Spurs' Trevor Tanner has little time for Cardiff, but then their 80-strong mob opted for a night in Swansea before their Worthington Cup Final rather than risk the Welsh capital. Cardiff also boast of taking 1000 lads to a Worthington Cup game at Spurs in 2002 and running the home firm ragged across North London. [see TOTTENHAM in *Hooligans 2*] Those larger firms who did battle with Cardiff in the 1980s and 1990s have considerably more respect for the Soul Crew. "My opinion of Cardiff is that, unlike most firms, they got better as the years went on," said one Birmingham Zulu.

Certainly Cardiff have been one of the largest firms in Britain over the past fifteen years, with mobs numbering over 800 on many occasions at home and away. Sometimes their sheer weight of numbers meant opponents offered little resistance or fighting simply occurred with the police. It is true that Cardiff have not been as organised as others,

especially at home; the lack of resistance offered to visiting Hull, Barnsley, Middlesbrough, Stoke and Manchester United mobs in recent seasons is testament to that. Away from home they have often relied on numbers rather than organisation. However, on their day Cardiff can be a match for anyone. The ferocity with which they took apart Millwall in August 1999 and then took 700 lads to The Den a few months later is evidence of this. How many other firms can say that they caned the full Millwall mob? More recently, they took West Ham in London, and few have ever gone through the East End with the ease that Cardiff did.

"All I can say that in season 2004/05 they came to Wolves in big numbers and were game as fuck," said Wanderers' Jenko. "We had a massive firm out, 500 easily, and it was like the old days with lads from both sides about from morning till night. Before the game there were little groups having it all over, and afterwards it was crazy with both lots trying to get at each other for what seemed like ages. Later on in the night I got a few calls from some of their known faces who said, and I quote, 'Wolves were game but we shaded it, and you backed off twice.' Well I disagree with that. It may have looked like the 200 who went at them as they came out of the ground backed off, but they were just running to try to get at them from another position. Are they invincible? No, no fucker is. Are they game? Yes. They are probably one of five firms in the country that every man and his dog will turn out for."

Further reading: *Soul Crew*, David Jones and Tony Rivers (Milo Books)

CARLISLE UNITED

Ground: Brunton Park
Firm: Border City Firm
Rivals: Wigan, Burnley

When an alcohol-ravaged drug addict is arrested at a crack house and appears in court on charges of possessing heroin, it rarely makes the national papers. This was not the case on 3 July 2005, as a 34-year-old man left court having pleaded guilty and been put on a twelve-month rehabilitation order and told to pay £43 costs. For this was Paul Dodd, ex-leader of the Border City Firm, England's self-acclaimed No.1 hooligan, and his time was up.

"Doddy was a game lad," recalled Davie who was a member of the firm when Carlisle hit the headlines on the release of Paul Dodd's autobiography, *England's Number One*. "The trouble was he loved all the media attention and because of this a lot of lads blame him for the demise of our firm. With all the hype surrounding him and the book at the time, the police were on our case and, although he revelled in it, many decided to get out of the firing line and have never returned."

Dodd certainly liked attention. He claimed to have started going to Carlisle matches at 14 and by the time of its release in 1998 also claimed to have amassed 17 convictions for football disorder. The tabloids were impressed and soon he had surpassed Nottingham Forest's Paul Scarrott as Public Enemy No. 1 in hooligan circles. The tabloids pursued him on a rollercoaster ride of notoriety; the problem with Dodd was he did not know when to stop the ride and ask to get off.

"He really did believe he was the number one hooligan in Britain," laughed Davie. "The truth is he was game but not a hardcase, he was not even a big, intimidating lad, so very few people took him seriously. He used to play up to reporters and, for a few pints, would tell them anything they wanted to hear. That was the start of the slippery slope for him and he went from ale to soft drugs to the mess he is today."

Long before Dodd's memoirs put his Carlisle mob on the map, they were regarded as a small but prickly firm. Situated in the north of England, like Darlington, Hartlepool and Middlesbrough to a degree they lived in the shadow of illustrious northern giants Newcastle and Sunderland. But these places were hard, rough areas and football was one escape from the drab lives most of the working class males lived during the 1970s and 1980s.

The Popular End was where the home fans who liked a fight would congregate, also known as the Scratching Pen, and few visiting firms took it. As Dodd recalled in his book, even the mighty Boro failed. "They came in, about 50 of them and just managed to chant 'Boro boys we are here' before Carlisle steamed down into them and kicked them over the perimeter wall."

After a spell in the top division in the early

Paul Dodd, England's self-styled Number One hooligan, photographed in June 1998.

Seventies, Carlisle soon returned to the lower reaches of English football. After meeting the likes of the north-east's "big two", they found it hard to take rivals like Hartlepool and Darlington seriously; even Workington were a better outfit scoffed Dodd. It was the likes of Burnley, Blackpool and Wigan who became rivals off the pitch and, throughout the Eighties, most games against these sides involved battles home and away. Of them all, Burnley did the best at Carlisle, even taking the home paddock on one occasion, a day on which, Dodd moaned, "a lot of our lads let the side down."

Needless to say, the northern rivals were less impressed with Dodd's comments. Andy, from Darlington, said, "I think over the years, the Darlo-Carlisle games have more often than not been a letdown. The games are played on Boxing Day or New Year's Day, meaning that there's no proper turnout on either side. There was a time when a good mob went to Carlisle via Newcastle in the late Eighties and had it with the Geordies around the station area. I don't remember much ever happening at Carlisle. They flatter to deceive. The only time they seemed to do anything at our place was when they ran into the town from Feethams and turned over a few market stalls. We'd all left by then, thinking nothing was going off. We couldn't believe it when we heard they'd made an effort. I worked the door at the Speedwell near the train station on match days in the mid-Nineties, when there was a strong rumour that Dodd's mob were going to turn out in force. Fuck me, they brought twenty lads if that, none of them up for it. I know they had a few active with England, that's about it, I don't rate them because we have never seen them."

Hartlepool rate them marginally better. A member of their Blue Order firm said, "We don't think highly of Dodd and them really, there is no major history between us, but about five years ago we played them there on the opening day of the season and arrived unannounced, which gave them a shock. For some reason they expected us to give it legs because we were outnumbered, but after trading a few punches we casually strolled off. They resorted to throwing bricks, cones and sticks and there was plenty of trouble, with a lot getting nicked. The return match at ours was over the Christmas period. They failed to turn up giving feeble excuse that they were all hungover from the festive period. In years gone by they had a good, big squad. Today I think they live off that reputation. In a small way they are our next rivals after Darlo."

Being so close to the Scottish Border, Carlisle have a very strong contingent who follow England, and the Border City Firm are as patriotic as most when it comes to following the national team at home or abroad. It's the same with clubs on the Welsh border like Shrewsbury and Bristol City; all have firms who follow England and in some cases are more passionate following their country than their club side.

It was on a trip to Hampden Park in 1987 when the BCF first emerged on the England scene, well represented in one of the first hooligan mobs England had taken north of the border. A number of their lads were arrested and held in custody after fighting before the match. A well-known Carlisle hooligan was stabbed as he made his way to Glasgow central station after a court appearance in an incident which, although at the time was low key,

was to be the catalyst for one of the most horrific football hooligan battles in the 1980s.

The return fixture, twelve months later, was at Wembley Stadium and the Carlisle lads had been a full year in planning their revenge. They knew that the large Scottish support, the famous Tartan Army, would pass through their town and travel alongside the BCF all the way to London. According to Dodd, "We had been waiting all year to get back at the Jocks and we were dying for it."

They didn't have to wait long; 21 one of them driving down in a van had been on the M6 motorway for less than an hour when they pulled into Killington Lake service station at around 3.30 a.m. They found Scottish fans everywhere. According to Dodd, one of them, draped in a St Andrews flag, then "made the worst mistake of his life," remarking to a friend, "I hope there are some English bastards in here, I wanna kick some Sassenach arse."

Dodd and a friend immediately attacked them. "Then the Jocks who were in the cafeteria saw what was going on and began pouring out carrying trays, cups, plates, cutlery, anything they could get their hands on," he later wrote. "They began to back us out of the door and into the car park, we were soon under pressure because of the numbers and were about to be on the receiving end of a serious kicking. Then the rest of our lads came charging over, running the Jocks right back into the cafeteria. It was mayhem now, windows were getting put through, chairs were flying, bandits were getting turned over, just total madness."

In the ensuing carnage, eight Scots were slashed. Some were cut across the face while others had had their backs carved open. A Carlisle lad was also cut and another was knocked over the roof of a Transit van. The Carlisle firm then jumped back into their van and drove to the nearest hospital, at Kendal in the Lake District, to seek treatment for their wounded friend and to clean up. They then resumed their journey, only to see flashing blue lights at the next motorway service station they passed. Soon a police Range Rover was behind them, then two motorcycle cops appeared. They were told to pull into the next service area, at Charnock Richard in Lancashire. "My heart sank," wrote Dodd. "The whole area had been closed to the public and we had a police welcoming committee of around 30 officers. We were brought out of the van one at a time and marched over to where the Old Bill had parked their vans. Our injuries and clothing were inspected by several officers by the light of the van's headlights. The Cumbria Constabulary arrived and each of us was handcuffed and sent back up the M6 with the blue lights flashing all the way. This is when I realised just how serious our situation was ..."

Twenty-one members of the BCF were arrested and twelve, including Dodd, were charged and committed to Crown Court. Eventually nine of them were sentenced to a total of 22 years' imprisonment. The resultant media coverage made Dodd notorious overnight, and on his release from jail he was happy to bask in the limelight at both Carlisle and England matches. His crowning glory came when England's rioting thugs caused the game in Dublin against the Irish Republic to be abandoned. Some papers reported that he had taken part in the riot and some went as far to state he was one of the main ringleaders, though the facts suggest that he was not even there, having earlier been arrested for fighting with ticket touts.

Dodd's notoriety meant that many firms would turn up in Carlisle looking for trouble and Paul was on everyone's hit list, but the truth is that during many of the outbreaks of violence he was not present. Davie is sceptical about the true role Dodd played in the BCF. "Paul came and went but he was not the main lad by any stretch of the imagination. Paul Davidson was the lad we all looked up to and there were many more who were higher up the pecking order than Doddy."

One of Carlisle's most publicised battles was against Wrexham, when a total of twelve BCF and Frontline members were jailed after the Welsh firm attacked the home mob's pub, The Crescent. It was not so famous at the time but CCTV footage is shown on Bravo TV's *Street Crime* programme at least once a month. One Carlisle lad who was charged with the incident never made it to court as he hanged himself before going to trial in what was a tragic waste of life.

Davie explained, "At the time the Wrexham fight was big news, a couple of OB were sat across the road filming the pub when from nowhere came a mob of Wrexham and started attacking the boozer. It was Christmas come early for the OB and they just sat there and got the lot, gift wrapped on a plate. Loads were nicked for it and Wrexham had a few

Jocks with them which made it look like it was all arranged and at the time all sorts of silly sentences were being predicted. It was too much for one of the lads who had a load of personal problems and he hung himself. A few months later it went to trial and quite a few walked, he would probably have done so himself."

Carlisle, thanks to Dodd's media links, were soon national news and the firm were often talked about in the House of Commons. One MP was quoted during a discussion on banning orders saying, "One of the worrying aspects of football hooliganism is that some of the people convicted have, unfortunately, hailed from Carlisle. They were involved in some ghastly football violence. I said 'unfortunately' because Carlisle is next door to my constituency and one likes to think that we do not do that sort of thing up there. However, there was a nasty pocket of football hooligans in Carlisle." Dodd was loving it, he had his book published and opened a website hoping to make enough money to retire and live happily ever after, but it didn't quite work out that way.

"For years Paul had been selling his tales for ale money, and then a couple of local fellas, Iain McNee and Gordon Bradshaw helped him write and publish his autobiography," said Davie. But they soon fell out. "Paul ended up going into Iain's office to demand money, and when he got none he CS-gassed him. Before the release of his book, Paul was banned from Carlisle and then he was banned from all football grounds and from travelling abroad with England. He ended up doing what he did best, getting pissed. The book did him no favours and before long he hit the drugs and went the way of so many before him. The firm carried on and we have had some good and bad days at the office but the police have always been on our case and it's mainly down to the media hype surrounding England's number one."

The following press report shows that Carlisle continued to be active without Dodd, but also that the police had a zero tolerance stance against them. "Police in Cumbria have welcomed a court decision banning five Carlisle football hooligans from every ground in Britain. Five men admitted charges of disorder at Carlisle United's first home match against Hartlepool in August 2002. Cumbria Crown Court ordered the five to be banned from every UK football ground and also from following the England national team abroad for three years. They were also sentenced to between 100 and 200 hours' community punishment order and each have to pay £120 costs. They were involved in violence which erupted as fans walked from the match at Carlisle's Brunton Park ground. The police were forced to use CS gas spray and batons to try to contain the situation." Detective Constable Ian Hodgson of Cumbria Police welcomed the sentencing and said it sent out "a strong message" to other hooligans. Judge Barbara Forrester said it had been "a terrifying experience for people who witnessed the violence," and added, "You are all old enough to know better." Recently Carlisle was rated the third worst club in the league for violence. A spokesman for Carlisle United said the club was working closely with the police and the Football Intelligence Unit.

As well as being active at home, the firm continued to travel with England and again the police were quick to root out the hooligans in their ranks. Another report covered the arrest of BCF members on their way to Slovakia. "In the last few days, five people have been stopped at Manchester Airport, three at Stansted, two at Birmingham and one at Heathrow. The three stopped at Stansted, who are all Carlisle fans, have already been taken to court and given banning orders."

The club's fortunes were no better than the firm's and, after a few close shaves, they eventually lost their league status. This opened a legal loophole which forced a debate in Parliament. Carlisle MP Eric Martlew pointed out that the banning orders only applied to league matches, and not for games against non-league opponents. Calling for a change in the law, he said, "Carlisle United was relegated to the Conference from the Football League at the end of last season. There are more than sixty Carlisle fans who are banned from the club's ground and other so-called A-list venues. If we play the likes of Manchester United, these people cannot go. But if we are playing one of the non-league clubs, like Morecambe, then of course they could go. This is against the spirit of the law and I think we need to clarify it and, if necessary, get this loophole stopped as quickly as possible."

A spokesman for Carlisle United said the club backed Mr Martlew's bid to change the law and added, "At the moment we have the pictures of

sixty-four people at our ticket office of people who are not allowed into the ground. But if we play at a ground that has never previously been in the Football League, then these people can attend games. We agree with Mr Martlew that something should be done to prevent them from following Carlisle United."

Detective Constable Ian Hodgson, Cumbria Police's football liaison officer, said, "Carlisle's relegation from the league means it will be playing teams that were never in the league. Carlisle's status has therefore created a situation that may not have been originally envisaged."

The non-league was new to the BCF and they clashed at several grounds not previously visited as well as at the likes of Chester and Aldershot. They did so without "England's No. 1" who by then was involved in the drug scene in Carlisle. His arrest in July 2005, for possession of heroin, was a far cry from the front page news he was making while following England, but he still carried his hooligan status despite the fact that this event had nothing to do with football or hooliganism at all. The headlines read, "Number One Soccer Yob Held in Drugs Raid."

Notorious soccer hooligan, Paul Dodd, has been arrested in a police raid on a crack house. Dodd, 34 – banned from every football stadium in the UK – was caught with heroin and cannabis.

He was nabbed after cops swooped on a housing association property in his home town of Carlisle, Cumbria. Dodd admitted the drugs offences when he appeared before Carlisle magistrates.

He was given a 12-month rehabilitation order with £43 court costs. Dodd has been involved in violent clashes at home and abroad. In 1995, he was at the heart of the riot that led to an England match against Ireland in Dublin being abandoned.

He gloried in his loutishness in 1998 when he wrote the book, *England's Number One: The Adventures of a Serial Soccer Yob*.

Dodd even found himself on a list of famous people who live or have lived in Carlisle, though the fact that the same list contains Richard Madeley puts such "celebrity" into perspective. Poignantly, in his book Dodd remembered the time he was locked up with another infamous hooligan. "While in the cells I saw a familiar face," he wrote. "It was Paul

Scarrott, who at the time was England's most notorious hooligan. I had heard a lot about him but I have to say, what I saw did not impress me much. He wasn't a dresser like the rest of us and he just did not look the part. I think that the media had built him up and given him his reputation, which is also what they have done to me. Hopefully I have justified my reputation though and am looked upon in a different light."

Time may deliver a harsher judgment.

Further reading: *England's Number One*, Paul Dodd and Iain McNee (P.I.G. Books)

CHARLTON ATHLETIC

Ground: The Valley
Firm: B Mob
Rivals: Millwall, Crystal Palace
Police operations: Fabric

Organised hooliganism arrived at Charlton in the late Sixties and early Seventies when groups of skinheads began to gather under the old covered end. So common was the violence that the club was one of the first to declare steel-toe-capped boots an offensive weapon and refuse entry to those wearing them. The team flitted between the old Second and Third Divisions and trouble occurred at matches with the likes of Rotherham, Rochdale, Northampton, Brighton, Orient and Portsmouth. Arguably, their biggest success was getting into Arsenal's North Bank during an FA Cup fourth round clash at Highbury in January 1969.

"We had a mob and a half out that day," recalled one Charlton old-timer. "It was a day that went down in Charlton folklore. Arsenal won two-nil and the attendance was 56,560. About 500 of us went into the North Bank early doors and caused mayhem. We met early in the day at Woolwich Arsenal and got the train into town where we were joined by others at Lewisham and Blackheath. It was a top firm, all skinheads apart from one great big black geezer, Les. We made our way to Holloway Road and went on a bit of a shopping spree, not paying for anything as we steamed into clothes shops and got new Crombies and Harringtons.

"At the ground, all the faces were there, skinhead gangs from Woolwich, Charlton, Greenwich, Eltham and Lewisham. We went straight into the North Bank singing, 'Charlton!' Soon, Arsenal turned up and tried to get us out of their end, but it was not going to happen. We gave them slap after slap and the Arsenal were reduced to throwing sharpened pennies and little skittles at us, but we stayed firm and remained in their end, singing for the whole game. One well known Charlton head, Keithy Giles, was thrown out of the ground three times but was back in every time within five minutes. After the game we were ready for some Arsenal payback but they never showed. We went on a bit of a rampage. I suppose it was a one-off, but one-offs like that live with you forever."

Charlton have suffered against the so-called bigger clubs. In January 1976, there was serious fighting at an FA Cup game at home against Sheffield Wednesday. The Yorkshire club brought thousands down, and hundreds managed to get into the Covered End well before kick-off. Try as they might, there were just too many for Charlton to budge, so they waited until after the game, where it went off in the streets. "We couldn't believe their numbers," recalled Steve Lyons, better known at Charlton as Wing Nut. "There must have been 500 of them and most were skinheads. After the game they paid the price as we ran them down Anchor Lane, all the way back to their coaches. Looking down the hill from Charlton station, all you could see was a mass of bobbing heads being chased by our lot." Interviewed in *Terrace Legends*, Lyons cites this as his best battle.

Sheffield Wednesday, however, believe that they came out the clear victors and, more importantly, that the mob they fought that day was Millwall, not Charlton. Wednesday said there was a brief fight with Charlton before the game which lasted no more than a minute, largely because "to be honest Charlton weren't really up to much and were soon sent packing," according to one Sheffield lad. "A mob of 100 to 150 did start to gather close by but this was Millwall, they had their notorious black lad, Tiny, with them and looked a different class to Charlton. The fists and feet seemed to be flying for ages, though it was probably only five minutes or so, and we backed them off further and further away from the Kop, until eventually the Old Bill got in between us. I'd say we did them, but they'd probably disagree."

In 1977, their ground was virtually ripped apart after the visit of Chelsea. The game was held towards the end of the season and Chelsea's hopes of promotion disappeared as the south London side ran out 4–0 winners. Chelsea's fans wrecked the ground. A massive bonfire was lit on the terraces using newspapers and match programmes in an attempt to halt the game and shortly before the final whistle, Chelsea fans kicked down the wooden gates and poured out into the street. Cars were damaged and house windows were smashed as the rioting spread into the local neighbourhood. There was widespread condemnation and Chelsea were given a two-year ban on tickets for away matches.

The Charlton firm had no identifying name in the early days, they were just a group of mainly skinheads who gathered in local pubs and train stations to cause havoc. As time wore on they grew their hair, put on weight and became affectionately known as The Fatties. A few of the originals were still active in the late Nineties, though they tended to come out only for big games. Replacing them, in the early 1980s, was a younger group known as the B Mob. They were never the biggest firm around, with a hardcore of 30-40, but were tight-knit and violent. They boasted about holding their own against anyone when the numbers were even, including Millwall.

One veteran said, "The name originated from the wearing of balaclavas. There were no real top boys, it was just a case of name the meeting place, and see who turned up. Scooter mobs and various skinhead gangs were involved. I recall being told to take off my steel toe-cap Doc Martens and, at the end of the game, having to go across to the old police office in the West Stand car park with a dozen or so other skinheads to retrieve them. They did this in all weathers. Most of the skinhead gangs came out of the Greenwich Borough area, Woolwich, Plumstead and Eltham."

The B Mob had a very strong right-wing link with the National Front and, more especially, with the more violent and openly-nazi British Movement. Many were also involved in the British Movement's Leader Guard, their elite and most violent group. The right-wing link also led to a close friendship with Glasgow Rangers and Charlton lads would

often be found at big games north of the border or with Scottish lads over in Belfast.

Most firms play down the racist element in their ranks, at least to outsiders. Charlton however were proud of it. "For as long as I can remember, Charlton's firm has had links with right-wing organisations," said one lad. "They may have been card-carrying members of groups such as the National Front, British Movement and BNP, and some were even known to have links with Combat 18. B-mob lads have attended anti-IRA rallies alongside these groups and one thing is for sure, they are proud to be British. Most are staunchly Loyalist, with links to Scottish clubs such as Glasgow Rangers, Dundee and Motherwell."

Another still-active Charlton hooligan added, "CAFC have always had a large number associated with the right-wing. Monthly BM meetings were held at Welling in the Kent Library and were like a CAFC home game. A local skinhead music pub, the Crown and Cushion in Woolwich, which is now closed, was run by CAFC lads. A battle at a County Hall gig by the Redskins [a left-wing band] involved a large number of CAFC. Charlton had some of the main British Movement players, we had regular collections for the BM at games and the mob ran security at their meetings. This is one of the main reasons the Charlton mob has never had black members. Through the Movement, ties were established with Leeds, the Chelsea Headhunters, Feyenoord and Dundee."

Charlton's closest rivals are Crystal Palace and their mutual antipathy increased during the mid-Eighties after Charlton moved in with Palace for a few years. One Palace lad recalled the trouble between the two sides. "There have been numerous occasions through the years that it's kicked off between us, including at their main boozer three years on the spin in the early Eighties. It was two-one to Palace, I'm told. They were also attacked and done in an escort coming up Park Road near the away end at Selhurst Park in the early Eighties. We did them again in the play-offs at Selhurst Park in the mid-Nineties when around forty of us got on the pitch but they didn't want it, even though there were hardly any stewards. We caught them unawares and after the game plenty of slaps were dished out down Selhurst Road."

But the Palace lad does admit there were occasions that Charlton were the more impressive mob. "I remember their firm in 1989 like it was yesterday. I accidentally walked straight into them in the pissing rain one Saturday morning coming up Holmesdale Road and they'd brought a decent firm, 150-strong with what looked like some game fellas. I was quite impressed. On another occasion in the late Eighties, fifty Charlton got into the home stand at Selhurst Park. It kicked off for a good five minutes before superior numbers forced them on the back foot. The police restored control, rounded up the Charlton mob and escorted them around the pitch to the away end."

A Charlton lad has different recollections. "I and many Charlton lads of a certain generation hate anything to do with Palace. It all really got going as more than just south London rivals in 1985 when we had to share a ground and certain people in charge at 'Sellout' Park tried to stitch us up financially and force the club to dissolve or merge. In my twenty years of going to Charlton v Palace games I have never been on the end of a hiding and never had it on my toes. We have always taken decent numbers to them and had a good size firm at home for their visits, but it's been a case of the OB being on top.

"Phone calls were made one year as we gathered in Beckenham. One of theirs, supposedly one of the old Woolpack firm, was told we had a good sixty or seventy lads. He told us to go to a certain pub in Thornton Heath, near the ground. Ten minutes later he was back on the phone saying that OB were all over the area and to go to Crystal Palace station, some distance from Selhurst Park. We arrived thirty minutes later only to be met by more than twenty OB who escorted us to Norwood Junction. After the game that same number was called and he said that they couldn't get any lads together. The spooky thing about this is when we arrived at Crystal Palace station, one of our lads called him and asked him if it was a set up with the police. He denied it, but as our lad was on the phone we noticed a copper at the end of the platform speaking into a mobile and we swear he was in sync with the conversation at our end.

"In the mid-Nineties, we drew Palace in the play-off semi-final. We blew an early lead at home to lose 2–1 in the first leg and handed them the route to Wembley. After the game we gathered in a pub on the road from Charlton Village to Blackheath. We

knew Palace had come through from Blackheath station and this was their only realistic route back and we discovered they were drinking in the Royal Standard. Fifty of us went to a pub not far from there and we paid a couple of kids on bikes to go and see if the OB vans were still outside the Royal Standard, which they were. One of our lads then made the walk and stood across the road. They clocked him and asked how many we had, the usual bollocks. Our pub emptied and we got to the main junction where the OB had started moving Palace off towards Blackheath Common. Palace moved to the Prince of Wales, and, as luck would have it, the OB decide to bugger off thinking their work was done. But as we started moving towards the pub, the OB vans across the common came back, boxed us off and escorted us back to Charlton. Now those two stories may not be that interesting, but they prove a very valid point, Palace either don't fancy it with us or, worse still, have a grass in their camp.

"The last time I remember the two sets of firms getting it on for real was in the mid-Eighties at Selhurst when we were ground sharing. It was their home game and 60 to 70 B Mob lads, all with bleached hair and earrings, paid into the Arthur Waite terracing about ten minutes before kick-off."

The loss of the Valley in September 1985 had a disastrous effect on the B Mob. Few of the original lads made the switch over to Selhurst Park and it took some time for a new generation of younger lads to attach themselves to the group. In time it happened and as well as the big turnouts against Palace, 200 lads turned out for Chelsea in a key end of season clash in 1988, a match which sentenced the West Londoners to relegation.

At another game against their more illustrious neighbours, Charlton gained some respect. "Chelsea away in the 1986/87 season was one they will want to forget," said one Charlton lad. "It was kicking off all day, Earls Court tube and Fulham Broadway. Twenty main Chelsea faces got brave, paid into our end and stood on the right hand side where the fence met the old benches area. It kicked off five minutes into the game and was a right carry on. The Chelsea lads were top drawer and honours were about even, although a few Charlton were nicked and fined for their troubles. One story, true or not, was that West Ham wound Chelsea up the next season chanting 'Chelsea run from Charlton'."

The 1990s were a quiet decade for Charlton's hooligans but by 1999 a new generation of lads was emerging and some of the older B Mob returned to activity. Fights occurred at matches with Norwich, Portsmouth and Bristol City. The core remained a small 30, but many were seasoned veterans who could rely on each other.

One of Charlton's more recent fights was away at Norwich. Contrary to police reports, it was not pre-planned but a spontaneous clash after the two mobs came across each other in the same pub. "It was a bit of a strange one," said a Norwich lad. "We had never had any bother with Charlton, in fact I didn't know they had a mob until that day. I decide to go for a swift one after the game in the Clarence Harbour pub, near the ground. I didn't even know there were any Charlton in and I didn't really take a lot of notice of the dozen lads sitting in there. As I sat watching the results on telly out of the corner of my eye I saw two of our lot move towards the Charlton lot and attack two of them. One punched one in the head while the other booted the other in the head. It was a bit sneaky really.

"Before I had time to get off my stool the Charlton mob had smashed a table and one of the fuckers whacked me over the head with a table leg. I must have gone out for couple of seconds. I just remember a pair of big hands picking me up and dragging me to safety, claret pouring down my face. I ended up in the corner of the pub next to Tilson, our old spotter.

"By now Charlton were well tooled up and our lot were on the back foot. I needed to get out, as my head was pissing blood and thumping. I managed to stagger into the car park and another club-wielding caveman came at me and just as I was thinking, fuck this, I don't want another one, the Old Bill turned up, nicked him, and stuck me in an ambulance. I thought that was the end of my worries but as I sat in A&E waiting to have five stitches put in my head, the caveman walked in wanting to have a another go. The next thing I know is that I'm getting arrested. I thought, is this some joke? I've got a fucking hole in my head, the worst headache of my life and now I was getting taken to the cells."

Charlton's account is similar. They say no large firm travelled, just the normal lads who would be up for it if called upon. After the game about nine Charlton walked into the pub near the away end by the railway bridge. "No one was particularly looking for trouble," recalled one of them. "But as we stood watching the football results on the pub TV, we noticed seven to ten lads gathering by the main door, one wearing a Villa badge. A few minutes later one of them came tearing across the pub, swinging punches and connected with one of our lads, who was engrossed in the TV, while another kicked one of our boys as he's sat at a table. He later needed a few stitches as his whole bottom lip seemed to come away. They shouted, "Come on Charlton," and we all turned to see these lads giving it the bouncy come-on.

"Totally unprepared and at the back of the pub with nowhere to go, we broke up bar stools and lobbed them in their general direction. This carried on for a minute or two, when there was a turning point. A couple of their lads threw a pub table in our direction, which was caught one-handed by one of our bigger lads and he returned it. This shocked them and we then started to get on top and forced them back towards the pub door.

"Unbeknown to them, a handful of our lads had been outside the pub but could not get in because Norwich had locked the door. When one of the windows came in from the outside, Norwich went for the exit, only to walk straight into our other lads, with us following behind. Suddenly we heard a big shout and a scream. The landlord had gone upstairs and fetched down a shotgun and was aiming it in our direction and asking us politely to desist. Being the gents we are, we did. Most Norwich had gone by the time we got outside and the OB arrived, apart from one who had been twatted over with a lump of wood by the fella who'd received the mouth wound. The strangest thing then happened. The Charlton liaison officer walked over and told us he knew it was going to happen, as he saw us walk in and knew these Norwich lads were in there. One Norfolk officer even said he was glad this little firm had taken a slap as they had been targeting small groups of lads for a while and that one of them was wanted for stabbing an officer a few weeks previously. Funny old world.

"This all went to court but was thrown out by the judge, not before a classic line by a Norwich defendant in the dock who admitted, 'We started it, but Charlton took it too far.' We have had no real problem with Norwich since. We tried to call it on with them the following season but OB got wind of this early in the morning when an off-duty officer spotted a few well-known faces gathering. We met a few of their lads in Munich at the 5–1 Germany game as one of ours, a regular on the England scene, occasionally travels with them. They're all good lads and there's no hatred on our part. They are similar to us in that no one ever takes them seriously but they have their results."

Another lad remembered returning from a game at Forest in late 1997, and being refused a drink in Nottingham after a few scuffles with the locals. "About a dozen of us decided to stop off in Leicester," he said. "We were not particularly looking for a tear-up, and were unaware that Leicester were at home that day. We found an empty pub right by the station opposite the public foot subway. After 45 minutes of playing pool and chatting we decided to up sticks and find a livelier boozer. I said I'd catch up as I had a phone call to make on the mobile. While making the call in a side street I heard the familiar roar go up and the sound of breaking glass. As I ventured out to the main high street I saw our lads tearing up the road towards the train station with 30 blokes chucking beer glasses at them in hot pursuit. I wisely decide to take a step back as my pals had already passed me and I didn't fancy my chances with their 30 lads. I waited a couple of minutes up the road hoping they wouldn't clock me. As I approached the station these Baby Squad lads were gathered outside the main entrance, peering through the doors. I slipped in another door and noticed our lads standing at the back of the concourse with scaffold brackets and lumps of wood. When I asked what had happened they explained they had unintentionally stumbled across a Baby Squad boozer. They told the Leicester lads they were not particularly looking for a row but one fella accused them of taking the piss and the Baby Squad started tearing towards them, hurling bottles and glasses.

"At this point one of our lads declared, 'Bollocks to this, we've nowhere else to run, fuck it let's have it.' At that we all ran at the doors where the Leicester firm were waiting and burst through. This had the desired effect and they scattered. A few punches and scaffold brackets were thrown and suddenly the OB were on the plot, presumably following up the reports or CCTV from the high street skirmish a few minutes earlier. I get whacked with a truncheon by a WPc and both groups were separated. By now there were only about ten Leicester left, the others pissing off because of the OB presence.

"One of their lads then asked from the other side of the police line, 'Who the fuck are you?' When we told him Charlton, he replied, 'We thought you were Arsenal.' 'We only stopped for a drink,' we said. 'If you had told us you could have had one.' The Baby Squad questioner then leant across the OB line and shook the hand of the lad he was talking to and said, "Game lads, fair fucking play'. A few months later we heard from one of ours who knows some Leicester lads on the England scene that they were still pissed off with us, thought we had been taking liberties and warned us not to come back.

"Our first game of the 1998-99 season was at home against Man City. We were back in the Premier League after a play-off win. A few lads were drinking in a bar after the game with the doors open to the sunshine when we noticed twos and threes of Man City lads appear from a side road heading towards the station. Bizarrely, all were dressed in black Henry Lloyd rain jackets despite the 80 degree heat. They spotted us but kept on walking. A few of us called it on but they continued to head towards the station with a few more joining them minute-by-minute until there were about 20 of them.

"Fifteen of us gathered outside the bar and called on others who seemed more interested in their beer, when this mob turned around and headed back up the road towards us. We gathered in the middle of the road and spread out, this time we had the pint glasses and bottles. We waited until they picked up pace and got closer. Then the shout went up and we let them have both barrels. This stopped them for a second as they dodged the missiles, but they then picked them up and threw them back. There was a stand off with lots of bouncing going on when the OB wagons came screeching up the road and separated us. City got escorted back to the station and the OB didn't even nick anyone which made it a top end to the day.

"I am told that a similar thing happened the next season when Charlton chased a load of City back into a local social club with City claiming we were Millwall. This is a regular accusation when we get any type of result, no matter how big or small, even when we show with numbers."

The club's main rivals to this day are Millwall and Palace and while it was always an uneven hooligan match when Millwall were in town, the rivalry with them is of an unusual nature. "The rivalry with Millwall doesn't really exist," explained one lad. "They are not overly bothered about us as they see us as small fry, plus a lot of Charlton and Millwall lads drink together, work together and come from the same areas.

"I can't remember many results against Millwall but one year we were coming back from Bournemouth and jumped on a train to London Bridge to cause a bit of mayhem. As we left the station we met a big firm of Millwall. We stood back for a minute and then one nutty geezer picked up one of those metal boxes you used to buy the evening paper from, lifted it over his head, ran at the Millwall and threw it at them. We all steamed in and Millwall were on their toes. We chased them all down Borough High Street but we lost them, so we had a bit of a rampage and went back to the station."

Another veteran recalls that in 1970, Millwall took the Covered End. "There was a large off which then went all round the ground, with Millwall hunting down known CAFC faces and a number of people put in hospital. In 1973, there was non-stop fighting throughout a night match, and no CAFC will forget the time that the Bushwhackers were bushwhacked in the Iron Horse pub in New Eltham on a Sunday by a mixture of Charlton and British Movement boys."

One of the later rivalries to emerge was with Southampton and the two mobs clashed in November 2001, when 50 Charlton entered a pub full of Saints. Police were soon on the scene and escorted Charlton's mob to the ground. There was more trouble immediately after the game around the ground and back at the train station. But it was another match, the following April, that received national media attention. The Internet had become a vehicle for rival fans to wind each other up and in the weeks leading up to the match there was considerable Web traffic. On the day of the match, 15 young Southampton hooligans travelled to Maze Hill station an hour before the game for a pre-arranged meet with Charlton. The home side were represented by 30 lads, mostly in their thirties. It was

a one-sided contest, with Charlton unleashing a wave of bottles and glasses at their young opponents. The fight lasted two minutes and left three people requiring hospital treatment. Police knew nothing of it until it was well under way and by the time they arrived the two gangs were gone. "Fair play to the group that got off at Maze Hill," noted one Internet posting from a Charlton lad. "Don't worry about the result. At least you bothered to get off despite knowing there'd be no OB about."

Unfortunately for the two mobs, the station was covered by CCTV, which filmed those fighting, but it was the use of e-mail and mobile phone records that was to nail the organisers. Schoolteacher David Walker, from Stafford, was not actually present during the fight but was found to have posted several messages on an Internet forum prior to the match and made telephone calls to the alleged leader of the Charlton group, 32-year-old Spencer English. Twenty people were arrested in dawn raids a year after the fight, with the court eventually sentencing 17 to prison for a combined total of 38 years. The British Transport Police were euphoric. Det Insp Carl Skrzypiec said, "There is no doubt that many of these hooligans would have been organising fights at Euro 2004. It's a major success having them behind bars." The reference to Euro 2004 was aimed more at the press than any real police concern, but the message to the hooligans was direct enough: you can no longer get away with it.

One Charlton lad who was nicked for the fight said, "Operation Fabric, what a fucking nightmare. Ten of us were arrested in early morning raids across London and Kent in October 2002, and a similar number of Southampton lads were arrested for the same incident. Yet it was nothing much. It was all pre-arranged a few weeks before after a request was made by Saints to gain revenge for a dozen or so Charlton lads gaining the upper hand in a Southampton pub the previous November. Saints were basically outnumbered and outclassed at Maze Hill and a couple took a bad beating, fair play to them though, they must have known they would be outnumbered. The actual fight only lasted a few minutes, no members of the public were involved and no criminal damage caused, but unfortunately for those involved the British Transport Police threw their full weight behind it and it was said to be their biggest case. What didn't help was that, on the day, one of the Charlton lads claimed that the CCTV at the station did not work. He called it wrong."

Five Charlton fans and six Saints were sentenced at Kingston Crown Court to between one and four years for conspiracy to commit violent disorder. In May 2004, a further half-dozen were found guilty at the same court and received similar sentences. They split the trial due, they said, to the numbers involved, though many feel it was more to ensure that the news hit the headlines four weeks before the start of Euro 2004.

The fallout from the Maze Hill fiasco all but killed the mob, though they did enjoy the chance to see their team send Crystal Palace down to the Championship in 2005. "It is every fan's dream, beat your biggest rivals in a cup final or send them down," recalled one lad with glee. "Not many have done it but I'll tell you what, it's as good as it gets. We drew with them and they were down. I'll tell you something else as well, they didn't throw a single punch in anger. Imagine Liverpool sending Everton down, or Chelsea sending Spurs down, it would be a riot. Palace went home without so much as a whimper. Good riddance to them."

Further reading: *Terrace Legends*, Cass Pennant and Martin King (Blake Publishing)

CHELSEA

Ground: Stamford Bridge
Firms: Headhunters
Rivals: Spurs, West Ham, Leeds, Leicester
Police operations: Own Goal, Extra Time, Hungarian

No club has had more written about their hooligan element than Chelsea. Books, newspaper articles and television programmes have featured their exploits over 40 years. Heavily influenced by the fashionable Kings Road, the aura surrounding Chelsea and more recently the Chelsea Headhunters have given a cachet to its hooligans unique amongst hooligan groups. Millwall might have had brawn. Manchester United might have had numbers. West Ham might have had tactics. But Chelsea had a

certain style, and this was often exemplified by the men who led them.

* * *

The grin said it all. Beaming, the ten-year-old strode across the pitch. Chelsea at home to West Brom, in November 1955 and Mick Greenaway was the club's mascot for the day. He was Chelsea. He was to become a Chelsea legend.

No one has had more impact on the Stamford Bridge crowd than Greenaway. He formed the Shed, created songs that still resonate and was a father figure to future generations of hooligan leaders. He was born in June 1945, into a strong Chelsea family. His grandfather attended the first ever match at Stamford Bridge and his father was a regular during the 1930s. But the Chelsea of the Fifties was a far cry from the threatening bastion it became. There was little noise from the crowd and its support was drawn from middle-class London, in contrast to the dockers and factory-workers of the East End. Writers, actors and artists were drawn by its proximity to the West End. All that was to change and a young Mick Greenaway was partly responsible.

As a teenager, Greenaway began following Chelsea away before it became fashionable. A few dozen would sometimes go together, including the players' close friends and family. Greenaway didn't just watch Chelsea. In 1964 he travelled to Manchester to watch the Charity Shield between United and Liverpool. A more youthful football culture was emerging in the North West. "Ends" were being established and outbreaks of violence between rival supporters were occurring. All this was new to Greenaway and he loved it. He was especially impressed by the Liverpool fans, who had established the first Kop in the country and with it, songs, another first. When Chelsea travelled to Liverpool in the Sixties, facing almost certain relegation, the home fans sang, "Chelsea, Chelsea, get down, get down, get down," to the tune of Gilbert O'Sullivan's more well-known song about his dog. Travelling away convinced Greenaway of the need to form a Chelsea end, which he did by switching from the halfway line, where the young lads had begun to gather, to the South End, better known as the Shed.

The Kings Road was where things were happening, and before long fashion-conscious and increasingly confident young people found residence in the Shed. The most famous song was "Zigger, zagger, zigger, oy, oy, oy". Its origins are unclear; it may have been first sung at Stoke City by a fan called Zigger Zagger Pat, but was also heard for a short time at Liverpool. But it was Mick Greenaway who would make it famous. It soon became a rallying cry for Chelsea fans, on the terraces and in the streets. In the days before segregation it only took a quick rendition for Chelsea's hardcore to come together. The media would later claim it was a battle cry, a signal to fight, but Greenaway was always insistent that this was not the case.

Another song introduced by Greenaway was "One Man Went to Mow". On the way back from a trip to the States for an aborted Chelsea tour of Florida, Greenaway sat next to a man who was the worse for drink. Throughout the journey the man mumbled, "One man went to mow, went to mow a meadow," incessantly, adding in an odd line about his dog Spot. Early in the new season Greenaway began the chant and it quickly caught on.

The Shed was forming but it was still some time before the young lads who gathered behind Greenaway began to resort to violence. In fact, it took a few beatings for Chelsea to get organised. In September 1965, Everton fans invaded the Shed. The following month Chelsea had a torrid experience in Italy when they played Roma in the first round of the Inter-Cities Fairs Cup. A draw was sufficient to see the Londoners through after they had won the home leg, but Chelsea players were pelted with rubbish from the crowds almost throughout the match and two players were knocked over. By half-time the pitch was littered with orange peel, paper, coins and heavier objects. After the match the Chelsea coach was stoned by howling Roma supporters as it left the ground under police escort. The escort consisted of 30 armed police in four jeeps and more than 50 officers on foot.

Chelsea reached the semi-finals of the FA Cup in April 1966, and lost to Sheffield Wednesday. Many fans from both sides carried walking sticks and these were used to deadly effect throughout the game. A year later a Chelsea programme announced, "Starting today, flags and banners are banned from Stamford Bridge. So are sticks, which have become another source of disturbance, and possible danger, at recent home matches."

In April 1967, Chelsea reached their third consecutive FA Cup semi-final, this time against Leeds United. A fortunate Chelsea sneaked through but lost the final to Spurs. These two games were to signal the beginning of lasting hostilities with these clubs that continue to this day. [For more details, see LEEDS, and TOTTENHAM in *Hooligans 2*.]

Greenaway's name was becoming known well beyond the confines of Stamford Bridge. When Manchester United overran the Shed in November 1966, he was struck across the head with a crowbar. A year later it was the turn of West Ham fans to run amok, and again Greenaway was singled out for a severe beating. Chelsea fans rallied to his side and in future games he was always surrounded by several hardcases who were determined to protect him.

By the early 1970s Chelsea was arguably the most glamorous club in London and possibly England. An FA Cup victory over Leeds in 1970 was followed by a European Cup Winners Cup Final victory over Real Madrid. Chelsea won a replay 2–1 and Greenaway was there, in his natural position, leading the small contingent of away fans. He even joined in the on-pitch celebrations with the players.

He may have been the King of the Shed, but Greenaway was not a natural fighter. His role was more of a protective shepherd watching over his flock. During one trip to Forest in 1968, Greenaway was walking to the ground with a small entourage of fans and players' families when a human barrier of menacing home fans confronted them. Unperturbed, Greenaway stepped forward, lifted his walking stick about his head, and roared, "Zigger zagger," then marched ahead. The startled Forest fans parted and the Chelsea contingent walked through unharmed.

Chelsea face Martin King cannot recall Greenaway ever throwing a punch in anger but it is clear that he would never run away from trouble either. "He was a most unlikely leader," wrote King, "but I don't think he ever saw himself that way." Steve Hickmott described him as a father figure. His only conviction for football violence came in 1983 when Chelsea fans rioted at Brighton. One Sunday newspaper branded him Chelsea's hooligan leader and he was denounced by the club. This had a harrowing effect on a man who lived for his team. Greenaway stopped going to the Bridge. Following the death of Matthew Harding in 1996, Greenaway

Some of Chelsea's mob attempt to breach the thin blue line to reach Liverpool fans in a nearby paddock at a game at Stamford Bridge in the mid-Eighties.

led a slow rendition of "Zigger zigger" in the Imperial pub, Harding's local. He died in poverty in 1999 at the age of 54, but his spirit is still felt.

The Shed was born and soon leaders emerged. The first was Daniel Harkins, better known to Chelsea fans as Eccles. Chelsea was always made up of several small mobs, most based on estates in towns dotted around Berkshire, Surrey and Kent. Come match day, certain figures would emerge as leaders and during the Seventies the undisputed boss was Eccles. "To drop into a conversation that you knew Eccles made you special," wrote Chris "Chubby" Henderson. "Your mates would look at you with respect because you saw him in the street and he addressed you by name and you called him back by his real name, Harkins."

"General Eccles made a real impression on me," recalled Martin Knight. "I remember hearing his name as a first year at senior school, therefore by

1969 he was already a bit of a folk hero in football's urban mythology. His name was daubed in paint on a wall by the Nell Gwynn on the Kings Road for years and years. To meet him and, indeed, see him in action was like meeting an England player or a pop star. He was certainly charismatic and had a huge devoted following."

Chelsea's trip to Bolton in 1977 saw Eccles at his organisational best. He marshalled the troops on the football special heading north and even had a map of the Bolton end which he huddled over, planning the attack with his lieutenants. A few hundred Chelsea, on Eccles' instructions, sneaked on to the Bolton Kop in ones and twos and got in between the home fans, who abused the Londoners. The roar went up, Bolton scattered and Chelsea had taken their end. Eccles wasn't finished. Outside the ground he ordered a small mob to act as a decoy for the police while he led the main mob in search of locals.

He took a different approach to West Brom a few weeks later, waiting until the end of the match and attacking home fans as they left the ground. There was a quick tactical retreat when the bulk of West Brom poured out but, again under Eccles' orders, the small group of 50 Chelsea linked arms and marched towards the mob, causing them to flee. Other ends taken under Eccles's stewardship include Aston Villa's huge Holte End, Spurs' Shelf and Arsenal's North Bank.

Leading Chelsea alongside Eccles was a one-armed black man called Babs, whose stocky build and gameness more than compensated for his disability. For some outsiders it seemed incomprehensible that a black man should be such a prominent face at a time when the National Front and British Movement were consciously moving into football, and nowhere was this link believed to exist more than at Chelsea. "Babs was the Chelsea top boy in a world where white was right," admitted Chris Henderson, who himself was attached to the BM and the NF. But to Henderson and the other right-wing Chelsea, Babs was just that, Chelsea. He was not the only prominent black face around the club: Steff, Black Jim and Black Willy were others.

Babs was also a leading mover behind London United, an attempt by some skinhead-based London firms to unite under a common banner to attack northerners on Friday nights in central London. The idea emerged in 1975 and lasted a few years before Babs had a fight with Steve Woods, a leading West Ham face, and football rivalries took over.

Clothes were important to Babs and he always ensured that he was smartly turned out. He surrounded himself with a loyal and tight-knit group of followers who would operate independently of Eccles but normally came together during a match and certainly for post-match violence, especially away. While Eccles planned his capture of ends with military precision, and then only when he considered victory likely, Babs's group used more brawn than brain. It was Babs who led the taking of the Wolves' North Bank, an assault many at Chelsea did not believe Eccles would have made because there was no guarantee that victory was likely. The men often joined together but there was also sometimes considerable friction.

The North East was a particularly unfriendly region for London clubs to visit and it didn't get much worse than Sunderland. Chelsea had just been relegated to the Second Division and their first game of the new season was away at Roker Park. It had been six years since Chelsea had played there in the league, which meant for most of those who climbed aboard the train at Kings Cross at 7.30am on the morning of Saturday August 12 it was their first visit. Taking control in marshalling Chelsea on their arrival at Seaburn Station was Eccles, calm, thoughtful and above all, organised. His was the first mob to arrive and the need to keep everyone together in one tight little mob was paramount. A football special of 700 lads faced an equal number of locals. Suddenly, from the wings, more Sunderland emerged, screaming, shouting, baying for Cockney blood. Chelsea fought back and eventually ran the home mob.

Inside the ground, Chelsea took an early lead, which was the signal for more small outbreaks of violence. Sunderland pulled a goal back, then scored the eventual winner. Outside the ground, what seemed like thousands of home supporters began to gather, waiting for the Londoners to come out. Many of the Chelsea fidgeted nervously – until a young, skinny-looking lad with a loud mouth climbed onto a crush barrier and began to speak. "Look at 'em," he shouted, pointing to the Sunderland outside. "A bunch of fucking wankers. They're nothing, no-hopers, no jobs, no nothing. They live in fucking caves, this lot – can't even speak English. Let's get out there and kick shit out of them. Show 'em we're Chelsea and proud of it. We ain't scared of them – they're all bum bandits and they ain't even proper Geordies." His speech had the desired effect – the crowd roared in approval, and out Chelsea poured, with Babs, Eccles and Co. to the fore, and fought viciously – and eventually victoriously – against the massed hordes.

The young speechmaker's name was Steven "Hicky" Hickmott, and a terrace legend had been born.

In February 1976, Chelsea played Crystal Palace at home in the FA Cup. "The sad side of soccer shows itself yet again," opened an article in one newspaper. "And not surprisingly at Stamford Bridge, where Chelsea went down three-two to visiting Palace. Nine mounted police were called to the ground – for the first time at a football ground, to my knowledge – since the crowd broke the gates at Wembley in 1923. Chelsea decided to have identity cards after their supporters halted the match at Luton in August by invading the pitch. There would have been an invasion on Saturday as well but for the 8ft high protective barrier Chelsea erected two years ago."

The following season was arguably Chelsea's worst for hooliganism. The first match was at Leyton Orient, where a wall collapsed as 100 Chelsea fans invaded the pitch. The next away game was Millwall and there were dozens of arrests as the South Londoners attacked Chelsea from all sides within the ground. Seven days later there was fierce fighting inside and outside the ground at Plymouth. Chelsea steamed through the Plymouth end during the game but came under fierce attack afterwards.

There was less trouble at home games but Cardiff was an exception. Four thousand Welshmen travelled down and caused considerable damage to Stamford Bridge, including destroying the club's new scoreboard. There was also trouble at the home match against Wolves, with clashes on the underground and around the stadium. November 20 brought 34 arrests during Chelsea's visit to Notts Forest, which was accompanied by ten hours of disorder. Play was held up for four minutes as fans clashed inside the ground. After the match more than 200 police were used to contain further trouble. The subsequent court cases heard how the Chelsea fans "behaved like animals".

Chelsea travelled to Kenilworth Road on December 29 and once again there was trouble. The previous season Chelsea fans had invaded the Luton pitch in their hundreds, halted the game and caused widespread disorder. The level of violence was not the same but this was largely because most of the local pubs had been shut for the day and extra police were called in. Thirty houses and shop windows were still smashed after Chelsea fans reacted angrily to their team's four-nil hammering. Inside the ground some of the fencing which had been installed just before the match collapsed as 3,000 travelling fans surged forward, pressing against it. A few days later the local police admitted that the club had received an anonymous written warning about violence prior to the game. "If I knew how to make letter bombs, then this would be one," the letter read. "Your ground is going to be a bomb site when we finish. Try stopping us, 20,000 of us feel like me."

Trouble accompanied Chelsea to an FA Cup tie at Southampton, Millwall at home was unsurprisingly violent, and then there was Bolton away in the League, the game where Eccles oversaw the taking of the home end. The threat of further disorder caused Notts County to alter the kick-off of their home game against Chelsea as Notts Forest were also playing at home. The Football League initially refused but pressure from the club and the police convinced them of a rethink.

Chelsea's away match at Cardiff earned the head-line "Cardiff's worst day of soccer violence" in the *South Wales Echo*. Eighty-nine people were arrested and dozens injured after trouble before, during and after the game. Some of the worst disorder occurred inside the ground before a ball had been kicked. A policeman was showered with missiles and a firework was thrown from the Chelsea end, exploding on the pitch. Forty-seven arrests were made during the match as rival gangs battled on the terraces of the Grangetown End. Police moved in to make arrests, including one young Chelsea fan who was marched out in a half-Nelson. But the worst came when a Chelsea defender was booked by the referee shortly before half-time. Chelsea fans hurled bottles and beer cans into the Grandstand, where Cardiff supporters were sitting.

Four hundred Cardiff left the ground ten minutes before the final whistle and clashed outside with 200 Chelsea who had done likewise. "It would have taken an army to stop them," a police commander admitted. Trouble continued for an hour after as Chelsea hunted down their rivals in what police described as "the most prolonged period of violence we have seen during a Cardiff soccer match." And it still wasn't over. Police literally had to fight Chelsea fans back to the Welsh border. It took two hours for one train to travel the 14 miles to Newport and one carriage had to be taken out of service after the wheels were damaged by the excessive pulling of the emergency brake. "The Chelsea fans in the enclosure in front of the Grandstand were little better than animals," Cardiff's Chairman, Stefan Terlezki, declared. That view was echoed by many ordinary Cardiff supporters. "It was terrible," said one female pensioner. "It made me afraid to live here." She had lived close to the ground most of her life and had had her windows broken on four earlier occasions, but had experienced nothing like that day.

A frustrated Chief Constable of South Wales called for all future high-risk matches to be made all-ticket. "It has cost us and the rate-payers of South Wales hundreds of thousands to police Ninian Park in recent seasons," he said. "The time has come to ask whether we can carry on paying out vast sums of money to police what is virtually a pitched battle between rival gangs. If I didn't have a duty in the field of public safety I would seriously consider withdrawing all police support from future matches."

The home fixture against Millwall saw dozens more arrests amid scenes of complete chaos. "A policeman was stabbed outside the ground, and there were more than 30 arrests, and once again the question remains, 'what will happen to law and order if Chelsea face the big city First Division teams next year?'" opined the *Evening Standard*. "The hooligan problem has been with us for so long that there is now a definite feeling of blank submission hanging over observers in the Main Stand when the violence starts. I viewed the trouble 30 minutes before the game started on Saturday and felt nothing, just an acceptance that this happening was part and parcel of a Saturday afternoon. But on the terraces the mood of the hooligans seemed more vicious than normal and the mood of the police more aggressive. The fighting was awful."

Chelsea went to Charlton over the Easter weekend still clinging to the hope of promotion but a 4–0 defeat put an end to that. Chelsea's fans wrecked the ground. A massive bonfire was lit on the terraces from newspapers and match programmes in an attempt to halt the game and then, shortly before the final whistle, Chelsea fans kicked down the wooden gates and poured out into the street. Cars were damaged and house windows were smashed as the rioting spread into the local neighbourhood.

The fallout from the Charlton game was swift. Home Secretary Dennis Howell was appalled by the small fines handed out to those arrested at the match and urged tougher sentences. "The use of detention centres and attendance centres seems to have more merit than inadequate fines," he said. He was speaking after five people were handed out total fines of just £160. He demanded a full report into the violence and suggested that Chelsea fans would be banned from buying terrace tickets in the future, a penalty that had already been imposed on

Manchester United that season. The chairman of the bench defended his action: "It may be all right for Mr Howell to talk in terms of £1,000 fines. He should try collecting them." A week later, Chelsea fans were banned from attending away matches for two years.

Somebody obviously forgot to tell anyone about the ban. Chelsea's final away match of the season was at Wolves, and British Rail still laid on football specials to take Londoners to the Midlands. The police had anticipated the arrival of hordes of Chelsea and decided that it was better to allow them into the ground than to have them wandering the streets of Wolverhampton causing trouble. Five hundred officers were on duty but this did not prevent, in the words of Superintendent Roy Mellor, "The worst afternoon of violence at Wolves this season." There were 76 arrests and 23 people were injured.

The trip to Wolves wasn't undertaken without trepidation by Chelsea. Steve Hickmott remembered the feeling of dread as the Chelsea mob entered the infamous Wolves subway on the way to the ground. However, once they had survived the home onslaught in the subway, they carried out an all-too-familiar tactic of slipping into the home end in small groups. The roar went up from Chelsea leader Eccles and the North Bank was cleared. The final whistle marked the end of a dreadful season of hooliganism.

Hicky had established himself as the main Chelsea face by the end of the Seventies. Eccles and Babs virtually disappeared from the scene and, while Chelsea continued to be a collection of numerous mobs, Hicky was the man to follow if you wanted action. "Most people liked him but his style was different again from what had gone before," wrote the two Martins, King and Knight. "Not for him the glory of taking an end; he wanted the buzz of a definite confrontation and invariably got it. Millwall were called the Bushwhackers, but Hicky's mob were masters at turning up in unexpected places at unexpected times and confronting unsuspecting mobs."

One of these unsuspecting places was in the middle of Cardiff's Bob Bank, where he and his coachload appeared at a league game in 1980. Surrounded by thousands of Cardiff's hardcore, Hickmott pulled out an English flag and waved it about. The rest of the Chelsea fans, on the terrace opposite, cheered wildly but the locals were furious. They steamed into the small Chelsea mob and gave them a terrible beating. Hickmott and crew stood for as long as they could but numbers and punches overwhelmed them. When they were finally led around the pitch to the away end, they were treated to a heroes' welcome.

Hickmott's antics became legendary at Chelsea, his stunts as much as his fighting prowess. He was often seen wearing a bright red beret and at an away game at Swansea, a gorilla suit, though an iconic picture of the man was shot at an England Under-21 game in Turkey where he wore flying goggles. At one match at Sunderland, Hicky was marauding the streets, heading for an arranged meeting with locals, when a police van pulled up and asked if they were lost. Hicky played along and he and his small mob got a lift back towards the station, passing the numerous police lines set up to catch them. The policeman was obviously not local and Hickmott even had to assist him with directions. Just before they reached their destination, Hickmott asked to get out, pretending to be saving the driver from getting snarled up in football and shopping traffic. He had arrived early for the meet with Sunderland, courtesy of the police.

At a game at West Brom, Hickmott and a friend climbed onto the roof of the away terrace. For several minutes they entertained the away support, dancing and prancing about, to the horror of West Brom officials. Eventually even Hicky got bored and, in one last act, launched himself off the roof and into the crowd below. At an away game at Huddersfield in 1982, Hickmott's mob steamed into the home end, chasing off far superior numbers. Despite the best and most vicious efforts of the locals, the Chelsea group could not be moved. At the final whistle Hickmott stood on the edge of the pitch and shook hands with all his Chelsea compatriots.

Hickmott's coach trips became infamous. They started with a single coach taking himself and friends from his home in Tunbridge Wells, but before long the service had grown to several coaches picking up from points across London. Flyers were printed and tickets sold long before match days. There was even a song sung to the tune of "When Johnny Comes Marching Home".

When Hickey's coach goes over the hill, hurrah, hurrah,

When Hickey's coach goes over the hill, hurrah, hurrah,
When Hickey's coach goes over the hill,
And there's fifty-two geezers ready to kill,
And we're all going into their end, just to dish out some pain.

The police were slowly but surely coming to terms with hooliganism at Stamford Bridge. Though football intelligence officers were still some way off, local coppers were put on the North Bank turnstiles to weed out known faces. Chelsea's leaders responded by moving to the West Stand, through Gate 13. It took some time for the police to cotton on, but eventually they did, and hooliganism increasingly drifted out into the streets, on to the Underground and even into central London. Chelsea were joined in the Second Division by Leeds and the two sets of fans renewed hostilities dating back to the 1960s. There was also regular trouble at Derby, whose ground had been ripped apart by Chelsea in 1970, 1973 and again twice in the early Eighties.

The Eighties were the period of the leaflet, and Chelsea, like other big firms at the time, used it to mobilise their forces. Word of mouth had been sufficient in earlier years, but leaflets, like the naming of the firms, were now in vogue. For a match at Manchester United, Chelsea's mob decided to have a go at the infamous Stretford End. "Chelsea v Munich United," a leaflet circulated in the weeks before the game began. "Not to be missed. All-ticket at the Chelsea end so queue in an orderly fashion only at the Munich end. All the best lads, and good luck on our most important mission ever."

It was during this period that the name, the Headhunters, emerged. It began as a bit of a laugh after one Chelsea lad took the name from an employment company. A few calling cards were made, the media latched on, and the name stuck. Naming a mob bemused some of the older lads, but it was just another element of the new, fashion-conscious football casual.

Chelsea supporters were rarely out of the press in the early Eighties. During a home match against Leeds in the 1982/83 season, more than 200 arrests were made, with three-quarters being held in central London. The same season Chelsea invaded the Blackburn end with minutes of the game remaining, scattering their supporters on to the pitch. There was fighting in the seats during a Milk Cup game away at Tranmere and considerable press coverage of the nazi-saluting Chelsea fans at Notts County. Towards the end of the season there were violent clashes away at Wolves, Leeds and Burnley. The final away match saw Chelsea travel to Bolton where they rioted in the main stand. At the first game of the following season here were 125 arrests at Brighton and widespread disorder on the final day of the season at home to Leeds. The hooligans could hardly have scripted it better themselves, as their 5–0 thrashing of their most-hated opponents saw Chelsea promoted.

In Division One, Chelsea were back amongst London rivals West Ham and Spurs. However, some of the worst trouble occurred during a League Cup clash with Millwall. A few weeks later, a Chelsea reserve player was stabbed during a fight. The worst trouble that season was the home leg of the Milk Cup semi-final against Sunderland, which Chelsea lost 3–2 on the night and 5–2 on aggregate. Chelsea fans responded by invading the pitch and holding up play. More than 100 people were arrested and 43 injured, including 20 police officers. Coins and even planks of wood were thrown at police horses as they tried to clear the hooligans off the pitch. One Chelsea fan even chased Sunderland's goal scorer, Clive Walker, around the pitch. The FA ordered an inquiry but many in the media were unimpressed, especially after the fan who attempted to attack Walker was led away by police to the chants of "loyal supporter" from large sections of the crowd. One paper described the violence as a "vision of hell".

The continuing violence at Chelsea, coupled with Heysel, led to an increased determination on the part of the authorities to crack down on trouble. While Chelsea chairman Ken Bates ordered the erection of electric fences, the Metropolitan Police were briefing six officers whose job would be to identify and collect evidence on the hooligan ringleaders. The results of a six-month undercover operation were the arrests of Hickmott and several other alleged Chelsea hooligans. In what became a common feature of future dawn raids, the police proudly showed off to the press an array of weapons they had found. Among them were knives, darts and even a ball and chain. [For more on this operation, see POLICING in *Hooligans 2*]

During the subsequent court case it was Terry Last, rather than Steve Hickmott, who was said to be Chelsea's leader. Last, standing five feet four and with a slim build, seemed an unusual hooligan figurehead. A filing clerk with a law firm, avid bird-watcher and chess player, he was portrayed as the club's most dangerous supporter, an "articulate and intelligent field commander for the Headhunter group." Even the judge, when passing sentence, described him as a "tin pot leader whose arrogance knew no bounds" who had organised a "cauldron of violence" at Chelsea matches. By contrast, Hickmott was presented as his loyal sidekick. Last's portrayal owed something to the diary he kept of his days following Chelsea, in which he boasted of fights and looked forward with great eagerness to future confrontations.

Last and Hickmott both received ten-year jail terms and several others received shorter sentences. The judge praised the police operation and the Met quickly trumpeted their operation to other forces across the country as a model to follow. They were all made to look rather foolish when, a couple of years later, the convictions were quashed after doubts had been raised over the officers' methods of collecting information. This arose during a second trial of Chelsea hooligans, codenamed Extra Time, which focused on the next generation of Headhunters, led by Chris Henderson. Hickmott was released from prison, received a substantial payment in compensation and emigrated to South-East Asia. However, he never lost the bug nor was he forgotten. He returned for big Chelsea and England games and regularly sent postcards to Fulham police station, reminding them that he was a free man.

The removal of Hickmott *et al* reduced hooliganism at Chelsea but did not eradicate it. Chelsea fans attacked a tube carrying Everton fans during the home game in April 1987. Several windows were smashed, a flare was fired into a carriage, and as Evertonians fought back, they were attacked with baseball bats. The following season brought a pitch invasion during Chelsea's away game at QPR and trouble at Old Trafford. With the latter game close to the 30th anniversary of the Munich air crash, Chelsea fans launched a burning model plane on to the pitch. The Red Army got their revenge after the game as they hunted down Chelsea fans making their way to Piccadilly Station. Chelsea finished third from bottom, which meant the play-offs. A defeat to Middlesbrough was followed by wide-scale disorder at Stamford Bridge and further FA sanctions. The club was fined £75,000 and their terraces closed for the first four games of the new season.

The link between racism and Chelsea has been long documented but equally strongly denied by many of their hooligans over the years. True, they admit, many were loosely linked to the National Front and NF leaflets were found in their homes during police raids. True, they admit, racist chanting and even nazi salutes were features of Chelsea's terrace culture in the late Seventies and early Eighties, and true, many of their songs against Spurs were deeply anti-Semitic in nature. But, they contend, this was more about having a laugh and a desire to shock than true political allegiance. "Although the average white lad fighting at football might have stated that he hated blacks, he didn't really," argued Chris Henderson, in his book, *Who Wants It?* "We'd chant 'blacks out' during the day, then dance to the Motown sound of Elgin's 'Heaven Must Have Sent You' in the evening."

Of course, for some Chelsea, the racist chanting was just a "laugh" and the more it got a reaction, the more they did it. But their support did have a considerable racist element. Asian shops were attacked during an away game at Aston Villa in 1979, and a year later a mosque was attacked by 150 Chelsea hooligans in Luton. Four people were injured as bricks and bottles were followed up by punches and kicks and one man almost died. In April 1982, during an away match against Crystal Palace, Chelsea's first black player, Paul Canoville, ran on to the pitch on his debut to howls of booing from the crowd. He suffered the same fate when he made his home debut against Luton a couple of weeks later. Throughout the Eighties and Nineties, Chelsea have always provided Britain's fascist groups with hardcore support. This reached its peak with the shadowy neo-nazi group Combat 18. When C18 tried to capitalise on a British National Party council victory in Millwall in 1993, they found few takers in South East London, because they were, according to Millwall, "a Chelsea mob".

Henderson, who became a key face on the Chelsea terraces during the Eighties, is reticent about his past but was a leading face on the far-Right scene, both within his music and on the street.

His autobiography fails to mention the swastika tattoo on his upper body, though this could be embarrassment at it being the wrong way round. His contention that black fans stood shoulder to shoulder with card-carrying BNP members without taking offence at the songs is again plainly wrong. Martin Knight recalled one of his close friends, a black Chelsea lad, being appalled at the racist behaviour of some of the others. True, Chelsea had the likes of Babs in their ranks, but he had virtually disappeared from violence when the racist element took hold in 1979. There remains a core of the current Chelsea Headhunter mob who associate with the far-Right, though considerably less so than in the past.

One of the defendants in the Operation Extra Time trial was Stuart Glass, leader of the Hounslow mob. When people talk about Chelsea and the right-wing link, they are unknowingly talking about this West London firm. They were in the National Front in the late Seventies, with Glass himself as an electoral candidate in 1978, ran with the BNP in the Eighties and then, during the Nineties, were involved in Combat 18. Some of them were responsible for a racist attack that left a shopkeeper almost dead after he was attacked with a motorcycle chain, the racist chanting against John Barnes on the plane returning from Brazil in 1984, and the persecution of the Chelsea Independent Supporters' Association after their fanzine backed an anti-racist campaign.

Glass and his core mob became active in 1977 and were still around well into the Millennium. Amongst themselves they were known as the Northstandi Family, an Italian gangster pun on the North Stand which Glass and his group occupied, and the West London Deviants. The Deviants travelled the world together for football, politics, holidays and, most importantly, for sex. In addition to the John Barnes incident, they almost caused a diplomatic row when one of their group climbed up a floodlight at an England Under-21 match in Istanbul and, in front of several Government figures, dropped his trousers. Getting deported was considered an honour. On one trip to Cuba they refused to leave the airport until their passports were stamped "deported" after they had been arrested for fighting with an Argentinean football team.

The group thrived on adventure, even to the point of scouring the Foreign Office's list of destina-

CHELSEA FANS ARE STILL TOP OF THE RACIST LEAGUE!

CHELSEA fans are champions of the Racist League for the second year running.

Last year they were put at the top of the Racist League by the *Daily Star*. The *Star* called it the "League of Louts" and they said that Chelsea had the most "NF thugs" amongst their supporters.

This season Chelsea fans are still as racist as ever. Three supporters were kicked out of the Shed by the police during the friendly match against Arsenal. They were kicked out when the whole of the Shed end started to chant "Get that nigger off the pitch!"

West Ham and Leeds are close behind Chelsea in second and third place. West Ham fans were slagged off in *The Sun* newspaper last season because they were racists. *The Sun* said: "At *West Ham*, *fascist White louts threw bananas on the pitch at two Black players on the opposing side.*"

"THE LEAGUE OF LOUTS"
1. CHELSEA
2. WEST HAM UNITED
3. LEEDS UNITED
4. LINFIELD
5. BIRMINGHAM CITY
6. MILLWALL
7. COLERAINE
8. TOTTENHAM HOTSPUR
9. GLASGOW RANGERS
10. CARLISLE UNITED

The National Front's Bulldog *magazine carried a league table of racist hooligans in which Chelsea always figured prominently.*

tions best avoided by Britons. On one trip, to Colombia, they insisted on going to the cocaine-growing region. They stopped for liquid refreshment in a small hut along the way, only for their quiet drink to be interrupted by an armed gang of bandits who burst in demanding money and possessions. Glass looked up and knew that they were in trouble but before he had handed over his valuables another one of the Deviants, who had begun football fighting with Glass in 1977, reappeared from a visit to the toilet. Realising what was going on, he quickly introduced Glass as "Don Corleone Northstandi". With that he bent down and kissed Glass's hand. The bandits, clearly impressed with their important visitor, put down their guns and joined their guests in a game of dominoes. Not all their trips were so salubrious and the label Deviants was also well-earned. Most of them took in the red light areas in each city visited.

By the mid-Nineties, Glass and his crew were less active, but the return of Chelsea to European competition brought them out. The first round was in Prague, but due to the fear of crowd violence the

game was switched to Jablonec, 60 kilometres away. Four hundred Chelsea hooligans made the trip, including faces from across the decades. There was fighting in Prague the night before the game and a few minor scuffles on the day of the match.

Chelsea next travelled to Vienna, where again they won. The third round pitted them against Bruges, and coming only a week after England's ill-fated game in Dublin in February 1995, there was a siege mentality in the Belgian city. In true Belgian police style, everyone without a ticket, and many with, was treated as a hooligan and hundreds were rounded up and held during the game. In one incident, six Chelsea supporters, all aged over 30, confronted 200 of Bruges's crew. The startled Belgians couldn't believe the lunacy of these English as they launched their suicidal attack. Glass was picked up in one police swoop and thrown into an aircraft hangar with others, where water cannons were used to dampen their spirits. There was a commotion and Glass thought he had his chance to escape. Wearing his obligatory sunglasses, designer clothes and gold jewellery, he made a dash for the river despite his hands still being bound by plastic cuffs. Unfortunately for Chelsea's version of Steve McQueen, his escape was unsuccessful. As Glass scrambled across to the other bank, he emerged from the water to find himself staring at the feet of waiting coppers.

Chelsea's final foray into Europe was against the Spanish side Zaragosa in the competition's quarter-finals. The Deviants travelled over in a mini-bus, with a homemade "Hate Bus" sign stuck in the back window. "It was so stupid it was funny," recalled one passenger. "People came on with crates of beer and one person even brought a blow-up doll."

The excursion epitomised their mentality: a desire to shock, abuse and insult. "The thing about the Spain trip, it was only partly to do with football. It was just a group of blokes, like in *Men Behaving Badly*, but they had nothing on us. A weekend of going over there, getting really, really drunk, causing loads of trouble and shagging loads of dodgy birds. It was outside the parameters of normal life. It was mental. The football was just the excuse for going. The main reason why we wanted the team to win was so we could do it all again next month. It's a social thing, especially going away from home. You go somewhere like Spain and you know it's going to be brilliant. You go over in a pair of shorts and just be really obnoxious. That sounds really childish, but that's half the attraction I suppose."

The Operation Own Goal and Extra Time trials closed a chapter on Chelsea. Some defendants might have walked free, while others later had their convictions quashed, but several decided to call it a day. Chubby Henderson set up a bar in Thailand, while Hickmott moved to the Philippines. A few others continued as before but a new generation of top boys was emerging. On May 31, 1988, the Metropolitan Police received a report from *The Sun* newspaper that the new Chelsea leader was Tony Covele. Then in his late twenties, Covele had been known to the police for some time but never in the capacity of organiser. He had first been arrested at football in February 1978. A few years later he was convicted of overturning a police car and assault on two officers. In 1986, police intelligence suggested that he was the "financial director" for the Own Goal trial, during which he gave an alibi for one of the defendants.

More reliable information soon began arriving on the desk of Chelsea's football coppers, based at Fulham police station. In January 1991, a registered source named Covele as the leader of the Headhunters. He was named as organising a coach that was involved in serious disorder in Sheffield, being involved in a fight at Aston Villa on the last day of the season and then, during the close season, organising a trip to Edinburgh for a confrontation with Hibs. Three minibuses, packed with 30 Chelsea, left the Stag pub in Victoria and travelled via the West Midlands to Penrith. There, the group looted a knife shop and stabbed an off-duty policeman who tried to intervene. The plan had been to link up with Rangers and Hearts hooligans but they were never to reach their location, as the police were well aware of their intentions and had been tracking their movements from the moment they boarded their vehicles. It was when one of these vehicles suffered a puncture, just outside Edinburgh, that the police finally pulled them over. Hidden behind the panelling of all three vans were an assortment of weapons, including baseball bats, plastic lemons containing ammonia, smoke flares, smoke grenades, distress flares, knives and "CFC Headhunters" calling cards.

A year later another police intervention blocked another of Chelsea's close season trips. Covele and 30 others were prevented from entering Brighton.

In the car Covele was travelling in, police found a baseball bat, a knife and three shotgun cartridges. Covele's reputation was growing across the country. By the time England played Holland in a World Cup qualifier at Wembley in late April 1993, he had emerged as a key organiser, bringing together several smaller mobs under the leadership of Chelsea. This was most vividly demonstrated on a police surveillance tape, shot during the return fixture in Rotterdam, the following October. A three o'clock meeting time had been set for the railway station on the day of the game, and as Covele headed an 80-strong Chelsea mob, other hooligan leaders stepped forward to shake his hand. The combined numbers reached over 300 and within moments of Covele's arrival, England were off.

Better known to the general public was Andy Frain, otherwise known as "Nightmare". In 2000, he was sentenced to seven years' imprisonment following a BBC *MacIntyre Undercover* programme, and was immediately propelled into the national limelight. To many hooligans around the country, he was already infamous. Considered by police to be one of the most violent football thugs around, Frain has amassed 36 convictions and been to prison on numerous occasions. He had been involved in the KKK, National Front, BNP and Combat 18, but at the same time has had black mates at Chelsea and in Reading, where he lived. On the MacIntyre programme he boasted about slashing an off-duty policeman across the face during Chelsea's failed trip to Edinburgh to meet Hibs.

Two more recent Chelsea faces are the Sim brothers, known simply as "the twins". If Eccles was the organiser and Hickmott was the joker, Ian and David Sim were the muscle. Born in 1972 and brought up in Orpington, the Sims are two scary men. In April 1998, they were involved in violent disorder against Spurs in central London. Seventy-five Spurs had arrived early for the match at Stamford Bridge and by 11.15 a.m. were drinking in the Imperial Arms, a pub normally frequented by Chelsea on match days. Chelsea couldn't believe the cheek of their fierce rivals and in went the Sims, with one other Chelsea, for what they later told police was "some banter." The police intervened and the Chelsea lads were sent on their way. Shortly before kick-off, those Spurs fans with tickets went to the game while the remainder, about 40, drifted off to Gloucester Road. The groups reunited at Victoria after the game before moving off to the Argyll Arms, just off Oxford Street. Chelsea, meanwhile, had also mobbed up in central London and, according to witness statements, a phone call was made and a fight was arranged.

CCTV cameras caught the moment Chelsea attacked the pub. At the front were the Sims, with one of the brothers wielding a scaffolding pole. This, and bottles, were launched at the pub windows. Spurs steamed out of the pub and initially backed Chelsea off, but the Headhunters regrouped and charged back, driving their opponents back into the pub. The fighting lasted five minutes and was only broken up with the arrival of the Tactical Support Group. A few arrests were made, but many more followed after police studied CCTV footage and stills from one of their own photographers. Four people received head injuries, including David Sim, but only one accepted medical attention. The case came up at Southwark Crown Court and while the Spurs lads walked, the Chelsea lads were sent down, with the Sim brothers receiving the harshest sentences.

Chelsea, like so many of the big firms of the Seventies and early Eighties, are now a shadow of their former selves. Police operations and, more particularly, the growing popularity and gentrification of football have kept some lads out and persuaded others that the price of losing a coveted season ticket is too high. Chelsea no longer has the numbers it once had, with the police estimating a core of only 50-70. However, this group includes some of the most violent hooligans around. A betting man would think twice about backing another firm in a twenty-on-twenty fight.

In July 1996, a pre-season friendly between Reading and West Ham turned out to be anything but as dozens of men clashed outside Reading railway station after the game. The visitors were met by a combined force of locals and Chelsea, who took it as another opportunity to reacquaint themselves with their East End foe. In fact the fight had actually been arranged between two Chelsea and West Ham hooligans a few months before while both were in prison. Forty people were picked up by police and 13 needed medical treatment. The most badly hurt was a West Ham fan who, according to a local newspaper, was "slashed, punched and kicked by a gang brandishing knives and glasses." One shouted, "Cut his fucking head off,"

to the man wielding the knife. He was cut across his throat, virtually from one ear to the other, and had a tendon severed in his arm. His injuries required 368 stitches.

A poor quality CCTV tape of the attack led to charges against seven men for the incident including what police believed was the core of the Chelsea Headhunters, and there was no disguising the delight amongst some officers. Finally, they had their main targets on serious enough charges that would take them off the streets for several years. Their euphoria turned to disbelief and anger after the case was dropped at the trial. The slashing victim failed to appear and the CPS decided that the tape without the victim was not sufficient to secure a conviction. The accused walked out of court as innocent men.

Further reading: *Hoolifan*, Martin King and Martin Knight (Mainstream); *Armed For The Match*, Colin Ward with Steven Hickmott (Headline); *Who Wants It?* Colin Ward and Chubby Henderson (Mainstream); *White Riot*, Nick Lowles (Milo Books)

CHELTENHAM TOWN

Ground: Whaddon Road
Firms: Cheltenham Volunteer Force
Rivals: Kidderminster, Gloucester City

When Graham McNulty leaned forward to throw a plank of wood from the stand at Lansdowne Road, he had little idea that he was making his Cheltenham Volunteer Force (CVF) a household name. The 38-year-old managing director from Cheltenham became a figure of hate for the tabloid press in the immediate aftermath of the Dublin riot in February 1995. The image of the balding and overweight hooligan was reproduced in every national newspaper as a personification of the evilness of English hooligans.

The CVF was formed in the late Eighties when Cheltenham were still in the Conference. Two of the closest teams to them, Gloucester City and Kidderminster Rovers, were also in the Conference and there were several clashes between the three. While Cheltenham are (at the time of writing) now two divisions above Gloucester City, it was as recently as 1997 that the two were battling it out at the top of the Southern League. Cheltenham Town were promoted into the Football League in 1999 and joined by Kidderminster a year later and the rivalry was renewed.

McNulty's affiliation to Aston Villa was also widely reported in the media and in this he was not alone. Several early CVF figures also supported Villa, and a few even backed Manchester United. There were some instances where the split loyalties caused trouble within the group. There was also much made of McNulty's Loyalist and far-Right connections, an allegation which had some substance. "There was some degree of truth but most of it was blown up by the media. Like a lot of firms, we have a few lads who are into that sort of thing but the majority aren't too bothered either way," said one lad active today.

The publicly generated by the Dublin riot focused local attention on the group and for some of the lads the pressure became too much. This and changing personal circumstances for others led some to drop out of the CVF, while those that remained became increasingly inactive. Promotion into the Football League saw the emergence of a new layer of lads, though as ever a few of the original group will still come out for bigger games.

The decline of the original CVF was reversed with the formation of the Cheltenham Under Fives. "It was formed by the youngsters who were initially rejected by the CVF for being too small or too young," said one. "Over that time they have grown close to the CVF youth lads and had several run-ins with the Kidderminster Railway Army Youth and also a bit with Southend and Shrewsbury youth. Brentford turned up with about fifty lads and our main firm was waiting for them near the station. A few who were drinking near the Brentford boys were asked to go down and let the visitors know what was happening. Only the five lads in question saw a young Cheltenham spotter get the nut stuck on him by one of their older lads, and this didn't go down well with the Cheltenham boys, who decided they'd not wait for the meet at the station. The five CVF launched a few handheld flares into the Brentford mob who were leaving the pub, then steamed in. I don't know if the flares put the Brentford boys off, but our lot stood toe to toe against far greater numbers for a good two or three

minutes before eventually being forced back. A couple of lads lost caps, which I understand were later put on display in their main pub, but no one took the sort of kicking they should have done with the numbers involved.

"Another incident was with Plymouth and QPR outside our train station. We were at home to QPR that day and a meet had also been arranged with Plymouth's Central Element. Twenty-five of our lads found a nice quiet boozer where the Old Bill wouldn't find us and waited for Plymouth to come down from a match at Crewe. When the call came through that the TCE were there, our lot headed down to meet them and as we came over the bridge we saw the Plymouth boys and steamed into them. Within seconds they were on their toes around the corner. Only when our lads got round that corner did they find out the Plymouth lads had gathered an impressive armoury of bottles, sticks and, I don't know where they'd got it from, a fucking big Christmas tree which they started swinging at us. The Plymouth lads were game and weren't budging an inch, in fact neither side did for what seemed like ages, before a large group of lads came steaming out of a nearby pub. For a few seconds both our lot and the TCE stopped fighting, as neither of us knew who these lads were and probably assumed the other had stitched them up. It wasn't until these came steaming into us both and shouting in Cockney voices did we realise this was QPR's mob, who'd been waiting for the last train back and seen what was going on.

"Things became hectic then as, in the dark, nobody knew who was who, and I would not be surprised if lads were getting hit by sustained friendly fire from their own firm. The place was quiet, too, so the fighting went on for ages, a good five to ten minutes before the sirens could be heard and all three mobs backed away, leaving only a bad broken Christmas tree, one TCE lad missing an ear, and a couple of QPR unconscious for the boys in blue to clear up."

The police admitted they were caught on the hop and also claimed that the fight was organised over the Internet. They were called to the scene only when a taxi driver rang it through. "As I approached the roundabout there was a mob of about thirty to forty young white men," he told the local media. "They wore smart clothes and many wore Burberry baseball caps. I saw two people on the ground with a gang around them beating them with their fists, feet and stakes."

Cheltenham also clashed with Plymouth after an encounter at Whaddon Road. About 2,000 Pilgrims made the trip and the congestion caused the game to be delayed for 15 minutes. After the game, which Cheltenham won, a group of 30 Plymouth attacked the Cat and Fiddle pub immediately outside the ground. Police later claimed that this had been a pre-arranged fight but the home mob had not turned up. Slightly further away, 100 Plymouth barricaded themselves into the Sudeley Arms to escape the clutches of the law.

As recently as March 2005, Cheltenham have battled it out with Kidderminster. The local paper reported, "Shoppers looked on with horror as more than 30 booze-fuelled men punched and threatened police officers in Kidderminster before Harriers' crunch football clash with Cheltenham Town. Police dogs were used as officers tried to calm the abusive men, reportedly supporting Cheltenham. They threatened passers-by and threw punches at police officers between 12 noon and 1pm in New Road before being moved up to Aggborough in time for kick off. Traffic came to a standstill as some yobs were arrested face-down in the middle of the road, with police vans swerving across the carriageway."

A businessman throwing a plank of wood in Dublin and a few isolated skirmishes over a ten-year period is not the fullest CV in the world of hooligan gangs, but as is the case with many smaller clubs, the lack of police interference does leave the potential for disorder in the future. Another observable lower-division trend is that many older hooligans who were key figures at bigger firms now attend fixtures involving lesser-known clubs. This trend may force the authorities to keep a more watchful eye on the small teams as seasoned campaigners seek their terrace fix away from their original stamping grounds.

CHESTER CITY

Ground: The Deva Stadium
Firm: Beer Belly Crew, Chester Casual Army, The 125.
Rivals: Wrexham

Chester conjures images of an award-winning race-course, a historic city within ancient Roman walls,

and trendy wine bars catering to a well-heeled clientele. Not football hooliganism. Yet within walking distance of the landmarks that make Chester a destination for camera-clicking Japanese and Americans, lies Blacon, once a run-down, drug-riddled overspill area. It was from the heart of Chester's carbuncle, as it was once known to the middle class denizens of the city, that Chester City FC drew its first hooligan mob.

In the 1970s, Blacon was one of the biggest council estates in Europe; only Wythenshawe in Manchester and Broadwater Farm in London had more inhabitants on one estate in the UK, and the pubs in the area drew a clientele who were often not welcome anywhere else. From these pubs came a group who attached themselves to Chester FC and formed the first known hooligan group at the club. Years before Sheffield United formed the Blades Business Crew, Chester adopted their own BBC, the Beer Belly Crew.

In those days the main rivals to the BBC were, perhaps surprisingly, not Wrexham but Port Vale, and every time they visited there were major problems. Boris, a Chester veteran, said, "At that time, at most grounds you could walk around and watch the game from wherever you wanted. It was a headache for the police and it was years before they cottoned on that if you put the home lads behind one goal, the away fans behind the other, and locked a gate near the paddock, trouble inside the ground would be easier to prevent. People talk today about Stoke, but if you ask the old lads which club from the Potteries they had murder with, they will all come up with the same answer, Port Vale. Year after year they came in the home Sealand Road End and took it with ease. The old Kop, with no roof and very little else, was where most away fans went, but if Vale were in town it was safer for us to go in there, or maybe the paddock, which we called the Pop Side.

"We played them once in the Debenhams Cup, a tinpot competition for the clubs from the lower leagues who got furthest in the FA Cup. There was mayhem. They took the place and the game was stopped. It was so bad they never played for that cup again, and Debenhams were not happy about the bad press either."

In the mid-Seventies, Chester gained the tag of giant killers in cup competitions, and in 1975 they reached the semi-final of the League Cup, defeating Leeds and Newcastle on the way to a two-legged tie with Aston Villa. A crowd of more than 19,000 packed into Sealand Road for the first leg and Chester twice came from behind to earn a creditable draw. On the pitch, the likes of Nigel Edwards, Terry Owen, father of superstar Michael, and Derek Draper, a balding lower-league Bobby Charlton, put Chester on the map. Off the pitch, the gangs who came from Blacon and The Lache joined up to resist the Villa hordes.

One of them, Big Sammy, said, "The Villa game was not as one sided as they would like you to believe. In those days The Lache lads and Blacon did not get on and didn't even stand by each other in the ground, often charging each other if there were no away fans to fight, but for big games we had to forget about local gangs and join up. After the game we had a fair crack at them outside what is now HMV and then loads of bikers turned up and we gave them a real pasting. The trouble was we had to go there for the second leg and at Villa Park it was as dodgy as fuck. I'd be lying if I said Chester fans did not get a right going over."

These divides in the local support were always evident. Apart from the Blacon contingent, the Lache lads and the lads who came from the city, Chester also attracted a large gang from Deeside. Though it was a couple of miles over the Welsh border, most youngsters opted to follow Chester rather than Wrexham, that's if they were not lured to Anfield, Goodison Park or Old Trafford. City centre pubs were specifically for certain mobs. Some holed up in the Victoria on The Rows, while others drank in the Marlborough. Blacon's three pubs, the Byron, the Wagon and the notorious Highfield, were taken by locals. Visitors, regardless of who they supported, were sent packing, usually on the end of a kicking.

Being so close to Merseyside, it was inevitable that the casual scene would reach Chester and by the early Eighties a few shops had started to sell designer sports gear and Italian clothes. Many footballers from Everton and Liverpool left the mass-produced garment stores in Liverpool and spent hundreds in City Gate, one of the first outlets for Armani and other lesser known brands. Gino, the shop manager, was a local celebrity who always sorted people out with what they needed – so much so that after an undercover police woman filmed him in action offering to supply more than shirts and jeans, he left the area, never to return.

It was at this time that the first football casual firm formed at Chester. A lot of thought went into the name, the Chester Casual Army. However, after a couple of seasons, it was changed to The 125, the name of the super-fast train which was the preferred mode of transport in the days of few ticket collectors, Persil vouchers and student railcard offers. A local music producer was one of the firm's founder members and among 40-odd nattily dressed casuals who embarked on their first away trip in 1986 to Aldershot.

The group included Ginge, Boris, Greener, Ritchie, Gresty, Tommo and Shane, who were leading members for years, and also Doddy, the leader of a splinter gang, D Troop. A mixture of jail, banning orders, ASBOs and the dreaded smack, in the case of one of them, took their toll and few remain active today. During these years of Lacoste, high speed trains and higher strength powder, Chester were as active as most firms in the lower divisions and Ginge is keen to point out that they went to most grounds over the years and is happy to remember the bad days as well as the good as they all helped bond them together.

"I laughed when I read in one book that we are a club with no firm. We would always have fifty or sixty lads on the train to most places and on a good day, when the local nutcases and old pissheads came with us, we could pull over 100 with ease. We were never in people's faces like Wrexham. We went and, if there was trouble, we had it. It is no surprise those silly fuckers claim to have more banned than anyone else, they are not exactly the cleverest firm about.

"We have had a few results over the years. Take it or leave it, but both Millwall and Manchester United have come off second best in battles with Chester. Millwall was before my time, but in about 1979 they came into the centre with 150 and bumped into fifty Chester by the Town Hall. An old Chester legend, Conk Cannon, fronted them. He was famous for nutting people while wearing a crash helmet even though he had no motorbike with him. Millwall eventually steamed the Chester firm, but they kept coming back and, after a few good battles, when the Cockneys reached Lasky's, near the ground, they all clapped the Chester lads from the other side of the road.

"After the game a minibus full of Millwall hard men stopped and asked for the roughest pub in

Chester. They were directed to the Highfield, which was full of drug addicts, dealers, and local undesirables, and Millwall were smashed everywhere when they attacked the doors. There probably wasn't a football lad in the pub at the time.

"United came unstuck at Crewe station. We were coming back from Orient, where we'd had the cheek to front the ICF at Euston and had over 100 lads waiting for a connection when up rolled their firm. They thought we were Scousers and fired a flare into us but we steamed them and in the end they were saying, 'We're on our way to Blackpool to a rave, we're not football lads'. They were distraught, the big, bad superfirm being twatted by little old Chester.

"Other games at which we did well were at Brighton, Crewe (even though they mobbed up with Port Vale), Northampton (where Greener got a busted skull when a copper broke a truncheon clean over his head), Hereford more than once and Shrewsbury, who were destroyed in 1989 after taking us lightly." But at Sealand Road, Ginge admits that Sheffield United, Tranmere and Port Vale all "took the piss" more than once.

Another firm to take over the city was Blackpool, who turned up mob-handed at a league game weeks after one of their lads was allegedly stabbed at a midweek cup match. Ginge said, "We had played them in the cup earlier that season and a small firm of them had a go at us and came second. One lad was badly battered and had his arm broken. They claim he was stabbed, I don't accept that, but for the League game they turned up and slaughtered us. It was a fucking nightmare and they were all over us like a rash. We did go there a couple of times, everyone does, it's a weekend away. I don't know if it's because they don't rate us, but they have never turned out for us at their place and we always ended up fighting with other firms and pissed-up stag nights.

"The same goes for Tranmere. We have been there endless times and never seen them. I wish the same could be said for Newport and Darlington, but it can't. At Newport we got fucked when they thought we were Cardiff and one time at Darlington I honestly thought we were going to get killed. It was by far the moodiest place we ever went. Thirty of us walked out of the station and about 150 of them steamed into us. They were lawless, did not

care for the police, absolute nutcases. I am no lover of the police, but anyone there that day will tell you that but for them we would have been killed."

Most Eighties firms cite the rave scene and police operations for their eventual demise. Chester blame Currys, Toys R Us and the Frankie and Benny restaurant franchises. They are the chains that now reside where Chester City Football Club once stood, after crippling debts led to the 1990 sale of Sealand Road to developers. The club was homeless, and had to play home games at Macclesfield.

Boris admitted it was the lowest the firm had ever been. "It was one shit place to share a ground. At first, Wrexham was suggested as a ground share but some were not happy and said we should be playing in England. In the end the police opposed it, fearing trouble, so we ended up at Macclesfield. It is over an hour by car, through country lanes, a nightmare journey, so we went to the first game on the train and it took two fucking hours. You had to wait at Kidsgrove for ages. I never went again after that and I was not the only one. We turned out for a few away games but it died a death and The 125 was no more." One offshoot of the move to Macc, however, was the appearance of a youth firm of about 30 strong, formed by a lad from Deeside.

In 1992, Chester returned to their city and took up residence in the purpose-built Deva Stadium. It took time, but eventually 50 or so lads returned and Carlisle, Crewe, Stockport, Bradford, York, Doncaster and Peterborough all found themselves fighting a rejuvenated Chester mob. York even brought their own streaker to celebrate a visit to a new ground. "The location of the Deva was perfect," said Boris, "with plenty of pubs on the way and plenty of chances to bump into away firms, the council have done us proud."

The team, however, was performing poorly, and after two relegations Chester left the Football League and joined the Conference. Owner Terry Smith, an American businessman noted for his eccentric methods who at one stage even took over team selection and training, left, to be replaced by boxing promoter Stephen Vaughan, whose money kept the club alive, and soon they were back in the League. The Smith years had been an embarrassment to everyone connected with the club, with many stories circulating of highly unconventional behaviour from a man with a background in American gridiron.

One of the lads worked at the club as an odd job man and provided an insight into how it was run with Smith at the helm. "We were in administration and our manager, Kevin Ratcliffe, was paying bills out of his own pocket. One day, Smith asked us to move his desk to a bigger office and we could not believe how heavy it was. In a drawer was a load of coins and we asked him what he wanted to do with them. Typical Yank, he said they were nothing and we could do whatever with them, as he only used notes. For two years he had been slinging his change in this drawer and we took over three grand in pound coins to the bank."

The Conference brought new rivals and many lads went for days out at places never before visited. Young lads joined older firm members on trips to Halifax, Burton Albion and Southport, where the police helicopter was used for one of the first times at a non-league fixture. It was at old rivals Hereford where Chester regained their Football League status and Ginge was one of the jubilant firm members who was there. "The whole city went and we took the place," he said. "I expected more from them as we had met them earlier in the season at ours and we had attacked them at half ten in the morning with pool cues and bats, but they had nothing for us. It was good to get back in the League but we also had some good times in the Conference. I remember Tamworth being a bit dodgy when about fifty Zulus turned up after their game was called off. Stafford was the same when Stoke did likewise. We were rated on the non-league circuit and were number one on the hit list for most of the small town clubs we visited."

Today Chester's main rivals are Wrexham, just over the Welsh border. The 125 admit that for the last few years their neighbours have had the upper hand, mainly due to the numbers they can pull and the leadership they have within their ranks. But it was not always so one-sided, and reports from the two local papers, the *Wrexham Leader* and the *Chester Chronicle*, back up the claim that in the past Chester held their own against the Welshmen they refer to as "the Goats". The various reports prove that the police were right to oppose a ground share between the two clubs:

"Seven fans were arrested and Chester keeper John Butcher was twice hit by stones thrown from the crowd."

"Police were forced to scramble the force helicopter to monitor gangs' movements before a clash at Wrexham's racecourse ground."

"Wrexham magistrates sat for five hours at a special court dealing with hooligans after trouble at the local derby at Wrexham. Twenty-three of those charged are from Chester."

"Chester thugs caused hundreds of pounds worth of damage after ripping seats out of Wrexham's Border stand and throwing them at the police."

"More than 50 rival fans clashed with pool cues in a vicious organised mass brawl."

"Thirty-four hooligans were arrested in clashes before during and after an FA Cup tie at Chester. Twelve were charged with affray after fans rampaged down Watergate Street."

"Chester fans disgraced the club after causing widespread damage to Wrexham's racecourse ground."

"Wrexham fans were arrested after an attack on Chester fans who had infiltrated the Wrexham Kop."

"Fighting fans spilled on to the pitch and caused the Charity game in aid of the Bradford fire disaster between Chester and Wrexham to be stopped after just 13 minutes."

"Police were forced to form a 'thin blue line' to keep Chester fans from attacking Wrexham rivals at the city's station."

"Ten Chester fans admitted affray after attempting to attack Wrexham fans."

Indeed, with the added England v Wales hostility, Chester v Wrexham is one of the most hostile derby games in football today.

A leading member of the Chester gang was honest in his assessment of today's mobs but keen to point out that for years it was just as one-sided in Chester's favour. "Give the Goats credit, they are well organised and have got decent numbers. We have no real leaders like they do and can only pull a fraction of their numbers. Wrexham is a massive town, a rundown shithole in the main, so it's no surprise they have hundreds of Chav rats following them. Years ago, when it was even numbers, mob against mob, they could not live with us, they didn't even show for some games, and when they came with 200 fans we chased them all over town and back to the Crossville bus depot. We went there in our hundreds, smashed up the ground, fucked the police off and generally ran amok.

"Since we went to Macc, many lads have not been seen and this is where they get the upper hand. They have the organisation and keep turning up and calling it on. It's stupid really. Chester is not Wrexham, it is a high-class tourist city and is policed that way. You kick off in town and you get jail, it is that simple. They can run around their town, tagged up and who cares, it is a shithole and is policed to suit. Fines and ASBOs, and community service when they don't pay their fines.

"Take their top lads, Esso and Lynx. Top lads at football don't do what they do, which is spend months in jail for petty crimes. All they have in their lives is robbing and their precious Frontline. They need to get lives, they are in the forties, for fuck's sake. Last year they came here and had about 100, including loads of checked hat kids. We had sixty. They went miles away and smashed a pub's windows to bring attention to themselves. Why? They have had results in Chester, like smashing up the Post Office Club in full view of the CCTV cameras. Our young lads called it on and were made to look foolish, but who's doing the jail? Some of our older lot fronted them a few weeks later as they were sick of them stopping off and taking the piss, but did they bounce out of the station and have it? No, they stayed behind the police and now our lads are doing jail for it."

He has a point. Chester is well policed and Wrexham do seem to be on a suicide mission when they hit town. Recently, 19 Oxford fans were dawn-raided for allegedly fighting in Chester city centre and more than 20 Tranmere fans suffered similarly after arriving in Chester for a pre-arranged meet with Wrexham. Those who were involved in the Post Office Club rampage and station stand-off all received custodial sentences, as the courts let it be known there would be no room for hooligans and tourists in the same city.

CHESTERFIELD

Ground: Recreation Ground, Saltergate
Firm: Chesterfield Bastard Squad
Rivals: Mansfield

Chesterfield has much in common with the South Yorkshire town of Barnsley. It is a small mining town, has a close-knit community and a football team that has won very little. Whilst Barnsley's claim to fame was an FA Cup win in 1912, Chesterfield's main honour is the Anglo-Scottish Cup, won in the early 1980s. Another thing the two clubs have in common are hooligan followers well known in the lower leagues.

Long before the days of tracksuits and casuals, the Miners' Strike and even the Anglo-Scottish Cup win, Chesterfield's fans had fought major battles at numerous football matches. During the 1970s, before organised firms got involved, many of the smaller towns were invaded and taken over by bigger clubs with huge travelling support.

Craig, a founder member of the so-called Chesterfield Bastard Squad, watched as his home town was over-run by more illustrious teams' hooligan armies. "The Aston Villa visit to our place in 1971 is not a fond memory," he recalled. "They brought shitloads with them as they were on a bit of a downer and going through the leagues. Their mentality was that they would probably never visit our place again, so they stormed the pitch, smashed everything up and only the brave in our ranks got a slap. The same thing happened with Brighton, who were a biggish team at the time and came second to Villa that year. Again, they took the piss and were probably more clued up than us, but it woke us up to what was happening. To this day we continue to have a good, unhealthy rivalry with Brighton. At the same time, Palace were on the up. Unlike Villa there weren't many of them but they were big fellas and they knocked people about for fun."

Another lad recalled, "In the Seventies, Villa, Palace and Brighton massacred us. The worst was perhaps when Villa came in August 1970, shortly after their relegation from the First Division. Another big takeover was Sheffield Wednesday in September 1975. They swamped us and took over most of the ground but, as far as I know, never actually took all of the Kop. It was a lesson to us all that we simply could not live with the bigger clubs at the time. There were some big blokes from town who would have a go at holding the lads on the Kop together, but some mobs came in their hundreds. Still, legends were made, and to this day the blokes who stood and fought for the club when we were kids are still well respected by us all."

Craig shares that respect. "Before we came on the scene there were people out there who gave us the inspiration to do what we did," he said. "They were proper misters, blokes who absolutely loved a good fight and loved our town. They were just known as the Barmy Army and are still around today and respected by all. They lost some and won some; remember, in those days no place was undoable. The biggest compliment to them came from Millwall's Harry the Dog in a documentary when he said that Chesterfield were the only team to have done Millwall at home."

Chesterfield played Bristol Rovers at home for the final game on consecutive seasons in 1972 and 1973. There was mass disorder in the first game but the second was a lot quieter, as Bristolian Chris Brown described in *Bovver*. "To everyone's regret, Chesterfield itself was a big disappointment. We took their Kop and it seemed that their lads had learnt their lesson from the previous year and gave us a wide berth."

Another game that saw surprisingly little trouble was Chesterfield's home game against Glasgow Rangers. Rangers had a terrible reputation when travelling south of the border, but despite bringing 7,500 down to Saltergate there was little trouble. It was the first game Craig went to on his own without an adult. "I shit myself," he remembered. "Hairy jocks were all over, pissed, and they had to shut most of the town down that day. It was a sight to see. We drew one-all and for the return leg only 200 Chesterfield fans went to Glasgow but we beat them three-one at Ibrox to qualify for the final of the Anglo Scottish Cup. We beat Notts County three-two on aggregate to take the cup, after that I was hooked."

The first casual mob to take Chesterfield were Portsmouth in the early 1980s. At the time the Chesterfield mob was called the Farm Inn Service Team (FIST) after the local pub the lads frequented in their under-age years. Young lads, however game, were no match for the infamous 6.57 Crew, who taught them that if they were to compete with the best, local rivalries had to be put aside.

Soon after, the Chesterfield Bastard Squad was born. "The Firm was born around 1982 to a bunch of bastards from an estate called Newbold," said Craig. "All the originals come from this estate and were dragged up together by our fine parents who, if nothing else, made us proud of where we came from. As we all went to the match from an early age, we were well known throughout the area and got a bit of a rep as the next sure thing. Because of our reputation the girls always wanted to be with us for the buzz, but lads being lads, we treated them as any other sixteen-year-olds would, a quick shag and on we go. These lovely girls regularly called us a right bunch of bastards and the name stuck, although at first we were called the Newbold Bastard Squad, as we were pretty tight-knit. As time went on the firm got bigger and it seemed natural to let others join us and we became known as the Chesterfield Bastard Squad.

"Before we move on, the girls who gave us this fine name deserve a mention. Without them we might have had a shit name like the Carrot Crew [Mansfield Town] or something. They named us the Bastard Squad but they were as bad as us and we named them the EWS – the Evil Women Squad – and to this day we still go out together and laugh about all the things we used to and still do. Our feeder group is the Young Bastard Squad, which speaks for itself. There is also a new breed who are going to be a bit special, the Sons of the Bastard Squad, or SBS."

Their key rivals, unsurprisingly, are nearby Mansfield and there has been trouble between the two dating back to the early Seventies. Virtually every game between them in the Eighties involved disorder. Four police horses were required to contain fighting during an Easter derby in April 1985 at Mansfield, when fans met on the pitch after the referee sent off the Mansfield skipper. More than £1,000 of damage was caused to the ground, 16 fans were arrested and several people taken to hospital.

At Chesterfield's home match against Mansfield, on New Year's Day, 1988, the Bastard Squad attempted to attack away fans at the end. Chanting, "CBS, CBS," a group of 50 were moved on by police from harassing rival fans and two were arrested. At the subsequent court case both men denied belonging to the CBS and claimed that they were provoked after Mansfield fans threw pies at them. The two clubs met at Saltergate later in the year and again there was trouble. "There were empty glasses and bottles flying past me from behind," said publican Harvey Hill. "The Chesterfield lads were lobbing them out at the Mansfield lot. I had to go back inside. There was glass all over the road, the traffic had stopped and someone's car windscreen had been smashed." After the game, the CBS ambushed the Mansfield escort with bricks and stones as it was coming down an escalator from The Pavements to the bus station.

Some Mansfield and Chesterfield lads had mutual respect but Craig is not one of them. "Mansfield! They may have had some minor results around the country but they always come unstuck with us. They think they had a result when they stormed our shopping centre but in reality they just pulled up in vans and attempted to get up the escalators but the blue rinse brigade held them off until we arrived. To be fair, it was a decent bit of stuff and about the only time they have shown any bottle.

"We arranged to meet them at Bolsover when we were travelling to a game at their place and they didn't show, so we went into their town and had a good booze but no-one was to be seen. We had three sides of the ground and took the piss all day. One of their boys had my number and was giving it loads on the phone, but when it came to a meet no-one was around.

"We were also in Manchester for the Greece game and were on Deansgate when a couple of our lads walking in front bumped into about twenty 'scabs' who decided to do a bit of bullying. When they saw the rest of us, even though they still outnumbered us, they scarpered back into the pub like something out of a Harold Lloyd film.

"Some of the hatred shown to them is just the normal football rivalry stuff we see between most local teams, however there is something else which makes this more hostile than most, the Miners' Strike. This is a massive issue between Derbyshire and those scabbing bastards from over there. A miner at the time, I was on strike with the rest of the country, living on strike pay and the goodwill of the people of Chesterfield. Even Yorkshire and the rest of the country was out so what do the jellyfish do? They carry on working. This split communities and

families and will never be forgotten. Mansfield, along with the rest of Nottingham, helped keep Maggie in power and the worker on his knees.

"To let you know what these people are really like, they came in a bus to one of our clubs, the Aquarius, and during the night there were various fights. But at the end, when they were back on the bus, they got their wage slips out and waved them at us. Needless to say, everyone went nuts but the bus only had a few dents as they fucked off. No-one should forget what these people did to us. But the effect it had on the CBS was good as it made us stronger. Not all of us were miners and those that were not looked after those that were. The old ashtray came out a few times so that we could still go to away games."

During the Eighties and Nineties there were several crucial end-of-season games in which smaller clubs misbehaved beyond their usual level. One of the worst incidents was the visit of Bolton on the final Saturday of the 1987 season. Shoppers fled for cover as 300 fans engaged in running battles through the town centre. Glasses, bottles and bricks were thrown and several people were injured, including police officers who were attempting to break up the fight. Several shoppers reported hearing Chesterfield fans chanting "CBS" like Zulu warriors. Six Chesterfield fans were subsequently imprisoned and eight others fined. The six were taken down to a standing ovation from 20 supporters in the public gallery.

Many of Chesterfield's last home games of the season have been against clubs fighting relegation and this has led to incidents from some unlikely quarters. In 1984, Northampton travelled to the Derbyshire town needing a win to stave off relegation. This was achieved but not without rival fans causing major disorder. Ten years later the same situation occurred and again hundreds clashed.

"We needed results to go in our favour to stop us getting relegated to the Conference," recalled a Northampton lad. "We got beat four-nil but stayed up courtesy of other results. It went off as soon as we got there, outside a hotel up the hill near the station. We did the Chesterfield lot due to the fact we had far greater numbers, but the CBS were a very game bunch. They got it together and had a go despite us having a good 200, and there were little offs all the way to the ground."

Just before half-time, some Northampton came onto the pitch and raced over to the beckoning home fans. The entire away mob of 200 were soon fighting with the CBS and it lasted for five to ten minutes, largely because there were few police in the ground. Even the corner flags were being brandished as weapons. Play was suspended and there were 27 arrests. "Afterwards we marched back to the station and just took liberties all the way," said the Northampton lad. "But even though we had very large numbers we all said fair play for them coming time and time again and attacking the escort with a small but very game lot."

Craig has similar respect for Northampton. "We always had it with them and the only reason I can think of is they are up for it all the time. We have been there three times and had it every time. Once, we went in their stand and got sussed in their bogs as I was wearing some Cerruti bottoms and I don't think any of them had seen or heard of them at the time. So we were followed outside and at least twenty of them came bowling after me, my brother and a handful of others. We hopped it to the nearest fence, ripped it down and proceeded to thrash them with what turned out to be balsa wood. They soon got wind and got into us and we had to do one. They came to our place in the late Eighties and were in our main pub, swinging off the lights and climbing all over the place until we showed up and had a good row with them. In the end, we took our pub back and off they went."

In 1990, Grimsby came to Chesterfield having secured promotion to the Third Division, while Chesterfield needed the points to reach the play-offs. The match was interrupted for 13 minutes as rival fans clashed in the away end. The home side eventually won and the final whistle signalled a Grimsby pitch invasion during which their mob climbed over the fence at the home end to get at the CBS. There was more fighting outside the ground.

"Chesterfield had a small mob, headed by a black lad who was pretty game," recalled one of the Grimsby mob. "They were run numerous times and then, at about six o'clock, we were down to about fifty lads outside a boozer and the black lad turned up again. We thought he had come for another go but he hadn't, he was alone and wanted to tell us how much he respected our showing that day. He

was not touched by us and we ended up inviting him to join us for a pre-arranged fight on the way home in Scunthorpe."

Handing out restriction and exclusion orders to eight fans arrested, chairman of the magistrates Betty Dunn said of the day's events, "Chesterfield was not fit for normal citizens to live in." It was the first time any fans had been ordered to register at police stations at certain times, including during the World Cup. The exclusion orders banned them from every English and Welsh football ground. A total of 30 people were arrested and a further 29 ejected.

Grimsby are another firm Craig rates. "We used to love that place when we had to get off the train in the middle of a council estate. It was stupid really because that's when football specials were still running so they had no chance with 500 or more piling off the train. In the ground we had to share a Kop with them, with a fence in the middle and fishing net on the top to stop missiles. One year, they came in force, a couple of hundred strong and ran around all day with not much opposition. When we did get some together it was like the Wild West outside our famous Spire but they did us through numbers and having good lads."

Having beaten Grimsby, Chesterfield reached the play-offs, where they met Stockport County. After the events at the Grimsby match, a number of extra measures were put into place to limit disorder, including a noon kick-off, an all-ticket match, a request to licensees to shut their doors at 1.30 p.m., and the reinstallation of perimeter fencing, which had been removed at the beginning of the season in the wake of the Hillsborough Disaster. Explaining the decision, Chief Supt John Pearson said, "Pitch invasions were being attempted throughout the match by Grimsby fans and officers had to form a scrum in a vain effort to keep them out."

Yet there was still trouble at the two matches. "They are definitely one of the better outfits in my book, at least in the lower leagues," said a Stockport fan. "I nearly got lynched in 1984 by a firm of skins after a game where their keeper scored. We went for the play-offs with one of the best firms we've ever turned out but the twelve o'clock kick off fucked us up and we didn't even get a drink in Chesterfield. We were wrapped up even when we came out at half-time. They brought a top squad for the game at Edgeley of around 150. They had come in 1984 during their promotion season, and there was mither all day. Our lot went in the away end and fifty or so got ejected. There was loads of toe-to-toe fighting outside the ground and in the town centre."

Chesterfield failed to get promoted in 1990 and the two teams met again the following season. The fixture had become a bit of a grudge match and Stockport travelled in numbers to the County Hotel, where they were told that Chesterfield would meet them. "We waited and eventually in they came but we smashed them and ran them out of the pub," recalled the Stockport lad. "Little has happened between the two sides since but we have the utmost respect for them."

Another team who had a number of run-ins with Chesterfield was Fulham, and one Londoner can remember at least three occasions when trouble broke out. "The first was in the Eighties at Saltergate when it went off in the town centre after the game," he said. "A Fulham lad got a broken arm and leg and it was generally toe-to-toe for ages but Chesterfield got the better of it all. The second incident was again in the Eighties, but this time at the Cottage. It was a top of table clash we won one-nil. Chesterfield brought a monster mob, some Fulham had a pop in the away end and were chased out. Afterwards there was a massive off on Putney Bridge with running battles down Fulham High Street. About six years ago, seventy Fulham and a similar numbers of Chesterfield battled outside a hotel fairly equally until the Old Bill came along and led us to the train."

In the mid-Eighties, the CBS hit the headlines for violence with Coventry, who they weren't even playing. Hundreds of Sky Blues fans, many attached to the Coventry firm the Legion, stopped off in Chesterfield after an FA Cup tie at Sheffield Wednesday. Before long, the town erupted. The local paper reported that, at its height, more than 500 people were fighting and it took police more than two hours to bring them under control. At a special court the next day, nine men were jailed and seven fined more than £2,000 for their involvement.

"Coventry stopped off after being at Wednesday for a booze and an easy ride, which they had for about an hour due to the numbers they had," recalled Craig. "A few of our lads weathered the storm but got a bit of a kicking for it until news

spread around town and then everybody came together. Football lads, normal lads, blokes out with the wife, all the bouncers and even the local Hell's Angels who were in town, all came together and stormed into them in the big car park in the middle of town. It was absolute madness, one of the worst scenes I have ever seen. Some people that day got proper hurt and most were from Coventry. It went on for about two hours and even the OB got stuck into them, which was amazing as they usually batter us. To this day I have never seen people from our town stick together so much. We are usually at each other's throats for one reason or another, but that day was different and shows what can be done when daft local grudges are put aside."

In 1997, Chesterfield nearly made the big time. "We stormed through to the FA cup semi-finals in 1997, beating Bristol, Bolton and Forest on the way," said Craig. "There were good kick-offs in all of these, especially Forest, as they had a bit of a free run in the day due to the Old Bill taking most of our front line away on prevention charges. Just before the game ended with a one-nil victory for us we saw them all filing out, so off we went to greet them. As we forced the gates open we were greeted by a good 150 of them and both sides proceeded to have a really good go of it for about ten minutes. It was one of the longest free-for-alls that lads from either side could remember. In the end we did them and they will admit it, and it was even better as Mansfield had teamed up with them, so they got a slap as well."

Chesterfield played Middlesbrough in the semi and came within a dreadful refereeing decision from making the FA Cup Final, as David Elleray failed to see a shot clearly go over the line which would have probably given the underdogs a place at Wembley. Off the pitch the game passed off peacefully. "Neither us nor Boro had much in the way of firms out that day," said Craig. "It was a massive game for us, one you just don't get following the likes of Chesterfield. Most of our lot took sons or daughters with them, and Boro were the same from what I saw. It was one of the best games I have ever seen, 22,000 in blue and white going nuts, getting cheated and a home boy scoring in the last minute of extra time to make it three-all and force a replay. You could not make up days like that. Sadly, we lost the replay three-nil. We've had a few run-ins with

A group of Chesterfield lads enjoying a drink on an away trip.

Boro when they were in our league and in the cup a few years ago, everyone will agree they have got a hell of a firm on their day."

Another memorable Cup classic was at Anfield. "We had drawn Liverpool in the League Cup and off to Anfield it was to have a go at Souness [then Liverpool's manager] and his boys and, fuck me, we are only three-nil up before half-time," said Craig. "In the second half we went four-one up and were seriously going mad. I got coshed for daring to go on their hallowed pitch but they eventually brought it back to four-all at the end. At the time we were the first team ever to score four at Anfield (Southampton have done it since) and the scallies came for a nosey at the end but the numbers and adrenalin buzz sent them back up Annie Road sharpish, as we went nuts.

"In the second leg they came in numbers, all walking about like they owned the place and many of them came unstuck, although they were not what we had expected and brought very few lads. As a firm they were poor."

An NCIS report on the visit of Mansfield in 2000 stated, "A group of Mansfield supporters was joined by a large number of Nottingham Forest supporters. Chesterfield had a number of Derby and Leicester supporters within their group. The Chesterfield supporters, numbering in excess of 300, gathered at local public houses. The Mansfield supporters smashed windows in a local pub after they were refused entry. There were a number of small incidents reported in various pubs prior to the fixture involving Mansfield supporters.

"At about 2.15pm a group of 100 Mansfield and

Nottingham Forest supporters began to make their way to the ground. They were attacked by a group of Chesterfield supporters with stones and sticks. Police attended and order was restored. As the group of Mansfield supporters were being walked to the away end of the ground, a group of around 400 Chesterfield supporters confronted them. Police with batons drawn managed to keep the rival groups apart. The Chesterfield supporters were escorted to their end of the ground. Shortly before kick-off another group of Mansfield and Nottingham Forest supporters were escorted to the ground. This group of supporters confronted a group of approximately 200 Chesterfield supporters. Police were vastly outnumbered and had to use batons both to protect themselves and to prevent both groups causing a major public order problem. Eventually the Mansfield Group was escorted into the away end.

"During the match, both sets of supporters were shouting and baiting each other but when Chesterfield scored their fourth goal, 150 Mansfield supporters left the ground and made their way to the home end. On seeing this, the Chesterfield supporters left the Kop and ran to meet the Mansfield supporters. The Chesterfield supporters forced a large double gate open and a confrontation took place between the two groups. Police at the scene struggled to keep the groups apart until reinforcements arrived. The Chesterfield supporters were then forced back into the ground and the gates were shut whilst the Mansfield supporters were escorted away from the ground."

The following month, CBS confronted a mob of 100 Brighton fans during a top of the table clash. The groups threw missiles, including bottles and glasses, at each other, and it took the intervention of the police to restore calm. Brighton threw missiles at the referee and the linesman after Chesterfield's winning goal in injury time. There was further trouble in Chesterfield town centre after the match and ten people were arrested.

Seven days later, Chesterfield braced themselves for the visit of Cardiff City. Expectation grew in the days leading up to the game after the local paper reported on threats made on the Internet by both sets of hooligans. The police were relaxed about the fixture ahead of the match, claiming intelligence suggested only 800-1,000 fans were travelling up from Wales as opposed to the 2,200 Brighton fans who had arrived the previous week, and promised additional resources to prevent any disorder.

The police's best endeavours could not prevent trouble as rival groups clashed in a town centre pub after a group of 50 Soul Crew members were dropped off nearby. There was further trouble inside the ground, which surprisingly, had been made police-free. A hundred Cardiff fans forced their way into the sterile area between the two sets of supporters and threw missiles at their rivals. Police were forced to come into the ground and, with batons drawn, cleared the sterile area.

The following season, there was a far bigger clash between Chesterfield and Cardiff, with fighting before and after the Easter match. "We were under siege and reduced to giving out bandages and plasters to people with injuries," said the general manager of an Ibis hotel after fans clashed outside. "Window frames were ripped out and debris was strewn all over the car park. Visitors and wedding guests have gone away with a very bad impression of Chesterfield." The 140 police on duty, backed up by a Derbyshire force helicopter, fought to contain over 500 rival fans who clashed repeatedly throughout the day. Four CBS members were later jailed for taking part. Chief Insp Debbie Platt said, "We are experiencing an increase in football hooliganism in Chesterfield from both home and away supporters. Both sets of fans wanted to have a go at each other but due to police intelligence and tactics we were able to keep them apart from start to finish."

Sixteen people were arrested on the day but police promised to identify more through CCTV. The local paper, meanwhile, offered to name and shame offenders. Craig refused to give the Welshmen any credit for their efforts. "They got a shock that day. They brought a right team of lads for the pisstake but didn't realise that the CBS, YBS, SBS and anybody else that could walk was waiting for them in the pubs, on the street, everywhere. They gave a good account but were simply put in their place.

"Not long after that game I met a kid in Blackpool, who was asking how many lads we could get out. I told him fifty to 150, whatever the occasion, and he replied that Cardiff have 3-400. My response was, 'Yes mate, I know, but there's only two fucking teams in Wales, there are ninety-two in Blighty, and I would rather have 150 lads I can count on, not 400 of which two-thirds are clowns, living on a reputation built over the years by people who have long since called it a day.'"

Next up for Chesterfield was Hull City, and the two teams met at Saltergate in November. A hundred Hull arrived early and a brief clash in a pub left the windows smashed. Inside the ground the rival mobs baited each other until both invaded the pitch and fought. Play was held up for five minutes and the deployment of extra police and stewards contained the situation for the rest of the game.

Staff at NCIS were kept busy logging Chesterfield's season. Their return fixture at Mansfield in February 2001 featured another large police operation. The NCIS report noted, "At this game, Mansfield were supported by Nottingham Forest fans and Chesterfield by Leicester fans. The Chesterfield supporters gathered in a nightclub that had opened that morning purely for the Chesterfield fans. By 2pm the nightclub had approximately 600 inside. In a public house across the road were 300 Mansfield supporters.

"As the Chesterfield supporters were being escorted from the nightclub by a strong line of police, there were a number of confrontations outside the above pub. Attempts were made by Mansfield supporters to get at the Chesterfield group, but again they were held back. Following the game, when the Chesterfield supporters boarded coaches, a group of Mansfield supporters passed and both sets of fans began throwing cones, stones and bottles at each other and the police. A large police presence restored order. A number of Mansfield supporters then ran towards the bus station area where the Chesterfield supporters were waiting for a bus home. There were a number of fights between the two groups which resulted in arrests being made."

It was a top against bottom when Chesterfield hosted Lincoln City late in the season. The Derbyshire club were in third place while the visitors were only a point off last place. Shortly before kick-off, 15 Lincoln were confronted by 20 Chesterfield and in a brief fight one Lincoln fan suffered a broken nose. At the end of the match a group of 50 Lincoln went in search of the CBS but were rounded up by the police and taken to the train station. En route they were confronted by a smaller group of Chesterfield, including several who were serving

banning orders. They were soon joined by another 60 Chesterfield but police were able to keep the factions apart long enough to clear the area.

Chesterfield lost the game 2–1 but still went away to Hull in third place. Their hosts, meanwhile, had got into a play-off spot, so there was everything to play for when the teams met on the last Saturday in April. Hull's mob attacked Chesterfield at the away turnstiles and in the process collapsed the segregation fence. It took the deployment of horses and dogs to restore order. Police used CS gas and 15 people were arrested. Fears of trouble after the game diminished with a heavy downpour of rain. Chesterfield lost again but a final day victory against Halifax secured promotion, which was all the more impressive as the club had been penalised nine points for financial irregularities.

Reading was another club to come unstuck at Chesterfield in more recent years. One Berkshire lad recalled, "We went up in 2002 and had about fifty in the Golden Fleece from 11 a.m. We left to go to the ground and it went off briefly just around the corner from the pub and Chesterfield had the better of it. I ended up lobbing a sign and getting it thrown back at me before taking a bit of a kicking. They also stole some caps and one of our lads' phones."

It took a huge police operation to prevent trouble at Chesterfield's home game with Mansfield in January 2003. "We had gained a lot of intelligence about pre-planned clashes," claimed Chesterfield's football liaison officer, Graham Lamin. "By managing to find out where they were, we stopped the groups getting together." More than 100 officers were drafted in for the match and the force helicopter was again used to monitor fan movements.

Mansfield aside, the Sheffield clubs also feature high on the CBS hate list. "The only relationship we have with the Sheffield clubs is to fight with them every time we meet," said Craig. "Wednesday are the ones most lads like to have a pop at as we have played them so many times. In the Seventies and Eighties it was probably evens, but over the last decade or so they haven't even shown at home, never mind away.

"United are better and if I didn't hate Mansfield so much this would be the one for me. They reckon they have the best of everything in that city, the team, the women, the beer, and if you believe them even the sun shines in Sheffield every day. The truth is, they have won fuck-all and probably never will. Saying that, they have a top firm and there's no getting away from that."

In recent years Chesterfield have formed friendships with Derby, Manchester City and Leicester. Many of these have been developed over the years following England. Talk of alliances has been played down by both Derby and Leicester, but one NCIS document reports, "During one local derby with Mansfield, Chesterfield's mob was boosted by sizeable numbers of Derby and Man City. Mansfield, meanwhile, had a good 60 Forest with them. This is probably less to do with bigger firms holding the hands of smaller firms and more to do with the modern state of hooliganism and the increasingly limited chances of an altercation. Derby came through in numbers because they had heard Forest were doing likewise and it was an opportunity to become involved in general disorder."

Craig accepted that a friendship exists with Manchester City lads. "Links with City have been around for a long time, as quite a few lads from town have been big fans over the years and a few still go to many games. I would rather they stayed local, but at least they are not glory hunting with the likes of United and Liverpool."

Derby resent the common perception about their link with Chesterfield. "I'd hardly call them rent-a-mob," one Derby lad told us. "We've only been to a few games, really. There's always a load of Mansfield with the Red Dogs [Forest] and no fucker says owt about that. There have only ever been four or five Derby go up to Chesterfield and that's because we're from a town as near to Chesterfield as Derby, and ties with the old Brampton lot, who don't even go that much any more. I know they've got ties with some Leicester and Man City, but again they hardly bring an army with them because it'd go off with each other if they did. Apart from the odd Youth scrotes, and you get the same anywhere, Chesterfield are a decent lot on their day."

Derbyshire Police have cracked down on Chesterfield's hooligans in recent years. At the time of the 2002 World Cup, 13 were banned. By the 2004 European Championships, this figure had risen to 39. Despite the bans and police attention, Craig, however, is quick to claim that hooliganism in Chesterfield is not dead. "Chesterfield is a good

stop-off town, as it is on the main line to Yorkshire and the Midlands for many firms, and we can pull 100 with ease if the opposition comes announced. We have a tasty load of young lads coming through, all under twenty-five, who don't really care about the police or other firms' so-called reputations. We took 250 lads to QPR and every football lad in London sat up and took notice of us. We got to QPR and it was like, 'Facking hell where have you pulled that lot from?'"

COLCHESTER UNITED

Ground: Layer Road
Firm: Colchester Riot Squad, Barsiders
Rivals: Wycombe, Southend
Police operations: Euston

A military town, Colchester is not unused to drunken squaddies brawling with each other and the locals. There have even been instances of other mobs travelling to Colchester on their way back from Ipswich to have a go at the soldiers, and in 1979 a Stoke City fan was killed there after a brawl in a pub ended up with the landlord blasting him with a shotgun.

The Times reported that Colchester United had been warned about the behaviour of their own fans as far back as 1967. In the Seventies, Colchester hosted several matches against south-east London clubs Crystal Palace and Millwall, which were magnets for trouble. The worst reported incident was during the 1980/81 season, when Millwall thugs ran amok in the town. Eighteen were arrested and extra police were drafted in to cope with running street battles. Millwall also attacked the Wagon and Horses pub on North Hill, The Bay and Say, the Marquis and the George Hotel, before being chased by police to the ground. "At one stage there were more people watching the fighting around the town than there were at the football match," said a senior police officer.

Things have quietened down with London clubs, though there have been sporadic incidents since. Surprisingly, there has been little hostility over the years with nearby Leyton Orient. "My only recollection of their place was in the early Eighties when a group of Orient followed Colchester back to Liverpool Street and got battered," recalled one Colchester lad. "About ten years ago Colchester gave it the big one outside a pub on the way back to the station and steamed a few blokes, but then it started getting on top. Three lads were left to get done, including one who was a guest of ours and who got his face carved open."

At this time the local *Evening Gazette* also reported clashes with Barnsley, when fighting on the terraces caused the game to be held up for three minutes, and against Reading, when Colchester fans attacked the 50-strong away mob during the game. One disgruntled fan, a Mr Threeman, was quoted in the local paper saying, "This is all getting very annoying, while watching the fighting a lot of us missed the third goal."

Colchester's main rivals during this period were fellow Essex club Southend. "The rivalry goes back to the Seventies when I first started going to foot-ball," remembered the Colchester lad. "They always bring loads to us, but they hate us more than we do them. In the mid-to-late Seventies they had the edge, but during the latter part of that decade and the early Eighties, it was us. The first time that comes to mind was 1978, when 70 lads went down on a coach for a Friday night game. The trip became too lively for the driver who promptly fucked off and left them there. Southend were nowhere to be seen that night and a lot of lads had to walk the 20 miles to Chelmsford.

"We played them in the FA Cup in 1982 and there was fighting all through the match. The replay is where a lot of the hatred comes from. One of their main lads got slashed down his back and ammonia was sprayed into the wound. The rest of the time, Southend have had the best of it. We were in differ-ent divisions for fifteen years but in the last couple of years we have played them four times, three in the LDV Trophy and one a friendly. Let's say Southend have been the more aggressive."

In 1981, the visit of Sheffield United saw fighting spill from the terraces onto the pitch. Embarrassingly for the club, BBC *Grandstand* cameras were present and the country watched the events unfold. Away from the cameras, the streets around the ground were turned into battlefields as rival mobs clashed before the home side's five-two victory. Dozens of football hooligans and skinheads brandishing knives

and broken bottles terrorised afternoon shoppers at the town's Saturday market.

"All hell was let loose," said 70-year-old Mrs Kitty Wilmott, the Colchester market traders' liaison officer. "There were Colchester skinheads, Sheffield hooligans and soldiers involved in a 200-man brawl. One man had a hand rake which he was tearing down people's faces, and another had a big iron horseshoe attached to a chain, which looked very dangerous." Surprisingly, no arrests were made and a police spokesman said, "Saturday afternoon was busy and hectic but we got it all sorted out."

The FA Cup has been the scene of many of Colchester's fiercest battles. In the mid-Eighties they were drawn away at Bishops Stortford, and one lad later gave the following account: "Bishops Stortford away in the FA Cup was blinding. I remember turning up in their town on a Colchester double-decker bus. We had a motorcycle Old Bill escort and were waiting at some traffic lights when someone pressed the emergency exit button and about seventy of us steamed out into the streets. Old Bill put us in the George pub where we all had a drink till they decided to escort us to the ground. As we were walking along, someone gave the shout and we all steamed to their pub. As people were trying to get in they were trying to get out of the side where they were met by Colchester. At the game there were a few scuffles and people were getting chucked out only to jump over the stream and re-enter the ground. A shop was looted and leather jackets were going pretty cheap over the next couple of weeks."

The local newspaper took a less approving view of the events and designated the louts the "Scum of East Anglia". Its report went on, "Colchester fans were today branded as 'scum' after running riot through a town centre, leaving a trail of destruction behind them. The game was held up for two minutes after fighting broke out and nine people were arrested, all of them from Colchester." A police inspector told the paper, "They were charging around town and raided a leather shop, stealing over £2,500 worth of goods and staff were assaulted. They damaged pubs, motor vehicles, a bank window and a number of officers were assaulted. They are not supporters they are scum." The events of this day led to the formation of the Colchester Riot Squad.

Other big FA Cup ties included Exeter away, again

in the 1980s, when Colchester descended on the Devon town in numbers. Dozens of Colchester fans also invaded the pitch at a cup tie against Yeading. But the infamous Portsmouth hooligans caused the worst problems when their team lost 3–0 at Colchester in a tie during the 1982/83 season and they invaded the pitch. Home chairman, Jack Rippingale, was forced to arrange an "urgent" meeting with police, regarding their failure to control the 200 Pompey fans who were said to be "in an ugly mood".

Colchester's Army connections occasionally attracted hooligans who felt reasonably assured of a punch-up. Travelling supporters would often hang around the pubs after matches in the expectation of clashing with locals or squaddies. As already mentioned, in September 1979, a vanload of Stoke City decided to stop off in the town for a pub crawl on their way home from a game in Ipswich, partly to see friends in the Staffordshire Regiment, which was garrisoned in the town. At 9.30 p.m. the rowdy group of up to 20 Stoke fans entered the packed Robin Hood pub in the town centre. It was later alleged in court that they were chanting Stoke football songs and threatening locals. The landlord, Terry Calder, was not prepared to put up with any trouble and reached under the bar for his shotgun. As he tried to fire a warning shot into the air he stumbled and accidentally shot 29-year-old Brian "Coddy" Hughes in the back. The Stoke fan died. Calder was initially charged with murder but eventually convicted of involuntary manslaughter.

In a strange summing up, the judge obviously accepted that the incident was an accident but put it down to the landlord's inexperience with firearms. "You were wholly inexperienced with that shotgun and I accept that you did not have the experience necessary to understand what a truly lethal weapon it was," the judge said. It would have been interesting to see if he was as broadminded had it been a hooligan who had fired the fatal shot.

In 1985, Wycombe emerged as Colchester's new rivals. The teams met in the FA Cup and Colchester's mob received a kicking. The rivalry intensified when the clubs faced each other in the Conference in the 1991/2 season, with Colchester pipping their rivals to the title and consequent promotion. Wycombe were especially pissed off because Colchester won their home encounter by a highly disputed late goal.

An opportunity to avenge the 1985 beating came

in 1999 when more than 100 Colchester travelled to Wycombe for yet another vital game, this time with the Buckinghamshire side languishing in the relegation zone. "They got collared by Thames Valley's finest and locked in a pub before the game," said the Colchester lad. "Not much happened really but there were six arrests. The only flashpoint was afterwards when Colchester were locked in the ground, kicked the gates down and had a little skirmish with the Robocops. Colchester's claim to fame with Wycombe is they have had more fans nicked at Wycombe than anyone else."

Not all days out have gone according to plan. In 1992 Colchester attacked a pub-load of blokes but, rather than a rival mob, as Colchester obviously thought, the group was a touring cricket team from Sussex.

Ipswich should be fierce rivals, given their close proximity, but Colchester United have never attained a high enough league status to meet them. Matches between the two have been restricted to pre-season friendlies and, in the late Seventies, encounters in the short-lived Willhire Cup. The pre-season competition lasted for only three years before it was halted because of continual violence between spectators. Each year there was trouble between Colchester and Ipswich and during the pre-season opener in 1979, the game was held up when fighting fans spilled on to the playing surface. At the last meeting, at Portman Road, someone even set a toilet alight during rioting.

The Colchester Riot Squad was later replaced by the Barsiders, named after the bar the lads gathered at inside their favourite stand. They have continued to be active. In February 2004, Colchester played Southend in a two-legged semi-final of the LDV Vans Trophy. A police operation involving 100 officers was implemented after the rival mobs posted threats on various hooligan websites. Several postings talked of settling "old scores", while others described the game as a chance for a "big dance". The police preparations proved successful and there were only four arrests, all for minor incidents. A similar operation for the return leg, at Southend, again saw the game pass off peacefully despite police intelligence indicating that troublemakers were hoping to arrange a fight.

Thanks to the excellent intelligence, the police have taken a pro-active approach towards hooliganism at Colchester in recent years and a number of men have been imprisoned and banned from matches, including 15 banned for life by the club itself. At the time of England's crucial World Cup qualifier against Turkey in April 2003, Colchester had more fans banned than other any club in the area, and this increased in the run-up to the 2004 European Championships. In early 2005, nine Colchester fans were arrested at Euston Station after allegedly being involved in a fight on their way back from Milton Keynes.

COVENTRY CITY

Ground: The Ricoh Arena, formerly Highfield Road
Firm: The Legion
Rivals: Leicester City, Aston Villa
Police operations: Rama, Edit and Freetime

"Coventry are fuck all. They've got a shit team and shit support. Hitler had the right idea when he flattened the place. The only good thing to come out of Coventry was The Specials and that was ten years ago." With that short opening declaration, novelist John King dismissed Coventry City football firm in his best-selling *The Football Factory*. Other, non-fiction hooligan authors have been equally scathing.

Yet they are overly dismissive of a hooligan crew that, although not the biggest or fiercest of mobs, has seen its share of action over the years. Indeed, between 1999 and 2001, Coventry fans were involved in some of the most intense disorder anywhere in the country. So active were The Legion that West Midlands Police ran three operations against them simultaneously.

Coventry, a city noted for car manufacturing, is a blue collar city with many tough housing estates – in the early Eighties some elements of the media labelled it Britain's most violent city – and hooliganism has been a feature since the late Sixties, when local magistrates called for greater powers to deal with the unruly element among the club's fans. In the 1970s, many Coventrians were among the 40 arrested at a Midlands derby against Wolves, one of the largest tallies of arrests for a single game at that time. Matches against Wolves, Aston Villa and, especially, Leicester almost always saw disorder.

The visit of Chelsea in 1970 was described as the worst violence the city had ever experienced. At least 1,000 Chelsea fans ran riot after the game, and in one incident four police officers had to fight their way out of a mob of 500 fans who punched and kicked them. Windows were smashed in a trail of destruction that ran from the ground to the railway station. "It was disgusting," commented Superintendent Gerald Whittaker. "These fans were just like animals. We are fed up with this in Coventry."

"Soccer savagery," ran the front-page headline of the *Coventry Evening Telegraph* in early January 1973, following a home visit from Leicester. "About 600 fans rampaged through the streets surrounding Highfield Road after the match, throwing bottles and bricks and smashing windows as they went. A young Coventry fan had an emergency operation for a stab wound which pierced his liver. A 16-year-old Leicester girl was treated for a neck wound after she was hit by a flying missile."

A police operation involving 150 officers failed to prevent trouble inside and outside the stadium, though they were to later claim that the disorder would have been far worse if the fans had not been segregated within the ground. This segregation was in itself a consequence of previous disorder. One 17-year-old was convicted of using threatening and insulting behaviour for chanting, "Kill the coppers." Asked in court about his behaviour, the youth replied, "I just don't like coppers." The judge was not impressed and told him, "In different circumstances you could well need their help."

Residents were furious at the damage the supporters caused and the fear they instilled. The local MP, William Wilson, called for a meeting between residents, the police and the club, and went on to describe his attempts to buy a paper after the match. "I had to knock at the door so the owner could see who it was as the windows were boarded up. It was like a New York speakeasy."

Under intense pressure, the club and the city council knew they had to act. A few days later a campaign was launched to rid Coventry of soccer violence and vandalism. A meeting headed by the Lord Mayor and Coventry's manager and attended by the police, local residents and shopkeepers, drew up measures they believed would alleviate the problem. These included dropping visiting fans close to the ground by opening up a disused train siding near Highfield Road, the removal of potential missiles from the area, and stronger efforts by the police to identify the ringleaders. The Coventry boss identified most of the hooligans as being aged between 14 and 16 and he urged parents to come to the ground to take their children home. Another move to combat the problem was to photograph hooligans and circulate the pictures to other parts of the country where Coventry were due to play.

The local paper suggested much stiffer penalties were needed. "The city is entitled to expect a much tougher attitude by the magistrates," it said. "They should make it clear that soccer hooliganism will no longer be looked on as youthful high spirits but will always be treated as serious and offenders will be dealt with on that basis. The only really effective way to prevent a repetition of last Saturday's incidents is by stopping it at source. Indications elsewhere are that this will happen when troublemakers are deterred by the prospects of the risks they face." In a further move to reassure residents, the police promised to have an extra 50 officers on duty for home games.

A fortnight later, the new anti-hooligan measures were given their first test with the visit of the dreaded Manchester United. Thousands of fans began arriving as early as six in the morning. Despite there being more than 200 officers on duty, there was widespread damage to cars, shops and houses and 32 arrests were made. Fourteen of those arrested were under 17. While most were given bail, one 15-year-old was remanded in custody after his father refused to stand bail, saying his boy was beyond his control. During the match, the police had to contend with United fans climbing the floodlight pylons and fighting between rival fans in the home end. Three-quarters of those arrested were Man United fans, though none came from Manchester. The front line of the infamous Red Army, pictured in the following Monday's *Coventry Evening Telegraph*, looked like a school outing, with none of the youthful fans reaching even the shoulder of the police sergeant at the front of the escort.

Small outbreaks of disorder continued during the rest of the season and the police announced further measures to combat hooliganism, included videoing supporters to identify the hooligans within their ranks as they left the railway station and coach park. The problem was, as they undoubtedly discovered, you had to know who you were looking for, which was especially difficult when dealing with away supporters.

Coventry had a secret weapon in the fight against hooliganism in the shape of their club chairman, Jimmy Hill. The outspoken former footballer turned pundit made it a personal crusade not only to rid his club of soccer violence but also to give a lead to the rest of the country. In September 1980, he announced that his club was considering a system of registering all fans. He also decided to make his stadium all-seater, which he believed would turn the ground into a family-orientated arena and reduce the likelihood of hooliganism. The plans were unveiled less than 48 hours after England fans rioted in Switzerland in June 1981.

"The new beginning for the game in this country starts here today in Coventry," Hill proudly announced. "Football hit an all-time low on Saturday – on and off the field. And people have never been quite as depressed about things as they are now. But then suddenly I thought that the new beginning for the game can start in Coventry. The whole idea of all-seating is to rid the game of the hooligan element, and even the critics will surely see the justification of what we are doing after last Saturday. The tide has swung in favour of what we are doing, and this could be a pattern other clubs will do well to follow."

Hill received the immediate support of FA Secretary Ted Croker. "It is the only way, and I have been pushing for this for years. So I am thrilled to bits that Coventry are going ahead and bringing their ground into the 1980s instead of living with the relic of the Industrial Revolution. Football has to face realities instead of having its head in the clouds. I want to see hooligans out, and perhaps the rebirth of football in this country could have started by what happened in Basle on Saturday night and what Coventry are doing now."

For the plans to work there had to be full cooperation from the fans. This was certainly not apparent when Leeds United visited early in the new season. Leeds hooligans had long decided that seats were preferable to terraces, particularly when ripped out and used as missiles. Fighting inside the ground and the breaking of dozens of seats marred the Division One game. Magistrates came down very heavily on those up on charges, handing out fines of £500 for threatening behaviour and vandalism. Presiding magistrate Ron Ferrans warned that fighting would not be tolerated. "Coventry City have made great efforts to see that the ground is trouble free," he said. "Away fans must note that we are determined to protect the good name of the city."

The local paper urged even greater efforts by the club to rid itself of hooliganism. "Without barriers rival factions cannot be kept apart, or this can only be achieved with difficulty. There is nothing to prevent spectators running on to the pitch. So what is the answer?" It advocated refusing to sell tickets to visiting fans on match days.

Back on the news pages, though, nothing changed. "Brawling fans made a mockery of Coventry's claims that their Highfield Road ground has been hooligan-proof since it was made all-seater," reported one newspaper after Coventry's 4–0 FA Cup win over Oxford United in February 1982. "Police threw out several fighting fans during first half clashes, but trouble came to a head with about 15 minutes left. Officers moved into the 20,000 crowd to separate fighting fans but became swallowed up in a brawl involving about 100 supporters. In the end, a sudden rainfall halted the troubles."

TC, who spent many years running with the Legion, Coventry's hooligan firm, remembers Jimmy Hill as an innovative chairman. "Some of his ideas, like the Sky Blue Special, the first special train for supporters, were brilliant, but his idea to make the stadium an all-seated one in the early Eighties seemed at the time to backfire. Now, when you look at the way all Premiership and Championship stadiums are all-seater, again you have to say the man had a good vision. When Highfield Road went all seated in 1981, the capacity was reduced from 36,500 to 20,600. As well as the seats being introduced, the fencing around the ground was also removed. Jimmy Hill then came out with this classic statement at the time. 'It's harder to be a hooligan sitting down than it is standing up.'

"It was extremely naïve, as was proven over the next couple of years when pitch invasions became a regular occurrence and incidents inside the ground happened quite often. After the Leicester trouble and a couple of other incidents, the fencing was reinstalled on to three sides of the ground and, after more violence where Leeds and Manchester City fans both used seats as missiles, the seats in the Kop end were removed in 1985 and the terracing brought back. It takes more than some new seats to stop hooliganism. CCTV, better policing, better stewarding and improved segregation all contribute to fewer incidents inside football grounds, but Jimmy Hill wasn't too far away from achieving that."

In March 1984, it was the turn of Birmingham's Zulus to rip out the seats and fight on the pitch. Forty people were arrested. Six months later, Coventry played bitter local rivals Leicester City. Modern-day hooliganism was at its peak and the Leicester Baby Squad came looking for trouble. They were intent on getting into the West Stand, home of the Coventry lads. One Leicester lad casually wandered up to the stand's ticket office and asked to buy 107 tickets, claiming they were for his Loughborough-based company which was having a works day out. The staff didn't buy his story but another away fan tried the same tactic at an ordinary turnstile and this time it worked.

The game was only two minutes old when Leicester announced their presence and fighting began. It soon spilled on to the pitch and the teams had to be taken off as play was held up for seven minutes. At its peak, hundreds were involved in the fighting. There was further trouble after the game as fans clashed in the neighbouring streets and the city centre. One fan was pushed through a shop window.

The FA ordered an immediate investigation, not least because of the ease with which the Baby Squad purchased tickets for the home end. Partly as an attempt to pre-empt FA censure, Coventry announced that fencing was to be reintroduced at the ground, with the cost being passed on to spectators in the form of a ten per cent price hike. Four weeks after the pitched battle, the FA imposed a £1,000 fine on the club.

The following season saw the birth of The Legion, Coventry's casual mob, which continues to exist to this day. The name was thought up in the back of a minibus on the way to a Milk Cup game at Chester. Over the next few years, The Legion turned out big mobs against Forest, Birmingham and Leicester. Even into the 1990s, The Legion could still turn out numbers: more than 300 travelled to Spurs in 1997 and 250 to Leicester in 1999.

"The Legion was made up of lads from areas such as Bell Green," said TC. "At most home games the mob would sit in the Sky Blue Stand or Sky Blue

Terrace, next to the away fans, and after the match would usually meet at the old Vauxhall Tavern pub in Hillfields and wait for away mobs to walk past. Incidents both inside and outside the ground in the mid to late Eighties involved Leicester, Birmingham, Man Utd, Q.P.R, Portsmouth and Aston Villa. The London firms always brought up good followings that usually saw some trouble. The League Cup semi-final with Nottingham Forest in 1990 at Highfield Road saw one of the biggest Coventry firms at that time. There were seventy-two arrests as sporadic fighting took place between hundreds of supporters away from the ground after Coventry were knocked out. Forest always brought a good mob to Coventry."

Almost two years after Birmingham and Coventry clashed on the pitch at Highfield Road, the Zulus returned, again causing trouble. Three policemen were injured as Birmingham fans went on the rampage. A train was damaged and missiles were thrown at rival fans and the police. Eighteen people were arrested.

The following season was certainly Coventry City's most successful ever as the club won the FA Cup, beating Spurs 3–2 in the final. Along the way Coventry fans misbehaved everywhere. "Coventry took big firms to every round with lads from all over the City joining up," remembered another Legion lad. "It was a mixture of lads and beer boys." Two hundred Coventry and Derby fans battled it out inside the ground after the two sides met in the Cup. A mob of 80 stopped off in Stoke and battled with locals on their return from a match against Manchester United.

Nine Coventry fans were jailed after a mob of 500 rampaged through Chesterfield on their way back from the quarter-final victory against Sheffield Wednesday. In two hours of disorder, pubs were smashed up, bar staff slashed with broken beer glasses and several cars wrecked. Seven police officers were injured and 23 Coventry fans arrested.

The next few years were relatively quiet on the hooligan front. Firm measures from the club, poor performances on the pitch and the rave scene, which was very strong in the city, all played their part. It was during this period that many of the less flattering comments were written about Coventry's mob. But the violence never disappeared; one Tottenham thug gave up hooliganism after being slashed across the throat during a fight with Coventry's mob in the late 1980s.

By the middle of the Nineties, after a relative lull in hooliganism, a few new faces were coming through. In May 1996, Coventry needed a point to stay up from the last home game of the season against Leeds who brought their usual vibrant and violent set of supporters. At the end of the game – a goalless draw that meant Coventry stayed up – both mobs had a fierce battle on the pitch with Coventry being slightly outnumbered by their Leeds counterparts but still holding their own. It took police ten minutes to restore order and some lads received jail sentences for their part in the troubles. In 1998 Coventry beat Derby 2–0 in the FA Cup, the prelude to a fight between 100 Derby and 80 Coventry. By the end of the century, turnouts of 50 to 100 were usual for home games with bigger numbers out for the bigger matches.

As always, games against Leicester brought out some of the biggest mobs, as was the case in 1999, when Coventry were drawn away to their local rivals in the FA Cup. "There was a buzz around the city," recalled one lad. "During the week, some lads made the trip over to Leicester to check out the pubs and to see where everyone should meet once they got there. On the morning of the game, a good mob met up early at a shopping centre on the eastern side of Coventry and made their way over to Leicester in cars, vans and minibuses. We met up at the arranged pub and waited until we had a good 100-plus mob. On the way to the ground there were various scuffles as groups of Leicester tried to get at Coventry's mob but Coventry had the edge and no one was going to stop us.

"Disorder broke out by a petrol station where Coventry got the better of Leicester. Police tried in vain to control the situation and eventually got most of Coventry's mob to the ground. Inside the ground there were pockets of Coventry in the Leicester end and some scuffles. After the game, which Coventry won, it was much of the same as Coventry stayed together and had the better of the day.

"This goes to show how organisation and planning can still enable a firm to get into a city centre, stick together and get a result in another city."

Later that year it was Leicester's turn to make a show at Coventry, as an NCIS report noted: "A group of around 60 Coventry supporters were drinking in a local public house. They came out and started to walk up the road to where a group of about 60 Leicester supporters appeared, armed with bottles, pool balls and pool cues. Half way up the road the two groups met, the Leicester supporters threw missiles. A lorry making its way along the road had its windows smashed by flying bottles. Officers arrived and the groups were dispersed. The Coventry supporters in the Hare and Hounds Public House smashed the windows. After the match, Leicester supporters were escorted from the stadium to the railway station. Coventry supporters were hanging around trying to get to them, but due to the escort they were prevented from doing so."

The following season saw trouble at home to Middlesbrough, Manchester United, Aston Villa and Leicester City. When six Manchester United fans got into a pub where 50 Legion were drinking, disorder was the only outcome. A short time later this same group of Coventry clashed with 80 United fans before the game and there was further trouble inside the ground when the visitors scored their first goal. After the game the police escorted 50 United to a local pub but they were intercepted by Coventry and an exchange of missiles followed. After police managed to get United into the pub it was attacked by the home mob.

The Villa game, three weeks later, also proved difficult for the police as a group of 40 Villa Hardcore opted to stay in a city centre pub during the game. At 4 p.m., as 20,000 other people were enjoying the match, a 40-strong group of Coventry made an attempt to storm the pub. This time the police were on top of the situation and managed to keep the two factions apart.

Leicester and Coventry hooligans were obviously in contact with each other during the Midlands derby in December 2000, and two coaches bringing the Baby Squad stopped right outside the pub where 70 Coventry were drinking. A small fracas left both coaches damaged, much to the annoyance of the drivers, who decided to head straight back to Leicester without their passengers. As the police escorted the Leicester mob to the ground, Coventry regrouped and tried to confront them, but were beaten back. As tensions mounted, the police arrested 22 Leicester fans for breach of the peace but that did not prevent another 40 from leaving the match early and heading for another pub where

Coventry were drinking. In a brief battle, one Leicester fan received a nasty head wound after being hit by a glass. While some officers escorted Leicester back to the train station, others were left to keep the Coventry lads in place. Among the items dropped by the home mob before they could be searched were pool balls and CS gas.

The increasing trouble at Coventry was beginning to concern West Midlands Police, who have always considered themselves one of the most pro-active in the country. Consent was obtained for extra video surveillance of Coventry's next high-risk home game, against Tottenham. Footage shot there and CCTV from the earlier three games formed the backbone of Operation Freetime: twelve men were convicted, nine being sent to prison. The heaviest sentence was handed down to Miro Cann, a 22-year-old paint sprayer who was caught on video chasing Tottenham fans with a bottle, and later fighting. Eleven of the twelve were banned from all football grounds in Britain for six years.

While the police were slowly sifting through 150 hours of footage for Operation Freetime, the Legion continued. In January 2001, Coventry were drawn away at Man City in the Cup. The clubs had already played a trouble-free League fixture but this time Coventry's police intelligence officer picked up that a coachload of "targets" were travelling together. Greater Manchester Police were alerted and on the coach's arrival at Maine Road they video-interviewed everyone on board. The Coventry lads then made their way into the North Stand, but after Shaun Goater scored a late winner for Man City, they pushed their way into the Main Stand to confront their Manchester rivals. This was no mean feat, as they had to clamber over a couple of dozen rows. The ensuing fight was short, ferocious – and extremely unwise. Manchester Police had only to match up the stadium's CCTV footage with the video they had shot before the game to identify most of those involved. Operation Edit culminated in charges against another dozen Coventry fans.

While both groups were awaiting trial, Coventry played a home match against Portsmouth. There was widespread disorder during and after the game. The press reported that 140 of the infamous 6.57 Crew had made the journey seeking revenge for the "cowardly" beating of a well-known Pompey lad by some Coventry lads back in May 1993. Rob Silvester, co-author of *Rolling With The 6.57 Crew*, disputes this version of events. "It was the first time we had played Coventry since the incident, but it is also known that those who did [the beating] were not part of their football mob. There's no specific reason why it happened, it's just that once a season everybody picks a game to go to. Coventry was that game. And it was just a coincidence."

The fighting led to the third police operation, code-named Rama. Early in 2002, West Midlands Police and Hampshire Police released pictures of 35 people they wanted to interview. Many handed themselves in but several, including six from Coventry and one from nearby Rugby, got the early morning knock. Fourteen were subsequently charged with violent disorder. This came only a month after the twelve from Operation Freetime were sent to prison and two months after eight Coventry fans were imprisoned for the Manchester City fight. It was a bad few months for The Legion, much to the delight of the local police.

The police operations did not signal the end of the Coventry mob, however. More than 100 lads travelled up to Wigan in the 2003/4 season in revenge for being caught off-guard by their opponents at the home match. While tight policing prevented trouble, a new rivalry had been born. In the 2004/5 season, Coventry put together large mobs for Forest, Leicester and Derby. After the Leicester game, around 80 Coventry fans had a running battle with police in the city centre. A large Legion mob also went to Newcastle in the FA cup-tie in January.

"A lot of lads from around the country continually put Coventry down," remarked TC. "But on their day Coventry can get a good mob together and have been a match for most firms."

CREWE ALEXANDRA

Ground: Gresty Road
Firms: Railway Town Firm, Crewe Youth, Gresty Road Casuals
Rivals: Wrexham, Chester, Shrewsbury
Police operations: None

Any hooligan who went to Crewe in the "old days" will know that at times, like all places, it could be a bit "on top". Even as a stop-off on the way to and from places, a change at Crewe station could see outbreaks of violence, invariably involving the large, black doormen who patrolled the pubs in the area, but there was often a firm of local lads prepared to mix it too.

So although the Gresty Road Casuals are hardly a name to strike fear in the hooligan world, they exist, and if honesty won medals in the world of terrace culture, Crewe would take gold. In the interests of anonymity, we will refer to one of their number as HFC: Honest From Crewe.

"We are known as the Gresty Road Casuals probably because the ground is down Gresty Road," joked HFC. "It is made up of lads aged between eighteen and twenty-five, with the majority in their early twenties. There are a few older lads who can be seen drinking around the pubs before and after the game and for a big game they will have a fair few out, but they will never go looking for it like the younger lads do. They may be older they may be wiser but I wish they would back us up a bit more. Surely it must piss them off seeing fans from other towns come here and basically take the piss?"

On a good day the firm can pull out up to 40 lads, but this is the exception rather than the norm. Like many small towns within easy reach of larger conurbations, many lads in Crewe support other teams. With the largest railway link station in the country, it is easy for locals to pop on a train and go further afield for their Saturday afternoon fix. Plenty follow the Merseyside and Manchester clubs and a fair number go with Stoke City. Even some Chelsea lads live in Crewe. A more regular turnout is 20, though even this number has been increasingly difficult to achieve as police action and bans have taken effect.

The Crewe mob has not always been so small. "In the mid-Eighties we could turn out a good 100 lads, with about the same again making up numbers for big games," said HFC. "The hardcore turnout would be between fifty and seventy and in those days we were called the RTF, Railway Town Firm, and CYSC, a reference to Crewe Youth Club on Miriam Street. The different groups from various areas had their own disagreements and only came together for the big games against Wrexham, Chester, Shrewsbury, Stockport, Port Vale, Burnley and Rochdale. Stoke was a rival but they were far too big for us to compete with, even if the in-house squabbles were put on hold for the day."

Crewe's most active season was in 1987, when the old away end was shut. The Wrexham game stood out. "G", an older Crewe lad, remembered, "Five of us travelled from Sandbach before the pubs opened at eleven and headed for the town centre. Small groups of Crewe were forming up near the Junction and Angel pubs and around the market centre. A bit later we spotted a mob of twenty Wrexham heading into town so we headed back to the Junction to let everyone know and then went back into the market centre to wait. As the Wrexham lads approached, the pub emptied and we came out of the market centre straight into them. Neither side gave ground for a while until we eventually backed them off. One of them came back a few minutes later and started gobbing off. He didn't realise one of our lads was standing next to him and he got a can of lager on his head and a close visit to a shop window.

"We moved on at about one and headed towards the ground in small groups," said one Crewe lad. "About five of us bumped into quite a few Wrexham and had to get on our toes past the station. We went into the Royal at about one-thirty and met up with the main bulk of Crewe lads, a good 100, with sixty really up for it and the rest ready to back it up. The pub emptied as the main Wrexham train mob walked past and there was fighting on Nantwich Road and into Gresty Road. The OB lost control and were standing around watching as Wrexham were attacked as they queued to get in. Once inside there were two lines of OB on the Popside segregating fans, as the away end was shut for rebuilding. It seemed as though it was going off for the full ninety minutes as we pushed the lines of OB into Wrexham and they responded with the same, with the odd missile thrown back and forth. Anyone who did manage to get through was beaten back by OB rather than nicked, par for the course in those days. You could push through the thin blue line, give and take a few slaps, and be back with your own lot without getting three years' jail. If you went through once too often the worst thing that would happen was that you would get slung out, which was no great shakes as we were shit at the time.

"As we left the ground at the end we were suddenly hit by flying debris from above. Wrexham had managed to get through the far end of the Popside and onto the roof and were showering us

with all sorts. Some people were throwing it back but most were covering their heads and running out of range. We were eventually held by the OB on the corner of Gresty Road and pushed towards the back car park as they escorted Wrexham back to the station. Wrexham tried to get through the OB and nearly made it through until they drove a van at them and got them back into the escort. Apart from Chester, I think we were their nearest rivals at the time and they always brought a tidy firm. Eventually they were pushed to the station and we were forced further into the back car park and had no way of getting at them again.

"The police tailed us back into Cam Street, where we stopped and refused to move. With everyone pissed off about the missile attack that caused a few casualties, including normal fans, everyone charged. There was scuffling with the OB until their vans turned up and herded everyone towards town. We were determined to get something out of the day, so about eight of us got back to the station and had a bit of a go with similar numbers of Wrexham lads who had just been let out of the cells. The Transport Police turned up and put them on a separate platform. It wasn't exactly a riot but it was a decent show from our lads and we followed it on at the next match at Rochdale. We took a decent mob and had a load of trouble at a motorway service station on the way home with another coachload of fans. I still don't know who they were."

Other games that saw action that season were home fixtures against Stockport and Burnley, and then Wrexham away. "Burnley was mad," he recalled. "We were only young, but keen to make a name for ourselves and ended up outside the ground throwing bricks over the wall into their end after we had heard that they tried to torch the old main stand. Fuck knows if any landed on our intended targets, as we never stayed around long enough to see."

Crewe's most infamous FA Cup away day was at local non-league rivals Northwich. "Four of us from school caught the bus early and arrived in Northwich well before the main bulk of the Crewe firm," recounted G. "We had heard at school that there was going to be trouble, so decided to travel early so we could get in a good position to watch, rather than participate. When we got there we went for a walk around and were surprised to see loads of older blokes who looked pretty nasty. We kept our heads down and went into a café with a good view so we could see what was going on. The older lads drifted off and we later heard they were locals heading to Manchester to watch United or City.

"As Crewe fans started arriving, it looked pretty tense with police moving local youths away. All of a sudden, a large mob of Crewe appeared out of the back of Woolworth's, where they had gone on a rampage, throwing stock around and battering people. It was all a bit daft but in those days these things went on when everyone was pissed. We joined up with the lads and went for a walk around town where the local youths didn't offer much resistance and were soon scattered. We then headed towards the ground with large numbers of police following us everywhere. There were a few stand-offs but nothing major until we got to the ground. It had gone off in a pub on the corner by the ground and there were still quite a few arguments going on which our arrival didn't help.

"It also seemed like half of us had tickets for the Crewe end and half for the home end, so at this point we all fucked off in different directions and the police didn't seem to know what to do. We ended up in the home end and soon realised that there was a hell of a lot of Crewe in there. Northwich were giving it to Crewe on their main terracing on the far side of the ground. They were well up for it and were giving our lot a kicking, while loads of younger lads were launching rubble over the segregation fence into the Crewe fans who were trying to get through or over the fence. The away end was a three-step terrace behind the goal with a corner section that was higher up and built on rubble. A lad from school was led across the pitch with blood pouring from his head after being hit with a brick and the picture made the front page of the local paper. We were having our own little battle with some lads about our age who reckoned they were Man City and we were going at it when the police took us round the pitch and put us in the already overcrowded Crewe end. We were losing two-one, so we left early and the police put us on the first bus home. If we had stayed we would have had loads more fun as the police lost control after the game and Crewe took over the town."

The mob more or less died in the early Nineties, with only six lads keeping it together. At its lowest point the mob dropped to just two lads for one game, though HFC and his mate say they still got stuck in. In recent years a mob has re-emerged, but numbers are still small. "We have arranged a couple of big away days in the last couple of years," said HFC. "We took a good firm of forty to Wigan, had good numbers in the ground at Stoke last year and this season took more than twenty lads to Preston. Any off nowadays is regarded as a bonus and recently we had a good ruck with Colchester at home when about equal numbers clashed. Their minibus came past the pub we were in and one of our lads sitting outside slung a pint glass at it. They came steaming off the bus so everyone picked up what they could and launched it at the Colchester lads as they attempted to get in the pub. It was going off in the doorway when one of our lads picked up one of the big pub signs that you see advertising 'What's On' and launched it into them. It hit one lad on the knee and that was it, game off, and we backed them onto their bus. One of their lads was game as fuck, wouldn't give in, and threw a few suicide attacks at us before he had to run back to the safety of the bus. If his mates had been as game we would have been in trouble.

"Days like that are rare, and all we have to look forward to is our small firm bumping into similar numbers, which is not very often. Six of us did back off ten Sunderland lads, which was funny as they were giving it the large one and ended up making cunts of themselves. One of our best performances was actually a defeat but one that we are proud of. Eight of us travelled to Bradford and for four, all sixteen years old, it was their first outing. We clashed with twenty Bradford outside a Wetherspoons pub and almost instantly, the youngsters ran off. The four of us remaining stood and fought and, while we really got hammered, we held our own for a period and at one stage Bradford backed off.

"Today, our firm, although small, has re-emerged, but our main problem is the Old Bill. It's harder for us because it is a lot easier to spot half a dozen ring-leaders in a mob of twenty, and every time we seem to be getting something good together the bastards come and slap a couple of more lads with a ban and this exclusion order shit.

"The most recent game at Preston sums up the scene today. We took our massive mob of about twenty-five and were followed by undercover police who stood out like a boil on the end of your cock. Soon, we had three riot vans outside the pubs we used and when we were eventually escorted to the ground there were four more OB than us!"

CRYSTAL PALACE

Ground: Selhurst Park
Firms: The Whitehorse, the Wilton, the Nifty Fifty, Dirty Thirty/Under Fives
Rivals: Brighton, Charlton, Millwall, Manchester United
Police Operations: Backyard, 1987

Crystal Palace are overshadowed on the pitch by London giants Chelsea, Arsenal and Spurs, and off it by neighbours Millwall, yet their supporters are fiercely proud and over the years have been involved in their share of football violence. In 1977, thousands of Palace fans celebrated a win at Wrexham by rioting all the way from the ground to the station. Palace were aiming for promotion along with Mansfield and Brighton and Hove Albion, who from that season on became their most hated rivals.

One of their early feuds was with Arsenal and culminated in Palace taking the North Bank in 1980. The feud began in October 1979 when their supporters came to blows at Euston Station. Palace were away at Everton and Arsenal were travelling to Bolton. "We gave them some stick in the morning at Euston, and without being full of lager they took it," remembered one Palace lad. "Ten hours later, when we got back with both mobs slightly worse for wear, they were waiting for us and their mood had changed. We were on the platform when they came down and fronted us, thinking we would crumble, we were only little old Palace to them but we knew what was coming and were ready for them. They got battered and a few caught fire extinguishers on the head for good luck."

A few weeks later, Arsenal played at Selhurst Park. The London hooligan grapevine revealed that Arsenal were out for revenge, so over 150 Palace waited on the mud bank at the back of the Holmesdale end and watched the North London fans steam into the singers and scarfers at the bottom of the terrace. Palace then surged forward, catching Arsenal by surprise. The Gunners were forced to the front of the stand before being escorted by police around to the Whitehorse Lane end. Arsenal had a sizeable mob out that day. "There were so many that they stretched from the halfway line to our end," remembered the Palace lad. "After the game this huge mob were waiting and it was Palace's turn to take a kicking."

For the return fixture, a mob of about 100 made the short journey across the river and went into the North Bank ten minutes before kick-off. "We were standing at the top right as you look at the pitch and we let them know we were there. They came towards us and then went backwards very quickly and the whole end ran. Hardly any punches were thrown and the Old Bill surrounded us. Arsenal came back and started giving it the big one. We were taken out and round to the Clock End but our escort was double the original size, as Arsenal had joined in with us. We got in the Clock End and were walking in a little alley at the back which was about five feet lower than the top of the terrace. We copped it from above and behind but stood our ground. There was more trouble at Arsenal tube after the game and they also came back to Victoria but by then there were plenty of police to keep us apart."

Heading up most of the trouble during this period was the Whitehorse mob, whose name was taken from the away, Whitehorse Lane end. They emerged in the late Seventies and continued into the early Eighties. This firm consisted of various smaller gangs from the surrounding areas who would congregate either side of the away support and attack them through a small cordon of police.

Shortly after the North Bank conquest, Palace tried to take Spurs' Shelf but this was a move too far and only twenty found the courage to go in. It was clear that they were going to get a pasting so they let the police know that they were in the wrong end and were quickly escorted around the ground. A more successful operation was Palace's home game against arch-rivals Brighton in 1979. The previous season, thirty or forty Brighton had travelled to South East London in a lorry and ran ten or so Palace ragged. Quite unexpectedly, an opportunity for revenge presented itself when one Palace lad saw the same lorry as he was on his way to the ground. An ambush was arranged for after the game but when Brighton were slow to return it was decided to turn the vehicle over. Someone stuffed a rag in the petrol tank and up it went.

On a number of occasions in the late Seventies, groups of Palace would gather at East Croydon railway station to "greet" the passing Brighton train. Once, Brighton were returning from a match at Cambridge. "There were about thirty of us," remembers a Palace old-timer. "A train appeared on the platform at slower than walking pace and on the front was a big sign saying 'The Seagull Special'. In those days everyone went on specials, including the team and the firm. We thought it was Christmas. As it came to where the subway was, you could see loads of them leaning out of the doors and we got ready to bombard them with everything that wasn't nailed down. Then we noticed the front carriage was a luxury coach with the players and directors having a meal. It was too good to pass on, and as they drew level with us we put the windows in with a few litterbins. The doors started opening and little groups kept jumping off, having a go and getting back on. We kept going at them but made sure we had our escape route by the subway behind us. The train didn't stop and we held our own as they didn't want to get left on the platform and didn't have the sense to pull the cord."

In 1980, Palace played Swansea in the FA Cup. A draw saw the teams replay at Cardiff's Ninian Park. A mob of Palace lads travelled down in a minibus but a fight on their arrival against four Swansea saw one Welshman, David Williams, stabbed to death and another suffer five stab wounds in his back. Nineteen-year-old Barry Rondeau, from Mitcham in Surrey, was later convicted of murder and four others were jailed for their part in the fight. Rondeau told the court that he panicked during a skirmish. He said that he had got out of the minibus and saw one of his friends being attacked by a man wearing a sheepskin coat. He pulled his friend away and was then hit by the Welshman as he tried to return to the van. Instinctively he got a knife from the van. "He came for me," he told the court. "I leant back and I jabbed him a few times." He then claimed that as he was running away he was attacked by a second man and soon the two were rolling around on the floor. "I went down with him. As he went down I just jabbed him a few times to keep him down."

Rondeau said that he never intended to kill anyone but the court was not impressed, especially when it emerged that after the stabbings he went to the ground to watch the match. He was given a life sentence for murder but was acquitted of attempting to murder the second man. In passing sentence, Mr Justice Phillips said that it was time to call an end to such outbreaks of violence. "Such expressions as 'only football violence' are a lot of nonsense. It is time that it was all stopped."

Palace fans were again in the national press early into the 1981/2 season after a cup game at QPR. Clive Allen scored for Rangers and his post-goal celebration included a two-fingered salute at the away fans. Four Palace fans charged onto the pitch after him. One kicked him up the backside before being wrestled to the ground by stewards. Another fan was given a three-month jail sentence, suspended for two years, for kicking QPR keeper John Burridge in the back, "kung fu style". At the final whistle, mounted police had to break up fighting fans. Trouble continued outside the ground for at least another hour. The disorder received national media attention, not least from ITV commentator Brian Moore, who said it was the worst trouble he had witnessed at a football game.

In the mid-Eighties, the Nifty Fifty emerged. There were roughly 50 lads who ran together and they were the first casual mob at Palace. They stayed together until 1991 and were involved in numerous incidents, mostly away from home. Another group active at that time was the Wilton, named after lads who drank in the Wilton Arms pub in Thornton Heath High Street. On match days, this mob, numbering about 70, consisted of ex-Whitehorse lads together with other lads from the surrounding areas.

Palace's key local rivals are Charlton and Millwall, but games against Brighton have seen the fiercest clashes over the years. In the 1985/6 season, hundreds of Palace fans thrashed the club shop at Brighton and fighting broke out during and long after the game. At another match during the same period 200 Palace fans broke through police lines after the game to confront 100 Brighton who had gathered in a nearby park. Brighton put up fierce resistance but were soon overwhelmed.

One Palace lad remembers the day: "The Old Bill decided to hold us in the ground to stop us getting at the Brighton mob. All of a sudden the gates swung open and out we went and straight into Brighton's mob. To this day no one knows who opened the gates; it certainly wasn't Old Bill. I don't think Brighton were expecting this and they were backed off from the start. It was kicking off all over the place and ended up in the big park opposite the old Goldstone Ground. The Old Bill were totally outnumbered and were only able to watch as the two mobs went at each other. Although the Brighton that day were game they were over-whelmed and were chased across the park by us. The police came charging over on horses and gained some sort of order but all the way back to the station there were clashes between the Palace and Brighton firms, with loads of arrests and casualties on both sides."

Brighton were also regular visitors to Selhurst Park and on one trip they smashed up the Surrey Street market. The following season word went round that they were going to attempt a repeat performance. The South Londoners met in the Forum pub at 11 a.m. and before long it was packed. Brighton did not show, unlike the police, who turned up in huge numbers and escorted Palace to the ground. Close to the turnstiles the police disap-peared believing that the mob would continue into the ground but instead it turned round and hunted down Brighton, catching a good mob in a side street in Thornton Heath. While Palace had the numbers, Brighton had the use of several builders' skips.

Charlton and Palace mobs have fought on several occasions, though the antipathy is nothing like that held towards Brighton. A Palace lad remembers an encounter with Charlton in the 1980s. "About forty of the Nifty Fifty lads took it to Charlton outside the Goat House pub in SE25. At the time we were all in our late teens, early twenties, but all the same didn't budge an inch when we crossed the railway bridge and bumped into around seventy of Charlton's older B Mob. We could see the Charlton lads backing off from the start, which set the tone for the rest of the battle. Charlton began to run down the Penge Road with us just behind them and a big roar went up as we went at them. All down the Penge Road punches and kicks were traded between both sets, but each time we got the upper hand and each time had the Charlton lads on their toes.

"After two or three of these offs, with Charlton on the back foot in them all, they finally got their act together. Another twenty of them were waiting under the railway bridge down Penge Road and

when the tiring Charlton saw these it gave them a second wind, so to speak. Still, we were on a high so we ran into the Charlton under the bridge and it kicked off, with both sides going for it. This went on for about five minutes, only stopping as both sides regrouped, took a breather and then went at it again. Eventually the OB arrived in SPG vans and were swinging at anything that moved."

For many older Palace hooligans, a home game against promotion-chasing Portsmouth in 1984 was especially memorable. Thousands of Pompey fans had made the short trip up to South London and many went onto the pitch at the final whistle. A group of around 60 headed towards the Arthur Waite Stand, where most of the Nifty Fifty sat, and began taunting them. The challenge was accepted and after a short but fierce clash, the Pompey backed off. Fighting continued outside, with the Palace mob, now numbering about 80, running groups of Pompey.

As one Palace lad explained, having thousands of fans did not always guarantee a result off the pitch. "The numbers Portsmouth had that day were some-thing we could only dream of but we stuck together in our tight mob inside and outside the ground that day and although we will never claim to have done the 6.57 firm all over our manor, we could only fight what came at us, and those that did come across us came off second best."

A midweek away fixture at Oldham in 1987 saw about 30 Palace lads travel up. Near the ground they bumped into a similar-sized group of Oldham and a battle ensued. More and more locals began arriving, including some doormen, but the outnumbered Palace lads held their own even though some were seriously hurt, including one who was hit over the head with a paving slab.

If Brighton was a challenge that Palace boys would readily accept, Millwall was a different proposition. Millwall was Millwall, and Palace fans knew that they were out of their league. In October 1986, a game between the two at Selhurst Park was held up for seven minutes after 200 Millwall in the home end charged down the terrace, scattering Palace fans onto the pitch. A few Palace tried to fight back but were heavily outnumbered and in the words of one, "basically didn't know what hit them." After the game Millwall fans were involved in a fight with West Ham in which a young man was killed.

In 1987, forty of the old Nifty Fifty decided to have a go. Palace veteran 'F' takes up the story. "We met early and got the train up to New Cross. This mob was all N50 and although we were game, we also knew we could easily come unstuck with the numbers we had. As we were walking up the Old Kent Road we bumped into around thirty Wall lads, who came bouncing down the road with the usual shouts and threats. We felt confident and bounced up towards them. It kicked off and we were doing OK, no one was backing off from either side, but it was one of those where it stops and starts while lads trade insults. After a couple of minutes we realised that we were getting outnumbered, and fast. At Millwall, if anyone is daft enough to take liberties the whole place goes up and you see women and kids coming out of the flats and running amok, never mind their husbands. We could see lads coming out of shops, jumping off buses and coming out of the estates both in front and behind us.

"The Wall lads were getting confident and had us on the back foot. They were now a hundred strong and growing, and after our blood. As bricks and bottles rained down on us I'd have to say a bit of panic set in and no fucker knew what to do other than run. Two Old Bill on horseback were in the area and came galloping into the fray but any relief was short-lived, as one of them wished us luck and left. We just ran back the way we had come. There were even shopkeepers coming out onto the streets and tripping us over as we tried to escape and one of ours ending up in cauliflowers in a fruit and veg shop. Luckily most made it out of the place in one piece and there was some small vengeance extracted later as fifteen of ours got on the train at New Cross and bumped into ten Millwall, but over the course of the day it was a lesson learned." There is a saying bandied about the football hooligan world along the lines of "better to show and get done than not to show at all". It rarely applies in the bandit country known as Millwall.

The 1987 season was a busy one for Palace, on and off the pitch, and ended with an appearance in the FA Cup Final against Manchester United. There was trouble before the game when fifty Palace bumped into a mob of United at Baker Street tube. Bottles and beer cans were exchanged before one Palace lad pulled out a CS gas canister and used it on the United fans. The only problem was that he was

in the Underground at the time, so everybody else on the platform got gassed as well. The police turned up as people poured out of the station, eyes streaming. There was more trouble at Wembley as Palace clashed with small groups of Cockney Reds. At first Palace held their own, but within minutes the United contingent had grown to more than 100 and ran their opponents everywhere. It was the same after the match, with 150 Mancs running 50 Palace down Wembley Way. "It was a bit of a disaster outside the ground but looking back a good day was had by all," remembered F. "After the trip to Millwall, running around Wembley with a few hundred United after you was like having a jog around Hyde Park."

The increasing activity of Palace hooligans did not go unnoticed. In January 1988, the Metropolitan Police launched Operation Backyard to identify and apprehend the ringleaders. "Officers from the Territorial Support Group and other units began infiltrating the gangs of hooligans who claim to support Crystal Palace," reported the London *Evening Standard*. Almost four months later, on 27 April, 31 Palace fans were arrested in a series of co-ordinated dawn raids across South London. Those particularly targeted were the Nifty Fifty and the Wilton mob. On the same day, 15 West Ham fans were arrested in a separate operation. The Met heralded the raids as a breakthrough in their fight against hooliganism in the capital. "By arresting these men who wrongly call themselves football fans, our aim has been to break the back of a hard-core element who are bent on causing trouble," said Supt Bill Griffiths. Yet less than three months later, all the charges were dropped after concerns about the safety of the evidence collected.

The last game of the 1988/89 season saw the visit of Birmingham City and their infamous Zulu Warriors. Palace were trying to secure a play-off place and the Midlands team were trying to avoid relegation. Ian Wright's opener for Palace was the signal for the first pitch invasion, but rather than go for their opponents the Birmingham fans tried to attack their own players. "I told the Birmingham players to get off the pitch – their fans were actually trying to hit them," recalled Wright. The game was held up for twenty-six minutes as the referee took the players off for their own safety. Earlier, 300 Birmingham fans had turned up at the Crystal

Palace Recreation Centre, two miles from the ground, looking for a fight.

The actions of the Birmingham fans received widespread condemnation, especially as they came only four weeks after the Hillsborough disaster. What went unreported was the fighting between Birmingham and Palace fans, according to one Palace lad. "Palace and the Zulus were having a right old dingdong further back in the seats in the Arthur Waite Stand, with Palace more than holding their own. There was no way of us getting onto the pitch, as in those days there was a barbed wire fence at the front of the seated section as well as Old Bill whacking anybody who tried to get down to the terracing in front. After the game, at least 100 Palace lads mobbed up down Whitehorse Road and smashed every Brum coach and minibus that went by. As far as we were concerned, this was a bit of revenge for their pisstake in the ground."

Palace reached the play-offs but failed in the semi-finals. The following season, however, saw them at Wembley in the play-off final against Leicester. The Nifty Fifty met up in Victoria and travelled up to North-west London, but with no Baby Squad in sight they headed for a pub in nearby Neasden instead. With still no word about Leicester's movements and with kick-off 90 minutes away, the Palace mob headed for the tube and the short hop to Wembley. As the train pulled in it was full of Leicester – both fans and boys. "As soon as we entered the train it kicked off, with bottles cans and other weapons being thrown by both sets of lads," recalled one Palace lad. "We were trying to get the Leicester lads to get off the train but they were having none of it, so we decided if they weren't getting off we would get on. I remember the train doors opening and closing with some of our lads getting caught inside and them having to do a mad windmill until we prised the doors open and came charging back into the carriages. This went on for ten minutes, with the train driver shouting down the Tannoy that all he wanted to do was go to the match and could we all leave it out. Yeah right, we thought. In the end we heard sirens coming in the background, which was the signal to go offside. There were casualties on both sides, with blood running from more than a few heads, mostly Leicester's, although to this day it will be said by our lads how game the Leicester at Neasden were."

Five years after Palace's FA Cup Final appearance against Manchester United, two teams met in the semis at Villa Park. Tensions had been running high between the two teams after Eric Cantona's notorious kung-fu kick at a Palace fan, which led to the Frenchman being banned from football and given community service. As a coach load of Palace fans from the New Addington area of South London finished their drinks at the New Fullbrook pub in Walsall, five minutes from the ground, they were attacked with bricks and bottles by United fans who had torn down a nearby wall to get the ammunition. In the ensuing battle, 35-year-old Palace supporter, Paul Nixon, was hit on the head with a brick and then died after being crushed under the wheels of a coach. A second fan was seriously injured after being stabbed.

"I could see all the trouble outside the pub and ran out," recalled Neil Golden, a United fan who was drinking peacefully in the same pub. "The lad was lying face down in the middle of the road. He was covered in blood and unconscious. He had a huge gash in the side of his head but he was still breathing. I gave him first aid and tried to clear his airway but he started coughing up a lot of blood. I knew he was going to die. I held him in my arms and tried to comfort him and speak to him."

Golden told reporters that the trouble started not because of any Cantona jibe but after a bald-headed Palace fan was referred to as "Willie Thorne", the snooker player. "The Palace fans were singing 'Ooh aah, prisoner' [a jokey reference to Cantona, who was originally given a jail term], but the United fans just laughed. Then I heard one supporter say, 'Come on Willie Thorne, you and me outside,' and the place erupted. One of my friends was smashed in the face with a brick that came flying out of nowhere. He was rushed to hospital with a broken jaw. Another lad had to have his head stitched. There were quite a few lads on the coach with black eyes and bruising."

The police blamed alcohol for the violence. "We are satisfied that this was not a pre-planned meeting," said Detective Superintendent John Plimmer, who headed the murder investigation. "It was pure coincidence that the two factions met." Police had hoped rivals fans would have been kept apart, as each club had been instructed to enter the city on different routes, but with the other semi-final kicking off three hours before, thousands of fans arrived in Birmingham early to watch it on television. "We started to get incidents reported at ten a.m.," the officer continued. A total of 84 people were arrested throughout the day, including three who were questioned specifically over the death of Paul Nixon.

The game finished a 2-2 draw and the replay went ahead, again at Villa Park, four days later. The FA wanted both managers to make on-pitch pleas for calm before kick-off. Both Palace boss Alan Smith and United's Alex Ferguson were happy to oblige. "Manchester United fans have led the way over the past two decades in good behaviour and that's what we are asking for now," said Ferguson, with more optimism than accuracy.

Less conciliatory was Palace chairman Ron Noades, who called on fans to boycott the game. "We sincerely believe that the match should not be played so soon after the dreadful events of last Sunday and we are anxious to avoid any further incidents. People seem to think the Eric Cantona incident was the beginning of this, but this is not the case. Two years ago we had a very serious stabbing incident prior to a league game against Manchester United and that nearly led to the death of a Palace fan." The FA dismissed his calls and the game went ahead. The fans acted in a dignified fashion, unlike United captain Roy Keane, who stamped on Palace skipper Gareth Southgate. "It's not football anymore, it's WAR!" ran the headline in the *Mirror*. Palace's Darren Patterson was sent off with Keane for grabbing the United player by the throat.

The Nifty Fifty gradually shrank and then virtually disappeared, to be replaced in 1999 by the Dirty Thirty. This new group continues to be led by veterans of the Nifty Fifty but also includes about 40 younger lads who are known as D30 Youth or the Under Fives. The firm has a hardcore of 30-70 but can pull over 100-120 for cup, relegation and promotion battles and local derbies.

One noteworthy fight of recent years came when 50-60 Dirty Thirty travelled to Derby. A heavy police presence saw the Palace group cajoled, marched around half of Derbyshire and searched under Section 60. Only half were eventually allowed into the ground, with the remainder being told to return to London. Bored and angry, someone suggested stopping off in Leicester and waiting for the rest of the mob to meet them. On the journey down, a Palace lad rang a contact in the Leicester Baby Squad, and the two mobs fought outside a pub near the station. Anything that wasn't nailed down was used as weapons, even a butcher's sign.

"This is how it should be, a proper battle just like the good old days we are always reminded of, with lads from both sides having their own little toe-to-toes," remembered one young Palace hooligan. "At the end of the day it was us Palace lads who were the gamer of the two firms and we ended up running the Baby Squad through their own city centre. Not many firms can claim to have done that through the years." Not surprisingly Leicester have a slightly different account of the day.

D

DARLINGTON

Ground: Formerly Feethams, now the Williamson Motors Stadium
Firm: Sheddy Boot Boys, Bank Top 200, Wrecking Crew, GAFA (Game as Fuck Association), Under Fives
Rivals: Hartlepool

Darlington Football Club was formed in July 1883 after a meeting in a grammar school brought together local amateur and part-time teams who thought it was better to have just one club in the town. They did not get off to a great start, being hammered 8-0 by Grimsby in the FA Cup two years after their formation. In 1955, Darlington made history by playing in the first floodlit match in an FA Cup replay against Carlisle at Newcastle's St James's Park. Three years later, they joined the old Fourth Division and soon boasted their own floodlights. The lights were switched on for a home game against Millwall in November 1960 but an electrical fault caused a fire which gutted the West Stand. It was rebuilt to the same design but this time with a tin roof. The stand became known as the Tin Shed.

The first report of trouble was when Bradford travelled up in 1969. The club was not one of England's most successful and between 1970 and 1980 they had to apply for re-election to the League on five separate occasions. Their Tin Shed also developed its first serious hooligan mob. "The Sheddy Boot Boys were mainly between seventeen to twenty years old," said one of their early recruits. "They appeared at the start of the Eighties, as part of the bootboy/skinhead culture re-invented by the Madness and Specials era. This gang was thirty to forty strong, and many went on to become original members of the Bank Top 200. The idea was to gather in the Shed and because there was no segregation in those days you could walk right round Feethams and head for the away end in dribs and drabs to confront opponents."

The current mob is known as the Bank Top 200, after Darlington's railway station. It was formed during the 1984/85 season but its roots go back to the visit of Sheffield United in May 1982. Ten thousand Yorkshiremen travelled up to celebrate their club's promotion out of the Fourth Division. They were met in town by a group of young Middlesbrough lads, known as the "Joeys", who travelled in search of a fight with their South Yorkshire rivals. These lads were kitted out in the diamond Pringles, Lyle & Scott golf gear and Adidas Samba training shoes. The locals watched in awe at these smartly dressed casuals went in search of violence. There was no going back; the Sheddy Boot Boys had seen their day.

Early coach trips to Scunthorpe and Blackpool cemented the bond between the lads, and as the team improved on the pitch, so the fledgling Bank Top firm built the foundations that made them a rated firm in the coming years. It was in the 1984/85 season that Darlington really made their mark. The name Bank Top 200 was coined and the first calling cards were produced and handed out. The lads drank in the Boot and Shoe, the Pennyweight and the Boulevard and every home game was a big game, with the pubs packed with lads from all the main areas of town – Denes, Eastbourne, Branksome, Albert Hill, Haughton, Northlands, Mowden and Cockerton.

The memorable games of that season were the pre-season friendly against Newcastle, which ended with a Geordie firm being chased round town. Other outings included Tranmere, Blackpool, Rochdale, Bury and of course Hartlepool, which always meant trouble. The away match at Hartlepool saw the Bank Top travel the twenty-five miles to their rivals' ground in a fleet of taxis. They headed straight for the home end and it immediately kicked off, later continuing as a free-for-all on the pitch at full-time. Their growing prominence that season meant that opposition firms began to turn out in numbers when the Bank Top came to visit.

Hartlepool are their arch-rivals and rarely has a game gone by without some sort of trouble. In the Eighties there were pitched battles involving hundreds of lads, and while the numbers involved decreased in the Nineties the hatred and ferocity was no less intense. "Hartlepool's always been tit for tat, whatever anyone thinks," said Andy, one of the Bank Top lads. "Pool's always up for it at Darlo and vice versa. In 1985 we took 2,000 in total, not just lads, to Pool and paid in their end. I travelled through in an old Morris Oxford with one lad in the boot whilst others went in taxis, vans and cars. Once in their end it kicked off big style and I remember it well for all the wrong reasons, I got smacked on the button and put on my arse within minutes. At half-time there was a funny two-man pitch invasion by our main lads, expecting everyone to follow. We never! And at full time there was a quality toe-to-toe on the pitch, which was only broken up when they brought out the police dogs.

"We've had victories and defeats against the Moose Men and Blue Order [Hartlepool's mobs] and respect is due. It's an on-going thing. The last confrontation will have been when Darlo travelled back from Orient, meeting Pools at York, fighting on the train at the station and ending up with a load of arrests and bans dished out."

In early 1985, Darlington were drawn against neighbours Middlesbrough in the FA Cup. The match was at Ayresome Park and while there was a big turnout of the Bank Top and even some older boys, there was little trouble. Darlington have long had connections with Middlesbrough and many of the fans of both clubs are friends. However, when the game ended in a draw, the replay was to be a far more heated affair. For Darlington lads it was the biggest game in the club's recent history; for Boro it was simply a day to get through without humiliation – on and off the pitch.

"The word had gone out that we would have to be at our best for this one," recalled Boro lad John Theone in his book *The Frontline*. "As they are only seventeen miles away we took every man and his dog." Trouble started almost immediately as Boro fans began arriving. All over town fights were breaking out. "Some of our lads copped for it in isolated incidents but in the main we had them all over the place before the game," Theone added.

Darlington Football Club had seen nothing like it and the press was quick to report it the following day.

The Darlington v Middlesbrough derby was held up after fighting broke out between rival fans yesterday. Police made seventy arrests before kick-off – and more in the second half.

The teams waited on the pitch for a couple of minutes before referee David Scott, of Burnley, took them back into the dressing rooms. Police dogs and other police reinforcements arrived on the pitch as the running battles between rival supporters continued.

The trouble started when 20 or 30 Middlesbrough fans managed to get amongst the Darlington supporters. Women, children and older people were led weeping from the terraces as police tried to restore order.

The match kicked off 12 minutes late after police cleared about 200 fighting fans from the pitch. Police used truncheons to break up the fans who fought running battles on the terraces.

Officers with dogs were drafted in to quell the ugly scenes, but fighting continued with fencing and advertisements being ripped up to be used as weapons.

Boro lost the match 2-1 and the result was given added significance because it was a former Boro player who scored Darlington's second goal. Fighting continued after the game, with the adjacent cricket pitch used as the central battleground. Bodies lay motionless in the snow as hundreds of fans steamed into each other in a roaring, heaving mass. Boro came out on top, largely due to their superior numbers, but Darlington fought like Spartans.

The police, keen to be seen to have done a good job in the face of total chaos, claimed the violence was pre-planned. "The kick-off was the signal for them to start fighting," said a senior officer. As trouble had started well before the start of the game, and with 70 hooligans already under arrest before the "alleged" signal, it was a rash statement, but the claim stuck and the magistrates dealt with any arrested fans accordingly.

Two special courts were set up over the weekend to

deal with the huge numbers arrested. In the first, which sat on the Sunday, 35 fans were remanded in custody, 20 pleaded guilty and were given fines and a further 16 pleaded not guilty and were given bail. The following day saw another 60 in court. Darlington magistrates had never been so busy.

Darlington were drawn away to Telford in the next round and a good mob of Bank Top made the trip. After the excitement of the Middlesbrough game this cup tie brought them back to earth with a heavy dose of reality as they lost to the non-league team. The same year saw a number of arrests at an away game at York. Three hundred lads made the short trip and rampaged through the historic city, smashing shop windows and chasing locals.

Almost exactly a year after Darlington and Boro clashed in the Cup, the two sides met in the League and once again there was serious trouble. Sixty-four people were arrested and the game began twelve minutes late after more fighting on the pitch.

"We were well up for it," recalled one Darlo lad. "Having played them in the FA Cup in 1985 we knew what we expect and it was not a day for the fainthearted. It was the best turnout of lads at home in the Eighties by far, at a guess 350 to 400. We'd decided to meet up out of the way, at the Engineers Club to the north of the town centre at ten, so we'd be ready for an early influx of Boro, who at this time were running riot through the old Third Division.

"As it was, a Boro lad who'd lived in Darlo for a couple of years directed a small mob of Boro to North Road Station, meaning that fifty lads had to run our gauntlet as they made their way into town. When we made our way into the centre, our mob was split into various smaller groups, skirmishing with the huge Boro turnout at every turn. Over sixty arrests were made before the game, so you can imagine the scale of the violence. There were some slashings on both sides, and many beatings taken and delivered. But as Boro will tell you, the Bank Top lads did themselves proud that day." ·

The following season Darlington played at Derby. The Midland side had been relegated to the Third Division for the first time in over 20 years and this brought them into the Bank Top's sights. Along with Middlesbrough, they were seen as the big team in the division and Darlington were keen to take them

on. Three hundred lads made the journey down, the largest mob they had ever taken away. Little happened, largely because Derby's DLF were not expecting such a turnout and were not around. One Derby lad who was confronted by the away mob came out with the old chestnut, "If we'd have known you were coming, we'd have turned out."

Darlington's fortunes on the pitch faltered towards the end of the decade and they slid towards the Conference, but that didn't deter their firm. Trips away to Macclesfield, with a pitch invasion and news headlines, and Cambridge in the FA cup saw more decent turnouts. "Lunatic fringe in soccer battle" was how one newspaper reported clashes between sixty Darlington and the police during the game at Macclesfield. About 100 lads had made the journey to Cheshire in a combination of vans and cars and plotted up in town before the match. With no opposition around, they made their way to the ground and went into the home end.

Disorder had been predicted and many of the town's pubs had been ordered to remain closed until two hours after the game. National Front literature was found on several of those arrested and Macclesfield police praised the prior intelligence sent down by their colleagues in Darlington. "The information was so accurate that we knew if certain people attended the game there would be trouble," said one officer. Darlington manager Brian Little, however, did not see the fighting that day and said that in the six months he had been at the club he had not witnessed any. Yet one newspaper carried a photo of two bloodied Darlington men being led away by police, while another had the headline, "If that's league football you can keep it!"

Under the stewardship of Little, the club bounced straight back up and the following season were promoted as champions. The Bank Top could once again test themselves against bigger firms and there weren't many bigger than Birmingham, who they played away in August 1991. Forty Darlington lads were arrested after violence broke out in the city centre. Bottles and glasses were thrown at the Rainbow pub before the game and there were further disturbances in Dart Street, where Zulus wielding cricket bats and bricks attacked the away fans. One Birmingham fan was stabbed and a Darlington fan beaten senseless.

Calling cards dished out over the years by the hooligan followers of Darlington FC.

Later that night, Darlington fans clashed with locals at the Sinatra's nightclub. Police were called and then became a target themselves. Thousands of pounds worth of damage was caused, including the smashing of the club's front window, as the hooligans used chairs and bottles as weapons. One officer described it as amongst the most violent scenes he had ever witnessed. Thirty-one people were arrested for the nightclub incident, all but one from Darlington.

The euphoria on the pitch did not last long and the following season the club was back down in what was now the Third Division. The next few years were mediocre but by 1996 the club travelled away to Scunthorpe on the last day of the season needing a win to secure promotion.

There had been trouble a few weeks before, with the Easter programme bringing three potentially explosive games. The first, at home to Shrewsbury, saw the FA charge the club for not controlling its fans. Three days later, Darlington played at Carlisle and there was trouble during and after the game. At the final whistle Carlisle supporters charged onto

the pitch and some of the Darlington players were punched and spat at. Three away supporters were also arrested after police identified them contacting Carlisle hooligans by telephone to arrange a fight. However, after the game the three men were released without charge and taken to Carlisle railway station. A few days later, Darlington hosted Lincoln City and the club pleaded with their fans not to bring further shame on the club.

A sizeable contingent of Bank Top made the journey to Scunthorpe and the carnival atmosphere soon turned nasty as they clashed with locals inside the ground. Thirteen people were arrested and a further six ejected. The trouble twice spilled onto the pitch, first when the home team went ahead and then, later, when a Darlington goal was disallowed. Mounted police had to be brought onto the field to restore order. The team could only manage a draw and they lost to Plymouth in the play-offs.

The Nineties saw major fights with Northampton, during which a Northampton fan apparently had part of his scalp ripped off, to be placed on display above "Berties" bar, and a couple of home rows with Cardiff's Soul Crew, the second of which, in 1997, saw lengthy jail sentences for a few of the top lads. One of those jailed was Paul Thompson, the local British National Party organiser and later to be a candidate in a local council election. In 1993, Thompson had been imprisoned for his part in an attack on a left-wing bookshop in Durham. Another Darlington hooligan who became a BNP candidate was Robert Baines, though he stood under the name of Robert Bowman.

Down the years, Darlington lads have been well known on the England hooligan scene, excursions which would see them build links with the likes of Nottingham Forest, Mansfield, Boro and Chelsea. The 1987 game with Scotland at Hampden saw the Bank Top 200 take one of the biggest firms north of the border and they were well represented at Euro 84 in Italy, Mexico in 1986, Germany for Euro 88, Italia 90, France 98 and Euro 2000. Fifty Darlington lads were deported from Holland during the crucial World Cup qualifier in October 1993; one group of ten was picked up at 8 p.m. the evening before the game and the rest in dribs and drabs as the evening wore on. Crammed four to a cell, they were deported back to Luton airport and arrived back in King's Cross in time to watch the match. Meanwhile back home in Darlington, England's defeat sparked trouble in the town centre and fourteen shops and businesses were damaged as fans rampaged.

In 1997 the East Stand was knocked down and rebuilt, and while it certainly improved the appearance of Feethams, it saddled the club with crippling debts. With the club facing administration, George Reynolds, a former safecracker turned businessman, saved it, wiping out an estimated £5 million debt and overseeing the construction of a new ground, which they moved into in August 2003. The club was virtually reborn and the mood of optimism spread to the pitch, with the team once again reaching the play-offs in May 2003. Once again they lost, this time to Peterborough. Four months after the club switched to the Reynolds Arena, further financial problems saw them go into receivership. Eventually the club's creditors became the new owners and the ground was renamed the Williamson Motors Stadium after their main sponsor.

Bans, police action and age have taken their toll on the Bank Top and their outings are now few and far between. A number of younger firms have emerged over the years but none have the same reputation or history. Among them have been the Under Fives and their spin-offs, the Wrecking Crew and GAFA (Game as Fuck Association).

In 2004, The Bank Top had an old boys' reunion. "It was decided to hold a reunion in Doncaster, a place where we'd had a couple of bruising encounters in the halcyon Eighties days, and easily accessible by us," said Andy. "Beforehand a lot of older lads said they'd go, and then thought better of it. So there we were, a few of us in our forties now, on the station wondering what the fuck we were doing. Within the next hour or so, our numbers had swelled to 150, and we got two trains to Donny for opening time. A massive police presence at Donny station saw the majority of lads turned away as they had no tickets for the game, which was no surprise as they had no intentions of going.

"Most of us went back to York, where a lot of the lads jumped into taxis straight into Doncaster. The few who remained in York, maybe fifteen of us, decided to try the train again. Some made it, some were sent back to Darlo. We had the run of the town centre, eighty-strong, but were under the watchful eye of the police video surveillance and riot squad. As soon as a minor fight broke out in the pub, that was it, we were marched back to the station and fucked off out of there. But a good day out and loads of reminiscing."

A Donny lad later posted on one Internet site, "If Darlo turned out consistently like that, they'd be number 1 in the lower leagues, no problem."

DERBY COUNTY

Ground: Pride Park, previously the Baseball Ground
Firms: Pot-Bellied Lunatic Army, Derby Lunatic Fringe, The Orphans
Rivals: Nottingham Forest, Leicester, Leeds, Man Utd
Police operations: Cabby, 2004

Nearby Nottingham Forest may be Derby County's most despised rivals, but in the early Seventies they also hated Manchester United and Leeds with a passion, as the three clubs were among the best in England and matches between them could sometimes determine the title. Leeds won the championship in 1969, while Derby, under Brian Clough, won it in 1972, when the Yorkshire club finished runners-up. Leeds won it again in 1974, while Derby took the title off them the following year. Tensions increased when Clough fell out with his chairman and left to manage Leeds, albeit briefly. Trouble regularly flared up between their supporters, and in 1974 it spread to the pitch as Derby's Francis Lee and Leeds's Norman Hunter swapped punches and kicks as they left the field after been sent off. Millions watched their punch-up on *Match Of The Day*.

Manchester United were coming to the end of the Busby glory years but had the largest travelling support in the country and brought some of the worst violence ever seen in Derby. Cars were burnt out and shops attacked as 200-300 Manchester United skinheads rampaged through Derby city centre after their team lost 4–1 in the Watney Cup Final in August 1970. Terrified residents saw two out of every three houses along two streets attacked by away fans and amazingly only six people were hurt, although amongst the casualties was a two-year-old baby injured when the Reds attacked a bus.

Trouble had begun at the end of the game when away fans threw missiles onto the pitch and at police before steaming out into the streets. Ammonia-filled liquid bottles were squirted through police lines at Derby fans in the Popular Side. "Skinheads used their 'bovver boots' to kick in windows of houses and shops," reported the local paper. Intriguingly, the local police even suggested that Forest fans were behind the violence; though nothing more than anecdotal evidence was provided. The police came in for considerable criticism from residents who were furious that the mob was allowed to go around with any police in sight.

Six years later, Man Utd were again causing trouble at the Baseball Ground but this time Derby appeared eager to meet their challenge. Fighting broke out mid-way through the first half and the beginning of the second half was delayed as police cleared trouble at the corner of the Osmaston End and the Popular Side, known to locals as the Pop Side. At the final whistle, thugs began hurling bottles and beer cans. Police formed along the front

of the Pop Side, resulting in the 3,000 Derby on the Osmaston terrace being left to face the bulk of the 7,000-strong Red Army. Finally, the Pop Siders broke through the police lines and streamed onto the pitch to help their beleaguered brothers. It took the police ten minutes to restore order, only for fighting to break out on the terraces. Forty people needed hospital attention and at least 30 people were arrested.

A new format *Match Of The Day* turned into Brawl of the Day when the opening Saturday of the 1973 season saw Chelsea fans clash with locals. Hundreds fought on the pitch at the end of the game and all the way back to the train station. "Just before the final whistle, fans in the Chelsea section of the Pop Side began moving ominously towards the Derby element," reported the local paper. "Then, as players disappeared down the tunnel, they swarmed onto the pitch. Running fights broke out along the touchline with youths kicking, butting and punching. Fighting continued as supporters streamed out of the ground." Outside the station, police had to hold back a mob of 150 Derby fans from the departing Londoners.

The trouble sparked off an instant demand for fencing to be erected around the ground and the day after the violence the club met the police to discuss their options. "All over Europe, fences are up to keep spectators off the pitch," club secretary Stuart Webb told the press. "I don't really see that there is any alternative. We lost an average of 2,500 spectators per match last season. I am sure that the lunatic fringe is the reason for this."

The police also announced an increase in their crowd control measures but insisted that a lot was already being done. "We have established a command post near where the players come out," said Chief Superintendent Shelley. "We also have a new detention room under the Normanton Stand. Police scanners with binoculars are still keeping an eye on the crowd and plainclothes detectives and police also mingle with them." The following day, experimental fences were erected at the Baseball Ground to help the soccer chiefs and police make up their mind. "If it is reminiscent of a zoo," noted the *Derby Evening Telegraph*, "it must be remembered that the conduct of the supporters has been little better than animals."

The 1970s also saw trouble with local rivals Stoke

and Notts Forest. In March 1975, a Stoke supporter was stabbed in what was the worst trouble at Derby of the season. Trouble began after 200 Stoke fans arrived by train at 10.30 a.m., and soon they were joined by two more special trainloads of fans. As police attempted to herd the travelling army to the ground, one Stoke fan was stabbed by a solitary attacker. Fans fought on the terraces of the Osmaston End and after the match hooligans "ran wild" in the streets around the ground. "It was our hardest day of the season," said Chief Supt Harry Shelley. "Until now we've had trouble before the game, during the game or after the game. This Saturday we had a hard day from early in the morning till we eventually got rid of them. We were at full stretch."

The arrival of Manchester United for the first game of the 1976 season caused serious concern amongst police, the club and locals alike. The police cancelled rest days and shopkeepers boarded up their premises in anticipation of the 7,000 travelling Red Army. Two thousand were expected on three specials, two from Manchester and the other from London, with most of the rest coming by coach or private transport. A few hundred even arrived in Derby the night before. The landlord of one pub, the Barley Mow, told the local press, "The windows have been boarded up since last night. I shall be on the door with a couple of heavies but if the situation gets out of hand I shall have no option but to shut the pub down. I had a lot of trouble last year with windows being broken and graffiti being sprayed on the walls. Things got worse when British Rail withdrew football specials because it meant more motor coaches."

Their worst fears were exceeded. "There are no words that I can use to describe how terrible this whole incident was," Chief Supt Shelley told reporters. "This was not just one of those invasions of the pitch that occurs as the final whistle is blown. It was six or seven minutes after, when the teams had left the pitch. I had walked about fifty yards across the pitch when a number of Derby supporters ran across it, presumably to get away from the United fans. That was when the trouble started."

Fighting continued outside the ground and windows of houses in nearby streets were smashed and cars damaged by bricks. Trouble continued well into the night, with the last reported incident taking place at 10.45 p.m. when a group of Manchester youths attacked a Derby supporter. Sixty-five people were treated by the St John Ambulance inside the group and 19 needed hospital treatment, including three police officers. Twenty-two people were arrested.

The violence re-ignited the debate over fences and the issue was raised at a meeting a few days later between the club, the Football League, the Minister of Sport and the police. The local MP added his voice for stiffer action. "We need to get really tough, and if they are really going to get it in the neck they may be deterred. Fines mean nothing at all to them. They support each other and pay fines collectively. They have got to be sent to prison, and made to report to the local police station after their prison sentences every Saturday for the rest of the football season."

Just three days later, Derby fans were involved in trouble at Doncaster. Twenty-one arrests were made, 45 were ejected and ten locals were injured when fighting erupted straight after the game on a dimly lit park immediately outside Belle Vue. With no police to separate the fans, the scrap went on for a full ten minutes.

Many Derby people had had enough and organised a march from the roads surrounding the club to the council headquarters to see the Mayor. En route they picketed club officials from Derby and Manchester United who were meeting to discuss the recent disorder. The residents demanded stiffer penalties for those responsible and argued that fencing the ground would not solve the problem. A Residents' Committee chairman told the demo, "The fans are like animals. People in our street get spat on and sworn at after every game. Saturday's scenes were worse than Belfast. I was in the Army for twenty-four years and never saw anything like that."

Another resident told the press, "We need help. We need it desperately. We've had petitions and complaints to the council for three years now but no action has been taken to protect us." The protesters got a meeting with the club but emerged unimpressed. While officials expressed their sympathy they refused compensation for the damage caused. Webster promised further action. "People are terrified and frightened. When people are like this, something is going to happen. It is like a fuse on a bomb."

An FA inquiry cleared both clubs of any responsibility and infuriated the residents and their MP. "Manchester United fans already have a bad reputation. What concerns me is that we have 400-500 bloody maniacs at Derby," said the MP, dismissing the inquiry as a whitewash.

The club and Football League agreed to erect fences but six months later, with the visit of local rivals Stoke City, this had still not been implemented. When the game was marred by a pitch invasion that briefly held up play, Sports Minister Dennis Howell rebuked the club, but its secretary, Stuart Webb, denied a binding agreement had been made. He claimed that the League had issued guidance to every club but it was only a recommendation, and said that fences were unworkable because of fire safety. To offset criticism, the club also announced plans to redevelop its training centre and the Baseball Ground into a community sports and social centre. "The aim of this would be to give youngsters a closer tie with Derby County," Webb said. Neighbours tried to obtain a High Court injunction to prevent Derby County playing at the Baseball Ground. While the bid failed, the group continued its campaign. They welcomed restrictions on Manchester United fans travelling to away matches and said every team should have a similar threat hanging over it.

The hostility between Derby County and Nottingham Forest reached fever pitch in the mid-Seventies when Brian Clough became manager of Forest. If that wasn't inflammatory enough, when Forest travelled to Derby in their next league game, in January 1978, they were sitting pretty on top of the table. While the match passed off relatively peacefully, afterwards the Forest escort was ambushed by hundreds of home supporters. Thirty-three arrests were made and five police officers were injured as hooligans left a trail of damage in Shaftesbury Street. "Soccer fury erupts," ran the front-page headline in the *Telegraph*. Once again local residents took the brunt of the disorder, with one elderly man narrowly escaping a lump of concrete hurled through an upstairs window. The fighting spread to nearby waste ground as rival groups broke away from the police.

The first recognised firm at Derby was the Pot-Bellied Lunatic Army (PBLA), formed by older lads during the relegation season of 1979/80. Most of them had been involved in football violence since the skinhead days, but in line with developments elsewhere in the country, they now took a name. Their biggest turnout that season saw them lead the pitch invasion against Manchester City on the final day, and they were also behind trouble at Luton in the second game of the new season. Two Derby fans were among ten arrested after fighting in the streets.

During the same season, some young Derby fans tried to create a casual firm separate from the PBLA. It was originally to be the PBLA Youth but without the donkey jackets and scarves. In 1981 it eventually became known as the Derby Lunatic Fringe, a casual firm quite apart from the PBLA. Their presence was not welcome by the PBLA and there were a number of violent rows between the two until the older crew retired and the DLF became the pre-eminent firm. Their first calling card, "DLF FUCK YOU", was actually produced in 1980, two years before club secretary Michael Dunford denounced "the lunatic fringe that go out and cause trouble" after disturbances during a match against Newcastle in 1982. The hooligans happily accepted this as official recognition and perhaps it even spurred them on for what was to be their most active season.

"Kick-off day – the start of a nightmare," was how the local paper reported the fears of residents at the onset of the 1982/3 season. They had every right to be concerned, because the season was to witness the worst trouble in Derby's history. "I hope the football club goes bust and it will be the end of it once and for all," said one neighbour. Already in their minds was the impending arrival of Chelsea. When the Londoners had played the previous season, a resident was punched in the face as he stood in his doorway and several others had their property damaged, and local people drew up a petition calling on the police for greater protection.

While a few Chelsea were arrested there was no repeat of the violence, but New Year brought three big home fixtures the club could have done without. On January 8, they played host to Forest and there was trouble before and during the game. Police used horses to separate fighting fans outside the ground after 40 Derby charged into Forest fans as they were making their way to the ground. The DLF also attacked away fans in the Cambridge Pub in Dairyhouse Road. "There they go again," said an exasperated resident. By her side was an iron bar in case trouble got too close. "I'll use it if I have to," she told a local reporter. At the end of the game both sets of supporters stormed the pitch. Three police vehicles were damaged and nine officers injured.

The crowd control operation clearly did not work and for the arrival of Leeds, Derby fans were once again allowed onto the Osmaston terraces. However, away fans were still given the middle and upper seats in the stand, providing them with both ammunition and an easy target in the home fans below. Given Leeds's reputation as ground wreckers, this was not a wise move, and sure enough over 500 seats were ripped up and thrown at defenceless Derby fans. The trouble started even before a ball had been kicked when Leeds fans attacked vehicles and the police. Inside the ground fighting broke out in the Ley Stand between Leeds and the Rowditch pub crew, and later, after being bombarded with flying seats, a mob of DLF climbed into the middle tier of the Ossie Stand to mix it with Leeds. Derby veteran Richard Gray claims Leeds were run. "The whole lot of them ran out the back of the stand with the match still in progress. I counted sixteen major fights that day and I was fortunate to have been involved in thirteen of them."

The trouble received the usual condemnation. Derby chairman Mike Watterson branded Leeds fans a "disgrace to humanity" and said, "I have never seen anything like it. Women and children were led away with terrible injuries. They had come in peace to a football game and ended up being harassed, abused and injured by this bunch of lunatics from Leeds." He called for Leeds fans to be banned from every ground around the country. "We thought we were safe because we had only sold tickets through the Leeds Supporters' Club and Travel Club. We thought they were responsible people. They are the scum of the earth."

The FA ordered another investigation but with the arrival of Chelsea seven days later for a cup game, the club had little time to prepare its defence. Watterson considered banning the Chelsea fans but in the end decided against the plan. Keen not to be outdone by their Yorkshire rivals, Chelsea also played up in the ground, though the trouble did not reach the intensity of Leeds. Over 150 seats were ripped out and hurled after Derby scored 90 seconds

from time. Fortunately Chelsea had been allocated the entire Osmaston End and so most landed harmlessly on the pitch. Hours earlier, a large group of Derby brandishing steel poles had chased and attacked a small group of Chelsea fans.

Fearful of further FA action, the club chairman wrote a letter to every club that Derby had played so far that season asking for a report into any trouble involving his supporters. He hoped to prove that away fans had initiated the three worst outbreaks of violence and generally Derby fans behaved well. This failed to influence the FA, who held Derby partly responsible for the trouble against Leeds.

Derby were through to the next round of the cup – and were drawn at home against Manchester United. Eleven thousand United fans packed into the Baseball Ground on a late February afternoon but this time the police were waiting for them. A convoy of 54 away coaches was escorted straight to the ground, in a police operation that included six mounted officers from Greater Manchester Police on the streets of Derby. Despite a large DLF turnout, the heavy policing restricted trouble to a foiled pitch invasion by Derby fans and a few minor skirmishes after the game. Derby were out of the cup but the successful police operation was considered a result in itself.

The club finally acted to prevent the pitch invasions and eradicate the scenes of the previous season by erecting the permanent fencing they had made and experimented with several years before. This did little to stop trouble during the visit of Middlesbrough. It also had no impact on the behaviour of Derby's travelling army, and as their performance declined on the pitch so they misbehaved off it. There were to be two more outbreaks of disorder involving Derby that season. The first was in early March when the club travelled to Leicester City. Fifteen people were arrested after fighting outside the stadium. The final match of the season saw Derby away at Fulham and needing a win to stay up. Thousands of Derby fans celebrated once survival had been achieved by rushing onto the pitch. The game was forced to finish with 78 seconds still remaining as opposing fans were attacked and the away dugout destroyed. An exasperated FA ordered Derby to shut its terraces for the first two home games of the following season.

Derby carried their poor form into the following

season and as gates dropped so did the intensity of the crowd violence. One exception was when the club hosted Plymouth. Four hundred hooligans refused to leave the stadium after the final whistle and began throwing seats at rival fans and police. Trouble continued outside and seven police were hurt. One eyewitness told the local paper that it started with chanting and then as two groups converged they began throwing bricks at one another. Transport carrying Plymouth supporters was also attacked.

A year to the day since Derby fans had celebrated Division Two survival by invading the pitch at Fulham, the club was once again travelling away on the last day of the season facing relegation. This time they were at Shrewsbury and 3,000 made the short hop across the West Midlands. Shrewsbury won the game and their second goal was the signal for a Derby invasion. Over 1,000 swarmed onto the pitch and broke both goal posts while others ripped out over 300 seats. The players fled. Trouble spilled into the town centre, with shop windows being smashed and locals attacked. Some fans managed to break back into the ground later and laid out some of the broken seats to make the words DCFC and DLF. "Last Saturday was the day Derby deposited their human garbage on Shrewsbury," said the police match commander later. "The people of Shrewsbury were disgusted." Six police officers were injured and there was an estimated £9,000-worth of damage. Many who had previously visited the Gay Meadow ground wondered if there was that much there to damage.

Shrewsbury fans watched in a mixture of horror and awe at this naked display of violence and contempt for the authorities. At schools the following Monday, children showed off DLF calling cards that had been dropped around town. For many it was the first time they had come across organised mob violence, and it was to prove the catalyst for the birth of their own mob, the English Border Front.

Action was sparse in the Third Division for the battle-hardened DLF. Following the riot at Shrewsbury they faced increased club and police attention. However, a new division brought new opponents and the DLF exploited the smaller grounds with less surveillance and fewer police. A group of Derby infiltrated Bradford City's main stand and kicked off during the game, and before

long rival gangs were clashing throughout the ground. Twenty-nine people were injured, some by lumps of concrete torn from the crumbling terraces. There was also fighting in the stands as seats were ripped out and thrown onto the pitch. Thirty people were arrested and Bradford admitted that they had been expecting trouble in the Kop not in the main stand. Derby manager Arthur Cox condemned the scenes as "horrific" and managing director Stuart Webb called for a complete ban on travelling fans. Michael Dunford was less apologetic, blaming Leeds fans who had infiltrated the ground to attack Derby supporters.

Two hundred Bradford hooligans travelled to the Baseball Ground the following season. They clashed with 100 Derby but police were soon on hand to split up the warring mobs. In the chaos, a police inspector lost his hat in a scuffle and watched as it was set alight. There was some damage to cars and shop windows but trouble was restricted and aimed largely at the police, a point acknowledged by the Chief Superintendent. "A number of officers including myself had our clothing covered in spit," he told reporters. "I have got to send my mac in for dry-cleaning."

The DLF was still smarting from Forest's last performance at Derby and in June 1984 they teamed up with Leicester's Baby Squad to seek revenge in the close season. "Fans' clash like Ulster battle," declared the local paper as it reported fights involving 400 people in Nottingham city centre. When fighting began only five officers were in the vicinity, though they tried to stop the warring mobs by charging with truncheons drawn. Eventually they were joined by another dozen officers who held up the lads until reinforcements arrived. The Leicester and Derby groups were marched to the bus station, where two buses were hired to take them home. In the following days police rounded up some of those responsible and 63 people were convicted, 30 receiving custodial sentences.

Derby bounced straight back up and the DLF were once more pitted against the larger mobs, but the police were making confrontations increasingly difficult. When County played Forest in a Milk Cup tie in 1985, 400 police prevented widespread disorder, while an away game at Millwall also proved a non-event. The other big game of the season was the return fixture with Millwall. Trouble had been

The police move in as Derby County and Sunderland fans goad each other at Pride Park in February 2001.

predicted for weeks, officers were drafted in from across the county and alcohol was temporarily banned for the game. Three hundred Derby hooligans waited for the Bushwhackers to arrive, but none showed. Only 400 Millwall fans made the trip and all were well behaved in the stadium.

The DLF have a history of using local non-league fixtures to fight with rival fans, so when Burton Albion were drawn at home to Leicester City in the FA Cup there was a tangible sense of excitement, especially when the match was switched to the Baseball Ground. Burton Albion returned 1,500 tickets and many of these were snapped up by the DLF. Any alliance that might have existed the previous summer was long gone as East Midland hostilities were renewed. However, on the day, it was Leicester who sparked the trouble. The Burton goalkeeper was knocked unconscious by a missile and seats were ripped out of the Osmaston Stand by Leicester fans and thrown at their rivals.

Later that year Derby travelled to Leicester for what turned out to be an explosive night. "Riot: Thugs Hurl Firebombs at Police," was the front-page newspaper headline following the game. The summer had seen several British cities explode in violence and now it was the turn of Leicester. In probably the worst violence involving Derby supporters since the 1970s, fans clashed during five hours of trouble.

Trouble began five minutes before the end of the game when bricks and bottles were hurled at police as they attempted to clear 50 Leicester hooligans gathering outside the away end. The Leicester mob grew to 300 as away fans were escorted out. Despite a ring of police, more than 1,000 Derby fans broke away to confront them. Outbreaks of violence soon spread to a nearby shopping centre and the Highfield area of the city, where 100 local youths threw petrol bombs at the police. Cars were overturned and shops wrecked. Forty people were arrested and at the height of trouble over 500 police were deployed.

The next eighteen months were relatively quiet. In February 1986, 100 Derby fans ran riot in Uttoxeter on their way back from a game in Blackpool. The trouble lasted an hour as Derby fans clashed with locals and a cast-iron pipe was thrown through a glass door of a pub. Eleven months later, Derby fans fought locals in Chesterfield as they returned from a match in Grimsby. A car was over-turned and shop windows smashed. Twenty arrests were made when Derby and Leicester clashed in the Milk Cup, and twenty-three fans were arrested when Derby played hosts to Stoke. Given what had occurred before, these were minor events.

The relative peace was shattered in March 1987 with the visit of Portsmouth. While little of the trouble involved DLF or even Derby fans attending the game, it was another dark day in the history of the club. An attack by 60 Portsmouth fans on an amusement arcade frequented by the city's young Afro-Caribbean community led to four hours of disorder. A car was set alight, barricades set up, windows smashed and police officers badly hurt as local black youths retaliated. The police claimed that the attack was pre-planned by Portsmouth fans, a claim that has recently been strongly denied by the 6.57 crew.

Such trouble was now increasingly rare. The DLF still turned out but trouble was nearly always restricted to pub fights as CCTV cameras made of arrest much greater at grounds. However, the violence often involved weapons. A Stoke fan was stabbed and 23 arrested in a clash before the local derby after Stoke began hurling milk bottles at local youths. On the opening game of the 1988/89 season, ten people were arrested after a pub fight with Middlesbrough. "It was vicious," said one onlooker. "One of the yobs even had a crowbar." There was also a clash with Newcastle fans in a bar in April 1988.

The late Eighties saw several more fights with Notts Forest. In October 1987, 500 Derby and Forest fans faced off at a sports centre before their game. In the return fixture, Derby fans took refuge as 80 Forest fans using hockey sticks, pool cues and bricks attacked them at a pub. A few seasons later, the local paper reported that 100 Forest caused "numer-ous problems" in Derby, stoning cars and smashing windows before and after the match.

The Sheffield clubs, particularly Wednesday, also emerged as key rivals for the DLF. In November 1989, a Wednesday mob attacked 200 Derby in a pub, smashing a dozen windows and terrifying drinkers. The landlord described the attack as organised, as the pub was well off the beaten track. "It would take some finding. If you didn't know it you would have to be looking for it. They came through an alley and started throwing bricks. They smashed about twelve windows. One guy with his leg in plaster was knocking them through with his crutch." After the game, which Derby won 2-0, the violence got worse as rival fans tried to get at each other outside the ground. Derby were heavily outnumbered by a mob of up to 1,000 Wednesday. Wednesday switched attention to the police, causing several injuries to chants of, "Charge them!" It was not the only charging that happened that day and many appeared in court following the disturbances.

After several years of languishing in Division Two, which in 1992 was renamed the First Division, Derby finally found a team that could at least challenge for promotion. In 1994, the club reached the play-offs, and were drawn against Millwall. The first leg was heavily policed but the return fixture received national attention. A DLF member recalls what became known as the Battle of Surrey Quays.

"During the first leg Millwall had a top firm out in town but OB was on top of it so we exchanged phone numbers and we arranged a meeting without OB in London. During two weeks there were some contacts and finally the meeting point was agreed, which was outside Surrey Quays tube station around 6 p.m., just a few miles from the Den and in the heart of Bermondsey. Derby travelled by train and coaches in small numbers and we met first, early in the morning, in a boozer outside King's Cross-St. Pancras and hours later in a pub outside Waterloo. We were around 150-handed and travelled on the Jubilee Line to Bermondsey without OB.

"Surrey Quays station is between two Millwall pubs, the Caulkers and Surrey Docks Wetherspoons, where the Millwall firm was drinking, waiting for us. I was impressed with Millwall's massive numbers because I had never seen those kind of numbers at any club level. A good bit of toe-to-toe went on before OB arrived and we were escorted to the ground."

Derby lost in the play-off final. It meant they were back down in South London a fortnight into the following season. Tensions were running high between the two sets of fans and the media were all camped out at the New Den hoping to report their moral indignation at a repeat performance. Unfortunately, the hooligans were not prepared to follow the script and met at a prearranged location well before the match at Surrey Quays station and there were several minutes of running battles until the police arrived to restore order.

The Derby keeper, who had been attacked during the play-off encounter, was abused as he ran onto the pitch and gave the finger to home supporters. There was a moment of silence as everyone watched to see the Millwall reaction but there was none.

Hooliganism tailed off at Derby as the police tightened their grip. The DLF clashed with Forest in 1997 but this was the only incident between the two mobs after 1988. Many Derby lads received banning orders and others found it hard to obtain tickets for the East Midlands' derbies and were shut out of city centre pubs in Nottingham. In more recent years the police have taken to writing to known hooligans of both sides before games, advising them not to attend. "The police have won this one," said one DLF member. "Both groups try to put out some sort of presence but this is more of a show than a belief that there will be a good off."

With the lack of action against Forest, the two Sheffield clubs have emerged as Derby's key rivals and in the 2002/3 season they clashed three times. On the opening day of the season, 150 Sheffield United fans stopped in Derby on their way back from a game in Coventry and attacked two pubs where the DLF were drinking. The trouble spread to the streets where the gangs fought running battles. The police were unprepared, having stood their officers down after a peaceful home game against Reading. When they eventually mobilised enough forces they rounded up the Sheffield fans, searched them and videoed them one by one.

Three months later the DLF sought revenge when they travelled to the Steel City to play Sheffield Wednesday. Despite the police turning back a large number of Derby lads travelling without tickets, there were still enough to clash with United after they had returned from Nottingham. Adding to the melee was a group of Barnsley fans who had decided to stay for the fun rather than watch their team in Chesterfield. The main trouble occurred between 6 and 8 p.m. on Saturday in the Campo Lane area and a police helicopter monitored the movements of hooligans. Sporadic outbreaks of violence continued until the early hours. There was further trouble at Wednesday's return fixture, three months later, and an Ilkeston policeman was slashed after trying to break up a fight.

Later that year, Derby hooligans were involved in fighting at a boxing match in Rotherham after 200 supporters travelled to watch boxer Scott Haywood. According to a local newspaper, "Violence first broke out in the 1,000-strong crowd during the third round of the former amateur star's bout against Birmingham's Arv Mittoo at about 5 p.m. A tearful Mr Haywood jumped from the ring into the crowd to plead for his supporters to stop. The disturbance was quashed after Mr Haywood, who had sold tickets himself touring Derby pubs, renewed his calls for calm over the microphone. He continued the bout and won. But, after the match, fighting flared again and more than 90 police officers with tear gas and dogs were called to quell the trouble. The following boxing matches were cancelled. Mr Haywood, who was in his dressing room when the trouble started, said: 'I couldn't believe it when I saw what was happening. It was horrible. These people are not my fans, they are just idiots. It is a small minority spoiling it for everybody else. I don't know who they are, but I will find out and I don't want anything more to do with them. I could be banned for this. I haven't cried for years but I couldn't stop after this. I'm just distraught.'"

By the summer of 2004 Derbyshire police were confident that the banning of over 50 supporters in Operation Cabby had dealt a severe blow to the DLF's ability to organise and inflict violence. They were particularly pleased with the banning of twelve younger Derby fans attached to a youth firm, the Derby Orphans, following an away match at Walsall. The subsequent court hearing heard how the twelve taunted home supporters, gave nazi salutes and sang anti-Catholic slogans. Had the authorities taken on board a Derby MP's proposals in 1976 to jail all hooligans, there is a reasonable chance that the Orphans would never have been conceived.

DONCASTER ROVERS

Ground: Earth Stadium
Firms: Doncaster Defence Regiment
Rivals: Mansfield, Hull

The Doncaster Defence Regiment is not the biggest hooligan mob around but it is known as a tough little outfit. Their numbers reflect partly the poor fortunes of the team over the years but also many lads within the town are drawn to bigger nearby clubs, amongst them Leeds (Donny Whites) and Sheffield Wednesday. The relationship between these groups and the DDR has occasionally been fraught and there has been trouble with the Leeds group. During one FA Cup game at Everton in the mid-Eighties, a Donny White unrolled a huge Leeds Union Jack in the Park End in an attempt to wind up the Scousers from the safety of the fenced off enclosure. It caused outrage amongst the travelling Doncaster fans and the culprit was given a kicking, much to the delight of the Everton fans unable to get at him.

"I know they used to have a tasty thirty or so who used to do it with Leeds and they once mullered some Grimsby at a train station on the outskirts of Doncaster in the mid 1980s," recalled Barnsley fan Stewart. "Barnsley went there for a pre-season friendly in 1986 and it went off outside the train station before the game. We were 130-handed that day but one of the lads was run over on the by-pass when fighting broke out. A coachload of Donny were prevented from travelling to Wigan and they ended up in York ,where they carved up a couple of YNS [York Nomad Society] lads."

There have been a number of clashes with Mansfield over the years. In 1983, a Mansfield fan was left unconscious and 13 people were arrested after rival supporters clashed at a first round FA Cup tie at Field Mill. The injured man was caught in the middle of a group of Doncaster fans and was repeatedly kicked before police could rescue him. A Doncaster fan was also severely kicked and needed treatment from the St John Ambulance. "The sickening violence formed an unwanted support bill to the main action," reported the local paper. It went on to say that many ordinary fans would have been put off attending another football match for the rest of the season.

Doncaster's relationship with Mansfield worsened during the mid-Eighties, when a lot of lads were involved in the Miners' Strike. Mansfield, by contrast, drew its support from the Nottinghamshire coalfields, most of whose miners continued to work. Years later, in early 2003, there were 14 arrests when the two clubs met in Mansfield.

The DDR earned the respect of Cardiff's Soul Crew after the two mobs clashed in the early Nineties. In 1991, a small firm of 25 Doncaster travelled to Cardiff, at a time when many bigger crews wouldn't. After the game Cardiff caught part of the crew at the train station and fighting broke out. Cardiff returned the favour for the away match when 50 Soul Crew travelled up, but there was no sign of the DDR at home. "On another occasion some of us went up to Doncaster after we won promotion at Scunthorpe," remembered the Soul Crew's Tony Rivers. "There were running battles for ages. We came out on top but they still gave us a run for our money."

Hull have been another team to have clashed with Doncaster over the years. During one fight a Hull supporter was so badly cut up that he required dozens of stitches.

In May 1998, Doncaster were relegated to the Vauxhall Conference, where they were to remain for five years. They became known for having some of the more aggressive non-league supporters, occasionally terrorising small, sleepy towns unused to invasion by travelling fans. Then, in May 2003, a third-place finish followed by victories over Chester City in a two-leg play-off semi-final and then Dagenham and Redbridge after extra-time in the final took them back into the League. Within a year they were promoted again and were now in Division One.

"Doncaster also have a big rivalry with Scunthorpe," said Stewart. "There was an incident one evening at Doncaster's dog track when a coachload of Scunny lads turned up on a stag night. A load of Donny lads got wind of their presence, went down there, kicked it off big time and one of the Scunny lads was killed in the fight. A few weeks after that incident a coachload of Scunthorpe lads were stopped by the police en route to Doncaster and a search discovered axes and other weapons on board."

A mid-season friendly at home to Scunthorpe in November 2001 saw a clash before the game. Fifty Scunthorpe had gathered in Yates's Wine Lodge when a group of 25 Doncaster attacked them. A woman suffered a head injury and a man was also hurt as bottles and glasses were exchanged. A number of arrests were made. Three years later was Doncaster's first visit to Scunthorpe after they returned to the Football League and this time the police took no chances. Two days before the game, Sgt Brian Burns, of Scunthorpe Police, said, "The police presence will be strong, with staffing increased due to intelligence and the potential for disorder. This should ensure this fixture goes smoothly and police resources are able to respond to any developing tension."

Earlier that season, nine people had been arrested during fights between rival fans at the Carling Cup match between Doncaster and Grimsby, with trouble in the town centre and even on the pitch. In November 2003, the DDR clashed with York fans in the Golden Lion pub in Church Street. Two women customers were hurt and a party of elderly tourists was showered with glass and beer during the battle involving up to 30 fans. "I have been here four years and I have never seen anything like it," said the landlord, John Raw. "It was like something from the Wild West."

DUNDEE and DUNDEE UNITED

Grounds: Dens Park and Tannadice
Firm: Dundee Soccer Crew, Tannadice Trendies, Dundee Utility, Under Fives
Rivals: Aberdeen, Hibs

A local derby against town or city rivals usually brings out the worst in soccer violence, but not so in Dundee. The football hooligans who follow Dundee and Dundee United actually mob up together, and the only argument tends to be over deciding which opponent to face on any particular weekend. Fans of the two clubs have been battling since the early Seventies, particularly against Aberdeen, and by the early Eighties there were two mobs in town, the Dundee Soccer Crew, who followed Dundee, and the Tannadice Trendies, who followed Dundee United.

It was the emergence of the casual trend, and more specifically the birth of the Aberdeen Soccer Crew, that spurred them to better organisation and

bigger numbers. Yet the early casuals were in a minority and were widely disliked, even attacked, by other groups in Dundee.

"It was in the 1983/84 season that the Dundee Soccer Crew and Tannadice Trendies joined forces to form the Dundee Utility thugs," recalled one veteran. "Dundee just wasn't big enough for two firms and Dundee city centre could be a dangerous place, with everyone wanting to have a go with the casuals, so it was decided that two small mobs wasn't good enough. It was good to have the pick of two teams' fixtures; the only bad thing is that we probably didn't travel as much as we should have and there have been a lot of arguments about what team to follow."

Dundee's longstanding rivalry is with Aberdeen. They are in relatively close proximity and Aberdeen fans have to pass through Dundee on their way to or from virtually every game. This has meant trouble between the two sides was possible most Saturdays of the season. "One of the first incidents in around 1984 ended in a Dundee lad getting slashed across the hand in Castle Street, Dundee," said the veteran. "On New Year's Day, 1985, twenty-five very game Dundee ran into a huge mob of ASC outside a shop on Dens Road and the police had to break it up. One trip we made up there was in 1988 with twenty-two Dundee youth, the oldest being nineteen. This match marked the beginnings of the Under Fives, who were to become a significant force in the 1990s. We got in a few battles after the game, doing very well. The police seemed to be very lenient at the time, turning a blind eye to a few incidents at the station, which of course we appreciated. As a result, we began travelling more often and with greater numbers.

"By the mid-Nineties the Under Fives were in full swing and we started pulling good numbers to go up to Aberdeen, averaging fifty to 120 lads. From around 1993 to 1997 there was so much trouble between the two teams they started mass arrests whenever we came up. Eventually this took its toll on our mob and we were no more. A few lads tried to keep it going but failed.

"During our break between 1997 and 2002, word went around that Aberdeen lads were stopping off in Dundee on their way home from Glasgow as they thought it was now a quiet place for a drink. How things change. Later on, in town, after most of our mob had gone home, seven of us decided to go into the station for a nose to see if there were still any ASC hanging about. We walked along the tunnel into the station not knowing how many Aberdeen could be in there and when we got to the end of the tunnel we heard shouts and the sound of people running up the stairs. We backed off, worried how many they were, but when we realised there were only eleven of them we turned round and steamed right in. With Aberdeen legging it and one of them getting a kicking in the tunnel, this small battle between a handful of lads seemed to spark life back into Dundee's mob, though we knew they would be down with serious numbers for the next game."

Mobilisations for big away days came via the usual word of mouth but also an intermittent newsletter produced by the Utility. *Utility News* and "Utility factsheets" appeared in the mid-Eighties and mainly gave details for big away days. "AFC v DFC 22/3/86 Utility take note," opened one such flyer. "The trip to Tynecastle was well attended, but you all know we can do much better; for the following trip to Pittodrie we're looking for a full turnout … no excuses whatsoever. We have absolutely nothing to fear by going to Aberdeen, especially

DUNDEE UTILITY SOCCER CREW KICKING AND PUNCHING YOUR TOWN AND CASUALS TO PIECES 2004 – 2005 SEASON

A leaflet produced by the Dundee Utility Crew, a combined force of Dundee and Dundee United yobs.

with a full mob. Over the past couple of seasons a hard core of the firm have never missed a DFC game at Pittodrie. We know most of the ASC moves when they are at home, although when they are away from home they always tend to be full of the business, at home the ASC are cautious of being arrested, with the Utility at full strength we will go to Aberdeen and do what we want to do." Readers were given travel details and told to board the train quietly so as not to attract the attention of the police. Arriving in Aberdeen, the lads were told to head for a certain pub. The final instruction was to "memorise the information above, then destroy this newsletter."

Dundee were not alone in producing these flyers. A 17-year-old Aberdeen fan was sentenced to three months' youth detention for distributing flyers before the two teams met in a Scottish Cup semi-final in Edinburgh. Dundee were dismissed as wimps and urged to put up at least some resistance rather than their usual running away. Sheriff Muir Russell described the flyer as "an appalling document, clearly designed to incite violence".

In the 1980s Aberdeen clearly had the numbers over Dundee and generally bossed the show. However, by the early 1990s the Dundee mob had matured, while Aberdeen were still reeling from an attempted ambush of Hibs in 1986 that went badly wrong. The Under Fives had come to the fore and the contest with their rivals was more even. In March 1992, a mob of 50 Dundee, backed by seven Welsh visitors, were drinking in Clarkie's bar on Union Street when about the same number of Aberdeen appeared. Dundee piled out of the pub and forced the ASC back down the road. The police soon rounded up Dundee and escorted them to the ground but not before a huge Dundee Utility Union Jack was hung over a bridge en-route to wind up the locals.

Around 120 Dundee, most squashed onto an incredibly overloaded double-decker bus, met, as arranged, in the Malthill bar early to await Aberdeen's inevitable arrival. "The bar was tiny with two doors and our entire mob was crammed in," remembered one lad present. "We had a few lads outside keeping an eye out, then they came running in and shouted that they were here. Every one threw their drinks down and tried to get out the crammed pub, squeezing through one door. There were only around forty-five Aberdeen who did stand for a bit but when the other pub door opened and the full mob spilled out, they had no chance. They ran and didn't stop and we chased them for what seemed miles. All the way up to the ground the mob went crazy and smashed shop windows and gave kickings in side streets to Aberdeen lads. After the game the Old Bill were everywhere. We tried to get into town, but they just rounded us up on the grass with their motorbikes and stuck us on our coach at the beach boulevard."

The two other clubs that Dundee have repeatedly clashed with are Hibernian and Glasgow Rangers, and against both there have been victories and defeats. Dundee are the first to admit that between 1989 and 1993 their record against Hibs was embarrassing. Hibs' mob comprised many older lads and, though Aberdeen could probably still pull out greater numbers, the Hibs Soccer Casuals were the more feared, while Dundee were the poor relations.

It was against Hibs that most Dundee casuals believe they suffered their worst defeat. Before a home match in 1990, a small mob of no more than fifteen Hibs arrived at Dundee bus station and ran a bigger, but much younger, group of Utility. "Our average age must have been around sixteen," recalled one. "So when you're up against a mob like Hibs who were all older, experienced lads, you've no chance."

After a few years the battles became more even, with the same Dundee lads growing older, and the 1993/94 season saw the beginnings of a reversal of fortunes. The turning point came towards the end of the season when 50 Hibs travelled to Dundee, only to be backed off in the city centre. Dundee took it as a victory and Hibs, wanting revenge, called a planned fight when the clubs met again in Edinburgh on the first day of the following season. Dundee met up in a bar on William Street, having travelled down in small numbers to avoid the police. For added secrecy, only one or two Hibs lads knew the final meeting point and it was agreed that they would ring Dundee lads to confirm on the day. Dundee, by now, had up to 60 lads crammed into the bar but there was no phone call. Hibs had obviously decided to keep their own arrival secret and, unannounced, 50 came bouncing down the road. Four Dundee in the pub doorway raced out to meet them but it was no more than a token gesture and they retreated as fast as they had raced out. The

remainder of Dundee were oblivious to events outside until Hibs actually began attacking the pub. After the initial surprise, Dundee steamed out and a huge battle commenced in the street, with several Hibs and Oldham lads, with whom they were closely linked, being badly injured. The police finally arrived, arrested some Dundee lads and escorted the rest to the station.

The battle was not the sort of image the city was keen to present. Tens of thousands of people were in Edinburgh for the annual festival and many were caught up in the trouble. "I was very frightened," Italian tourist Paulo Evangelista told the local paper. "I came here to see the festival, not a street fight." Company director Ian McDonald concurred: "I came out for a quiet drink and ended up in the middle of a war zone. The boys were smartly dressed and came into the pub in ones and twos. You could feel the tension in the air and it erupted when somebody shouted, 'Hibs.' All hell broke loose after that and it was really ugly for five to ten minutes."

In another fight, before a Dundee United match, a lad known as Teardrops or Spiderman because of his extensive facial tattoos led the troops into battle. "This guy was nuts," laughed the veteran. "Above all, he hated Hibs with a vengeance." Thirty Dundee faced 30 Hibs and Teardrops steamed in shouting his usual battle cry, 'Canna fight, they canna fight.' Everyone else followed and, by the end, two Hibs lads were in hospital. After the game there was further trouble, this time between 80 Hibs and 200 Dundee. Each time the police thought they had contained the trouble it started somewhere else.

A week later the Edinburgh side were back in Dundee, this time playing Dundee. One hundred and fifty Hibs gathered in the Centenary pub and the one officer on the door could do little when 80 Dundee came up the road. Heavily outnumbered, the Utility were soon on their toes.

The casual fashion took off in Dundee a year or two after it emerged in Aberdeen. Despite their rivalry, there seems to have been a lasting respect for their northern rivals. The same could not be said of their attitude towards the west coast teams like Rangers, Celtic and Motherwell. Dundee Utility has had a right-wing element within its ranks but was never interested in the religious sectarianism of Glasgow. They also looked down on the small casual scene in Scotland's biggest city, as one Utility flyer revealed. "You are a disgrace to the name 'casuals', you wear the very best in second hand gear (Fred Perry, Bukta, Puma, Adidas, Kappa, Nike.) You want to give it up. It is rumoured that some of you religious bigots wear FILA. Very good but that went out last August, so get saving up your Giro's (or family allowance in your case) you poverty stricken peasants and buy yourself some decent 'casual' gear. But please, before trying any of these exclusive garments, have yourselves fumigated by Rentokil so that when we're browsing around we don't catch any of your resident Glaswegian diseases such as Ricketts, Typhoid, Rabies, AIDS, Black Death or Plague." It was signed off by, "City of Dundee Casuals (Best Dressed in Scotland)."

Over the years, Dundee has had fewer clashes with Celtic and Rangers than with Aberdeen and Hibs. The Old Firm clubs have swamped Dundee during their travels and, especially in the 1980s, were slower to take up the casual hooligan culture. However, there have been a few very violent incidents.

The worst against Rangers was a Monday night home match in 1986. Dundee's mob had gathered early, knowing that Rangers would walk up from the station. They hid among the bus shelters and doorways on the High Street with a view to ambushing their guests. The plan worked, with 50 Rangers being caught from every side by small groups of Dundee. A vanload of locals drove straight at the visitors and lads armed with hammers piled out of the back. To make matters worse, as the defeated Rangers group arrived near the ground, they were again attacked by Dundee, though this time with a foul concoction of oil and piss.

For a Dundee outing to Glasgow in February 1995, the lads hired a double-decker bus, but only 44 turned up. "Rangers had a good mob at the time and we were pissed off we didn't have a full bus, but regardless we decided to leave for Glasgow," said the veteran. "Our plan was to get off the bus in the Gallowgate, which is a Celtic area, and Rangers would come and get us. Rangers are well known for using weapons and we knew they would come tooled up. One of our other encounters with Rangers ended up with two lads getting slashed, so one of our lads decided it would be a good idea to take a flare gun. We got into Glasgow around three o'clock, found a pub, as we had no intention of going to the game, and sat tight. One of the lads

phoned Rangers to let them know we were there and they said they would phone back when they were on their way.

"We sat around drinking for what seemed ages and everyone was getting a bit impatient, until eventually they called to say they were on their way and we started getting ready. It was funny because we were in a Celtic pub and the barman knew why we were there and was sound. He even let someone break up a broken stool for us to use as coshes, but I remember him shouting to someone, 'Leave my fucking pool balls alone,' when they were stuffing them in their pockets. We went out, looking for Rangers but no show, so we headed back in. It was getting dark outside and still no Rangers, our bus was coming for us shortly so we decided to wait in the street in case it showed. The bus came and every one got on a bit pissed off that Rangers had shat it.

"I was at the back, upstairs, drinking my bottle when the bus started moving. As I looked out of the window, I could hear shouting and saw a lad with a yellow bin above his head running at the bus. Then I saw a mob running down the road behind him. It was Rangers. We piled down the stairs shouting to the driver to stop. Someone pushed the doors open and we all jumped out. Rangers were in the middle of the road carrying the biggest arsenal of weapons I've seen at a football match. It kicked of briefly but Rangers backed off.

"The lad with the flare gun pointed it at a Rangers lad, but I don't think the target realised what it was and said, 'What you gonna do with that?' Next thing, bang, the flare missed him and landed up the road, lighting up the whole street. Another flare went off and Rangers were running. We decided to get back on the bus, but as we did they came back. We got off and chased them again. This went on and on until suddenly the police were everywhere. They boarded the bus and found the flare gun down the back of a seat. They also found a sword lying on the road and a load of sticks that Rangers had dropped when we ran at them. They took the bus to the police station and nicked all forty-four of us. Most of us were released on the Monday but seven were held and charged with mobbing and rioting."

The fight was one of the most violent in Scotland for many years. Indeed, the police in Glasgow told the media that it was their worst incident in the city

Dundee United fans in Glasgow to see their team play Aberdeen in a Scottish Cup final clash in the street with a mob from Rangers.

since the introduction of the Criminal Justice (Scotland) Act in 1980. The police were initially coy over the weapons used in the trouble, saying only that, in addition to knives and coshes, "other bits and pieces of a more dramatic nature" were recovered. One newspaper reassured readers that they understood no guns were involved.

Trouble with Celtic has been much less frequent. Possibly the worst incident occurred just before the 2005 Scottish Cup Final, when 30 fans were arrested after a mini-riot. Police said that the disturbances in the Gorbals area were pre-planned. Another 16 fans were arrested as rival groups fought immediately outside the stadium.

Like many Scottish clubs, the Utility developed links with other Scottish and English mobs. During the 1980s it was Arbroath, and more recently a few Airdrie lads have joined up with them at Scottish games. However, the main Dundee link has been with Stoke City. Dundee met a few Stoke on holiday

around 1995 and decided to take a trip down to Wolves with them. After that, Dundee travelled down quite often and Stoke went up to Scotland a few times, mostly for cup games at Hampden.

One of the most ambitious trips down south was for 50 to travel to Stoke's away game at Millwall, but it never got off the ground. "The Millwall game was a set-up," explained one of the lads. "We met in a bar in Dundee and planned to leave from a nearby park to avoid the police. We left the pub and got carryouts for the bus. As we walked up we were all stuffing tins in our pockets. Then unmarked vans came into the car park with Old Bill jumping out of the back, shouting, 'Get your hands on the seats or you'll be handcuffed.' You could hear all the drugs and weapons being thrown under your seat from the folk behind. The police boarded the bus and said we had conspired to mob and riot in the Stoke and Millwall areas and we would be getting nicked. We were taken to the police station and held for six hours with some being done for drugs and weapons offences. A small number of lads also lost their clothes – they couldn't pick their bags up from the bus as they had stuff they shouldn't have in them. To my knowledge only a few Dundee made it down, where there was a massive operation in London and no trouble."

"Police thwart rent-a-mob football mob," screamed the front page of the local paper. "A terrifying alliance of Scottish and English football hooligans threatened havoc at Millwall's clash with Stoke on Saturday. Thugs supporting Dundee United were intercepted and arrested as they tried to make their way to London on Friday. They had allegedly been recruited by the Stoke supporters to help with the planned chaos. Tayside police were tipped off by the National Criminal Intelligence Service and moved to stop them making the trip to London. Acting on the same information, police in London stopped 300 Stoke fans without match tickets at Wembley and Baker Street tube stations and escorted them to and from the game in police coaches. Lewisham Chief Supt Ken Chapman said: 'You do get these unholy alliances between certain football clubs and it makes our life difficult.'"

In recent years, police in Scotland have got a lot tighter around football and Dundee is no exception. "They really got on top in '97," admitted one lad. "After years of getting away with doing what we wanted, fifty lads got locked up in one go for just walking down the road in Aberdeen. They would nick known faces for just being there. This happened a few times, big mobs getting arrested for nothing. Then, to make things worse, we got our whole mob nicked up there for fighting with a fucking pool team. We were waiting for the ASC after the game when someone started arguing over a game of pool. Next thing, pool balls and cues were flying about the pub.

"We had a break, then came back in 2002 bigger and stronger than before, only to find the Old Bill was even more clued up than ever. Mobs could go a whole season only getting one battle. We seemed luckier than most and got a few battles but we also had a good few lads nicked and by the end of the 2004/5 season our numbers had dropped from more than 100 to around fifty. Then the final straw was the recent Scottish Cup Final [against Celtic – see above]. We have had the mob decimated like this before but got it together again. This time I'm not so sure that we can do it again."

Ɛ

EVERTON

Ground: Goodison Park
Firms: Scallies, Snorty 40
Rivals: Middlesbrough, Manchester United, Chelsea

It was described as the worst football violence ever to take place on Merseyside, and the most sustained attack on Liverpool's police since the Toxteth riots more than 20 years before. The *Liverpool Echo* front page news on 21 February 2005 was a wakeup call, not only for the so called "super firm" from Manchester but also to the police and authorities, that serious football violence was alive and literally kicking at Everton Football Club.

"As Manchester United fans were escorted from Goodison Park they were met with a torrent of bricks and bottles as they reached Everton Valley and Scotland Road," said the report. "Despite there being around 35 police vans just yards away, dozens of trained police dogs and the force helicopter hovering above, the hooligans were not put off. The assault was as ferocious and sustained as anything seen in Liverpool for decades."

Chief Insp Chris Armitt told the paper, "Around 300 rival supporters appeared and there was a violent and large-scale confrontation. Officers intervened and came under attack. The rival fans were ripping up fences and picking up bricks and throwing them at the crowd. Obviously it was a slow process to move the crowd along Scotland Road and the bombardment lasted for a full hour, I have been in this job for some time and I can say it was the worst football-related violence ever seen in Liverpool."

During the violence, 33 supporters were arrested and held overnight at separate police stations before being released on bail. Assistant Chief Constable Mick Giannasi said, "We are anticipating a significant number of post-incident arrests. This was an orchestrated incident and there were known football hooligans at this game."

The trouble was no surprise to the lads at Everton or United, but the media attention made hundreds of Chav-like hooligans all over the country sit up and take notice that Everton were still a hooligan force to be reckoned with. Meanwhile, old school veterans from the bigger firms probably scoffed at the headlines and remembered that visits to Goodison were often that eventful.

The city of Liverpool was perhaps more influential in the emergence of modern football hooliganism than anywhere else in the UK. Much has been written about the emergence of the casual fashion in Liverpool in the late Seventies, with the wedge haircuts and brand-label sportswear. But the first stirrings of the youth sub-culture that was to attract, involve and criminalise tens of thousands of British youth over the next three generations was first noticeable 20 years earlier. With football success being dominated by the cities of Manchester and Liverpool during this period, and the post-war boom bringing a big increase in disposable income for young people, travelling away with your team became a new phenomenon. And nowhere was this craze bigger than with Everton, whose fans, together with neighbours Liverpool, earned a reputation as football's worst train wreckers.

As far back as March 1956, *The Times* reported, "A British Railways official today described damage done to a number of trains by Liverpool football enthusiasts returning from the Everton v Manchester City match at Manchester on Saturday, as the worst in the history of the railways. He listed damage done to the last of six football excursion trains which arrived at Liverpool at 11.20pm: eight door windows smashed, five side windows smashed,

14 pictures broken, two mirrors cracked, one whole door missing, another door damaged, a door handle missing, dozens of light bulbs removed, several compartments heavily bloodstained, luggage racks pulled from the walls as though people had been swinging on them, and a number of slashed seats."

This was not an isolated incident. Throughout the late Fifties and early Sixties, Everton fans were notorious for demolishing train carriages, with one paper even describing them as the "Merseyside maniacs". Their impending arrival in towns and cities around the country was met with apprehension. "Shopkeepers lock up when Everton are in town," noted one local paper in November 1964.

In early October 1963, Everton fans had again hit the national news for damage they had caused to trains. Ten out of eleven coaches on a train carrying Everton supporters back from a match in Birmingham were badly damaged and had to be withdrawn from service. Windows were broken, light bulbs removed or smashed, light fittings ripped out, fire extinguishers emptied and even a lavatory pan torn out. Fed up with this continuing problem, the *Liverpool Echo* reported that a top level BR meeting had discussed the possibility of withdrawing all football specials in and out of Liverpool. The following day, attention turned to the schoolboys whom the authorities believed were behind the vandalism. One idea was to abolish the half-fares on the specials in a bid to discourage teenagers posing as schoolboys. In the end, as was so often the case with the way the authorities dealt with football hooliganism, the tough talk did not lead to action and a couple of months later the press were yet again reporting on vandalised trains transporting Everton fans back from matches.

In the autumn of 1963, football disorder was still a rare occurrence outside Liverpool and Manchester. On the pitch, ill-discipline was also a growing problem, as Everton manager Harry Catterick remarked in mid-November, "The game is being spoiled by ill-temper. Whether it is due to the amount of money successful teams and players are getting; whether the generation now playing has different standards from ours, I don't know. Perhaps it is a bit of both. Where you find a man getting ill-tempered you can be almost sure he is bound to lose his effectiveness."

Catterick was speaking about football in general,

though his intervention came shortly after an Everton home defeat against Blackburn Rovers that saw the referee book three Everton players and send off a fourth. That, coupled with the fact that no opposing player was booked, so incensed the home crowd that the officials had to shield their heads from garbage hurled at them as they left the pitch. Thousands of Evertonians congregated outside the players' entrance chanting, "We want the referee," and it took mounted police to clear them away.

A few days later, the Chief Constable of Liverpool City Police and the club chairman met to discuss "anti-missile precautions", including the erection of barriers behind the goals, a semi-circle enclave about 16 feet deep between the goal and the fans, and appeals to supporters over the public-address system. "Barring the crowd from the terracing immediately behind the goals would not necessarily by a permanent feature," noted the *Liverpool Echo*, "but it is felt by authority that some action should be taken now to offset the behaviour which is occasionally characterising matches." The paper concluded that while the club would lose revenue from several hundred fans, "this would be a small price to pay for effective action against the few who are tempted to throw things."

The moves to restrict hooliganism did not mean the club escaped censure from the Football Association. Only a day after the club announced its plans to erect barriers and create enclaves behind the goals, the game's governing body threatened the club with ground closure if further trouble occurred. "We have received two strong letters from the Football Association following incidents at home games against Tottenham Hotspur and Blackburn Rovers," a downbeat but defiant club chairman, John Moores, told the press. "The first made us responsible for the throwing of a dart, though we have no evidence that it was thrown by one of our spectators, and we have received many letters from supporters saying that the missile was thrown during the interval when Brown, the Tottenham keeper, was not even on the pitch. The second letter, even firmer in tone, followed misbehaviour of some supporters at the Blackburn Rovers game." While Moores reiterated that no Everton supporter had been prosecuted in the previous 20 years, he was anxious to act to prevent further trouble with the FA.

"Because we are anxious that Everton's good name should remain because we realise that further unruliness might lead to the FA closing the ground, we have taken the precaution of erecting barriers behind each goal in the hope that we shall get the co-operation of all our loyal fans in ensuring there is no further trouble. To call it a fence is wrong, we are not fencing our followers in; we are erecting barriers immediately behind the goals and barring a small section of the terracing to spectators. We have asked the football authorities for any ideas they might have on helping us to solve a problem that affects other clubs as well as ours, but so far they have not come up with any concrete suggestions."

The move was applauded by *Echo* sportswriter Leslie Edwards. "It would be fitting if the city which first gave the game goal nets (through a brainwave from the then City Engineer, Mr Brodie) should also be first to introduce effective measures against missiles, as they have come to be known."

The FA inquiry into repeated crowd trouble at Everton reported back a few days later and the club was issued with a £100 fine and ordered to post notices around the ground warning fans of future behaviour. The committee was also satisfied that missiles were thrown at the match with Blackburn Rovers, and had it not been for the action already taken by the club, the FA punishment would have been more severe.

A few days later, Chelsea manager Tommy Docherty was struck in the face by a missile thrown by an Everton fan. More objects were thrown when Everton played away at Fulham but this time it was two Blues players who were on the receiving end, including outside-left Derek Temple, who was hit on the back of the head by a metal staple.

From this period right up to the Heysel Disaster, Everton gained a reputation as one of the most active hooligan gangs. The antics of hundreds of lads that followed the club all over the country marked them as a major player in the unlicensed sport which, for over 30 years, did more harm to the reputation of British football than any of the lager-fuelled, chair-throwing antics that came to guarantee headlines for wannabe thugs all over Britain.

Whilst few clubs brought large away followings to Goodison, most games away from home saw large numbers of Evertonians following their team.

Goodison was something of a fortress, off the pitch at least, and while it was common practice for away fans to attempt to take home ends all over the country, very few bothered setting foot on to the Gwladys Street End. The notable exception was Millwall, but it was hardly the most successful day in F-Troop's riotous history.

"As a 17-year-old Millwall fan lay in Walton hospital with a stab wound in his right lung today, a team of detectives was looking for the knife gang who stabbed him and 10 other Millwall supporters," reported one paper. "Kevin Stoker, of Stepney, had an emergency operation at the hospital and was seriously ill for a while, although today the hospital said his condition was slightly improved. He and the other fans were attacked at the Gwladys Street end of Everton's Goodison Park ground on Saturday, before the start of the Cup match between Everton and Millwall. Four other stab victims were treated in hospital and kept overnight. Detective Chief Inspector Frank Jones was today leading the hunt for those responsible. He said, "We have searched the Goodison Park ground for weapons which may have been used."

One of the stab victims told reporters, "A lot of Everton supporters charged towards us. Some of ours tried to get at them and the rest tried to get away. I turned away and felt a sharp pain in my back. Somebody obviously had a knife. A couple of lads said they had seen screwdrivers and a hatchet. This is the first time I've ever been to Merseyside. I never thought anything like this would happen to me."

After press reports about the stabbings, substantial away followings became rare at Goodison and, with the exception of Man United and the North East's big two, Newcastle and Sunderland, only Wolves, Bolton, Leeds, Spurs and Forest brought numbers of note right up until the late Seventies, when segregation was introduced in the Park End, making the place safer, inside the ground at least. Soon, most clubs would bring a smattering of supporters, although very few came as a mob and fewer still looked for trouble.

Goodison's dangerous reputation had much to do with the belief that many Everton hooligans used knives. This fear had some substance; indeed Merseyside street gangs were notorious for their antics with blades. The introduction of the easily hidden Stanley craft knife, a terrace "trend" which both Everton and Liverpool used to their advantage for years after it appeared in the early Eighties, gave the Scouse football firms a special notoriety. But their hooligan rep was not based solely on slashings. Mobs of hundreds, bladed and otherwise, roamed the streets around the grounds on a match day. Liverpool was a hardened city riddled with poverty and crime, and with that came scores of youths hell-bent on taking out their frustrations on anyone who showed on their patch.

Failure on the pitch throughout the Seventies did little to discourage the Goodison faithful and the club retained an impressive support. With the exception of a couple of seasons in the late Eighties when attendances in general hit a slump, Everton averaged 36-38,000 fans for home games and were well-supported on their travels. During the mid Seventies and early Eighties their away support was made up of a hardcore of about 2,000 and the majority of those were regarded as lads or at least game blokes who would fight if necessary. With Everton being the poor relation in the race to fill their trophy cabinet, the majority of hangers on, fun supporters and glory hunters ended up at Anfield, leaving Everton's "firm" free from the kind of support which might crumble if it came on top.

However, others were now turning out to face Everton with increasing enthusiasm. Suddenly, places like Aston Villa, Stoke, West Brom, Derby and Bristol City saw mobs await the hated Scouse hordes and many places that once were regarded as "jollies" now turned nasty. Yet through to about 1979 there were few occasions when the cockiness of Everton's away following was seriously dented. Many of its away mob were streetwise scallies or hardened dockers, so the ingredients for violence were always present. Throughout the dark days of pitch invasions, end infiltration and mass disorder, Everton gave at least as good as anything the rival mobs had to offer.

Frequent trips to London were regarded as easy with the exception of West Ham. Everton did not take the numbers to Upton Park as they did to the other capital grounds – but claim they never hit the lows of the Reds across the Park, whose special train for a West Ham away game was once cancelled when only 14 had turned up at the time of departure.

Things did, however, sometimes go wrong. At least four games during the mid-Seventies saw Everton's mob come a poor second. The first was a trip to Leeds. Elland Road was never easy but on this day it was shocking, as Steve, who travelled all over the country in those days, recalled. "On this trip we all got a coach. It was an eye-opener and the last time I bothered using that method of transport. We pulled in at the last service station on the M62, kicked the fuck out of the outnumbered Huddersfield Whites, robbed all their scarves and did the service station, knowing the police response would be non-existent, given that we were ten minutes from the ground. Back on the coach, happy days so far. The tricky bit on approaching the ground was to avoid the fuckers on the motorway bridges dropping slabs through the coach skylights. That was always a worry at Leeds according to the coach driver, which dented our enthusiasm a bit. We got off at the main coach park adjacent to the rugby ground and mingled with all the bruised up Huddersfield Yokes, who now seemed to be in the majority. Where the fuck was everyone?

"We queue up for the Cowshed End, as we called it, and it was a double-click in and a brisk walk on to the terracing just in front of the South Stand. All the Leeds lads on the right were fenced in but with the minor detail of a gate left open at the top. I could never understand that.

"Half an hour into the game we were two down and the Leeds lot have been steadily coming through the gate at the top, ready for a rumble in our centre. Big mistake, as there must have been fifty-odd dockers complete with regulation donkey jackets ready for anything. The result was five-two to Leeds but a complete whitewash for the Scouse dockers.

"We all file out, the Dockers' Army go left, we go right and so do fucking hundreds of Leeds. We approached the rugby ground and by now their faster pace means that we are five minutes behind them as we reach our destination, huddled together and well down on numbers, while all of their boys are waiting across the road, tying the laces on their eight- and ten-hole Dr Martens, and more worryingly the cunts are all smiling.

"Anyone without a Leeds scarf was fair game. We were totally outnumbered in the heady days of the mass charge and got slaughtered at the top end of the coach park. We were all late teens or early twenties, they all had fucking kids our age. Some of the lads ran into the park, some broke for the motorway. Oh the fun of running into different mobs around the coaches in all the mayhem, everyone gets a dig, no time to recognise who's punching who, just got to find your coach amongst the hundreds that are parked up, hilarious looking back at it, but few thought so at the time.

"Finally we got on the coach only to realise six of us are missing. We picked up two on the motorway hard shoulder, one with a size ten Doctor Martens sole firmly imprinted on his forehead, and fuck the missing four, we're off home. Two days after the game we found out that one of the four was in a Leeds hospital with brain damage after the kicking he took. And they moaned when we chased them down Priory Road with hammers and a hatchet in the return game at Goodison!"

Cardiff City away in the FA Cup in 1977 saw Everton turn up in numbers, but most of South Wales was out for them and during fighting before, during and after the game, the home firm came out on top. Steve was one of the many Evertonians who arrived in Cardiff unaware of the reception awaiting them. "It was a four and a half hour trip on the ordinary train for the lads who did not want to go on the special. It's safer on the special but there is an ale ban and at the end of the day we were Everton, so fuck the escort and the fact the special gets you there safely. Bad move.

"We got to Cardiff General and were the proverbial lost sheep, standing out a mile and no-one had a fucking Scooby where to go or who to ask. Just outside the station was the main bus stop and someone with no idea and less brains walked over and asked some six foot Taff where the ground was. That was the second bad move of the day. He laughed through several missing teeth, grunted that the walk to Ninian Park was a long one, about thirty minutes – and within seconds we were hit from three sides. One of our lot poleaxed one of them with a full tin of Newcastle Brown and we were off. If you got away, great; if you didn't you were fucked. Unfortunately for me, I was never the best sprinter in the world, especially in Monkey boots that were a size too big, and I ended up standing and took option two: I got fucked.

"It was not all bad. After a first-class kicking, the Blue Birds picked me up and told me we had done better than Tottenham, who had run all the way to the ground in the previous round, and took us to

the pub. The Craddock Arms was obviously their local and I was introduced to Veggie from Barry Island and the rest of the crew who had ambushed us. I was well treated to pints of Brains all day, which helped the sharp pain in my balls wear off. After some commotion, two police birds came into the Craddock and to this day I have never seen two coppers virtually stripped, fondled and badly manhandled. They offered no response, they seemed to love it. It was a madhouse and next up was a lad with a wooden leg dancing on a table.

"Off we went to the game and at the ground, fuck me, it was alive with Everton. However, the Cardiff lot are coming through the same entrance as us and it's quite obvious that no Scouser has ever been further south in Wales than Rhyl and they're all under the misapprehension that this place is just as soft as the North Wales seaside resort.

"I walked up to the Bob Bank where all the Everton were congregated, feeling kind of smug that my new Welsh mate, Veggie, will watch my back. He was not impressed that the away following had taken the end, decided that there were too many Scousers about and kicked off within seconds. The Bob Bank at Cardiff ain't intimidating but it is open plan. Five thousand Everton were on there and a lot fewer Cardiff. No contest you might think; you'd think wrong. By half-time we were one-nil up but a few hundred down. All through the game they keep coming. One lad asked me for help as there was a Cardiff fan looking for him with a knife. They creamed us on the day. After the game there was nothing worse than looking at all our lads at Cardiff Central, a few metres from the ground, taking the piss from the safety of a fenced off station, all on the specials back to Lime Street. It was time to take a deep breath, keep your fucking head down and start the thirty-minute walk of death back to Cardiff General."

A game with a similar outcome was at Newcastle on a Good Friday, or "Bad Friday", as the *Daily Mirror* put it after fighting fans caused the ref to stop the game. The press bore some of the blame however; a report in the *News of the World* a week earlier had claimed Everton were taking 9,000 to the game, which meant that the whole of Newcastle turned out to meet them. Phil was a Newcastle fan who witnessed the carnage that day. "The *News of the World*'s 9,000 was obviously a misprint as there weren't even 900 Everton there. There were gaps in the fences the entire length of the East Stand and people used to go through them to move throughout the ground and some claim that lads working in the ground had sawn bits off the fence to make the gaps bigger, ready to attack the Scousers.

"It was one of those games when you knew it was going to go off, as loads of Geordies had mingled with the Everton lot well before kick off, then the Gallowgate End piled through, too. It spilled onto the pitch and the game was held up. I lost no sleep as in those days Goodison was as bad as it gets for away fans, and when I listen to some of the lads who represent today's so-called top mobs, I piss myself laughing. Most of today's crews wouldn't last five minutes with the gangs of old from Everton, Newcastle and beyond."

The same year Everton beat Manchester United 3–0 in the quarter-final of the FA Cup at Old Trafford. By the time the third goal went in and United's dreams of the final were gone, the ground rang with the sound of, "We'll see you all outside." They were true to their word and it was probably the worst trip to United that Everton ever endured. They would fare far better in years to come, however.

The away following was not deterred by the odd hiding and the chant of "What's our name? EVERTON!" was heard around the country. The away support grew and there was an air of invincibility about both Scouse firms once the casual scene hit Merseyside after a couple of raids on foreign soil by the Reds. According to Andy Nicholls, co-author of this book, there is little mystery about the emergence of the so-called scally or casual look: "Liverpool were in Europe every year, they robbed all the shops that stocked the sports clobber, copied the wedge haircut from a weirdo pop singer, the Asian market traders supplied the straight Lois jeans and 'bingo', the casual was manufactured. The look gave both the red and blue firms a cocky air of invincibility and both clubs' trendy armies thought that they were the cock of the land, never mind the cock of the North."

Hubris, however, can lead to nemesis, and for Everton it came on the first day of the 1978/79 season when hundreds of fans, many having swapped scarves and boots for Fred Perry and Stan Smith, left Lime Street and headed for Chelsea. After a pretty uneventful afternoon, the tube journey back to Euston turned into a nightmare when at Kensington High Street they were ambushed and suffered what is still regarded as the worst off-field result they have ever received.

It was later rumoured that Chelsea had a contact working at the station, and as the train pulled in and the doors opened, the power was turned off, leaving nowhere to go for the train and passengers alike. A massive onslaught followed, leaving scores of Everton fans injured, several with stab wounds. Token resistance was put up as the organised London firm, consisting of Chelsea thugs backed by hordes of punks and skinheads, indulged in a bit of "Scouse bashing".

For the return game, leaflets were distributed urging every street gang, urchin and consenting male with a decent punch to congregate at Gerard Gardens and seek revenge for "Kenny High Street". Only a huge police operation, which in 1978 was rare, prevented serious disorder. Although Chelsea did not bring great numbers, they did show, leaving the matter of retribution on hold for another season. It was reported in the local papers that over 500 hooligans had congregated two hours before the kick off, but were dispersed by squads of police acting on a "tip-off". A police spokesman was quoted as saying, "There could have been what can only be described as an organised attack." A picture was released showing an armoury of weapons confiscated at the match, which, despite the huge police presence, saw eight Londoners end up in hospital.

Chelsea's relegation that season to Division Two meant it would be a few years until Everton's chance to get even. After a few years passed Chelsea were duly promoted, having caused havoc across the country, and the fixture computer allocated the second Saturday of the season for the trip Everton's mob had wished for since the humiliation five years earlier. However, it was selected to be the first live match on terrestrial TV, following a new deal set up with the FA, which meant it was moved to a Friday night. This, if anything, helped the Everton mob, as it meant that the large number of normal supporters would watch from the comfort of their armchairs, leaving a hard-core mob at the game.

More than 400 Everton met at Euston but Chelsea were nowhere to be seen, and even a half-hearted attempt to enter the home seats did little to stir their interest. A win for Everton saw a minor Chelsea attack on the huge away end, occupied by fewer than 600 Evertonians, which was quelled when a couple of flares were sent into the Londoners, at least announcing to the watching millions at home that Everton's boys were in attendance. By the time the Scousers returned to Euston it looked like all the hype about revenge, and even Chelsea's credibility as a hooligan force, was in question. However a few unknown faces appeared on the station forecourt and announced that Chelsea were mobbed up and waiting in a couple of pubs near King's Cross, having decided to avoid police detection and wait for the chance of trouble away from the ground.

The majority of police had already left, leaving the several British Transport Police to watch in disbelief as hundreds of lads slipped through a side door and marched en masse the short distance to King's Cross. It was not long before Chelsea showed a large mob, but short of the numbers Everton had pulled. Armed with scaffolding poles, flare guns and gas, they launched a ferocious attack, steaming in from all angles. One was knocked out when a metal bin was planted over his head, then left for dead as his face and body were cut and slashed with a knife. The Chelsea tried to regroup but were unprepared for Everton's numbers, and were gone by the time the police had returned to find Euston Station refilling with jubilant Evertonians. "It was a long journey home, on a cattle train unfit for humans, but nobody minded," said one of the Everton firm.

That season ended in glory for Everton as they claimed their first Championship for 14 years, and off the pitch they took large mobs to every game. As well as Chelsea, the main opposition that season, Manchester United, Manchester City, and Leeds United in the cup, were all visited and overcome. However, the firm was truly spanked at QPR, a wake-up call to the Merseysiders that London, regardless who you are playing, is a dangerous place if you're not on your guard.

Arguments still rage within the Everton mob about this embarrassing encounter. Some say it was a Chelsea mob after revenge for King's Cross, others blame it on a firm prominent at the time who came from the White City Estate, but the fact is that Everton went looking for trouble and were ambushed by a huge mob of Londoners in west London, including many coloured youths near the estate. They were heavily armed, a huge bottle of

ammonia was smashed into the Everton lads as they went into battle, flares were fired, and before they could regroup they were chased back towards the station. A couple were stabbed and slashed, but while knife wounds heal once the stitches are removed, hurt pride takes longer and some still cringe when the incident is mentioned.

Hooligan pride was restored at Spurs, where Everton won 2–1 and virtually clinched the Championship on their nearest rival's home ground. Hundreds of Yids were waiting on Seven Sisters Road and the Everton firm of about 400 decided not to chance their arm and began following police advice to take the alternative route to Northumberland Park station. It was a night when reputations were made and a young lad, "Spike", began making clucking noises as the masses walked within the safety of a huge police escort, deriding his own fans for being "chicken". Within minutes, hundreds had taken the bait and, to the amazement of the Tottenham police and the huge Spurs firm, Everton ploughed up Seven Sisters to chase them off and claim their second victory of the night.

They were heady days for the club and the firm. In his book *Naughty*, Mark Chester recounted his experiences whilst with the formidable Stoke mob against the Blues that season. "After we attacked a pub near the ground, had we turned the corner and gone down County Road we would have come under attack from every angle. We had taken the initiative but were struggling in the end. It's no stroll in the park at Everton. In the corresponding fixture, Everton stormed all over the town centre and took the piss all day."

The aftermath of the Heysel Disaster in 1985, which led to a ban on British clubs in Europe, was a bitter pill for Everton FC. On the pitch, many believed they were ready to mount a serious assault on the European Cup, whilst off it, trips to Europe saw hundreds revel in the activities enjoyed for years by their rivals from across Stanley Park. Everton fans' behaviour had generally been impeccable in Europe, apart from one trip to Dublin, when they actually hijacked an Irish Sea ferry and tied up the captain.

After the tragic events in Brussels, many Everton hooligans decided enough was enough and "retired" from the scene. Dwindling numbers were reduced further when many Scousers got "loved

A mounted policeman attempts to clear the pitch during mass fighting between Everton and Southampton fans at an FA Cup semi-final at Highbury in 1984. More than 100 were arrested.

up" on pills and started travelling to raves in obscure places instead of the likes of West Ham away. This was the second time drugs had hit the mob; a few years earlier, the emergence of heroin on the streets of Merseyside saw many strong lads who were respected at the match return from a pre-season break stones lighter and wretched after becoming hooked to the brown. Many didn't return at all.

Still, a hardcore remained and lads who survived the lure of skag or Ecstasy are still at the forefront of the Everton firm, many of them in their late thirties and early forties. It was due to this hardcore that, during the Nineties, when most clubs' mobs were non-existent or only active for local derbies, Everton rekindled a reputation off the pitch. Major

disorder occurred at Manchester City when the Dry Bar, a City stronghold, was attacked, and in just a couple of months violence erupted in the streets of Leicester, Newcastle, Bristol City and Middlesbrough, as old firm members came out of the woodwork, having ditched the pills for the "charlie". Indeed, so popular was the white powder among them that the firm was nicknamed the Snorty 40 by a well-known Sheffield United fan who made frequent trips to Goodison and witnessed the lads in action with their fists and noses.

One major incident which made national headlines during this period was when the Wimbledon team bus was burnt out on the eve of a crucial relegation match at Goodison. After so-called hard-man Vinny Jones was reported to have said he was not concerned about sending Everton down, as their fans were hardly hostile, the bus was torched in the car park of the Lord Daresbury Hotel. "We are treating the incident as suspicious," said a police spokesman. The Blues won the game 3–2 after being 2–0 down, and the coach incident was not the only one regarded as suspicious, as those who witnessed the goalkeeping display of Hans Segers will confirm.

Whilst on the decline, violence never went away, and given the occasion old heads would still turn out in force. This was evident whenever Everton played Middlesbrough; a feud has existed between the two mobs for over two decades. A full complement was also always on parade for big FA Cup games. There cannot be many clubs whose fans celebrate with a trademark pitch invasion as much as Everton have done over the years, and at Highbury in the FA Cup semi-final against Southampton in 1984 the celebrations turned into one of the worst riots ever filmed on national TV at a football ground.

After a late winner in extra time, hundreds of Blues swarmed onto the pitch and pockets of fighting broke out before the game restarted. At the final whistle the pitch became a battlefield as mounted officers tried in vain to clear the playing surface of brawling mobs. A total of 75 hooligans were arrested, the majority of them from Merseyside, and around 100 people were injured. A team of ambulances ferried the injured to hospital, including ten police officers, one of whom was treated for knife wounds. Most of those arrested received fines at Highbury Magistrates Court. Five years later, 29 Everton fans were dealt with more severely and were jailed for a total of two and a half years after they attacked the Woodbine Pub on Blackstock Road before a game at Arsenal in December 1989.

The same season that Everton reached their first FA Cup Final for 16 years, 68 Everton fans were arrested at Villa Park after another semi-final riot and ten years later, despite a 4-1 victory against Spurs at Elland Road, 80 Everton thugs clashed with the Yids on the pitch, and officers were led away having been sprayed with CS gas. Spurs' world famous striker Jurgen Klinsmann complained to police that he had been punched when he tried to flee the pitch at the end of the game.

One surprising upturn in violence has been between the Everton and Liverpool mobs, not only on derby days but on other occasions in the city centre. Traditionally, encounters between the two sides were passionately contested but not overtly violent, and when there was trouble it was usually away from either ground and fuelled by disappointment and defeat rather than hatred. Indeed, large gatherings of Evertonians on the Kop and Liverpudlians on the Street End were frequent, though not always approved of by all.

A distinct cooling of relations in the past few years seems to be down to the lack of respect the younger members of the two mobs have for each other. Years ago, large numbers from both groups would join forces at Lime Street Station and take on visiting firms and even travel to the tougher away games to support each other off the pitch. This is now a distant memory. Liverpool blame Everton for the start of the hostilities, accusing them of breaking a minute's silence in memory of the Hillsborough Disaster ten years after the tragedy. It did happen, though Evertonians say nobody could have been more supportive than their club and fans towards the disaster victims and their families. They say the "divorce" goes back much further and stems from Heysel; they blame the behaviour of Liverpool fans for the subsequent ban on British clubs and its detrimental effect on Everton as a force in European football. Elements among both sets of supporters hit new lows when a memorial statue to Everton legend Dixie Dean was twice covered in red paint, and on each occasion the Hillsborough Memorial was vandalised a day later in apparent retaliation.

The past five years has seen disorder at both Goodison and Anfield, and at night the city centre is heavily policed. Late one night, gangs clashed after a match on the very weekend that dignitaries were visiting the city to decide whether Liverpool would be made European City of Culture. Merseyside's Chief Constable was contacted about the trouble, resulting in the force helicopter collecting him from his garden. From the sky he witnessed firsthand how hostilities were stretching his men to their limits, allegedly while still in his pyjamas.

He apparently gave stiff instructions to smash the gangs, targeting leading members from both sides. Soon, letters were issued to known hooligans warning them not to attend certain games and to stay out of the city centre. Gradually, after years of collecting evidence, the police were given the go-ahead to take out injunction orders on several "Category C" hooligans, classed as the worst kind.

Many banning orders have been secured since Liverpool was granted the Capital of Culture title. "In a 400-page document used in the court case against me, a total of fifty-four Everton targets' names were blanked out," says author Andy Nicholls. "I contested the ban despite twenty-one football-related arrests and being named as target two in the top secret dossier, but magistrates were unsympathetic towards 'Everton's hooligan author' and handed me a two-year exclusion order from not only designated football grounds where Everton or Home International countries were playing, but also from Liverpool city centre, or the L1 to L32 postal addresses, when Everton, Liverpool or Tranmere play. Not wanting to miss an opportunity to put their own house in order, Everton Football Club banned me for life from Goodison Park."

After a hastily arranged board meeting, an Everton spokesman said, "After a lengthy meeting with the board of directors, it was decided that Andy Nicholls is not the sort of person we want associated with Everton Football Club." Sergeant Ian Millar, the football liaison officer for Everton FC was more pointed: "After months of dedicated undercover police work costing thousands of pounds, we have finally prevented a very dangerous thug from attending any football matches." Nicholls responded on a local radio station: "Many thousands of pounds have been wasted during this operation to ban me. All Merseyside Police had to do was go into W.H.Smith's and buy my book for £15. Everything I'm guilty of is in it."

Everton's following have often been accused of racism, and the club itself had a poor record of picking black players: just one had turned out in an Everton shirt since the war until a few celebrated imports joined the white-only gathering at Everton's Bellfield training ground during the mid-Nineties. This lack of ethnic mix was also evident on the terraces and in the stands at Goodison Park, and even today, whilst most clubs have hundreds of coloured and Asian fans, Everton's support seems almost exclusively white. Despite that, two coloured lads were prominent firm members in the Seventies and Eighties, and were highly regarded by their fellow hooligans.

"The club could probably have done a lot more to rid themselves of the racist tag but chose not to, so at the end of the day they are as much to blame as the bigots in the crowd," said Andy Nicholls. "One point that is important to make though is that at no time did Everton have large group membership in any of the right-wing parties such as the NF and the BNP, in fact on many occasions recruitment campaigns were halted when they came under attack from locals who took offence to skinheads in flying jackets leafleting outside Goodison. On the negative side, the same misfortune befell members of the left-wing groups who attended, drumming up support for the Anti Nazi League."

During the Sixties, an influx of Catholic connections meant that to many, Everton were also regarded as a "Catholic club". However, it has never been regarded as an issue to any of the firm members. Neither Celtic or Rangers have been made welcome and both clubs have been visited pre-season by huge Everton mobs. Indeed, Liverpool's friendship with Celtic may, if anything, have turned some Everton supporters towards Rangers, indicating the fickle nature of such allegiance. During the Eighties, a large number of Everton thugs attacked a pro-Republican march in the city centre shortly after the death of hunger striker Bobby Sands, and some of Everton's firm have attended the Orange Lodge parades in Merseyside for many years. These instances counted for nothing when Rangers arrived in 1997 for Dave Watson's testimonial; the *Liverpool Echo* reported on its front page that fighting had marred the occasion and over 70 people had been arrested.

Despite the lure of drugs and organised crime, or the deterrent of repressive police measures, Everton kept a firm together when many of the bigger clubs were unable to, and in July 2002 were involved in some of the worst rioting seen by an English club abroad for many years. Before a pre-season game at Anderlecht, 100 Everton fans clashed with 300 locals an hour before the game in Brussels and after the match more than 500 visitors broke through police barricades and rampaged back to the city centre.

At one point, the police fled, leaving behind riot

clothing and batons which were used against them. Despite several attempts to control the visitors, the police were eventually forced into a retreat which included the water cannon being switched off and reversed for a mile at speed as gangs surrounded it and attempted to attack the driver with metal poles and fencing.

Certain trips continue to attract the hardcore element. One was away to Wolves towards the end of the 2004/05 season. Evertonian Gee tells it as he saw it: "Travelling with Everton away from the main mob can have its advantages, less attention from the OB and less chance of getting collared with a section 60. Word had gone round that there would be a proper turnout for this one. No messing. Upon arriving in the Midlands, I was told the vast majority of ours had been rounded up and were under the keen eye of West Midlands' not-so-finest. While making our way up to the ground, you knew it was, at some point, going to go off. The West Mids OB were clocking everyone and anyone's grid. They seemed like they were on a bit of a hair trigger. Upon reaching the ground and seeing little more from Wolves than a few Burberry clad, acne-ridden Brummies shouting, 'Scouse cunts' – and the blokes weren't much better – it seemed like it would be a day like many others, a victory for the OB. Indeed the OB seemed very keen to flex their muscles and mark their territory, attacking Everton fans with batons and dogs.

"They were, however, less vigilant when a mob of our lot broke away later and made their way to the Asda car park, where a mob of Wolves were waiting to give us some Yam-Yam hospitality. Initially, Everton had a slight problem getting lads through the fence to engage in the fun, however once the numbers began to even out there was only one way it was going. Wolves did have some game lads but the mob Everton had out that day were different class. Plenty of old faces were all up for it and they were soon run. Call it re-grouping, call it backing off, call it what you will, they legged it.

"As the OB got everyone back to the station, the quality of this mob really hit home. Regardless of what the Burberry-clad glue sniffers may like you to believe, on our day Everton are more than a match for anyone, as Man United were to find out on February 20, 2005."

Events after the United game made national news headlines, but to the lads there was no shock or horror about it at all; they had all known it was going to happen. Gee included. "This game and the atmosphere were a throwback to the good old days, or bad old days, depending on what you do at the football. The traditional rivalry between both clubs had been compounded by the fact that the Mancs had signed Wayne Rooney from Everton and today was the day the prodigal son was to return. The atmosphere that Saturday evening for the Cup game was unbelievable. Practically everyone who has ever showed for Everton was there, except for some silly cunt banned for writing a book! And everyone was baying for blood.

"As we got beat, the mood leaving the ground a little early was one of bloodlust. Word had got round that, like the halcyon days of the Eighties, the Manc escort would be given the necessary attention as it reached Everton Valley. A group of United's finest had avoided their escort and managed to make their way up there, a move normally to be commended by the lads. However, on this night, in this atmosphere, it was not the brightest thing to do. As they approached the Valley pub there were about a dozen Everton outside. The Mancs bounced up and it went off. The pub emptied and soon the Mancs were well and truly on their toes. Wave after wave of Everton waded in. Some of the Mancs were very game, but you expect that of them. Anyone who says they are just numbers is full of shite. However, while the first ten or so Mancs wanted it, and indeed got it, the ones behind them were like rabbits caught in headlights.

"I honestly believe some of the ones who were in the break-away firm expected to do what United have done on many occasions, turn up and run the show. But it didn't go their way at all. They were clambering over each other to escape. After several minutes the police actually started to realise what was going on and tried to make their way up, restore a bit of order and get the Mancs back in the main mob. However, the main mob of United did not appear too bothered about breaking the escort, happier to be getting back to Limey. And who can blame them?"

Further reading: *Scally*, Andy Nicholls (Milo Books)

EXETER CITY

Ground: St. James's Park
Firms: H Troop, the Sly Crew
Rivals: Plymouth, Cardiff, Newport
Police operations: Offside

Exeter's football hooligans have had a hard time of it. Nestling between the cities of Plymouth and Bristol and close enough to South Wales to be regarded as derby material by Cardiff City, their historic city is surrounded by bigger clubs with considerably bigger mobs. Exeter's tiny ground has often been overrun by other clubs, but a mob can prosper in the face of adversity. Exeter has never had the numbers to take on the Soul Crew or Central Element in their entirety, but it did develop a tight little group that could hold its own against equal numbers.

As far back as the late 1960s, the national press was reporting trouble in Exeter, with arrests at matches against Plymouth. The 1970s continued in similar vein. In August 1970, after a League Cup home match against Bristol City, 24 youths, including one girl, appeared in court after fighting broke out on the terraces. The following season, 18 people were arrested after trouble during the visit of Bristol Rovers.

The early mobs at Exeter were the H Troop, a group of lads who came from Heavitree, and the Tea Stand, named after lads who would gather at the tea stand at the end of the Cowshed, closest to the away end. "This was always good sport as the football wasn't always the best," remarked one of the few Exeter lads still around from the early days. The memorably named Sly Crew was born in 1986 during a meeting in the Queen's Vaults, a pub frequented by local lads who were up for a fight. Trouble had followed the club for some time and now the lads wanted a name. While some of those present went for the Sly Crew others preferred the Anti-Welsh League, because of Exeter's rivalry with Cardiff, Newport and Swansea. Predictably those clubs took exception to the name, but that was the point. Calling cards were produced and AWL chants were regularly heard at games against Welsh teams.

The AWL eventually faded away, leaving the Sly Crew as Exeter's recognised firm. The regular drinking hole remained the Queen's Vaults, a large underground pub with no windows and only one

way in and out, making it an ideal defensive location. Local gangs from across the city would congregate here before games, leaving their differences at the door. The police also appeared content to let everyone gather there; better, they thought, to keep everyone together than disperse them around the city.

During the 1980s, when the club played Wolves, Plymouth and Cardiff, the Sly Crew could muster 60-80 lads, but this dropped to 30-60 during the 1990s. This was due in part to a change of personnel within the group, with many of the older lads switching to National Front activity and others slipping into the rave scene. Today, with local rivals Hereford and Aldershot, 40 is considered a good turnout.

Plymouth is considered the main event and over the years there have been several confrontations, mostly in Exeter but also in central London at England matches. In 1987, Plymouth fans staged repeated charges against Exeter fans following their 1–0 away victory in a pre-season friendly. One eyewitness said, "The City fans were all dispersing quietly after the game when, all of a sudden, a crowd of Argyle fans charged up York Road yelling, 'Kill them, kill them.'" As police attempted to round up the Plymouth fans, a second group who had travelled up in cars were battling with Exeter lads in a number of locations.

In March 1996, police made 24 arrests after trouble between rival fans erupted before the derby. Further trouble was averted after police ejected some Plymouth fans who had got into the Exeter end. The local paper carried a vivid photograph of rival fans fighting.

Other noteworthy clashes occurred at home against Bournemouth, Port Vale, Swansea, Chelsea and Hereford. Chelsea's visit was in a pre-season friendly in August 1981, and their supporters ran amok, causing serious damage to the Quay Club. Water pipes were ripped out in the men's toilets and bloodstained tissues and broken glass littered the floors. The decision to invite Chelsea drew severe criticism. "We managed to keep clear of the recent [Brixton] riots but it seems the football club wants to start its own," said the press officer for Exeter Liberal Party.

"Here we go again," was the headline in the local paper in September 1990, when the visit of Swansea led to violence between rival fans. A policeman who went to apprehend two hooligans causing trouble in a local shop was "throttled" as they tried to escape.

The Sly Crew were not great travellers and rarely turned out more than once or twice a season. One outing was the short trip to Torquay, in April 1990, when 60 Exeter lads "rampaged" through the town centre. A week later, 30 fans were involved in serious fighting during Exeter's home match against Stockport. "I was brought up in a pub and I have seen lots of fights, but I have never seen anything like that," said landlord Tracy Emery. "There were Exeter and Stockport supporters in here drinking and it was all right and everything was quiet. Then suddenly glasses and bar stools were being thrown everywhere."

Perhaps the most serious consistent trouble involving Exeter has been when hosting the supporters of Cardiff. In April 1987, more than 100 Exeter fans bombarded Cardiff fans and their vehicles with bricks and rocks. A police operation, codenamed Offside, identified 40 local men who took part. More recently, in August 2000, Cardiff travelled to Exeter for the opening game of the season. The Soul Crew brought a mob that was good enough to take on most hooligan firms and was simply too big for Exeter. Rather than attempt a suicide mission and be decimated one game into the new season, the Sly Crew picked off small groups of visitors and, during a number of small skirmishes, 11 people were arrested.

Despite having little reputation across the country, the Sly Crew, like most lower and non-league sides, will always turn out for a plum FA Cup tie. Twice over the past few seasons they have been handed such draws. Although the home tie with Everton was a relatively peaceful morning kick-off, the game against Manchester United in 2004 saw the biggest away following in the club's history. Despite numerous posts on the internet following Exeter's remarkable draw at Old Trafford, claiming

they did equally well off the pitch, few Mancs give the Sly Crew any credit. Fran, a United hooligan, said bluntly, "Fucking Exeter, who's gonna turn out for them? They had thousands of fans out and we saw about thirty lads all day. When we clocked them after the game they looked terrified. Even the police let them walk about knowing that as long as they kept their mouths shut they were in no danger, they were given a walkover. Down there we never saw a firm. They claimed a result on the Net? Don't make me fucking laugh."

Exeter has also developed a nasty rivalry with Bournemouth, and while the fights have never involved large numbers, they have often been violent affairs. In 1993 it took the intervention of Bournemouth manager Alan Ball, who darted onto the pitch to plead with twenty Exeter fans who had come on to the playing area, to defuse a potential flashpoint. Meanwhile, Bournemouth lads have said that they respect the Sly Crew. A couple of seasons ago, Bournemouth fans ran across the pitch to confront Exeter lads in the Cowshed stand as their team went down 2–0. Four fans were banned from football grounds for a year. Although St James's Park is regarded as a tinpot ground, the CCTV works just as well as the system at Old Trafford, and the culprits were easily identified and brought before the courts.

Exeter's mob continues today but is younger and smaller than the group that was around in the Eighties. In February 2002, they were involved in a serious brawl before a game at Oxford United. Police, who described the disorder as "significant", eventually separated the two groups before giving the fans an escort to the stadium. In May 2003, Exeter were relegated from the Football League, despite winning their last three games of the season. That reduced the already small crowds and deprived the Sly Crew of local opponents, which could see the death of the firm altogether.

F

FALKIRK

Ground: The Falkirk Stadium
Firms: Falkirk Fear
Rivals: Airdrie

Fan power has been more crucial to Falkirk's survival than most. Faced with liquidation and certain closure, the club was only saved by a group of supporters who established a Trust to financially support it. Formed in August 2002, the Brains Trust has raised over £250,000 and helped to develop the club on a community basis.

Off the field, the Falkirk Fear made their own waves over the years. Not the biggest group around, they nonetheless earned a decent reputation. There have been regular clashes with Airdrie, including one match which saw 15 in court.

Fifteen thousand Falkirk fans travelled to Ibrox in April 1997 to see their team beat Celtic 1–0 in the semi-final of the Scottish Cup. Away from the ground there was trouble as Falkirk fans set off CS gas in an underground station. "It was very busy and, as usual, people were pushing on whilst other people were coming off," remembered one onlooker. "The next thing I can remember is all hell breaking loose. From over my shoulder I could see what I thought was a fire extinguisher going off. My eyes started streaming and there was a big cloud of gas. I could hardly see."

Falkirk opened their new stadium with a pre-season match against Dundee in July 2004. What was supposed to be a carnival atmosphere was overshadowed by fierce fighting between rival gangs before the game. The local paper later claimed that the fight was arranged over the Internet, with rival fans swapping phone numbers to keep in touch during the day.

One Dundee fan recalled the melee: "We outnumbered them seventy to thirty, but it was one of the best battles there's been in Scotland for years. We met in a pub not far from their stadium. It was an ideal place. We all arrived at different times in mini-buses and met in this pub near the ground. The pub was set back from the road with a park behind it. It was planned for them to come from their pub over the grass and it would kick off in the middle of the park. We hung around for ages waiting but no Falkirk appeared. We started doubting them and some lads were saying we should go to them. We were stood at the side door of the pub getting ready to go to them when we heard a shout go up, 'There they are.' At that moment Falkirk came running at us, tooled up with bricks and bats and whatever else they could find on the road. One of the Dundee lads came running out the side door of the pub with a pool cue and started smashing Falkirk lads with it. The fight went on for around five minutes with Falkirk lads lying on the road everywhere. There was even a Falkirk lad lying in a back garden.

"Eventually they all legged it with a small battle ensuing on the main road. Next thing all you could hear were sirens. We all ran back in the pub, the police cars couldn't get in the car park for Falkirk lads lying unconscious in the street. Respect to them, they were as game as they come. We all got rounded up thinking we were jailed but the OB just seemed to want us out of there and let us go without arresting anyone."

The authorities were predictably outraged. Chief Inspector Donald McMillan said, "We will be cracking down hard on any organised violence. We will be using every method of intelligence gathering we can and on the day we will target it – and target it hard. There is no place to hide." His comments had a hollow ring given that the trouble had already happened, several people had needed hospital attention and yet no-one had been arrested.

The Fear have also clashed with the likes of Motherwell's Saturday Service, and like many of the Scottish casual gangs, have their own website, falkirkfear.co.uk, with photos, press reports, a forum for posting messages, and links to similar sites.

FULHAM

Ground: Craven Cottage
Firms: SW6, Thames Bank Travellers, Green Pole Boys, H Block, Fulham Youth Crew
Rivals: QPR, Brentford

Fulham supporters have the highest income per head of any in Britain, and that probably accounts for the sparse hooligan history at the club. It has never had the fan base of Chelsea or even the sprawling White City estate of QPR. Instead, it draws its support from Kensington and Chelsea, the richest borough in the country, Putney, and out into Hammersmith. SW6, the postal code for the area, was the name of their first mob.

That is not to say that there has not been trouble at Fulham; rather that it has not been on the scale of many other clubs. In October 1967, for instance, the club warned its fans about their behaviour and around the same time Fulham were involved in a major disturbance with Leeds. By the Seventies, fights occurred regularly, though few of them were organised. Most of the trouble would happen in the pubs off the Fulham Palace Road. "It was more some mates who often fancied a fight and would go for it if the team was renowned," said one younger Fulham supporter. "They weren't too organised and were about fighting rather then running the opposition." The next mob at Fulham was the Thames Bank Travellers, a largely skinhead group who travelled away on overnight coaches drinking heavily and tabbing. On one occasion a group of 20 to 30 Thames Bank Travellers went to an away game at Swansea. In the car park near the ground they clashed with a much larger group of Jacks. "They did it for the sheer hell of it; it was suicidal but apparently worked well."

QPR has always been Fulham's key rivals though for much of the last thirty years this has been a rather one-sided hooligan contest. It was not uncommon for QPR to bring mobs of several hundred to Fulham but there was little to fight. Given the close proximity of the two clubs there has been surprisingly little trouble. Fulham supporters tend to look down on QPR as their poor relatives, as their chant 'you all play in a tin blue pot' clearly demonstrates, though many were forced to eat humble pie when they were forced to move into Loftus Road, while QPR's mob rarely register their West London rivals as any real opponent.

The last major attempted confrontation between the two sides occurred during Fulham's promotion season of 1999/2000. The home fixture saw a group of twelve QPR get into the Fulham end but, according to Fulham, they were quickly repelled. For the return fixture, Fulham boast of walking down Shepherds Bush with a mob of 120 and clashing with QPR outside the Green Bar until police horses arrived to separate the groups. The fight was short but fierce, and several people were injured.

Fulham have had a much less complicated relationship with Chelsea; they simply don't fight them. This is somewhat surprising given the long history between the two. Fulham is London's oldest football club and in 1905 property developer Gus Mears invited the club to reside at the stadium he had just built at Stamford Bridge. Fulham declined the offer and instead Chelsea FC was formed. There was a clash before the two teams met in the Premiership in the 2003/4 season but true to form it was a mob of QPR fighting Chelsea rather than Fulham.

It has not been uncommon for Chelsea's mob to turn up at Craven Cottage to have a go with Fulham's opponents. This was certainly the case in 1993 when Cardiff played there on the first Saturday of the season. Four hundred Soul Crew arrived knowing that Chelsea were their real targets. Inside the ground their numbers were swelled by another 3,000 Cardiff fans and unsurprisingly they took over much of the ground. Thirty Cardiff got into the Fulham end and the game had hardly begun when trouble erupted. The few Fulham on the packed terrace were supplemented by a few Chelsea hard cases and for a while the rival groups fought toe to toe. The explosion of violence in the Fulham end was the green light for hundreds of Cardiff fans, many of whom scaled the fences and went to their

Mirrorpix

A young fan in the terrace attire of the day is arrested on the pitch by at least five police officers during a 1-1 draw between Fulham and Liverpool in 1967.

comrades' aid. The Fulham and Chelsea mob knew they stood no chance and backed off, leaving the Welshmen in control. Play was halted for almost thirty minutes as police, managers and even Labour Party leader Neil Kinnock appealed for calm. There were further clashes between Cardiff and Chelsea later that evening and several Cardiff received the early morning knock and subsequently jail.

Fulham were again aided by Chelsea for a home game against Everton some years later, as one fan recalls. "Before the game some Fulham lads fancied a ruck, as they were getting fed up with pissed-up Scousers taking liberties on their turf. They met some Everton lads who they thought were their firm and took them by surprise, and there was a bit of a toe-to-toe before police intervened. About ten minutes later Everton's real firm turned up, about eighty of them, and there were no takers. During the game coins, bottles and other things were

chucked from the Everton end and at the end a few Fulham went round but police kept us back. We knocked them out of the Cup when we were renting Loftus Road and they were all over the place, in our seats and even had a few hundred locked out all trying to force the gates in. It was mad. It's strange really, Everton always seem to come down in a firm whereas Liverpool don't." Everton, however, consider it one of the softer London trips.

Another match where Fulham linked up with lads from other mobs was the away trip to Brighton. Both sides were trying to gain promotion from the Third Division and 5,000 West Londoners made the trip. The core of Fulham's mob that day was sixteen lads, with nine being drawn from Chelsea, West Ham, Rochdale and Aston Villa. Opposing them were 30 Brighton, but despite being outnumbered, the heavy firepower the outsiders gave Fulham allowed them to gain the advantage in the early exchanges.

Brighton were backed off into a pub and one of the visitors threw in a gas grenade. Fulham finally got into the pub, where the fighting continued. Brighton were turning the situation around as reinforcements arrived, and Fulham were helped by the appearance of the police. Unbeknown to the lads, police officers from Fulham had witnessed the whole affair and several people were arrested, though the case against them later collapsed in court.

The rivalry with Brighton stemmed from following England abroad, where the two mobs met and took an immediate dislike to each other. In 1996, Fulham travelled down to the south coast and gassed and flared the Nightingale pub outside Brighton station. For the return fixture, Brighton came and mixed it with Fulham on the Palace Road and then with QPR in Hammersmith.

In March 1998 Fulham did hit the national press after the death of 24-year-old Matthew Fox during a fight at Gillingham. There'd been little love lost between the two teams since a 23-player brawl in a fixture a couple of years before; an added ingredient was that both teams were going for promotion. Tensions were high inside the ground and missiles were exchanged, with one supporter even believed to have used a sock stuffed with coins to attack his rivals. Gillingham won the game 2–0, with the second goal coming in the final minute. Unfortunately both sets of fans were let out simultaneously and a fight between two small groups broke out in a neighbouring street almost straight away. Matthew Fox received a single punch to his neck and died almost immediately.

Thirty-year-old Barry Cullen was later convicted of manslaughter and sentenced to four years' imprisonment after admitting to throwing the punch that killed Fox. It was a tragedy for everyone concerned. During interviews Cullen told detectives: "Those few seconds ended a man's life and I cannot say how sorry I am to this man's family." The judge added, "You said yourself you were devastated – and so you should be. Instead of moving away from the violence you ran towards it. That young man had not threatened you in any way. You punched him on the head with considerable force and you had that very large keeper ring on your finger. Death was almost instantaneous."

Such incidents deter some hooligans but not others. During an away game in Europe, about 70 Fulham lads travelled to Hadjuk Split. "The lads were enjoying a quiet beer by the harbour soaking up the sun," said one of them. "But as the kick-off approached, small groups of Split fans began to gather. With two hours to go, thirty locals began throwing bottles from a small square. Fulham came out of two bars and steamed into them, backing them off up the road until they turned and legged it down a network of small streets. The police, backed by Fulham Old Bill, came in hard and the Split fans tried to bully ordinary fans later in the evening but the day was a top result for Fulham. By the time we got home the internet had pictures posted of the fighting: the locals had filmed the whole thing. One thing needs to be made crystal clear, it was not England on tour or a Fulham/Chelsea mob, it was 100 per cent Fulham."

Fulham's firm today has a core of 40 lads, though as they are quick to assert, they have seen over 100 turn out in recent years. The current mob is called "H Block" after a section of the ground and all are between 20 and 40 years old. A younger mob called Fulham Youth Crew has formed in the past few years. Over the years, about 40 lads have been banned, though at the time of writing about ten were still excluded. It is not a club known for its hooligan problem, and its hooligan website shows that despite being an established Premier League team, its forum is dominated by hostility towards Brentford. Fulham's reputation as a family club is backed up by the lack of trouble inside the ground's "neutral" section. It is the only such area in the Premiership where home and away fans freely mix, although at most games the smattering of away fans are joined by day trippers and tourist fans rather than out and out Fulham supporters. There was trouble against Arsenal in there but one contact was quick to point out that it is an area "full of scarf wearing fans so any infiltration by firm lads would almost certainly lead to arrest."

Another Fulham lad was honest about their situation. "Unless it's a grudge game against some club we have history with, it's pointless turning up looking for trouble, as there are so few of us and we stand out a mile. Most fights we get involved in are just spontaneous kick-offs when visitors large it in the bars, thinking there is no opposition. A perfect example was when about ten of us went through to the game with Leeds last year. We entered a bar near the ground, where we were recognized as cockneys and a scuffle broke out, which spilled onto the road. A group of coppers ran over and began nicking everyone. We acted daft and pleaded our innocence, claimed we were locals having a drink and were let off with just the Leeds lads being locked up. Cue the classic line from the Old Bill: 'These bloody hooligans should know there's no one to fight with at Fulham.' It is a term used by the police and visiting fans alike and not something we agree with, but it does come in handy at times."

G

GILLINGHAM

Ground: Priestfield
Firm: Gillingham Youth Firm
Rivals: Millwall, Brighton

Gillingham should have a tough following. The only football league club in Kent, its catchment area encompasses the Medway towns of Chatham, Margate, Thanet, Ramsgate and Gillingham itself. Until 1987, Chatham was home to the Royal Navy dockyards, and the other seaside towns are in parts rundown, violent and home to people from across the British Isles drawn to cheap bedsits and low-paid seasonal work.

Yet it seems Gillingham has never had a major firm. There have been reports of trouble at matches going back into the 1970s, but except for the death of a Fulham fan in 1998, Gillingham hooligans have hardly ever hit the national news. Why? One word, perhaps: Millwall. Many of the harder lads across the Medway towns either had previously lived in South East London or simply gravitated towards them because of their reputation. There are also a smaller number of Charlton fans who live in the area.

Gillingham's hooligans have also struggled to find a serious rival. They are not threatening enough to be a major problem for Millwall, while Charlton, Crystal Palace and even Brighton are more preoccupied with each other or rivals much further afield. One rivalry was against Swindon, whom many Gillingham fans felt had scuppered their hopes of promotion on several occasions. In the Eighties this spilled over on and off the pitch. A 23-player brawl in the tunnel led to Swindon pressing charges after one match. In 1987, the first leg of a promotion play-off saw serious trouble in Gillingham town centre when Swindon attacked a mob of locals and several people were imprisoned.

The Eighties also saw repeated violence at home matches against Brighton, which peaked in 1987. Two hundred Brighton fans arrived on masse by train and made it onto the home end before being forced off the end by the police. Brighton fan Nick was at the match and said, "For whatever reason we turned out a fantastic firm that day. We marched up the road to their end and it turned into a riot. Police were injured and when it spilled outside it was mayhem. A firm of our lads got a vantage point above the street and every time the police charged they were forced back by a hail of milk bottles and bricks. Gillingham had a go back but mainly from behind the police lines; simply they neither had enough bodies or bottle to come near us that day. The fallout was that loads were arrested and for the first time ever ten lads who were convicted were handed life bans from the club. One copper who we spoke to after said it was the worst trouble they had had there apart from a visit from Chelsea, which will do for us."

A few years later, Brighton were homeless and for a couple of seasons ground-shared with Gillingham. It was embarrassing for the Hove lads, who for years had sung "In your Gillingham slums". Whilst there was very little trouble between locals and the few Albion faithful who bothered to make the trek for "home games", many of the local residents were amazed the police had sanctioned the short term lease agreement.

Another south coast visitor during the early Eighties was Portsmouth, and while hundreds of 6.57 Crew made the trip, their focus was on a possible clash with Millwall in central London later in the day. "The time we had it with Gillingham was unlucky for them, as we knew we would be meeting

Millwall at Charing Cross that night, so everyone was out for it," recalled Eddie of the 6.57 Crew. "Gillingham turned a mob out after the game and basically were taken to pieces. Very few would live with that mob, let alone fucking Gillingham. It taught them a lesson as I have never seen them turn out since."

Other mobs stumbled across Gillingham. Both Steve Cowens (Sheffield United) and Shaun Tordoff (Hull City) recall small clashes in Gillingham after league matches. Both were quite dismissive about Gillingham's mob but there were certainly people who would have a go. The general hooligan view of the club is summed up by Hogger, a well respected Bristol City fan: "We would go to places like that just for a day out, we had no agenda with them and they never showed against us. It was the kind of place we would seriously take the piss at."

Not all mob leaders are as dismissive of the place, however. "At Gillingham a mob of Stoke were turned over, and turned over quite badly," recalled a well-known Stoke leader. "It was a Tuesday night game in about 1996 and very few bothered going. Fifteen lads, consisting of mainly youth, were with three or four main faces who went by car and met with a few Stoke who were working in London. Nothing went on before, during the game or after so they holed up in a pub near the ground and began to enjoy themselves. They must have been spotted, as just before last orders a firm of Gillingham bounced in, all tooled up, and Stoke basically took a shoeing. It was a lesson learned and one which the younger lads will remember for a long time. Regardless of who you are, regardless of what your reputation is, always have respect for the area you are visiting. If you don't there will be an element who are proud of their club and will utilise any opportunity that arises to let more notorious mobs know that they are not allowed to take liberties."

Gillingham struggled financially in the Nineties. As they stared extinction in the face, Paul Scally bought the club for £1 (though some people insist it was just 1p). At most clubs, Scally would have become an instant hero but not at Gillingham, where their relief at being saved was tempered by the knowledge that their saviour was a Millwall fan who had publicly stated his desire to own Millwall. Though he has largely rebuilt the ground, he found himself in hot water with the fans and a £10,000

fine from the Football League after he bet on Manchester City to beat Gillingham in the 1999 play-off finals. His relationship with supporters soured further when he banned the head of the supporters' club from attending home matches for not handing over the rights to the domain name of his website.

In March 1998, a promotion clash at home to Fulham led to fighting between rival fans after the game during which 24-year-old Matthew Fox was killed. The Fulham supporter had been struck on the head by a punch thrown by 30-year-old Barry Cullen and died later in hospital. Cullen was quickly arrested, pleaded guilty to manslaughter and was sentenced to four years' imprisonment. One newspaper reported that an anonymous Fulham fan had issued threats to avenge the death. It was even claimed that Fulham hooligans were set to link up with Southend fans for Gillingham's visit a week later and that this tie-up was established through neo-nazi groups. There was no firm evidence to back up this claim and Essex Police dismissed it out of hand. Gillingham, meanwhile, issued a warning to all its supporters to be careful when travelling to away matches in case of revenge attacks. The game passed off without incident, much to the relief of everyone.

Gillingham's next game was at home to Luton, another promotion contender. Police were much in evidence and again there was no trouble. "The spectators were well behaved and we would like to thank them for that," said Sgt Martin Cunningham of Kent Police. The match had begun with a minute's silence for Matthew Fox and the attitude of the home fans greatly impressed Scally. "This was always going to be a difficult game given the circumstances, but the atmosphere was as good as could have been expected. I am delighted at the way Gillingham fans conducted themselves. Gillingham fans do not have a poor record of behaviour and, to keep things in perspective, what happened to Mr Fox was tragic but also isolated."

Gillingham missed out on the play-offs on an inferior goal difference, with Fulham, ironically, taking the final place. The following season they did manage to go one step further but lost in the Wembley final to Manchester City on penalties. By now a new mob had emerged at the club, called simply Gillingham Youth Firm. Most were teenagers or in their early twenties. A large mob travelled up to London for the play-off final and there was a small rumble at Baker Street, but the Kent hooligans had been followed closely by police since arriving at Victoria. "The whole of Medway came out," recalled one fan, "though many did not go to the game."

It was third time lucky as Gillingham was eventually promoted into the First Division in May 2000, defeating Stoke City and then Wigan. Promotion saw them up against bigger teams and bigger firms and this acted as a catalyst for their young mob.

Fights over the next few years were few and far between. A mob of the Youth Firm attempted to attack a small group of Bristol City at one home game, unaware that another 100 were having a toilet stop around the corner. The new mob hardly terrified the First Division but the 27 Gillingham arrests during the 2000/01 season were more than at bigger clubs such as Palace (11), Huddersfield (26), West Brom (24) and Wolves (25). In September 2001, Gillingham attacked Rotherham fans outside the ground. The police intervened and escorted the visitors back to the railway station, where they were attacked again. It was not to be Rotherham's day; later, on the train home, they were attacked by Sheffield United fans.

More recently, Gillingham were "turned over" on their own patch by Crystal Palace, and one of the Palace lads was quick to point out it was the younger lads in the firm who did the damage. "We took a firm of about seventy to theirs a few seasons back but it was mainly a piss-up. No-one had tickets so we sat outside some boozer in Gillingham surrounded by OB and getting on it. A few of our youth fronted a firm of Gills lads who thought they were up for it but were not and soon ran. There is no history between us, so to speak, a few small offs through the years, certainly nothing major, so why they fronted it that day no-one knows."

Today, the firm hardly exists. A few continue to turn out but there has been little trouble at Gillingham for a couple of seasons. Severe beatings at the hands of Portsmouth and Wycombe in recent years persuaded many of those involved to pack it in. A few of those still around are also active in the BNP and National Front but an attempt to large it over a small group of Asians at a bus stop saw them come off worst.

But probably the single most important reason for their demise has been their continual feeling of inferiority to Millwall. "Some Gillingham lads will never admit that they have been turned over by any club other than Millwall," one lad told us. "Gillingham's youth firm might have been turned over by Wycombe but most of the lads will swear it was really a Millwall firm."

GLASGOW CELTIC

Ground: Parkhead
Firms: Celtic Soccer Casuals
Rivals: Rangers

In ancient Rome, the fans who packed the Coliseum to watch gladiatorial combat divided themselves into two opposing camps, the Greens and Blues. More than 2,000 years later, equally fierce contests take place at least four times a year in Glasgow. The Irish question appears to be, very slowly, resolving itself but in those couple of square miles around Parkhead and Ibrox, the war is still alive and kicking. The Irish Tricolour is still waved during pro-IRA songs at one end of the ground, while the Union Jack flies and the "Billy Boys" screams out from the other. It is a rivalry still filled with hate, passion – and violence. It is the Old Firm, the greatest city derby in the world – at least as far as Scottish fans are concerned.

Celtic and Rangers did not always hate each other. Back in the 1880s, when Celtic was formed, there was a close relationship between the two clubs. They invited each other to watch English opposition at their respective grounds and, in 1893, even agreed that Celtic Park should be the venue for the Glasgow Cup Final and that the takings would be divided equally. Bill Murray argues, in his book *The Old Firm*, that the closeness was due to shared financial interests. "The two clubs had sound financial reasons to support each other in those early days, as they whittled away at the pre-eminence of Queen's Park and threatened the position of the amateurs in the SFA."

But money was also a factor in the growing split along religious, sectarian lines. Both clubs drew support from a deeply divided city: Celtic from Irish Catholics and Rangers from the larger Protestant community. Encouraging and expanding their support base meant reinforcing the respective clubs' identities, something helped by the stiffening in religious zeal of both club owners, more so at Rangers than Celtic. By 1894 the first incidents of trouble were reported and, two years later, the *Scottish Sport* reported that bad blood had crept into the game. On the first day of 1898, Celtic hosted Rangers at Celtic Park and with the game balanced at one each, home fans stopped the match with a pitch invasion. Four years later, another game at Celtic Park was described by one journalist as "one of the most disgraceful exhibitions that has ever been witnessed in a Scottish football arena." He went on to ask, sarcastically, why, if rat pits were illegal, were such games tolerated.

At a Scottish Cup semi-final in March 1905, a Celtic riot brought an end to the match when their club was two-down. "This was the infamous Quinn-Craig game," recalled Murray. "Quinn was ordered off after appearing to kick the Rangers fullback. A section of the spectators broke through the fence, taking iron-spiked palings with them as weapons, and set upon the referee." A Celtic director was hit by a stone as he attempted to appeal for calm and the game was eventually abandoned after a restart led to another attack on the players.

Economic development and the clamour for home rule in Ireland intensified the Old Firm rivalry. In 1912, the Belfast shipbuilding firm, Harland & Wolff, opened a base in Glasgow. It was known to have strong Protestant leanings, to the point where it consented to allowing Catholics to be violently driven out of its Belfast yard, and drew its workforce almost exclusively from Protestant, Rangers-supporting Govan. It became a magnet for Orange Order sympathisers, many of whom had moved to Scotland during the preceding ten years. On the other side of the divide, the increasing agitation for Irish home rule mobilised the Scottish Catholic community and reinforced their own sense of identity. This translated itself into even greater Old Firm violence, which set a pattern. Arrest tallies of more than 100 people were quite common during the inter-war period.

The sectarian divide came against a backdrop of gang culture. The Penny Mob ruled the Townhead and East End in the 1890s, their name coming from the amount they levied shopkeepers. In the early 1900s there were constant battles between the San Toy Boys (Protestant) and the Tim Malloys, a collec-tion of Catholic gangs who united to face a common rival. Tim was an anglicised name for Taigs, or Catholics, while Malloys was rhyming slang for the Bhoys, the name commonly associated with Celtic fans. Police reports of the day reveal the extreme violence of the opposing gangs, whose members were generally in their twenties and thirties.

The First World War ended the Tim Malloys, but its dominance within the Catholic communities was taken up by the Baltic Fleet, and many Fleet gangs continue in some form today. On the Protestant side came the Billy Boys, who plied their violent trade at Ibrox. After the 1930 Cup Final between Rangers and Partick Thistle, the Billy Boys fought the South Side Stickers and the Liberty Boys with bricks, sticks, bottles and other missiles. Another gang was the Redskins, known to have more than 2,000 paid-up members. Collectively, all these groups were better known as the Razor Gangs.

The gangs culture, coupled with the religious sectarianism, spread trouble into other football matches. In April, 1920, Celtic were forced to close their ground for four weeks after fans stormed the pitch during a match against Dundee and attacked the referee. One Dundee player was struck over the head and another carried off unconscious. In 1922, a Celtic game at Morton produced widespread disorder. The Celtic fans arrived in a huge convoy, blowing bugles and waving Sinn Fein flags, and were met by Morton fans, many of whom were drawn from a strongly Loyalist estate. Celtic needed a point to win the title and fighting broke out inside the ground during the first half, and then, with their club a goal down, there was an explosion of rioting that forced the players to flee for safety. The players returned and Celtic scored the equaliser they needed.

Sectarian differences could be put aside, as was graphically illustrated when Celtic and Rangers fans united in rage during the 1909 Scottish Cup Final replay. The game ended in a draw but to the bewilderment of the crowd and the players, the referee took the players off for another replay rather than take the game into extra time. A report in *The Times* read, "There were angry shouts from all sides, demanding that the game should be continued. The bolder section of the crowd led the way into the arena and a break-in all round took place. The crowd made for the passage by which the players had retired, and in a moment the police were engaged in a hand-to-hand struggle with the encroaching thousands. Stones and bottles were thrown, and the police drew their batons. A free fight near the Eastern goal created a diversion but off in that direction the crowd applied themselves to pulling down the posts and nets. This piece of destruction was accompanied by cheers, a rush was made for the other goal where the same performance was gone through. The framework of the ground roller, which was lying on the track, was then seized on, and with it a few roughs began to plough up the pitch.

"The appearance of the mounted police caused a section of the crowd to scatter, and a baton charge cleared the stand. The mounted men were received with a shower of heavy stones, planking was torn from the framework of the roller, and with it and stones they were knocked about unmercifully, one man being hurled from his horse. Attempts were also made to fire the large stands, but the police frustrated them. In the struggle a constable was kicked into insensibility by several roughs. The fire brigade arrived, but the mob jumped on the hose, and prevented the water from flowing. It was not until 7.30 that the ground was fully cleared and order restored, after three hours of rioting."

Trouble between Celtic and Rangers continued relentlessly in the post-war period. Virtually every game during the 1950s and 1960s resulted in trouble. The gang culture continued but had evolved. The traditional family-based gangs had lost ground during the war while the religious-based gangs, like the Billy Boys, became more dominant.

The emerging youth culture in the 1950s, including teddy boys and rockers, came to Glasgow but had that extra hard edge which linked gang mentality, heavy drinking, fighting and football. These more youthful gangs were given their chance to dominate with the post-war slum clearances and the building of huge housing developments containing a high proportion of young people, many of whom carried knives. It was this hardman ethos that gave rise to the soccer violence of Celtic, Rangers and indeed Scotland fans in the Sixties and Seventies. Another phenomenon that originated in Glasgow was gang graffiti. The phrase "XXX Rules OK" first appeared in the city in the Fifties and was copied by football mobs in England years later.

Celtic fans continued to cause trouble in the Scottish League. In 1961 there was trouble at the Cup Final against Dunfermline. A year later Celtic fans rioted and held up play for 20 minutes in their Cup semi-final against St Mirren. Hundreds spilled out onto the pitch as their team were losing, some clearly under ten years of age. Some commentators claimed it was a deliberate attempt by the fans to get the game abandoned and so force a replay, a charge the Celtic chairman denied. "What can Celtic do to control the all too frequent outbursts by a section of their fans?" asked the *Daily Record*. A number of possible solutions were presented, including banning children from big matches, closing certain parts of the ground to young people and increasing patrols by official attendants. The St Mirren manager even suggested that fences and moats should be considered. The City's Lord Provost was despondent and called for a meeting of clubs, police and the SFA. "For years we have been trying to paint a more pleasant image of Glasgow for the world. And in a few moments all our work is undone," he despaired.

Celtic played Liverpool in the semi-final of the European Cup Winners' Cup in April 1966, in what most papers dubbed the "Battle of Britain". The first leg in Glasgow passed off without major incident, with Liverpool's fans earning praise from the police, railway officials and coach operators. Celtic fans did not receive the same accolade, with bottles thrown at away supporters after the game. Thousands of Glaswegians travelled to Merseyside five days later for the eagerly awaited return fixture but their excitement soon turned sour as Liverpool ran out 2–0 winners and Celtic fans rioted. The spark was a disallowed Celtic goal minutes before the end of the game. Celtic supporters ran onto the pitch, fought with police and hurled bottles into the Liverpool crowd. Twenty people were rushed to hospital and one St John Ambulance man described it as the worst night of violence in 30 years of attending football.

Even before the game there were signs that the party atmosphere could get out of hand. Scottish fans had begun gathering in central Liverpool from early morning and many were drunk by lunchtime. Large groups wandered through the shopping streets chanting and a few apparently helped an unsuccessful bank robber escape the pursuing police.

Bailie Shinwell, Glasgow's most senior magistrate, was furious at "the bestial minority who sully the good name of Glasgow". He went on. "Every decent person in Glasgow was brought into disrepute by those who could be classified as nothing more than cheap, fanatical hooligans who should be barred from every game." The *Glasgow Evening Times* also expressed its shock. "Poor Glasgow suffers again for the sins of its football hotheads," it complained. "Even Liverpool, with a reputation as the home of the bad boys of the English circuit, claims never to have seen anything like the fury and bad sports-manship of a section of Celtic's following. That the notorious Kop should be able to get up on its morally reproving high-horse and chant 'Hooligans, go home' is a measure of Glasgow's shame."

Less than two years later, Celtic travelled to Newcastle for what one police officer called "a night of sheer, simple hooliganism and vandalism". More than 200 coachloads of supporters arrived in the city on Saturday, many already drunk. Fifty-seven people were arrested and 61 treated in hospital. Superintendent John Martin said, "Mobs of young hooligans were running amok through the city, breaking shop windows and sometimes stealing from shops. They were trying to force their way into dance halls, public houses and other places of enter-tainment. Between 7pm and 1am we had about 100 emergency calls."

Events in Northern Ireland, coupled with a resur-gence of street gangs in the late Sixties, led to an upsurge in trouble at Old Firm games. There were stabbings and 23 arrests when the clubs met in January 1970. In August 1972, further violence led to a meeting of city magistrates, police and clubs to discuss ways of ending the hooliganism. Whatever was discussed at the summit meant nothing on the terraces as a year later there was a repeat of the disorder that had marred so many previous fixtures. A journalist for *The Times* recounted, "As Celtic scored their second goal, the far end of the ground erupted in a sea of green and white. Behind me, at the Copeland Road end, there was an eerie silence from the red, white and blue crowd, then it too erupted. A hail of beer cans and bottles arced through the air. Some landed on the turf behind the goal as ambulance men and photographers scat-tered. But dozens more cascaded on to fans on the lower part of the terracing. In a desperate bid to

escape injury, hundreds of fans scrambled on to the pitch. Police reinforcements rushed to the scene and made dozens of arrests as fans roamed on to the pitch. But for some of their fellow fans that match had already ended abruptly – as blood flowed from head and face cuts." The Celtic goalkeeper had to flee, the game was held up for several minutes and there were 80 arrests.

Once again the clubs, magistrates and police met to discuss solutions, but once again the meeting broke up without agreement. Rangers' general manager Willie Waddell said it was the first outbreak of trouble for two years and dismissed it as an isolated incident. Others were less impressed with the blasé attitude and accused both Rangers and Celtic of contributing to the terrace hooligan-ism by their continued institutionalised religious sectarianism.

"It's a waste of bloody time. Nobody was prepared to admit that it is bitterness between a certain section of Catholics and Protestants that is the root cause of all this trouble," said Bailie Albert Long. "Whether they admit it or not, Rangers are a Protestant team and Celtic are a Catholic team and they are trading on this religious bitterness. If it did not exist, and if it was not engendered by the atti-tude of the clubs, Rangers and Celtic would just become two ordinary clubs." Bailie Long was the only one to defy the "no comment" ban imposed on everyone at the two-hour meeting in the Glasgow City Chamber. "We were told that everything was in confidence. But that's part of the trouble. Nobody's really interested in bringing it into the open. I think the whole affair should have been made open to the Press. We might have been able to throw some light into the dark corners. There has to be some very plain speaking before we can ever find a solution. They tried telling us it was a social problem. It's nothing of the sort.

"When it was suggested that Rangers sign a Catholic player, the club said that they would run the club the way they wanted to. It was not a matter in which anyone outside could interfere. I pursued the point of the Eire flag at Parkhead, suggesting it was provocative and pointless. The Celtic chairman said that the Tricolour was not offensive. I wanted Celtic to remove the flag and Rangers to make a public statement disassociating themselves from any religious or semi-religious

Celtic and Rangers hooligans fight on the terraces while the game goes on at an Old Firm match in August 10, 1968.

organisation, but they both evaded the issue," he added.

The meetings made little difference and violence continued unabated, though trouble at Celtic matches not involving Rangers did begin to subside. There were, however, exceptions. Towards the end of the 1978 season, Celtic travelled to Easter Road, Edinburgh, and their fans disgraced themselves, both inside the ground and then when hundreds rampaged through the streets of Edinburgh. Thirty arrests were made, 24 of them inside the ground, after supporters invaded the pitch holding up the game for four minutes. One resident, who had lived in the area for 26 years, described the trouble as "the worst I have seen in the time I have lived here. It is always the Celtic and Rangers fans who cause trouble. The people who live near the ground are

terrified to leave their homes on a Saturday because of these hooligans. If these Glasgow fans cannot behave themselves, they should be banned."

A few months later came a match south of the border that would result in what one observer called "the most disgusting scenes ever witnessed at Turf Moor". In mid-September 1978, Celtic played at Burnley in the Anglo-Scottish Cup. The match was temporarily abandoned as home fans poured on to the pitch to avoid the missiles being thrown by the Celtic supporters. Sixty people were injured, including two police officers. Twenty fans were taken to hospital, most requiring stretchers. The trouble began after Celtic fans reacted angrily to a Burnley goal. Fencing dividing the two sets of fans was torn down as the away fans tried to get into the home enclosure. Dozens of bricks were thrown, as well as bottles filled with urine.

"Trouble had been brewing throughout the game," reported the local paper. "The police who had realised they would be unable to confine the Celtic fans to the away team enclosure, had set up a second line of defence at the railings separating the Bee Hole end from the Longside. They were fighting a battle they were bound to lose, and after about half-an-hour there were sufficient Celtic fans on the Longside for them to attempt a takeover bid. They were quickly repulsed with chants of 'They'll never take the Longside,' but the scene had been set." When the Celtic fans tried again, ten minutes before the end, they were more successful, scattering the home supporters on to the pitch. Even then, they continued to be hit by flying missiles.

The home of Celtic's hardcore support was "the Jungle", a long section of terracing down one side of the ground that was home to fervent, vocal and ferociously partisan Glaswegians. It became one of the most famous, and intimidating, "ends" in football. Any rival crazy enough to enter the Jungle was taking his life in his hands, and few ever did. Infiltration would have proved almost impossible unless the interlopers wore green and white, because every fan in the Jungle was expected to display his or her colours, something that hindered the growth of a "casual" firm at the club.

Casual culture came to Glasgow in 1984, several years after it had been adopted by Aberdeen and Motherwell. Before long, the Celtic Soccer Crew was formed, though it never matched their Rangers rivals, to say nothing of Aberdeen or Hibs. There was widespread hostility towards the casuals from other Celtic fans, even to the point of violence. As far as the older Celts were concerned, Celtic fans wore their colours and proclaimed their allegiance. These effete-looking youngsters in their tight jeans and sportswear were not welcome. The young casuals, for their part, looked on the archaic "bears" with disdain – but some trepidation.

The arrival of the Celtic Casuals coincided with a number of incidents abroad or at European games. The Glasgow clubs were the first British teams to take large groups of supporters abroad. For Celtic's European Cup Final in Lisbon in 1967, a guide book was brought out to help travelling supporters. (In 1987, many Rangers fans were so keen to get to

their European Cup tie in the Soviet Union that they joined the Glasgow branch of the Communist Party, as a pre-arranged Party tour to the country took in the city that was then out of bounds to other fans.)

These foreign trips often brought trouble. A pre-season friendly against Cliftonville in Northern Ireland in August 1984 was abandoned after police opened fire on supporters with plastic bullets. Trouble flared among Cliftonville fans after only 20 minutes as they chanted anti-RUC and pro-IRA slogans. Eventually, baton-wielding police reinforcements drove a crowd of almost 2,000 of the 8,000 supporters out of the ground. The match was abandoned after 75 minutes with Celtic winning four-nil, but the trouble continued in the streets and a fire was started near the main gates. The police denied they had been heavy-handed, insisting that it was they who had been attacked. Among the weapons used against them were iron bars, a scythe, sledge hammer and petrol. At least 35 were injured and one RUC officer had his firearm stolen.

Despondent Cliftonville vice-chairman Jim Boyce said, "It was meant to be a wonderful occasion but it turned into a disaster." His counterpart, Celtic chairman, Desmond White, slammed the RUC for heavy-handed tactics. "Half the Cliftonville supporters are also Celtic supporters. I don't know what sparked it off , but there were far more police in the ground than necessary. The fans were watching a fun game until the riot police appeared. I watched in horror as supporters were kicked and baton-charged by policemen in combat gear."

Three months later, the club's home European Cup Winners Cup tie against Rapid Vienna was halted for 15 minutes after an amazing fall-out over a disputed penalty awarded to Celtic. A bottle was thrown on the pitch from the home end, and Rapid substitute Rudolph Weinhofer fell down as if badly injured, claiming that it had struck him in the face. He lay motionless for nearly ten minutes as teammates and Rapid officials besieged the bewildered Swedish referee. Eventually the penalty was taken but missed, but by that stage Celtic were 3–0 up and 4–3 ahead on aggregate, and the game was theirs, or so they thought.

"Throw Celtic out," was Vienna's rapid reaction to the match, as both clubs were hauled before UEFA's disciplinary committee. Meanwhile there was an increasingly bitter war of words between the clubs and their respective media. TV footage showed clearly that the Rapid player had not been struck by the bottle but that did not stop him flying out of Scotland with his head bandaged. The film footage was backed up by a Red Cross Ambulance worker who was present on the night. "In my opinion, there was absolutely nothing wrong with Weinhofer. He did not have a mark on him. I saw him going down, but he wouldn't let anyone near him. Eventually I was allowed to see him and he was fine."

The UEFA committee met ten days later and punished both clubs. Celtic were fined £4,000 for the two bottles that landed on the pitch and Rapid Vienna £5,000 for the conduct of their players. Rapid's Reinhard Kienast was banned for four games for striking Tommy Burns, and their coach, Otto Baric was banned for three for throwing a bottle onto the pitch. Weinhofer's claim that he was hit by a bottle was dismissed out of hand. A jubilant Celtic claimed that they had been "exonerated" and that justice had been done.

A week later Celtic heard the shock news that they had, after all, to play the match again after new evidence was given to UEFA's appeal committee in Zurich. The Austrian club now argued that Weinhofer was hit by a small, unidentified object, possibly a coin. The player was forced to leave the pitch, leaving the club with just nine players, as one had already been sent off. "The new ruling shocked and puzzled Scottish football," noted the *Daily Record*.

Manchester United's Old Trafford was the venue for the replayed game but Rapid Vienna's 1–0 victory was accompanied by more crowd trouble. The Austrian goalkeeper was attacked, as was the goalscorer as he left the field. It all made a mockery of the plea by the Celtic manager before the game to restore the image of the club, which he said was more important than the result. Two Celtic supporters were imprisoned for three months and the club was fined £18,500 and ordered to play its next European game behind closed doors.

The CSC hit the headlines in November 1987, when a gas bomb was thrown into the home end at a match at Hibs. More than 100 people were injured as thousands emptied from the terraces to escape, many blinded, choking and vomiting. The bomb was thrown midway through the second half and exploded on impact. Mounted police were brought in to clear the pitch and the game was suspended for 16 minutes. Forty-five people were taken to hospital and five needed to stay in overnight.

Thirteen-year-old Stephen Johnstone was standing on the terrace next to the pitch when the bomb exploded. "I saw everybody just panicking," he said. "So I did the same myself. I said to my friends, 'Run, just run,' and started running. People were trying to get over the fence and police were getting their truncheons out and just hitting everyone until someone shouted, 'It's teargas, it's teargas.' Then they tried to help them out."

"Work of morons," ran the headline of the *Daily Record* editorial. "Scots may have been tempted to feel smug as they watched English teams banned from Europe because of their fans. Complacency ended at Easter Road on Saturday." The following day the same paper ran an exclusive after the man who threw the gas bomb rang them up to claim credit. "I have no interest in football," he told them. "I go to games to fight." He claimed that he and other Celtic Casuals had purchased 50 CS gas canisters and intended to cause further disruption at other games. Unfortunately for the young man, he left a trace which the paper immediately passed on to the police, and provided the paper with its front page story the following day. "Tear gas: Men held."

The CSC dwindled as the police cracked down and ordinary fans turned on them even more viciously than before. Neil, a Wrexham fan whose Frontline mob forged a friendship with the CSC, was amazed by the way they were treated by their own fans. "We went up there a few times and they came down to us but it was a crazy set up at their place," he said. "Their casuals were hated by their own fans, it's as simple as that. We went to a game at Hearts and we were in a pub when a huge mob of Celtic walked past, spotted us and turned on us in seconds. They were by the windows chanting, "Casuals, casuals, fuck off home." The CSC firm could not compete with the number of drunken scarfers Celtic had. We went out with them in Glasgow a few times and, as the numbers dwindled, Rangers terrorised them in the clubs and pubs. Casuals were accepted at Ibrox and formed a major part of the hooligan force that was Rangers, but the CSC were on a hiding to nothing at Parkhead and many just fucked it off from what I saw during the few years we went up there."

By the late Eighties, Celtic's fan base had been

transformed. The once bad boys of Glasgow had now become one of the most popular teams in Europe, including England. Backed by their huge Irish Catholic following, which had established itself all over the world, Celtic's popularity contrasted with the continuingly sectarian Rangers, in much the same way as the followers of the national team had become the mirror image of the hooligan English. Everyone wanted to play Celtic. They brought fans and guaranteed a bumper gate. In the immediate aftermath of Hillsborough, it was to Celtic that Liverpool turned for a benefit match.

Whereas Rangers were the pariahs of English clubs following a spate of trouble, Celtic came to England for numerous pre-season friendlies. But, while the CSC was not too active, the simple presence of Celtic was a magnet for trouble. In 1987, several people were arrested after fighting between rival fans after a match with Arsenal. In July 2002, police had to break up 100 rival Middlesbrough and Celtic fans at Ayresome Park after they invaded the pitch during a testimonial for Tony Mowbray, Celtic's former Middlesbrough defender. In 1994, 200 Birmingham and Celtic supporters clashed outside the Dubliner pub before a pre-season friendly in the Midlands. Bricks and bottles were exchanged, five people were injured and 12 were arrested.

The CSC attempted to make a comeback in the 1990s but were even more marginalised than before, and have created few headlines in recent years. The exception was games against Rangers, which continued to be marred by sectarian violence. In May 1999, more than 100 fans were arrested as Rangers clinched the League title at Parkhead. A number of fans invaded the pitch during the match and the referee's head was cut by a flying coin. Running battles took place outside the ground and in Glasgow city centre between rival fans.

In October 2002, there were 40 arrests and the fighting extended to the Ibrox pitch, with rival players trading punches. In years gone by this would have been shrugged off and swept under the carpet, but such behaviour was now unacceptable. The Scottish Parliament got involved and began the process of outlawing sectarian singing and displays. The clubs promised to play their part but old habits die hard.

In late April 2005, 20 were arrested at the last Old Firm clash of the season. There was trouble before and after the game and there were also reports of disorder between rival sets of fans throughout the country. A riot broke out on the Troon to Larne ferry service as rival fans clashed on their return journey to Northern Ireland. Up to 100 people were reported to have been involved, and riot police were forced to board the ferry to quell the disturbance.

Bill Aitken, an MSP for Glasgow, said, "This behaviour is disgraceful and paints a bleak picture of the tribalism which still persists in Scotland. People need to be reminded that it is only a game and not part two of the battle of the Boyne. But, frankly, I fear that the Old Firm games are just an excuse for some people to indulge in mindless violence." One look at the statistics for arrests and injuries over the years indicates that Mr Aitken may be correct in his assessment of the rivalry between the two Glasgow giants.

Further reading: *The Old Firm*, Bill Murray (John Donald)

GLASGOW RANGERS

Ground: Ibrox Park
Firm: Inter-City Firm, Her Majesty's Service
Rivals: Celtic, Aberdeen, Hibernian, Motherwell

"Johnnie Stark was a product of the Gorbals. Tall, broad-chested, and with dark, sullen eyes he looked like a fighter – and he was. Johnnie liked women – and women liked him. For their sake, and for any other reason that seemed good to him, Johnnie was ready to fight. There were no Queensberry rules in the Gorbals, and when violence erupted, any weapon was used..."

Alexander McArthur and H. Kingsley Long's portrayal of a brutal razor gang leader of 1930s Gorbals, *No Mean City*, reflected the society from which Glasgow Rangers drew its support. Vicious, gang-dominated and uncompromising, they were communities where violence and religious attachment ruled the streets. Their people had been all but abandoned by wealthier society, and so they created a parallel civic structure where the "hard men" ruled the streets and hope was simply a distant dream. *No Mean City* shocked and infuriated

Scottish society, and the Glasgow Central Library refused to stock it when it first appeared. Uncomfortable as it was, the book was an accurate portrayal of the underbelly of Glaswegian society and the likes of Johnnie Stark, the Razor King, were all to be found on the terraces of Ibrox.

A real life Johnnie Stark was Billy Fullerton. Born in Bridgeton 1906, he went on to lead the Bridgeton Billy Boys, the most famous of all Glasgow gangs. In 1924, Fullerton scored the winning goal in a local football match only for his opponent, a Catholic, to attack him with a hammer. The call went out for the wrong to be avenged and within weeks he had amassed an army of 800 men. The Billy Boys were born and for the next decade they terrorised opponents at football matches and at the regular Orange Walks. Their influence continues to resonate across Ibrox to this day.

Hello! Hello! We are the Billy Boys.
Hello! Hello! You'll know us by our noise.
For we're up to our knees in Fenian blood,
Surrender or you'll die.
For we are the Bridgeton Billy Boys

From the mid-Sixties until the late Nineties, every trip into England brought mayhem. In August 1967, fans were forced on to the pitch at Highbury to avoid injury during a visit by Rangers when dozens of Scots began launching bottles into the North Bank. Several people required hospital treatment, including an eleven-year-old boy who needed twelve stitches to a head wound.

In May 1969, Rangers played Newcastle in the semi-final of the Fairs Cup. The Geordies ran out winners but the match was chiefly memorable for the anarchy before, during and after the game. "Fifty terrifying minutes in a policeman's life, on the night the Scots went daft," was the headline in a Newcastle paper. "It was a night of the jagged-edge bottle, the sharpened stick, the boot, the fist and the head. The violence that took place was quite simply utterly outrageous."

The paper went on to give a blow-by-blow account of how the trouble unfolded, from 6.45 p.m., when all seemed peaceful, to well after midnight when the last police and ambulance siren went quiet. In between, thousands of Scots ran amok. Hundreds marched through the streets chant- ing Loyalist songs in what the local paper described as "a Durham [miners'] big meeting atmosphere without the motive. By nine, most pubs had closed and most of those that attempted to remain open were wrecked. There were reports that drunken Rangers fans were climbing on tables and bar coun- ters to 'conduct' howling choruses of abuse, directed not only at Newcastle United but anyone who stood for officialdom. Meanwhile, gangs wandered around the streets looking for locals to attack. At 11pm they took over the Marlborough Crescent bus station and weaved unmolested between the bus queues, shouting obscenities and abusing women. They got away with it simply because the police by then were busier elsewhere.

"As the night wore on the incidents piled up rapidly. Shortly before 11pm, when most Rangers coaches were due to leave, the incidents grew uglier. Hordes of supporters marched towards Marlborough. One youth, stripped to his waist, physically molested every woman he met en-route to the bus. Under normal circumstances, each inci- dent would have merited a police charge. But, safe in the midst of his laughing group, his actions were unnoticed, except by his victims. He left one teenage girl in tears, crying for a policeman. None was avail- able. It took a middle-aged woman – and drunk herself – to restore some sanity. A Rangers supporter peered into her face and remarked: 'I've seen better looking sheep.' She removed her shoe and hit him with it, then commenced to chase the entire group through the station."

During the match, dozens of Rangers fans had climbed up the floodlight pylons and others perched on the rooftops of neighbouring buildings. One newspaper seller said, "I have never seen anything like it in all my life. They're going daft." The news- paper agreed. "It was as good a sentiment as any to express what happened on the night that the streets of Newcastle erupted. They went daft." Even their own chairman branded his fans "lunatics" and, stung by the fallout from the game, the Rangers board held a special meeting to discuss the trouble associ- ated with the club. In addition to extra stewards who would point out troublemakers to the police, the club considered using a Klaxon to drown out the anti-Catholic singing. It was also agreed that young people would be segregated in special enclosures.

The same year saw Rangers take over Leeds in a

similar way. Even Glasgow Rangers' greatest triumph, victory in the final of the European Cup Winners Cup, was overshadowed by their violent supporters. Their 3–2 victory over the Russian side Dynamo Moscow in the final in Barcelona, Spain, left 150 people injured, 15 Scots in custody and thousands of other fans stranded. The day began badly and steadily got worse. An eighteen-year-old fractured his skull when he fell from a second-storey window while celebrating his arrival in Barcelona. Later, 120 Rangers fans wrecked a hotel bar. The violence reached a climax during and after the match, when Rangers fans poured on to the pitch on three separate occasions, hitting an opposing player over the head with a bottle and fighting with the police. The first invasion came after Rangers took the lead on 23 minutes and then again when a second was scored. The final invasion, by most of the travelling support, occurred at the final whistle. Bottles and wooden seats were used as weapons. When the riot ended, all eight of the stadiums bars were wrecked, hundreds of seats had been ripped out and more than 2,000 bottles lay strewn across the pitch. Legend has it that some Spanish police drew their sidearms, only to run before the Rangers hordes.

The Russians were understandably furious and demanded the result be cancelled. The Dynamo coach claimed that two-thirds of the 25,000 Scottish contingent who stormed the pitch were "completely drunk" and that his players were terrified and this affected their performance. His views were backed by the Russian Football Federation, who claimed that the conditions "were abnormal because of the frequent interference by fans". In a telegram to UEFA, both the club and the Russian Federation demanded the match be replayed.

There was mixed reaction back home. The Lord Provost of Glasgow quickly condemned the hooligan element, but one Scottish police sergeant who had accompanied the fans on their trip described his Spanish counterparts as "a cowardly, atrocious bunch". He said that they had allowed the fans on to the pitch only then to baton charge them off. The British Consul-General, the country's highest ranking diplomat in the city, personally apologised in the measured understatement of the British diplomatic service: "A number of visitors from the United Kingdom showed various examples of behaviour which demonstrated a lack of consideration for the host city."

UEFA held an inquiry, admitting that it was the first time in European club football history that such a protest had been put in "when the final is over". When the committee did finally issue a statement, a fortnight later, there was universal condemnation for the behaviour of the Scottish fans. However, with Spanish police reports not having arrived, any possible action was delayed, much to the annoyance of the Russian club, who had cancelled a trip to the United States in case they were required to play again. Eventually the Glasgow side were banned from European competition for two years – but the result stood.

While the Barcelona riot received acres of the headlines, back home Rangers fans had been involved in bother for many years. In 1960 they caused havoc in the border town of Berwick during a Scottish Cup tie. The following year there was trouble at a European qualifier at Wolves, while the 1963 Scottish Cup Final was marred with chanting about the dying Pope, and later that year the fans disgraced themselves during the minute's silence to mark the death of US President John F. Kennedy. In October 1965, Celtic fans had to cut short their lap of honour to mark winning the League Cup after a Rangers invasion. Towards the end of the decade a number of games, including matches at Leicester and Dundee, were halted due to bottle throwing. "Very little of this was new," commented Bill Murray, in his book *The Old Firm*. "What was new was that such behaviour was getting greater publicity through television, and the changing climate of public opinion was refusing to tolerate it."

Less than three months after Barcelona, Rangers fans brought more shame on their club. At a pre-season Cup game against Hibs they battled with police on the pitch and traded religious insults with their rivals. Police confiscated several umbrellas with sharpened points. But the real violence erupted after Hibs skipper Pat Stanton scored in the fifth minute of first-half injury time, and when the whistle finally went hundreds poured on to the pitch. Hibs scored two more goals in the second half and there were further pitch invasions. A train carrying Rangers fans home was also wrecked.

Rangers promised to get ruthless with the hooligans. Three days after the trouble, the club announced plans to make Ibrox an all-seater stadium, a ban on alcohol within the ground and extra stewards and police. There was also a promise to end all party songs and obscene language but, of course, nothing was mentioned about the club's own anti-Catholic policy, which many considered the root of the problem.

Alongside all this chaos outside Scotland, Rangers continued their hostility against neighbours, Celtic. At every game there were major ructions and dozens injured and arrested. The 1971 New Year's Day match was one of the darkest days in British football; a crush resulted in 33 deaths and 500 injuries. Rangers were losing the game and hordes of home supporters began leaving the ground, but with a minute to go, Rangers equalised, and many of the departing fans heard the roar and rushed back. One fan stumbled and a domino effect caused carnage. The tragedy was no fault of Celtic fans but their subsequent joke of "the orange crush" only hardened the bitterness between the two sets of fans.

The European ban did little to reduce the propensity of Rangers fans to drink to excess and brawl. In October 1974, a little over two years on from Barcelona, Rangers fans ran amok in Manchester before a game at Old Trafford. They came in their thousands, many arriving in the early hours of the morning, and literally took over the city. There was undoubtedly the added incentive that United was supposedly a Catholic club, but for most of those who travelled down, it was just another invasion south of the border.

"The only safe place for us at our age was the Stretford End," recalled Tony O'Neill, then a fledgling United hooligan, in his book *Red Army General*. "Packed into the Stretford, we looked across the pitch at this mass of swaying blue. It was awesome, a scene you dream of being in. I hadn't seen an away following that big. The noise, energy and raw emotion coming from them set your hair on end. You knew it was going to blow. The game went by in a blur and the talk was of going to the city centre as there would be loads more trouble. I heard tales of gangs of United trying to take on the Jocks before the game and it seemed to me things had not gone our way. For once in my life, I thought the better of it, and my little gang decided to make our way home. We passed the Scoreboard End, where the Jocks were still locked in. You could hear them

pounding and screaming to get out and it was only a matter of time before they kicked down the gates. I could actually see the gates buckling and knew that if I was there when they flew open, I'd be for it."

Two years later, Rangers caused havoc in Birmingham before, during and after a friendly with Aston Villa. Trouble began in the city hours before kick-off as Rangers fans poured in on overnight trains and coaches. A 21-year-old woman was hit on the head by a bottle as she walked home, and another person was stabbed in the stomach. With Rangers fans on the rampage, police were forced to close 50 city centre pubs.

At half-time, Rangers fans tried to take the Holte End. Bottles, cans and other missiles were thrown onto the pitch, and when the 50 police on duty inside the ground moved onto the Holte they immediately became targets. Nine minutes into the second half, Villa went 2-0 up and the game was held up as Rangers poured onto the pitch and attacked Villa fans throughout the ground. The game eventually had to be abandoned. Ninety-nine people were arrested and 50 people were injured, including a number of Rangers fans.

Pub owners and shopkeepers were furious that the match had been held in the first place. "Rangers fans have a diabolical reputation and there was no need for the match to take place," said Horace Stokes, a publicans' union spokesman. The Villa chairman said that his club could take none of the blame; he thought Glasgow Rangers fans had reformed. Instead he claimed that the trouble was the fault of the police who allowed hundreds of Rangers supporters to arrive in the city early in the morning. His comments were attacked by local politicians who believed he was abdicating responsibility for stewarding and segregation.

The police remained silent in the immediate aftermath, preferring to study video footage, the first time CCTV had been used at Villa Park. But Home Secretary Merlyn Rees demanded a full report. "We shall certainly be looking at the whole question of these matches which become excuses for almost a drunken rave-up," he said, questioning the early arrival of the special trains, the drunken state of the Rangers fans who disembarked and poor segregation inside the ground. "The referee told me that when he arrived at the ground two hours before the game there were about 200 fans climbing into the Holte End."

The Glasgow Rangers game was to have national implications as a debate started about segregating supporters. One club chairman predicted "the complete segregation" of rival supporters, with home fans forced to use one end and opposing fans the other. The Chief Constable of West Midlands Police briefed a senior official at the Home Office and there was even the suggestion of closing pubs close to football grounds. Eventually, Villa manager Ron Saunders broke his silence: "The birch should be reintroduced and there should be stiffer jail sentences. It's a joke to fine these people." Only five of the 55 arrested were convicted and the maximum jail term given was six months.

Many Scottish commentators turned on Rangers' religious sectarianism, a mood that had been building for several years. The *Daily Record*, the *Glasgow Evening Times* and even the Protestant *Sunday Post* all voiced their opposition to the club's continuing ban on Catholic players. While there were no obvious religious overtones to the violence in Birmingham, there was a general consensus that the anti-Catholic stance encouraged "the bigoted, lunatic fringe of their so-called support". Football writer Ian Archer, of the *Glasgow Herald*, was one of their fiercest critics: "This country would be a better place if Rangers did not exist. They are a permanent embarrassment because they are the only club in the world which insists that every member of the team is of one religion. They are an occasional disgrace because some of their fans, fuelled by bigotry, behave like animals." After years of denying an anti-Catholic policy even existed, a shaken Rangers chairman, Willie Wadell, finally promised that a Catholic would be signed, if he was good enough. The press applauded but nothing changed. It was to be another decade before the first Catholic would don the Blue shirt.

Possibly the worst Old Firm clash in recent times occurred in the full gaze of the nation during the 1980 Scottish Cup Final. Celtic scored the winner in the final minute and, as their fans poured onto the pitch in celebration at the end, they were met by a furious Rangers mob. "Showers of bottles, stones, and cans rained down on to the field," reported the *Daily Record*. "Battling fans, armed with iron bars and wooden staves ripped from terrace frames, created the most violent and ugly scenes seen at

Hampden in more than 70 years. Mounted police with batons drawn galloped across the pitch, separating the rival fans and herding them back to the terracing." The trouble lasted almost an hour and the final toll was 160 arrests, with a further 50 being held outside the ground.

The shockwaves from the televised chaos were felt throughout the footballing world. Clubs, football authorities and police all attempted to shift the blame on to one another and the Government demanded both an explanation and an answer. *Daily Record* sportswriter Alex Cameron was in no doubt where the blame lay, and in a comment piece he laid into Glasgow Rangers. "How long must we wait, Rangers? How many more disgraceful riot scenes have to be endured before Rangers honour a promise which could make a start towards ending the bigotry bedevilling Scottish football? The louts from both ends of Hampden who soiled the Cup Final with savagery were motivated by hate. Forget, for a moment, the arguments about who started the mayhem, or how it could have been prevented. The root cause is religion. And while no one would suggest that one club is solely to blame, Rangers stubbornly refuse to do their part in a modern way to start the long and difficult process of removing this horrible barrier. This can only be kicked off when they sign Catholic players as they promised to do after rioting in Birmingham … Rangers raised this as an issue themselves and in doing so openly conceded that their unwritten policy of religious apartheid played a significant part in sordid crowd trouble. The Ibrox club have sidestepped their responsibilities and broken a promise. Surely they cannot keep on doing so."

A bitter war of words followed in the days after. While supporters' groups pinned the blame on inadequate policing, the Secretary of State for Scotland, George Younger, the Scottish FA and the police pointed the finger at Celtic players for their post-match celebrations. "It is the police view that had Celtic not acted as they did, the invasion of the pitch might not have occurred," the Minister told Parliament. His comments were immediately shouted down by his Labour opponents, many of whom were also equally furious that drink was blamed, when the match was sponsored by a brewery! Labour preferred to point to the religious bigotry as an explanation.

The clubs were predictably split over the police response. While Celtic's manager, Billy McNeil, defended his players, Rangers issued a terse three-sentence statement agreeing with the police findings. Three hours later, Celtic hit back with a vicious riposte to both Rangers and the Scottish FA. They dismissed Rangers' criticism as "appalling", and said that any attempts to ban both clubs from the competition the following year would be the death of Scottish football. The police were accused of being almost "non-existent" inside the ground when the trouble started. Responding to the allegations of religious bigotry, the Celtic chairman said, "At least we play anyone of any colour or creed as long as he plays football. Had two players been fit on Saturday, we would have been playing seven Protestants and four Catholics. But, despite criticisms, we will continue to fly the Irish Tricolour because of the associations related to the origins of the club."

One immediate casualty of the affair was the police's low-profile policy, which had characterised policing of matches in Scotland until then. Also, all drink was banned from Scottish football grounds and this appeared to reduce disorder within the stadia for the following few years. A study of the effects of the ban was carried out by academics at Edinburgh and it showed that arrests and incidents of violence were down.

With Rangers and Celtic pre-occupied with one another, changes were happening in the Scottish football culture that largely by-passed Glasgow. In 1980, the Merseyside-led casual fashion was adopted in Aberdeen, and a couple of years later by Motherwell and Dundee. It would take a while for the fashion to appear on the Ibrox terraces. One Rangers fan, Burlington's, recalled, "There were 'trendies' in Scotland's largest city but it was not until late 1984, some four years after the birth of the Aberdeen casual, that Rangers had its first casual mob. Our Inter City Firm was a direct take-off of the more infamous West Ham crew, while Rangers' other gang, Her Majesty's Service, originated from the Southside of the city and took its name from the Loyalist nature of the fan base.

"In those early days, the Rangers mobs were young and inexperienced. The average age was just sixteen, putting them at a distinct disadvantage against the older and more streetwise Aberdeen and even Motherwell gangs. However, as time went by these young lads grew up and remain at the core of the group even today. The casual scene first made real headlines in Glasgow after an Old Firm game in 1984, with the headline 'Cavalry Charge' on the front page of the *Evening Times*. This was accompanied by a photograph of 400 or so Rangers in Celtic Park complete with the ski hats of the time. After the match 'The Battle of Janefield Street' took place outside with police horses and dogs among the injured. Strange as this may be, but the Celtic Soccer Casuals had decent numbers and not a bad crew up until the CS gas incident at Easter Road in 1987 [see GLASGOW CELTIC]. The aftermath led to their firm being depleted by the usual police hassles. Prior to this there were various scuffles between the two teams' casuals, some of which were pretty nasty, and took place in Glasgow city centre even on days when neither club had played. The Gallowgate, a traditional Celtic haunt, saw plenty of battles after Old Firm games, as did outside Ibrox in Govan."

Hooliganism at Celtic declined in the late Eighties, and while clashes between rival groups continued around Old Firm fixtures, this was as much sectarian bigotry as football thuggery. The emerging Rangers casual firm looked further afield for their football fix. "The main rivals to us were Aberdeen Soccer Casuals and the [Hibs] Capital City Service," said Burlington's. "Both of these firms provided great opposition to us for the best part of twenty years. If you speak to lads from both firms I am sure they will agree that there have been some legendary tussles over the years. During the Eighties, CCS were our main rivals, mainly because they were closer than Aberdeen and tickets for Easter Road were easier to get than those for Pittodrie. Back then going on a train for up to four hours to get sent straight back due to having no ticket was not appealing The ASC fell away a little in my eyes after the jailing they suffered in 1986 [see ABERDEEN], which is natural. This is where Hibs picked up the mantle. The CCS were constant visitors to us from 1987 to 1994 and we had many good rows over the course of this time, some won, some lost, as is the norm. Before 1986, Aberdeen was by far the biggest and best mob in Scotland, with some huge numbers coming to Ibrox in the 1984/85 period. From 1995 to 2005, the ASC and ICF were almost the only two mobs in Scotland doing anything of note at all. Dundee

Truncheons at the ready, police officers tackle unruly fans of Glasgow Rangers fans at White Hart Lane, where their team was playing Tottenham Hotspur in a testimonial match for Paul Miller in August, 1986.

Utility were also appearing in the early 1990s as a force of sorts, however this didn't last."

There was a sectarian and hooligan rivalry with Hibs. They were viewed by Rangers' fans as "Edinburgh Celtic", so there was a long history of trouble between the supporters. But during the Eighties, as both mobs emerged as major players in Scotland, this took on a more competitive dimension. "We naturally wanted a crack at what we perceived to be one of the top mobs and when we got a result, it was a scalp worth collecting," said Burlington's. "During the peak of the casual scene, between 1984 and 1989, neither firm could claim to be dominant. We and Hibs both got turned over on occasions. The tide did change in a major way with other reasons coming into play later in the 1990s, like the Scottish

National Firm [an allegiance of various Scottish soccer gangs between 1996 and 1998]."

Everything was up for grabs on the final day of the 1985/86 season. Hearts needed to win at home to Dundee to take the title, otherwise it would go to Celtic. Rangers needed a win at home to Motherwell to get into the UEFA Cup, and, just to make things even more exciting, Graeme Souness was being introduced as their new manager. Motherwell came to Ibrox with a tidy mob of 150-200 lads, which often would have been enough, but not that day, not against the massed casual ranks of Rangers.

Events off the field were to prove an inspiring introduction to one Rangers lad who, almost 20 years later, continues to go with the ICF. "A dozen of us, all thirteen to fifteen years old, dressed in jumbo cords, Kickers and Next jumpers, headed into town and caught the subway to Ibrox. The whole of Ibrox was buzzing with the arrival of Graeme Souness, but it was also very busy with Rangers casuals milling around Ibrox Underground waiting for any Motherwell to appear. The game saw a crowd of just 20,000, unimaginable by today's gates, and there was the usual banter and bravado between the two sets of fans. Rangers won and clinched a UEFA spot and out poured the fans.

"We headed round to the back of the Broomloan Road Stand and saw a sea of casuals, all Rangers, waiting for Motherwell to come out of the ground. Motherwell didn't shy away either. It kicked off instantly, police got knocked over, their horses went berserk and, of course, sirens were going ten to the dozen. What a buzz this was, unbelievable. I was hooked, as were most of my pals. The adrenalin was pumping. This day was spoken of for weeks and months by all of us. It was the start for all of us to go to the footy every chance we could."

Aberdeen have been Rangers' most consistent hooligan rivals and probably the only one to last into the new Millennium. Burlington's believes that one clash, in 1987, finally marked the arrival of the Rangers casual mob. "The match at Pittodrie was memorable in so many ways. The ASC were still the best firm in Scotland and Rangers hadn't won the League for nine years and this was a chance to finally win it. Again the Rangers support was huge and at full time a 1–1 draw with a Terry Butcher header was enough to give us the championship. We all piled on the pitch, expecting the ASC to follow, but for whatever reason there was no real sign of them other than 100 or so at the corner who were soon chased back into the stands. Rangers' firm must have been 200 to 300-strong. Outside, the ASC were more than a little fucked off at their pitch being taken on national TV and went for it big time. For the next hour or two it went off all over Aberdeen in smaller scale scuffles. That in my opinion was a bit of a coming of age for Rangers' ICF."

Not all Rangers' fights have been against the big boys or even been victories. Like many large firms, they have suffered setbacks in the most unusual of places. Burlington's explained, "Rangers have actually come unstuck to Kilmarnock, of all firms, back in 1994, when twenty of our lads embarked on the train only to be met with more than double the numbers and a decent Killie firm. This was later paid back with a mob of ninety of us, in May 1995, a week or so after we had claimed yet another League title. A thunder flash fired down London Road in Kilmarnock greeted our arrival from the train. Killie put up some resistance but the Rangers mob was too much for them on this occasion. Strangely, the Killie firm were never seen again by us after that day.

"St Johnstone's Fair City Firm (FCF) came to Glasgow in 1989, on the day of the Hillsborough tragedy. They were almost dispatched on arrival at Queen Street Station, then later at Celtic Park. I have since spoken to ex-members of the FCF who reckon that was the day their firm ceased to exist, as they had near on 100 lads but were largely overwhelmed by a very good Rangers firm. We have also had various scuffles with Falkirk Fear, Airdrie Section B, Morton MSC, and St Mirren's LSD, to name but a few of the lesser lights who, on their day, could provide a day's fun."

The Loyalist leanings of Glasgow Rangers are well documented and so it is no surprise that the Rangers ICF have repeatedly been involved in political events away from football. Most of this has occurred within Scotland, with the mob coming out to oppose Republican marches in Glasgow and Edinburgh, such as the Bloody Sunday and James Connolly parades. The ICF have often linked up with the CSF of Hearts, another Loyalist-linked club, and with smaller groups from teams like Morton. Opposing them was an alliance of football hooligans from Celtic, Hibs and the far-Left group Red Action. In recent years the police have had the events tightly controlled but the Eighties and Nineties saw numerous disturbances, with the last major clash taking place at the Connolly march in Edinburgh in 2000.

The Loyalist influence was obviously a major factor in the trouble that marred the club's European tie with Bohemians of Dublin in 1984. The Irish club ran out winners but it was the violence that grabbed the headlines. Disorder broke out at half-time when Rangers fans clashed with police at one end of the ground and continued until well after the final whistle. While praising the Irish part-timers, Rangers' manager, Jock Wallace, slammed his own violent supporters. "We don't want them," he said. "They are a disgrace to the club. They are ruining the name of Glasgow Rangers and we'd prefer it if they stayed away from our games."

The ICF has also travelled further afield in support of the Loyalist cause. In January 1993, dozens of Rangers lads went to London to join up with hundreds of other football hooligans and Loyalists in an attempted attack on the annual Bloody Sunday march. Organising was the fledgling nazi group Combat 18 and the Ulster Defence Association, and it was part of a wider strategy to take the fight to the British mainland and in particular to antagonise the British Irish Catholic community. Whether the Rangers' lads knew it is unclear, but the intention of the organisers was to kick off a riot in Kilburn, the heart of London's Irish community. It was only the arrest of 396 mainly football lads out of a total mob of 600, that prevented it happening.

Many of Rangers' opponents, particularly Celtic fans, have pointed to an intrinsic link between Rangers' Loyalism and fascism. While it would be totally inaccurate to brand an entire fan base as fascist, the link between the two has been present for almost 70 years. Billy Fullerton, leader of the Billy Boys, was a section commander for the Fascist Party and had 200 men under his control. In 1926, the Billy Boys were hired by Conservative politicians to smash the General Strike and trade union and Communist Party meetings were attacked. Fullerton even launched a Scottish branch of the Ku Klux Klan, though it is hard to think of anyone other than Catholics fulfilling the role of the blacks in the American Deep South. Bill Murray, in *The Old Firm*, says that neither the Fascist Party or the KKK really took off, and perhaps this sums up the relationship. For a few, sometimes high-profile, Rangers' fans, the far-Right has been politically attractive. Most however, are not really bothered.

In more recent decades, elements of the ICF have also been linked with fascist groups such as the British National Party and Combat 18. For some this was a natural extension of their own Loyalism but for others this increased when the Rangers' mob formed an alliance with a far-Right clique within Chelsea's mob. While some Rangers lads are quick to play down the extent of this, saying that while there was general sympathy, few could be called politically active, many links clearly exist. Several ICF followers have stood for the BNP in General and European elections, while others have signed nomination papers and been named in the media.

The Loyalist and right-wing sympathisers of the ICF found a common bond with a Chelsea element and the two mobs have been closely linked for 20 years. This bond was formed in 1985 when Rangers played a fundraising match at Chelsea for the victims of the Bradford fire. The following year, ironically on Valentine's Day, Chelsea played a match at Ibrox and a large contingent of Chelsea made the trip and the two mobs mixed freely. Not everyone was so impressed. Many of the Chelsea lads carried large quantities of counterfeit money and local shops were swamped with the dodgy notes. Since the mid-Eighties, Chelsea and Rangers have formed an alliance and lads from both sides travel to each other's big games and on more political trips such as to Northern Ireland.

The annual fixture at Goodison Park, home of the supposedly Catholic Everton, became better known as the 'NF-Orange' connection. During the 1994/95 season, when Chelsea were back in Europe for the first time in more than 20 years, several Rangers lads were deported from Belgium and also made the journey with them to Austria and Spain.

"White Hart Lane in 1986 cemented our friendship with Chelsea," recalled Burlington's. "The Yids had always been a rival of Chelsea and Rangers took a big firm and huge support down, which was supplemented by a big Chelsea contingent. Outside the ground before the match, the Yids were run ragged, even Rangers scarfers joined in. The police locked the doors but a firm of Rangers and Chelsea managed to unlock them and as soon as they got in launched a full attack at the Yids. The Spurs mob were simply not in the same league as us that day and were humiliated on their own soil, much to the delight of our mates from Stamford Bridge."

Four years later, Rangers planned to link up with the Headhunters for Chelsea's pre-season friendly at Hibs. Three minibuses of Chelsea travelled up intending to meet Rangers and Hearts before seeking a confrontation with the Hibs CCS. However, Chelsea had an informant within their ranks and the police knew their plans. As the Headhunters entered Scotland, their vehicles were pulled over and everyone was arrested. An arsenal of weapons was discovered, including a wide selection of knives that had been taken during a raid on a shop in Cumbria the night before. A few Rangers decided to carry on into Edinburgh but without the presence of the Headhunters the game passed off quietly.

The link with the Headhunters might have solidified the ICF's links with the far-Right, but there were signs the club's sectarian grip was loosening. The turning point came in 1986 when Graeme Souness was appointed player-manager. Rangers had not won the title for several years and crowds had dropped to as little as 20,000. They were not only miles behind Celtic, but had also been overtaken by Aberdeen and, to a lesser extent, Dundee United. Rangers were intent on revolutionising their under-achieving team. Souness was a known Conservative and a royalist, but he was also a winner. One of his first signings was striker Maurice Johnston, the club's first known Catholic player. Some fans reacted with horror and ripped up their membership cards, but as the first of nine consecutive League titles were won, the uproar subsided. The taboo had been broken. Souness also signed Mark Walters, the club's first black player, who, ironically, was wanted by Everton to become their first black signing. While again there were bigots who disapproved, the player soon became a firm favourite. Rangers fans even began to take delight in highlighting the racism Walters faced at the hands of Celtic supporters.

The mould was broken but it could never be removed. The glee of Rangers supporters when Paul Gascoigne playing an imaginary flute on the pitch, shades of the Orange marching bands, and Andy Goram posed for photographs with a Loyalist banner, showed how ingrained, if unthinking, the Loyalist link was. In more recent years, leading Loyalist terrorists, including the notorious Johnny "Mad Dog" Adair, have occupied executive boxes at Ibrox.

The trouble at White Hart Lane meant that no English clubs were willing to organise "friendlies" against Rangers for several years. Their next trip south of the border was to Sunderland in 1993, and again there was widespread disorder. A coach of ICF travelled down knowing that others making their own way independently would swell their numbers. "The coach arrived at around eleven a.m. and everybody walked into the city centre for a few beers," said Burlington's. "We sat in a pub and had a Union Jack flag with 'Rangers ICF' across it, hanging from the window, which was unusual for us as we normally preferred to keep a low profile. A few more beers were sunk in

another pub across the road and I went to the toilet. While in there I heard a bit of a commotion coming from the bar and, as I stepped outside, there was blood everywhere.

"Apparently a group of Sunderland lads came in, got lippy, then someone who is now dead slashed a few of them. I disagree with the use of weapons, but if you go into a pub of rival lads and try to take the piss then you take what's coming to you. The police were on the scene very quickly and after a while let everyone carry on towards Roker Park. By this time our numbers were more than 100 and everybody was fairly hyped up. A small altercation happened with a few lads fighting with a few Rangers barmies. When that was over, we found ourselves walking up a main street with a lot of pubs, and a lot of Sunderland lads outside them. Without a word we charged in and, to a man, they legged it. The police got in the middle and one grabbed a Rangers lad, who pushed him away and told him to fuck off. The copper hesitated and soon Rangers were all telling the police where to go and walking round Sunderland like we owned the place.

"Some looted shops in between the odd skirmish with a less than up for it Sunderland firm. As the ground got closer, the coppers got more desperate to contain what could only now be described as a riot. We eventually went into the match in our own time and when we came out we were ferried back on the buses and escorted straight out of Sunderland. There were in the region of 100 arrests, the first of which at eight a.m. The papers were full of the trouble for a few weeks and the police arrested a few for the slashings but, as usual, they got it completely wrong. That was without doubt one of the maddest days, not so much for the fighting with Sunderland but the lawlessness."

If the trip to Pittodrie in 1987 was the turning point in Rangers' relationship with the ASC, then a match against Hibs in 1994 marked a change in fortunes with the CCS. For many years, Rangers had come off second best to a mob that was arguably the "best" in Scotland. In 1994, the ICF and the CCS agreed a meeting in Slateford, a suburb of Edinburgh on the Glasgow train line, and 22 ICF made the trip. They faced a mob of 100 Hibs. There was only going to be one winner but the defeat acted as a catalyst for Rangers to organise and prepare for revenge. Fortunately, said Burlington's and his mate, Blue, Hibs did not appear at the next meeting at Ibrox. "It was a relief, as I'm convinced one of them would've been killed that day with the weaponry and lads Rangers had out," said Blue. Since then, the clashes between the two have been few. The Scottish National Firm irreversibly split the Hibs mob – because some adamantly refused to join up with Rangers and Hearts – and when, in 2005, Rangers won the title at Easter Road and brought more than 100 experienced lads, mostly aged 30-45, there was no Hibs mob around.

The trips to Hibs have had their lighter side, said Burlington's. "One of the funniest tales was when fifty of us were on a service train coming back and someone threw a lighted newspaper at someone else. As expected, this escalated and soon everybody was searching for newspapers to light and launching them at each other. The next thing an announcement came over the train, 'Can the ICF please refrain from trying to set fire to each other and the train.'"

In July 1997, thousands of Rangers fans made the trip to Goodison Park for Dave Watson's testimonial. They were joined by several Chelsea faces and, during outbreaks of violence throughout the day, 77 people were arrested, the majority of them Rangers fans. The following year Rangers played at Tranmere's Prenton Park against Irish club Shelbourne. There was trouble outside the ground after a Rangers lad tried to make off with the cigarette machine in the Mersey Clipper pub. "It was the first time I have seen a mounted copper in a pub," said Burlington's. After the game there was sporadic fighting with locals on the way back into Liverpool.

Most of Rangers' biggest recent battles have been while playing in Europe, in particular against the Dutch teams of Feyenoord and PSV Eindhoven. Jim "Jinks" McTaggott, a leading face in the ICF, received a life ban from Ibrox after being imprisoned for four weeks after the European Cup match in Eindhoven in 1999. Three years later he was back in the Netherlands, this time for a match in Rotterdam against Feyenoord. He recounted the story in a recent book, *Top Boys*. "I'd have to say Feyenoord [was] very intimidating. Many Feyenoord fans lined the route for the escorted Rangers fans

coming in, throwing fucking everything at all the buses, banging windows, fucking all sorts, really nasty atmosphere, terrible, terrible. It was a fucking awful day. Loads of them had bottles and bricks aimed at all the fans. The worst atmosphere at an away ground definitely."

Rangers' main rivalry, Celtic aside, continues to be with Aberdeen. Trouble occurred at matches at Pittodrie in October 2000 and again in February 2002. On the latter occasion, fighting spilled onto the pitch and the match was held up for 20 minutes. The last encounter between the two mobs was a chance meeting at a railway station.

General hooliganism at Glasgow Rangers is now rare, largely because of the increasingly tough court sentences and better policing, but also because of the lack of Scottish opposition. "At Rangers these days we have a hardcore of forty lads who will show rain, hail or shine, but it has to be said, games are picked out now as opposed to days gone by when it was fairly constant activity," said Burlington's. "But there is always some sort of representation of lads at Rangers games at home, away domestically or in Europe where we have had many great fights as well."

The Good Friday Agreement and the reduction in violence in Northern Ireland has done little to reduce the Loyalist sentiments of Rangers fans. A recent BBC *Panorama* programme revealed the lingering sectarianism of the Old Firm and exposed a continued reluctance by Rangers to act. The violence might have greatly reduced but the hatred remains. In October 2003, as Roy Keane waited to lead his Manchester United team-mates out at Ibrox, he heard the "Billy Boys" being sung by thousands in the crowd. A man who had stated his desire to play for Celtic, he knew that he was in for a tough old evening.

There was a certain symmetry to the match. Twenty-nine years after Rangers fans took over Manchester, the Mancunians got their revenge. "There were 5,000 Reds in Glasgow by the time the pubs opened," recalled Eddie Beef, a leading United face. "We were everywhere and they were nowhere." United's main mob, over 400-strong and dressed in black, deliberately occupied some of Rangers' main pubs from early morning onwards, and routed all opposition throughout the day. The wheel had turned full circle.

GRIMSBY TOWN

Ground: Blundell Park
Firm: Park Street Mafia, The Nunsthorpe Lads, Ice House Lads, Scartho Lads, Grimsby Hit Squad, Cleethorpes Beach Patrol
Rivals: Scunthorpe, Lincoln
Police Operations: Trapper

Grimsby Town FC hasn't seen much glory over the years but some great players have graced the black and white stripes. Matt Tees, Graham Taylor, Clive Mendonca, Nigel Batch, Kevin Drinkell and, more recently, Ivano Bonetti, may not be household names, but they are remembered with affection and pride by the Mariners faithful. However, the local lads believe that, despite the lack of success on the park, off it, they can rely on another, unofficial section of the club to gain success: the Cleethorpes Beach Patrol. There have been other similar elements among Grimsby fans in the past, like the Grimsby Hit Squad, the Nunsthorpe lads, the Scartho lads, the Icehouse lads and the Park Street Mafia, but they have come and gone, while the Beach Patrol has stayed.

Even among those in the firm, there is uncertainty about the origin of their name. One view is that it came from a gang of local lads who used to hang about on Cleethorpes promenade and who got up to the usual drinking and fighting. Another story is that it started with youths who used to torment security guards on patrol at a nearby maternity unit, getting involved in chases and clashes with them. Whatever the true history, all agree that the CBP has been the dominant mob over the years.

"Back in the heyday of football violence in the 1980s, all the groups combined could create a mob of between 300 and 400," said veteran S-Grimsby. Andy Nicholls, the co-author of this book, confirmed this in his autobiography, *Scally*: "When Everton were arguably at their best, Grimsby were the best firm from the lower divisions to come to Goodison. They went in the Blue House early, like lots of mobs did, Boro, Villa, Newcastle and Sunderland had all pulled the same stunt but Grimsby took more shifting than all of them." The Grimsby hooligan scene has died down, but CBP of 2005 could still muster up to 250, usually for derbies against Lincoln City or Scunthorpe United, and more if they were to meet Hull City.

For a club which, for so long, has languished in the lower divisions, Grimsby could produce big turnouts, but they have still been heavily outnumbered on occasions. The visit of Leeds in 1982 was the opening game of the season and Leeds's first in the old second Division. A 600-strong Leeds mob travelled down on the Friday night and caused mayhem. A warehouse was broken into and became their hotel for the night. Pubs and cars were damaged and locals didn't know what had hit them. More Leeds descended on the town at daybreak and a mob of more than 400 ran the Cleethorpes Beach Patrol up and down the sands. "It was one of only two occasions that Grimsby have been well out of their depth and run ragged all day long," said S-Grimsby.

Eight years later, it was Grimsby's turn to wreak havoc, this time during a visit to Chesterfield. A mob of 400 made the journey and the Chesterfield Bastard Squad couldn't cope. "That day Chesterfield couldn't quite live with the mob that Grimsby took. There were offs in graveyards, with some Grimsby lads shamelessly digging out headstones to throw at the Chesterfield lads, a market stall was emptied of all its fruit and veg which were used as missiles, and a visiting fair was trashed by the rampaging mob."

On any other Saturday the trouble would have hit the national press, but on this day Grimsby was again in the shadow of Leeds as the newspapers concentrated on two days of Yorkshire mayhem in Bournemouth. Even so, for Grimsby lads this day will never be forgotten. "In recent years I have revisited Chesterfield to watch Grimsby Town and taxi drivers have told me of their memories and their shock at the trouble Grimsby caused that day."

The following season, Grimsby lads were involved in a serious clash at home with Stoke City. Rival mobs fought throughout the day, with Stoke at one point attacking Grimsby's pub, the Imp. S-Grimsby was in the thick of it again: "There was a vicious forty-a-side taking place with both mobs having shouts of a victory. It was a an old-style Eighties battle."

In one nasty incident, Stoke's mob, the Naughty Forty, were gaining the upper hand when a couple of Grimsby lads arrived armed with the contents of a garden shed. The Stoke group were forced to back off, one receiving a nasty injury to his head from a pair of shears. Plenty of action was still to come and when the game finished, the banter between Grimsby's lads, to the left of the away end, and Stoke was getting more and more tense. Both sides spilled on to the pitch and a 100-a-side battle commenced on Blundell Park.

"We put up a very good fight that lasted the best part of fifteen minutes," said S-Grimsby. "Stoke narrowly edged it, eventually backing us off to our home end and out of the gates. The excellent book about the Naughty Forty by Mark Chester claims the pitched battle was their easiest fought victory of the day. I think that's debatable." He added that the respect remains, even fifteen years later. "We happened to bump into the Stoke author and his mates at the recent England v Wales game in Manchester and I must say, they looked after us. There were only six of us and nearly 100 of them and the quality of Stoke's lads was visible for all to see, they really are a class mob, with good numbers, good organisation, a lot of respect for each other and, most of all, they are all game as fuck. For me they are definitely in the top three mobs in this country."

Recent years, especially the late Nineties, have seen the terrace culture quieten down at Grimsby, but at the home fixture against Huddersfield in 1999 the silence was well and truly broken. The Huddersfield Young Casuals arrived early, but instead of going straight to Cleethorpes, as many firms did, they left their train at Grimsby town centre and took over the main streets with about 120 lads. It took about two hours for the police to realise that they were there and so began the long trek to Blundell Park, which is actually in Cleethorpes. The word spread amongst locals, and slowly a mob was put together. At this stage it was no more than 40-strong and nothing happened before the game, but contact was made during it and the two sides agreed that Huddersfield would board the train at Cleethorpes, where they would be undoubtedly taken by the police after the game, but they'd get off again at Grimsby Town Centre where the CBP was gathering.

At the final whistle, the plan was put into action and the HYC split into two groups. The first, sixty-strong, was escorted out of the ground under a heavy police presence and put on the train to West Yorkshire, which allowed a second, more important group to slip out of the ground undetected and head into Grimsby. An hour after the final whistle, this mob boarded the train at Cleethorpes and made the short hop to Grimsby, without the police and into the arms of an expectant home mob. The CBP were drinking in the Huxters, right outside the station, and as the Huddersfield train pulled in, the pub emptied and everyone bowled over.

"There was a tense, momentary stand-off as both sides squared up to one another in the knowledge that whoever charged first would take casualties. Finally, a ten-strong group of Grimsby made the first move and in seconds the rest of the Grimsby firm followed and there was a nasty toe-to-toe with their opponents. The Huddersfield mob was forced to back off but this was largely because most of them were still platform-side and could not get through to the station forecourt. The police eventually arrived and a few were nicked on the spot." The local paper ran an account of the fight under the headline, "Hooligans plan battle", and police raids followed, but despite the fight being caught on CCTV, the cases were thrown out for insufficient evidence.

Although the firm was in the main inactive, the CBP clashed twice with Man City, most recently in early 2000 when two rival mobs of 25 apiece met in a car park in Cleethorpes. Seaside towns like Cleethorpes often attract trouble as visiting fans take the opportunity for a boozy weekend, while the locals are used to fighting with drunken holidaymakers.

In 2001 the CBP were surprised by the appearance of around 30 Crystal Palace lads. There was no history between the two clubs and no prior warning. The small Palace group left the match early and decamped in a pub on Freeman Street. They were initially shadowed by the police but managed to give them the slip by sneaking out of the back door and making their way to Grimsby town centre. Waiting for them was a slightly smaller group of CBP and there were running battles through the streets. No clear winner emerged and a few CBP were arrested, some for racially abusing some of the black Palace lads.

The following season, a leading Grimsby lad was woken at eight in the morning by a phone call from Palace informing him that they were on their way. By eleven a small CBP mob had gathered in town, but as the clock ticked away there was no sign of the Londoners. As two o'clock approached, they received another Palace call to say that their train had broken down. Most of the Grimsby gave up and headed for the ground, leaving a handful behind.

"We finally found out that they were in People's Park," recalled S-Grimsby. "It was a great place to meet but was also a fair distance from where we were in Cleethorpes. At this point we were struggling for numbers due to a lot of lads becoming tired of waiting and going to the game. We told the fifteen or so lads left to get into town, while we drove past People's Park to see what Palace had out. Sure enough, there they were, about thirty of them, including some big black lads who were prominent the previous season. And most of them had tree branches in their hands. For a laugh, three of us got out the car and called it on. When they got within distance, we ran back to our car with thirty lads waving branches and logs in hot pursuit. I was glad the driver didn't stall the car. The lads in town were told but before a proper Grimsby mob could get to the park, the police arrived, gathered up Palace and marched them back to the train station. A small mob of Grimsby made a half-hearted attempt to get at Palace, but it was a poor effort on our part and, once again, Palace earned a lot of respect."

In 2003, Stoke again put in an appearance with a nasty but impressive mob of N40 getting into Cleethorpes by ten in the morning. However, because of a new membership card scheme at Stoke, aimed at stamping out hooliganism, the police were sending back all those without tickets. One coach was turned back, but the police failed to spot a smaller group of 20 Stoke still in Cleethorpes. The locals had noticed them and before long 60 CBP attacked the pub where the Stoke were drinking. "With the numbers heavily stacked against them, all they could do was guard the doors of the pub which they did quite well with the help of various pool balls, stools, ashtrays and glasses", said S-Grimsby. "This resulted in the pub taking quite a hammering with a lot of smashed windows and one young Grimsby lad receiving a wound to his head courtesy of a pool cue."

Later that season, 40 Brighton made the trip up to Humberside for the last game of the season. They travelled on the Friday night but their presence almost instantly attracted attention, including that of S-Grimsby. "A few of us caught wind of this and informed other lads and before long I was taking part in the best row I've ever been in", he said. "A five-minute off ensued in the middle of the road along the seafront in a proper old-style football row with brief breaks for breath of a few seconds. The most satisfying thing about this result was the fact we had exactly twenty-three lads, the vast majority in their early to mid twenties, whereas Brighton were all big old school, well into their thirties. Despite spells where we looked edgy, we eventually pushed them back through the double doors into the pub. Interestingly, we were later told by Brighton that they had another thirty lads in the boozer who wouldn't come out. Whether that's true or not, we'll never know."

Grimsby's most active recent season was 2003/04 when the team was in Division Two. Although the days of them pulling 400 at home and taking big numbers into enemy territory were a distant memory, a small but violent gang had formed that season. "We travelled quite a lot," said S-Grimsby. "We got to Peterborough twice with fifty lads, the first time bumping into a mob of Chelsea on their way back from Leeds and having it with them for five minutes down a dodgy back street, with neither side budging an inch until Chelsea pulled a blade out and the OB turned up. We went to Luton with a good twenty lads on a minibus and chased an unexpected mob of Luton 200 yards. Three mobs of eighty visited Chesterfield, Oldham, and local rivals, Doncaster, in the Carling Cup, nothing happened of note but at least we were putting the firm back on the map."

The problem with putting your firm "on the map" is that the police are keen to have a look at the map at regular intervals and late in 2004, they raided the homes of a number of Grimsby and Scunthorpe lads after a clash following Grimsby's match at Stockport. Operation Trapper, set up after a hundred rival fans fought street battles, led to almost 40 arrests.

H

HARTLEPOOL UNITED

Ground: Victoria Park
Firms: Hartlepool Wrecking Crew, the Greenies, the Moose Men, Blue Order
Rivals: Darlington

"We were out of the doors the moment they opened. Thirty lads wearing Sergio Tacchini, bleached jeans, Trimm Trabb trainers and Lacoste if you had a bit of dosh. Our adrenalin was sky high, excitement and apprehension creating the best buzz possible. We had arrived in Darlington. A few police were mingling around the station but they soon drifted away and we were left to our own devices as we sauntered across the cricket pitch close to the ground. Eyes flicked left and right, the occasional lad almost walking backwards to protect our rear. Darlington were nowhere to be seen but it was only a matter of time. To the football world Hartlepool and Darlington is not Rangers v. Celtic but to us it is far more important and the feeling was mutual. To keep it simple, we fucking hate each other.

"The word went round, Darlington were here, about ten of them in our end. The cheeky fuckers. They stood there goading us, waiting for the inevitable. We had the numbers but they had the front. The two mobs stood opposite one another trading verbal, feet bouncing, fists clenched. One of our lot beckoned Darlo to come forward, one did and crack, he was sent flying. Encouraged by that we charged forward, everyone went in even the shirts. The small Darlo mob attempted to make a hasty retreat but four or five got caught good and proper. One lad had his arm of his Ellesse tracksuit ripped off and held aloft triumphantly by a Pool lad. A few years earlier it was the dog's bollocks if you managed to nick a scarf from your hated rival and tie it around your waist, but a sleeve from a £200 tracksuit top was a much better trophy and really did piss the poor bastard off! It was a symbolic sign of victory that earned a huge cheer from our end but we knew that Darlo would not take this humiliation lying down.

"After the game all hell broke loose. We steamed out of the ground and into the Darlo mob gathered expectedly on the cricket pitch. One lad came up to me and looked down disdainfully: 'Tacchini is shit.' My mate pointed out that unlike the Darlo Ellesse number, it had two sleeves and then whacked him, he scarpered as the rest of the lads came pouring out. Everywhere we looked there was fighting. Small groups of police tried to separate the crowd but initially with no success."

Darlington v Hartlepool was always the same in the 1980s. The fixture spelt trouble. When Darlo went to Hartlepool a couple of years later, a well known Darlington lad was thrown through a shop window and another was punched over a wall, with a drop of about 12 feet.

The hatred continues to this day. Philly Bailey, a veteran of Hartlepool's Blue Order mob, told the author of *Top Boys*, "A few years ago Darlington brought a top firm over, they were nicknamed the Milk Bottle Firm after they turned up in Hartlepool town centre and bombarded the Pool firm with hundreds of the fucking things before the game. It was a proper old-school battle and as always they were up for it." Another major fight between the local clubs came thanks to the fixture computer. Hartlepool were at Barnet and Darlington were at Orient. The rival firms ended up battling all the way home, with fighting continuing when both mobs had to get off at Darlington. Many were arrested and placed on five-year banning orders.

Many others towns were raided by Hartlepool,

A large contingent of Hartlepool's Blue Order gather to pay their respects to a friend killed in a road accident in Holland.

and during the early Eighties several firms who travelled away with the team in their own groups. "You had the Greenies, a set of lads who drank in a pub called the Greensides, they were a well game bunch and looked forward to nothing else but a good piss-up and a good punch-up," remembered Jon and Liam, two Hartlepool lads. "Then we had a group who called themselves the Hartlepool Wrecking Crew, these were a bunch of lads from the Manor area, quite a scary place at the time. These lads used to do what most firms were doing in the early Eighties and that was smashing up the odd boozer, car windows, etc., unlike the Greenies who were more sensible yet still as mad for a fight."

In about 1988, a group of lads decided to form a firm called the Moose Men. It should have been the

Noose Men, after the old story of Hartlepool folk hanging a monkey during the Napoleonic Wars because they thought it was a French spy, but the calling cards they had printed were misspelt as the Moose Men, and the name stuck. The group was formed by 15-20 lads who went to as many games as possible, to "have a laugh and cause plenty of mayhem".

They had notable away battles at Carlisle, Darlo, Peterborough, Rotherham, Sheffield United, and Hereford. Major kick-offs at home included Preston, Darlington, Birmingham, Carlisle, Sheffield United, Middlesbrough and Cardiff, but one remembered more than any was the home game against Burnley, which brought the Moose Men face to face with the fearsome Suicide Squad. One of the Hartlepool lads told the story:

"We were all out, anticipating an early Burnley arrival. We knew they'd be coming, Burnley travelled everywhere and had decent respect from all the lower league firms. It had got to two-thirty, half an hour before kick-off, a few of the hangers on split from us and it was the normal fifteen who we knew we could trust. We decided to walk around the ground and have a quick pre-match drink. We were walking past the long alley which separates one side of the ground from the other, then we heard something, 'Su, Su, Suicide' – and again. About twenty Burnley turned the corner, we were face to face with the enemy, about 100 metres apart. They stopped, all went quiet, then they went into their coat pockets and pulled something out – gumshields. They placed these in their mouths and grinned at us, like a middleweight boxer awaiting his new challenge. At that time I think we all felt nervous, outnumbered and up against Division Four's most fearsome firm.

"As they started to walk towards us, one of our lads shouted, 'Right, fuck this, we're at home, let's get into them.' He ran towards the first lad and tried something which looked like a karate kick but was basically a wild swing with his leg. Amazingly the Burnley lad turned on his heels but was stumbling as he tried to run. We saw the chance and charged at them. Most of his mates turned quickly and were off up the road towards the away end. The one at the back received a few hefty kicks up his arse as he staggered away, and it was only later we found out that the lads we'd bumped into were a few of the main lads but they'd drunk themselves silly on the way down and by the time we'd seen them they were far too pissed to fight."

By the early Nineties the rave scene was taking its toll and the firm disappeared, but after a few years of poor attendances and inactivity a few younger lads decided to get things going again. They called themselves the Blue Order; a play on the Orange Order from Ulster, although some say it was a spin-off from the band New Order.

The Blue Order's first outing was the FA Cup game away at Hereford. The game had been switched to the Sunday, so a group of 30 Hartlepool lads decided to make a weekend of it and spend the Saturday night in Worcester. It was the first time that some of the group had been away together and it proved to be a bonding experience. "There were a few minor skirmishes with locals but the night brought us all together as a tight group," said Jon from Hartlepool. "On the Sunday our lads were up early, and made the short hop to Hereford. They parked up in a hotel by ten and finally settled in a pub near the ground. The lads were buzzing. They had noticed a few police spotters but they still expected an onslaught. It never came, but it was not for the want to trying. A few old Hartlepool lads who travelled down by train reported later that Hereford were out with a big mob. The Pool lads knew it was only a matter of time."

Liam, another of the Blue Order, continued the story. "The game was a non-event and we lost, with us playing shite as usual. When the final whistle went 300-400 Hereford fans invaded the pitch, including a sizeable mob making their way towards us. A few Pool lads took to the pitch to confront them and serious fighting erupted on the pitch and in the stands. We stuck together and held them off, but it was real hand-to-hand stuff, helped no doubt by the complete absence of police inside the ground. The Blue Order was born."

A year after the Blue Order was formed, Hartlepool played host to Aberdeen in a pre-season friendly. Two hundred and fifty Aberdeen fans made the journey and their number included about sixty Aberdeen Soccer Casuals (ASC), who infiltrated the home terrace. Within five minutes of the game kicking off fighting broke out with local fans and while no one was arrested, 30 Aberdeen were thrown out of the ground and the match was held up for five minutes while fans were taken off the pitch.

Over the next few years the Blue Order had rucks at Swindon, took 100 to Carlisle and surprised Hull with 120 lads. They have clashed home and away with Mansfield and always travel across to Darlington, though the days of guaranteed trouble are long gone. In the 2002/03 season, Shrewsbury turned up with a firm and put up a good fight, rare in the days of increased surveillance and police intelligence. Few enemy mobs venture so far north these days.

With the 2004 European Championships in Portugal approaching, Cleveland Police targeted numerous football hooligans, including at Hartlepool. They identified 30 key targets attached to the club and sought banning orders for as many as possible. Detective Sergeant Ian Fawcett, one of the officers spearheading the football unit, said,

"We are building up a data bank of names of trouble-makers and we will actively be seeking banning orders preventing them from heading to the championships."

The police action took its toll. A number of the main Hartlepool lads have been banned and others have dropped out.

Further reading: *Top Boys*, Cass Pennant (Blake Publishing)

HEART OF MIDLOTHIAN

Ground: Tynecastle
Firms: Gorgie Boys, the Casual Soccer Firm
Rivals: Hibs, Celtic

Lord Tebbit to the House of Lords: "My Lords, one of the wonderful features of this House is that a debate on football hooligans can embrace an exchange of the kind we have just heard on the 17th century interpretation of Magna Carta ... Because statements of one kind or another about football seem to be *de rigueur*, I shall plead guilty to having once attended a professional football match. It took place, I think, in 1953, in Edinburgh between Hearts and Hibs. The experience led me to conclude that I never wished to attend another football match in my life. Perhaps I may say that hooliganism at football matches did not start only in the last twenty years."

The Tory peer was not the only person to be shocked by the ferocity of the Edinburgh football mobs. In the 1970s, many Scots fans rated the followers of Hearts as the most formidable in the country, "Never mind us or Rangers," said a Celtic veteran, "Hearts all seemed to be big, tough blokes who were absolutely fearless. They were worst, no doubt about it." The taking of ends was their speciality, even against the Old Firm giants.

Like Rangers, the club's followers were identifiably Protestant in their religious sympathies. Hearts fan and author C.S. Ferguson recalled getting on the Gorgie Sons of William supporters' bus to go to Dumfries as a youth, and being in awe of the characters on board. "The bus had a hard reputation and we were well out of our league. We just sat at the front and tried to look inconspicuous all the way

down there," he related in his evocative memoir *Bring Out Your Riot Gear, Hearts Are Here!*

Hooliganism was endemic among the club's followers. "Basically, if you followed Hearts away regularly at that time, you would probably end up in some sort of trouble, somewhere along the line, whether you liked it or not," wrote Ferguson. But in 1981, Hearts were relegated from the top division, and to an extent the worst of their behaviour was behind them. They continued to be a force, but now the likes of Falkirk, Motherwell and Ayr United could be guaranteed to fight back, while Edinburgh was divided by rivalry between various youth movements, especially mods and skinheads.

The Hearts hardcore in 1981 were largely skinheads or wedge-heads in green flight jackets, but always with club scarves. Their number included Wattie of the Edinburgh punk band The Exploited. They tended to attract support from the estates to the west of the city – including the feared Broomheads Skins – while Hibs came more from the east and south sides. Hearts also drew support from the new town of Livingston, but as is frequently the case, there was tension between the Livi punks and skins and the Edinburgh lads, sometimes resulting in spilled blood. A cup game against Queen of the South became irrelevant when the Livingston and Edinburgh mobs tore into each other in the Hearts end, then turned on the police.

The 1981/82 season ended in a riot when Hearts failed to clinch promotion at home to Motherwell. Gorgie fans in the Shed turned on the police and three officers spent the night in hospital with head injuries. Then, in the summer of 1982, Leeds United – and some of their Service Crew – arrived for a pre-season friendly. The more discerning Hearts fans noticed that some of the Leeds were not wearing colours. This was their first exposure at Tynecastle to English casuals. The small mob of Leeds came out at the end and gave at least as good as they got against a Hearts welcoming committee. By coincidence, the first organised mob of Hearts hooligans to travel, in the pre-casual days, were themselves known as the Service Crew.

A benefit match in the name of Tom Hart, the recently deceased Hearts chairman, against Hibs a few days later saw mass disorder and led to calls for Hearts fans to be banned from travelling – and this was before the season had even begun. Visits to

Rangers and Celtic in cup games that season saw Hearts more than hold their own, particularly at Parkhead, where they went mad after Celtic's Danny McGrain had broken a Hearts player's leg and then another of their players was sent off in dubious circumstances. A return to the Premier League saw Hearts get "done" at home by Rangers, something that had been unthinkable for many seasons.

A visit from Aberdeen and their now casually dressed mob further influenced the fledgling Hearts dressers. By the summer of 1984, with casual culture finally hitting the Scottish newspapers, a single-figure group called the Casual Soccer Firm appeared at Hearts, first showing themselves at Dundee United, where they were chased by a much larger group of Dundee's "Tayside Trendies". So few in number were they at the time in Edinburgh that the Hib and Hearts casuals happily mixed outside football, swapping fashion tips.

The pendulum swung further away from Hearts with the advent of the casuals. After years of domination, the Gorgie Boys faded away as a new generation of hooligans emerged, which within Edinburgh was dominated by Hibs. The Hearts Casuals Soccer Firm (CSF) would for most of the next 20 years play second fiddle to the Hibs' Casual City Service crew. Indeed for a while it seemed Scotland's capital would follow the example of Dundee by forming one united mob, but the first outing of the two mobs together was a disaster, leaving bitter recriminations. A Scottish Cup semi-final between Dundee United and Aberdeen in Edinburgh saw the two mobs unite again, but Hibs later accused their city rivals of bottling it and a bitter feud broke out. Hibs distributed a letter announcing that they would never link up with Hearts again.

The first Edinburgh derby of the 1984/85 season saw Hearts fans invade the pitch at Easter Road. Twelve fans were arrested inside the ground, 20 Hearts fans were treated mainly for cuts and bruises – caused by rocks and coins thrown in the terracing – and there were a further 42 arrests after the game. Even the Hibs goalie was struck on the head, with a large marble. Hearts Chairman Wallace Mercer attacked the way in which police handled the trouble, claiming that if they had lined the pitch at the Hearts end of the ground there would have been no invasion. "I am not making excuses for the idiots and hooligans but we must work in conjunc-

tion with police to make sure that officers are used sensibly and strategically," said Mercer.

This was the last advertisement the city needed, at a time when thousands of tourists were enjoying the Festival. "The summer reputation of Edinburgh as a city to enjoy yourself in and the good name of Hearts as a soccer club on the crest of a revival are both in tatters today, disgraced by an outbreak of soccer violence as shocking as it is sinister," commented the editor of the local paper.

"There are grave implications ahead. Hearts have just won their way back into Europe, and if they export that kind of off-the-field performance to Paris next month, they drag the whole image of Scottish football down with them. New standards must be set in the new season. Hearts must stamp on the trouble and do it now. Whatever solution is found, it must be tough and fast. There is altogether too much at stake."

If anything, the situation got worse. After a home game against Celtic, by which time the CSF had come under attack from their own anti-casual "scarfers" in the Shed, Hearts were threatened with an appearance in front of the Scottish FA's disciplinary commission. By late March 1985, Edinburgh was a city on the edge. Aberdeen had just visited Easter Road and clashes between their fans and the CCS almost saw a Hibs fan killed. There were unpleasant scenes inside the ground and the day was widely reported in the press. At around the same time, Aberdeen played in the cup at Tynecastle and the Hearts and Hibs casuals teamed up to attack them. All of this coincided with broader concerns over hooliganism, coming only days after Millwall fans rioted at Luton.

The following week was the Edinburgh derby and fear was growing within the football establishment. Five days before the match, the Hearts chairman met senior police officers to draw up crowd control measures for the match at Tynecastle. The meeting was given extra impetus with the emergence of a letter circulating around Hearts fans which gloried in recent crowd violence in England and urged defiance of segregation measures at the Edinburgh ground. It was signed off, "Casuals – Soccer thugs – Firm but handy." The club and the police laughed off the leaflet and the CSF generally as the product of "ten to 15 individuals", but behind the scenes both were preparing for the worst.

Four days before the match, the *Evening News*

said the city's football fans were "on trial", while Hearts again called for organised hooligan groups to stay away. The police announced that plain-clothes policemen would be on duty inside the ground and the video crowd surveillance system would be in operation. Hearts also announced plans to meet their Hibs counterparts to ensure both sets of players were "aware of their responsibilities". The authorities continued to play down expectations of trouble but the day before the game the *Evening News* ran its third front-page story of the week:

HOOLIGAN! HOOLIGAN! HOOLIGAN!

Isolate them tomorrow at Tynecastle. Football has taken a hammering in recent weeks at the hands of the hooligans. It must stop. The Hearts-Hibs derby match at Tynecastle tomorrow is an obvious target for them – a big crowd, a tense match, and the kind of atmosphere they love to exploit. They must be prevented from ruining what should be a great sporting occasion. They must be stopped from killing the game.

The police can only do so much. The clubs can only do so much. But you, the fans, the great majority of real, responsible supporters, can do much to help.

…The game cannot take much more of the kind of disgraceful incidents witnessed at Easter Road last Saturday. Hibs were fortunate to emerge with little more than a warning.

Neither they nor the game of football are likely to be so lucky if there is a next time.

The future of the clubs and the very game itself lies with you, the fans.

The game still belongs to you. Right now it needs your loyalty, and your positive help to isolate and rid the terraces of the louts.

Make a start tomorrow.

After all the build-up, the game was cancelled due to snow, and rearranged for the following Tuesday. In the event despite 24 arrests, police announced themselves pleased with the result. The bulk of the arrests came after the game when mobs squared up in Gorgie Road. "In view of the particular circumstances affecting the game and the background, we were fairly well pleased with the way it went," a police spokesman said.

Hearts' mob, especially their casuals, were less than pleased. For the first time in memory, Hibs had got the better of the fighting at the derby game, and it emphasised the shift in off-pitch power between the two sets of hooligans. Some Hearts fans even began to attend Hibs matches because there was a greater chance of a ruck. The Hearts casuals did, however, finally gain ascendancy over their own scarfers – who tended to mock them with the words, "Jam tarts [Hearts] and casuals don't mix" – by fronting them at a home game and forcing them to back down.

Small casual gangs now sprang up all over the city – the Tufty Club, the Hyvots Dressers, the Muirhouse Casual Firm, the Saughton Chosen Few – and inter-gang fighting became a feature of the city's nightlife. One of their biggest joint turnouts was in October 1985, when 250 made the trip to Celtic. Around 150 Celtic casuals were waiting for them in George Square and running battles broke out

The CSF continued throughout the rest of the Eighties, with the casual scene hitting its peak north of the border and headlines such as "CASUALS TERROR HITS CITIES" in the *Sunday Mail* after one particular day in which 300 of the CSF fought with Celtic in Glasgow while Hibs and Aberdeen went at it in Edinburgh.

Like Glasgow Rangers, Hearts' Protestant-inclined hooligans have had links to both Loyalist and far-right groups like Combat 18 and the BNP. They have repeatedly linked up with Rangers to attack pro-Republican marches, and during the early to mid-Nineties some of them travelled to London for Combat 18 and Apprentice Boys events. Their best known right-wing face is Warren Bennett, currently the British National Party's head of security and personal minder to its leader, Nick Griffin. Bennett has a long history with Hearts, and has been imprisoned in Holland and deported from France. He has become a particular hate figure for the *Daily Record,* which regularly plasters him across its front pages.

Sectarianism in Edinburgh never reached the levels of Glasgow but did add an extra spice to local derbies and matches against Celtic. In a match at Tynecastle in October 2002, fans fought running battles in the neighbouring streets after a game marred by sectarian chanting and banners. The home fans' songs of "Rule Britannia" and "No

Surrender to the IRA" were met with a volley of pro-IRA songs, despite the Celtic chairman's pre-match plea to refrain. A female steward was assaulted, 20 people were ejected or arrested and police were forced to ring a large group of fans in the dying minutes to prevent a pitch invasion. After the match, hundreds clashed as Hearts ambushed Celtic fans on the way to their coaches. At a more recent match, this time at Celtic Park, 14 Hearts fans were arrested for religious and race hatred offences.

During the Nineties, the Hearts lads were strong supporters of the Scottish National Firm, but their limited size and strength always made them bit players. The decline of the SNF marked a decline in hooliganism in Scotland generally and Edinburgh specifically. However, in recent years a younger generation of hooligans has emerged. In March 2002, police dogs and CS spray were used to separate fighting groups at the Edinburgh derby at Easter Road. There was further trouble after Hearts' 5-1 win at Easter Road the following August. Forty rival fans clashed in the streets, though this time the police were on hand to record some of the trouble and several homes were later raided. The violence, which also saw a pub attacked by 50 hooligans before the game, increased fears that hooliganism was returning. "We know exactly who is involved and a number of ringleaders have been charged and more will be in the future," said Chief Superintendent Charlie Michie, commander of C Division, which takes in Tynecastle stadium. "Many of them are mature individuals who are sad and misguided and we will make Edinburgh an unwelcoming place for those types."

The police's optimism appeared well-founded when later that season they thwarted a pre-planned fight before Hearts' home visit by Celtic. A tip-off revealed that the rival groups planned a pitched battle in the Balgreen area of the capital but a large police presence prevented the disorder. Inside the ground, Hearts supporters were restricted to taunting rival supporters with Nazi salutes and obscenities. However, the game confirmed that hooliganism was re-emerging at Hearts, with a younger generation linking up with older lads returning to the scene.

"Guys that used to run about ten to fifteen years ago are back on the scene because they miss the violence and the fighting and want to get involved

again," a football intelligence officer told the local paper. "It's very worrying that men who should know better are becoming involved in extreme violence. This younger group are coming through at the same time as the older ones are re-establishing themselves. With their links to extreme right-wing groups, it's obviously a concern."

Further reading: *Bring Out Your Riot Gear, Hearts Are Here*, C.S. Ferguson (Terrace Banter)

HIBERNIAN

Ground: Easter Road
Firms: Young Leith Team, Capital City Service, Baby Crew
Rivals: Hearts, Aberdeen, Motherwell

Hibernian's casuals were left licking their wounds following a visit of Aberdeen in March 1985. Four hundred Aberdeen Soccer Casuals had rampaged through their city, their streets, and their club. One of their own was lying in a critical condition in hospital and several others were nursing serious injuries. Worst of all, the ASC were laughing.

That home game would prove the catalyst for what became the most feared soccer firm in Scotland. They might not have been the first, nor are they today the same force, but between 1988 and 1994 the Capital City Service (CCS) dominated Scottish hooliganism. There had been mobs at Hibs in the Seventies, such as the Young Leith Team (YLT), but these were in the pre-casual days and were area-based. The CCS emerged towards the end of 1984, shortly after casual fashion arrived in Edinburgh, and was citywide. For a Skol Cup final in 1991, the CCS took more than 400 lads to Glasgow, though its usual turnout was half that. This was a sizeable firm for a club with an average crowd of less than 10,000.

When Aberdeen came to town early the following season, everyone knew there would be trouble. The ASC who travelled down on the train knew it. The CCS, who were mobbing up at the back of the Waverley Centre, knew it. And the police knew it. But it was not until after the game that the serious skirmishing started, with Hibs attacking the ASC escort from all sides and the Dons lads fighting back all the way to the train station. Then came the incident that made the fight infamous: the launching of a petrol bomb at the Aberdeen ranks.

"There are certain things in your life that you never forget; first pets, marriages, deaths and the birth of your first-born," wrote Dan Rivers in *Congratulations, You've Just Met The Casuals*. "To that I would like to add something else; the sight of a petrol bomb flying through the air towards you." The explosion of a Molotov cocktail marked a new chapter in Hibs–Aberdeen rivalry.

At the same fixture later in the season, a shipping flare was fired into the Aberdeen mob. Two coachloads of ASC were attacked as they arrived for one game in the capital, with the CCS emptying the contents of a bar through their windows. In 1987, an ASC lad was severely stabbed, and in reply a mob of more than 600 lads travelled to Edinburgh for the next game, where a huge police operation prevented any chance of mass disorder. Confrontations after this became more difficult as police cracked down, normally by turning around coaches or throwing the lads off trains. When the two groups did meet they were fairly evenly matched.

A trip up to Aberdeen was remembered by "Cameron C. Strachan" in the recent book *Casuals*. In an attempt to avoid police detection, the CCS agreed to meet at Edinburgh's Waverley station at 6 a.m., but it proved too early and only 20 turned up. An hour later their numbers had doubled and though many felt they still had too small a mob, they decided to head north. "We realised that we would be vastly outnumbered and we would all have to go bananas as soon as we met them," recalled Strachan. This they did when coming across a pub full of Aberdeen.

"Aberdeen's top boys were there and must have been raging," said Strachan. "Some of them came out of a side door. 'Come on!' they shouted. Our mob duly obliged and one of my mates put his hand inside his quilted, baseball-style, Pop 84 jacket as if reaching for a blade, although he didn't have one, shouting, 'Come on Dons,' to a group of their lads. They backed off. We looked to the other end of Union Street to see another mob of Aberdeen. Half of us ran towards them, the rest stayed baying at their boys in the pub. They were in disarray at both ends of their city's main street. 'CCS, CCS,' we

chanted." The police finally led away the Hibs mob, all sporting "cheesy grins".

Since their formation, the Hibs casuals have been known by a variety of names, including the Hibs Inter City Service and Hibs Soccer Trendies, both of which were used in their earliest days. Another name was the Hibs Bender Crew, after the Newcastle mob of the same name with whom they had a link. There was even a girl section who called themselves the Lassie Soccer Trendies; to many of the CCS, they were more commonly known as the Gobblers. A further name that did the rounds was The Family, which was an elite group of their top boys. The name obviously had Italian Mafiosi connotations, which no doubt added to the aura of the firm. "I'll tell you why we're called The Family," one leading CCS lad told an academic. "Because, see that boy there; if he got kicked out of his house tonight, he'd have about sixty places to stay. We look after one another. And if anybody has a go at a Hibs boy, we're after him."

Another offshoot of the CCS was the Baby Crew, or, as it was known when it was first formed in 1985, the Blackley Baby Crew after the club's manager, John Blackley. Involving boys and girls too young to get into pubs, the BBC loitered around Princess Street during school holidays and weekends, hanging about outside a Wimpy and quizzing anyone dressed "trendy". Anyone from Hearts, Rangers or Celtic was liable to be punched or "taxed".

In keeping with most Scottish firms, Hibs formed alliances with English clubs. Their first was with Newcastle, and in the spring of 1987 a group of 20 preferred a St James's Park match against Leicester to watching Hearts fans celebrate winning the title. Their city rivals only needed a point from their game with Dundee and, even if they failed to obtain that, their nearest challengers, Celtic, required a five-goal margin over St Mirren. "Before the match Hibs and Newcastle's younger lads fronted the Leicester mob and had the better of them, with Hibs at the front," remembered Strachan. "Newcastle's older lads missed the confrontation and weren't too happy that Hibs had enjoyed more action than them, but the younger lads had been happy enough at the time.

"During the game, word spread of extraordinary events north of the border. Hearts were down by two goals and Celtic were five up. The Hibs lads started jumping up and down singing, 'Lost the league, lost the league, lost the league,' smashed the backs off the seats in the process, then used them as Frisbees. Newcastle followed suit and hurled bits of blue plastic seats through the air and half the Newcastle end sang, 'Lost the league, lost the league, lost the league.' Hearts lost the league and the Hibs lads had whetted their appetite for journeys south."

The relationship was not to last. Later that year the two mobs clashed at the Scotland and England international and that ended their friendship. The CCS developed an alliance with Oldham's Fine Young Casuals which was arguably the most infamous collaboration in British football hooligan history.

"In 1985 there was a pre-season tournament on the Isle of Man, between Oldham, Hibs, Stoke and Bury," said Oldham old-timer Carl Spiers. "Stoke had the biggest firm of lads, followed by Hibs, then Oldham, and not surprisingly Bury had none. Hibs and Oldham lads got on well and had some great piss-ups and stuck together throughout the weekend whilst Stoke did their own thing, as Stoke do. A few Oldham and Hibs lads swapped addresses and kept in touch and a year later Oldham played Hibs in a pre-season friendly at Boundary Park at a time when the FYC had just been formed by a small mob of sixteen and seventeen-year-old casuals. These lads were run ragged by the Hibs Casuals after the match, as none of the older Oldham firm had taken Hibs seriously and did not bother turning up. Later that night a few Hibs lads stayed in Oldham, a friendship was made and both firms have visited each other and stayed over many times.

"Oldham lads have been invited to some really tasty Scottish encounters with Hearts, Aberdeen, Celtic and Rangers, and likewise Hibs have been involved with some of Oldham's best encounters against the likes of Leeds, Spurs, Villa, Man Utd and Man City. But perhaps the best example of an Oldham-Hibs connection was in 1994 when Oldham played Bolton at Burnden Park in the FA Cup quarter-final. A mob of more than 100 lads went on the train via Manchester Victoria. This mob included twenty of Hibs' finest, but when the train arrived in Bolton it was met by the whole of Bolton constabulary and they searched each and every one of us. Some of the stuff the Hibs lads offloaded was awesome, I have never seen so many weapons hit the deck.

"Very few of us had tickets for the game and the cops made the rest of us go back to Manchester. When we got back we were told that United's main firm were in a well known city centre bar, which we stormed. We trashed the pub and hammered the few Reds who bravely fought, it was a right result for us and for the next hour we wandered around Manchester unchallenged. One of the lads had this mad idea of hijacking a double decker bus and going back up to Bolton, so we did. We all piled on to this bus and told the driver to get to Bolton ASAP and not stop. After we had a whipround for him, he deposited us right in Bolton town centre where we remained until the game was finished. We then met Bolton's firm head on and it was another result for the Oldham-Hibs connection, although quite a few Oldham and Hibs lads got nicked. The OB ran us out of town at about 6.30pm, but by then we had done the damage."

In August 1990, some crazy soul decided to organise a pre-season friendly at Millwall, a fixture that screamed violence. The CCS were at their peak and their members awaited this clash with relish. Almost 200 Hibs met up late on the Thursday night and boarded several coaches for London. Fuelled by drink and pills, this was the crème de la crème of Scottish hooliganism. Unfortunately for them the police had got wind of their plans and as the lads waited patiently to board their coaches the police arrived and waved the transport away. Frustrated but not deterred, dozens opted for alternative methods of transport. Some took the train, others ordinary scheduled buses and a few even flew.

They arrived in London a few at a time and the mob was a good 90-strong by the time it made its way to Millwall. Walking down the Old Kent Road the group began to sing, "We thought you were hard, we were wrong," and, "Hibees Family." Then they attacked a Millwall pub, fighting with a few hardy Londoners outside, putting the windows through and overturning a car. Nearer the ground, a breakaway group of 25 Hibs apparently got the better of another confrontation with an equal number of Millwall.

Millwall's furious reaction inside the ground did little to disguise their humiliation. A thousand made a feeble attempt to have a go at the Hibs fans but, despite their verbal threats and aggressive posturing, their moves came to nothing. The 300 Hibs fans were taken out of the ground under a police escort of almost equal size. For the CCS, who had seen their transport drive off without them in Edinburgh, it had been a long and expensive day but value for money.

The rave scene hit Edinburgh in 1988 and soon many of the CCS were avid partygoers, with a couple of the lads launching their own night at one club. Ecstasy might be the love drug but the appearance of large numbers of Hibs Casuals at clubs also brought trouble, especially against Motherwell's mob, and the two travelled to each other's clubs with increasing frequency. There were several Hibs arrests after clashes at a club in Motherwell in April 1989, and a few days later the CCS attacked their rivals en route to the Morecambe Weekender. A CCS casual was a member of an Edinburgh band during this period called the Guitar Casuals. Trouble followed them around and before long they were banned from most venues.

In the late Eighties, Hibs had a nasty feud with Dunfermline that included several incidents away from matches. One Hibs lad was attacked on at least three occasions, two leaving him needing hospital attention. The wife of the same casual was also threatened with weapons and the petrol bombing of the family home. The CCS decided to retaliate. On the evening of 7 September 1990, a mob of 30-40 travelled to Dunfermline. Many wore balaclavas, most carried weapons. They headed to The Well nightclub and went straight for the front entrance, where they managed to smash the outer door but couldn't get past the heavily fortified inner door. Armed with axes, swords, iron bars and sticks, they made their way round the back where they steamed through the bar but still couldn't get into the disco.

A beer keg was hurled through a window, and as some of the disco crowd began leaving through the front they were confronted and attacked by a small group of Hibs. Three managed to get away, seven others were caught. One Dunfermline lad was struck up to 30 times with an axe and other weapons. Friends had to literally hold his back together until the emergency services arrived. He underwent four hours of surgery. A woman police officer who saw his injuries fainted at the sight. Another man was stabbed in the shoulder and struck over the head with a chair.

Two men were convicted of the assault eleven months later. Andy Blance and Ivor Levine were sentenced to five years and four years respectively for mobbing and rioting, attempted murder and three charges of assault. Cases against two other men were found not proven. The judge told the court that their behaviour could not be tolerated in a civilised society. Blance denied his involvement in the attack, claiming that he was working in a pub in Inverkeithing, and produced five witnesses to support his claim. A prosecution witness, however, claimed that he had disappeared from work for about 35 minutes at the time of the attack. Blance was convicted on an eight to six margin. He had 41 previous convictions, including a two-year stretch for assault, and the prosecution produced evidence that he had been personally attacked in the on-going feud with Dunfermline.

Then there was the small matter of the media. The period between the attack and the trial saw unprecedented media interest in the CCS, with virtually every Scottish paper running some sort of exposé on the group. While this might not have had a direct impact on the outcome of the trial, it did create the sense of a gang completely out of control and worthy of police action. First off the mark, only days after the incident at The Well and an Edinburgh derby at which there were 36 arrests, was the Glasgow-based *Evening Times*, which ran the front-page headline, "Exposed: The casual thugs who bring terror to Scots football." It went on, "An Edinburgh solicitor is thought to be a leader of the Hibs Casuals. Police also think another is 41 years old and some are 20 to 30. They are the brains behind the trouble and use teenagers as front-line troops. There is also evidence of a rank structure in the Casuals. Members are given specific tasks by the leader who selects more aggressive members to be known as the Frontline. They are responsible for organising fights and collecting 'taxes'. Others organise travel or the printing and distribution of leaflets and calling cards." The paper's information came from a police report into the mob. The solicitor and his sidekick were alleged to be homosexual, and it was stated that a 20-year-old drove around in a three-year-old Mercedes while others hired vans for away matches.

This article was followed by another in Edinburgh's *Evening News*. In a three-part investigation the paper gave readers a unique insight into the sinister organisation behind the CCS. "Hibs' Casuals' campaign of terror is run with military-style precision," the paper announced. "They boast of being able to muster around 240 fighting members for a 'rumble' within a few hours. They call on members from seven 'family' zones in Dalkeith, Penicuik, Leith, Niddrie, Corstorphine, Inch and Tollcross. And midnight training exercises are carried out Army-style in Princess Street. At the sound of a whistle, gang members, all wearing identical track-suits, dash into side streets. A few minutes later they regroup. Casual leaders claim the exercise is to 'keep the mob under control' before a fight." Readers were warned of the dangerous casuals hidden within their own communities. In what appeared more like a public health warning, the article opened, "We all know a Hibs casual. He may be your neighbour or the quiet young man who drinks in your local, or he may even deliver your letters each morning. Despite a catalogue of atrocities over the past two years Hibs casuals for the most part live normal lives. Most are in employment, they dress smartly and are well groomed, they have girlfriends and enjoy having a meal and going to nightclubs. But when Saturday comes, they shed their respectable image and go looking for trouble. The Casual is a terrifying Jekyll and Hyde figure, were-wolf who turns into the beast as the clock strikes midnight on Friday."

The media also highlighted the mob's alleged criminal links. The *Evening Times* claimed to have seen a police dossier on the CCS which stated that the mob was involved in drug-dealing, robbery, extortion and prostitution. Some time later the *Daily Record* splashed the headline "The match day drug dealers" across its front page. "The rave drug Ecstasy, usually sold in discos, is being pushed on Scottish football terraces by soccer thugs." The article went on to claim that the Hibs Casuals organ-ised a big slice of the Edinburgh Ecstasy market. The scale of the drug problem in Scotland was mentioned, including the size of the largest seizures and police fear of an ecstasy factory being estab-lished in the country, but offered no direct link with the CCS other than a police quote that several Casuals had been prosecuted for dealing. This was quite different from proving the CCS ran part of the city's drug trade. Many of the CCS leaders ridiculed the paper's claims in a more sober interview in

Scotland on Sunday. The article's author concluded that some individuals might get involved in crime, "because they are people who would be involved regardless". The academic, Richard Giulianotti, who spent a considerable amount of time studying the group, questioned whether any major drug baron would risk his empire by getting involved in high-profile street fights.

The *Evening Times* also claimed that the group took over doors at city centre pubs. "Casuals have also intimidated publicans into allowing them to work as bouncers in their bars. If the publican refuses, their cars are usually smashed. Casuals often stage mock fights in bars to set up attacks on police and sometimes video the violence." The door and protection racket theory also stemmed from a feud that the CCS apparently had with Westland Securities, an Edinburgh-based security firm that ran many of the pub doors in the city. Its offices were smashed up by the casuals, its boss was threatened and a number of doormen were attacked. The theory was that this was an attempt to push them aside and take control of the doors themselves. About 30 of the CCS were doormen and a few of the lads ran nights in various clubs across the city. The CCS, however, claim the clash with Westland was simply due to the security firm barring many of their number from pubs and clubs in the city.

The imprisonment of Blance and Levine and the media spotlight did not stop the CCS. A large mob travelled to Belgium for a UEFA cup match at Anderlecht and there was trouble in Brussels. There were also two clashes with Aberdeen in the 1992/93 season. The first was in Aberdeen when 50 Hibs battled with 70 Aberdeen in the city centre. Later in the season, 200 rival fans clashed in Edinburgh. The police, however, had obviously had enough and the following season they impounded the coaches carry-ing the ASC lads.

Trips to Glasgow were often lively affairs and this didn't just include matches at Ibrox and Parkhead. One of the biggest mobilisations was the Skol Cup Final in 1991 for which 400 CCS made the trip. Hibs travelled by train for games against smaller clubs such as Airdrie and St Mirren; this often led to trouble at the stations. At a match against St Mirren, 80 Hibs went into the home end and clashed with a similar number of locals. They then stopped off in Glasgow on the way home and came across a large mob of

Celtic, one of whom threw a CG gas canister into their midst. As the rest of the Hibs crew set off in pursuit, the police appeared and rounded them up. Instead of the usual herding them into the station, they called up reinforcements, transported the hooligans to a local police station and nicked them all. Fifty-five CCS were charged with breach of the peace, though the charges were all later dropped.

During the early Nineties, the casual scene dropped off in Edinburgh. Some embraced rave but more were probably dissuaded by a more concerted police action. There was also a frustration amongst many of the CCS that so few firms would travel to Easter Road for a confrontation. This, by the mid-Nineties, included even Aberdeen. One academic has suggested that the main reason for the decline in hooliganism at Hibs was the changing attitudes of other supporters. Being a football casual was out of fashion.

With no football firms to fight, the CCS kept their hand in at concerts held in the city and there were skirmishes at most high-profile gigs. The worst was at a Madness concert in 1993, with fighting before the group even got on the stage. A report on the website *Skinhead Nation* read, "At the Madness gig the CCS provided an awesome display of violence that has made Hibs Casuals the most feared crew in Scottish football and one of the most notorious mobs in British football. Despite having only a small fraction of firm members in the 8,000 crowd, every time the CCS chant went up, they became as one and charged into any group who wanted to know."

Kenny, a ticket tout from the North West of England, agreed that at the time concerts in the City's Playhouse were "moody". He said, "At a time when everyone was getting loved up it went west at some places, the worst being Edinburgh. It was always on top if a gig was on a Saturday. About half past six a couple of dozen lads would turn up, immaculately dressed, with girls in tow and start casing the area. The girls would be up and down the queue, finding out where groups of lads were from, then they'd run back and tell these total headcases who was who. They were the best dressed headcases I have ever seen though, and they would terrorise any groups of lads they didn't know. Basically, they were a headache for the spivs. It's hard enough earning a living without a load of kids wanting to fight anyone not in the mob."

Hibs follower Andy Blance, jailed for five years after a brutal attack on Dunfermline fans in a nightclub.

In many ways the CCS was a shadow of its former self when the Scottish National Firm, an alliance of rival football gangs, was established in the 1990s. The idea of an alliance with Protestant Rangers and Hearts would never have been discussed during their heyday. In the event it still divided the Hibs mob, with some refusing to have anything to do with what they saw as a Loyalist-led mob while others saw it an as opportunity for the Scots to become a major force on the international front, especially because they faced so much hostility from the ranks of ordinary supporters. Foreign-based hooligans were one thing, but taking on their own Tartan Army required numbers. The SNF proved to be short-lived, and its legacy at Hibs was that the mob would never be the same again. Most of the early CCS leaders dropped out, with some ending up in jail and at least one very prominent figure, known as Big James, relocating to Thailand.

However, another generation of hooligans appears to be coming through at Hibs. In early 2003, the local paper reported that the CCS had launched an Internet site "which celebrates violence and allows gang members to exchange information". This coincided, it said, with fears at the club and the police of a rebirth of football casual gangs. The paper estimated that the CCS now had a hardcore of 30-40. There was also trouble at a game at Hearts, with a very short clash and exchange of bottles. Hibs' win over Hearts at the beginning of the following season was also marred with trouble. There was a pitch invasion at the final whistle and rival supporters clashed after the game at Easter Road.

In August 2004, the club hosted a pre-season friendly against Leeds United. There was a small fight between Hibs lads and an older group of Leeds Service Crew on Easter Road, just outside the ground. While not on the scale of the Eighties clashes against Aberdeen, it did signal that hooliganism remained a problem. A few weeks later it took a large police operation to stop a fight between Hibs and Dundee. Football violence, it seems, is far from over at Hibernian.

Further reading: *Casuals*, Phil Thornton (Milo Books)

HUDDERSFIELD TOWN

Ground: McAlpine Stadium
Firm Names: Cowshed Enders, Khmer Blue, Kenmargra, The Pringles, Huddersfield Young Casuals, Huddersfield Youth Squad
Rivals: Leeds United, Bradford City

Huddersfield Town were sitting pretty on the top of the First Division in 1965, the day football hooliganism first came to town. Defending their 100 per cent home record against fourth-placed Manchester City, the air of excitement that had been building in the days leading up to this game gave way to chaos. Thousands of City fans swelled the 31,876 crowd, Huddersfield's biggest for years, and many of them were out for trouble.

"Despite loudspeaker appeals, dozens of toilet rolls were thrown into the goalmouth," reported the local paper. "At half-time about 5,000 spectators swarmed on to the pitch to change ends for the second half."

It appeared that toilet roll throwing had been a feature at Maine Road for a while but it was new at Huddersfield. Club directors were particularly worried that this new hooligan craze might spread to their own supporters, who behaved themselves impeccably during the game. A police officer told the press that there had been no trouble from Huddersfield supporters. "We only needed two policemen to keep an eye on them."

The club's fears were realised within 18 months as the first Huddersfield mob emerged. Known as the Cowshed Enders, they took their name from the stand where the young lads, skins and boot boys, tended to congregate. It was a covered end behind one of the goals at the old Leeds Road ground, and their leader was Ainley, who liked a song and the odd pint or ten before kick-off.

One of the biggest battles during this era was the FA Cup clash at home to Bolton in 1976. Peter Reid scored the game's only goal for Bolton. The visitors were managed by former Town boss Ian Greaves, and a highly pressured Cup atmosphere saw fighting before and during the game. Police made 21 arrests, most inside the ground, and St John Ambulance staff treated 29 people. After the game a 58-year-old Bolton supporter collapsed and died. One small boy told the man in charge of the St John Ambulance operation that iron bars were being thrown about in the Cowshed End until the police separated rival fans.

The Cowshed Enders emerged in 1967 and lasted for about ten years until they were replaced by the Khmer Blues, who lasted from 1975 to 1979. The name was a play on Pol Pot's Khmer Rouge regime in Cambodia. That was Huddersfield at its lowest point, with the team relegated into the old Fourth Division. The Khmer Blues also reflected a change in fashion in the town, as punks replaced the earlier skinheads of the Cowshed End. Huddersfield was regarded as a punk town, and the Sex Pistols played their last-ever UK gig there on Christmas Day, 1977.

The top of the table clash with Portsmouth in October 1979 pitted the punks of Huddersfield against the skinheads of Portsmouth. Thousands made the long journey up as first faced second, with many arriving at ten in the morning, already drunk. More than two dozen fans were arrested. "These people cannot be called football supporters, they simply want to cause trouble and spoil the game for others," said Supt Peter Coddington, the officer in charge of the police operation. "There was a big crowd of about 16,500 and 16,000 behaved themselves perfectly and should be complimented. Unfortunately there were 300 from this area and 200 from Portsmouth who had no intention of watching the game and between them caused trouble in the ground. Rival gangs chased each other across the terraces and I had to bring in three police dogs, who did a wonderful job."

Club secretary George Bins said part of the problem was that both sets of fans were wearing blue and white, so it was hard to segregate fans. "We do try to keep them apart and a large number of Portsmouth fans did get in at turnstiles where they were not expected."

Portsmouth won the match and leapfrogged Huddersfield to the top of the table. Both clubs were eventually promoted that season but the violence of that day ensured that trouble would be a regular feature when the two sides met during the 1980s.

By now a new mob had emerged at Huddersfield, called the Kenmargra, named after the only coach company that would transport the more boisterous of the club's supporters. The regulars on the coaches were big drinkers who loved a ruck. For these lads ale was far more important than fashion, and Huddersfield as a town lagged well behind the newly emerging fashions in the north-west. One leading figure in the group was known as Small. He was young, black and as hard as nails.

In November 1981, a match away at Millwall was seen by many of the Kenmargra as an opportunity to test their mettle against the toughest around. Many went tooled up, not that it did them much good. Police were alerted to their presence after staff at a motorway service station found their shelves emptied during a short stop along the M1. Other calls to the emergency services were made when a mass brawl broke out on the car park involving the Kenmargra lads and a coachload of Barnsley Reds who were on their way to watch Manchester United play Liverpool in the League Cup Final. The fighting was short but nasty and one United fan was stabbed. The Millwall-bound coach was eventually halted after further calls were made by other motorists, complaining that beer cans were being lobbed at them out of the coach windows.

When Thames Valley Police finally stopped the coach, they found stolen goods, knives and forks from the service station, a kitchen knife, a hammer and a small machete hidden on board. No-one admitted ownership of these weapons, so the police arrested the entire coach and transported them to Bletchley police station. Under questioning, one lad admitted to stealing the cutlery, saying he needed it as he was moving into a new flat. So, with at least a culprit, the police allowed the rest to go, but only on the condition they headed back north.

The club distanced themselves from the group, saying that the coach had been privately hired. "We have very tough restrictions on the people we take to away matches," said the club's commercial manager, Maurice Porter. "The people detained by the police on the way to the match are not the sort of supporters we want. They don't go to every game and they simply cause trouble." Despite the incident, there was still trouble after the match when Millwall fans attacked Huddersfield supporters and coaches, and one driver was injured when his front windscreen was smashed.

Another trip where the Kenmargra lads enhanced their reputation was at Cardiff in March 1983. At the start of the season, Huddersfield had hosted their Welsh rivals, who arrived early and took over the Crescent pub near the railway station. Nothing much happened, as there was a police cordon placed around it, but Town lads were annoyed that the police had allowed the Cardiff to stay there all lunchtime with their flags and banners draped everywhere. It was decided that when the away game came around, Cardiff would be visited and the lads would not be sneaking in the back door.

One Kenmargra lad said, "With it being a Tuesday night match, we set off early and arrived at around teatime, making sure the driver, who was always obliging, stopped right outside their pub. As we pulled up everybody piled off, chanting, and went straight into their pub. Fighting broke out in seconds and spilled into the street and running battles continued whilst the police fought to regain control of the situation, eventually making several arrests. We had made a point and were finally escorted to the ground. After our attack on the pub we knew there would be trouble outside, even with a large police presence. Fighting broke out as soon as we neared the car park and continued for several minutes. As we pulled away from the ground, Cardiff fans appeared on nearly every street corner and for thirty minutes we were constantly on and off the coach, fighting with different groups, until eventually we were on the motorway. That was mainly down to our driver, 'H', who took us to most matches; he must have been sixty then and treated us like his own boys, and knew what the deal was. You could always count on H to get you there and back, well, most of you."

However, for a League Cup tie at Arsenal they were forced to use a new coach company. "Due to problems related to using Kenmargra and the high profile of the game, we had trouble obtaining a coach for Arsenal away in the cup so we ended up using SKJ Coaches," said Kenmargra's Paddy. "We were supplied with a brand new twenty-seven-seater for the match on the proviso that no alcohol would be allowed on board. However, the driver wasn't that bothered and by the time we hit London the atmosphere on the coach, fuelled by drink and other substances, was electric. I can't remember the match but we lost and afterwards everybody was up for it.

"We had parked in an area used by both sets of supporters and decided to hang around and wait to see what happened. Eventually, there was only us and what appeared to be three coaches of Arsenal fans left in the car park. We decided to target the first coach and attempted to get in through the front and emergency doors. Unfortunately, the coach turned out to be full of police on their way back to the station and they soon piled off and scuffles broke out as we attempted to get back to our coach. We managed to get out on to the main road but traffic hold-ups meant everyone was soon out of the coach again and fighting Arsenal fans who were celebrating outside pubs along the route.

"After a while we noticed that the police coach we'd had the confrontation with was now behind us further back down the road, so we piled back on the coach and told the driver to drive and not to stop. We had only gone a few hundred yards when the driver hit the brakes and one of our guys went through the windscreen on to the road in front of the bus, while at the same time the police bus rammed into the back of ours and a copper came partly through the windscreen of their coach and the back window of ours. Police reinforcements and an ambulance arrived. The coach, which had been new in the morning, was now a foot shorter, with no windscreen or back window and the door had to be held shut with a Town scarf. For all that happened, no-one was arrested, however we were given a police escort nearly all the way home to Yorkshire."

It was at an FA Cup game in the early 1980s that Huddersfield's hooligans first became aware of the changing fashion. A trip to Tranmere brought them face to face with the casuals. "Loads of effeminate looking lads, all with wedge haircuts and Slazenger V-necks," remembered Paddy. "This was Tranmere's crew and they were well game despite being massively outnumbered." Two months later Huddersfield played host to Millwall in the return fixture to the aborted motorway trip and again the new youth fashion was much in evidence, with even the players sporting the wedge haircut.

Within a year the new look started to become commonplace in Leeds and was being picked up in the smaller towns to the north and east of Huddersfield, where support was split between the two clubs. Places such as Brighouse, Elland, Cleckheaton and Mirfield provided the nucleus of Town's first lads to adopt the look. The initial conversion saw box leathers, cycling shirts, Slazengers, Kickers and Pods all popular, topped off with a wedge, or in a couple of cases, full-on Phil Oakley-style fringes. Over the next three years, the regulation look was to change with startling regularity as the lads played catch-up with the pacesetters of the bigger city clubs. Designer sportswear became the vogue and the next firm to emerge at the club, in 1982, was called the Pringles after the ubiquitous knitwear. The name was actually coined by the older Kenmargra and the firm lasted about six years.

In January 1983, Huddersfield were drawn at home in the FA Cup against Chelsea, then arguably the most feared hooligan mob around. Trouble before and during the game saw 16 people charged with threatening behaviour, one with possessing a kitchen knife, and one with causing criminal damage. After the game, fans hurled bricks and cans at parked cars, and a further four Chelsea were arrested after trouble at a Chinese takeaway.

The casual fashion took off among growing numbers of young lads in Huddersfield, but not everyone was impressed. While some scurried off to Leeds and Manchester to acquire the latest trainers and sports tops, a small group from the outlying town of Holmfirth looked on at these town "puffs" with disdain. In the autumn of 1983, the tensions came to a head and clashes in Huddersfield town centre on a number of consecutive Fridays led to the police providing an escort for the last bus back to Holmfirth. In May 1984, things almost came unstuck for the Huddersfield lads as they found themselves outnumbered by the Holmfirth boys during an away match at Middlesbrough. It was only the intervention of some Boro lads, who offered to back up Huddersfield, that averted serious trouble. The feud continued well into the 1990s.

Chelsea might have been bad but worse was to come in the shape of Leeds United. It was, in the words of the police, the club and the local paper, by far the worst trouble in Huddersfield ever. A week earlier, Leeds had rioted at Barnsley, and the knowledge of that disorder had heightened what was already a tense build-up to the bitter local derby. The clubs had not played each other for a while but history suggested that there would be trouble. Hundreds of extra police were drafted in from across West Yorkshire to patrol the ground and the routes to and from the town centre. Town centre publicans were advised not to open at lunchtime.

The best planning failed to prevent mass disorder. "Thugs bombard police and crowd in soccer mayhem," screamed the front page of the local paper. "Police and club officials were today counting the cost of the worst-ever hooliganism at Huddersfield Town. In a terrifying display of violence, notorious Leeds United supporters clashed with home fans and police before, during and after Saturday's derby match." In all, 65 fans were arrested and more than 20 people, including three policemen, were injured. Thousands of pounds of damage was caused to the ground and parked cars and even first-aid volunteers were pelted with missiles. The blame for most of the trouble was laid at the feet of the thousands of Leeds fans, who were described as "hostile and atrocious" by Superintendent George Calligan, the man in charge of the police operation.

Among the weapons found were ball-bearings, a full brick ripped from a perimeter wall, sharpened coins, seats torn from the main stand and lumps of metal.

The second half was delayed by six minutes after a hail of missiles rained down on the pitch during the interval. A plea from the pitch by the Town chairman and a Leeds director failed to stop the trouble, and Town manager Mick Buxton vacated the dugout ten minutes before the end because of the violence, claiming that he could no longer concentrate on the game. Club secretary George Binns said the violence was premeditated, well-organised and nothing to do with football, and

added that there was little clubs could do when faced with such an organised threat. He even dismissed an identity card scheme as unworkable and restrictive to our civil liberties. After the game there were running battles in Leeds Road and towards the town centre.

By 1986 the Pringles had given way to a younger generation of hooligans, the Huddersfield Young Casuals, a name which has stuck to this day. Near-neighbours Bradford remained Huddersfield's bitter rivals, the enmity being exacerbated by the death of a Bradford lad during a late night fight outside Bradford Interchange station and the decision by Bradford to play a few of their home games at Leeds Road after fire destroyed part of their ground. "Bradford became a virtual no-go area at one point, as we discovered when attending a New Order gig at St George's Hall," recalled Paddy in the book *Casuals*. "While four coachloads of Mancs and a mob of Leeds were 'tactically avoided' by some of the Section Five [from Bradford] loitering outside, a handful of Town lads were picked off at the Interchange afterwards. One lad ended up having to jump on a Halifax bus to escape injury after having his suede jacket slashed down the back."

Huddersfield also had a number of clashes with Manchester City in 1987 and 1988. One lad recalled, "It was greeted with joy when we got them in the FA Cup third round. We all agreed to meet in town about half ten and City were already there. We went into the pub and more lads kept coming in saying, 'They're all over the place'. It seemed that every train that pulled in brought another thirty City lads with it. As far as fighting goes, it was one of the best days ever for Town. You did not seem to go more than twenty minutes without a battle. Quite a few City were so cocky they were walking round in groups of seven and eight. There weren't 100 police to guard you in those days, it quite literally went off all day. The walk to the ground felt like going to an away match, as City were just coming at us from every angle and every street. They probably had a good 300 to 400 about. The match ended two-all, so it was off to Maine Road for the mid-week replay.

"We got into Manchester and had very little trouble before the match. After the game, a nil-nil draw, it was a different matter. Outside the ground we were straight at it with City. The police cordoned quite a few of us off and put us back on coaches to

Victoria. Twenty lads escaped and made their own way through Moss Side, subjected to quite severe beatings on the way. When they arrived at the station – the train had been held up for them – it was like a scene from *The Warriors.* They were covered in blood and their shirts were ripped apart, but they were still laughing about walking through Moss Side, saying it was a piece of piss.

"The next replay was back at Leeds Road and there was a noticeable police presence. After the match, Town got it together in the old car park outside the away end and as soon as City came out, Town went straight into them. Several cars were missing bits which were launched at City. Town did fairly well on that occasion, actually backing City off into the away end."

That was not the end of the feud. Several years later, a mob of 80 travelled over to Bury, normally a hooligan non-event. They met some City lads en route and it was agreed that they would have a mob ready for their return. After the game, the Huddersfield lads jumped into taxis and headed into Manchester, and before long were fighting with City in Piccadilly Gardens. A Huddersfield police spotter was present and allegedly told the lads that they had "five minutes max to get it on". A fierce toe-to-toe broke up after a couple of minutes when more police arrived, which was fortunate for Huddersfield because a large mob of City was heading towards them at speed from up the road.

In 1989, there was disorder on the streets of Huddersfield after a Cup game against Nottingham Forest. A large Huddersfield mob had travelled down to the East Midlands for the first leg and now the challenge was being reciprocated. One hundred and fifty Forest arrived mid-afternoon and there was almost instant trouble. Forest clashed with Huddersfield along Kirkgate, Leeds Road and in Wakefield Road, where a pub was badly damaged. Eleven people were arrested. "Fair play to them," said Forest veteran, Nick Stevenson. "They were a game firm."

The Forest game might have proved that Huddersfield could mix it with the better-known hooligan firms; it also coincided with a defining change for the mob. Huddersfield's proximity to Manchester meant that the rave scene soon took a strong hold in the West Yorkshire mill town.

Forest went on to play Liverpool in the semi-final in a match rendered irrelevant by the deaths of 96 Liverpool supporters. To the surprise of some Huddersfield lads, a group of Scousers decided to stop off for a drink on the way home. Incredibly, given the appalling events of that day, the two sets of lads decided to have a fight. It was a day and a night that no-one was going to forget, as another Huddersfield lad recalled.

"This was probably the night that a lot of our lads realised that you could get seriously hurt doing what we do. It was the day of the Hillsborough Disaster and it was a night that a few of our lads grew up. It was about eight o'clock when one of the lads said that there were quite a few Scousers in Yates's at the bottom end of town. As these lads may have lost mates in the disaster and probably did not know yet if they had or not, it was probably not a wise decision to go down. When we got to Yates's a few of the lads had been talking to the Scousers who said that they were up for it, if Town wanted it.

"As we got to Yates's they came driving past in cars, slammed on and jumped out. What followed was quite unbelievable. They must have been outnumbered by at least four to one by Town but we were not prepared for the array of weaponry that came with them. I remember going into one, smacking one, being grabbed by the throat and his mate shouting, 'Cut him, cut him.' Luckily for me, being nineteen but looking about fifteen, one of the other lads said, 'Leave him, he's only a kid.' By this time my top had been dragged off and one of them had it in his hand. Cheekily I asked for it back. What was going on around was amazing. There were lads with baseball bats, knives, axes and one distinct piece of weaponry that was fashioned like a stick with a diamond shape with blades on. They were not only standing Town, they were giving it out big time. One lad got hit full in the face with a brick and just carried on. Obviously that brand of powder had not reached so far inland as Huddersfield.

"Eventually, they ran us all over and lads were just glad to get out of the way of the weapons as quite a few had been hurt. Most notably they got one black lad down on the floor and actually swung the axe at him, though luckily they missed and took a great lump out of the road instead. I admit that I was as scared as I have ever been at an incident. I think quite a few of us grew up that night and realised that we had not quite enough to play with the big boys as we got well and truly done by far lower numbers."

Huddersfield has always had a mixture of white and black lads in their firm and while this has caused no problems within the mob, it has irritated mobs with more right-wing leanings, especially at England matches. In 1995, 100 made the journey to Dublin for the "friendly" cup-tie that was to prove anything but. Huddersfield never made it, after clashing with Stoke on the train ride over to Holyhead.

"As we were changing trains," said one of Huddersfield's black lads, "we got on to a carriage full of Stoke lads, who seemed amazed that, being born in England, holding the same passport as them but being of a different colour, this did not instantly disqualify a person from following England. 'Who brought the spooks?' was one of the lame remarks to come our way. On hearing this, one of the Town lads put both his index fingers behind a Stoke lad's eyeballs and gouged them, leaving him screaming in agony.

"Fighting erupted in the carriage and it is not the easiest thing to fight in such a confined space so a lot of lads were taking blows from all angles, not all necessarily aimed at them. At times it was a struggle to move, let alone throw a decent punch. The Transport Police were more or less already on the scene and after the clash they decided that we were the aggressors and cleared a carriage for about thirty-five of us at the front of the train. There was no doubt in my mind that it was going to go off again as soon as we reached Holyhead. As the train pulled in to the port we knew that we would possibly have to front a train full of lads. There was a fair bit of conversation along the lines of 'just do it' and 'don't fucking move'. The police line was not the most co-ordinated.

"Two of their lads came round the corner, giving it the old arms outstretched gesture. We just waltzed through the police line and went into them. The ones that were coming from behind them had nowhere to go so it was chaos. A few lads got food from a vending stall and threw it about. The police, after being so lax, went into 'if it moves, hit it' mode and they backed us off to the point where we started from. That was really the end of it. To add insult to injury, the captain of the ferry refused to take us and it was a long journey back to town that night. At least the rail company agreed to refund

our fares as long as we left our names and addresses with them. That was the day British Rail found out that John Smith is a popular name in Huddersfield."

A couple of years later, during an England match in Poland, Huddersfield again took flak for the presence of black lads in their mob, this time from Aston Villa. Villa had a strong right-wing following, with many of their leading faces also involved with Combat 18, and by the 1990s had begun to travel abroad with England in large numbers. The incident that followed is remembered by some of the lads who travelled on what they described as "the maddest train journey of our lives".

"About ten of the older lads flew out to Berlin to meet up with a good twenty HYC in the Sports Bar for a few bevies before getting the sleeper train up to Katowice. The atmosphere was good as we walked from bar to bar with various mobs, including good lads from Exeter and Wolves, until some div sprayed gas in a bar just to see if it worked. Before you could say 'Who won the war?' we were rounded up by heavily armoured paramilitaries and marched around the city before being shunted into what seemed like a deliberately deserted railway station. By now people were getting pissed off. This became more apparent when Villa's mob, about forty wannabe C18, started eyeing up two of our black lads and muttering about doing Huddersfield. Things eased off, however, when one of Town's main lads confronted Villa's main mouthpiece with a few pushes to the chest and a generous offer of a one-on-one, which was declined.

"The tension remained high on the train and became even more so when our guards got off and we crossed the Polish border. Once in Poland we were in real bandit country and at every station we were ambushed by window-smashing scruffs or baton-wielding police. At one of the first stations we pulled into our compartment door was flung open by Villa armed with bottles who asked the older lads if we were gonna do Huddersfield with them. We glanced at each other, got up and, being careful not to let our accents give us away, followed them.

"Villa were proper buzzing about what they were going to do to these 'Yorkshire nigger-lovers' until we reached the other end of the train. They then saw what Huddersfield lads were capable of. Town had taken the fight to the Poles and were fucking them all over the platform and down the track. Villa thought it wise to turn around and walk back down the train, not to be seen until much later.

"About two in the morning, I was woken by the sound of bottles smashing all around us. I then received my first ever gassing. A small group of Poles had sneaked down the banking and across the tracks and, once the train was in motion, began attacking. Some of our lads had steamed down the carriage, struggling under a barrage of bottles and rocks and somehow managed to rip open the windows. Gradually, the Poles were forced back as more lads awoke and Polish ammo ran short. Then our mates from Villa showed again. This seemed much more like their kind of row as the opposition was already unconscious.

"We arrived at our destination at about 6.30 in the morning with just about every window shattered and the floor swimming in blood, piss, beer and broken glass. Later that day people told us that Villa reckoned they'd done us on the train. We can only assume that they dreamt it while the real battling was going on. They also made the mistake of claiming to have done West Ham the previous season. What West Ham said to them at that match we don't know, but Villa were not seen again that weekend."

In 1996, 76 Huddersfield were arrested at a match at Wolves after an allegedly pre-arranged fight on the outskirts of Wolverhampton. Police reported that two coaches, one a 52-seater and the second half the size, set off from Huddersfield for a pub a few miles from their eventual destination. It was later alleged that everyone had been told exactly what awaited them and if anyone had any doubts they had to leave now. None did, and the two coaches continued the short distance to the agreed fight location. As their coaches pulled up, Wolves came bounding out of the pub, throwing whatever makeshift weapons they could.

The fighting continued, despite many of the lads realising that the police were videoing the whole event. Wolves stood for a short time before being backed off up the street. As Huddersfield attempted to storm the pub the police arrived in droves and began rounding up the away fans. A few slipped into the local estate but, given they didn't have a clue where they were, they all returned to the waiting police expecting to be taken to the ground.

Wolverhampton police station was their actual destination, where they were held for several hours before being returned home under a heavy escort. The police eventually charged 30 people for the fight but the cases collapsed, as the video evidence was inconclusive in many instances and in others the police were shown simply to be incompetent or exaggerating their version of events. The evidence was so detailed that many Huddersfield were convinced that they had an informer within their ranks and the finger of suspicion fell on one lad who was soon excluded from future ventures.

It was never proved if the person blamed was actually a "grass", but the police operation at the Wolves game was a wake-up call, and any new faces were subsequently greeted with extreme caution. The lad who was singled out has never been accepted back into the firm.

Despite the arrests and pending court cases, the HYC were not put off, and in February 1999, an FA Cup game with Derby County saw the worst trouble at Huddersfield since the Leeds game of the mid-Eighties. Trouble between rival fans broke out after Derby took the lead and when police entered part of the stand occupied by the HYC to eject some supporters, they became the target. A number of arrests were made and police were injured during the trouble, one quite badly after he was knocked unconscious. Huddersfield's mob had joined the cross-border craze and was boosted for the day by eight Aberdeen lads.

A month later there was more trouble in Huddersfield, this time with the visit of Birmingham City. The local paper reported "serious disorder" in the town centre after the game, with rival gangs involved in running battles. Police made seven arrests. Police on horseback tried to keep the rival gangs apart, but clashes continued on Gasworks Street, St Andrews Street, Northumberland St, Brook Street and St George's Square. Five of those arrested were from Birmingham and two from Huddersfield. For many Huddersfield lads this was their best encounter against a mob who would always show.

In the FA Cup the following season, Huddersfield were handed a plum tie at home to Liverpool. Tickets were snapped up almost as soon as they went on sale and, despite the game being live on television, every nutter from the area turned out for a piece of the action. Nothing much happened before the match, as all the main pubs were packed to the rafters with lads who only come out for such big games. "The match itself was an injustice," recalled one Huddersfield lad. "Town had the better chances but were unable to convert and Liverpool's higher league status told in the end. As the match was drawing to a close we noticed quite a few Liverpool lads leaving the away end so we all left our seats and confronted them on the steep stairs outside the ground, them being at the top of the stairs and us being at the bottom. Town went straight into them and the same black lad from the previous incident with Liverpool, who flits in and out of the scene, seemed to be on a mission to rid himself of his demons.

"Town did very well, ending up at the top of the stairs. The police quickly quelled this outbreak and after the game ushered us through back streets towards town, which turned out to be convenient because we walked straight into the Liverpool escort at the roundabout by the carriageway. We seemed to hit them head on. From then on the police lost control as a few of our lads went straight into the escort, one of them receiving a cracking right-hander from one of the Liverpool lads. This was followed up by one of our lads giving him a crack back. It was just going off and Liverpool seemed to be backing off, caught a bit unawares. The police got it back under control and ushered Liverpool to the side of the carriageway and kept us separated.

"I am in no way saying that we would do Liverpool as a whole, but a lot of big city clubs that come to small towns like Huddersfield seem to think they can take the piss, bring fifty lads and it will be a stroll in the park. Really, they ought to know that, with it being a big match for us, we would have well above the normal turnout. Everyone wants to make a name for themselves so in a few years time they can sit telling tales about how they cracked so-and-so from whatever club."

There is a refreshing honesty to Huddersfield's own history of their mob. In interviews for this book they acknowledged a far larger number of defeats and downright hidings they received at the hands of others than any other club. This is not to say that they have been turned over every week, but that winning and losing fights is part and parcel of their lives.

Contrasting footballing fortunes had kept Huddersfield apart from Leeds in the League for well over a decade, so when it was announced that Leeds were coming to town for a pre-season friendly in August 2000, many eyebrows were raised and a huge police operation was put in place. But it was not enough, as a police report on the match makes clear: "Leeds fans travelling to Huddersfield were attacked upon arrival at railway station. During this disturbance BTP [British Transport Police] officers were singled out for attack. The Huddersfield fans made it clear to BTP officers that when no West Yorkshire Police were present they would be attacked. After the match sporadic fighting outside station when again BTP came under attack. Officers with batons drawn and dog section repelled this attack. The Huddersfield group stated to officers that they were aware that BTP had few officers on duty and that they would be attacked when the opportunity arose."

A month later, Huddersfield were at home to another long-time rival, Manchester City. Thirty-four people were arrested at this match and there were several injuries, including one to a young boy. Gangs clashed in Huddersfield town centre before the game after City lads arrived several hours before kick-off. There was further trouble along the way to the ground and also afterwards. "This was probably the start of police really clamping down and going into full Eastern Bloc-style policing," recalled Paddy. "There were quite a few minor incidents during the day, as it was a night match, but the full-on stuff came after the game. City came out of the away end all mobbed up and the hundreds of police on duty could not contain them. They were breaking out of the escort and scuffles were happening all over the place. As they neared town, the fighting got worse as Town got together."

Christmas 2001 provided an opportunity for Huddersfield to re-acquaint themselves with Stoke City, though it was the visitors who grabbed the headlines. Hooligans from Stoke's Naughty Forty and Under Fives firms fought the HYC throughout the day. In the worst incident, Stoke fans smashed up and set fire to the White Hart pub, causing extensive damage. Police were later to claim that the trouble would have been far worse if it had not been for their strong intervention and boasted of intelligence that suggested the gangs had planned to confront each other before the game which led them to deploy 16 mounted officers.

Sean Lithgow, landlord of the White Hart, spoke of his terror as thugs began chanting, "Let's burn the pub down." He said, "We shouted last orders at 1.50 and they went berserk. Some of them were throwing bottles and glasses and they then set fire to the snug area. They threw a chair on the gas fire and the chair set alight. We put it out with fire extinguishers and there was a lot of smoke. The police were outside waiting for the fans to come out. We are never having fans in here again."

The newest mob at Huddersfield is the Huddersfield Youth Squad. Formed in 1999 for the visit of Liverpool in the FA Cup, this group of "youngsters" emerge as one of the main groups. "There were about fifteen of us at the start, all good lads who have stood together through thick and thin and are still here today, even though we know full well that prison is a real possibility, more so than it was in the early days," said a founder. "Since we formed, the Youth Squad numbers have swelled to fifty, though we are sometimes back down to fifteen. For the first few years we travelled everywhere, no matter what the numbers were. We sometimes got a row and sometimes got run. Most times we just went for the crack and whatever happened, happened, but in the main we showed up. Since then we have all become good mates through adversity. Down the years we have taken a lot of shit off the older lot but I think they respect us now and know we are willing to put ourselves on the line."

One Youth outing was Huddersfield's away match at Hull in 2004. They met at a quiet local pub in Huddersfield, arriving separately in taxis and before long their numbers had swelled to almost 100. They set off in a fleet of minibuses for Hull, stopping on the edge of the city to link up with one of the biggest mobs Huddersfield had put together for many years. A couple of Hull lads turned up with the news that they had 150 in the city centre, so Huddersfield drank up and re-boarded their transport. However, the police were on top of events and after only a few minutes they surrounded the buses, took everyone off, searched them and allowed only those with tickets to continue, and then only directly to the ground. But afterwards there was a serious clash in the car park, which one Huddersfield Youth described as "the nastiest brawl of my life".

HULL CITY

Ground: Formerly Boothferry Park, now the KC Stadium
Firm: Mad Young Tigers, Kempton Enders, Hull City Psychos, Silver Cod Squad, The Minority
Rivals: Middlesbrough, Leeds, Sheffield United

Until 2004, the British police used the Epicentre computer network to record incidents and circulate intelligence on hooligan activity. Established by Interpol, Epicentre was little more than the police's version of the hooligan website *In The Know*. Most postings could be viewed by anyone with access to the system's password and much of the material was little more than gossip and rumour. Football Intelligence Officers were encouraged to record any incident involving trouble or mobs of more than 50 lads. Some officers enjoyed the process more than others and lost no time in recording events at their club, however trivial. Others were conspicuous by their silence, including the FIO from Hull.

"Why aren't there many postings from Hull?" one fellow FIO was overheard asking at an annual get-together. "I thought your mob was really active?"

"What's the point?" came the reply. "If I recorded every incident involving fifty lads or more, and general fights, I'd do nothing else apart from post reports."

Hull is a working class city built around the docks, the Merchant Navy and the fishing industry. It is an often forgotten, unglamorous place that was largely rebuilt after the Second World War. In its tightly packed terrace streets and the sprawling estates of Bransholme and Orchard Park, a youth gang culture was born that quickly became attached to Hull City Football Club. For a period in the early 1970s, and again from the mid-1990s onwards, Hull could mix it with anyone in the country, though like the city, they rarely received the "credit" they deserved.

Hooliganism arrived in Hull a little later than at some other clubs, but in 1969 it came in the form of hobnail boots worn by their opponents. During a home match against Crystal Palace, a dozen of the away contingent surged at the home crowd, scattering them. "One was waving a knife about, another a chain, and as boots and fists connected, Hull City's South Stand lost its innocence," remembered veteran Hull hooligan Shaun Tordoff, in his terrace classic *City Psychos*. A short time later, Hull received another painful lesson in the new language of the terraces, this time at Middlesbrough's Ayresome Park. Hull lost the game 5–3, and trouble kicked off shortly after the break when the home fans swapped ends and proceeded to steam into the away fans, who were oblivious to the switch. "This huge surge of Boro, many wearing miners' safety helmets and heavy steel-toe-capped boots, came straight at Hull, now down to about forty in number, pinned us against the back of the stand and gave us a good hiding," recalled another Hull lad.

The beatings galvanised the young hard men at Hull and before long the Monte Carlo Mob emerged. The skinhead fashion had taken hold in 1969 and young mobs were often linked to youth clubs and cafes. The Monte Carlo was a café off Osbourne Street, close enough to the railway station to confront opposition fans, but slightly off the beaten track so as not to draw the attention of the police. They were a violent crew and soon gained a massive reputation in the town, marked out by their unique tattoos: a black boot, with a number underneath to show your standing in the gang.

Number One was the legendary Sinbad. "Sinbad's lads were usually at the forefront, clashing with greasers," recalled another Hull lad, describing the regular city centre brawls on a Saturday. "It was normally smash, bang, wallop, with greasers running all over, battered and bruised, and the Old Bill arriving ten minutes later with Sinbad long gone. Sinbad's reputation went before him and he wasn't looking to win any popularity contests. He was a bit secretive, a cut above us really. He was heavily tattooed, with a gold earring, long before it became a fashion necessity. He didn't mix freely and was usually seen with three or four other lads, also heavily tattooed. They had hundreds of stars on each arm and hand. Sinbad also had the famous bovver boot marking with Number One underneath. He was from a large, well-known Hessle Road family, very muscular in build and usually dressed in faded Levis and Doc Martens; a fearsome looking character, not to be crossed."

By 1970 Hull was gaining in confidence and muscle, which was just as well because in August the club drew Manchester United in the Watney Cup and running battles took place across the city. There was further trouble near the ground and inside, where hundreds were ejected and every cell space was occupied.

There was more trouble over the next few weeks, at matches involving Bolton, Birmingham and Sheffield United. Hull was also beginning to export trouble and, later that season, as the team battled for promotion, there were two serious outbreaks of disorder. The first was a promotion clash at Sheffield United when about 10,000 Hull fans made the trip, leading to the comment by player-manager Terry Neill that "at times a stranger in the ground would not have known which was the home team." There was trouble on and off the pitch, and some Hull coaches were badly damaged after the game. "Battle of Bramall Lane," was how the *Hull Daily Mail* headlined the story.

The second match was a couple of weeks later when Hull were away at Bolton, where skirmishes broke out almost as soon as hundreds of Hull disembarked from the trains. It could have been a lot worse had it not been for trouble at Bolton a few weeks before with the visit at Leicester; fearing a repeat, the police managed to herd the Hull fans away from the main shopping streets and straight to the ground. However, rival gangs still managed to fight in the centre circle of the pitch. Twelve fans were arrested, mostly juveniles from Hull. The trouble was widely reported in the national media and even on the BBC's *Grandstand*, but despite this, Lancashire Police claimed to have been pleased with their operation. "It could have been far worse," one officer remarked, ominously.

It was around this time that the hardcore of Hull fans moved ends within their ground. For many years they had been based in the South Stand but now they switched residence to the old Railway End, known to locals as the Kempton. It had a low, echoey roof and was darker and more forbidding. It was also more difficult for the police to control and before long the lads in the new home called themselves the Kempton Fusiliers. Their main group was from West Hull, split between the Hessle Road, Anlaby Road, Gypsyville and Boothferry estates. The most notorious were the Monte Carlo Mob, the Orchard Park Estate Boys, the Gypsyville and Boothferry Skins, the East Hull Boys and the lads living around the Avenues area. "Inter-gang rivalries between these different factions meant it was sometimes volatile at home games, especially if the away fans were few," said Tordoff. "But away from home everyone closed ranks and fought for the cause."

Hull still lacked the organisation of more established mobs. At Sheffield Wednesday in December 1971, a small group of Hull got into the home section of the Leppings Lane End believing they would be soon joined by hundreds more, but Wednesday lulled them into an ambush down the entrance tunnel, away from the gaze of the police. And it didn't end in the ground, they had to run the gauntlet to get back to their coach which was surrounded by Sheffield lads banging on the windows, baying for blood. "It taught us that you didn't mess about with Wednesday, or if you did, you had better go with plenty of game lads," said a Hull veteran.

For the return fixture, on the final Saturday of the season, Wednesday travelled up in their thousands having already been relegated. Their fans ran amok. In the worst incident, a local man, dressed in a sheepskin coat and sporting a Hull City scarf, threw a Wednesday fan through a shop window, causing extensive back injuries. Hull got their revenge after the game but the fighting continued long after the away fans had left for home. Hundreds of Hull ran through the shopping streets, smashing windows and kicking over displays. The craze of snatching scarves as trophies caused considerable displeasure. One Wednesday fan sent a scarf back to the club that had been stolen from a ten-year-old girl by his brother. "It may be impossible to return the scarf to its owner," wrote the "true Wednesdayite", "but I hope that you can give it to someone who deserves it and all Wednesday fans will not be judged alike."

Hull's lads might have considered the Sheffield teams, Sunderland, Bolton and even Forest as their main rivals, but fixtures against clubs closer to home also featured considerable violence. In August 1972, 200 Hull boys joined up with York City to confront Grimsby. At a pre-season friendly at Scarborough at about the same time, hundreds of Hull battled it out with locals along the seafront. Trouble continued inside the ground and more than 50 fans were arrested.

An FA Cup game at Stockport in 1973 saw perhaps the most widespread disorder involving Hull during this period. The film *A Clockwork Orange* had captured the imagination of football louts across the country, and Hull was no different. "The Stockport game is one of perhaps half a dozen matches that have gone down in folk legend among the followers of Hull City, and perfectly encapsulates the mindset of the early Seventies hooligan," wrote Tordoff. "We wanted to be different. We wanted to shock, as well as frighten our opponents. Some lads were seen at games wearing bandages, bandana-style, emblazoned with the term 'MAD' copied from the popular American magazine of the same name. Then a few lads brought some glitter, spray-painted their Docs silver or gold, and soon everyone looked like roadies at a Sweet concert. The look was finished off with silk scarves tied to their heads, Indian-style, and a few even went to the extremes of painting their faces, inspired I suppose by Stanley Kubrick. This hybrid of a bootboy was unleashed on an unsuspecting public at Stockport County." Eight hundred outlandish-looking hooligans travelled over the Pennines that day, and for eight hours Stockport was a town besieged.

The following Saturday, Hull were at home to West Ham. Everyone came out for a chance to have a go at the infamous Hammers. Many met at 10.30 and waited for the Londoners to arrive, but when they did they were given a police escort straight to the ground. That didn't stop a group of 15 Hull fans, who normally followed Manchester United, getting into the away end. There was a short but vicious fight but overwhelming numbers forced the Hull lads to retreat. They regrouped after the game and the rival gangs clashed again with the police occupied elsewhere. In the city centre, West Ham fans were indiscriminately attacked.

The City lads felt invincible. The youngsters who had emerged in the late 1960s had within three years become seasoned veterans. All this changed on 10 February 1973, in what became known as the "Battle of Dock Street". Returning from an away match at Burnley, some of the Hull lads went for a drink in the city centre. The previous week there had been some fighting between rival Hull gangs and two lads had been arrested. This time the police were out in force, waiting for something to happen. It did: in a vicious gang fight, one lad was stabbed through the lung and almost died.

The authorities cracked down hard and several key leaders were given long prison sentences. This precipitated a fall-out within the Hull ranks, with the Hull Reds, followers of Man United, being blamed for the trouble, though they insisted that they were the victims. Feelings toward the Hull Reds soured further a short time later when Hull played the recently relegated United. "Rumours circulated that the Orchard lads were meeting up with other Reds to come and do City," recalled the leader of the Hull Reds. "It was complete bollocks, but a few people with old scores to settle made us out to be bad bastards. After this, the rift never really healed. None of us went again."

Hull's mob disintegrated. From the thousands who would once fight for their club, only a hardcore of a few dozen remained. The demoralisation was compounded when a succession of clubs took liberties in Hull's end, among them Forest (twice), Sheffield Wednesday (again), Sunderland and Manchester United. The average age of the main lads dropped to as low as 16. There was virtually no trouble at away matches as the entire effort was put into defending their own turf from too regular incursions. To compound the young mob's mood, the club's performances were increasingly dreadful.

Adversity often unites, and gradually the young mob began to grow up. After a number of comprehensive beatings, their resilience showed through and with it came better tactics. They knew they could not compete with the large mobs but were determined that no one would take their end again. Even the mighty Chelsea were spotted and attacked before they could group, most opting to escape over the barrier.

New Year's Day 1976 confirmed the rebirth of hooliganism in Hull, when a coachload of young lads, drawn from a few local mobs, travelled together to a match at Blackpool. The most important connection was that between West Hull and the Selworthy mobs, largely brought about by three brothers who had grown up near the ground but moved to the sprawling Bransholme estate and introduced the two mobs to one another. The brothers' reputation ensured that there was no rivalry. It was from this group a few years later that the Hull City Psychos were born.

The hard days were still not completely over, as a game at Tranmere, in August 1978, proved. There had been little indication that the home fans were intent on trouble, but Hull's growing confidence was dented a few minutes before the end of the game when 100 Tranmere burst into their end

armed with sticks and rocks. "Led by oldish blokes in their late twenties, they were well organised and knew exactly what to do," recalled one Hull lad. "They laid into any City fans they could spot, bricking some and kicking and punching anyone between fifteen and thirty in what seemed a well-rehearsed attack."

Hull dropped back into the old Fourth Division and though crowds plummeted, the lads were still returning. The team had won a pathetic eight games out of a possible 46 and crowds were averaging just 3,000, yet the notoriety of the City Psychos was growing, helped in part by a "Psycho newsletter" produced every few months. It related terrace battles and talked up forthcoming fixtures. "The language was quite colourful but would nowadays be considered juvenile and innocent," said another Hull lad.

Two matches in 1981 confirmed Hull's revival. The first was an FA Cup tie at Spurs at which a lot of the older lads who had been inactive for a while returned. Spurs ambushed the Hull coaches but the visitors more than held their own in running battles before and after the game. Then, in August, Hull played Bradford City. Again, a coachload of Hull were attacked by missile-throwing locals as they arrived. Another group managed to get into the Bradford end but the police moved in to prevent major trouble. After the game a group of Bradford skins were attacked.

Segregation had long ended the ease with which fans could move around the ground, but in the pre-police intelligence days it was still possible to catch opponents by surprise. Twenty paid in to the Chelsea end when the two clubs met in an FA Cup replay in 1982 but they misjudged where the London mob might be and the element of surprise was lost. With greatly superior numbers, Chelsea charged forward, but Hull held out until the police arrived. Some Chelsea, meanwhile, had slipped into the South Stand and in a brief fight one was dispatched from the seats into terracing below.

In another change in tactics, Hull ditched the highly visible coaches in favour of Luton and Bedford vans. Whereas once police would simply be waiting on motorway slip roads to escort the coaches straight to the ground, the boys could now enter towns and cities unannounced. This was to work at both Sheffield United and Oxford in the early Eighties.

Punches and kicks fly during a fight between the casuals of Hull City and Bolton Wanderers at a match in March 1984.

In May 1984, Hull went into the last game of the season needing to beat Burnley by three clear goals to secure promotion out of Division Three at the expense of their fierce rivals, Sheffield United. Among the thousands of Hull fans who made the journey were 150 top lads, but to their surprise they were to face not only locals but a small group of Blades who had come to celebrate their own team's promotion. Hull won the game but only by two goals and for the angry Hull mob, everyone was considered fair game.

The 1984/85 season is considered one of Hull's busiest off the field, with big games against Derby, Bradford, Wigan, Doncaster, Brentford and, above all, memorable cup ties against Tranmere, Brighton and Southampton. One of the fiercest battles all season was the home game against Lincoln. Of all the local teams Hull played during the Eighties, only Lincoln could be guaranteed to put in an appearance. A small group of Hull were battered by locals and were only saved from a worse beating with the arrival of a removal van transporting another 50 lads. The tables were soon reversed and first the opposition and then their cars were dealt with.

Another big game that season was against the recently relegated Derby County. Three full coaches of lads planned to arrive late and pay in the home end. Their plan failed, but Derby knew they were around and the atmosphere during the match was tense. At the final whistle, the Hull lads broke through a line of police forces and fought with Derby up and down the street and on the fringes of a nearby estate, in particular a small group of black youths who stood their ground longer than the rest.

An FA Cup tie away at Tranmere gave Hull a chance to avenge the pasting they received six years previously. Five hundred lads made the journey. They arrived early and took over several of the pubs around the ground. In most, the locals fled, but in one case they stood and fought. It was nasty, neither side gave an inch and a Hull lad was knocked unconscious with a glass ashtray. The fighting only stopped with the sound of approaching sirens. There was further trouble inside the ground, as Hull rushed Tranmere in the seats and the Merseysiders fought back strenuously.

Hull finished third and began the 1985/86 season in Division Two. Their first away match was a plum tie at Leeds and while 300 lads made the short trip a strong police presence ensured the game passed off quietly. The same could not be said of other matches that season, especially those against long-standing rivals Sheffield United and Middlesbrough. Boro arrived in a fleet of vans and parked up on the edge of town, well away from the inquisitive eye of the law, and walked towards the city centre. Rumours had been flying around of possible sightings all day, so when this news of their arrival came, only a small group of 20 Hull were dispatched to investigate. The mobs clashed but Hull were heavily outnumbered.

For the return fixture, a fleet of six vans and two coaches made the short trip north. Fighting kicked off almost as soon as the lads disembarked, with half going right into town and the remainder heading for a known Boro pub where one lad went in to offer the home mob out. As the locals poured out they were met with a hail of missiles. Boro were pinned in the pub but it wasn't long before reinforcements arrived and soon complete chaos broke out. There was more than a little relief amongst the heavily outnumbered Hull lads when the police arrived. One group of Hull didn't get much further after police searched their van and discovered a fireman's axe, a weighted cosh, Stanley blades and some Hull City calling cards. Twenty-two Hull fans were arrested and charged under Section 5 but the charges were eventually thrown out after the judge queried how two officers could possibly have signed off all the charge sheets.

Hooliganism declined in Hull during the late Eighties and early Nineties. This was less to do with the rave scene but more to do with a poor team and second-rate opposition. The drop-off nationally was most felt in the top flight where all-seater stadiums and the newly formed Premiership, coupled with the lasting impact of the police undercover operations, dissuaded many old-school hooligans. In years gone by Hull's home matches against the likes of Liverpool and Chelsea would have guaranteed mass disorder, but not in the new age of football. Even away cup games against top flight clubs proved quiet. Hull took huge mobs to Newcastle, Villa, Derby and Bolton, only to encounter even greater numbers of replica-shirt-wearing "normals".

An exception was Birmingham, who never failed to put on a show, and on a visit to Hull they headed straight to the Silver Cod pub near the ground. "We knew Birmingham were in the Silver Cod and that would be our next stop," said a Hull lad. "We made out as though the main section were going straight on towards the ground but, as we approached Cod from the opposite side of the road, we all bolted across, barged through the doors, and steamed right in. There wasn't any time for posturing outside, it was now or never. The Birmingham lads didn't fuck about either; we were met with full resistance as they hurled stools and glasses and all manner of fixtures and fittings. The Zulus took a few casualties but they were game lads right up to the arrival of the police.

"Satisfied that they'd taken care of business, Hull swarmed out of Cod. It was going off down the road with another group of Birmingham and we all aimed for the action. I could see that a couple of their boys were Rastas and one was being dragged around by his dreadlocks. A couple of his mates came to his aid and managed to get him away before the arrival of our main firm. They retreated to the car park, where they had larger numbers. A group of thirty Zulus, many hooded up, stood apart to the left. These looked the part. They waited until Hull followed the retreating Brummies on to the car park and then came at us from the side … You could always rely on the Zulus to make things interesting."

The Hull mob became known as the Silver Cod Squad, after the pub that was normally their match day base, or sometimes simply The Minority. As a result, the Cod became the focus for enemy attack, with fights occurring inside it with Plymouth, Huddersfield and Crystal Palace. One of the fiercest battles there was against Stoke City in 1986, the first time the two clubs had played one another for nine years. Stoke arrived early and were drinking in the Cod when the locals launched a counter-attack. Stoke took several injuries, including one lad who was blinded after being hit by a glass ashtray.

Others who occupied the Cod were followers of Blyth Spartans, in Hull for an FA Cup tie. Few locals believed that Blyth would bring a mob and so they were unprepared. Of course, the away following included a contingent of Newcastle lads. They set up base in the Cod and dished out a few slaps to anyone in their way. Even after Hull regrouped and attacked, the Geordies held firm.

By the mid-Nineties, Hull's numbers began increasing again and so did the frequency of disorder. The catalyst for this revival was the final game of the 1996 season when Hull hosted Bradford City. Hull were already relegated but Bradford still had the chance of promotion. To make matters worse, the visitors were given the South Stand, the traditional home of Hull's hardcore.

There was a major pitch invasion even before kick-off as more than 150 Hull fans swarmed from the North Stand towards the Bradford supporters in the South. Mounted police were brought in to prevent further trouble and a flare was thrown from the South Stand. The match kicked off on time and within minutes the home side were ahead. With the game only ten minutes old, a Bradford equaliser precipitated another pitch invasion. Both sides clashed on the pitch as police officers raced on in a desperate bid to separate them. The players were told to keep in the middle of the pitch as Bradford city manager Chris Kamara appealed to the thousands of away fans. It took almost ten minutes for order to be restored and eventually the game continued.

The start of the second half sparked further trouble as fighting broke out on the terracing. Young fans were seen being led away in tears while older supporters were taken out with blood streaming down their faces. Hull's chairman later revealed that the match commander was seconds away from abandoning the game after another pitch invasion followed Bradford's next goal. "Fortunately, common sense prevailed so we could get the game going," the chairman said. There was further

trouble at the final whistle as Hull fans prevented the away supporters from leaving the ground.

Police intelligence that Bradford would bring no more than 2,000 fans was clearly wrong – they had 5,500 at the game. The club announced that anyone arrested and convicted for the disorder would be banned for life, while the local paper ran with the front page headline, "Shame on City." More than 50 Hull fans were convicted and banned following the game.

Hull City settled down in the bottom division, having to content themselves with derbies against Mansfield, Lincoln, Doncaster and Scunthorpe. They would regularly take a couple of hundred lads away to these towns but it was hardly the glamour ties of Chelsea or Manchester United. Still there were some battles, such as Lincoln in the 1999/2000 season, and Scunthorpe, who made a surprise appearance, in numbers, at Hull.

By the late Nineties, Hull's travelling army was a shadow of the mobs that travelled away in the Seventies or even to the likes of Tranmere in the Eighties. There were still plenty around for really big games, as was evidenced by the 700-800 mobilised for the visit of Leeds in a pre-season friendly in 2002. A combination of less attractive games, bans and poor opposition all contributed to declining turnouts, but Hull simply didn't need really big mobs anymore. Many of the teenagers who cut their teeth on the terraces of the early Seventies continued to be active in the late Nineties but were now seasoned veterans who had formed a tight bond and were considerably older and bigger than most of their opposition.

Some of Hull's best fights in recent years have been when some of these older lads were caught in the lower division towns against much bigger numbers. Chesterfield, Carlisle and Shrewsbury all found this to their cost between 1999 and 2001. A trip to Shrewsbury exemplifies this point perfectly. Only 15 Hull made the trip where they successfully confronted a mob of 50 of Shrewsbury's English Border Front. "Years before, we had been young men battling older, harder opponents," reflected Tordoff. "Now the roles were reversed and I know which side of the fence I'd rather be on. Age does make a difference. Younger firms will only stand a chance against an older foe if they outnumber them and even then it would be touch and go. We found the best way to tackle older groups was to try and break them up, isolate a few and then attack, but it is hard to do that to a firm like Hull's. We stay together and fight together; we're in it together. That comes with years of experience and knowing who is by your side, and if you've experienced that you're a lucky man."

Hull's status as one of the best mobs in recent years was clearly evident on the Friday evening of 2 March 2001. One hundred and twenty took the day off work and travelled six hours down to Cardiff for a night match. They drank in Cardiff city centre and, after the game, ran the small Cardiff crew in the car park outside the ground. The home mob was caught unprepared.

Another Friday night game brought Hull back into the national headlines when a pre-season friendly at home to Middlesbrough was overshadowed by violence. "After catching the locals off guard, Boro left an empty Silver Cod and moved down the road to a pub called Tam Tams," said Tordoff. "A seething mob of Hull arrived from Beverley Road, where they had been waiting for Boro, and proceeded to move towards Tam Tams. Boro poured out and, after a small skirmish, a stand off ensued with the police between both sets of supporters. Boro took up residence in Tam Tams whilst a growing number of Hull stood outside Cod, waiting for movement. As a double decker bus arrived to pick up the Boro Frontline, a large mob of Hull ran at a line of police and bombarded them with bricks, forcing the police to retreat. A second surge was met with more police resistance and the mob broke up into smaller numbers. Boro were taken to a local park where they remained until the match was over or, as the police put it, were left there in the interests of public safety.

The *Hull Daily Mail* was supplied with a video shot by a local resident from which they reproduced a number of stills of the fighting. "Name Them," demanded the front page headline. An accompanying comment piece urged readers to help police "track down the thugs who brought shame on our city". It went on, "No doubt many of the morons were feeling pleased with their exploits over the weekend. However, little did they realise their every move was being captured on video by a resident living nearby. The tape has been handed over to the *Mail*, and we are today joining forces with Humberside Police in an attempt to bring the hooligans to book. There is only one place for people like that – behind bars. So, please, if you know who any of these thugs are please pick up the phone, call the police and name them." Local people responded and 18 Hull supporters received prison sentences and were banned for life from the new KC Stadium.

Moving to the purpose-built stadium, and successive promotions, have breathed new life into Hull City FC. Back among the second-tier of English football, and with a potentially massive support base, the omens are good for success on the pitch. It is all a long way from Sinbad and the Monte Carlo Mob, but the authorities should be wary of thinking that the "Minority" has yet disappeared.

Further reading: *City Psychos,* Shaun Tordoff (Milo Books)

I

IPSWICH TOWN

Ground: Portman Road
Firms: Ipswich Punishment Squad, North Stand Boys
Rivals: Norwich

Ipswich's followers have a bad press among football "lads" around the country. Their fans are dismissed as "tractor boys" and their mob is laughed at as a joke. There are few newspaper reports of violence involving Ipswich Town and fewer stories about the successes of their hooligan outfit, the Ipswich Punishment Squad. But, like every other club, they have had hooligans and have a history.

As far back as December 1968, 14 fans were arrested after an Ipswich home game against West Bromwich Albion. What was different about this incident, as opposed to previous outbreaks of violence in Ipswich was that it involved home fans.

"In the past we had trouble mainly from visiting fans but, unfortunately, their behaviour now seems to have rubbed off on local lads," said a police spokesman.

Ipswich were one of the surprise teams of the 1970s and early 1980s. Under the stewardship of Bobby Robson, and with the Continental talents of Arnold Muhren and Frans Thijssen, coupled with home stars like Terry Butcher, Alan Brazil, Russell Osman and John Wark, they won the FA Cup in 1978, the UEFA Cup in 1981 and were runners-up in Division One in both 1981 and 1982. Success brought them European football, but it also brought trouble.

In November 1973, Ipswich reached the last 16 of the UEFA Cup by beating Lazio 6–4 on aggregate. The second leg was in Rome and the Italian fans responded to their team's defeat by targeting the visiting team. Bottles, cans and bits of wood were thrown on to the pitch and several Italians attempted to confront the referee. Bobby Robson was indignant, especially after one of his players was attacked in the tunnel at the end of the game. "What upset me so much was that first of all I could have brought back five or six seriously injured players," he said. "And worse still, someone could have been killed after the match. We had to carry David Best into the dressing room. I locked the door but they were banging on it, trying to get in. On top of that, as one of their players went berserk in the tunnel, their officials stood by watching. The same man who injured Johnson in the first leg – and he had eight stitches in his groin – chased him off the field afterwards. He had to run for his life. If this is football at this level, I don't think we want any more of it."

Off the field, the 200 travelling Ipswich fans also had a miserable time. Italian riot police fired tear gas into the crowd, a fan's Union Jack was ripped down and burnt and the team coach was stoned. After the game, Lazio fans surrounded an ambulance and ripped open the doors in the belief that the referee was hiding inside.

Most of the early trouble at Portman Road came from visiting London clubs, whose fans saw a trip to East Anglia as a bit of beano. In December 1974, 36 fans were arrested before, during and after the home game against Spurs. Twenty-eight of these were from London, eight were local. Most were charged under the Public Order Act. They included two 17-year-old girls from London; one was charged with carrying an offensive weapon, and the other with threatening behaviour.

Two seasons later, Spurs were again the cause of disorder, with trouble before and after the match at Portman Road. Of the 26 arrested, all but three were from London. Shoppers were subjected to abuse as hundreds of Spurs fans paraded through the town

An ill-fated attempt by Ipswich Town to 'take' the Den in New Cross, south London, during an FA Cup tie ended with a ferocious assault by Millwall thugs on the visitors, many of whom were forced to leave the ground early.

centre. Police were also called to supervise the travel of 50 Spurs supporters who kicked off trouble on a local train from Chelmsford. There was also trouble the previous evening as many Spurs fans arrived early. A group of 15 Spurs were turned away from the Falcon pub, where they had caused substantial damage on their last visit, and the pub's DJ suffered three fractured fingers when a window was slammed shut on his hand after he had told Spurs fans to stop throwing bottles. The local paper placed the blame on drink and backed MPs' calls to ban the sale of alcohol at football grounds. The fear of possible violence at the home match against Chelsea the following season caused the club to erect crash barriers.

Very occasionally, Ipswich exported trouble. Bristol Rovers' Chris Brown recalled Ipswich taking Bristol City in a game that led to 17 arrests. A more surprising incident occurred at an away FA Cup tie at Millwall, which turned out to be one of the most violent days at the old Den.

In March 1978, a mob of Ipswich fans travelled to South London intent on trouble and infiltrated the home end. Maybe they were unaware of the home club's hooligan reputation, maybe they were drunk, maybe they were very brave, whatever the reason, they were very stupid. Their presence caused a huge, angry and brutal backlash from Millwall fans. The final spark for the major trouble was when a 24-year-old Ipswich fan, David King, ran onto the pitch holding aloft a scarf and chanting, "Ipswich for the Cup." King jeered and taunted Millwall fans who responded by running on the pitch in an attempt to attack him, but ended up fighting with the police.

Millwall were later to exact their revenge by hunting down and attacking Ipswich fans within the ground. So ferocious was the onslaught that 200 Ipswich fans felt forced to leave the ground early. The game was featured on *Match of the Day* and the images of battered and bloodied Ipswich fans spilling on to the pitch as punches and missiles rained down on them were watched by millions that Saturday night.

There was further trouble after the game. During a fight on a train, several Ipswich thugs threw a Millwall fan off, and he narrowly avoided death when he landed only inches from a live rail. One 23-year-old Ipswich fan, a court heard, leapt from one train, sprinted across the track and climbed on to another platform to join in the attack. The accused told magistrates that he had been provoked because of missiles that had been thrown at him. "Most of my mates are in hospital after being beaten up. I'm sorry for the trouble I've caused but I came out of the ground early because we were attacked there." The court's public gallery had to be cleared after many of the football fans packed in there giggled and laughed at comments made during the hearings. A furious magistrate ordered police to throw them out, saying, "This is a serious matter that I am dealing with, not an amusement. It is not funny and if they find it so they can enjoy it outside."

One of Ipswich's most consistent opponents has been Arsenal. There were regular clashes at Portman Road throughout the Seventies but this became even more intense after Ipswich beat Arsenal in the FA Cup Final in 1978. When Arsenal travelled to Ipswich the following season, hundreds of their supporters were bent on trouble. It coincided with a revival in Arsenal's hooligan mob and in the ensuing melee 58 people were arrested.

"Ipswich meant nothing to us," remembered one Arsenal fan. "They were regarded as a small-time club in a small-time town with no hooligan mob worth bothering with. The year they beat us in the Cup changed all that; they somehow won one-nil. The following year we decided to go down there and the majority of us were penned in the corner of the away end. It was a shit section and the thick wire fence segregating us meant you saw very little action if the ball was down that end. They were taunting us about the Cup Final and a few simply climbed over the wall and went into their section and it went off. A few more joined them and in minutes half the Arsenal lot were in there. Many were arrested and the scenes were shown on TV. From then on they always seemed to turn out for us and we had trouble every time we went there for years afterwards. Every town has local hard men and nutcases and they all must have come out of the woodwork when we went there, as I don't know any other club who ever saw a punch thrown at Portman Road."

The Arsenal fan was right. Very few of the many lads interviewed for this book experienced any bother at Ipswich. The few that did remembered the occasional outbreak of vandalism by their own fans and very little else, although one Villa fan did admit

to getting a hiding there. "The worst pasting I ever took was at Ipswich in the late Seventies. As you do after a load of lager, a mob of Villa lads went round to their end and we thought it would be breeze in the park. I'm not ashamed to say we got put on our arses, which proves it can happen anywhere."

One Newcastle fan complained about the way the police treated them on their visits to Suffolk. "The two times I've been there, the police had the bars closed because we used to terrorise the locals. It was a bad place for us and we always lost the match. The police used to hate Newcastle down there in the Eighties, and basically couldn't cope. The pitch was always one of the best to play football on, it's a shame we couldn't play football."

Such was the club's belief that no hooligan problems would arise at Ipswich in the mid-Eighties that they came up with a bizarre system of segregating home and away fans. Those with tickets for the away end were situated behind the goal. To their left were the Ipswich followers and along the far side of the pitch, in the upper tier of the stand, were the away fans with seat tickets. This meant that the couple of thousand away fans had to walk through thousands of home fans to reach their transport with no escort, while the fans in the standing section were escorted by police. In theory it was OK, as the belief that the fans paying extra to sit down would hardly be of a troublesome nature. However, as trends changed it was soon the thugs who went in the seats. After several high profile games ended with chaos in the streets after the match, the club did a quick rethink and relocated away fans.

The club's main rivals are East Anglian neighbours Norwich, and over the years this as been the one game guaranteed to bring lads from both sides out. It was always a major headache for the police. In April 1980, 16 people were arrested after the teams met at Portman Road. After a few seasons apart, the clubs met again in the Milk Cup semi-final. The first leg was at Ipswich and there was considerable violence after the game when 150 Norwich were ambushed by an equal number of Ipswich. Sixteen people were arrested.

At the second leg, even Norwich were impressed with what Ipswich brought. John, a Norwich thug at the time, said, "I went for a nose in a pub called the Woolpack, as some young lad told me they had landed early, and I was fucking amazed with what they had with them and made a swift exit. A couple of seasons later things got a bit out of hand when blades were handed out before we were due to meet them and one of their lads was cut up outside the old cattle market, which wasn't for me. Another time there, we were split up and ended up roaming around the Whitton Estate. We were bombarded with stuff from the flats and it's an experience I never want to repeat."

The hatred between the two mobs peaked in 1999, when the police received information that Norwich fans had made petrol bombs for their derby fixture against Ipswich. A search of wasteland near the train station found two Molotov cocktails. A bomb disposal team dealt with the situation.

In recent years there have been only sporadic incidents of violence. At a home game against West Ham in October 2000, 40 Ipswich supporters taunted and goaded their opponents outside a pub where the Londoners were drinking. Police held the West Ham group in the pub and the Ipswich lads then confronted police, who used batons and CS spray.

Some of the worst violence for many years occurred during the visit of Portsmouth in April 2003, when Pompey fans drinking in the Drum and Monkey pub in Princes Street, a regular haunt for visitors, were attacked. "A bloodied Ipswich Town fan was rushed to hospital amid the worst scenes of football violence in the town for years," reported the local paper. A mass brawl developed involving dozens of fans from both sides and spilling out into the street. Windows were broken and furniture destroyed and paramedics were called upon to treat several walking wounded. The most seriously injured man was taken to Ipswich Hospital suffering facial cuts. But, despite eyewitness reports that he was covered in blood, a police spokesman said his injuries were not serious.

"More than 30 police officers descended on the scene and quickly brought the situation under control. Town fans were separated from their Portsmouth rivals and physically herded across the street into Riley's snooker club. A tense hour-long stand-off across Princes Street was relieved after police escorted a group of Portsmouth supporters to the railway station. Drum and Monkey landlord Dave West described the scenes as 'totally out of control'. He said, 'The windows alone will cost thousands of pounds and then there's the furniture. I've only been here ten weeks. We are really upset with these football hooligans. All we are doing is trying to provide a service for people and they have let us down.' Inspector Martin Barnes-Smith said the fighting followed seven arrests during the game after supporters clashed."

Days like that are few and the Ipswich lads blame the lack of opposition rather than the claim that they don't have a mob. "No-one is saying we are anywhere near as good as even the most average of firms in the league, but to say we have nobody is utter bollocks," claimed one. "The problem is, because of our family club reputation, very few, if any, firms come here looking for trouble, and on the odd occasion we travel, firms complain that they never expected us to show. Everton came one year for some reason and we will never agree what happened. Our shout is we arranged to meet them at a certain time, we had numbers that day, and some of our lot who saw them admitted they looked impressive. But they marched around town, whacked a few youth who were a bit too impatient and brought OB into play. They then complained when a couple of their lippy lads got their noses bust after the game. They came again the year after for revenge. Let it drop. A coachload of balding bouncers in their late thirties looking for us three hours after the match ended, what's all that about?"

Despite the efforts of the minority, there is no doubt that Ipswich pride themselves on being a family, trouble-free club. They even refuse sponsorship from independent club fanzines because bad language is used in them. In recent years the club has consistently had one of the lowest arrest rates in the top two divisions, and the mayor of Helsingborg and the head of police in Milan both praised the club's fans for their behaviour in the UEFA Cup. It's music to the ears of the club, the local police and the overwhelming majority of supporters, but not the kind of praise the local hooligans want to hear.

K

KIDDERMINSTER HARRIERS

Ground: Aggborough Stadium
Firm: The Railway Army
Rivals: Cheltenham

Kidderminster Harriers does not have a hooligan problem. That's the official line that the club and the media peddle, and they have a point. During the 2003/2004 season there was not a single arrest at their ground, leading one national newspaper to describe them as "the stars of the Third Division" in an article about disruptive football fans.

Of course, that is not the complete story. Kidderminster Harriers, like every other football club, has a hooligan group and it is called the Railway Army. In November 2000 they were involved in a fight in Kidderminster when the club played Burton Albion in the first round of the FA Cup. An NCIS log described how 30 Burton fans, many of whom were actually Derby County hooligans, were attacked by the Railway Army as they were being escorted back to the train station. The local paper went into a bit more detail, stating that as trouble had been expected many locals were unimpressed with policing on the day.

"Police have defended their action to let football thugs into the town after fighting broke out on Saturday. Pub licensees were shocked to find about 30 hooligans on the rampage after Kidderminster Harriers' clash against Burton Albion despite prior warnings thugs were expected. Nine were arrested after fighting broke out outside the Farmers pub,

Comberton Hill, at about 5pm and trouble flared as police and hooligans had a two-hour stand-off at the railway station. The yobs, mainly Derby County 'fans', refused to board one train but finally left under police escort at about 9pm.

"Kidderminster Police duty inspector Ian Massey explained the police were powerless to prevent the thugs from entering the town. He said: 'We received intelligence reports they were coming but were powerless to turn them away. It would be an infringement of their civil liberties.' Police spotters identified troublemakers and those causing offences were arrested. Insp Massey said: 'Although there were a number of ugly scenes these were caused by a minority of people. There were no reports of serious injuries or extensive damage.'"

Railway Bell landlord Bill Campbell, one of many licensees who closed their doors on police advice, was aghast the hooligans were allowed in town and incensed it took four hours for them to go after fighting broke out. "The police talk about civil liberties," he said. "What about our civil liberties and all those people who were frightened on the hill? The police had riot gear. Why didn't they just steam in and get rid of them?"

The club's trouble-free tag vanished the season after being hailed as an example to all. In March 2005, there was serious disorder during Kidderminster's home clash with local rivals Cheltenham. Police dogs and baton-wielding officers were required to restore order after the local commander admitted that the situation had got out of hand. Four arrests were made.

L

LEEDS UNITED

Ground: Elland Road
Firms: Service Crew, Infant Hit Squad, Intensive Care Unit, Very Young Team.
Rivals: Man Utd, Sheffield Utd, Chelsea
Police operations: Wild Boar

It was a dramatic fall from grace. No team has the right to remain in the top flight, but Leeds United's rapid decline startled their own supporters as much as it amused their rivals. Between 1965 and 1975, Leeds had won the League twice, been runners-up five times, and finished either third or fourth in the remainder. They had twice won the Fairs (now UEFA) Cup, played two more European semi-finals, won two FA Cups, and lost two finals. In May 1975 the club reached the European Cup Final, and their fans still complain that poor decisions by the match officials cheated them of victory. It marked the pinnacle of the Glory Years, but also the beginning of the decline.

Within a few years, most of their star players had retired or moved on. Don Revie was a memory and Leeds were struggling. The fans continued to sing, "We are the champions, champions of Europe," to the amusement of many, as they had never actually won Europe's number one prize, and this highlighted their decline. The only saving grace for Leeds fans as they watched their team draw 3-3 away at West Brom, a result that confirmed their relegation, was that Manchester United, for all their money and bluster, had failed to win the League for fifteen years.

Violence had accompanied Leeds for many years. In January 1970, Leeds fans took Stoke City's home end, much to the fury of local supporters. Sixty-one people were taken to hospital, with 14 detained, many with serious head injuries. In the same year they were forced to play four games behind closed doors after fans ran onto the pitch and attacked the referee. A couple of years later they took the kop at Sheffield United. When the *Daily Mirror* launched a "League of Shame" in May 1973, Leeds finished seventh, with 181 arrests at Elland Road. Police announced that they were happy that hooliganism was declining, but the following year arrests leapt to 239 and Leeds were up to third.

In 1975, their fans rioted in Paris following a 2-0 defeat to Bayern Munich and the club was banned from European competitions for two years. Leeds fans attacked German supporters before the match, then Peter Lorimer's disallowed goal marked the beginning of several hours of violence. A German TV operator lost an eye and a TV camera was wrecked. Hundreds of seats were ripped up and thrown as missiles at police and rival fans, windows were smashed and private property damaged. Leeds had only recently been fined for the misbehaviour of their supporters in Belgium.

Domestically, Leeds fans battled their way across the country, clashing with Manchester United and City, Cardiff, the Sheffield and Merseyside clubs, and were universally despised. In January 1981, a seventeen-year-old fan died when Leeds were ambushed by Spurs in London, an incident that led to a long-running feud between the two firms. The following season, national news headlines accompanied Leeds's troublesome support after they clashed with West Ham's ICF both home and away. Relegation followed the Yorkshire club's worst season for many years, and around the country rival fans cheered their demise.

As they slipped down into Division Two, their mob, the Leeds Service Crew – formed in 1980 and named after the local service trains they took in preference to the heavily policed special trains – was to earn national, even international, notoriety. In doing so, they also almost brought the club to its knees.

Leeds marked their departure from Division One at West Brom by ripping apart the Midlands club's ground. Thirty-four police officers and 13 fans were injured as an estimated 3,000 Leeds hooligans pulled down the nine-foot-high security fence. To shouts of, "Kill them," they clashed with police on the pitch and outside the ground. Both clubs were subsequently cleared of responsibility for the violence, but the FA ordered Leeds to print a warning to their fans in every programme that season, advising them of the consequences of future misbehaviour. A relieved Leeds chairman, Manny Cousins, admitted to being "happy with the result".

The FA's warning fell on deaf ears. Only two weeks after the verdict on the West Brom disturbances, Leeds were misbehaving again. Their first game in Division Two was at Grimsby. Six hundred turned up in Cleethorpes the night before and, as *The Sun* reported, went on "an orgy of drinking, looting and fighting, and turned a quiet seaside resort into a town of terror." FA Secretary Ted Croker said he was furious – but did nothing. "The FA intends to take strong action against persistent misconduct by fans," he said, impotently. Grimsby Town were not impressed and withheld Leeds's £16,000 match fee to cover repairs to their damaged ground.

There was despair at Elland Road after the Newcastle game in October when two Newcastle players, including England star Kevin Keegan, were hit by missiles, and the FA ordered yet another inquiry. The next home game saw a plea to fans in the match programme: "The future of Leeds United Association Football Club hangs in the balance. This in no way exaggerates the position and must not be taken as an idle threat. Despite repeated pleas and warnings, the mindless actions of a minority of the club's so-called followers last Saturday have placed an enormous degree of uncertainty over this great club. We know from comments received in the last few days that many true supporters deplore what took place at the Newcastle game. We would ask for the help and cooperation of everyone who has Leeds United at heart – and we appreciate that this is the majority of our supporters – to help rid this

club of the 'scab' element who, although small in number, have caused so many problems and whose loathsome actions now place the very existence of Leeds United in jeopardy."

In the New Year, Leeds fans were again in the national news as they ripped up more than 500 seats inside Derby's Baseball Ground and there was no disguising the seriousness of this latest outbreak of disorder. Derby chairman Mike Watterson said: "What happened today was not just a disgrace to football, it was a disgrace to humanity. I've never seen anything like it in my life, these people are worse than animals." *The Times* back page headline summed up the severity of the situation. "Riot that could be the end of Leeds United," it read.

Two months earlier, following the Football Association inquiry into the Newcastle missile-throwing incident, the club had been forced to close its terraces for two home games. Chairman Manny Cousins said that United, with debts running at £2 million, could not afford the cost of ground closure, and fearing the worst after the Derby riot, the club returned 1,200 of the 1,600 tickets it had been given for the following week's FA Cup game at Arsenal. The London club understood Leeds's motives but knew that they were flawed as ticketless away fans desperate to see the game would now be forced to get access to the home end. Their fears were confirmed when rivals clashed inside the ground. The Leeds board also made a direct appeal to the Government for stiffer sentences against hooligans.

Once again Leeds had an understanding FA to back their corner, with Ted Croker publicly sympathising with their plight and accepting that the club was doing all it could to stamp out the hooliganism. And Leeds officials were again smiling when the FA investigation reported that although both Leeds and Derby were guilty of failing to take reasonable precautions to control their fans, they were let off with a severe warning of a harsher punishment for any future misbehaviour. "It is a very difficult problem and difficult to find a solution," said FA Chairman Bert Millichip.

Hopes of bouncing straight back into the top flight were fast disappearing and, as most of the recognisable players left Elland Road to be replaced by unknowns, Leeds fans settled for another season of mediocrity. The club was stuck in the shadow of Revie and the choice of successive Leeds managers –

Billy Bremner, Allan Clarke, Eddie Gray – who had all played under the Great Don did little to bring in a new era.

The new season started fairly quietly, even when Portsmouth turned up with 300 lads in October. In what was an occasional criticism of Leeds from the larger firms, the home hooligans were nowhere to be seen before the game. "I was very disappointed with Leeds," remembered Portsmouth 6.57 veteran Rob Silvester. "What I had heard before I went was that we were going to encounter a lot of trouble." However, he admits that when Leeds went to the south coast the following season, the Yorkshire mob went right to the Pompey turnstiles, a rare feat.

At around the same time, Leeds clashed with Sheffield Wednesday before an away fixture, and attempts by 200 Leeds to start trouble away at Middlesbrough was only stopped by the quick use of police dogs. In November, a missile thrown by Leeds fans floored Carlisle's goalkeeper and darts were among the items retrieved from the pitch.

The Eighties saw a number of violent clashes with Chelsea, with whom Leeds fans had had an enmity since the mid-Sixties. The clubs met in an FA Cup semi-final and an outclassed Chelsea side won by a single goal. Leeds fans believed they had been robbed by what appeared to be a good goal, through a Peter Lorimer free-kick, which was disallowed after the referee judged an encroachment by the Chelsea wall. Revenge was reaped the following season on and off the pitch. Leeds hammered Chelsea 7-0 and there was an even more comprehensive defeat on the terraces, with many Londoners literally fleeing for their lives. The mood was soured still further by some strong words by Don Revie to the waiting press; in response, one Chelsea fan sent the Leeds manager excrement in the post. The two sides met again in the 1970 FA Cup Final, which the Londoners won in a replay.

This hatred spilled out onto the terraces as the two big clubs under-performed in Division Two and the respective hooligan firms vied for the position of England's worst. While West Ham and Millwall were arguably more violent and organised, the Service Crew's hatred of them never reached the levels set aside for Chelsea. The rivalry was given extra spice through the pages of the National Front's *Bulldog* magazine; with both sets of hooligans having sizeable NF support (which West Ham and Millwall did not) they competed for the title of the most racist in the country.

For Leeds, any away trip at Chelsea was one to mob-up for and the Service Crew put out a leaflet calling for their supporters to make an extra special effort for one match. "These leaflets are for the loyal supporters of Leeds United FC, not the Christmas trees who sing Chelsea here we come in the safety of the Gelderd then do not show on the day. We are not ground wreckers. This sort of incident just attracts more pigs and other trouble such as the FA inquiries, which Leeds United do not want and cannot really afford. The Service Crew do not need a police escort. WE are the hardest in the land and have proved this everywhere. SCUM, YIDS and even WEST HAM have had to be honest and admit this. It was The Service Crew who stood at Upton Park and the market. No other team in the land has done this to West Ham. Scum ran all over the place. Yids are scared to go there, in fact all cockneys fear West Ham, but LEEDS don't. We fear no-one in England. The Service Crew always stand together. Today we will show Chelsea what we think of them ..." It was signed, "Dave, Leeds United Service Crew, National Front."

Police detained 120 Leeds fans on the way to London, but many more made it to the capital and, by chance, bumped into Chelsea's mob at Piccadilly underground station. The Chelsea firm had been prowling the West End without success before deciding to head to Stamford Bridge for a drink. What happened next was described by the *News of the World* as "The Bloody Battle of Platform Four". Chelsea ripped into the Leeds, even chasing some of them off the end of the Tube platforms and into the dark of the tunnels.

There was further humiliation in 1984 as Leeds crashed 5-0 to a rampant Chelsea in a match that saw their fierce rivals promoted. The home fans taunted their northern rivals and stormed the pitch on two occasions. Despite the entreaties of "Dave's" pre-match leaflet, the Leeds responded in trademark fashion, ripping up seats and hurling bottles at the police. A plank went through the electronic scoreboard at the visitors' end. Well over 100 people were arrested, and while Leeds may have come off worse in the tube station fight, their ground-wrecking activities would draw many of the next day's headlines – although one jibe aimed at Leeds by the Headhunters was that their electronic scoreboard couldn't fight back.

If the Leeds United board had hoped the worst was behind them, they were sadly mistaken. The first game of the 1984/85 season was away at Notts County and played against the background of a Miners' Strike in full flow. "It wasn't just the 'mindless few' who were out for trouble," a shocked journalist reported afterwards. "Three or four thousand Leeds 'fans' were set on causing trouble."

The season brought derbies galore, and in the space of three weeks in October, Leeds played Sheffield United and Middlesbrough at home and Barnsley and Huddersfield away. Leeds directors would later complain about the clustering of such potentially explosive games but, as always, this was after the event. While the Blades brought a tidy mob of 300 to Leeds, and there were clashes before the match, the fixture went ahead without major disorder. The same could not be said of the trip to Barnsley, where thousands of Leeds fans waged a pitched battle with rival supporters and the police. Corner flags became improvised javelins and bricks and stones were hurled at a stand containing disabled supporters. "Morons" and "Animals" were just two of the newspaper headlines the following Monday. "These people make miners' pickets seem like gentlemen," said a police officer.

A week later, Leeds fans were rioting again, this time after their side lost away to Huddersfield. Home fans were bombarded with lumps of metal and gobstopper-sized ball bearings. Thirty-four seats were ripped up, windows smashed, doors battered in and the stand's toilet destroyed. Outside the ground, eight cars were damaged and 65 Leeds fans were arrested.

Distraught Leeds manager Eddie Gray had no answers. "I don't blame anyone for staying away from matches when you have trouble such as we experienced on Saturday," he said. "I feel sorry for genuine supporters but there is no way that you could say the trouble on Saturday was being caused by a minority." He announced that his wife and children would not be attending any more away matches. For a family that had Leeds running through its blood, this illustrated how bad things were.

The club was desperate to avoid further trouble but knew it was on borrowed time and risked financial ruin if its doors were closed to fans again. Describing the troublemakers as "vermin", a new club secretary announced a raft of measures to combat hooliganism. A meeting was held between the club, the supporters' club and the police. Away tickets, it was agreed, were only to be sold to members of the official supporters' club and season ticket holders, and lines of police were to be positioned inside Elland Road to break up large groups of fans and identify troublemakers.

The Service Crew's response was made clear a month later when they stopped an away match at Oxford. Six-foot-long planks were ripped from a TV gantry and hurled onto the pitch and the Oxford goalkeeper was struck on the head by a missile. Eddie Gray came close to pulling off his players and conceding the game.

The Service Crew were out for revenge when it travelled to Sheffield in March for what was the first visit to the Steel City since 1978. Leeds arrived mob-handed but Sheffield were waiting with 600 lads, the numbers bolstered by a leaflet drop around local pubs in the preceding few weeks. After skirmishes before and during the game, and the obligatory seat throwing, the real action took place in the city centre afterwards. Even the Blades Business Crew, normally dismissive of the "vandals" and "seat throwers" of Leeds, acknowledged their Yorkshire rivals' prowess that day.

The final game of the season was away at Birmingham, home of the notorious Zulus. Everyone knew that this was the big one, a battle between two of the country's worst hooligan gangs. The fears were realised almost as soon as the first ball was kicked and it was only a matter of time before the two baying mobs got at each other. The half-time whistle was the signal for battle to commence and as the players departed down the tunnel, hundreds of fans from both sides swarmed onto the pitch. Bricks, bottles and planks of wood were used as improvised weapons and, when those had been exhausted, it was back to feet and fists. The police tried in vain for over half an hour to separate the crowds but the second half still began 42 minutes late. Fighting continued well after the match, with an estimated 4,000 people involved. The Chief Constable of West Midlands Police described it as the worst incident of its type in his career.

The carnage left terrible casualties. A fifteen-year-old Leeds fan from Northampton, attending his first game, was killed after being crushed by a collapsing wall. Another 500 people, including dozens of police officers, suffered some kind of injury. The trouble received widespread coverage and once again, the club was in the dock. Yet an even worse tragedy befell football that day, when a devastating fire at Bradford City's ground killed 56 supporters.

It was British football's darkest day, shortly to be followed by the Heysel Disaster in Belgium. The Government were forced to intervene and set up an inquiry into crowd violence and safety under the stewardship of Lord Popplewell. Yet again fate smiled on Leeds after the judge announced his findings. Both clubs were fined just £5,000 by the FA for not controlling their supporters, and Leeds became the first British club ordered to sell tickets only to fans who identified themselves. *The Times*'s verdict of the punishment was typical. "The FA response is totally inadequate," it boomed. "It flexed its puny muscles and delivered a blow of customary stunning weakness." There was palpable relief at Elland Road.

The Service Crew was under the media and police spotlight and the new ticket restrictions meant that they found it increasingly difficult to get large numbers into grounds. But they found a way when they played at Millwall three months into the new season. There was a chill in the air that November afternoon as hundreds of Millwall thugs awaited the arrival of Leeds. The clubs had not played each other for several years and the capital's meanest wanted to remind the mob of Yorkshiremen who were the top boys. Leeds took a mob of 500 down but were still outnumbered by Millwall, who swarmed out of the pubs as they arrived, bombarding them with bricks and bottles. Police appeared to withdraw as the trouble began, only to return to arrest the injured littering the street. Trouble continued throughout the game and four officers were injured, one struck in the face with a brick. Leeds fans were once again banned from attending away matches but hooligan-fatigue meant that this incident received no more than six lines in the *Yorkshire Post* and nothing in the evening paper. The people of Leeds, and its journalists, were getting tired of reporting more bad news.

The rest of the season passed with little incident and it appeared that the ban on away fans was working. Violence, of course, did not disappear from home games, and in August 1986, a mob of 40 Birmingham fans attacked a Leeds pub, chanting "Zulus" and letting off CS gas, and two people were

stabbed in the ensuing fight. However, this was an isolated incident and, in September 1986, the ban on Leeds fans attending away fixtures was lifted.

The timing could not have been worse. The first fixture was away to Bradford, now temporarily housed at the Odsall Stadium following the awful fire at Valley Parade sixteen months earlier. Some Leeds followers appeared to have little respect for their close neighbours and even less for the victims of the dreadful fire. Two minutes into the game, a chip van was set alight and pushed down the terrace as hundreds of Leeds fans clambered over the fences in an attempt to confront the terrified Bradford supporters. Leeds fans then turned on the police with bricks and bottles. Bradford won the game 2-0 in front of an almost deserted ground.

Another day of violence, another FA Inquiry. "The louts of Leeds have got away with it for far too long," opined the *Daily Star*. "They have terrorised the terraces, tormented town centres and driven away many decent, honest followers of football. Too often they have been let off the hook. We are sick to the back teeth of the prattling of a succession of managers, directors and administrators who have told us, 'It's only a minority.' That 'minority' has been involved in thirteen savage incidents over the last forty months. Today, we regret to say, the authorities have only one course open to them.

"Leeds United MUST be closed down."

Leeds, yet again, were the pariahs of football, so it must have been with some trepidation that West Bromwich Albion, the scene of the 1982 relegation riot, welcomed them a few weeks later. Their fears were confirmed when Leeds fans used petrol from the club mower to burn down a shed. Seventeen arrests were made and a further 19 people were ejected.

The third round of the FA Cup saw Leeds drawn away at non-League Telford United, and although it should have been the minnows' biggest day, West Mercia Police refused to let the game go ahead, forcing Telford, against their wishes, to concede home advantage. Sports Minister Dick Tracey called it a "sad day for football".

Many people by now had had enough. Around the ground the local Trades Council launched an anti-fascist fanzine in a bid to drive the National Front away as racism had long been a problem among a section of Leeds fans and appeared to get worse as their performances declined on the pitch. Racist chanting mirrored the increase in misbehaviour of Leeds fans and it wasn't uncommon for thousands of home supporters to abuse black players. Michael Brown was just 16 when he played his first game for Shrewsbury Town, away at Leeds. It was a torrid baptism as stand after stand took turns to abuse him. Finally, to great applause from what appeared to be a majority of the crowd, the Kop took its turn. Brown recalls walking back into the changing room at half-time expecting moral support from his teammates. No-one said a word, leaving him to ponder whether he was playing in a different match. Nevertheless, he played a blinder and Shrewsbury won the game 3-2. When the youngster was substituted near the end of the match, many Leeds fans joined the 130-strong away support in clapping him off in appreciation.

The Service Crew were often central to this racist chanting and many were supporters of the National Front. In 1985, Sheffield United travelled to Leeds to be met with a large contingent of the Service Crew giving the visitors a Nazi salute. The Blades had dozens of black lads within their ranks and, as a mark of solidarity, began applauding them individually. "Our response was to get our black lads high up on their colleagues' shoulders," wrote Steve Cowens. "They mockingly sieg-heiled back at the Leeds masses. I admired their guts. Then in a show of respect to our black Blades, all 300 of our boys packed into the 4,000-strong following, sang a tribute to each one of them, to the tune of the 1978 pop hit, 'Black Betty'."

Away from public view, the police were putting together the final elements of an investigation to take out the hooligan ringleaders. The changing mood coincided with the club's best season for years. They reached the semi-final of the FA cup and the Division One play-off final against Charlton, though Leeds were eventually to lose this 2–1 after being ahead with five minutes of extra time to go. An attempt by some of the crowd to rip up the terrace fittings was met by jeers and chants of "You are the scum of Elland Road." It seemed that even their own fans were sick of the continual wanton vandalism.

Operation Wild Boar was run out of a former county council premises close to the West Yorkshire Police training school in Wakefield. Four police offi-cers infiltrated the Leeds mob during the 1986/7 season and catalogued what they saw. Conscious of the difficulties other undercover operations had faced and knowing that two involving Chelsea and West Ham had been thrown out of court, causing great embarrassment to the forces concerned, officers involved in Wild Boar were in constant contact with Crown Prosecution Service lawyers and senior officers.

Heading the undercover team was Sgt Mick Fickling, known to Leeds fans as David "Simmo" Simpson, a window cleaner who did not work much himself because he had young lads working for him. With him was 33-year-old Paul "Gibbo" Gibson, otherwise known as DC Paul Crehan. Bearded and more than 13 stones, he was easily spotted by his shoulder-length flowing hair, flashed with gold streaks. He passed himself off as a South Yorkshire poacher and even supplied the lads with the occasional rabbit or wood pigeon. He was once arrested at Bradford Interchange station, reinforcing his apparent credibility. In late 1987, with the undercover work completed, police raided the homes of eleven Leeds fans, aged between 17 and 30, and charged them with conspiracy to commit affray.

Fickling was the main prosecution witness the following spring. He told the court how he identified the person who he believed was the ringleader and deliberately manipulated himself into the young man's presence and befriended him to the point where the man, later identified as David Brown, confided in him. The racism of the Service Crew was a major element in the nine-week trial. Fickling described travelling away with the group to a match at Ipswich, where he saw 23-year-old Martin Pickard assault a black man, and later boast, "I battered that nigger over there." Another defendant was described as shouting, "Come on nigger. My mate smacked you in the mouth. Come on cunt. Have you got any bananas? I'll cut your liver out." Then more Leeds fans joined in, and a racist chant went up. The man continued to shout abuse at the opposing fan. "Hey, nigger, you're dead boy. You are one dead coon."

Fickling also described a fight in a South London pub before Leeds's away match at Crystal Palace. He said that there was a bang outside the pub and someone shouted, "There's a team of niggers outside." The sergeant said that 21-year-old Patrick Slaughter rushed to the doors of the pub shouting,

"Come on Leeds, everybody out and into them." While some of the attackers ran off a group of five black men came running towards them brandishing knives and bats. Slaughter shouted, "Stand Leeds, stand," but the group ran back into the pub, armed themselves with bar stools and glasses and then went back into the street in search of their attackers.

Cross-examining the officer, lawyers for the defendants claimed that the policeman had "provoked" the fans. The court was even shown a photo of him raising his fists alongside other Leeds fans. "I suggest you were attempting to provoke the group into some action," said barrister Benjamin Nolan. "I have to suggest to you that you were acting as an agent provocateur." Fickling strongly denied this.

Six weeks into the trial, the judge learnt that some of the jurors were worried about reprisals. After the acquittal of two of the defendants, one jury member was overheard saying, "There's no way I am going to say guilty to anything in there." There was a demonstration of applause from the public gallery. During a meal later that evening, yet another juror said to one of the many reporters looking for an exclusive insight into the goings on, "I know we aren't supposed to talk about the trial but can I just say that we are frightened. You can cut the atmosphere in the court with a knife."

The judge showed little sympathy. "A society's only safeguard is a police service prepared to do its duty and juries prepared to do theirs", he declared. His pep talk did the trick and the following day the jury returned guilty verdicts on five of the defendants – David Brown, John Milner, Martin Pickard, Patrick Slaughter, and a 17-year-old boy. The rest were acquitted.

The ringleader of the group was 26-year-old "Para Dave" Brown, the self-styled general of "Para's Little Army". The son of two Salvation Army officers, he joined the Parachute Regiment as a bandsman in 1979 and later progressed to their medical wing. His experiences in the Falklands, where he had treated injured comrades under heavy fire at Goose Green, and the murder of an uncle serving in the Royal Ulster Constabulary four days before he set sail to the South Atlantic, brought on post-traumatic stress disorder. Milner, aged 23, was described as the gang's banker and organiser of a coach known as the "One Punch Battalion Battle Bus". The warehouseman collected money for future trips and kept a log of the Battle Bus trips. Patrick Slaughter was training to become a lawyer and had just passed his second year exams at Huddersfield Polytechnic.

Brown, Milner and Slaughter were all sentenced to four years' imprisonment. Pickard, aged 23, described as a thug but not a ringleader, was given two and a half years, and the teenager got fifteen months in youth custody. The judge simply could not comprehend football hooliganism and at the end of the trial he reminisced about his childhood watching Burnley. "When things did not go as planned on the pitch, men would throw their cloth caps in the air. That seemed to do the trick."

Former Service Crew followers dismissed the trial as an unnecessary waste of time. Interviewed in the *Yorkshire Evening Post*, one veteran claimed the Service Crew was dying anyway by 1985. "If the police had moved in earlier then they would have dropped on a goldmine," he said. "There would have been hundreds of real aggro merchants. But most of the SC lads have gone now. There are still elements left, but it's just the name that sticks. The SC as such was years ago. There are offshoots like the Intensive Care Unit, which is about the biggest now, and the Very Young Team, and there are some hard men left. Being in the SC was something to do on a Saturday. It was like a drug. Once you've been involved in aggro it is hard to get it out of your system."

The violence never totally disappeared but it certainly became less frequent and less intense. This had much to do with a changing atmosphere within Elland Road, a more stringent ticketing policy and a general decline in hooliganism at the time. That was until the 1989/90 season, when Leeds United fans once again made national news on a scale not seen again to this day. No amount of police intelligence and government guidelines can influence the fixtures computer and that season it allocated the Yorkshire masses a seaside resort game over the May Bank Holiday weekend. A trip to Bournemouth, with the bonus that United needed a point to win promotion to Division One, was the kind of fixture hooligans dream of. Despite receiving a ticket allocation of 2,000, more than six times that number made the journey on a sunny holiday weekend, most in the knowledge that they were unlikely to see the game. Being there was all that mattered.

Bournemouth awaited their arrival with trepidation. The police had twice asked for the game to be rearranged, but the Football League bizarrely refused both requests, so the town boarded up as hundreds of officers were put on standby. Only one pub remained open that Friday night as Leeds fans began pouring in, and before long that too was closed, as someone set fire to a cigarette machine. Fighting between police and a couple of hundred bored Leeds fans continued well into the night and later Leeds supporters claimed that the local constabulary did not help matters by roaming the beach late on, moving people who were trying to sleep. With hindsight the police actions hardly fostered good relations between the two groups and set the tone for the rest of the weekend.

The following day was more of the same – much more. Several hours of drinking was followed by several hours of clashes with police outside the ground. Between 2-4,000 Leeds fans, depending on which paper you read, charged hundreds of police before turning and fleeing the advancing cavalry. This ebb and flow continued for hours. The only break in proceedings was when one side or the other upped the intensity of the battle. For Leeds, it was when a rumour went around that the police had run over and killed a fan, and for the police, it was when two fans came out from behind a tree, took a mounted officer off his horse with a branch, and the whisper went round that he had been stabbed to death. Some Leeds fans were clearly out for trouble, but there was also a confrontational policing strategy that did little to defuse the situation. Added to the existing tension was lingering ill-feeling towards the police for their role in the Miners' Strike. "Yorkshire miners," was the repeated chant of hundreds of Leeds.

Kick-off arrived and still the trouble continued. It was only when Leeds went 1–0 up that the seriousness of the events outside the ground became apparent to wiser heads. Here was Leeds United Football Club, on the verge of its greatest achievement for years, and hundreds, if not thousands of fans, were battling with police. Some of the older Leeds supporters began to berate the younger lads. "What do you think you're fucking doing?" one former Service Crew member screamed. "We're going to get kicked out of the League because of you idiots."

The newspapers were full of condemnation of Leeds. "It's WAR!" blared the headline in one. "Leeds fans go berserk at police," was another. "Leeds scum are back," said the *Daily Mirror*. "Kick them out," demanded the chief sportswriter of the *Daily Star*. "Leeds United should be stripped of the Second Division Championship and deducted enough points to prevent them being promoted," wrote Bob Driscoll. The article was accompanied by a photo of Bournemouth players fleeing the pitch as riot police, with several dogs, tried to contain the thousands of Leeds fans pouring on to it. Another paper reproduced a photo of a Leeds fan sticking the boot in to a policeman who lay motionless on the ground.

The *Yorkshire Evening Post* captured the desperation and frustration felt by most Leeds fans: "The greatest day in the history of Leeds for the last eight years, and it had to end like this. Savage scenes of thuggery by a mindless minority wrecked for thousands of true fans the glorious moment when their team made it back to Division One. For the hooligans, the Battle of Bournemouth was not about cheering their team to glory on a sunny day. For this tiny minority it was a chance to use the fist and the boot. It left more than twenty injured and 120 arrested, and it left in serious doubt the question of England teams playing in Europe."

Other English teams were not at the front of Leeds' fans minds when they digested the disorder on the south coast. The survival of their club was again at stake. As three courts began hearing the cases against those arrested, the Labour Party demanded a full inquiry into the "ineffectiveness" of national police intelligence. The Government responded by hinting at "special measures" against Leeds United, while Bournemouth's Tory MP demanded that Leeds be denied promotion – perhaps not realising that would have meant them visiting his town again the following season.

The club was predictably defensive and a rearguard action was mounted by chairman, Leslie Silver. "After Hillsborough when there was a terrible disaster and a major loss of life, nobody was drummed out of any competition," he said. "Fortunately, here, there was no loss of life. Some sympathy should be extended to Leeds. We've tried to ensure there were no problems." Many in the football world felt disgust in Silver comparing the mindless violence at Bournemouth to the horrific disaster that claimed the lives of 96 Liverpool supporters a year earlier. The Leeds supremo remained unrepentant. Even in the days before the Premiership millions poured into the game, top-flight football was the key to his club's survival.

Leeds were lucky that the tabloids also vented much of their spleen at the football authorities who had rejected police advice to rearrange the fixture. In an editorial, the *Mirror* laid the blame firmly at the doorstep of the Football League: "The Bournemouth soccer riot was predictable, predicted and avoidable. Only the Football League turned a blind, and now blackened, eye to the warnings. Yesterday, the League's President, Bill Fox, said, 'with hindsight we have to regret that we did not give the police request any consideration.' What English football, and towns like battered, bruised and bloodied Bournemouth, need isn't hindsight from the men who run football, BUT FORESIGHT. And if they aren't up to the job, they should make way for a controlling supremo who is, before there are more smashed shops and looted pubs, serious injuries or even death."

By the following day, the paper had turned its focus on Leeds. "Twenty ways to make Leeds yobs pay", ran the headline over a two-page story. The suggestions ranged from making Leeds fans pay a £1 levy for every home game, the money to go to the south coast side, to armbands being worn by players as a mark of respect to soccer. The paper joined the chorus who believed that Leeds had set back the chances of English clubs returning to European competitions.

The League was in a difficult position. It had to be seen to act against Leeds, but it too was culpable. As the authorities contemplated their next move, the FA hinted at a total ban on United fans travelling to away games. This was instantly attacked as punishing the majority of well-behaved fans, and also impractical. Chief Supt Dave Clarkson, who oversaw a virtually trouble-free Elland Road, described any such ban as futile. "It would not work because it would not stop fans from going to games," he said. "They would get tickets somehow and that would ruin any plans for segregation."

Lucky Leeds eventually received no more than another ticking off from the football authorities. They were now back in the big league and the racism and violence that accompanied the club during its dark days in Division Two were, it was hoped, distant memories.

* * *

There is no team Leeds fans hate more than Manchester United. The enmity extends beyond simple Pennine rivalry and dates back to the 1960s when the two teams were at the top of British football. In 1965, 1970 and 1977 they met in FA Cup semi-finals, with the first going to a replay, the second going to two replays and the third being finished in one go, but with only one goal separating the teams. With Leeds dominating English football in the late Sixties and early Seventies and United's Red Army emerging as Britain's premier hooligan group, it was probably only natural that the two sets of fans would loathe each other.

In truth, Leeds seemed to hate Man Utd more than the other way round. Leeds had no immediate local footballing rivals, while the Manchester club had City and, of course, the Scousers down the road. The Yorkshire club also suffered a number of high-profile soccer defections to their fierce rivals – Joe Jordan and Gordon McQueen in the Seventies, then, spectacularly, Eric Cantona. More recently Rio Ferdinand and Alan Smith journeyed west along the M62, which did as much for cross-Pennine relations as Adolf Hitler did for world peace.

Most games between the two clubs brought trouble and that was certainly the case in 1972 at Elland Road. Shortly before the final whistle, as the gates were opening, a large group of Leeds charged the away end. Manchester fans were run back to the city centre, where they were hunted down and attacked, and a train ferrying United supporters home was bricked 100 yards out of the station in what was clearly a planned ambush.

In October 1975, Leeds once again hosted Man Utd. There were pitched battles in the streets from 11 a.m. until 6 p.m. and 60 supporters of both sides subsequently appeared at magistrates' court. "The battle of Leeds United was fought on the football ground, in the side streets, and the broad main streets of the city as warring gangs went on the rampage," said prosecutor Ian Pollard. "Police manpower was stretched to the limit. There were 365 officers on special duty with eighty-four inside the ground and 281 outside. They had to deal with battles involving ones and twos, running battles through the streets and pitched battles involving several hundred on each side throwing bricks and stones at each other. Frantic pedestrians had to scurry for safety as bricks whizzed about their ears. They heard the sickening thud of boot against body as those involved were either thrown or beaten to the ground and kicked mercilessly."

The visitors came off worse on that occasion, but two years later Manchester United got their revenge as they ran the Yorkshiremen ragged at the third FA Cup semi-final between the two clubs in 1977 at Hillsborough, Sheffield. The host city was on high alert and erected two ten-foot steel fences at a cost of £6,000. Police feared the worst and put 1,200 officers on duty, with 160 inside the ground. The Reds won, reaching their second consecutive final, and police claimed the match passed off relatively peacefully – though there were still 100 arrests. At one point during the game the police had to form a human barrier between the rival fans as segregation failed.

A *Times* journalist watched the ensuing trouble: "At one stage a fight broke out at the top of the terrace. Against the skyline it was possible to see a long weapon crashing down on somebody's head, although I could not see who was hitting whom, the people around me seemed to know. The fight created an almost hysterical atmosphere among the people outside and when the police arrived on the top terrace the group on the ground burst away, charging down the main Penistone Road.

"The explanations of academics and sociologists, and even some sports ministers, seemed difficult to accept as one watched the breaking of windows, the vandalising of parked cars, urinating in gardens, charging in hundreds down back streets of terraced houses and terrorising local residents. Perhaps what I saw was unrepresentative but what took place was on a large enough scale to be very disturbing. It is not just the cost in policing and lost trade that a neutral city like Sheffield has to pay, but the frightening tyranny of virtually uncontrollable youths."

Leeds's relegation brought an end to matches against Manchester United for eight years, but when the two sides met again in August 1990, little of the venom had been lost, though it was clear that in the intervening period fans from Manchester had

found new rivals, whereas they were still top of Leeds's hate list. This grew to hysterical proportions in 1992 when Leeds sold Eric Cantona for just £900,000. The Yorkshiremen had just won the League Championship and with Manchester United still without a title win in 25 years, there was justified hope that the balance of power was shifting back across the Pennines. What was even sweeter for Leeds fans was that they had pipped their bitterest rivals, fondly referred to as "the Scum", to the title on the last day of the season. Cantona's defection meant that the police were on full alert for the arrival of Manchester United at Elland Road following the French star's transfer and there was much trouble before and after the game.

Only a minority of Leeds fans were involved in fighting but virtually all of them had a pathological hatred of MUFC and "stand up if you hate the Scum" still resounds around Elland Road during matches. During the 1990s, even David Beckham and his Spice Girl wife, Victoria, became the target of many anti-Man Utd songs, although this had little discernible effect on their rivals, unlike the repertoire of "Munich 58" songs that were favourites amongst a Leeds element. The hatred of anything Manchester received national media attention when a section of the Leeds crowd at their away fixture at Blackburn in January 1994, booed during the minute's silence in memory of Sir Matt Busby, who had recently died.

In 1996, there were 40 arrests after clashes between rival gangs and in September 1997, the *Yorkshire Post* ran a front-page headline, "Bloody face of soccer hatred" after yet another incident. It was accompanied by a picture of a fan with blood pouring from a head wound. The police spoke of a "frightening" atmosphere outside the ground. In 2001, the two mobs had a prearranged meet outside Rochdale as Man United fans were travelling over to Bradford City and Leeds to Man City, but police intelligence prevented a major disturbance.

More trouble followed at Elland Road less than two months later as thugs fought in a side street near the ground and a Manchester police spotter was struck on the back of the head. It was not all bad news for the police as another spotter filmed the battle and to the delight of the authorities several main faces from both firms were identified from the footage clashing with fence poles and other weapons, including a wheelie bin. Two of those subsequently convicted were nephews of former European Cup winner Brian Kidd, who had been assistant manager to Alex Ferguson before moving to Leeds (via Blackburn) as assistant manager.

Even worse trouble came at the same fixture the following season, when 250 Manchester lads clashed with 150 Leeds outside the ground. In many of the latter clashes, the Manchester firm came off best, but in their last encounter, in the spring of 2004, with Leeds facing relegation once again, more than 200 Leeds walked through Manchester city centre hours before the game without facing any trouble. Manchester United's mob was not the force it had been, and Leeds were signing off on a high. After all, no one knew when they would be playing each other again.

* * *

In April 2000, two Leeds fans were stabbed to death in Istanbul hours before their team played Galatasaray in the semi-finals of the UEFA Cup. What should have been a wonderful night for the long-suffering Leeds fans turned out to be another dark day in the club's history. While the behaviour of a few Leeds fans was deemed disrespectful to many in Turkey, there was never any suggestion that Christopher Loftus and Kevin Speight had done anything wrong at all. In a clear sign of hypocrisy, the game was allowed to continue (with Leeds players given an escort onto the pitch by shield-carrying riot police) and the Turkish team received little sanction.

When Galatasaray flew into Yorkshire for the return fixture, tensions were running high and away fans were banned for their own protection. That didn't prevent hundreds of Leeds fans attempting to attack the away team coach. The *Yorkshire Evening Post* later ran a rogues gallery of 29 men wanted for the trouble, several of whom were later imprisoned.

Across the country, football fans showed respect for the Leeds fans who had died – but not Manchester United. During their visit to Old Trafford in October, the Yorkshire team were greeted with Galatasaray flags and throat-slitting gestures. Some Leeds fans responded with loud chants about the Munich air disaster. Hostilities between the two sides resumed, though perhaps not with the same intensity as before.

England's game against Turkey in a crucial Euro 2004 qualifier at Sunderland's Stadium of Light in April 2003 now became another potential flashpoint. The hooligan grapevine was rife with stories of rival firms putting aside their differences to allow Leeds to seek revenge. Police intelligence suggested as many as 500 Leeds intended to make the journey and there were even rumours that a small group from Batley were going "tooled up" with the intention of killing a Turk. The match itself passed off relatively peacefully, though not without huge police panic. Large groups of Leeds had been reported to be on the move early that morning, but then vanished from the police radar. There was an anxious wait in Sunderland as police searched high and low for the missing Service Crew. Finally, at about 5 p.m., a mob of 100 Leeds was rounded up after marching through the main shopping area. At the ground, another mob of Leeds had arrived just in time for the appearance of coaches ferrying Turkish supporters. A few were attacked but it was nothing the police could not handle. Five Leeds fans were later jailed for the assaults.

The long-trailed truce also didn't materialise. Forest joined up with Newcastle to attack Sunderland and, in the biggest clash of the night, 100 Middlesbrough old boys charged 150 Sunderland. Trouble started in town and continued to a crossroads outside the ground. The intensity of the fighting shocked many, but for the local police it was an ordinary day. When their spotters debriefed after the game, the incident was not even noted by the match commander.

* * *

The Premiership years saw continued Leeds violence. A gang of sixty attacked Boro lads with bottles and CS gas, 300 attacked a pub of Sheffield Wednesday fans at the home fixture and fifty damaged a Sheffield tram before attacking fans. Fighting occurred against Notts Forest, Newcastle, Huddersfield, Bradford, West Brom and Spurs. At a pre-season friendly against Hull in 2003, 80 Leeds travelled by train and clashed with Hull outside the station. The newspapers reported the largest-ever police operation at a Hull match and fighting also broke out at several other locations around the city. Most of these events were brief small-scale skirmishes well away from the ground, but the number and intensity of incidents increased into the new Millennium. By August 2003, Leeds United topped the national list for banning orders and a year later a British Transport Police survey noted that Leeds fans had caused more trouble on the trains than any other club.

A new generation of hooligans was emerging, many of them connected to the Infant Hit Squad, the youth wing of the Service Crew who produced their own calling cards:

IHS

Infant Hit Squad.
No battle – No Victory.
Britain's Elite Young Casual Firm.
"Nothing personal just business as usual"

The IHS battled with Bradford's Ointment gang at Leeds's main train station and was involved in trouble at a Worthington Cup match at Sheffield United. "I know there's a game set of lads starting to hang around Leeds again," said one ex-Service Crew member at the time. "Back in the 1980s there was the Very Young Team, who were the up-and-coming

coach. On any other day, in any other city, this would have been an almost invincible mob – but not on that cold Sunday afternoon in Ninian Park. Massed before them were literally thousands of Cardiff, youths and men, baying for their blood. It was more than Cardiff v Leeds or even England v Wales, it was the Soul Crew v the Service Crew and everyone knew there would be trouble.

At half-time a police spotter approached one of the main Leeds faces and enquired about the lads' intentions after the game. "Don't worry," he was told. "We are not going to start anything, we've got 500 good lads here, and obviously we'll fight if attacked, but we'll be murdered if we start on them." Cardiff won 2–1 and approximately 1,000 of their followers came onto to the pitch to taunt the Leeds contingent. Police from both forces agreed that a Welsh defeat would have resulted in far more serious problems. Outside the ground, Leeds fans complained to a BBC TV crew about the unpleasant behaviour of the Cardiff fans. The irony of their treatment, given the behaviour of the Service Crew over the years, was not lost on neutrals.

Leeds United fans attempt to attack visiting Cardiff supporters outside Elland Road.

ones; with the passage of time some of the VYT ended up as the top boys." Inspector Cameron Young, of the British Transport Police, confirmed the emergence of this new group. "In the last six months the presence of the Leeds hooligan fraternity has been noticeable. There also seems to be more young fans turning up."

But one especially tense fixture was an old boys' reunion on a grand scale. Four to five hundred lads, many of them ex-Service Crew, made the long journey to South Wales in 2002 for an FA Cup tie at Cardiff. Half went by train via Hereford, with a similar number going straight to the ground by

At the time of the Cardiff game Leeds were top of the Premiership but a dreadful run of results saw them tumble down the league and once again find themselves in the old Second Division. While crippling debts threatened the club's future on the pitch, off it things seemed quieter, with few reports of disorder. An exception was their continuing feud with Cardiff City, the results of which were reported by the *Yorkshire Post* in August 2005:

Football hooligans who join in mass violence against the police were given a stern warning by a judge yesterday – expect to go to jail.

Sentencing 15 men involved in terrifying clashes after a Leeds United game earlier this year, the Recorder of Leeds, Judge Norman Jones QC, said courts will not tolerate football violence from binge drinkers or anyone else.

"This was an horrific incident. Had it not been for the cool courage and discipline of the police officers it could have ended with tragic consequences."

The judge handed out custody orders to 14 of the defendants involved in violence after the home clash with Cardiff City in January, including a soldier, and a 21-year-old man, whose barrister said had previously played for both Leeds United and Bradford City.

Judge Jones told the last defendant at Leeds Crown Court, given a community sentence, it had been "touch and go" whether he joined them in jail. Orders were imposed on all 15 banning them from football matches.

He said violence was the "blight" of English football for many years, resulting at one time in English clubs being refused access to European competitions.

"It was not spontaneous violence, but violence organised and triggered by those whose interest was not the game, but fighting. For some time it had been hoped that the curse had been largely removed. This incident indicates that it has not been entirely eradicated."

He warned prison sentences would follow for those who attack the police. "The courts have a duty to protect the vast majority of decent fans from violence. They have a duty to protect English football from the stigma of violence. They will not shirk from that duty."

Before the match on January 15, the judge said, there was ill-feeling by a section of Leeds supporters towards Cardiff fans, arising from an earlier cup match when Leeds fans were injured.

Police became aware of attempts by some fans to create a situation where the Cardiff fans could be attacked, with messages appearing on a website exhorting Leeds fans to violence, and decided to prevent that.

A large force of officers with a mounted contingent were amassed. Cardiff fans were segregated at the match, and afterwards kept back while Leeds fans dispersed.

The judge said he accepted there was no evidence those in court were involved in planning the violence that followed, but they had joined in when about 400 so-called fans gathered outside Elland Road, and a chant went up, "Let them out."

CCTV and police cameras captured the scenes for 45 minutes, as bricks, stones, bottles, glasses, traffic cones and coins were hurled at officers.

There were eight mounted charges to disperse crowds, and at one stage missiles were thrown across or at the M621. Four officers and four police horses suffered minor injuries.

Several of those involved were identified following a publicity campaign. All 15 defendants admitted affray.

The years when their team were regarded as the cream of English football seem a long time ago and their fans may no longer be the wreckers of old. Yet ask any residents who lived in the towns the Yorkshiremen invaded during the Seventies and Eighties, and they will remember it as if it were yesterday.

LEICESTER CITY

Ground: Filbert Street
Firm: Long Stop Boys, Market Traders, Baby Squad, Young Baby Squad
Rivals: Derby County, Nottingham Forest, Coventry, Chelsea
Police operations: Lion, Hawk

The best-behaved fans in the country is an accolade that no hooligan would want, but that was the position of Leicester City when the *Daily Mirror* published a "League of Shame" in May 1974. Over the course of a season, only 26 people had been arrested at Filbert Street; Manchester United topped the poll with 343. The low figure was put down to a new get-tough policy from magistrates, and the level of arrests hardly made Filbert Street the most feared of venues for visiting fans.

The *Mirror* accolade was slightly misleading. It covered only Leicester's home matches and did not include ejections from grounds. Arsenal also had only 26 arrests yet their mob was considered one of the toughest around. And Leicester fans had been involved in trouble that season. In August 1973, British Rail cancelled a football special that was supposed to take them to Liverpool after they had smashed up a train taking them to Ipswich just 48 hours before. Three coaches were wrecked and the other eight extensively damaged. A BR manager told the press, "It was wanton, apparently premeditated vandalism."

The first recognisable mob at Leicester was the Long Stop Boys, so-called after a pub they frequented. They emerged in the early to mid-Seventies, superseding the unorganised bootboys who had been causing trouble with visiting fans since the late 1960s. The Long Stop Boys occupied the middle of Pen 3 in the Kop, and liked to do their own thing rather than mix with the masses, but were infrequent travellers.

Leicester fans were not the worst around but that did not make them immune from the violence of others. An October 1977 visit by Aston Villa was a day of humiliation for the Long Stop Boys. Villa infiltrated the Leicester Kop and chased the locals down onto the pitch, throwing missiles and punches at anyone in their path. The game was held up but their club secretary was quick to defend his supporters. "I was down on the pitch within a minute or two and many of the people were there because they were scared and for no other reason," said John Smith. He went on to say that the appalling scenes at least showed why fences were wrong. "If the innocent had not been able to get on the pitch there might have been many more casualties." As it was, 23 people needed medical help.

Within a few years another mob had appeared at Leicester, the Market Traders. They were just that, tough lads off the market who all knew each other and didn't look like typical football fans, so they could often get stuck into opposing fans without attracting attention from the police. They were to drive around at home games in Transit vans picking off rivals. They were joined about this time by several emerging coach crews named after the pubs they frequented, such as the Blue Moon, the Horsefair, and the Invincible.

The key period for Leicester was 1980-2. In 1980 they were back down in the First Division. Many coaches stopped going away but a small hardcore emerged known as The Firm, including a contingent

from the Dominion pub in Glenfield. They were about the only lads going away looking for trouble at that time. In 1981, a few younger lads appeared, mainly from the Thurnby Lodge area, attracted by the trouble and also the emerging casual fashion. By 1982 they outnumbered the slightly older Firm lads, though they teamed up together.

The Baby Squad was born after Leicester's away match at Leeds in 1980, when this young, casuals mob stood and fought alone against the Service Crew. An increasing number of young casuals had been attending Leicester games for a while but until that day they had been unorganised individuals in the shadow of the older lads. "Against both superior numbers and ages, these casually dressed heroes battled with the Yorkshire legions until the result became a victory in favour of the sartorial East Midlands teenagers," remembered JB, a Baby Squad veteran. "The phrase 'Baby Squad' was coined to reflect the age of the Leicester City followers and is still used to the present day despite some 'Babies' having now reached middle age."

Although the Baby Squad attracted members from all parts of Leicestershire, most of its followers came from Knighton, Eyres Monsell, Saffron Lane, Nether Hall, Thurnby Lodge, Beaumont Leys, Thurmaston, Coalville, New Parks, Saint Matthews/Marks and Hinckley. Most were from working class backgrounds. Research by Leicester University into the Kingsley Lads, a component part of the Baby Squad, revealed that the occupations of 23 key members included two drivers, one barman, one slaughterman, three bouncers, one bookmaker's assistant, three factory workers, one milkman, one apprentice printer, one apprentice electrician, one builder's labourer and eight unemployed.

Throughout the Eighties, their numbers fluctuated between 200-400. Football culture was fashionable and even George Michael sported a Fila BJ tracksuit on the large poster in the window of Ainleys. However towards the Nineties and thereafter, numbers dropped to a hardcore of around 80. The reasons for this, including the rave scene, were the same as in other towns, plus many changes in sentencing at Leicester Magistrates from a £50 fine to virtually certain imprisonment, and increased police harassment.

Other Midlands teams generally constituted

Leicester's rivals and it was with Derby County that the Baby Squad saw most conflict. In March 1983, they fought the Derby Lunatic Fringe outside the ground following a 1–1 draw. Yet despite their rivalry, the two firms put aside their differences and came together for a joint assault on Notts Forest. In June 1984, a mob of over 150 Baby Squad and DLF travelled into Nottingham, in what was coined in one newspaper as the Derby-Leicester Alliance. A leading Forest lad was having a stag night, and while the Nottingham lads were taken by surprise they had the numbers on hand to repel the attack. Over 400 people were involved in the fighting at its height.

The brief friendship between the two groups was absent when Leicester played Burton Albion in the Third Round of the FA Cup. Burton decided to cash in on the tie and held it at Derby's Baseball Ground. Burton had returned 1,500 tickets and these were quickly snapped up by the DLF. Fighting broke out between Derby and Leicester inside the ground and a few dozen seats were ripped up, but what caused most controversy was when the Burton keeper, Paul Evans, was hit by a piece of wood when the game was 1–1. Evans was concussed but continued playing. Leicester scored two goals shortly after, and the Burton keeper had little recollection of either. He was violently ill at half-time and a doctor declared him unfit to continue. Leicester went on to win 6–1.

After FA deliberation, the result stood. Ironically the match referee was Brian Hill, no stranger to on-pitch aggression. In 1977, he was linesman in a Millwall v Ipswich match when a fan ran onto the pitch to attack the referee, and he had been struck by a missile during a match at Norwich City.

The summer of 1985 saw disturbances in many inner cities. The media portrayed them as exclusively "black" riots, but this was far from the case. In Leicester many young lads, white and black, were happy to fight the police if the opportunity arose. And it did, on the evening of 10 October 1985, as the growing hostility between Leicester City and Derby County erupted into mass disorder that lasted into the early hours.

Trouble began five minutes before the end of the game at Filbert Street, when bricks and bottles were hurled at police as they attempted to clear 50 Leicester hooligans gathering outside the away end. The Leicester mob grew to 300 as away fans began to be escorted out and, in three groups of 100, they attacked the away fans from several directions. Despite a ring of police, more than 1,000 Derby fans broke away to confront their attackers. The ruckus spread along Waterloo Way and London Road, while quite some distance away, another group of Leicester youths ran through the St Martin's shopping centre, attacking shops and breaking windows.

As the police finally managed to escort most of the Derby fans to the railway station, Leicester regrouped and launched an attack on the station from another direction. According to the *Leicester Mercury*:

A mob of 80 youths responded with a hail of bricks, bottles and any loose object they could get their hands on. Officers were sent in and the mob responded by smashing their way into Highem Chemist. They threw the shop till through the window and virtually tore the shop apart.

The police decided to tighten their grip on the youths and a group of officers in full riot gear charged about 50 youths, where the youths turned over two cars in the street and set them on fire.

They advanced in phalanxes of five behind their riot shields into the maze of flats in nearby Pluxo Court. But their opponents launched a hail of broken bottles and then melted away into the shadows.

The damage continued with an attack on the row of shops in the precinct next to Highfields Community Centre on Melbourne road. The chemist, supermarket and butchers were all attacked and windows smashed before police in riot gear forced the youths further and further back.

The turmoil spread to a nearby shopping centre and the Highfield area, where 100 youths overturned cars, looted shops and threw petrol bombs at 60 police in riot gear. Leicester was a city in shock. Forty people were arrested, dozens injured and at the peak of the riot 500 police officers were on the street.

The club was quick to deny any responsibility, highlighting the good atmosphere within the ground and stressing that not a single person had been caught on CCTV throwing a missile during the match. "While accepting that football is used by hooligans as a cover for their activities," a club statement read, "the unfortunate events on Thursday evening confirm our contention over many years that football is not the cause of hooliganism, merely the unwilling recipient of society's problems."

Not since Villa rioted in 1977 had trouble spilled into the city itself. Coming so soon after the inner-city riots, and with Highfields containing a sizeable Afro-Caribbean community, both residents, the city council and the local newspaper were quick to link the riots to race. Indeed, the editorial of the local paper went out of its way to praise the restraint of local people in the face of outside agitation.

Highfields saw more trouble the next night, though this was more copycat in nature and involved much younger people. Petrol bombs were again thrown, a car set alight, an office equipment centre damaged by fire and police vans stoned. Police estimated that about forty lads were involved, some as young as ten. "What should send a chill in the heart of every parent is they were mere school children," noted an indignant editorial in the *Leicester Mercury*. "Why weren't they fast asleep in bed, tired and content after homework and a little television?"

Many newspaper reports of the riot noted the mixed ethnicity of those causing trouble. This was not a one-off but reflected the rare, mixed nature of the Leicester hooligan mob. "Throughout the mid-Eighties, a large group of predominantly Afro-Caribbean youths from the city, dressed in the obligatory Burberry golf jackets and Deerstalker hats, would travel alongside the original Baby Squad members in pursuit of likeminded individuals for a spot of Saturday afternoon jousting," said JB. While some of these later dropped away, the Baby Squad remained a mixed mob.

Coventry City were another Baby Squad target, and in 1984 the two mobs fought on the pitch. Amongst weapons used during the ensuing battle was the corner flag, a photo of which made many a tabloid the following day. Coventry manager Bobby Gould came onto the pitch to appeal for the fighting to stop but nobody listened.

In early February 1988, a large contingent of Baby Squad travelled to Stafford to watch their local boxer Tony Sibson's world title bout. Many arrived without tickets but had little difficulty sneaking in to the Leisure Centre where the fight was taking place. Unbeknown to them when they set off on their journey another mob, West Ham's ICF, were

also attending the event to follow East End fighter Nigel Benn, who was on the same bill. It didn't take too long for a major brawl to break out, with the Baby Squad letting off canisters of CS gas. The out of ring fight hit the national press.

In the local paper later that week, a journalist caught up with the jubilant Baby Squad. "We really stuffed the ICF this time," boasted one of them. "They wanted a pop and we gave it to them. We went to see Sibbo but the ICF were an extra bonus." Asked about the gas, the journalist was told that serving soldiers stole canisters "while on manoeuvres" and that "they had plenty more where this lot came from. We've got flares and air bombs and the odd canister of CS gas. We use it to cause diversions."

The readers were given an insight into the Baby Squad, its origins, numbers and organisation. "To avoid detection, squad members have now formed splinter groups with names like the MMA (Matthew and Mark Alliance), BIF (Braunstone Inter Firm), TRA (Thurnby Republican Army), and the ICHF (Inter-City Harry Firm). One Leicester hooligan, who gave his name as "Derek" explained the smaller groups. "As soon as you get collared now and they know you are Baby Squad, you are guaranteed six months at least. That has put the wind up people. So now we stick in small groups with people we can trust and get together when we have to."

"The Thurnby Republican Army was predominantly an offshoot of the Baby Squad comprising gentlemen from the Thurnby Lodge Estate," remembered JB. "Not content with purely a Saturday afternoon adrenalin rush, they travelled around the city and county making their presence felt to the locals and could often command significant numbers for these 'tourist' visits. The wall facing Costa's Fish Bar in Oadby still displays the initials of TRA nearly twenty years on since their visit to the sleepy Leicestershire suburbs."

To say that there is no love lost between Leicester and Chelsea is a gross understatement. For many supporters of the London team only Spurs will rank higher in their antipathy. There have been clashes between the two sets of supporters for almost forty years, though the intensity of the hatred has grown since Chelsea received a real spanking in 1994. Chelsea fans Martin King and Martin Knight made their views of Leicester well known in their book

A fight breaks out among spectators during the Worthington Cup final between Leicester City and Tottenham at Wembley Stadium, after Tottenham fans had illegally obtained tickets located in the Leicester City section of the ground.

The Naughty Nineties: "They rate themselves, that's for sure. Love getting on the blower and mouthing off to other mobs. They're the wannabes of football hooliganism. But they've never been rated by anyone else, really. A bit of a fucking nuisance, but that's about it. It is hard to show respect for a firm who won't travel."

Another Chelsea face, Steve "Icky" Hickmott, also had a pop at them in his book *Armed For The Match*. "They were sneaky. Never a mob of them until 20 of you get detached in some backstreet with dirty net curtains and pastel-coloured front doors."

Trouble was first reported between the two in the late 1960s. Reports of disorder twice made the national press in the Seventies, both times involving Chelsea taking liberties at Leicester. In May 1989, Chelsea took 10,000 to Leicester to celebrate promotion to the top flight. After the game, all four streets surrounding the ground witnessed battling males in possibly the largest clash at Filbert Street since Villa in 1977. Twenty-seven people were arrested and dozens injured. Fortunately for both clubs, this was the same day as the Hillsborough tragedy and so was overshadowed in the media. "They came to cause trouble," ran the headline in the *Leicester Mercury* although the article was relegated to page five because of the Hillsborough disaster.

For more than half an hour, pitched battles between rival gangs of supporters raged in the Filbert Street and Walnut Street areas of the city.

The police team, which was concentrated around the other end of the ground where the majority of Chelsea fans were standing, was completely outnumbered by more than 100 fans before reinforcements arrived. The police had drafted in mounted officers, dog handlers, special constables and other officers from all over the county.

Broken house bricks and other missiles were hurled at opposing gangs and the police, telephone boxes and bus shelters smashed.

Darren Smith, one of Leicester's top boys, remembers the game well. "It was the Friday night and the house phone is ringing non-stop and it's the lads. 'Fucking Chelsea are here, they're fucking here already!' It was a mental day, a bit naughty to be honest. They had a huge firm but we were about 200-handed after the game and seven or eight Chelsea were stabbed or slashed."

Leicester became a hate team for most Chelsea lads after the battle of Granby Street in 1994. A mob of Chelsea travelled to Loughborough before a league game and settled in a pub while deciding what to do. An exchange of phone calls led to a promise by Leicester that they would travel the fifteen miles out of town to meet them. Chelsea waited. As the minutes ticked away they made further calls, only to be told that a couple of Leicester were on their way over to the pub. *A couple?* thought Chelsea, in a mixture of disgust and bemusement. The Londoners were told that the police were around but that Leicester would arrive at the first opportunity.

As kick-off approached, some Chelsea became restless and headed off to the game, leaving 50 behind. The game ended and still Leicester had not shown. Some of the Chelsea decided to cut their losses and head back home before the night was too long gone. The remainder – 27 of their top firm – went into Leicester to find the Baby Squad. No sooner had they got out of the train station than they were attacked on all sides by Leicester. The Chelsea backed against a wall and took a severe beating from what one of them later called "the slimiest mob in football" until police rescued them.

Two years later, the sides were drawn together in the FA Cup. Fifty Chelsea travelled up by coach and they claim that they ragged Leicester outside the ground, while another 20, operating separately, got tickets for the home end. With a clash looking likely after Chelsea went 2-0 up, the police escorted the small mob out of the ground to a local pub where they could watch the rest of the game on TV. Fifteen minutes later, Leicester announced their arrival with a brick through the window. The front door then went in and the pub was virtually destroyed, but Chelsea succeeded in keeping the Leicester mob out – though not without taking serious casualties.

Portsmouth remember Leicester turning up on a number of occasions at Fratton Park. One of these trips was in 1993, when a large number of Baby Squad travelled south by road to renew old rivalries with the 6.57 crew. "Leicester took it to an unprepared Pompey both before and after the match, resulting in resounding successes for the visitors," recalled JB. "Remembered by myself for a casually dressed Pompey lad standing at the door of the bookies pretending to check his fixed odds whilst holding an upside down TV guide."

The early Nineties saw the Baby Squad at arguably their most active. While some of the larger firms suffered from undercover police operations or defections to the rave scene, the Baby Squad held their numbers together. The opening day of the 1991/92 season saw about 100 Leicester fans invade the pitch at Swindon. Two weeks later, they ran amok at Southend. Police arrested 27 fans after fighting, first in the Foresters pub on the seafront, where the situation was not helped by two Baby Squad members dancing on the roof, then in pubs and clubs throughout the seaside town. "This is the worst trouble we've had for a long time," said a local police inspector. "A minority of Leicester fans acted disgracefully. We won't tolerate this loutishness."

A couple of months later, Millwall travelled to Leicester – and when the Wall go looking for trouble, they invariably get it. Their Bushwackers made their way to Leicester by train and congregated in the Rutland and Derby pub on Millstone Lane. Only yards away, in the Nags Head, drank the Baby Squad. Within minutes, a full-scale battle ensued – and was filmed by Leicestershire Constabulary. A few weeks later, as part of Operation Lion, 18 people were arrested. Twelve people subsequently received custodial sentences.

The final game of the season was at home to Newcastle. It was a vital fixture for both teams, with the home side needing a win for automatic promotion and the visitors needing the points to remain in Division One. Over 22,000 fans packed into Filbert Street, and as the game kicked off there was a carnival atmosphere, with confetti and balloons greeting the players. Hundreds of Leicester supporters had blue and white stripes painted on their faces while others sported the "rooster head" hairstyle of City's striker Kevin Russell, and a charity fun run was staged around the pitch.

The joviality stopped almost as soon as the whistle blew. The home crowd was stunned into silence when the visitors scored shortly before half-time, a goal that precipitated three pitch invasions and signalled the opening of hostilities. It was the turn of Leicester fans to storm the pitch when Steve Walsh equalised for the Midland side and the fans believed that they were almost there. But the game was to end in disaster for Leicester as Walsh put the ball into his own net in injury time. The home fans held their heads in their hands while the jubilant Geordies, having seen their side stay up, swarmed onto the pitch. It took 60 officers in full riot gear to separate supporters on the pitch. In the midst of the trouble, one leading Baby Squad member decided to have a one-man sit-down protest in the centre circle. Thirty-three people were arrested, most from Leicester.

At the headquarters of Leicestershire Police, an incident room was set up and Operation Hawk was launched to sift through hours of CCTV footage to identify culprits. In the end a number of hooligans received custodial sentences of between one and nine months.

The next few years saw the emergence of a new breed of casual within the county who were significantly younger than the original participants and were known, not surprisingly, as the Young Baby Squad (YBS). With crisp Stone Island jackets and hair spiked with gel, their aim was to emulate the feats of past years and carry the name forward into the future.

Hostilities were renewed with Derby in 1995 when the two mobs clashed in the Woodgate area of Leicester. "After an incident earlier in the season, every single past or present member of the Baby Squad turned out on a Wednesday evening in order to prepare a welcome for our visitors from further up the M1," said JB. "Huge numbers walked from the city centre to Woodgate to confront the DLF, who were drinking in a pub. They stood their ground before becoming overwhelmed and having to take cover in an Indian supermarket where they flung tins, Pot Noodles and loaves of bread at the Leicester hordes before legions of police arrived."

Yet of all their Midlands rivals, it is Villa who are held in the highest respect by the Baby Squad. "From the waste grounds of a Birmingham estate to Leicester city centre late on a Saturday evening, they have always endeavoured to become involved in the action," said JB. One such incident was a brawl at the Crows Nest pub after Leicester's home fixture in 1997. "Full credit to a certain well known Villa face who was far from shy and put one or two of ours on the floor before receiving his dues. The local paper called the incident a 'disgrace' and called for the participants to be banned."

The numbers of incidents involving the Baby Squad has diminished but they still exist. For a big game they can still pull out over 150 lads, though most games see far fewer. The mob has been affected, like most have, by a recent swathe of banning orders. Veterans look back on some serious fights and some comedy moments. "I remember a firm of Tractor Boys on their heels from a marauding group of Baby Squad dressed in full Hare Krishna regalia during the game against Ipswich Town in 1991," said JB. "Then there was the sight of a coach load of Baby Squad travelling to Watford in fancy dress. Due to a costume oversight the bald wigs had to be replaced by the ends of ladies' tights."

Darren Smith, aka "Coalville Daz", bemoans the fact that the Baby Squad have never had the respect they deserve. "Through the decades we have had rows with everyone, all the major firms, West Ham, Boro, Chelsea, we always turned up at Pompey and even today we can pull 200 at home for a decent game. People say we never travel, mainly Chelsea, but we have been there, and there is no shame in picking your away games in today's climate. Basically people hate us, not rate us."

Further reading: *Top Boys*, Cass Pennant (Blake Publishing)

LINCOLN CITY

Ground: Sincil Bank
Firm: Clanford End Boys, Lincoln Transit Elite
Rivals: Hull, Mansfield, Scunthorpe

If ever a hooligan firm has punched above its weight, it's the Lincoln Transit Elite.

Lincoln is a town of less than 86,000 people, including just over 18,000 males aged between 14 and 46. A town with such a small adult male population would not be expected to have a hardcore football mob, but over the years they have earned a reputation even among some of the bigger and more active firms: leading figures at Portsmouth, Sheffield United, Hull City and many other clubs have described vicious little encounters with the Lincoln Transit Elite, especially at Sincil Bank.

Another set of supporters who are well aware of the dangers of Lincoln are Mansfield. Since the 1970s, the two sets of fans have fought home and away. In November 1976, vandals put through the windows of the Lincoln team coach moments before the team boarded it after the game. The driver was showered with glass and his face was badly cut. It marked a low point in a day marred by violence during the game. The next season, Mansfield ambushed a coach carrying Lincoln lads. The away fans retaliated by disembarking and going on the rampage. Thirty-five Lincoln fans were arrested and dealt with by the courts.

In 1980, Lincoln dished out a battering to Mansfield when the clubs met in the league shortly before Christmas. The local rivalry was made worse by the fact that both clubs were near the top of the table. Mansfield brought thousands of fans down and there was trouble beforehand as they were picked off by small groups of LTE, but the real disorder occurred during the game when hundreds of Lincoln poured onto the pitch from three sides and confronted their opponents. Mansfield fans had clothes ripped off their backs and some had their shoes thrown in the Sincil drain, which became a point of mockery for the rest of the season.

Mansfield fan Anthony Strouther was one of the victims that day. He was leaving the ground when Lincoln streamed on to the playing surface and he was hit in the face with a half-brick. "It was terrifying," he later recalled. "There were women and children screaming and these Lincoln fans running riot. God knows where the police were. Nobody stopped them charging across the pitch." His mood was not helped when the police refused to give him any transport home after he had made a statement at the police station, and all this after he'd had to visit the local hospital for treatment. "I had to fork out £17 for a taxi home," he complained. "The whole day was nightmarish. It's the last away match I'm going to."

Lincoln travelled to Mansfield for one of the last games of the season but there was little trouble between the two sets of fans as different Mansfield mobs appeared more intent on fighting each other. Lincoln were promoted late that season and it was another ten years before Mansfield had to run the gauntlet there again. This time they were far more prepared (see *Hooligans 2* for a fuller account). In the intervening years the clubs met at Mansfield in the FA Cup, another good day for the LTE. There have also been clashes between the two at matches in 1992 and more recently in 2003.

The early Lincoln mob was called the Clanford End Boys, named after the terracing where they stood. It has since been renamed after the two Lincoln fans who died in the Bradford fire. Two big confrontations in the Seventies were home games against Sheffield Wednesday and Stoke, where visiting fans turned up in huge numbers and ran amok. In the early Eighties, the Lincoln Transit Elite was born. It evolved out of the CEB but was run by younger lads who were much more fashion conscious.

The LTE was in its infancy when it had the first of three serious clashes with Sheffield United. A pre-season friendly in August 1982 saw Lincoln run a surprised and ill-prepared Sheffield mob. A month later the sides met in the league and United this time came prepared. A hundred of their main lads travelled through on the train – and the moment they came out of the station, Lincoln appeared. "They poured across the road at us, with a few glasses and bottles thrown our way," wrote Sheffield face Steve Cowens. "Then everybody was into them in a flurry of fists and boots, neither side budging." The police finally appeared in numbers and Sheffield were escorted to a pub some distance away. Within the hour, Lincoln re-emerged with bottles, pool cues and glasses, some going around the pub to attack through the beer garden; they were repelled with a volley of slates stockpiled in the yard.

The clubs were drawn together again early in the following season and it was another day of violence. Even more United hooligans made this trip and again they were met by Lincoln at the station, but this was only a prelude to the main act. The police divided the mobs briefly but they fought again in the main shopping centre. "Soccer fan battle 'terrifies' OAPs," ran the headline in the local paper:

Nearly 50 old people cowered in terror last night as soccer hooligans fought a running battle with bottles, glasses and iron bars outside a home for the elderly in Lincoln.

Many had to be led to the safety of an upstairs room as more than 200 rioting supporters turned the lower High Street into a battleground.

"The old people were absolutely terrified," said Mr Matthew Littlewood, husband of the warden at the home for the elderly at St. Botolph's Court.

Eight people were arrested before, during and after the match. A mob of 200 Lincoln attacked United in the Golden Eagle pub, smashing seven windows in their attempt to force their way in. One United fan was cut in the face by flying glass while another was hit on the head with a brick. Despite the numerous incidents spanning several hours, the local police claimed to the press that they had the situation "fairly well under control".

Lincoln's main rivals are Hull City, though there are conflicting interpretations of who has come out on top in these encounters. Hull fan Shaun Tordoff, author of City Psychos, recalls a number of clashes between the two mobs since the early Eighties. While conceding that Lincoln is the only one of Hull's local rivals to regularly turn out, he records Hull victories on both counts. The first was the opening day of the 1984/85 season when Tordoff and a few others found themselves in a tricky situation in a pub before help arrived in the form of a 50-seater coach containing the bulk of the City Psychos. "Within seconds," he remembers, "the tables had turned. Aided by some 'borrowed' scaffolding poles from a lorry, the lads began to rearrange and refurbish the front of the pub, along with any cars unfortunately parked nearby."

The second match was an away fixture in the 1999/2000 season, which he describes as the "highlight of the season". Two coachloads of Hull lads managed to evade a police round-up and parked several miles from town. "I think we surprised the local lads by turning up mob-handed from seemingly nowhere." However, the police and their dogs were out in force and there was little chance of a fight. Disorder did occur after the game as 100 Hull slipped out early and met a Lincoln mob brandishing weapons. "They stood there with an impressive armoury: coshes, bats, pool cues, chains and metal bars. They were out to do real damage. Now I think they were expecting us to do a runner. We did – straight into them, and after some fierce fighting, which at one point stopped to let some of the Lincoln lads drag away two of their comatose mates, we had them backing off. Demoralised and bruised, the Lincoln limped back to their pub and locked themselves in."

Lincoln strongly contest this version of events. "The Hull book doesn't tell the whole story of the day," says LTE lad SD. "They were run or done twice that day, with one of their main lads taking a trip in an ambulance. Before the match they came about seventy-handed and seven ran one of our spotters down the high street on his own. Our boozer emptied, which stopped them in their tracks, with Lincoln coming out of everywhere. We backed them off, with one of the main lads needing hospital treatment after being knocked out with one punch. The incident mentioned in the book was actually seventy-five Hull onto fifteen LTE, so they would come out on top with them odds.

"During the 2002/3 season we went to the KC Stadium and ran them after the game. Every time I went to Hull in the Eighties we ran them if we got near them, but they will always deny this."

In February 2004, 74 Hull lads were arrested after what police described as "serious violent disorder" at the Barbican Hotel, a pub opposite Lincoln train station frequented by the LTE. Pub furniture, bottles and glasses were all exchanged in the fierce clash between the two sides before the police arrived and made the arrests.

Lincoln's other key rivals are Grimsby and the two had a serious ruck in 1989, as MM remembers. "Twenty-one of our finest went in cars, parked up near a fish factory, had a beer, then strolled to the ground. What happened next takes some believing but it is true, as ten of the lads have given the same account to me. They first had a do with about the same number, then had a do with about fifty, then had another do with about eighty or so and they have all said that they did them each time and were fighting all the way to the ground. Lincoln did have casualties but kept going. According to Grimsby this never happened. They keep telling everyone that they ran us after the game but all they ran was a group of eighteen-year-old lads going to their first away game."

The Lincoln lads are the first to admit that they are poor travellers. If the away game is not a local derby or on a direct train route from Lincoln, they are unlikely to go. The exception to this was the odd trip down to London, which the lads would try to do once a season. The lack of away travel has been put down to the difficulty of hiring several minibuses for one day, especially when the police would go round cancelling their bookings.

In 1985, Lincoln played Derby for the first time in several years. It was close enough to be considered a derby, and the Derby Lunatic Fringe was a rival mob worth turning out for. The away game was held in early November and seventy-five LTE made the trip, many of whom were already prevented from attending games at the Sincil because of a strict membership scheme run by the club. In the police they found a determined opponent, and with intelligence suggesting that the LTE were travelling in numbers, a large operation was organised. The police rounded up Lincoln near the ground before they could cause any trouble, and held them there until after the game. The drivers of the numerous vans were made to go back to their vehicles and ordered to drive directly to the ground to pick up the rest of the mob. Under a heavy police escort, they were herded out of town.

The home fixture, in mid-April, was much more explosive. Over 500 Derby hooligans were part of the 3,000 East Midlands invasion of Lincoln, and there was trouble before, during and after the match. Travelling with Derby that day were a contingent of Leicester thugs, and together they were known as the Derby/Leicester Alliance (DLA). "One of our top lads had a do with a Leicester lad on the pitch after the game," remembers MM. It was a torrid day for the Lincoln lads. "We got run out of the ground and never really got together to have another go. It went off all day all over the place, with lads from both sides getting hammered." Despite that, he says it was "a good day really".

Lincoln's largest crowd of the season witnessed fighting all around the ground and even on the pitch, largely as a result of hundreds of Derby fans pouring on to the playing surface in an attempt to confront the home crowd. Lincoln's vice-chairman told the local paper, "We have gone to a lot of expense on improving the safety and security on the ground. Behaviour like this causes a lot of inconven-

ience for everyone concerned." Most of the trouble was pinned on Derby fans, but coming so soon after their riot at Shrewsbury a few months before, County were quick to spread the blame. Their club secretary blamed poor segregation and said the violence did not just involve Derby fans.

The Lincoln Transit Elite hit the national headlines after 200 locals fought running battles with the police in the early hours of New Year's Day, 1987. What started with a small scuffle shortly after midnight ended up with running battles across the town. "There were a lot of lads in a line and they were provoking and goading [the police]," reported a local journalist. "The police were all in a line and were charging the lads, who were throwing bottles and bricks. The police were ducking but some got hurt. One was in a mess and covered in blood and they carried him off, and there were various youths in the same state."

The trouble quickly spread as revellers poured out of pubs to help their friends. Five minutes after the trouble erupted, five officers were trapped against a shop window and attacked by lads chanting, "LTE." Mick Kemp was one of 23 police officers injured after he was struck in the face with a brick. A long-serving bobby, he described the Lincoln riots as worse than the Miners' Strike or the Toxteth riots. "At Orgreave [a power station where 13,000 miners battled with 8,000 police] there was a buffer zone of fifty yards between us and the crowd and we could just about see what was happening. But here it was too dark and we were being attacked from two sides at once – it was just a matter of time before getting hit." Whilst the officer was obviously shaken, many policemen in Liverpool would dispute his claim about Toxteth.

Kemp's commander, who had not been in the front line or hit with a brick, still called the riot the worst trouble the town had ever seen and implied that it was pre-planned. "Half-bricks were thrown at police officers," Supt Malcolm Rollinson told the press. "People do not walk around with half-bricks unless they intend to cause trouble." He admitted that he had no idea about who did what or even why. "We need the help of the public on this." His appeal was backed by a councillor who called on parents to "shop the yobs". Seventy officers were on duty in Lincoln that night and another seventy were drafted in from across the region. They arrested thirty-seven people on the night and the Home Secretary called for a report on the trouble.

Despite police claims that the riot was planned and orchestrated by known Lincoln hooligans, the LTE lads disagree. "The New Year riots were not organised at all but were started by two coppers getting heavy handed with certain people," said SD. "Many of the lads were not LTE but because a large number of the ones nicked were, they say it was all premeditated. Two coppers took a proper hiding, and this involved some football lads, they were recognised as officers from the match who used to hassle everyone, wrong place wrong time scenario. The rest of the riot was a bit of drunken mayhem and payback. Most put it down to the general public's hatred towards the police and the way they go about duty in town. There is no denying football lads got involved; some happily did and revelled in it due to the shit a certain sergeant had handed out to a few lads in the previous couple of seasons. It fucked it up for us though, and was the demise of the firm for many years due to some of our best lads getting between two and six years.

"That's the sign of the times we live in, these incidents happen all over the country, every weekend in the big cities, but for a place like Lincoln it was massive news and when the police proved that football lads were involved the sentences handed out trebled overnight. Where's the justice in that?" he bemoaned.

The LTE were again involved in trouble away from football when, in September 1990, they clashed with police at the 5th Avenue club. The trouble kicked off when police were called to deal with a small disturbance at the nightclub, but it soon escalated. As the police tried to arrest three men they thought were responsible for the trouble, which included the vandalism of the club's toilets, they were confronted by a mob of up to 50 lads, backed up by another 100 on the fringes. As the LTE clashed with police outside, others threw beer glasses and bricks at officers from upstairs windows. The windscreen of one police van was smashed, four other police vehicles were damaged and several officers were taken to hospital.

In recent seasons the Lincoln Transit Elite has emerged as one of the busiest firms in the country, and by 2004 they were second in a national table of arrests. During the 2000/01 season, they clashed at a pre-season friendly with Grimsby Town. Before the game, 25 Grimsby tried to attack a pub where the LTE were drinking, while afterwards, it was the turn of Lincoln to attempt an ambush of their visitors. "The rival groups had been in contact with each other throughout the day via mobile phone," noted a police report. In early November a group of 25 LTE tried to attack Chesterfield hooligans at the train station, while on Boxing Day, rival Lincoln and Scunthorpe hooligans clashed in the High Street in Lincoln. Towards the end of the season the return fixture at Chesterfield saw violence before and after the match during which one Lincoln fan suffered a broken nose.

The 2002/03 season opened with an early away game at Boston. Greeting their Lincolnshire rivals into the Football League, 75 LTE travelled through and kicked off with the police inside and outside the ground. There was further trouble at matches against Hull and Plymouth, and the play-offs saw major disorder against Scunthorpe involving several hundred people [see SCUNTHORPE in *Hooligans 2*]. More recently, a clash between Lincoln and Hull fans in a pub outside the train station while the game was being played led to 74 arrests.

For the final away game of the 2004 season, 250 LTE travelled down to Bournemouth, a huge turnout for a firm that rarely travels in numbers. The seaside beano was given an extra twist by allegations that Bournemouth had bullied a few ordinary supporters at Lincoln earlier in the season. Eighty travelled down on the Friday to make a weekend of it, while another 160 travelled overnight, arriving in the seaside town early on Saturday morning. Their football intelligence officer was caught completely off guard and it was only the huge deployment of riot police that prevented a major clash between Lincoln and 150 Bournemouth.

"We had Robocops with us all day. At one stage our escort was sixty cops and eight vans," remembered DD. "Nothing really happened before or after the game except for Bournemouth throwing glasses at us outside the Queens Park pub and after the game a stand-off between us and the Old Bill on the field near the ground, where a couple of their lads got put on their arses."

In 2005, an LTE reunion saw 70 travel to Yeovil, all but ten of them over 30 years of age. It may have taken years for other clubs' hooligans to recognise

Lincoln as a football firm, but the police were not so tardy. In the autumn of 2004, NCIS rated them as the most active firm in the country, something the LTE themselves took pride in. Such notoriety, however, can lead to a greater police presence at games and anyone charged with a football-related offence may find the gang's high hooligan rating used against them in court.

LIVERPOOL

Ground: Anfield
Firm: The Ordinary Mob, the Urchins
Rivals: Manchester United, Everton

At least two matches that have influenced the whole of British football, and football hooliganism, over the past 30 years have involved Liverpool. The shadows cast by Heysel in 1985, and Hillsborough in 1989, changed the game. They had an even greater impact on the psyche of Liverpool Football Club, its supporters and the hooligans. No-one escaped the fallout.

Research suggests modern, post-war football hooliganism may have begun in Liverpool. It was at Anfield where the first end, the Kop was born. It was on that Kop that the vibrancy and music of the city in the 1960s first translated itself into football songs, against a backdrop of confident and stylish bands, such as the Beatles, who made smart appearance cool and perhaps laid the early foundations for the emergence of the football casual. This flare was mixed with a strong gang culture, sometimes sectarian in nature, which had been imported with the thousands who had moved to the city from Ireland in the 19th century and west Scotland during the 20th. The similarities between Liverpool and Glasgow included poverty and high unemployment, which in turn led to a heavy drinking culture and a readiness to reach for a weapon, the flipside of the city's renowned wit. There was also a long history of political militancy, which in turn led to a distrust of authority and a willingness to fight it.

In March 1958, 20 people were arrested at Liverpool's FA Cup match at Blackburn and several people were taken to hospital, including one police officer. There was also damage to three football specials returning fans to Liverpool. Fourteen windows were broken, a door pulled off, 60 lamps stolen and three electric fittings destroyed.

Trouble on trains became a recurring problem for British Rail. From the mid-Fifties, supporters of Liverpool and Everton wreaked havoc on the transport system, vandalising their own carriages and ambushing incoming ones. In 1963, officials from both clubs were forced to make public appeals to their supporters to stop damaging trains. The following year British Rail decided to cancel all football specials from Liverpool after repeated warnings about hooliganism. "British Railways can no longer tolerate the disgraceful behaviour of Merseyside maniacs calling themselves football supporters," a BR spokesman said.

By the mid-Sixties, violence had become a common feature at Liverpool matches, particularly those against northern rivals from Manchester and Leeds. In April 1966, young Liverpool supporters were reminded that they still had a lot to learn when their city was overrun by Celtic in the semi-final of the European Cup Winners' Cup. By contrast, Liverpool fans had been generally well behaved during the first leg in Glasgow. Liverpool fans were considerably more confident when they went back north a month later for the final against Borussia Dortmund at Hampden Park. Their supporters spilled onto the pitch after Roger Hunt equalised for the Merseysiders. Several arrests were made and the police were forced to ring the Liverpool terracing for the rest of the game.

Over the next few years, Liverpool supporters were involved in trouble at Arsenal, Spurs, Leeds, both Manchester United and City, and Birmingham. Twenty-three arrests was considered a successful day by the police after Liverpool's visit to Ipswich in 1975. Five football specials took thousands of Reds to East Anglia, where they were joined by hundreds who had made their way overnight independently. From daybreak Liverpool youngsters were wandering round town in the face of an obviously worried local population.

Anfield was a particularly unpleasant place for away fans. The Scouse wolfpacks didn't just give you a beating, they would slash you and take your money and even your clothes. Colin Ward in *Steaming In* recalled the horrors of a London team visiting Liverpool. "Fans were robbed of their clothes, stabbed and hunted down. It was violence for violence's sake." Unsurprisingly, few mobs turned up on Merseyside in numbers. Birmingham or Leeds sometimes would, but rarely with more than 100 lads. One exception was Manchester United, who regularly came in large numbers and boasted that in the mid-Seventies they generally had the upper hand, having been on the receiving end at similar fixtures in the early part of the decade. United also claim to have run Liverpool ragged at the 1977 FA Cup Final, as well as ruining their dreams of a Treble.

Peter Hooton, editor of pioneering fanzine *The End*, charted the rise of the casual culture in Liverpool, though it was never referred to as such at the time. He claimed that the changing music scene, away from punk, arrived more quickly on to the Merseyside terraces than elsewhere because a greater number of clubbers in Liverpool also attended football, so the style crossover from nightlife to Saturday afternoon was quicker. The wedge haircut symbolised this new fashion. "On Merseyside, the wedge became a mainstream, popular haircut and, allied to the continuing success of Liverpool FC, an undeniable sense of superiority set in with Scousers," he argued. "Fans of other teams and non-Scousers everywhere were treated with contempt, especially in regard to their fashion sense."

It was no coincidence that the young "scals", "trendies" or "dressers" began to emerge in 1977, the year of Liverpool's first European Cup triumph in Rome. The travelling thousands came into contact with a far more fashion-conscious country and found many new clothes labels, which were quickly adopted (if not always paid for). This in turn reinforced their sense of superiority or one-upmanship over their English rivals. Long before it became fashionable to tour Europe on student passes and visit places like Austria and Switzerland rather than Magaluf or Benidorm, scores of Liverpool thieves made the theft and re-sale of Continental fashions, watches and jewellery their main form of income, and the many European matches the Reds were involved in were a bonus rather than an excuse to travel. The easily forged Trans Alpino rail tickets available at the time were used and abused, and a £30 ticket and a few felt pens could see you travel all over Europe for a month.

One favoured destination, Switzerland, was described by seasoned traveller Nicky Allt, in his book *The Boys from the Mersey,* as "Christmas come early" and "the big Scouse warehouse". Many of today's notorious Merseyside criminals cut their teeth on the club's European tours, where in-store security was often notably more lax than in the UK and thousands of pounds could be netted on a single trip. Even when the Continentals wised up to the marauding Scousers, they kept one step ahead, and each trip was regarded as an "earner" for many. Stolen credit cards, reversible magnets to remove security tags, and holdalls lined with silver foil to prevent alarms being triggered were all tools of the trade.

Many of the lads who travelled Europe became known as the Annie Road mob, as they congregated in the Anfield Road end of the ground. Soon violence was becoming a major concern for the club and local police as the mob attacked away fans situated in that part of the ground.

Liverpool built a specific pen for away fans in 1978 at a cost of £500,000. The biggest difficulty was when other clubs under-estimated the number of travelling fans. On one occasion, a club visiting Anfield suggested that 2,500 fans would attend, when in fact 10,000 arrived. In a bid to co-ordinate better control over their supporters, Liverpool appointed an executive liaison officer to work with other clubs, British Rail and the police to ensure the minimum fuss when Liverpool travelled away. He was also responsible for monitoring the movement and behaviour of Liverpool fans in Europe.

It was about this time that the boys from the Annie Road came together and small mobs from all over the city joined forces on match days. As well as the robbers and blaggers, the mob had many pickpockets amongst their number, but they mainly consisted of out-and-out hooligans, such as the notorious Breck Road crowd, who cared less about "earners" than battering away fans.

The emergence of the Anfield Road end and the casual scene in tandem saw the tables turn in Liverpool's on-going war with Manchester United. A particularly violent encounter was the 1979 FA Cup semi-final at Maine Road. The game ended in a draw and there was even worse trouble at the replay at Goodison, with United fans getting picked off across the city.

Steve, a well-known Red, remembered the evening well. "It was a night of pure hatred, the complete night was evil," he said. "There were golf balls with nails in getting chucked from one end to the other and kick-offs all over the ground as Mancs were sussed out with ease. We'd had a bit of a rough ride at Maine Road on the Saturday and it was payback time. In those days we were mates with the blue lot and when Jimmy Greenhoff scored the winner for them late on, we left the ground to be met by hundreds of lads outside waiting for United. The bizzies let them out and I have never seen an onslaught like it. They were systematically hunted down and destroyed. I saw grown men crying and pleading for protection, but in those days the bizzies offered none. I think that is when the real hatred between us and them started."

Several of Liverpool's most violent clashes in the late Seventies were with teams from Birmingham. In September 1978, at an away match against Birmingham City, five police officers and 30 fans were injured as rivals threw darts, bricks, bottles, and coins at each other, and there were 48 arrests. A couple of seasons later there was a violent tit-for-tat with Aston Villa. Villa took a battering at Anfield in 1980 but more than got their revenge when Liverpool travelled down for the return fixture. Six Liverpool fans were cut up by a leading Villa face who had previously been hunted and taunted by Liverpool fans because he was black (see ASTON VILLA).

Another Red, Paul, remembered, "I was involved in a good kick-off with Villa in the green seats of the Annie Road in 1985, when one the Urchins slashed one of theirs in the face before the game had even started. Villa always tried to come into the 'green seats' around that time but usually came unstuck. If you're going to talk about Liverpool in the early to mid-Eighties, you've got to mention the green seats in the Annie Road, which were always a hotbed of tension and usually action."

Liverpool didn't have one homogeneous mob, but rather a collection of up to ten small firms. These groups would mob up together for big games but there were many occasions of them fighting each other, even away from home. "The funny thing is, our boys actually had ongoing rivalries with three other sets of Liverpool boys from Anfield, Bootle and the St John's estate in Huyton," said Paul. "At various times little bits would kick off and we'd find ourselves trading digs with fellow Reds on the streets of Willesden or Leeds or wherever." *En masse*, they tended to be known by the collective term the Ordinary Mob – because they travelled on "ordinary" rather than football special trains – or the Yankee Mob, after the bar outside Lime Street Station where they often gathered.

Liverpool were the most consistent team in Europe during the 1977/85 period. Every foray to the Continent brought reports of trouble and arrests. Most was fairly low-key, a bar fight or a few arrests for thieving, nothing too serious. In May 1981, thousands of Reds made the short hop over to Paris for yet another European Cup Final. "Rioting Reds Fans Banned by Hotels," ran the front-page headline in the *Liverpool Echo* on the morning of the game. Several local hotels had closed their doors to the English after a riot at the Hotel Normandy in which 30 fans were arrested after they rampaged through corridors and fought in the streets outside. Fire extinguishers were let off, carpets slashed and cans of paint used to daub Liverpool slogans on hotel walls and escalators. "Some people on the third floor were throwing bottles out on to the road and urinating on passers-by," said the hotel's deputy manager. "They were behaving like animals."

The trouble came after several hours of fighting between Liverpool and local French youths. Two French youths were stabbed, one slashed across the throat with a Stanley knife. "Apparently only a few lads had paid for the rooms, the rest were dossing down on the floor," said one Liverpool fan. Even before the trouble, the authorities had been concerned at the thousands of Liverpool fans arriving for the final, against Real Madrid, without tickets. Only 12,000 tickets were allocated to Liverpool but an estimated 30,000 made the trip.

By the afternoon of the match, more than 100 Liverpool fans were being held, mostly for trouble in the red-light area after battles with riot police, but the majority were soon released after the payment of small fines. One Red was taken to hospital after being struck by a knife. "We were in the McDonalds café, sitting at our tables, when a gang of French lads came in and started showing flick knives and razors. One lad at another table told them to get out because he wanted no trouble and as he put his hand up he was slashed across his wrist," described a witness. Meanwhile, the British Foreign Office apologised to their French counterparts for the trouble.

The *Liverpool Echo* carried a very mixed message when Liverpool next appeared in a European Cup Final, this time in Rome against local team Roma. "The Ecstasy and the Agony," read the front page. "Red Army celebrate but 30 are hurt in Rome thugs' ambush." Liverpool won the game in a penalty shoot-out and the Italians were not happy. Hundreds streamed out of the stadium and attacked the departing Liverpool fans with knives, sticks, and bottles. More waited in the giant coach park and ambushed the English fans as they arrived back for their transport. Thirty Liverpool fans needed hospital treatment, five for stab wounds.

The Italian media was clear who were the perpetrators of the violence. "The gravest aspect is that the English did absolutely nothing to provoke the violence. They were extremely well behaved," said *Il Messaggero*. "Manhunt against the English" was the front-page headline in *La Republica*. "The Romans did not demonstrate the calm and self-control, typical English characteristics," said the *Corriere Della Sera*. It went on, "It was a night of vile, blind violence that disappointment cannot justify." The British Embassy came to the same conclusion and praised Liverpool fans: "The Liverpool fans behaved as everyone expected them to and maintained their good reputation," said a spokesman.

Liverpool supporters were not in fact blameless. Earlier in the day, the police had confiscated 50 knives from them in the city centre. Ten Italians went to hospital, one having been struck with a hammer. One of the most violent incidents occurred over the River Tiber, where rival gangs fought a pitched battle. However, the memory of this game, and the viciousness of the Italian onslaught would remain strong when Liverpool met Juventus in the European Cup Final twelve months later.

The following season, Liverpool once again met Manchester United at the semi-final stage of the FA Cup. Many of United's huge mob, estimated at up to 800, left their train when it stopped a short distance outside Lime Street Station and walked along the tracks and through a tunnel to chants of, "War, war." They then steamed out of Lime Street and scattered the Scousers waiting nearby. And this was only the advance United army.

Not surprisingly, Liverpool have their own version of events. "They brought a tidy firm that day, they

had to after being destroyed a few years earlier, but to claim they ran amok is laughable," said Steve. "They were in the Enclosure before the game and were well and truly spanked out of there. After the game they fared better than the last time, but to be honest they could not fare any worse. They also blurt on about the replay at Maine Road saying we were done in, total bollocks. They were all on the pitch celebrating when we marched back through Manc land via Moss Side, which we turned upside down with no resistance."

Liverpool have had few other major rivals over the years. "We only had eyes for Man U and to a lesser extent Man City. I think it is in the Scouse make-up that we look down on everyone else anyway, so going anywhere else in the country felt the same, whether it was Villa or Sheffield Wednesday," said Paul. "Wednesday provided a brief rivalry in the mid-Eighties but it was nothing like on the scale of Manchester United or City. Our little crew did have a rivalry with what we were told were Wednesday's top boys for a while after we took the piss in a big way in 1984. We took their main boozer without so much as a struggle and they virtually ended up begging us to get out, while we just laughed them off. They tried a half-hearted revenge mission the following season by turning up at the wrong pub in Huyton and being abusive to one man and his dog and the bar staff. So at the away game, we went back to the Burgoyne Arms and again took over the bar and pool table, although this time they did exchange a few hooks."

The club's defence of their European crown saw Liverpool once again reach the final, where they were up against the Italian champions, Juventus, in Belgium's Heysel Stadium. The events of that day, and the deaths of 39 people, have been copiously documented and investigated, but little of the information released has come from those actually involved in the trouble. None of the people interviewed for this book sought to justify their actions and all admitted that the price paid was a terrible one, but their reflections on what occurred give a slightly different perspective from the bloodthirsty lunatics that we were presented with in the media.

The finger of suspicion was initially pointed at the National Front, courtesy of the Liverpool chairman and *The Sun* newspaper. "Six Soccer Nazis boast: We

The Heysel Disaster in 1985, in which thirty-nine fans met their deaths, marked a watershed both in British football and in the activities of hooligans following Liverpool FC.

did it," was a front-page headline two days after the match. "Six Nazi soccer thugs who support Chelsea boasted of causing the shameful European Cup Final carnage," it went on. "The vicious gang surrounded Liverpool chairman John Smith just after the disaster and announced that they were members of the National Front. They admitted throwing bricks and concrete at the Juventus fans which started the stampede. Mr Smith said on his return, 'They were boasting that they caused the trouble. They were very pleased with their actions of that evening.' The club chairman said the thugs told him they were Chelsea fans."

The Sun provided other "evidence" to support the claim. "Loyal Liverpool fans and club officials say they spotted NF members in the Brussels stadium where the disaster happened. Flags daubed with Chelsea NF were seen being brandished at the ground. Bedraggled Liverpool fans returning home spoke of skinheads with Cockney accents posing as Liverpool fans and former Liverpool manager Bob Paisley revealed that NF supporters penetrated the ground's VIP section." Liverpool Football Club did not wish to comment on the claims that before the game £150,000 worth of jewellery had been stolen by their fans in a planned raid, or that the night before the game there had been clashes and robberies in bars all over the Belgian capital.

The Sun also brought in a psychiatrist to assist the readers in understanding the "evil mind of a soccer hooligan". The soccer yob was, the paper's expert claimed, "oversexed, socially frustrated and always on the lookout for violence. He also has a low intelligence, but wants to feel important. He might have a girlfriend and a satisfactory sex life but an over-abundance of male hormones in his body have the side-effect of producing aggression." Dr Glenn Wilson, of the Institute of Psychiatry, also partly blamed the parents, whom he described as "sloppily permissive". He argued that part of the problem was that "Britain hasn't had a good bloodletting for forty years, since World War Two ended."

In truth, Heysel was a tragedy that could have happened in many football grounds on many occasions. Every time a football mob appeared at the back of a stand and charged forward, scattering the home fans on the pitch, there was the potential for serious injuries, even deaths. Poor or even non-existent segregation, bad blood between Liverpool and Italian supporters, and ineffective policing also played their part. "People must believe that if any of the big clubs who had a firm in those days was in Heysel they would have done the same as us," said a Liverpool hooligan who was arrested for his involvement in the tragedy. "I know it is a whinge but that ground was a shithole and the police were shit-scared. The segregation was a joke and I admit we went through it. The ICF, the Mancs, Chelsea and, despite what they say, Everton would all have done the same."

As the British Government promised a crackdown on "soccer thugs" and UEFA imposed a ban on British clubs playing in European competition, the police, helped by a willing media, pinned the responsibility on some of Liverpool's main hooligans. "I was nicked for it and know firsthand the problems it caused in Liverpool," said one. "Imagine being in bed and the police come and say, 'We are arresting you on suspicion of causing the death of thirty-nine people at the Heysel Stadium.' Your life is in bits. We did some jail over there but were very lucky, I accept that. At the time, imagine how it felt, thinking you may have to do twenty years in a foreign jail for just doing what we all had done for years at the match. No one wanted anyone dead, but you can't turn the clock back. It finished it for me at the football.

"Afterwards it was weird. When I headed for a game, some people would turn away, some would curse and spit at you, and some would want to buy you a drink, like you're a hero. None of the lads I know wanted any of that. Some of those charged were Liverpool hooligans, some were just lads on the piss and others were just beauts who got caught up in it. I don't know many who bothered after that

and with the police and all the bad press, lots fucked it all off for good. Heysel finished Liverpool as a top football mob."

Another veteran Liverpool hooligan, Graham, claimed that most of the trouble came from ordinary but drunken fans rather than hardcore hooligans. He is also annoyed that the Italians were portrayed as innocent victims. "There were plenty of Italians out there looking for trouble," he insisted. "On the day of the match we joined hundreds of Reds on the main drag in Brussels, sitting having a beer from early doors. Even at ten in the morning it was chocker, so we moved off and found a quiet bar. Soon a coachload of Italians pulled up down the road and when it unloaded we realised it was all lads. They started walking down with scarves over their faces and we thought, here it comes. We stood up and the next minute they turned and ran, as another mob of Reds had clocked them and were running over to give us a hand.

"That set the tone for the day. After the year before, when loads of ours were stabbed in Rome, all the lads with no tickets stuck together as a mob because we knew they had mobs out looking for it. Even as we went into the ground, a Scouse copper stopped us and warned us to go into the next section, as someone had been stabbed in block Z, where some had tickets for. Outside Z there were holes in the fence and the wall where people had kicked their way into the ground. Inside, we stood by the fence separating us from section Z; it was what we did at most grounds to have a nose at the other mob. Stuff was being lobbed both ways and some fireworks came over that seemed to change the attitude of everyone. Some charged, the Belgium coppers disappeared, the fence got pulled down, and as soon as some lads got through, the Italians ran. The rest is history.

"When it happened, I looked at the lads running through and none of the real lads were involved, it seemed more like the barmies were at it. It was ages before the game and any of the lads with tickets were still in town on the rob or on the ale. The one thing that anyone will tell you is that nobody realised that anyone had died until much later on. Once the rumours went round, Italians were kicking off all over the ground and we knew it must be bad.

"Lads came in before kick-off and told us that

loads were dead and there were moody mobs of Juventus outside, so after the game we came out and the Belgium Paras had turned up and escorted us to town. We found a bar full of the real Yankee Crew and no-one could believe all those people were dead. There was no gloating. I know Liverpool get stick for trying to blame everyone else, but this was our firm and apart from a few who didn't have tickets and had gone up early to bunk in, no-one else was even in the ground when it happened. A Swedish TV crew came in to interview lads and someone said, 'Don't say fuck all, you will only be on TV saying I killed some Eyeties.' Then one lad said to the crew, 'This was practice for when we play the Mancs next season.' Very few found it funny."

Overnight, Liverpool's mob was no more – except for really big games like United. In February 1986, Liverpool hooligans attacked Manchester United players as they arrived at Anfield for a League game. A teargas spray was fired at the players as they attempted to step off their bus, injuring 22 people. Bricks and stones were also thrown. "It was pure hatred," said United chairman Martin Edwards. "When you have to sit and watch a crowd like that, it makes you think that, after Brussels, they do not feel an ounce of remorse. I have never seen such abuse. It was frightening. A brick was thrown at the coach, but luckily it hit a stanchion first. Otherwise it would have hit Mark Hughes. He could have been killed."

Chelsea v Liverpool also had its share of trouble. There was fighting on the terraces during an FA cup tie at Stamford Bridge, and when Liverpool took thousands down to the capital in 1986 for a game at which they clinched the League, there were running battles after the game and Liverpool claim they ran Chelsea off Edgware Road.

Four years after Heysel, another tragedy befell the club when 96 people were crushed to death at Liverpool's FA Cup semi-final against Nottingham Forest at Hillsborough. Notwithstanding the twisted reporting of *The Sun*, which Merseyside has still not forgiven, the fans themselves were not at fault, though it still had a deep impact on what remained of the Liverpool mob. Football violence seemed offensive against the background of what occurred in Sheffield. Paul was one of those who lost interest. "Hillsborough ended it all for me," he said. "I was a bit disgusted with myself and, along with a few others, began actually buying tickets and behaving

myself. Any semblance of a Liverpool firm died that day in 1989 and did not resurrect itself until well into the 1990s."

Steve similarly felt the disaster marked the end of his hooligan career. "By then, fighting at the match was on a down anyway and the deaths made loads more realise it was not worth it. It was nothing to do with trouble and fans, but still the press angled it that way and it scared a lot of people. Some lads carried on, but lots have never bothered since. We have lads at games, just not in one big mob. If there is a reason to turn out they do, but apart from Manchester, give me a good reason to risk jail for a fuck-all incident."

There was another factor at play too. Liverpool was fast becoming the main conduit for the importation of both hard and soft drugs to the north of England, Scotland, Wales and parts of the Midlands. Many main football heads began to pursue the riches of organised crime, and curtailed their terrace activities when they could no longer risk arrest for something as pointless as football hooliganism. Their criminal lives led them in a different and altogether more sinister direction, though they would reappear for particularly attractive trips: according to HM Customs and Excise, a small group of major traffickers chartered an aircraft to fly to London for one cup final. "If we'd had a ground-to-air missile we could have taken out the entire top tier of Liverpool's drug dealers," remarked one officer ruefully.

Then, in January 1995, Liverpool played away at Birmingham City in the FA Cup. The game ended as a disappointing goalless draw but afterwards Liverpool supporters' coaches were bricked and stoned by Blues. Liverpool's mob was out in force for the return leg, knowing full well that the Zulus would be travelling up. The result was 20 people arrested after street brawls, fights and stabbings before and after the match. Three fans were taken to the Royal Liverpool University Hospital with knife wounds but all were later released. Trouble flared outside Sam Dodd's wine bar and the Albert pub, but the biggest confrontation was in Anfield Road. A spokesman for the Merseyside Police football office said, "We had extra officers because it was a cup tie and there were plans to cope with all eventualities after the game. We dealt with an unusually large number – dozens – of disorder incidents around the football ground. We regret it is not possible for everyone to just enjoy the match and go away quietly."

In September 1998, Liverpool were out for revenge against Manchester United, who had badly turned them over the previous season. It resulted in one United man having his throat cut, an incident that caused fury among United's main heads. "We went in cars and a few of them did get cut," said a Liverpool hooligan who is still active. "We were tooled up because we had to be. Don't believe the spin merchants that say they fight fair, they have loads of blade men." It was a bloody encounter that received considerable press coverage, and twelve people were arrested. Two mounted officers were knocked to the floor and attacked as police battled to restore order. Inevitably, innocent fans were caught up in the trouble, including 17-year-old Ian Bagot, who needed forty stitches after he was hit with what doctors believed was a knuckle-duster.

Two seasons later, a coachload of Liverpool hooligans travelled over again but this time the police, acting on a tip-off, intercepted them. On board they found knives, iron bars, CS gas and knuckle-dusters. Among the Liverpool fans was Peter Lyons, who in August 2002 received a three-year banning order from all football grounds in the country. Magistrates heard that he had caused trouble at home and abroad. He and Gary Ferguson, who was also banned, were arrested in Kiev, Ukraine, before a UEFA Cup game for damage caused to a bar and acting aggressively towards locals. The court also heard that Ferguson "waved his genitals at police and behaved like a monkey in a cage".

Policing of Liverpool-Manchester United games did not always please ordinary fans. There was criticism after officers body-searched children, some as young as twelve, on the coach where the weapons were found. One fan told the media he had taken his son to the match as a special treat on his 14th birthday. "The police searched David and made him take his shoes and socks off after we got off the coach. He also had to give his name and address. It was a very frightening experience for him. I spent £40 on the two tickets for the match, plus £10 for the coach fare and we were not even allowed to see the game. I am now going to seek legal advice."

Another fan, who took his twelve-year-old son, described it as his worst experience at football. "The police treated us like animals. I have travelled all over Europe following Liverpool and have never been in trouble. I will never go back to Old Trafford. It was very frightening for my son and the other children on board. A lot of them were crying." The police allowed the coach to continue into Manchester but all on board were refused entry to the game.

The return fixture at Anfield also caused a furore, after several people complained of being indiscriminately attacked by riot police attempting to clear four pubs after serious disorder had broken out between rival fans. A local solicitor, representing some of the complainants, described the police's actions as "quite outrageous". The trouble broke out more than five hours after the end of the game. Five people were charged and two police officers injured.

During the last few years, a mob has begun to re-emerge at Liverpool for matches other than Manchester United. "Three years ago, they turned up about sixty-strong at ours," said a West Brom lad. "There were no younger lads, just the older lot. Fuck knows why they came to Albion but we were very impressed all the same. Whilst the game was going on, one of ours shouted, 'They're fucking here!' Fifteen of us came running down the stairs and they were bouncing up and down, dishing out some slaps. I got a good whack off one. The police came and pushed them back as more Albion came and our numbers swelled to more than forty. We made one last charge but the Old Bill baton-charged us back, and that was the end of that. Liverpool later went to Wolverhampton and robbed the till of their main boozer, the Albert."

There was also trouble at Millwall, where Liverpool played in the Coca-Cola Cup in the autumn of 2004. Sixty-eight seats were ripped out in the away end and four supporters ejected. Police had to put on riot gear to prevent Liverpool supporters reaching the pitch, and a disabled supporter at the edge of the field was injured in the melee that overshadowed the visitors' 3–0 win. Liverpool fans claimed that they had been provoked by home fans singing about Hillsborough but this was strenuously denied by Millwall. Joe Broadfoot, a board member of the Lions' Trust, Millwall's official supporters' club, said, "I did not hear any chanting about Hillsborough, nor did anybody around me, so it has come as a bit of a surprise to hear Liverpool fans claiming this. I think they are making an excuse for the events that took place in their end of the ground. If there was chanting, why did the TV microphones not pick it up, and why did none of the security staff hear it?"

This view was echoed by the club's chairman, Theo Paphitis, who claimed his club was the innocent party. In a statement published on the club's website, Paphitis said, "The facts are that Liverpool fans clashed with riot police in the lower tier of the North Stand and appeared to be attempting to get at Millwall supporters. The suggestion is that they were provoked by chanting referring to the Hillsborough tragedy, but there was no chanting of this nature that was clearly audible to the majority of people in the ground. Naturally, if any such chanting did occur it is deplorable and in the worst possible taste." Rather, he argued, it was the presence of a Liverpool supporter in the home end which caused the initial trouble.

"Mind yer car, mister?" has been a saying heard around Anfield and Goodison for decades. Years ago it was often a ploy used by the street urchins to suss out away fans, who were then followed and systematically beaten. Today it can be a lucrative business for youngsters who patrol the streets on a match day. Such are the earnings available, many gangs of young kids on mountain bikes are under the supervision of local criminals and do the collecting and harassing for a set wage. Many a foolish motorist has returned to his car having politely told the kids "no thanks" to find a damaged or sometimes burnt out motor, and in some cases no motor at all. There is an old joke that does the rounds about one motorist who, when asked if he wanted his car minding, pointed out to the local scallies that there was a huge Alsatian occupying the back seat, to which one youngster replied, "Can it put out fires and change wheels?"

Such became the problem with car minding that the police made sweeps on a match day and estimated that one gang was collecting between £400 and £1,000 every game. "A young hooligan who threatened to damage football fans' cars unless he was paid a 'minder's fee' is banned from going anywhere near Liverpool's stadia on matchdays," reported the *Liverpool Echo*. "Thomas Young, of Stanley Road, Sandhills, has caused problems around Goodison and Anfield for the last 18 months. Now he is the second youngster in six weeks to be ordered to stay away from the grounds whenever the two clubs are playing. Liverpool Magistrates Court heard 15-year-old Young was a member of the same gang as Patrick Garrett, also 15, who was handed an anti-social behaviour order (Asbo) in May for intimidating fans into handing over cash. Young admitted taking money to mind cars during football matches as well as driving a stolen car, hurling abuse at an off-duty policeman and his girlfriend, damaging a lamp post and throwing eggs at a home. He was issued with an Asbo banning him from entering roads to the south of Goodison Park in the period two hours before to two hours after Everton or Liverpool home games."

While teenage car minders and touts mix freely at Goodison and Anfield, the same cannot be said of the two clubs' hooligan members (see EVERTON for details of their fallout). Liverpool's Steve said, "You know the score now, no relationship. We blame them and vice versa. You paint the [Hillsborough] memorial, we paint Dixie [Dean's statue]. It's fucking sad. I know it's mostly down to the kids but Everton want to take a back seat. All these threats that the doors will come in are getting boring. Pack it in. It will go off one day and we will all be sorry in court when the bizzies are laughing at three and four years being handed out. That town now is bang on. Why bother?"

The days of both sets of fans teaming up to attack Mancunians and chanting "Merseyside" together have gone, and the report in the *Echo* following a recent derby indicates they will never return. "A total of 33 arrests were made when violence flared after the Merseyside football derby at Anfield on Sunday, which Liverpool won two-one. During Sunday evening's disturbances, a police horse suffered a nine-inch cut on the flank when police tried to stop Everton supporters attacking Liverpool fans passing the Blue House pub near Goodison Park. The police horse was injured when Everton fans began hurling glasses and bottles at Liverpool fans. Everton spokesman Ian Ross said because the trouble did not take place at Anfield but near Goodison, the football clubs should not be blamed for the violence. He said, 'The arrests are hugely regrettable but they were well away from the stadium and the question is whether this is a football problem or a problem in society.'"

Mr Ross was also quoted in the *Echo* when it reported the tit-for-tat attacks on memorials at both grounds. "Vandals ruin derby party," ran the headline. "Football fans were left shocked after vandals daubed paint on memorials at Anfield and Goodison Park. The Hillsborough Memorial on Anfield Road was targeted days after the 14th anniversary of the disaster in which 96 Liverpool supporters lost their lives. Blue paint was splattered across the memorial which was surrounded by flowers from victims' families. In another incident in the build-up to Saturday's derby match, the statue commemorating Everton's Dixie Dean was covered in red paint and graffiti. Liverpool and Everton today condemned the vandalism. A minority of fans were also criticised after a number of fights in the city centre in the aftermath of the game. At Goodison Park shocked groundsmen found the Dixie Dean memorial had been daubed with red paint just hours before the derby. Club spokesman Ian Ross said, 'It would appear to us that this was an act of malicious vandalism rather than one of football-related hooliganism.'"

Liverpool's recent forays into Europe have probably seen more trouble than domestic games, as the English team's reputation brought out locals keen for a fight. In February 2001, a Liverpool fan was stabbed before an away game with AS Roma, their first meeting since the infamous European Cup Final in 1984. Two other Liverpool fans suffered head injuries as rival gangs clashed in central Rome. This was merely a sideshow to the main battle, which took place between Roma fans and the police, in response to a Roma fan having been thrown down steps at the previous week's game by police and lapsing into a coma. "AS Roma fans attacked police with little bombs, bars, stones and flares," said one Italian fan. "Two police vans were burnt out, as well as a couple of cars and motorbikes. Police first tried to react with tear-gas, but had to take refuge inside the Curva Sud."

At Liverpool's Champions League game at Basel, Switzerland, a joint mob of Swiss and Germans attacked the Brits. One Liverpool fan was injured and 19 arrested before the game. A petrol bomb was hurled into the McDonald's, injuring a 35-year-old fan, and causing head injuries, lacerations and bruising. One hundred people were involved in the attack and a local police spokesman said, "During the fight the fast food restaurant was set on fire,

chairs and other objects were smashed into windows and the entrance door was completely demolished." Many of the rival hooligans had met up in Zurich, three hours away, before making their way into Basel for the clash with the English.

During the 2004/05 season, Liverpool struggled in the Premiership but excelled in Europe. They strolled past Grazer AK, Olympiakos Piraeus, Monaco, Deportivo La Coruna and Bayer Leverkusen, setting themselves up for a quarter-final against Juventus, their first encounter since Heysel. The first leg was at Anfield and the Merseyside club, fans, council and police did everything they could to show respect for the people who had lost their lives 20 years before. A huge friendship flag unveiled inside the ground, coupled with a minute's silence, emphasised Liverpool's attempts to say sorry and also to conduct the present encounter in a dignified and friendly manner. Most visiting fans appreciated the gestures, though a contingent refused and booed during the minute's silence while making obscene hand signs.

It was always going to be the game in Italy which the police most feared. A huge operation was put into place involving some 1,000 armed officers and hundreds of extra stewards. The tensions were raised by idiots on both sides using the Internet to make threat and counter-threat, but there was none of the violence that many had feared. During the game, however, Liverpool fans became the targets of literally hundreds of makeshift missiles thrown from the home end. "Stones, flares and seats rained down on travelling fans as gangs of Italian hooligans clashed with police at the Stadio delle Alpi," one paper reported. Many in the Turin crowd obviously refused to forgive Liverpool for the events of Heysel. A banner in the Curva Sud, home of the local Ultra, read, "(It is) easy to speak, difficult to pardon." Another said, "We can't forget." A third carried the date of the Hillsborough disaster complete with writing scrawled underneath saying, "There is a God." The police did little to help inside the ground, casually standing back as Italians entered a sterile zone to launch their missiles. The Liverpool fans by comparison behaved impeccably, even earning the praise of the British Consul.

With the tie won, Liverpool next edged past Chelsea to clinch a place in the final. Twenty years after Heysel, they were back in the European Cup Final but the chosen venue caused concern for UEFA.

"Liverpool's visit to Istanbul for the Champions League Final will involve the biggest security operation mounted by UEFA in 49 years of European club competition," reported the *Echo*. "The Turkish authorities are launching a huge security operation in response to requests from UEFA to do all they can to ensure a trouble-free night. UEFA spokesman William Gaillard said the event is the 'most important, complex operation we've staged' ... Chief Superintendent Dave Lewis of Merseyside police said, 'They will be able to congregate in Taksim Square and we would make our usual appeal to them to be on their best behaviour at all times, and to remember they are ambassadors for their club and the city'."

In the event, the final passed off peacefully – and euphorically for the Scousers – and after an amazing win, many Reds went home via Bulgaria. At the resort of Golden Sands in the Black Sea town of Varna, however a barman was attacked and left in a coma when a paving slab was dropped on his head, once again bringing the behaviour of Liverpool fans back into the spotlight. Michael Shields, an 18-year-old engineering student, was arrested in his hotel and charged with the attempted murder of 25-year-old Martin Georgiev, who had asked a group of Liverpool fans to quieten down as they smashed bottles and chanted outside the bar where he worked. Despite receiving a confession from 20-year-old Anfield electrician Graham Sankey, faxed by his solicitor to Bulgaria, Judge Angelina Lazarova refused to allow it to be submitted as evidence. Sankey confessed to the crime after he and his family received threats upon his return to Merseyside, but asked to be tried in Britain rather than be extradited to face trial in Bulgaria. The confession was not accepted by the Bulgarian courts and on July 26 Michael Shields, still protesting his innocence, was sentenced to 15 years for attempted murder.

Today Liverpool's mob is a shadow of its former self, and the days of 400-strong firms leaving Lime Street on the ordinary to Euston or Manchester Piccadilly are a distant memory for many. They do however still have a hardcore of about 50 hooligans who come out for the bigger games and can pull on many more, according to one lad. Having smaller numbers and with the media spotlight the club attracts, it is inevitable that any known thugs will be targeted and, as was the case at Everton once the

city gained its capital of culture award, police were ordered to take out known leaders in a bid to stamp out the violence which was gradually creeping back into the city's football fraternity.

The *Liverpool Echo* took great delight in splashing across its front page the story of how one thug surprisingly accepted a three-year ban when the police took a civil case out against him, even though he had never been convicted of football hooliganism. Stephen Jeffers, 31, from Mile End, Everton, was named as a Liverpool ringleader and police backed this up with 36 intelligence reports linking him with violence. Among them were pictures of Jeffers at the head of a gang of Liverpool supporters who confronted Birmingham fans, at the front of a gang of known trouble-causers fighting with Manchester United fans before the Worthington Cup Final in Cardiff in 2003, and as a passenger in a car which drove into Southampton fans. Jeffers's solicitor, unsurprisingly, branded the action "draconian", adding, "The evidence is all hear-say and would not stand the test of a criminal trial."

Another Reds fan who made the papers was Tristan Berry, who was stopped by police at Liverpool airport as he tried to board a plane to Madrid with other fans on his 20th birthday. Berry appeared before magistrates in Liverpool and agreed to a football banning order for three years. He had previously been sentenced to a year in jail after he was convicted of firing a burning flare into the crowd in the Reds' pre-season match at Aberdeen in August 2003.

Liverpool veteran Graham accepts that the Urchins are no more. "The name may live on but most of the original Urchins are finished. It's mainly lads from the north side running it now, who are trying to get us noticed again. It's a tough process though when you've got to build from scratch. To be fair we had a tidy mob developing until Walton Lane [police station] started clamping down. That's pretty much it on the domestic scene, but Europe's a different matter. Who can forget the thirty Liverpool going toe-to-toe with 150 Marseille. It went backwards and forwards for a good five minutes before sheer weight of numbers meant we had to retreat."

Nicky Allt, who travelled everywhere with Liverpool during their glory days, has like most former Annie Road Enders, no desire to turn the clock back. "But there are hundreds of balding fortysomethings in designer clothes still looking for trouble today," he told the *Liverpool Echo*. "I think they're desperate to be like young kids again. It's a joke. With the lads in their twenties, it's more about letting off steam. There are few, if any, other outlets for them to do so and they know no better. I think the police have things under control these days, not least because a lot of people are scared of being caught on CCTV."

LUTON TOWN

Ground: Kenilworth Road
Firm: The Oak Road, The Harry's, Castle Bar, The Hockwell Ring Steamers, The Migs, The Riffs, MI2s
Rivals: QPR, Leicester and Watford
Police Operations: Spoonbill

Luton, an unremarkable town 30 miles north of London, has traditionally been home to large immigrant communities, housing vast numbers of Scottish, Irish, Afro-Caribbean and Asian settlers amongst its inhabitants (*this section has kindly been contributed by Luton fan Richard Stewart*). In the early Eighties it was also the birthplace of the Mig Crew, a hooligan group linked to Luton Town FC, nicknamed "The Hatters" after the local millinery industry that flourished in the 18th century. In 1905, with the hat trade all but extinct the club moved into its current Kenilworth Road ground, in the same year Vauxhall Motors left South London for a new plant in Luton, to become the town's main employer. They were later joined by Electrolux, SKF and others in the light engineering sector, each of them contributing towards Luton's bleak industrial landscape. Now owned by General Motors in Detroit, Vauxhall recently ceased car production in Luton with the loss of some 2,000 jobs, whilst the football club *still* talk of relocating to a new stadium on the outskirts of town.

This was not Luton's only experience of accountants pulling the financial plug. During the 1930s, the council, with the support of grants from the 1936 Housing Act, began a slum clearance programme. Changes to the Act in 1957 strengthened the powers of local authorities to clear and redevelop areas of bad housing, giving rise to large-scale building proj-

ects in Farley Hill, Stopsley, Limbury and Leagrave, which substantially increased both the size and population of the town.

By 1975, enthusiasm and funding for social housing had dried up, and Luton fell into decline. A supply of cheap housing and plentiful work continued to draw an itinerant workforce, drafted in to keep the wheels of its burgeoning manufacturing industry turning. In the late Seventies, Luton was one of several towns mopping up a mass exodus from London but the ensuing decade's lack of investment saw the town's council estates and high rise blocks fall into disrepair, creating ghettoised communities and a breeding ground for low-level petty crime and gradually more serious criminality.

Operation Swamp in 1981, with ill-conceived stop-and-search measures handed to police by the Conservative Government, provided the spark for the Brixton riots. The fever of revolt proved contagious and by the summer had seized many parts of the UK. The run-down neighbourhoods of Lewsey Farm, Hockwell Ring and Marsh Farm simmered uneasily in a potent brew of poverty and mistrust for the police. On 11 July 1981, three months after Brixton, black and white youths banded together for three days of rioting. Police joined politicians in labelling these copycat riots, but the causes were consistent for every city and town buckling under the weight of the new economic order. For some members of the Migs, this was their first time donning a balaclava and the start of a long-running battle to outwit the Bedfordshire Constabulary.

This coincided with Luton winning promotion to the First Division under the stewardship of a youthful David Pleat. Although Luton had no shortage of gangs at that time, what it lacked was an organised mob attached to the club. The team's success on the pitch acted as a magnet for the various local factions, all vying for "top firm" spot. The club had a good crop of players, including Paul Walsh, Brian Stein, Mal Donaghy and Ricky Hill, and were strengthened with the acquisition of Paul Elliot, Steve Foster and Mick Harford as well as talented youth players coming through the ranks. Pleat earned his spurs during this period and the Migs were busy too, cementing their reputation as a gang to be reckoned with.

The High Town district of Luton was the borderline for Stopsley and Stockwood schools. As a large number of up and coming punchers lived on or near the down-at-heel Butterworth Path Estate, these schools forged a natural affinity and it was from this embryonic coupling that the Migs emerged. Turn right at the far end of High Town Road and you would stumble upon a dark and dangerous nightclub called Mollies. They were known to turn a blind eye to under-age drinking, as lads from both schools discovered, and because the club was strategically positioned within a brick's throw of the train station, Mollies soon doubled up as the fledgling Migs HQ. Their gang name came from the Russian fighter jets, but it also stood for Men in Gear, denoting a strict adherence to football's discerning dress code.

Our earliest run-ins took place when the Mollies boys, aged roughly between 13 and 18, powered by a mixture of bravado and the whiff of Paco Rabanne, journeyed to nearby towns for a weekly punch-up. Wheathampstead and Harpenden were the two main ports of call, and heavily outnumbered by natives, we carried the lofty albeit misguided notion that somehow, we were custodians of Luton's honour. Exam revision couldn't compete with this infinitely more engaging weekend ritual. After a solid tear-up, we avoided the attention of the Old Bill and, charged with alcohol and adrenaline, returned to base with tales to tell and war wounds to exhibit. It was these unruly invasions that fashioned a basic manifesto which the Mig Crew would expand upon over time.

We learned a lot during our first season in top flight; hosting the big teams was a valuable learning curve. Most clubs were putting firms together as casual culture gradually ousted the dated bootboys from grounds around the country. Out went the burgundy cardies and waffle trousers, replaced by sportswear that seriously tested both the resources and resourcefulness of our little brigade. This was a genuinely grass roots movement, completely word of mouth. You clocked who wore what and the way they organised themselves as well as perfecting the finer details, the all-conquering football gait. We watched in awe, soaking up the knowledge in the process. A clear separation from both ordinary fan and bootboy developed; we wanted nothing to do with either. Our agenda was more sophisticated than that of the hooligans preceding us, and for an all too brief moment, this changing of the guard went unnoticed by the authorities.

The club had their own learning curve to navigate. The penultimate fixture of the 1982/83 season was a Monday night game at Old Trafford and a 3-0 defeat against Man United looked certain to send Luton down. The final game came five days later, again up in Manchester to face City, themselves positioned marginally above the relegation zone. A Man City victory or a draw would be enough to seal Luton's fate, a Luton win would put City down.

On the morning of the game a huge contingent of Luton arrived at the station, decked out in orange scarves and flags and straw boaters. In this sea of scarfers a few stood out, wearing diamond cut Pringles, Lyle & Scott roll necks, Lois jumbo cords and Nike tennis shoes. In order to distance ourselves from the rabble we travelled by coach, allowing us the freedom to rob Keele service station blind and licence to go on walkabout in small groups before the game.

Tension was high all day and Maine Road basked in brilliant sunshine. With just four minutes remaining, Raddy Antic hammered in the only goal, throwing Luton a lifeline that simultaneously consigned Man City into the abyss. The massed home fans, many who jibbed in free for the last 15 minutes for the celebratory end-of-season pitch invasion, suddenly faced a very different prospect. The atmosphere darkened as the Guvnors attacked several Luton players at the final whistle, an affront that was quickly forgotten. Nothing could detract from the result and we savoured this great escape on our long journey home.

A combination of factors culminating with this game gelled to see the Migs emerge strongly for the 1983/84 campaign. Although young, many still in their latter years of school, we had the bug. As the contest for supremacy on the park warmed up we were driven by off-pitch battles, cultivating a habit that would consume our lives.

The local derby came against Watford, but was always regarded as a non-event by the boys. The Migs' fiercest rivalries developed with QPR or Leicester and both fixtures rendered much action over the coming years. We also saw the main London clubs as a great challenge and one we felt duty bound to confront. Any firm taking the trouble to visit would be pleasantly surprised; turnout for home games was a feature at Luton and virtually guaranteed until the late Eighties.

Our first trip to QPR came in November 1983, and numerous skirmishes with them followed over the years. The Leicester grudge began the following season after they came down mob handed for a Tuesday night Milk Cup fixture; well dressed, well organised and well up for the row. We were due to play them shortly afterwards at Filbert Street and the Mollies Planning Committee swung into action. Paddy W, a charismatic and street-smart hustler, was responsible for travel arrangements, laying on two coaches with more travelling by train. Paddy possessed a flair for leadership and was highly influential at Luton. A few of the older black faces (the Potty Chops) had a rude boy styling that infused the Migs language and dress sense, Paddy perhaps more than others due to the respect he commanded. The Baby Squad had also built a decent reputation, but after the game our two coachloads stood firm and gave a good account. We left Leicester feeling that we had cancelled out their prior encroachment and any meeting between the clubs became a keenly fought contest. It was hard to say if either firm ever definitively came out on top, but both would claim to have edged it.

Meanwhile, in the high-rise flats of Marsh Farm, something else was afoot. To make a few quid, cash-strapped tenants could be persuaded to hire out their homes for all night "blues". Furniture was ferried out by day, making way for the giant speaker stacks and crates of beer. When the switch went off, the DJ operated in darkness save for the light on his trusty 1200s and the party started. The bass-line thundered throughout the block, but as these dances were dangerously packed, any police intervention was deemed a risky call.

The main players at that time were Soul Incorporated, Positive Force, Lovelite and Masterock. The latter was a rig with which DJ Scooby and a youthful Matt "Jam" Lamont learned their craft, and behind it was the enigmatic Aubrey B, a figure largely credited with introducing matchday tactics to the firm. Exodus have continued the town's love affair with the sound system, albeit to a different beat, though certain members of this collective had ties with Luton's football gangs of the Eighties. These gatherings were the stamping ground for many of the black football crowd, but the music and ample supply of puff attracted a number of Migs as well. Getting mashed on a Friday night was probably not that clever if we had an early meet Saturday morning, but somehow we always made it to the station on time. The mid-morning hair of the dog and the anticipation of the day ahead perked everyone up.

Cross-pollination in our socialising and newly found employment helped to swell the ranks of the Migs, who by now were recruiting from neighbourhoods like Dallow Road, Farley Hill, Marsh Farm and even the outlying areas of Harpenden and Bedford. The Migs were principally blue collar and work was just a means of supporting our passions: clothes, drink, drugs and going to the match. Few saw their job as anything more significant than this because, leaving school in 1983 or '84, we were presented with uncertainty and fairly limited prospects. If validation was not forthcoming in our careers, then we would find acceptance elsewhere and football culture was on hand, offering alternative opportunities to shine. Society frowned upon the antics of what they considered working class oiks, but this had zero effect on us. We had the swagger and an arrogance that transcended such triviality. In truth, we saw ourselves as a different league from the ordinary Joe, or to give them their correct name, the "Muggy Bone-Head".

Tony Blair prefers to brand his oil-grabbing aggression in Iraq as policing global security, whilst the pro-hunt brigade insist fox hunting is about pest control. Similarly, we found ways of justifying our publicly unacceptable behaviour, but in stark contrast to the aforementioned, we upheld the principle of a fair fight. Our quarry was equally keen to get it on and irrespective of the folly behind certain missions, we were all there by choice. We were cast as social pariahs because our arguments were settled with fists and feet, yet unbeknown to us, Reagan and Thatcher spent those very same years taking societies apart, bullying the developing world in the name of economic gain. The red tops roundly applauded their strong arm tactics on the front pages whilst hysterically denouncing us as scum in the sports section, dismissing our well-orchestrated manoeuvres as mindless thuggery. Getting togged up and travelling to the heart of enemy territory and then out-smarting the Old Bill to have a square go with their main chaps may have simply been us playing out a latent perception of war and religion. Ask any boxer to describe the adrenaline rush a fight gives them and it helps paint a picture on this vexed aspect of masculinity. Throw in everything else that came with enlisting in a football gang and it was not hard to see why the casual frontline was mobbed with the alpha males of every town signing up for action.

Close to the ground sat a factory called Propafloor, and with several "faces" on the payroll, it became a fertile breeding ground for the Migs. Whilst we were far from an Identikit group, the make-up consisted largely of builders, electricians, factory hands, mechanics and shop workers; occupations that left us scope to pursue outside interests. There were exceptions to the rule, such as the trainee lawyers who proved useful and broadened the dynamic. The characters who occupied this world were far more diverse than we recognised at the time, encompassing everyone from the mad traveller types who worked on the motorways through to our university set. It highlights the glue this culture had, pulling in and holding such disparate strands together. Through networking, alliances were formed and enemies made. The rationale was a familiar one: you're either with us or against us.

The Blockers Arms on the High Town Road, now called The Well, was another popular haunt for the Migs. For a later drink we frequented a dive called Strokes, where a measure of Northern Soul was often accompanied with a black eye courtesy of the sovereigned-up bouncers. Throughout these establishments a common theme ran – a relaxed management when it came to illicit activities. Wherever the Migs went, trouble closely followed. Lighting the fuse could be an innocuous affair to the uninitiated; a careless, wide of the mark comment, any lingering glance misconstrued as "staring out", or simply the bad luck to bump into the wrong person. Trading punches became an inevitable consequence of a night on the town, either one-on-one straighteners or larger scale rucks. These were very aggressive times and with so much testosterone to discharge, it was little wonder we were not welcomed in many pubs and bars.

Predictably, there would be in-town disputes and at the back end of '83 an envoy from Lewsey Farm arrived at Mollies to settle a beef with the Migs, resulting in a street brawl that spread across Midland Road. These local rivalries would be set aside for match day, when a united front was called for, but the menace of unfinished business proliferated and could flare up without warning. Luton's other firm of note were an older crew called the Riffs, a well respected and very game outfit who took their cue from the Migs. On a good day, with a big turnout from the Luton Blacks, the Migs and Riffs combined, the mob might be up to 350 strong.

But it was not always big numbers that got the best results. For long periods, the hardcore Migs – those who were there week in, week out – numbered around 50. They often had their finest hours with a smaller head count. It has been recognised by the military in something they call the Rule of 150. Armies never have more than this number in any unit as it has been shown to decrease efficiency during battle. The explanation is two-fold. Firstly, hierarchal leadership diminishes under such numerical dilution, but perhaps more relevant is the fact that peer pressure takes on less significance in larger groups. In a small, tight collective we all monitored each other, forcing everyone to face their responsibilities to the crew. The point was not lost on TR, widely regarded as the Migs' top boy, who on one nocturnal raid made everybody pair up. The idea was that you kept tabs on your designated partner to make sure they did not bottle out; if you were in it, then you were all the way in it. A similar thing happened sub-consciously on match-day, and the smaller the mob, the more this applied. Of all the quaint rituals that were associated with football, *losing your bottle* was the number one cardinal sin.

Pre-match started with an early drink in Mollies, allowing us to monitor the train station. There would be little groups gathered in several pubs across town, as other small pockets scanned the town centre. This was long before the advent of mobile phones, but should an away firm materialise, a welcome party swiftly rallied to greet them. Word travelled like wildfire once the enemy appeared on the horizon.

Another favoured drinking den on match day was in the town centre. The top level was a pub called Toby's, but stairs at the back led to Breakers, a naughty West Indian drinker. The firm would split in two, either going downstairs for a game of pool and a smoke as the rest remained on stand-by in Toby's. It was a bit close to the police station for comfort, but its dual exit and entrance offered an element of surprise and our boys could quickly mobilise or disappear as the situation dictated. In a shifting political climate, the police had become very wary of black establishments and Breakers was normally given a wide berth despite its close proximity to the main nick, another reason the lads congregated there.

The route from train station to stadium took twenty minutes to walk and was scattered with the paraphernalia of a football hooligans' playground: large dual carriageway for stopping traffic with pitched battles, fences for the one-handed vault, a flyover that announced your arrival to opposing firms and a sprawling, run-down shopping centre with lots of flat space for a decent off. Around the ground lay a warren of alleyways and the crumbling West Side Centre at the foot of Kenilworth Road, whilst pretty redundant for shopping, was just the thing for ambushes. The ground itself was in the Asian stronghold of Bury Park and shops on the Dunstable Road paid a heavy price, as it was often the flashpoint for warring firms.

The layout of neighbouring streets offered numerous possibilities for meeting the away firm before they were finally taken to the train station, which tested the patience and mettle of the police. If you were unable to get at them near the ground then the cat and mouse would begin, as we'd break off into smaller groups looking for ways to rush the escort en route. Led by Aubrey, Masterock's eccentric Yardie and obsessive tactician, we pulled off the perfect pincer movement against Tottenham one year behind the West Side Centre, before it was eventually torn down to make way for a casino.

March 13, 1985, was Black Wednesday for the club, as Luton Town hosted Millwall in the FA Cup. In short, the town was demolished by an enormous Millwall herd, strengthened by mercenaries from Tottenham, Chelsea and Arsenal. If we'd had a full mob out we would have still been swarmed, but our plight was compounded by a below par showing from the Migs and the missing personnel brought the question of commitment sharply into focus. It left us an insurmountable task and resistance on the night came in small and unexpected pockets. To rub salt into the wounds, Luton were then portrayed as a small "family" club who did not deserve such unprovoked aggression. The story went national, with repeated footage of shell-shocked pensioners greatly magnifying the embarrassment.

The repercussions of that night would have far

wider implications for the Migs than anyone could have imagined. The club's chairman, David Evans, decided that Luton would never again witness the spectre of hooliganism, and by the following season had instigated a ban on all visiting supporters. With the outcry surrounding the riot, it was not difficult for Evans to push through the legislation needed to implement such a ban, and Thatcher, post Heysel, talked of extending this policy to all league clubs. Without a trace of irony, the clamour to reintroduce the birch rose and this inconsistent thinking spoke volumes about the political establishment of the day. The away-fan ban came on the back of the club's decision to lay a new plastic pitch, and these controversies together combined to make Luton just about the most reviled team in the country in 1985.

The Millwall invasion punctuated the 1984 Miners' Strike and the Broadwater Farm riot of October 1985 that culminated with the murder of PC Blakelock, hacked to death in the line of duty. The soaring levels of violence threatening the thin blue line brought about a seismic governmental rethink and the passing of successive crime bills that greatly enhanced police powers. Images of pasty faced plod holding onto their helmets and ducking behind a flimsy plastic shield or running around with flapping tunics and only a stick or an Alsatian for company have now been firmly relegated to the past yet perfectly encapsulate a brutal and bloody era. Nowadays, the towering lumps who pass themselves off as Dibble, armed to the teeth and with a taste for zero-tolerance, must surely rate as the most fearsome mob in the land.

Football supporters have for many years served as guinea pigs for government efforts to restrict personal freedoms, and in the aftermath of the Millwall riot, debate surrounding the merits of fans carrying compulsory ID cards raged in political circles. 2005 finds the electorate awaiting a delayed announcement on ID cards for all ... now that's progress. If you find yourself engaged in what are deemed illegal activities, it is then naive to bemoan your lack of rights. As a hooligan, all rights were instantly traded in; we knew it and the Old Bill certainly knew it. But what about the normal fans there solely for the match? They were caught up in the heavy-handed policing and have historically been treated appallingly by the clubs they help keep alive.

Whilst we cannot be held responsible for this shabby treatment dished out by the club, we ought to acknowledge the impact our actions were having on others. Despite the talk of "we only ever had it with our own", the Migs rampaging through packed town centres on a Saturday afternoon undoubtedly terrorised ordinary people. This collateral damage was unintentional and left a bad taste, but never enough for us to knock it on the head.

Millwall's notorious mob carved their name in history that night and if this came as a wake-up call for the authorities to act, then the glare of television also relayed a harsh lesson for the Migs. To our credit, we learned from it and came through the adversity stronger and more focused than before. The truth is not many clubs could muster anything like the numbers to answer that Millwall army, but in response, the Migs became more compact, shrinking in size in order to weed out the riders. As the 1985/86 season began, we took matters more seriously and with no visitors to entertain, our attention turned to away games.

Early that season Aston Villa was earmarked. The morning arrived and less than 30 gathered at the station, but regardless, we travelled with confidence in our small yet handy crew. The day started well when we realised that our train changed at Leicester, who were setting off to London for their game against Arsenal that afternoon. It went like a dream, as we caught the Baby Squad napping. I'm not sure they realised their numerical superiority, but we forced them out of their own train station and scattered them in the surrounding streets. We even managed to catch our connecting train without anyone getting nicked, so were already on a high by the time we arrived in Birmingham. As soon as the ticket office opened we bought seats for the home end before departing the area to keep a low profile and fuel up on Dutch courage. On returning to Villa Park, we tried to avoid drawing attention to ourselves, but still managed a few minor scrapes, which we easily had the better of.

Mission accomplished; we had made it into their seats but were disappointed to find that they had no boys in this end. It seemed their chaps still stood on the terracing of the Holte End, whereas most firms had switched from behind the goals into seated areas away from the divs. At Luton, in our efforts to stay one step ahead of the local plod, we went from

the K2 scoreboard end, onto the Maple benches (where Paddy would "bust his moves" and lead us through an array of silly songs such as "Sing a Bit Louder Now", bemusing home and away fans alike) before finally ending up in the pricier Wing Stand in search of our foe. To give Villa the benefit of doubt, perhaps they hadn't expected a show from us, but at half-time, being 3-0 down and with no Villa Youth in the vicinity, we left the ground to prepare for the main event. Foolishly it turns out, as we were picked up by the Old Bill, who herded us onto a train. They got off a few stops down the line, so we left the train at the following station, bang in the middle of nowhere. We didn't have a clue where we were headed, but were just glad to be free again.

The police soon found us again and we were taken in four police vans to New Street Station, only this time we had the pleasure of their company all the way to Oxford, a good way off their patch. It had been a long and eventful day, with the unexpected bonus of our breakfast rendezvous with Leicester. Other notable excursions that season saw big turnouts for Oxford and Southampton, as well as taking up position in the home seats at Tottenham and QPR. There was also a three-legged FA Cup tie against Arsenal, with one of the games ending in a pitched battle at a nearby park, where one of Arsenal's main lads was stabbed before mounted police eventually broke things up.

The Arsenal games created a particular problem, as some of our boys had started running with the North London club, an obvious conflict of interest. A couple also went with Chelsea, and when either game came around tension would rise as it was unclear where loyalties lay in certain quarters. Despite the friction, there was an upside; the adoption of new tactics employed by these bigger clubs. We were certainly more sussed and organised as a result of innovations introduced by those fraternising with London clubs. That said, a rift developed which at its low point threatened the unity of the Migs, the very thing that gave them their edge.

The next season saw Luton disqualified from the Milk Cup after refusing Cardiff City tickets in line with their away fan ban. The FA Cup draw followed and David Evans, thinking of the cash register, caved in and allowed visiting supporters for the first time since the ban. Liverpool came, and after two 0-0

A composite CCTV image, released by Hertfordshire Police, of Luton Town and Watford fans fighting on the Vicarage Road pitch before a derby game.

draws, the tie was emphatically won at the third time of asking at Kenilworth Road. Dalglish had a moan about the pitch, but that was academic once the draw was made – QPR at home! We couldn't have asked for better.

The past two seasons had seen clashes with them at St Pancras, with us winning the first one but then getting battered the following year. Starved for months of testing visiting mobs, we were eager to make home advantage count once more. We had a huge turnout, as evening fixtures always seemed edgier than Saturdays and the magic of the cup also applied to firms. Fighting broke out sporadically on either side of the game, but on the whole a large police presence kept the rival firms apart. There were, however, six reported stabbings and a spate of arrests, news of which reached the national papers.

Fleet Street was outraged to learn that, despite what the club had endured, their own fans could be responsible for crowd trouble, and singled out the Migs as having tarnished the good reputation of Luton Town FC. Finally the shame of the Millwall walkover had been exorcised, in the *Daily Express* of all places.

There being no home games to concern ourselves with, the crew were increasingly drawn into feuds with local gangs instead. The Migs were never short of a battle, be it the trips to Tropicana nightclub or Pink Elephant in Dunstable to see off out-of-town coach parties, or on-going skirmishes with the BPYP, an Asian firm we often tangled with. There was also an incident at a wine bar called Charlie Brown's which saw the Migs cross the path of an Irish family connected to it. Things were spiralling out of control and for the unfortunate, this resulted in prison sentences for a variety of offences.

Full scale offs were becoming rarer, replaced instead by smaller, fiercer battles. The level of violence grew ever more intense and incidences of serious injuries were on the up. Weapons were a distinct feature now, so people were getting badly done. In the back pocket of every self-respecting hoolie would be a rolled up newspaper; once folded correctly, a copy of *The Sun* became as hard as an iron bar. This was a trick practised back in the Forties by South London gang the Elephant Boys, possibly the reason it was dubbed the Millwall Brick. There were craftily concealed Stanley blades, Lemon Jiffy or Vicks bottles filled with ammonia and golfing umbrellas with sharpened tips – you had to have your wits about you to contend with the new armoury.

In any event, it was during these turbulent times that the club enjoyed their greatest success, reaching the semi-final of the FA cup in 1985 and finishing ninth in the league a year later. David Pleat departed acrimoniously for Tottenham, replaced by the in-house appointment of John Moore who took Luton to their highest ever top flight finish of seventh before resigning. The next season under Ray Harford, the club won its first major silverware, beating Arsenal 3-2 in the Littlewoods Cup Final as well as reaching the FA Cup semi-final. With the away fan ban still in place, it was the club's excellent form in cup competitions that held the first generation Migs together for what was probably another two seasons.

The main action came in the cup runs, with a home and away tie at QPR, followed by a quarter-final visit from Portsmouth. The police took much of the sting out of this potentially volatile clash with the 6.57 Crew using Operation Spoonbill, a series of dawn raids at 17 addresses across town. Brandishing trumped-up conspiracy to cause disorder charges, which were subsequently watered down, they achieved the disruption they had set out to. TV cameras accompanied the police, so images of hooded hoods being led away were splashed all over BBC News, much to our amusement.

These were a mad few years in which we survived the traumas of puberty, the funerals of some good lads, the Bushwhackers and Steve White's ineptitude in front of goal. By 1988, things were changing

quickly and for a sizeable number casual culture seemed to have lost its momentum. There were many reasons behind this, but what cannot be under-estimated was the effect the away fan ban had at Luton. Of course, the inconvenience of doing bird, allied to the fact that sentencing had become draconian for football-related offences, put many off. Others simply had enough of wandering around for two hours in post-match drizzle without so much as an "E-I-E" shouted in anger, due to the more effective policing and crowd control. Yet more moved on as it was no longer what they signed up for. The whole basis for the Migs was to break away from the crowd, to behave and dress differently from the herd. Watching the Beautiful Game's rise in popularity and its inevitable commodification, being *football* no longer felt like the secret society that it had started life as.

Hard as it was to accept, the over-riding feeling was that life on the firm had run its course and now was the time to broaden our horizons, from which point the Migs splintered off in many directions. Some jumped ship to acid house as punters, DJs or dealers. For others, more serious crime beckoned and they stepped onto the lower rungs of that ladder. Lifestyle changes and the ending of our teenage years may have called for a move out of town, either to London or to work abroad. A few just stopped going to football altogether. This left the hardcore Migs to take things underground, where it was very much business as usual; in a dawning age of peace and love they remained fiercely committed to the cause.

In commerce, there have been rafts of studies to pinpoint what constitutes the successful entrepreneur. They suggest a marked tendency for risk-taking, and that those studied thrive on adrenaline. Others even suggest a very thin line dividing the entrepreneur and the psychopath, as the two share remarkably similar characteristics. Risk-taking and the adrenaline rush formed the engine of our peculiar social phenomenon and this could explain why so many from the football scene went on to carve out successful careers, turning up in the creative industries, running their own businesses, becoming authors and publishers and so on. Adrenaline junkies who were spurred on as a result of the one-upmanship instilled by terrace culture, they simply transferred their guile and adjusted to fresh challenges. On the other side of that thin divide sat the psychopaths.

This signalled the end of a chapter, though not of course the whole story. The Migs may have taken varied paths, but the network remained intact. It lurked out of view for a time before events gradually conspired to draw people back to the match following a few seasons' hiatus. Thinner on top, thicker of waist, the hooligans steadily reclaimed the turf that was once theirs. In the Migs' case, local boxer Billy Schwer's dramatic rise to WBC Lightweight and IBO Light Welterweight world champion brought many old faces out of the woodwork, especially those based in London. However, due to a previous run-in involving some of the lads, Billy was not popular with the inner circle and was therefore unable to fully unite them, although the sense of re-union that pervaded his fights was tangible. Beneath the surface, momentum was gathering pace, and by the Nineties a rebirth of the Migs was well underway. Reinforced by an influx of young guns and with a promising splinter group, the MI2s, under their tutelage, the second coming had arrived. Britannia rode the crest of a wave as its shores were being steadily bombarded by Italian and Colombian imports. Stone Island and cocaine had already seeped into casual consciousness during the previous decade, but it was their increased availability and patronage that would once more transform the football landscape.

* * *

The MI2s, sometimes referred to as the "Babies", started with around a dozen youths and grew in two years to 35-40 who ran their own minibuses and coaches. Not all of the older Migs welcomed them but the main man was encouraging and they travelled with the older lads for a couple of seasons.

For one trip, they took their own minibus to Swansea. "We headed into town early before the older lot, but got collared straight away by the OB," said one. "They escorted us in with horses and then stuck us in the middle of an empty car park and ordered everyone off the bus. It was a bit of a battle bus and there was all sorts of weapons and other shit on there, even some golf balls with the George Cross and 'Migs' on. We all got off the bus one by one and they were searching everyone. We were

thinking we were properly fucked. People had stuffed these golf balls down their pants and one of them fell out the bottom of someone's jeans and rolled across the car park stopping at one of the OB's feet. He bent down, picked it up and was like, 'What's this then? Have you got Tiger Woods stashed in there too?' And of course he wasn't far wrong, but somehow we got away with it.

"There was about 150 Migs there, split between those in their mid-thirties and us lot in our late teens and twenties. It must have looked like a load of dads taking their sons along for the ruck. We tried to have it all day, but it only went off bits and pieces. It was a good early mission for us though and was worth it to see the Taffies faces when some of the black boys got up on the fences and waved their wallets at them. At Luton the crew has always been multi-cultural. That's one of the things I love about Luton and the mob. We're all about the same thing."

The MI2s' first outing as a separate unit was Graham Taylor's final game as Watford manager, which was their last home game of the season, against Tranmere. Ten drunken Babies decided on the Friday night to go to Watford the next day, and spent the Saturday drinking in their rivals' town centre. "We were in the Robert Peel when one of their lads came into the bar in his Stone Island and went to the barman, 'Who the fuck are that lot?' and he said, 'I dunno, but none of them have got scouse accents.'

"When we left and were heading up the road, the same geezer was outside and asked, 'Are you lot Tranmere then?'

"'Are we fuck. We're Luton!'

"And he was like, 'No way. You're taking the piss,' and shot straight back in the pub. He must have thought it was Christmas, New Year and Easter all come at the same time. 'There's ten Luton outside!' Forty of fifty of them came out, but we stood our ground and had it with them properly for about two minutes."

Another violent trip was Cambridge for a Friday night game. "We terrorised them all night; they couldn't compete with us. Thirty of our Babies turned up at twelve o'clock and were straight on the lash. We ended up bashing a load of students on the Green. We were walking across the park and they called it on: 'Come on then. Who the fuck are you lot?' And we went across thinking it might be

Cambridge's boys, but it was a load of students and we ended up running them across the park for the fun of it. Then the OB drove in, so you had all these vans bouncing around with bodies scattering everywhere. And there on the other side of the green was our own PC Palmer going, 'Bashing students now is it? Whatever happened to you lot?'"

In November 2001, Luton took one of their biggest firms for years to Mansfield. "I had met some Mansfield at an England game in Athens and we heard that they had a good firm and some Forest went with them too," said the MI2 member. "So when we went down into the Third Division, the talk went round and the trip to Mansfield was on.

"We turned up there at ten o'clock in the morning, 150-handed. I'll never forget, coming out of the station, I looked back up the road and it was full from side to side – all you could see was lads. We got put in a pub, but it was going off all day. In the end Mansfield didn't really compete with us, and we were expecting a lot from them. The ratio was about three-to-one old Migs to younger MI2s, a really good mixture.

"On the way back, a few of us decided to get off the train at Leicester and ended up drinking in a bar opposite the train station. There were a few rugby lads in there and it was a right good crack – music, dancing, people on the stage being idiots. Then when we went back down to get the last train home, there was a couple of Leicester lads on the platform. A few words were had and they said, 'Right, we'll be back in a minute.'

"We got out the station and Leicester were pouring out of this pub. At first it was a good battle, until the numbers began to tell and we got backed off a bit. The next thing, we got it together and we ran them down the dual carriageway and gave it to them proper."

Police mounted a massive operation for the game at Watford in 2002, and 16 Migs ended up going to prison. "There was three of us from the younger lot who ended up doing a bird for it. We started off in Euston with a good hundred boys and the OB thought we were Man City going to Arsenal, but when we started walking back to Euston Station they were like, 'If they're Man City why are they going back to Euston?'

"We all got off the train at Bushey to try and meet Watford and the OB were trying to get us back on the train. Next thing a couple of lads got down on the tracks and started throwing rocks at the police and that was it – everyone was going, 'Come on, we're Luton, we do what we want.' We ran across the tracks, over the fence and out the station. The OB didn't know how to handle us.

"We tried to break off in splinter groups and keep away from the main escort, but in the end it didn't work out like that. Eventually most of us were herded up and walked to the ground with the rest, with little bits going off with the OB all the way.

"Outside the ground we made more of an effort to break through the police. A few Watford came up behind them for a little show. We wanted it, they didn't.

"People were saying, 'Fuck it, if we can't get them out here, we'll just do them in the ground instead.' I don't suppose anyone really thought that would happen, but everyone went in the ground and straight down to the front. There was almost no OB in the ground, and everyone started going, 'There's no OB, let's go on the pitch.' And the next thing you know, everyone's gone on the pitch and I was thinking to myself, I am right on way line, what am I doing? I am having a tear-up on the pitch and it's live on telly! I knew for a fact as I was coming off the pitch, and it's been going off and there's Watford lying there, I am going to prison for this. But how many teams go on the pitch and have a full-scale battle? It just doesn't happen nowadays.

"Watford didn't come out at all at first. We were on their pitch giving it, 'Come on, come on,' and a couple of lads had jumped in their end and were having it, but then we had been there a couple of minutes and nothing was happening. So we said we'd better get off and as we were walking back down the other end, some Watford finally decided to jump on the pitch behind us. Then when everyone realised that Watford had come on, that's when we went on for the second time and Watford got bashed and run properly."

Meanwhile, 15 of the older Migs had managed to do their own thing and forced a large crowd of Watford back into a pub in the town centre. "By coincidence, this happened at the same time as we were doing our thing at the ground. The police actually thought that we co-ordinated it with the pitch invasion, which is a load of bollocks. If you tried your hardest to sort something out like that, it would never come off in a million years. But they said it was a conspiracy and that the older lads had rung us from the pub and said, 'Well, all the police are here, so you go on the pitch now.' What a lot of bollocks.

"So I knew from that moment on that I was going to get a knock over that. It was always going to come. Six months later at half six in the morning, it did. Sixteen of the Migs ended up going to prison for it, six for the taking of the pub and ten from the pitch invasion, with an age range from nineteen to thirty-eight. We all ended up in Bedford Prison together at first and it wasn't exactly a laugh but if you're going to go to prison you might as well go with fifteen of your mates.

"I got eleven months so I only served about four and then got my tag. I've got a seven-year ban, which hurts because this is the first time Luton have been doing well in ten years and I would love to be going. But even more than that, I used to go to every England game and now I can't go to any. But the Baby firm is still thriving and can pull between eighty and 100."

Further reading: *Casuals*, Phil Thornton (Milo Books); *Top Boys*, Cass Pennant (Blake Publishing)

Acknowledgements

Special thanks go to all those people who helped with volume one, especially M, Seth, Fordie, Stuart and Brian, Smithy, Andy, Ian, Raver, Del, Nick and Lorne, Mel and Essy, Hogger, Craig and TD, Benny, Hammers, Matt, Les, Davie, Simon, Simmo, Annis, Mallow, Steve, Jake, Boris, Gav and Bernie, Craig and Carl, Lee, Matt, Kalvin, Jibber, Wallie, Andy, Mike, Matty, Larry, Gee, Gruff, Steve, Franno, Paddy, Tim, Ian, Liam, JB, John, Tony, Paul, Ste, Graham, the three LTE lads MM, DD and SD, John O, Tuse, Richard Stewart and the dozens of other people we interviewed but who wished to remain anonymous.

In addition, we would also like to thank the authors of other "hooligan" books who helped to chronicle this period or have given us contacts and suggestions. They include: Cass Pennant, Chris Brown, Steve Cowens, Dave Jones and Tony Rivers, Mark Chester, Paul Debrick, Shaun Tordoff, Callum Bell, Jay Allen and Dan Rivers from the ASC, Rob Silvester, Nicky Allt, the Martins King and Knight, John Pulling, Andrew Porter and Colin Ward.

Lastly but most importantly (*writes Andy Nicholls*), to Nia, thanks for sticking with me when the doors were surrounded during various police operations to snare the "dangerous author".

Index